T0336851

Advanced Research on Cloud Computing Design and Applications

Shadi Aljawarneh
Jordan University of Science and Technology, Jordan

A volume in the Advances in Systems Analysis,
Software Engineering, and High Performance
Computing (ASASEHPC) Book Series

An Imprint of IGI Global

Managing Director:	Lindsay Johnston
Managing Editor:	Keith Greenberg
Director of Intellectual Property & Contracts:	Jan Travers
Acquisitions Editor:	Kayla Wolfe
Production Editor:	Christina Henning
Development Editor:	Courtney Tychinski
Cover Design:	Jason Mull

Published in the United States of America by
Information Science Reference (an imprint of IGI Global)
701 E. Chocolate Avenue
Hershey PA, USA 17033
Tel: 717-533-8845
Fax: 717-533-8661
E-mail: cust@igi-global.com
Web site: http://www.igi-global.com

Copyright © 2015 by IGI Global. All rights reserved. No part of this publication may be reproduced, stored or distributed in any form or by any means, electronic or mechanical, including photocopying, without written permission from the publisher. Product or company names used in this set are for identification purposes only. Inclusion of the names of the products or companies does not indicate a claim of ownership by IGI Global of the trademark or registered trademark.

                    Library of Congress Cataloging-in-Publication Data

Advanced research on cloud computing design and applications / Shadi Aljawarneh, editor.
      pages cm
 Includes bibliographical references and index.
 Summary: "This book shares the latest high quality research results on cloud computing and explores the broad applicability and scope of these trends on an international scale, venturing into the hot-button issue of IT services evolution and what we need to do to be prepared for future developments in cloud computing"-- Provided by publisher.
   ISBN 978-1-4666-8676-2 (hardcover) -- ISBN 978-1-4666-8677-9 (ebook) 1. Cloud computing. I. Aljawarneh, Shadi.
  QA76.585.A3775 2015
  004.67'82--dc23
                          2015015765

This book is published in the IGI Global book series Advances in Systems Analysis, Software Engineering, and High Performance Computing (ASASEHPC) (ISSN: 2327-3453; eISSN: 2327-3461)

British Cataloguing in Publication Data
A Cataloguing in Publication record for this book is available from the British Library.

All work contributed to this book is new, previously-unpublished material. The views expressed in this book are those of the authors, but not necessarily of the publisher.

For electronic access to this publication, please contact: eresources@igi-global.com.

Advances in Systems Analysis, Software Engineering, and High Performance Computing (ASASEHPC) Book Series

Vijayan Sugumaran
Oakland University, USA

ISSN: 2327-3453
EISSN: 2327-3461

MISSION

The theory and practice of computing applications and distributed systems has emerged as one of the key areas of research driving innovations in business, engineering, and science. The fields of software engineering, systems analysis, and high performance computing offer a wide range of applications and solutions in solving computational problems for any modern organization.

The **Advances in Systems Analysis, Software Engineering, and High Performance Computing (ASASEHPC) Book Series** brings together research in the areas of distributed computing, systems and software engineering, high performance computing, and service science. This collection of publications is useful for academics, researchers, and practitioners seeking the latest practices and knowledge in this field.

COVERAGE

- Software engineering
- Network Management
- Computer Networking
- Enterprise Information Systems
- Performance Modelling
- Storage Systems
- Human-Computer Interaction
- Distributed Cloud Computing
- Engineering Environments
- Metadata and Semantic Web

IGI Global is currently accepting manuscripts for publication within this series. To submit a proposal for a volume in this series, please contact our Acquisition Editors at Acquisitions@igi-global.com or visit: http://www.igi-global.com/publish/.

The Advances in Systems Analysis, Software Engineering, and High Performance Computing (ASASEHPC) Book Series (ISSN 2327-3453) is published by IGI Global, 701 E. Chocolate Avenue, Hershey, PA 17033-1240, USA, www.igi-global.com. This series is composed of titles available for purchase individually; each title is edited to be contextually exclusive from any other title within the series. For pricing and ordering information please visit http://www.igi-global.com/book-series/advances-systems-analysis-software-engineering/73689. Postmaster: Send all address changes to above address. Copyright © 2015 IGI Global. All rights, including translation in other languages reserved by the publisher. No part of this series may be reproduced or used in any form or by any means – graphics, electronic, or mechanical, including photocopying, recording, taping, or information and retrieval systems – without written permission from the publisher, except for non commercial, educational use, including classroom teaching purposes. The views expressed in this series are those of the authors, but not necessarily of IGI Global.

Titles in this Series

For a list of additional titles in this series, please visit: www.igi-global.com

Intelligent Applications for Heterogeneous System Modeling and Design
Kandarpa Kumar Sarma (Gauhati University, India) Manash Pratim Sarma (Gauhati University, India) and Mousmita Sarma (SpeecHWareNet (I) Pvt. Ltd, India)
Information Science Reference • copyright 2015 • 429pp • H/C (ISBN: 9781466684935) • US $255.00 (our price)

Achieving Enterprise Agility through Innovative Software Development
Amitoj Singh (Chitkara University, Punjab, India)
Information Science Reference • copyright 2015 • 350pp • H/C (ISBN: 9781466685109) • US $225.00 (our price)

Delivery and Adoption of Cloud Computing Services in Contemporary Organizations
Victor Chang (Computing, Creative Technologies and Engineering, Leeds Beckett University, UK) Robert John Walters (Electronics and Computer Science, University of Southampton, UK) and Gary Wills (Electronics and Computer Science, University of Southampton, UK)
Information Science Reference • copyright 2015 • 519pp • H/C (ISBN: 9781466682108) • US $225.00 (our price)

Emerging Research in Cloud Distributed Computing Systems
Susmit Bagchi (Gyeongsang National University, South Korea)
Information Science Reference • copyright 2015 • 447pp • H/C (ISBN: 9781466682139) • US $200.00 (our price)

Resource Management of Mobile Cloud Computing Networks and Environments
George Mastorakis (Technological Educational Institute of Crete, Greece) Constandinos X. Mavromoustakis (University of Nicosia, Cyprus) and Evangelos Pallis (Technological Educational Institute of Crete, Greece)
Information Science Reference • copyright 2015 • 432pp • H/C (ISBN: 9781466682252) • US $215.00 (our price)

Research and Applications in Global Supercomputing
Richard S. Segall (Arkansas State University, USA) Jeffrey S. Cook (Independent Researcher, USA) and Qingyu Zhang (Shenzhen University, China)
Information Science Reference • copyright 2015 • 672pp • H/C (ISBN: 9781466674615) • US $265.00 (our price)

Challenges, Opportunities, and Dimensions of Cyber-Physical Systems
P. Venkata Krishna (VIT University, India) V. Saritha (VIT University, India) and H. P. Sultana (VIT University, India)
Information Science Reference • copyright 2015 • 328pp • H/C (ISBN: 9781466673120) • US $200.00 (our price)

www.igi-global.com

701 E. Chocolate Ave., Hershey, PA 17033
Order online at www.igi-global.com or call 717-533-8845 x100
To place a standing order for titles released in this series, contact: cust@igi-global.com
Mon-Fri 8:00 am - 5:00 pm (est) or fax 24 hours a day 717-533-8661

Editorial Advisory Board

Associate Editors

Rajkumar Buyya, *University of Melbourne, Australia*
Anna Goy, *Universita' di Torino, Italy*
Ryan K. L. Ko, *HP Labs Singapore, Singapore*
Maik A. Lindner, *SAP Research, UK*
Shiyong Lu, *Wayne State University, USA*
Yuzhong Sun, *Chinese Academy of Science, China*
Ray Walshe, *Irish Centre for Cloud Computing and Commerce, Ireland*

International Editorial Review Board

Sanjay P. Ahuja, *University of North Florida, USA*
Junaid Arshad, *University of Leeds, UK*
Juan Caceres, *Telefónica Investigación y Desarrollo, Spain*
Jeffrey Chang, *London South Bank University, UK*
Kamal Dahbur, *NYIT, Jordan*
Ravindra Dastikop, *SDMCET, India*
Sam Goundar, *Victoria University of Wellington, New Zealand & KYS International College, Melaka - Malaysia*
Sofyan Hayajneh, *Isra University, Jordan*
Sayed Amir Hoseini, *Iran Telecommunication Research Center, Iran*
Gregory Katsaros, *National Technical University of Athens, Greece*
Mariam Kiran, *University of Sheffield, UK*
Anirban Kundu, *Kuang-Chi Institute of Advanced Technology, China*
Sarat Maharana, *MVJ College of Engineering, Bangalore, India*
Manisha Malhorta, *Maharishi Markandeshwar University, India*
Saurabh Mukherjee, *Banasthali University, India*
Giovanna Petrone, *Università degli Studi di Torino, Italy*
Nikolaos P. Preve, *National Technical University of Athens, Greece*
Vanessa Ratten, *Deakin University, Australia*

Jin Shao, *Peking University, China*
Bassam Shargab, *Isra University, Jordan*
Luis Miguel Vaquero Gonzalez, *HP, Spain*
Chao Wang, *Oak Ridge National Laboratory, USA*
Jiaan Zeng, *Indiana University Bloomington, USA*
Yongqiang Zou, *Tencent Corporation, China*

Table of Contents

Preface xix

Acknowledgment xxxii

Chapter 1
An Entrepreneurial Approach to Cloud Computing Design and Application: Technological
Innovation and Information System Usage 1
    Vanessa Ratten, La Trobe University, Australia

Chapter 2
Using Cloud Computing for E-Government: A New Dawn 15
    Thamer Al-Rousan, Isra University, Pakistan
    Shadi Aljawarneh, Jordan University of Science and Technology, Jordan

Chapter 3
Supply Chain in the Cloud: Opportunities, Barriers, and a Generic Treatment 24
    Goknur Arzu Akyuz, Atilim University, Turkey
    Mohammad Rehan, Atilim University, Turkey

Chapter 4
System Benchmarking on Public Clouds: Comparing Instance Types of Virtual Machine
Clusters 37
    Sanjay P. Ahuja, University of North Florida, USA
    Thomas F. Furman, University of North Florida, USA
    Kerwin E. Roslie, University of North Florida, USA
    Jared T. Wheeler, University of North Florida, USA

Chapter 5
Approaches to Cloud Computing in the Public Sector: Case Studies in UK Local Government 51
    Jeffrey Chang, London South Bank University, UK
    Mark Johnston, Julian Campbell Foundation, UK

Chapter 6
A Mechanism for Securing Hybrid Cloud Outsourced Data: Securing Hybrid Cloud 73
    Abdullah El-Haj, University of Jordan, Jordan
    Shadi Aljawarneh, Jordan University of Science and Technology, Jordan

Chapter 7
Optimal Resource Provisioning in Federated-Cloud Environments 84
    Veena Goswami, KIIT University, India
    Choudhury N. Sahoo, KIIT University, India

Chapter 8
Towards Future IT Service Personalization: Issues in BYOD and the Personal Cloud 102
    Stuart Dillon, University of Waikato, New Zealand
    Florian Stahl, University of Münster, Germany
    Gottfried Vossen, University of Münster, Germany

Chapter 9
User Preference-Based Web Service Composition and Execution Framework 118
    Bassam Al-Shargabi, Isra University, Jordan
    Omar Sabri, Isra University, Jordan

Chapter 10
Cloud Security Engineering Concept and Vision: Concept and Vision 139
    Shadi A. Aljawarneh, Jordan University of Science and Technology, Jordan

Chapter 11
Fairness-Aware Task Allocation for Heterogeneous Multi-Cloud Systems 147
    Sanjaya Kumar Panda, Indian School of Mines Dhanbad, India & VSS University of
        Technology Burla, India
    Roshni Pradhan, VSS University of Technology Burla, India
    Benazir Neha, VSS University of Technology Burla, India
    Sujaya Kumar Sathua, VSS University of Technology Burla, India

Chapter 12
Submesh Allocation in 3D Mesh Multicomputers Using Free Lists: A Corner-Boundary
Approach with Complete Recognition Capability 171
    Saad Bani-Mohammad, Prince Hussein Bin Abdullah College for Information Technology,
        Al al-Bayt University, Jordan
    Ismail Ababneh, Prince Hussein Bin Abdullah College for Information Technology, Al al-
        Bayt University, Jordan
    Motasem Al Smadi, Prince Hussein Bin Abdullah College for Information Technology, Al
        al-Bayt University, Jordan

Chapter 13
Cloud Computing in the 21st Century: A Managerial Perspective for Policies and Practices 188
    Mahesh Raisinghani, Texas Woman's University, USA
    Efosa Carroll Idemudia, Arkansas Tech University, USA
    Meghana Chekuri, Texas Woman's University, USA
    Kendra Fisher, Texas Woman's University, USA
    Jennifer Hanna, Texas Woman's University, USA

Chapter 14
Bio-Inspired Private Information Retrieval System over Cloud Service Using the Social Bees' Lifestyle with a 3D Visualisation..201
    Hadj Ahmed Bouarara, Tahar Moulay University of Saida, Algeria
    Reda Mohamed Hamou, Tahar Moulay University of Saida, Algeria
    Amine Abdelmalek, Tahar Moulay University of Saida, Algeria

Chapter 15
Performance Management on Cloud Using Multi-Priority Queuing Systems 229
    A. Madankan, Yazd University, Iran
    A. Delavar Khalfi, Yazd University, Iran

Chapter 16
An Efficient E-Negotiation Agent Using Rule-Based and Case-Based Approaches.........................245
    Amruta More, Maharashtra Institute of Technology, India
    Sheetal Vij, Maharashtra Institute of Technology, India
    Debajyoti Mukhopadhyay, Maharashtra Institute of Technology, India

Chapter 17
Domain-Based Dynamic Ranking 262
    Sutirtha Kumar Guha, Seacom Engineering College, India
    Anirban Kundu, Netaji Subhash Engineering College, India
    Rana Dattagupta, Jadavpur University, India

Chapter 18
An Approach on Cloud Disk Searching Using Parallel Channels...280
    Saswati Sarkar, Adamas Institute of Technology, India
    Anirban Kundu, Netaji Subhash Engineering College, India

Chapter 19
Data Intensive Cloud Computing: Issues and Challenges 305
    Jayalakshmi D. S., M. S. Ramaiah Institute of Technology, Inida
    R. Srinivasan, S. R. M. University, India
    K. G. Srinivasa, M. S. Ramaiah Institute of Technology, India

Chapter 20
A Key-Based Database Sharding Implementation for Big Data Analytics 321
    Sikha Bagui, University of West Florida, USA
    Loi Nguyen, Development and Technology Center (NETPDTC), USA

Compilation of References 346

About the Contributors 377

Index...386

Detailed Table of Contents

Preface xix

Acknowledgment xxxii

Chapter 1
An Entrepreneurial Approach to Cloud Computing Design and Application: Technological
Innovation and Information System Usage 1
Vanessa Ratten, La Trobe University, Australia

The design and application of cloud computing services is inherently entrepreneurial as it is constantly evolving as a result of technological innovation. This chapter focuses on providing an entrepreneurial approach to understanding change in the cloud computing context by highlighting the importance of innovative system usage. The chapter discusses how cloud computing services are creating a ecosystem of mobile commerce applications that is changing the way consumers, businesses and the government collects, disseminates and stores information. These changes have given way to entrepreneurial service innovations in the cloud domain that are a result of consumer demand for more current and relevant technological innovations. This chapter addresses the role of entrepreneurship in technological innovations by focusing on marketing and learning applications that are unique to cloud computing services. The future research suggestions from this chapter stress the importance nature of being entrepreneurial to encourage technological innovation in the cloud computing context.

Chapter 2
Using Cloud Computing for E-Government: A New Dawn 15
Thamer Al-Rousan, Isra University, Pakistan
Shadi Aljawarneh, Jordan University of Science and Technology, Jordan

For the last two decades, e-government has attracted government around the world to itself. Today almost every country in the world has developed and implemented e-government system in some form or another in order to reduce costs, improve services, save time and increase effectiveness and efficiency in a public sector. With increasing generalization of technology access by citizen and organizations, e-governments across the world face a major challenge in keeping a pace with ever changing technologies and offer an efficient, effective and transparent way of offering its services. Cloud computing is becoming an adoptable technology for many countries. The concept of cloud computing becomes important for each e-government, facilitating its way of work, increasing its productivity and all that leading to cost savings. It will likely have a significant impact on the e-governments in the future. In this paper, we analyzed cloud computing and its applications in the context of e-government.

Chapter 3

Supply Chain in the Cloud: Opportunities, Barriers, and a Generic Treatment 24

Goknur Arzu Akyuz, Atilim University, Turkey

Mohammad Rehan, Atilim University, Turkey

Cloud concept is directly related with the beyond-ERP integrity and collaboration across a number of heterogeneous Supply Chain (SC) partner infrastructures. The technology enables partners to form a collaborative SC community without the burden of significant IT investment. Cloud applications offer significant opportunities from SC perspective, and the assimilation of the Cloud Technology is not complete yet in the Supply Chain domain. It also involves various barriers from implementation perspective, as well as the concerns related with vendor lock-in, security, reliability, privacy and data ownership. This chapter provides a comprehensive coverage of the opportunities and barriers as well as the generic treatment from SC perspective. It also highlights how the cloud technology represents a perfect fit with the ideas of 'Collaborative Supply Chains', 'Business Process Outsourcing' and 'long-term strategic partnerships', which are the key themes characterizing the Supply Chains of today's era. This chapter reveals that the intersection of the topics 'Cloud computing' and 'Supply Chain' is a promising area for further research. Further studies in a multi-partner setting with respect to a variety of configurations, case studies and applications, as well as the security, reliability and data ownership issues are justified.

Chapter 4

System Benchmarking on Public Clouds: Comparing Instance Types of Virtual Machine

Clusters 37

Sanjay P. Ahuja, University of North Florida, USA

Thomas F. Furman, University of North Florida, USA

Kerwin E. Roslie, University of North Florida, USA

Jared T. Wheeler, University of North Florida, USA

There are several public cloud providers that provide service across different cloud models such as IaaS, PaaS, and SaaS. End users require an objective means to assess the performance of the services being offered by the various cloud providers. Benchmarks have typically been used to evaluate the performance of various systems and can play a vital role in assessing performance of the different public cloud platforms in a vendor neutral manner. Amazon's EC2 Service is one of the leading public cloud service providers and offers many different levels of service. The research in this chapter focuses on system level benchmarks and looks into evaluating the memory, CPU, and I/O performance of two different tiers of hardware offered through Amazon's EC2. Using three distinct types of system benchmarks, the performance of the micro spot instance and the M1 small instance are measured and compared. In order to examine the performance and scalability of the hardware, the virtual machines are set up in a cluster formation ranging from two to eight nodes. The results show that the scalability of the cloud is achieved by increasing resources when applicable. This chapter also looks at the economic model and other cloud services offered by Amazon's EC2, Microsoft's Azure, and Google's App Engine.

Chapter 5
Approaches to Cloud Computing in the Public Sector: Case Studies in UK Local Government 51
Jeffrey Chang, London South Bank University, UK
Mark Johnston, Julian Campbell Foundation, UK

Cloud computing refers to a scalable network infrastructure where consumers receive IT services such as software and data storage through the Internet on a subscription basis. Potential benefits include cost savings, simpler IT and reduced energy consumption. The UK government and local authorities, like commercial organisations, are considering cloud-based services. Concerns have been raised, however, over issues such as security, access, data protection and ownership. This study attempts to investigate the likely impact of cloud computing on local government based on a conceptual framework and case studies of four London borough councils. It reveals that the concept of cloud computing is new and not clearly understood. Local authorities, who face further cuts in government funding, welcome a cloud-based IT infrastructure which may lead to considerable savings. Yet local government is conservative, so with their risk-adverse attitude local authorities are more likely to adopt a hybrid approach to implementation.

Chapter 6
A Mechanism for Securing Hybrid Cloud Outsourced Data: Securing Hybrid Cloud 73
Abdullah El-Haj, University of Jordan, Jordan
Shadi Aljawarneh, Jordan University of Science and Technology, Jordan

The existing research related to security mechanisms only focuses on securing the flow of information in the communication networks. There is a lack of work on improving the performance of networks to meet quality of service (QoS) constrains for various services. The security mechanisms work by encryption and decryption of the information, but do not consider the optimised use of the network resources. In this paper the authors propose a Secure Data Transmission Mechanism (SDTM) with Preemption Algorithm that combines between security and quality of service. Their developed SDTM enhanced with Malicious Packets Detection System (MPDS) which is a set of technologies and solutions. It enforces security policy and bandwidth compliance on all devices seeking to access Cloud network computing resources, in order to limit damage from emerging security threats and to allow network access only to compliant and trusted endpoint devices.

Chapter 7
Optimal Resource Provisioning in Federated-Cloud Environments 84
Veena Goswami, KIIT University, India
Choudhury N. Sahoo, KIIT University, India

Cloud computing has emerged as a new paradigm for accessing distributed computing resources such as infrastructure, hardware platform, and software applications on-demand over the internet as services. Multiple Clouds can collaborate in order to integrate different service-models or service providers for end-to-end-requirements. Intercloud Federation and Service delegation models are part of Multi-Cloud environment where the broader target is to achieve infinite pool of resources. This chapter presents an optimal resource management framework for Federated-cloud environments. Each service model caters to specific type of requirements and there are already number of players with own customized products/ services offered. They propose an analytical queueing network model to improve the efficiency of the system. Numerical results indicate that the proposed provisioning technique detects changes in arrival pattern, resource demands that occur over time and allocates multiple virtualized IT resources accordingly to achieve application QoS targets.

Chapter 8

Towards Future IT Service Personalization: Issues in BYOD and the Personal Cloud...................... 102
Stuart Dillon, University of Waikato, New Zealand
Florian Stahl, University of Münster, Germany
Gottfried Vossen, University of Münster, Germany

Cloud services are ubiquitous today and increasingly used for a variety of purposes, including personal and professional communication, social networking, media streaming, calendar management, file storage etc. In recent years, a fast evolution of cloud services from private applications to corporate usage has been observed. This has led to the question of how private and business cloud services can be dual-accessed through a single device, in particular a mobile device that is used as part of a BYOD (Bring Your Own Device) policy. This chapter considers the issues that arise from a consolidation of private and professional applications when accessed from a single device and introduces the term "personal cloud" to characterise such situations. It also surveys recent work in the field and finally presents an approach to cloud governance from a business perspective focusing in particular on security tokens, hardware keys and smart containers, thereby providing a glimpse into the future of IT service personalization.

Chapter 9

User Preference-Based Web Service Composition and Execution Framework................................. 118
Bassam Al-Shargabi, Isra University, Jordan
Omar Sabri, Isra University, Jordan

the motivation behind this chapter is that Service Oriented architecture issued to compose an application as a set of services that are language and platform independent, communicate with each other, Therefore, user preferences rules in web service composition process plays crucial role and has opened a wide spectrum of challenge, In this chapter, an agent for composing web services based on user preferences was introduced to fulfill a certain process, where the user preferences are essential for determining which web service are to be selected. In other word, the agent designed to maintain the following function: an intelligent web services selection and planning based on user preferences(such as price or availability), along with web services execution, tracking and adaptation.

Chapter 10

Cloud Security Engineering Concept and Vision: Concept and Vision 139
Shadi A. Aljawarneh, Jordan University of Science and Technology, Jordan

The research community found that a software system should be evolved once every few months to ensure it is adapted to the real-world environment. The system evolution requires regularly amendments that append, delete, or alter features. It also migrates or converts the software system from one operating platform to another. These amendments may result in requirements/ specifications that were satisfied in a previous release of a software system not being satisfied in the subsequent versions. As a result, software evolutionary changes violate security requirements, and then a system may become vulnerable to different kinds of attacks. In this paper, concepts and visions are presented to avoid/minimize the Cloud security issues.

Chapter 11

Fairness-Aware Task Allocation for Heterogeneous Multi-Cloud Systems 147

Sanjaya Kumar Panda, Indian School of Mines Dhanbad, India & VSS University of Technology Burla, India
Roshni Pradhan, VSS University of Technology Burla, India
Benazir Neha, VSS University of Technology Burla, India
Sujaya Kumar Sathua, VSS University of Technology Burla, India

Cloud computing is rapidly growing for its on-demand services over the Internet. The customers can use these services by placing the requirements in the form of leases. In IaaS cloud, the customer submits the leases in one of the form, namely advance reservation (AR) and best effort (BE). The AR lease has higher priority over the BE lease. Hence, it can preempt the BE lease. It results in starvation among the BE leases and is unfair to the BE leases. In this chapter, the authors present fairness-aware task allocation (FATA) algorithm for heterogeneous multi-cloud systems, which aims to provide fairness among AR and BE leases. We have performed rigorous experiments on some benchmark and synthetic datasets. The performance is measured in terms of two metrics, namely makespan and average cloud utilization. The experimental result shows the superiority of the proposed algorithm over the existing algorithm.

Chapter 12

Submesh Allocation in 3D Mesh Multicomputers Using Free Lists: A Corner-Boundary Approach with Complete Recognition Capability 171

Saad Bani-Mohammad, Prince Hussein Bin Abdullah College for Information Technology, Al al-Bayt University, Jordan
Ismail Ababneh, Prince Hussein Bin Abdullah College for Information Technology, Al al-Bayt University, Jordan
Motasem Al Smadi, Prince Hussein Bin Abdullah College for Information Technology, Al al-Bayt University, Jordan

This chapter presents an extensive evaluation of a new contiguous allocation strategy proposed for 3D mesh multicomputers. The strategy maintains a list of maximal free sub-meshes and gives priority to allocating corner and boundary free sub-meshes. This strategy, which we refer to as Turning Corner-Boundary Free List (TCBFL) strategy, is compared, using extensive simulation experiments, to several existing allocation strategies for 3D meshes. In addition to allocation strategies, two job scheduling schemes, First-Come-First-Served (FCFS) and Shortest-Service-Demand (SSD) are considered in comparing the performance of the allocation strategies. The simulation results show that TCBFL produces average turnaround times and mean system utilization values that are superior to those of the existing allocation strategies. The results also reveal that SSD scheduling is much better than FCFS scheduling. Thus, the scheduling and allocation strategies both have substantial effect on the performance of contiguous allocation strategies in 3D mesh-connected multicomputers.

Chapter 13

Cloud Computing in the 21st Century: A Managerial Perspective for Policies and Practices 188

Mahesh Raisinghani, Texas Woman's University, USA

Efosa Carroll Idemudia, Arkansas Tech University, USA

Meghana Chekuri, Texas Woman's University, USA

Kendra Fisher, Texas Woman's University, USA

Jennifer Hanna, Texas Woman's University, USA

The constant changes in technology has posed serious challenges to top management teams, employees, and customers on how to collect, store, and process data for competitive advantage and to make better decisions. In this chapter, to address this issue, we present the managerial perspective of cloud computing that provides the infrastructure and/or tools for decision making in the 21st century. Since the year 2000, the interest in cloud computing has had a steady increase. (Mason, 2002) Not only has cloud computing substantially lowered computing costs for corporations, it continues to increase their abilities for market offerings and to access customers' information with ease. Cloud computing has allowed managers to focus more on their business plans and bottom line to enhance competitive advantage.

Chapter 14

Bio-Inspired Private Information Retrieval System over Cloud Service Using the Social Bees'
Lifestyle with a 3D Visualisation.. 201

Hadj Ahmed Bouarara, Tahar Moulay University of Saida, Algeria

Reda Mohamed Hamou, Tahar Moulay University of Saida, Algeria

Amine Abdelmalek, Tahar Moulay University of Saida, Algeria

In the last decade, a new paradigm had seen the light named Cloud Computing, which allows the delocalization of data and applications on a dematerialized infrastructure accessible from Internet. Unfortunately, the cloud services are facing many drawbacks especially in terms of security and data confidentiality. However, in a world where digital information is everywhere, finding the desired information has become a crucial problem. For the purpose to preserve the user privacy life new approaches and ideas had been published. The content of this chapter is a new system of bio-inspired private information retrieval (BI-PIR) using the lifestyle of social bees, which allows both to find and hid, the sensitive desired information. It is based on a multi-filters cryptosystem used by the server for the encryption of stored document and the retrieval model using a combination of filters by 3 types of workers bees (Purveyor, guardian and cleaner), the queen bee represents the query, and the hive represents the class of relevant documents. We have tested this system on the benchmark MEDLINE dataset with panoply of validation tools (recall, precision, f-measure, entropy, silence, noise, and accuracy) and a comparative study had been realized with other systems existed in literature. Finally, a 3D visualization tool had been developed in order to make the results in graphical format understandable by humans. Our objectives is to improve the services quality of cloud computing.

Chapter 15

Performance Management on Cloud Using Multi-Priority Queuing Systems 229

    A. Madankan, Yazd University, Iran

    A. Delavar Khalfi, Yazd University, Iran

Cloud computing is known as a new trend for computing resource provision. The process of entering into the cloud is formed as queue, so that each user has to wait until the current user is being served. In this model, the web applications are modeled as queues and the virtual machines are modeled as service centers. M/M/K model is used for multiple priority and multiple server systems with preemptive priorities. To achieve that it distinguish two groups of priority classes that each classes includes multiple items, each having their own arrival and service rate. It derives an approximate method to estimate the steady state probabilities. Based on these probabilities, it can derives approximations for a wide range of relevant performance characteristics, such as the expected postponement time for each item class and the first and second moment of the number of items of a certain type in the system.

Chapter 16

An Efficient E-Negotiation Agent Using Rule-Based and Case-Based Approaches 245

    Amruta More, Maharashtra Institute of Technology, India

    Sheetal Vij, Maharashtra Institute of Technology, India

    Debajyoti Mukhopadhyay, Maharashtra Institute of Technology, India

The research in the area of automated negotiation systems is going on in many universities. This research is mainly focused on making a practically feasible, faster and reliable E-negotiation system. The ongoing work in this area is happening in the laboratories of the universities mainly for training and research purpose. There are number of negotiation systems such as Henry, Kasbaah, Bazaar, Auction Bot, Inspire, Magnet. Our research is based on making an agent software for E-negotiation which will give faster results and also is secure and flexible. Cloud Computing provides security and flexibility to the user data. Using these features we propose an E-negotiation system, in which, all product information and agent details are stored on the cloud. This system proposes three conditions for making successful negotiation. First rule based, where agent will check user requirements with rule based data. Second case based, where an agent will see case based data to check any similar previous negotiation case is matching to the user requirement. Third bilateral negotiation model, if both rules based data and case based data are not matching with the user requirement, then agent use bilateral negotiation model for negotiation. After completing negotiation process, agents give feedback to the user about whether negotiation is successful or not. Using rule based reasoning and case based reasoning this system will improve the efficiency and success rate of the negotiation process.

Chapter 17

Domain-Based Dynamic Ranking 262

Sutirtha Kumar Guha, Seacom Engineering College, India
Anirban Kundu, Netaji Subhash Engineering College, India
Rana Dattagupta, Jadavpur University, India

In this chapter a domain based ranking methodology is proposed in cloud environment. Web pages from the cloud are clustered as 'Primary Domain' and 'Secondary Domain'. 'Primary' domain Web pages are fetched based on the direct matching with the keywords. 'Primary Domain' Web pages are ranked based on Relevancy Factor (RF) and Turbulence Factor (TF). 'Secondary Domain' is constructed by Nearest Keywords and Similar Web pages. Nearest Keywords are the keywords similar to the matched keywords. Similar Web pages are the Web pages having Nearest Keywords. Matched Web pages of 'Primary' and 'Secondary' domain are ranked separately. A wide range of Web pages from the cloud would be available and ranked more efficiently by this proposed approach.

Chapter 18

An Approach on Cloud Disk Searching Using Parallel Channels 280

Saswati Sarkar, Adamas Institute of Technology, India
Anirban Kundu, Netaji Subhash Engineering College, India

In this chapter, Cloud disk searching technique is going to be proposed. Cloud based searching mechanism shows the utility of indexing, balancing, and data storage in cloud. The Chapter exhibits complexity of cloud based searching algorithms in real-time scenario. The proposed cloud based disk searching technique using parallel channels is searching data in less time consumption. Comparison graphs have been demonstrated for time difference realization in cloud. Parallel concepts have been introduced to facilitate searching the cloud. Sequential and several parallel situations have been compared using time graphsLoad balance monitoring, data searching and data accessing in less time have been introduced in this chapter.

Chapter 19

Data Intensive Cloud Computing: Issues and Challenges 305

Jayalakshmi D. S., M. S. Ramaiah Institute of Technology, Inida
R. Srinivasan, S. R. M. University, India
K. G. Srinivasa, M. S. Ramaiah Institute of Technology, India

Processing Big Data is a huge challenge for today's technology. There is a need to find, apply and analyze new ways of computing to make use of the Big Data so as to derive business and scientific value from it. Cloud computing with its promise of seemingly infinite computing resources is seen as the solution to this problem. Data Intensive computing on cloud builds upon the already mature parallel and distributed computing technologies such HPC, grid and cluster computing. However, handling Big Data in the cloud presents its own challenges. In this chapter, we analyze issues specific to data intensive cloud computing and provides a study on available solutions in programming models, data distribution and replication, resource provisioning and scheduling with reference to data intensive applications in cloud. Future directions for further research enabling data intensive cloud applications in cloud environment are identified.

Chapter 20

A Key-Based Database Sharding Implementation for Big Data Analytics 321
Sikha Bagui, University of West Florida, USA
Loi Nguyen, Development and Technology Center (NETPDTC), USA

In this chapter, we use MySQL Database Cluster to demonstrate and discover the capabilities of key based database sharding and provide the implementation details to build a key based sharded database system. After the implementation section, we present some examples of datasets that were sharded using our implementation. The sharded data is then used for data mining, specifically association rule mining. We present the results (association rules) for the sharded data as well as the non-sharded data.

Compilation of References 346

About the Contributors 377

Index 386

Preface

Do not worry about your difficulties in Mathematics. I can assure you mine are still greater. -Albert Einstein

The corresponding book publication summarizes the recent research papers on Cloud Computing design, technologies and applications entitled, "Advanced Research on Cloud Computing Design and Applications."

This book summarizes some current trends in the Cloud Computing such as Cloud services, applications and technologies, and explores one key area of growth: Cloud computing. To illustrate the role of Applications and Services in the growth of Cloud computing industries, a number of examples focusing on the learning, government and security are used. Recommendations for future areas of IJCAC journal are presented.

This book is intended for researchers and practitioners who are interested in issues that arise from using technologies of cloud computing advancements. In addition, this book is also targeted to anyone who wants to learn more about the cloud computing research advancements in design and applications. Cloud computing has become a hot topic in recent years and people at different levels in any organization need to understand cloud computing in different ways.

BOOK DESCRIPTION, MISSION, AND OBJECTIVES

This book focuses on advanced research in the practical applications and the theoretical foundations of Cloud Computing, through presentation of the most up-to-date advances and new directions of research in the field from various scholarly, professional, and practitioner perspectives. An interdisciplinary look at Cloud Computing, including engineering and business aspects, such book covers and encourages high-quality research exposition on such topics as virtualization technology, utility computing, SaaS, and Grid Computing, as well as web services, SOA, Web 2.0, and Services Computing.

Cloud Computing marks a significant change of IT service delivery from on-premise installation to virtualized, on demand, and pay as you go approach. From an IT service provider's perspective, Cloud Computing means delivering the IT capability to the massive users with highly dynamic and virtualized resources. From an IT user's perspective, Cloud Computing means enjoying the Cloud services with extremely low cost without the burden to build IT infrastructure by one's own. The recent rushed announcement of the Open Cloud Manifesto (OCM) confirms that even those late to the party see it as a major sea change in the industry.

Cloud Computing covers both the traditional enterprise IT services and new massive consumer IT services. Examples in the formal case include upgrading traditional data center with virtualization technologies, realizing fast production level infrastructure topologies through private Cloud. Examples in the later case include search Cloud service (Google), e-Business Cloud service (Alibaba in China).

The main mission of this book "Advanced Research on Cloud Computing Design and Applications" is to be the premier and authoritative source for the most innovative scholarly and professional research and information pertaining to aspects of Cloud Applications and Computing. Such book presents advancements in the state-of-the-art, standards, and practices of Cloud Computing, in an effort to identify emerging trends that will ultimately define the future of "the Cloud." Topics such as Cloud Infrastructure Services, Cloud Platform Services, Cloud Application Services (SaaS), Cloud Business Services, Cloud Human Services are discussed through original papers, review papers, technical reports, case studies, and conference reports for reference use by academics and practitioners alike.

This book is intended to reflect new directions of research and report latest advances. It is a platform for rapid dissemination of high quality research / application / work-in-progress articles on Could Computing solutions for managing challenges and problems within the highlighted scope.

The objectives of this book are multi-folds, including,

1. Establish a significant channel of communication among Cloud Computing researchers, engineers, practitioners and IT policy makers;
2. Provide a space to publish and share the latest high quality research results in the area of Cloud Computing;
3. Promote and coordinate international collaboration in the standards of Cloud and Utility Computing to meet the need to broaden the applicability and scope of the current and future research of Cloud Computing.

Topics to be discussed in this book include the following:

- Technology & service
- Application
- Architecture
- Standard
- Management and optimization
- Cloud engineering
- Business

WHAT THIS BOOK COVERS

In this book, we will present the current state of cloud computing research advancements on design, and applications. So that we will summarize each advanced research, its influence in the science of cloud computing and applications and the marketing feasibility as follows:

Chapter 1: An entrepreneurial approach to cloud computing design and application: Technological innovation and information system usage.
Vanessa Ratten.

The design and application of cloud computing services is inherently entrepreneurial as it is constantly evolving as a result of technological innovation. This chapter focuses on providing an entrepreneurial approach to understanding change in the cloud computing context by highlighting the importance of innovative system usage. Cloud computing services are creating an ecosystem of mobile commerce applications that is changing the way consumers, businesses and the government collects, disseminates and stores information. These changes have given way to entrepreneurial service innovations in the cloud domain that are a result of consumer demand for more current and relevant technological innovations. This chapter addresses the role of entrepreneurship in technological innovations by focusing on marketing and learning applications that are unique to cloud computing services. The future research suggestions from the chapter stress the importance nature of being entrepreneurial to encourage technological innovation in the cloud computing context.

Importance of the chapter and the area: More research is need on the entrepreneurial approaches to cloud computing as there have been a lot of security issues surrounding the storage of online information that has made its future applications contingent of the proper application of this technological innovation. This chapter is important because cloud computing is continually emerging as an innovative technology that derives its benefits from information system usage. The usage of cloud computing design and application will change depending on the entrepreneurial approaches that developers, businesses and consumers take towards creating better security and knowledge features.

Marketing feasibility: This chapter has good marketing feasibility because most businesses and consumers are using cloud computing in some way and this will increase as cloud computing enhances its security and privacy features in the future.

Chapter 2: Using Cloud Computing for E-Government: A New Dawn.
Thamer Al-Rousan and Shadi Aljawarneh.

For the last two decades, e-government has attracted government around the world to itself. Today almost every country in the world has developed and implemented e-government system in some form or another in order to reduce costs, improve services, save time and increase effectiveness and efficiency in a public sector. With increasing generalization of technology access by citizen and organizations, e-governments across the world face a major challenge in keeping a pace with ever changing technologies and offer an efficient, effective and transparent way of offering its services. Cloud computing is becoming an adoptable technology for many countries. The concept of cloud computing becomes important for each e-government, facilitating its way of work, increasing its productivity and all that leading to cost savings. It will likely have a significant impact on the e-governments in the future. In this chapter, we analyzed cloud computing and its applications in the context of e-government.

Importance of the chapter and the area: E-government refers to government processes in which information and Communications technology (ICT) play an active and significant role for efficient and effective governance, and for making government more accessible and accountable to the citizens, businesses and other governments. Information and Communication Technologies are the key factor for global society development. Innovations in information and communication technology are always there in order to increase productivity, to change the way we work, to grow business economy, to share global knowledge and to have automated business processes and communications. One important innovation in information and communication technology is cloud computing.

Cloud computing is an emerging computing paradigm that promises to provide opportunities to deliver a diversity of computing services in a way that has not been experienced before. The use of cloud computing in e-government has many benefits, such as cost savings, scalability, integration, reusability of services, or high availability, which make cloud computing interesting for many areas.

Marketing feasibility: This chapter discusses the cloud computing and its applications in the context of e-government and identify the key factors that make cloud computing attractive to the e-government scene. This chapter has a good marketing feasibility because it explains the critical needs to adopting the cloud computing on e-government. The Cloud architectures will help the government to reduce operating costs and increase end user satisfaction levels. Government's ministries, interested in the environmental pollution and involved in the "Go green" projects, collaborate with each other through cloud computing, using a common infrastructure, platform and applications and delivering cost-effective services to the public. All of these efforts can drive the growth of the economy and government productivity.

Chapter 3: Supply Chain in the Cloud: Opportunities, Barriers and a Generic Treatment.
Goknur Arzu Akyuz and Mohammad Rehan

Cloud Computing is gaining momentum and receiving more and more interest in the literature as a very recent IT paradigm. By offering flexibility, cost reductions, platform independence and on-demand service, cloud paradigm opens up tremendous opportunities from Supply Chain (SC) perspective. However, extant literature reveals that adoption and assimilation of the technology is not mature in SC domain as yet. There exists significant barriers regarding the assimilation, and cloud-based modelling initiatives are only recent. To fill this gap, this study discusses cloud computing from SC perspective, and proposes a generic representation based on cloud philosophy. The proposed representation is a conceptual, flexible and customizable one, utilizing the cloud benefits in a multi-partner setting. Contribution of this study lies in comprehensive treatment of the intersection of cloud computing and SC topics, as well as providing a generic representation.

Importance of the chapter and the area: Cloud concept is directly related with the beyond-ERP integrity and collaboration across a number of heterogeneous Supply Chain partner infrastructures. The technology enables partners to form a collaborative Supply Chain community without the burden of significant IT investment. Cloud applications offer significant opportunities from Supply Chain perspective, and the assimilation of the Cloud technology is not complete yet in Supply Chain domain. It also involves various barriers from implementation perspective, as well as the concerns related with vendor lock-in, security, reliability, privacy and data ownership.

Hence, the chapter is important by providing a comprehensive coverage of the opportunities and barriers as well as the generic treatment from Supply Chain perspective. It also highlights how the cloud technology represents a perfect fit with the ideas of 'Collaborative Supply Chains', 'Business Process Outsourcing' and 'long-term strategic partnerships, which are the key themes characterising the Supply Chains of today's era.

Therefore, the intersection of the topics 'Cloud computing' and 'Supply Chain' is a promising area for further research. Further studies in a multi-partner setting with respect to a variety of configurations, case studies and applications, as well as the security, reliability and data ownerhsip issues are justified.

Marketing feasibility: The study addresses both Supply Chain and IT domains, provides a generic treatment, and contains technical as well as managerial perspectives. Thus, the authors believe that the chapter will be appealing to a large profile of audience from both domains, including researchers and practitioners. Anybody dealing with ERP add-ons, Strategic Supply Chain Management and outsourcing, as well as cloud technology in general can benefit from this chapter. Therefore we think that the chapter has significant marketing potential.

Chapter 4: System Benchmarking on Public Clouds: Comparing Instance Types of Virtual Machine Clusters.
Sanjay P. Ahuja.

There are several public cloud providers that provide service across different cloud models such as IaaS, PaaS, and SaaS. Benchmarks have typically been used to evaluate the performance of various systems and can play a vital role in assessing performance of the different public cloud platforms in a vendor neutral manner. Amazon's EC2 Service is one of the leading public cloud service providers and offers many different levels of service. This research focuses on system level benchmarks and looks into evaluating the memory, CPU, and I/O performance of two different tiers of hardware offered through Amazon's EC2. Using three distinct types of system benchmarks, the performance of the micro spot instance and the M1 small instance are measured and compared. In order to examine the performance and scalability of the hardware, the virtual machines are set up in a cluster formation ranging from two to eight nodes. The results show that the scalability of the cloud is achieved by increasing resources when applicable.

Importance of the chapter and the area: The cloud is an emerging platform that is taking shape as more vendors offer services and researchers delve deeper into how to use it and how to measure the level of services offered in a vendor agnostic manner. Currently, reliance is placed upon the specifications that each cloud vendor publishes to judge price and performance comparisons. Performance is the one of the key factors for any enterprise when determining the true benefits of cloud computing. Benchmarks have typically been used to evaluate the performance of various systems and can play a vital role in assessing performance of the different cloud platforms in a vendor neutral manner. Benchmarking would allow enterprises to perform transparent and insightful comparisons to see how various types of applications run on different clouds with various kinds of instance configurations. The goal of cloud benchmarking is to help developers predict the behavior of the targeted application and help users to know the performance offered by the target applications for comparison with other offerings. Benchmarking in the cloud computing world can help establishing a baseline of user's application ability to support business requirements. Many vendors/cloud providers do not reveal the details about the implementations of the services provided by them. So it helps organizations or end users to review the benchmarks and decide which cloud provider is better suited to their needs.

Marketing feasibility: This chapter has excellent marketing feasibility. Cloud computing is experiencing dynamic growth with even governments adopting it to save costs. Smartphones and tablets are bringing cloud-based applications, such as Facebook and Twitter, onto mobile devices. With the amount of data increasing exponentially dependency on the cloud is increasing. Need is growing for cost effectively processing and archiving huge amounts of data to the cloud for all content types—social media feeds, health care records, scientific data, financial data etc. Studies have shown that cloud computing has a role in stimulating the economy and creating jobs. The economic appeal from cloud computing partly stems from the ability for enterprises to convert capital expenditures to operational expenditures and the pay-as-you model. There is a need for the researchers to evaluate the performance of various cloud offerings using vendor neutral benchmarks. Research into new benchmarks for the cloud is growing.

Chapter 5: Approaches to Cloud Computing in the public sector: Case studies in UK Local Government. Jeffrey Chang and Mark Johnston.

Cloud computing refers to a scalable network infrastructure where consumers receive IT services such as software and data storage through the Internet on a subscription basis. Potential benefits include cost savings, simpler IT and reduced energy consumption. The UK government and local authorities, like commercial organisations, are considering cloud-based services. Concerns have been raised, however, over issues such as security, access, data protection and ownership. This study attempts to investigate the likely impact of cloud computing on local government based on a conceptual framework and case studies of four London borough councils. It reveals that the concept of cloud computing is new and not clearly understood. Local authorities, who face further cuts in government funding, welcome a cloud-based IT infrastructure which may lead to considerable savings. Yet local government is conservative, so with their risk-adverse attitude local authorities are more likely to adopt a hybrid approach to implementation.

Importance of the chapter and the area: Cloud computing is an emerging area that has received a lot of attention lately. While an increasing number of studies on cloud computing have been focused on commercial organisations that are moving to a simpler cloud-based IT infrastructure and saving costs, little research has been carried out from the public sector's perspective. However, public organisations are facing unprecedented economic challenges and funding cuts. They have just the same need as private sector organisations to transform their current IT structures to more cost-efficient ones. Cost efficiency is one of the benefits cloud computing promises. The chapter is important because it begins to fill the gap in the current cloud literature and identify the critical factors when local government considers cloud-based IT services. Future research needs to continue to address this important area.

Marketing feasibility: The chapter would attract a wide range of readers, from academic researchers in the subject area to decision makers within public sector organisations. The findings of the study bring an understanding as to why UK local authorities would consider cloud and what approach and implementation methods they might employ. The perception and experience garnered from UK local government in this study, and the recommendations made, are applicable not only to other local authorities but more widely to other public sector organisations both in the UK and around the globe.

Chapter 6: A Mechanism for Securing Hybrid Cloud Outsourced Data: Securing Hybrid Cloud. Abdullah El-Haj and Shadi Aljawarneh.

The existing research related to security mechanisms only focuses on securing the flow of information in the communication networks. There is a lack of work on improving the performance of networks to meet quality of service (QoS) constrains for various services. The security mechanisms work by encryption and decryption of the information, but do not consider the optimised use of the network resources. In this chapter the authors propose a Secure Data Transmission Mechanism (SDTM) with Preemption Algorithm that combines between security and quality of service. Their developed SDTM enhanced with Malicious Packets Detection System (MPDS) which is a set of technologies and solutions. It enforces security policy and bandwidth compliance on all devices seeking to access Cloud network computing resources, in order to limit damage from emerging security threats and to allow network access only to compliant and trusted endpoint devices.

Chapter 7: Optimal Resource Provisioning in Federated-Cloud Environments: Optimal Resource Provisioning in Federated-Cloud.
Veena Goswami.

Cloud computing has emerged as a new paradigm for accessing distributed computing resources such as infrastructure, hardware platform, and software applications on-demand over the internet as services. Multiple Clouds can collaborate in order to integrate different service-models or service providers for end-to-end-requirements. Intercloud Federation and Service delegation models are part of Multi-Cloud environment where the broader target is to achieve infinite pool of resources. This chapter presents an optimal resource management framework for Federated-cloud environments. Each service model caters to specific type of requirements and there are already number of players with own customized products/ services offered. They propose an analytical queueing network model to improve the efficiency of the system. Numerical results indicate that the proposed provisioning technique detects changes in arrival pattern, resource demands that occur over time and allocates multiple virtualized IT resources accordingly to achieve application QoS targets.

Chapter 8: Towards Future IT Service Personalization: Issues in BYOD and the Personal Cloud.
Stuart Dillon, Florian Stahl and Gottfried Vossen.

Cloud services are ubiquitous today and increasingly used for a variety of purposes, including personal and professional communication, social networking, media streaming, calendar management, file storage etc. In recent years, a fast evolution of cloud services from private applications to corporate usage has been observed. This has led to the question of how private and business cloud services can be dual-accessed through a single device, in particular a mobile device that is used as part of a BYOD (Bring Your Own Device) policy. This chapter considers the issues that arise from a consolidation of private and professional applications when accessed from a single device and introduces the term "personal cloud" to characterise such situations. It also surveys recent work in the field and finally presents an approach to cloud governance from a business perspective focusing in particular on security tokens, hardware keys and smart containers, thereby providing a glimpse into the future of IT service personalization.

Chapter 9: User Preference based Web Service Composition and Execution Framework.
Bassam Al-shargabi and Omar Sabri

The main motivation of using Service Oriented architecture is to compose an application as a set of services that are language and platform independent, communicate with each other, Therefore, user preferences rules in web service composition process plays crucial role and has opened a wide spectrum of challenge, In this paper, an agent for composing web services based on user preferences was introduced to fulfill a certain process, where the user preferences are essential for determining which web service are to be selected. In other word, the agent designed to maintain the following function: an intelligent web services selection and planning based on user preferences (such as price or availability), along with web services execution, tracking and adaptation.

Chapter 10: Cloud Security Engineering Concept and Vision.
Shadi Aljawarneh.

The research community found that a software system should be evolved once every few months to ensure it is adapted to the real-world environment. The system evolution requires regularly amendments that append, delete, or alter features. It also migrates or converts the software system from one operating platform to another. These amendments may result in requirements/ specifications that were satisfied in a previous release of a software system not being satisfied in the subsequent versions. As a result, software evolutionary changes violate security requirements, and then a system may become vulnerable to different kinds of attacks. In this chapter, concepts and visions are presented to avoid/minimize the Cloud security issues.

Chapter 11: Fairness-Aware Task Allocation for Heterogeneous Multi-Cloud Systems.
Sanjaya Kumar Panda, Roshni Pradhan, Benazir Neha and Sujaya Kumar Sathua.

Cloud computing is rapidly growing for its on-demand services over the Internet. The customers can use these services by placing the requirements in the form of leases. In IaaS cloud, the customer submits the leases in one of the form, namely advance reservation (AR) and best effort (BE). The AR lease has higher priority over the BE lease. Hence, it can preempt the BE lease. It results in starvation among the BE leases and is unfair to the BE leases. In this chapter, the authors present fairness-aware task allocation (FATA) algorithm for heterogeneous multi-cloud systems, which aims to provide fairness among AR and BE leases. We have performed rigorous experiments on some benchmark and synthetic datasets. The performance is measured in terms of two metrics, namely makespan and average cloud utilization. The experimental result shows the superiority of the proposed algorithm over the existing algorithm.

Chapter 12: Submesh Allocation in 3D Mesh Multicomputers Using Free Lists: A Corner-Boundary Approach with Complete Recognition Capability.
Saad Bani-Mohammad, Ismail Ababneh and Motasem Al Smadi.

This chapter presents an extensive evaluation of a new contiguous allocation strategy proposed for 3D mesh multicomputers. The strategy maintains a list of maximal free sub-meshes and gives priority to allocating corner and boundary free sub-meshes. This strategy, which we refer to as Turning Corner-Boundary Free List (TCBFL) strategy, is compared, using extensive simulation experiments, to several existing allocation strategies for 3D meshes. In addition to allocation strategies, two job scheduling schemes, First-Come-First-Served (FCFS) and Shortest-Service-Demand (SSD) are considered in comparing the performance of the allocation strategies. The simulation results show that TCBFL produces average turnaround times and mean system utilization values that are superior to those of the existing allocation strategies. The results also reveal that SSD scheduling is much better than FCFS scheduling. Thus, the scheduling and allocation strategies both have substantial effect on the performance of contiguous allocation strategies in 3D mesh-connected multicomputers.

Chapter 13: Cloud Computing in the 21st Century: A Managerial Perspective for Policies and Practices. Mahesh Raisinghani, Efosa Carroll Idemudia, Meghana Chekuri, Kendra Fisher and Jennifer Hanna.

The constant changes in technology has posed serious challenges to top management teams, employees, and customers on how to collect, store, and process data for competitive advantage and to make better decisions. To address this issue, we present the managerial perspective of cloud computing that provides the infrastructure and/or tools for decision making in the 21st century. Since the year 2000, the interest in cloud computing has had a steady increase. (Mason, 2002) Not only has cloud computing substantially lowered computing costs for corporations, it continues to increase their abilities for market offerings and to access customers' information with ease. Cloud computing has allowed managers to focus more on their business plans and bottom line to enhance competitive advantage.

Chapter 14: Bio-Inspired Private Information Retrieval System over Cloud Service using the Social Bees' Lifestyle with a 3D Visualisation.
Hadj Ahmed Bouarara, Reda Mohamed Hamou and Abdelmalek Amine.

Recently, a new kind of web services had seen the light under the name of Cloud Computing, which represents the dematerialisation of software, systems and infrastructures, based on the virtualisation techniques. In other hand, the users of cloud services starting to ask about their privacy protection.The content of our work is a new system of bio-inspired private information retrieval (PIR), composed of four steps: the authentication to ensure the identification of authorised users. The encryption of stored documents, by the server using the multi-filter cryptosystem based on the life of workers bees. The retrieval model using a combination of distances by social worker bees, where a document must pass through three filters controlled with 3 types of workers, the bee queen represents the query, and the hive represents the class of relevant documents. Experimentation and comparison phase using MEDLINE dataset. Finally, a 3D visualization step in order to make the result in graphical format understandable by humans as a 3D cube. Our objectives is to improve the response to users' needs.

Chapter 15: Performance Management on Cloud Using Multi Priority Queuing Systems: Performance Management on Cloud Using MPQ Systems.
Ali Madankan and Ali Delavar Khalafi.

The process of entering into the cloud is generally in the form of queue, so that each user needs to wait until the current user is being served. In this model, the web applications are modeled as queues and the virtual machines are modeled as service centers. There is no Virtual Machine live migration involved in this model which makes it much simpler than some existing models. It has shown how the queuing model, M/M/K model is used for multiple priority and multiple server systems with preemptive priorities. To achieve that the paper distinguish two groups of priority classes that each classes includes multiple items, each having their own arrival and service rate. It derives an approximate method to estimate the steady state probabilities with an approximation error that can be made at the expense of some more numerical matrix iterations. It can derive approximations for a wide range of relevant performance characteristics, such as the expected postponement time for each item class and the first and second moment of the number of items of a certain type in the system.

Chapter 16: An Efficient E-Negotiation Agent using Rule Based and Case Based Approaches: An E-Negotiation Agent.
Debajyoti Mukhopadhyay, Sheetal Vij and Amruta More.

Research in the area of automated negotiation systems is going on in many universities. This research is mainly focused on making a practically feasible, faster and reliable E-negotiation system. The ongoing work in this area is happening in the laboratories of the universities mainly for training and research purpose. There are number of negotiation systems such as Henry, Kasbaah, Bazaar, Auction Bot, Inspire, Magnet. Our research is based on making an agent software for E-negotiation which will give faster results and also is secure and flexible. The negotiation process can be transformed into rules and cases. Using these features, a new automated negotiation model for agent integrating Rule based and Case based reasoning can be derived. Cloud Computing provides security and flexibility to the user data.. Using rule based reasoning and case based reasoning this system should improve the efficiency and success rate of the negotiation process.

Chapter 17: Domain based Dynamic Ranking.
Sutirtha Kumar Guha, Anirban Kundu and Rana Dattagupta.

In this chapter a new method is proposed to rank Web pages in cloud environment. Web pages from the cloud are clustered as 'Primary' and 'Secondary' domains. 'Primary' domain Web pages are fetched based on the keywords. 'Primary' Web pages are ranked based on Relevancy Factor (RF) and Turbulence Factor (TF). Relevancy of the Web pages with respect to the user query is measured by Relevancy Factor. Impact of the user query towards similar Web pages is measured by Turbulence Factor. It is observed that a Web page, having relevant information with respect to the user query, may not have matched keyword with respect to the user query. Those Web pages are covered by 'Secondary' domain concept. 'Secondary' domain is constructed by Nearest Keywords and Similar Web pages. Nearest Keywords are the keywords similar to the matched keywords. Similar Web pages are the Web pages having Nearest Keywords. Matched Web pages of 'Primary' and 'Secondary' domain are ranked separately. A wide range of Web pages from the cloud would be available and ranked more efficiently by this proposed approach.

Chapter 18: An Approach on Cloud Disk Searching using Parallel Channels.
Saswati Sarkar and Dr. Anirban Kundu.

The authors propose a cloud disk searching technique in this paper. Proposed cloud based searching mechanism shows the utility of indexing, balancing, and data storage in cloud. The paper exhibits complexity of cloud based searching algorithms in real-time scenario. Comparison graphs have been demonstrated for time difference realization in cloud. Parallel concepts have been introduced to facilitate searching the cloud. Sequential and several parallel situations have been compared using time graphs.

Chapter 19: Data Intensive Cloud Computing: Issues and Challenges.
　　Jayalakshmi D. S., Srinivasan R., S. R. M., Srinivasa K. G., M. S. M.

Processing Big Data is a huge challenge for today's technology. There is a need to find, apply and analyze new ways of computing to make use of the Big Data so as to derive business and scientific value from it. Cloud computing with its promise of seemingly infinite computing resources is seen as the solution to this problem. Data Intensive computing on cloud builds upon the already mature parallel and distributed computing technologies such HPC, grid and cluster computing. However, handling Big Data in the cloud presents its own challenges. This paper analyzes issues specific to data intensive cloud computing and provides a study on available solutions in programming models, data distribution and replication, resource provisioning and scheduling with reference to data intensive applications in cloud. Future directions for further research enabling data intensive cloud applications in cloud environment are identified.

Chapter 20: A Key Based Database Sharding Implementation for Big Data Analytics.
　　Sikha Bagui, Loi T Nguyen.

As the digital revolution heralds into a new era with Big Data on the cloud, the idea of centralized data storage has to be modified to accommodate availability, scalability, reliability and manageability. Higher performance and lower cost become a major challenge. This can be addressed by leveraging on database sharding. With database sharding, the database is divided into smaller chunks or shards across multiple data nodes in the cluster. We used MySQL Cluster for database sharding. Then we used the sharded partitions to perform data analytics, specifically the association rule mining algorithm of data mining. Association rule mining is used to find frequent patterns in large datasets. We ran the association rules using WEKA's Apriori algorithm and presented the association rules for the sharded partitions as well as the non-sharded data. From the association mining results we can see that the partitioned datasets give us rules that the whole dataset was not able to produce.

FUTURE TRENDS IN CLOUD COMPUTING RESEARCH ADVANCEMENTS IN DESIGN AND APPLICATIONS

Analysts say "the global market for cloud computing will grow from $40.7 billion in 2011 to more than $241 billion in 2020" from Source: Forrester Research, "Sizing the Cloud", April 2011.

It should be noted that the Mobility: Over 80% of the Fortune 100 is deploying or piloting tablets with sales expected to increase by 123%. Where as Storage: Nearly 40% increase expected by 2012 in backing up to/storing data in the cloud. Each day, AWS adds the equivalent server capacity to power Amazon when it was a global, $2.76B enterprise (circa 2000).

According to Economist Intelligence Survey October 2011, The cloud landscape is evolving. In 2010, (i) Peak of market hype on cloud computing -- driven by cost savings and IT efficiency gains. (ii) Security, availability and vendor lock-in are top of mind concerns for CIOs. (iii) Sandbox/ trial implementations of non-critical applications emerge: Testing enterprise-readiness.

In 2015, (i) enterprises expand focus of cloud as a driver of business innovation. (ii) Cloud computing will play a significant role in shaping client value propositions. (iii) Enterprises will look at cloud to drive innovation across the eco-system. (iv) Cloud will be increasingly looked to drive collaboration and reduce business complexity.

Looking at each trend also highlights future research topics. For example, to take advantage of industries, practitioners and governments need to further develop Cloud applications and services and continue to invest in research and development. Metrics are needed to measure the impacts of these investments. How should organizations build trust to achieve collaborative applications and services? What are the legal implications of collaborative Cloud-based commerce, learning and government? Note that the Next generation Cloud provisioning models rely on advanced monitoring and automatic scaling decision capabilities to ensure quality of service (QoS), security and economic sustainability.

Most papers in this book are worried regarding the customer's fears from using cloud applications and so how to calm these fears from using Cloud applications and services in future. Here I would like to mention some reasons that let the customer's fears are increased:

- The phone's customers might be shocked especially from the phones that rely exclusively to communicate with the company's servers to the keeping and data handling. So that the question is; what happens if I stop company's servers for work or faced major problems preventing them from working? But the truth is that regardless of the capacity and capabilities of the company that manages these servers, the potential collapse of the system is taken place in everywhere and at any moment, and then this meltdown happens. Thus, the second question, could the cloud computing fail? To overcome this big question another article will discuss this as a part of future work.
- Reputable companies attempted to mitigate the customer fears by confirming that the cloud model is secure, the cloud services is protected, the data centers and hosted servers are encrypted and the communication channel between the customer and the cloud resources is secured and then it is protected from any kind of attack. However, the attackers claimed that the cloud resources are penetrated much more easily than the non-cloud environment. For instance, Sony stated that the customer's credit card data is a secure, but the attackers claimed that the customer's credit card data are selling online. So that who inform us the truth and what is the level of protection we believe it does!!! If Sony is telling the truth about encrypting the data, it seems that the level of encryption is not sufficient well.
- Due to lack of control over the Cloud software, platform and/or infrastructure, Academies and practitioners stated that a security is a major challenge in the Cloud.

A summary of the recommendations of this book:

- Importance of the transition from traditional to Cloud in the sense that interested.
- Developing strategies and solutions to the problem of research by linking traditional relationships and concepts that facilitate access to information. For example:
  - Architectural Design for Cloud applications and services
  - How to implement the Cloud applications and services.
  - Cloud computing for large scale applications
  - Cloud technologies for P2P, services, agents, grids and middleware
  - Cloud technologies for software and systems engineering

- ◦ Cloud for E-government
- ◦ Databases, IR and AI technologies for Cloud
- ◦ Social networks and processes on the Cloud
- ◦ Representing and reasoning about trust, privacy, and security
- ◦ Cloud computing techniques and approaches
- ◦ Frameworks for developing Web applications
- ◦ Security issues for Web applications
- ◦ Scalability issues and techniques
- ◦ Applications that illustrate interesting new features or implementation techniques
- ◦ Performance measurements of Cloud applications
- ◦ M-commerce applications, issues, and security

FEEDBACK

This book contains a large of information from many resources on a large variety of topics in the cloud applications and computing. I have tried to be accurate as possible, but there could be errors. Please send your feedback to me shadi.jawarneh@yahoo.com.

Acknowledgment

The editor would like to acknowledge the help of all the people involved in this project and, more specifically, to the authors and reviewers that took part in the review process. Without their support, this book would not have become a reality.

First, the editor would like to thank each one of the authors for their contributions. Our sincere gratitude goes to the chapter's authors who contributed their time and expertise to this book.

Second, the editor wishes to acknowledge the valuable contributions of the reviewers regarding the improvement of quality, coherence, and content presentation of chapters. Most of the authors also served as referees; we highly appreciate their double task.

Shadi Aljawarneh
Jordan University of Science and Technology, Jordan

Chapter 1

An Entrepreneurial Approach to Cloud Computing Design and Application:
Technological Innovation and Information System Usage

Vanessa Ratten
La Trobe University, Australia

ABSTRACT

The design and application of cloud computing services is inherently entrepreneurial as it is constantly evolving as a result of technological innovation. This chapter focuses on providing an entrepreneurial approach to understanding change in the cloud computing context by highlighting the importance of innovative system usage. The chapter discusses how cloud computing services are creating a ecosystem of mobile commerce applications that is changing the way consumers, businesses and the government collects, disseminates and stores information. These changes have given way to entrepreneurial service innovations in the cloud domain that are a result of consumer demand for more current and relevant technological innovations. This chapter addresses the role of entrepreneurship in technological innovations by focusing on marketing and learning applications that are unique to cloud computing services. The future research suggestions from this chapter stress the importance nature of being entrepreneurial to encourage technological innovation in the cloud computing context.

INTRODUCTION

Cloud computing is a technological innovation that provides a computing platform for every business that has software, hardware and infrastructure (Ratten, 2014). As a rapidly emerging technology trend, cloud computing has developed as more information needs to be stored in a mobile electronic data format (Ratten, 2015). The advantage of the internet for storing information is that it enables convenience, flexibility and anonymity (Freestone & Mitchell, 2004). The concept of cloud computing has been

DOI: 10.4018/978-1-4666-8676-2.ch001

Copyright © 2015, IGI Global. Copying or distributing in print or electronic forms without written permission of IGI Global is prohibited.

around for a long time but only recently has it been mass marketed to consumers and businesses (Harauz, Kaufman & Potter, 2009). Cloud computing services have been referred to as Infrastructure as a Service (IaaS), Platform as a Service (PaaS) and Software as a Service (SaaS) (Morrell & Chandrashekar, 2011). Cloud computing comprises a wide range of internet applications including providing information and configuring servers (Moch, Merkel, Gunther & Muller, 2011).

Cloud computing enables the outsourcing of technology infrastructure in order to manage information systems, protect data and enabling people to gain access to information process intensive activities by lowering the barrier to entry (Ratten, 2013a). The large cloud computing service providers including Amazon, Yahoo and Salesforce have the ability to provide massive data management and data mining services that a small company would not be able to do by themselves (Bradshaw et al., 2011). This has lead to cyberinfrastructure being built upon a service orientated architecture that is based on grid and utility computing (Vouk, 2008). The cyberinfrastructure enables a large amount of electronic information to reside in a large data centre that is managed by a third party and accessible at any time or geographic location with an internet connection (Bradshaw, Millard & Walden, 2011). The use of on demand services is a key differentiating feature of cloud computing, which has evolved from the increase in the number of e-commerce transactions occurring (Osterman, Iosup, Yigitbasi, Prodan, Fahringer & Epeman, 2010). Globally many businesses have increased the commerce they conduct on the internet and with this large physical data centres have been built to handle the increased internet traffic and data flow (Ratten, 2013b). At the same time cloud computing has progressed as a way for businesses to store data without facing large capital hardware outlays and for outside companies to manage information software systems (Armbrust, 2010). This paper defines cloud computing as a "platform that is able to dynamically provide, configure and reconfigure servers to address a wide range of needs ranging from scientific research to e-commerce".

Cloud computing enables a person to access information stored electronically from any location (Lu et al., 2003). This advantage of increased independence to store electronic data enables the transfer of information and better communication (Altschuller & Benbunan-Fich, 2009). Part of the appeal of cloud computing is that it enables access to material previously only available in hard copy format thereby increasing a person's mobility to communicate. Mobile commerce has further increased a person's access to electronic information in a free-space environment without physical conduit technology being used (Aungst & Wilson, 2005). Mobile commerce is increasingly being used for business purposes and cloud computing is a major part of future growth within the industry as it is an alternative to face-to-face transactions. In conjunction with mobile commerce, cloud computing integrates electronic data storage into business processes thereby forming part of the electronic commerce industry (Vaquero, Rodero-Merino & Moran, 2011).

An ethical issue has been raised by cloud service providers managing information in the event of cybertheft or system crashes (Sasikala, 2011). Other ethical issues facing cloud computer services include privacy, anonymity, liability, reliability and government surveillance (Jaeger et al, 2008). Despite the advantages of cloud computing, there are ethical issues related to different international laws occurring in countries around the world. This has lead to a growing divide between the current usage of cloud computing services and the laws governing its applications (Vaquero, Rodero-Merino & Buyya, 2011). The ethical issues raised by cloud computing is an area that merits more attention because of the increased usage by both consumers and businesses. Educational institutions including various universities around the world have been partnering with large technology companies such as IBM and Google to provide a solution to these ethical issues created by the educational and research information found on cloud servers (Jaeger et al., 2008). This paper focuses on the intersection of ethics and entrepreneurship conducted by people intending to adopt cloud computing services. In the paper, the nature of cloud computing as a technology innovation and how it is adopted will be considered. By focusing on the ethical issues created by cloud computing services, this paper will attempt to solve potential ethical dilemmas before they progress.

This paper is structured as follows. First, the paper discusses the role of cloud computing services. Next, a literature review of technology innovation theories is stated that includes the variety of perspectives researchers have taken to understand how a person adopts a technology service. Then the theoretical framework of the paper based on social cognitive theory is highlighted. This leads to a section on research propositions for technology marketing, entrepreneurial intensity, ethical behaviour, learning expectancy and perceived outcomes. Finally, the benefits for practitioners and research suggestions for focusing on ethics and entrepreneurship in helping to understand how a person adopts cloud computing services are stated.

BACKGROUND

Global changes made possible through electronic commerce have changed the way people conduct business (Coombs et al., 1987). The online environment has created a new wave of technological innovations, which have impacted the way people interact with the environment (Cantisani, 2006). People access electronic information on a daily basis thereby forming part of their decision making processes (McMahon & Cohen, 2009). The online environment has resulted in more knowledge and information being acquired that helps people decide how to use a technological innovation (Chiu et al., 2008). Often people choose whether to adopt a technology innovation based on the perceived benefits of the service (Scholnikoff, 2001). This adoption decision about a technology innovation is further influenced by a person's social group (Li et al., 2007). A person's social networks enable knowledge dissemination about the technology, which influences the rate at which the product is adopted (Lin & Huang, 2008). Furthermore, as a person is exposed to more information about a technology, they may learn new behaviours (Ratten, 2011). A person's behaviour may change as they are influenced by their social network, which can include family, friends and work colleagues (LaRose & Eastin, 2004). This form of social learning can be in response to information stimuli that changes the way a person behaves (Harris et al., 2005).

In the learning literature there are the behavioural and cognitive models that help to explain adoption rates (Bandura, 1989). The main focus of the behavioural model is that a person will react to information by solving problems and creating solutions (Schiffman & Kanuk, 2000). In contrast to the behavioural model, the cognitive learning approach focuses on a person's response to information as a result of environmental conditions. The cognitive learning model to explain technology adoption is used in this paper to understand a person's behavioural intention to cloud computing. There are a number of theories in the cognitive learning approach to explain technology adoption including the technology acceptance model, theory of planned behaviour, theory of reasoned action and social cognitive theory, which will now be discussed.

The technology acceptance model focuses on understanding the reasons why a person will use a technology (Venkatesh & Davis, 1996). Within this model, the rate of technology adoption behaviour is understood by focusing on the perceived ease of use and usefulness (Davis, 1989). The model was one of the first models to explain the role of the internet in affecting how a technology fits within a person's lifestyle (Chan & Lu, 2004). By focusing on a person's perceptions of a technology the model takes a simplistic approach to describe the reasons why a person uses a technology (Taylor & Todd, 1995).

The theory of planned behaviour is one of the most commonly referred to theoretical frameworks to understand a person's actions in adopting a technology innovation (Ratten, 2008). The theory focuses on the actions and steps a person goes through in adopting a technology. There is an assumption within this theory that a person goes through a rationale thought process in conducting their behaviour (Ratten, 2008). Due to this assumption the theory does not take into account unplanned behaviour that is a result of impulses or opportunities. This presents a limitation for the theory as it omits serendipity that may occur in the adoption of a technology (Mathieson, 1991). Furthermore, the structured and formalised approach of the theory lacks integration of learning and environmental changes that affect the ability of a person to use a technology. Some people do not pre-plan their behaviour, which affects the practical value of this theory. As a person's behaviour differs depending on their geographic location, there are inherent difficulties in applying this theory to all demographics (Ajzen & Fishbein, 1980).

The theory of reasoned action extends the theory of planned behaviour by including unplanned actions in technology adoption behaviour. The theory still has a formalized approach to understanding behaviour by taking into account the role of social networks and other people's attitudes in the evaluation of technology innovation (Fishbein & Ajzen, 1975). The theory is commonly used to explain and predict adoption behaviour in technology that has a discrete number of steps when a person starts to use the service (Chan & Lu, 2004). By incorporating reasons why a person will adopt a technology the theory includes a variety of behaviours influenced by internal environmental factors but does not include many external environmental conditions such as advertising and marketing (Ratten & Ratten, 2007).

Social cognitive theory includes internal and external environmental factors thereby incorporating elements of the technology acceptance model, theory of planned behaviour and theory of reasoned action. People learn through different environmental factors that impact the skills they acquire from adopting a technology (Compeau et al., 1999). Social learning includes both individual and group behaviour that determines the actions a person takes (McCormick & Martinko, 2004). Social cognitive theory is a type of social learning as it demonstrates how an individual learns from their social group, which in turn influences their own behaviour (Pincus, 2004). Due to the complex nature of human behaviour, people will adopt behaviour based on their cognitive processes (Bandura, 1986). The key focus of the theory is that it acknowledges the role events and experience play when a person learns about a technology (Kock, 2004). A person's future behaviour thereby results from their interaction with the environment (Ratten, 2008). The advantage of social cognitive theory over other technology adoption models is that it incorporates unplanned actions that result from interacting with the environment.

This paper is premised on social cognitive theory as it incorporates a number of other elements of prior technology innovation models. Social cognitive theory is helpful in analysing the antecedent factors to a person adopting cloud computing as a result of their ethical and entrepreneurial behaviour. This paper utilises social cognitive theory to answer the following research question: What influences a person's decision to adopt cloud computing? The next section will discuss the theoretical framework of the paper, which is based on social cognitive theory.

THEORETICAL FRAMEWORK

The theoretical framework of this paper focuses on social cognitive theory in order to understand the different environmental factors influencing a person's decision to adopt cloud computing services. Technological innovations such as mobile data storage devices and portable internet enabled devices have increased the popularity of cloud computing services. This has lead to more people intending to adopt cloud computing as a way to save time and money. Rycroft (2006) focused on the time efficiency of technology innovations that have been made possible by increased research and development efforts placed on understanding how a person adopts a technology. A person's entrepreneurial proclivity is a time saving behaviour that affects the way they adopt a new service (Lundvall & Borros, 1999). This form of entrepreneurial behaviour is likely to consist of risk taking and forward thinking activity that helps a person see the benefits of a technological innovation.

Technological innovations including cloud computing services require a person to learn about the outcomes associated with the technology that may be innovative but at the same time involve potential unethical activity. This paper utilises social cognitive theory to understand the relationship between a person's internal environmental factors (ethical behaviour, learning expectancy, entrepreneurship proclivity) with external environmental factors (technology marketing, outcome expectancy). By proposing that both internal and external factors affect a person's decision to adopt cloud computing, this paper recognises that a person essentially learns through social and intrinsic motivational efforts. Each of these environmental factors will now be discussed and a set of research propositions stated to see how they influence a person's intention to adopt cloud computing services.

Ethics

Ethics is an important aspect of the internet as cyberspace has a different environment to the physical realm (Johnston & Sohal, 1999). Ethical behaviour includes the beliefs or standards a person has, which helps them to decide what to do and how to feel (Freestone & Mitchell, 2004). Ethical internet behaviour has been referred to as "netiquette" because it refers to behaviour that is expected when a person uses the internet (Albers-Miller, 1999). As behaviour on the internet can be difficult to punish, some people argue that unethical actions on the internet can be ethical if it provides an overall benefit to society (Freestone & Mitchell, 2004). This has led to internet related unethical behaviour occurring due to people being given unprecedented access to information and knowledge in a digital format.

There have been few studies examining a person's ethical attitudes to cloud computing services, due to a variety of ethical debates existing about how to determine ethical behaviour. As cloud computing services affect a person's decision making abilities about what is right or wrong, the large amount of confidential information stored electronically can have potential ethical dilemmas. This means that a person who has ethical internet behaviour will be more likely to use technological innovations that allow them to determine their own actions. Therefore, this leads to the following proposition:

Proposition 1: A person's ethical orientation will influence their intention to use cloud computing services.

Perceived Outcomes

The perceived outcomes a person perceives resulting from their behaviour influences their intention to conduct new activities (Bandura, 1986). This expectant attitude influences the behaviours a person foresees from using a technological innovation. The adoption rate of technological innovations is facilitated by a person determining that the service will become widespread in the business marketplace. This leads to a person perceiving that their actual outcomes will be beneficial when they use the technology and this motivates others to also adopt the technology. Previous research by Henry and Stone (1999) found that the perceived outcomes of a service largely determine whether a person adopts a technological innovation. Therefore, as cloud computing has a number of advantageous benefits including time and cost savings, it can be expected that an important indicator of a person learning about the effects of cloud computing will be influenced by potential outcomes. This leads to the next proposition:

Proposition 2: The more perceived outcomes a person has about technological innovations, the greater their intention will be to adopt cloud computing.

Entrepreneurial Intensity

Entrepreneurial elements form part of a person's adoption behaviour as they determine innovation, proactiveness and risk taking activity (Lee & Petersen, 2000). Behaviour that has an entrepreneurial capability helps a person decide whether to engage in competition that influences their degree of engagement with a product or service (Miller, 1983). Previous research on adoption behaviour in technology has revealed that entrepreneurial intensity helps to understand how a person will adopt a technological innovation (Ratten, 2008). Entrepreneurial intensity can influence the way technology innovations are disseminated to people. Cloud computing is a technological innovation that has not widely been used in a business setting. This means that some people will perceive it risky before understanding the benefits of adopting the service. People with an entrepreneurial proclivity towards trying new things will likely adopt technology at a faster rate as they realise how it can be used successfully. This leads to the next proposition:

Proposition 3: A person with a higher level of entrepreneurial intensity towards technological innovations will adopt cloud computing services faster.

Learning Expectancy

Learning about new products and services involves a person placing value on the propensity to create and use knowledge (Ratten, 2011). This form of learning behaviour is part of a person's decision making criteria when evaluating how quickly they will be able to learn about a technological innovation (Woodward et al., 2007). Learning can involve a variety of behaviours from collecting and sharing information to disseminating information amongst a person's friends and colleagues. A person with more accumulated knowledge will be better able to evaluate ethical internet usage such as inappropriate use of material, access to sensitive information and illegal downloading . As learning about the potential access to confidential social or pirated information made available by a technology can take time, it is important that a person focuses on the learning capabilities of the innovation. Therefore, the next proposition is:

Proposition 4: The greater a person's learning expectancy about a technological innovation, the more willing they will be to adopt cloud computing.

Technology Marketing

Marketing about technology can take a variety of different forms from internet advertising, television advertisements, magazine articles, promotional activities and word of mouth communication. Marketing is an important way to communicate information about a technology that can fasten the rate of adoption. People respond to marketing campaigns through their behaviours that are aimed at a person adopting the product or service. The exposure to technological innovations through marketing efforts is aimed at encouraging people to use the technology as part of their overall behaviour (McCormick & Martinko, 2004). By focusing on technology as a social status symbol, marketing can affect different types of people to adopt the innovation.

Demographic characteristics can further influence adoption rates by marketing efforts being placed on different types of advertising mediums such as traditional print media or more technologically advanced online media (Sheth et al., 1999). The effectiveness of this marketing will be tied with emotional elements associated with the technology such as ease of use and usefulness that make a person more willing to use the technology innovation (McCoy et al., 2007). Cloud computing services have only recently been marketed to individuals as a way to save time and money accessing important information. The ethical nature of information stored in cloud computing services means that technology marketing can help impact a person's decision to adopt cloud computing. This leads to the next proposition:

Proposition 5: The more a person is exposed to technology marketing, the more likely they will be to adopt cloud computing services.

SOLUTIONS AND RECOMMENDATIONS

As cloud computing is emerging as a significant technology trend there are a number of implications for managers and practitioners stemming from this paper. As more people are expected to use cloud computing services, this means the way people adopt technological innovations is important for businesses involved in cloud computing. From a managerial point of view, a firm needs to assess the way a person adopts cloud computing services in order to consider ethical behaviour. Managers should consider how cloud computing services are innovative developments that create value in their organisation. In this way a firm can motivate employees to use cloud computing services as a mechanism to develop their business services. Managers should take into account the learning capabilities of people to adopt cloud computing and the outcomes that derive from using this technological innovation. The use of cloud computing services can be facilitated as a way to market new products and services to existing customers.

FUTURE RESEARCH SUGGESTIONS

Cloud computing services are expected to reshape information technology processes in the next couple of years (Sasikala, 2011). This means that future research should examine how enterprising individuals are adopting cloud computing through innovative business practices such as setting up online document storage or educational programs. More work is required on how the large technology companies such as Amazon and Google are meeting the outcome requirements of cloud computing to see whether smaller technology companies are providing different types of ethical guidelines on the use of their services. An interesting research avenue is to investigate how technology start-ups and new ventures are marketing cloud computing to deliver more innovative applications that speed up the rate at which people are adopting cloud computing services.

Empirical and case study research should be conducted on how different types of industries from education, tourism and financial are adopting cloud computing. Longitudinal data on how existing storage systems are converted into cloud data should be undertaken in order to bridge the gap between theoretical perspectives of technology adoption and how it is utilised at a managerial level of inquiry. In addition, developing better ethical practices by cloud service providers merits further attention in order to focus on the marketing innovations made possible by cloud technology services.

CONCLUSION

As more people utilise cloud computing there has been an increased emphasis on understanding the adoption process of this technological innovation. This paper has discussed the importance of ethics and entrepreneurship in affecting a person's decision to adopt cloud computing services. The literature on technology innovation was reviewed with social cognitive theory being found to be the most suitable framework for this paper. A number of propositions were then stated that showcased the importance of consumers learning about the privacy and security features of this technology. As cloud computing services are likely to continue to gain ascendancy in the business marketplace, this paper has stressed the importance of the adoption process of technological innovations.

REFERENCES

Ajzen, I., & Fishbein, M. (1980). *Understanding Attitudes and Predicting Social Behavior*. Englewood Cliffs, NJ: Prentice-Hall.

Albers-Miller, N. D.Albers –Miller. (1999). Consumer misbehaviour: Why people buy illicit goods. *Journal of Consumer Marketing*, *16*(3), 273–287. doi:10.1108/07363769910271504

Altschuller, S., & Benbunan-Fich, E. (2009). Is music downloading the new prohibition? What students reveal through an ethical dilemma. *Ethics and Information Technology*, *11*(1), 49–56. doi:10.1007/s10676-008-9179-1

Armbrust, M., Stoica, I., Zaharia, M., Fox, A., Griffith, R., Joseph, A. D., & Rabkin, A. et al. (2010). A view of cloud computing. *Communications of the ACM*, *53*(4), 50–58. doi:10.1145/1721654.1721672

Aungst, S. G., & Wilson, D. T. (2005). A primer for navigating the shoals of applying wireless technology to marketing problems. *Journal of Business and Industrial Marketing*, *20*(2/3), 59–69. doi:10.1108/08858620510583650

Bandura, A. (1986). *Social Foundations of Thought and Action: A Social Cognitive Theory.* Prentice-Hall.

Bandura, A. (1989). Human agency in social cognitive theory. *The American Psychologist, 44*(9), 1175–1184. doi:10.1037/0003-066X.44.9.1175 PMID:2782727

Bandura, A., & Adams, N. (1977). Analysis of self-efficacy theory of behavioral change. *Cognitive Therapy and Research, 1*(4), 287–310. doi:10.1007/BF01663995

Bradshaw, S., Millard, C., & Walden, I. (2011). Contracts for clouds: Comparison and analysis of the terms and conditions of cloud computing services. *International Journal of Law and Information Technology, 19*(3), 187–223. doi:10.1093/ijlit/ear005

Calder, B. J., Philips, L. W., & Tyhout, A. (1981). Designing research for application. *The Journal of Consumer Research, 8*(September), 197–207. doi:10.1086/208856

Cantisani, A. (2006). Technological innovation processes revisited. *Technovation, 26*(11), 1294–1301. doi:10.1016/j.technovation.2005.10.003

Carusi, A., & De Grandis, G. (2012). The ethical work that regulations will not do. *Information Communication and Society, 15*(1), 124–141. doi:10.1080/1369118X.2011.634015

Chan, S., & Lu, M. (2004). Understanding Internet banking adoption and use behavior: A Hong Kong perspective. *Journal of Global Information Management, 12*(3), 21–43. doi:10.4018/jgim.2004070102

Charlesworth, A. (2012). Data protection, freedom of information and ethical review committees. *Information Communication and Society, 15*(1), 85–103. doi:10.1080/1369118X.2011.637572

Chiu, C., Hsu, M., & Wang, E. (2008). Understanding knowledge sharing in virtual communities: An integration of social capital and social cognitive theories. *Decision Support Systems, 42*(3), 1872–1888. doi:10.1016/j.dss.2006.04.001

Chonka, A., Xiang, Y., Zhou, W., & Bonti, A. (2011). Cloud security defence to protect cloud computing against HTTP-DOS and VML-DOS attacks. *Journal of Network and Computer Applications, 34*(4), 1097–1107. doi:10.1016/j.jnca.2010.06.004

Compeau, D., Higgins, C., & Huff, S. (1999). Social cognitive theory and individual reactions to computing technology: A longitudinal study. *Management Information Systems Quarterly, 23*(2), 145–158. doi:10.2307/249749

Coombs, R., Saviotti, P., & Walsh, V. (1987). *Economics and Technological Change.* Rownam & Littlefield.

Davis, F. (1989). Perceived usefulness, perceived ease of use and user acceptance of information technology. *Management Information Systems Quarterly, 13*(3), 319–339. doi:10.2307/249008

Fishbein, M., & Ajzen, I. (1975). *Belief, Attitude, Intention, and Behavior: An Introduction to Theory and Research.* Reading, MA: Addison-Wesley.

Freestone, O., & Mitchell, V.-W. (2004). Generation Y attitudes towards e-ethics and internet-related misbehaviours. *Journal of Business Ethics, 54*(2), 121–128. doi:10.1007/s10551-004-1571-0

Godding, P., & Glasgow, R. (1985). Self-efficacy and outcome expectations as predictors of controlled smoking status. *Cognitive Therapy and Research, 9*(5), 585–590. doi:10.1007/BF01173011

Harauz, J., Kaufman, L. M., & Potter, B. (2009). Data security in the world of cloud computing. *IEEE Security and Privacy*, (July/August), 61–64.

Harris, P., Rettie, R., & Kwan, C. C. (2005). Adoption and Usage of M-Commerce: A Cross-Cultural Comparison of Hong Kong and the United Kingdom. *Journal of Electronic Commerce Research, 6*(3), 210–224.

Henry, J., & Stone, R. (1999). The impacts of end-user gender, education, performance, and system use on computer self-efficacy and outcome expectancy. *Southern Business Review, 25*(1), 10–16.

Herbig, P., Koehler, W., & Day, K. (1993). Marketing to the baby bust generation. *Journal of Consumer Marketing, 10*(1), 4–9. doi:10.1108/07363769310026520

Hesseldahl, A. (2010, February 22). The iPad: More than the sum of its parts', $270 more actually. *Business Week,* 24.

Jaeger, P. T., Lin, J., & Grimes, J. M. (2008). Cloud computing and information policy: Computing in a policy cloud? *Journal of Information Technology & Politics, 5*(3), 269–283. doi:10.1080/19331680802425479

Johnston, K., & Johal, P. (1999). The internet as a 'virtual cultural region': Are extant cultural classification schemes appropriate? *Internet Research: Electronic Networking Applications and Policy, 9*(3), 178–186. doi:10.1108/10662249910274566

Keppel, G. (1991). *Design and Analysis: A Researcher's Handbook* (3rd ed.). Englewood Cliffs, NJ: Prentice-Hall.

Kim, B. C., & Park, Y. W. (2012). Security versus convenience? An experimental study of user misperceptions of wireless internet service quality. *Decision Support Systems, 53*(1), 1–11. doi:10.1016/j.dss.2011.08.006

Kock, N. (2004). The psychobiological model: Towards a new theory of computer-mediated communication based on Darwinian evolution. *Organization Science, 15*(3), 327–348. doi:10.1287/orsc.1040.0071

Kuratko, D. F., & Goldsby, M. G. (2004). Corporate entrepreneurs or rogue middle managers? A framework for ethical corporate entrepreneurship. *Journal of Business Ethics, 55*(1), 13–30. doi:10.1007/s10551-004-1775-3

LaRose, R., & Eastin, M. S. (2004). A social cognitive theory of Internet uses and gratifications: Toward a new model of media attendance. *Journal of Broadcasting & Electronic Media, 48*(3), 358–372. doi:10.1207/s15506878jobem4803_2

Lee, S. M., & Peterson, S. J. (2000). Culture, Entrepreneurial Orientation, and Global Competitiveness. *Journal of World Business, 35*(4), 401–416. doi:10.1016/S1090-9516(00)00045-6

Leymann, F., Fehling, C., Mietzner, R., Nowak, A., & Dustdar, S. (2011). Moving applications to the cloud: An approach based on application model enrichment. *International Journal of Cooperative Information Systems, 20*(3), 307–356. doi:10.1142/S0218843011002250

Li, Y., Liu, Y., & Ren, F. (2007). Product innovation and process innovation in SOEs: Evidence from the Chinese transition. *The Journal of Technology Transfer, 32*(1-2), 63–85. doi:10.1007/s10961-006-9009-8

Lin, C., & Huang, C. (2008). Understanding knowledge management system usage antecedents: An integration of social cognitive theory and task technology fit. *Information & Management, 45*(6), 410–417. doi:10.1016/j.im.2008.06.004

Lu, J., Yu, C., Liu, C., & Yao, J. (2003). Technology acceptance model for wireless Internet. *Internet Research. Electronic Networking Applications and Policy, 13*(3), 206–222. doi:10.1108/10662240310478222

Luftman, J., & Zadeh, H. S. (2011). Key information technology and management issues 2010-2011: An international study. *Journal of Information Technology, 26*(3), 193–204. doi:10.1057/jit.2011.3

Lundvall, B., & Borras, S. (1999). *The globalising learning economy: Implications for innovation policy.* Luxembourg: European Union.

Malaviya, P., Kisielius, J., & Sternthal, B. (1996). The effect of type of elaboration on advertisement processing and judgement. *JMR, Journal of Marketing Research, 33*(4), 410–421. doi:10.2307/3152212

Malhotra, N., Hall, J., Shaw, M., & Crisp, M. (1996). *Marketing Research: An Applied Approach.* Sydney: Prentice-Hall.

Mathieson, K. (1991). Predicting user intentions: Comparing the technology acceptance model with the theory of planned behaviour. *Information Systems Research, 2*(3), 173–191. doi:10.1287/isre.2.3.173

Matsuno, K., Mentzer, J. T., & Ozsomer, A. (2002). The Effects of Entrepreneurial Proclivity and Market Orientation on Business Performance. *Journal of Marketing, 66*(1), 18–32. doi:10.1509/jmkg.66.3.18.18507

May, R., Masson, M., & Hunter, M. (1991). *Applications of Statistics in Behavioral Research.* New York, NY: Harper and Row.

McCauley, J. M. (2011). Cloud computing- A silver lining or ethical thunderstorm for lawyers? *Virginia Lawyer, 59*, 49–54.

McCormick, M. J., & Martinko, M. J. (2004). Identifying leader social cognitions: Integrating the causal reasoning perspective into social cognitive theory. *Journal of Leadership & Organizational Studies, 10*(4), 2–11. doi:10.1177/107179190401000401

McCoy, S., Galletta, D. F., & King, W. R. (2007). Applying TAM across cultures: The need for caution. *European Journal of Information Systems, 16*(1), 81–90. doi:10.1057/palgrave.ejis.3000659

McMahon, J. M., & Cohen, R. (2009). Lost in cyberspace: Ethical decision making in the online environment. *Ethics and Information Technology, 11*(1), 1–17. doi:10.1007/s10676-008-9165-7

Miller, D. (1983). The correlates of entrepreneurship in three types of firms. *Management Science, 29*(7), 770–791. doi:10.1287/mnsc.29.7.770

Moch, R., Merkel, A., Gunther, L., & Muller, E. (2011). The dimension of innovation in SME networks- A case study on cloud computing and Web 2.0 technologies in a textile manufacturing network. *International Journal of Innovation and Sustainable Development, 5*(2/3), 185–198. doi:10.1504/IJISD.2011.043067

Morrell, R., & Chandrashekar, A. (2011). Cloud computing: New challenges and opportunities. *Network Security, 2011*(October), 18–19. doi:10.1016/S1353-4858(11)70108-8

Murphy, G. B., & Tocher, N. (2011). Gender differences in the effectiveness of online trust building information cues: An empirical examination. *The Journal of High Technology Management Research, 22*(1), 26–35. doi:10.1016/j.hitech.2011.03.004

Nunnally, J. (1978). *Psychometric Theory*. New York, NY: McGraw-Hill.

Osterman, S., Iosup, A., Yigitbasi, N., Prodan, R., Fahringer, T., & Epema, D. (2010). A performance analysis of EC2 cloud computing services for scientific computing. *Cloud Computing, 34*, 115–131.

Pincus, J. (2004). The consequences of unmet needs: The evolving role of motivation in consumer research. *Journal of Consumer Behaviour, 3*(4), 375–387. doi:10.1002/cb.149

Ratten, V. (2008). Technological innovations in the m-commerce industry: A conceptual model of mobile banking intentions. *The Journal of High Technology Management Research, 18*(2), 111–117. doi:10.1016/j.hitech.2007.12.007

Ratten, V. (2011). Ethics, entrepreneurship and the adoption of e-book devices. *International Journal of Innovation and Learning, 10*(3), 310–325. doi:10.1504/IJIL.2011.042083

Ratten, V. (2013a). Social e-entrepreneurship and technological innovations: The role of online communities, mobile communication and social networks. *International Journal of Social Entrepreneurship and Innovation, 2*(5), 476–483. doi:10.1504/IJSEI.2013.059322

Ratten, V. (2013b). Cloud computing: A social cognitive perspective of ethics, entrepreneurship, technology marketing, computer self-efficacy and outcome expectancy on behavioural intentions. *Australasian Marketing Journal, 21*(3), 137–146. doi:10.1016/j.ausmj.2013.02.008

Ratten, V. (2014). Indian and US consumer purchase intentions of cloud computing services. *Journal of Indian Business Research, 6*(2), 170–188. doi:10.1108/JIBR-07-2013-0068

Ratten, V. (2015). International consumer attitudes towards cloud computing: A social cognitive theory and technology acceptance model perspective. *Thunderbird International Business Review, 57*(3), 217–228. doi:10.1002/tie.21692

Ratten, V., & Ratten, H. (2007). Social cognitive theory in technological innovation. *European Journal of Innovation Management, 10*(1), 90–108. doi:10.1108/14601060710720564

Rycroft, R.W. (2006). *Time and technological innovation: Implications for public policy*. Academic Press.

Sasikala, P. (2011). Cloud computing: Present status and future implications. *International Journal of Cloud Computing, 1*(1), 23–36. doi:10.1504/IJCC.2011.043244

Schiffman, L., & Kanuk, L. (2000). *Consumer Behavior* (7th ed.). New Jersey: Prentice-Hall.

Scholnikoff, E. B. (2001). International governance in a technological age. In J. De la Mothe (Ed.), *Science, Technology and Governance*. New York: Continuum Press.

Sheeshka, J., Woolcott, D., & MacKinnon, N. (1993). Social cognitive theory as a framework to explain intentions to practice healthy eating behaviors. *Journal of Applied Social Psychology, 23*(19), 1547–1573. doi:10.1111/j.1559-1816.1993.tb01047.x

Sherif, M., & Sherif, C. W. (1967). *Attitude, Ego, Involvement and Change*. New York: John Wiley.

Sheth, J., Mittal, B., & Newman, B. (1999). *Consumer Behavior: Consumer Behavior and Beyond*. Austin: Dryden Press.

Sinkula, J. M., Baker, W., & Noordewier, T. G. (1997). A framework for market-based organisational learning: Linking values, knowledge and behaviour. *Journal of the Academy of Marketing Science, 25*(Fall), 305–318. doi:10.1177/0092070397254003

Snowden, S., Spafford, J., Michaelides, R., & Hopkins, J. (2006). Technology acceptance and m-commerce in an operational environment. *Journal of Enterprise Information Management, 19*(5), 525–539. doi:10.1108/17410390610703657

Sparks, J. R., & Pan, Y. (2010). Ethical judgments in business ethics research: Definition, and research agenda. *Journal of Business Ethics, 91*(3), 405–418. doi:10.1007/s10551-009-0092-2

Tamasjan, A., Strobel, M., & Welpe, I. (2011). Ethical leadership evaluations after moral transgression: Social distance makes the difference. *Journal of Business Ethics, 99*(4), 609–622. doi:10.1007/s10551-010-0671-2

Taylor, S., & Todd, P. (1995). Understanding information technology usage: A test of competing models. *Information Systems Research, 6*(2), 144–176. doi:10.1287/isre.6.2.144

Vaquero, L. M., Rodero-Merino, L., & Buyya, R. (2011). Dynamically scaling applications in the cloud. *ACM Siqcomm Computer Communication Review, 41*(1), 45–49. doi:10.1145/1925861.1925869

Vaquero, L. M., Rodero-Merino, L., & Moran, D. (2011). Locking the sky: A survey on IaaS cloud security. *Computing, 91*(1), 93–118. doi:10.1007/s00607-010-0140-x

Venkatesh, V., & Davis, F. D. (1996). A model of the antecedents of perceived ease of use: Development and test. *Decision Sciences, 27*(3), 451–482. doi:10.1111/j.1540-5915.1996.tb01822.x

Vouk, M. A. (2008). Cloud computing- issues, research and implementations. *Journal of Computing and Information Technology, 16*(4), 235–246.

Woodward, B., Davis, D. C., & Hodis, F. A. (2007). The relationship between ethical decision making and ethical reasoning in information technology students. *Journal of Information Systems Education, 18*(2), 193–202.

Yang, C., Liu, S., Wu, L., Yang, C. & Meng, X. (2011). The application of cloud computing in textile order service. *International Journal of Digital Content Technology and its Applications, 5*(8), 222-233.

Yu, J., & Cooper, H. (1983). A quantitative review of research design effects on response rates to questionnaires. *JMR, Journal of Marketing Research, 20*(1), 36–44. doi:10.2307/3151410

KEY TERMS AND DEFINITIONS

Cloud Computing: A computing platform that is accessible in any geographic and time format.

Cloud Platforms: Cloud services that can be configured and reconfigured on demand.

Cloud Services: Infrastructure, platform or software that is accessible via a variety of computing devices.

Cyberinfrastructure: Service orientated architecture that is based on grid and utility computing.

Mobile Commerce: Electronic information in a free-space environment.

Mobile Data: Information stored in an easily transmittable format that provides convenience for users.

On-Demand Services: Internet applications that are accessible depending on consumer needs.

Chapter 2
Using Cloud Computing for E-Government:
A New Dawn

Thamer Al-Rousan
Isra University, Pakistan

Shadi Aljawarneh
Isra University, Pakistan

ABSTRACT

For the last two decades, e-government has attracted government around the world to itself. Today almost every country in the world has developed and implemented e-government system in some form or another in order to reduce costs, improve services, save time and increase effectiveness and efficiency in a public sector. With increasing generalization of technology access by citizen and organizations, e-governments across the world face a major challenge in keeping a pace with ever changing technologies and offer an efficient, effective and transparent way of offering its services. Cloud computing is becoming an adoptable technology for many countries. The concept of cloud computing becomes important for each e-government, facilitating its way of work, increasing its productivity and all that leading to cost savings. It will likely have a significant impact on the e-governments in the future. In this paper, we analyzed cloud computing and its applications in the context of e-government.

1. INTRODUCTION

It is beyond doubt that the use of Information and Communication Technology (ICT) has good impact on performance of businesses (Khazaei and Misi,2010). Keeping a successful implementation of e-business into account, governments decided to employ ICT in public affairs to improve the effectiveness and efficiency of public sector organizations in the form of providing best possible information and services to citizens, businesses and other governments under what is called e-governments (Alford, 2009).

E-government can be viewed as the use of emerging information and communication technology services like World Wide Web(WWW), internet and mobile phones to deliver information and services

DOI: 10.4018/978-1-4666-8676-2.ch002

Copyright © 2015, IGI Global. Copying or distributing in print or electronic forms without written permission of IGI Global is prohibited.

to citizens and businesses(Jeanna et al.,2009). E- government helps simplify the working procedure of government mechanism by providing better services, more transparency and accountability, and instant response to end users. It also helps in better information dissemination by providing accessibility of different web services of e-government regardless of geographical and language barriers. The ultimate goal of the e-government is to increased public services in an efficient and cost effective manner(Hashem et al., 2013).

Every day the expansion and complexity of the e-governments is being observed, so that the size of their computational data is increasing daily. Increasing demands for information and service by the citizens and continuous advances in technology which puts governments under pressure to be innovative. One of the new inventions is cloud computing where information and computing services are provided as utilities (Lee, 2010).

Cloud computing is a result of continuous research in virtualization, distributed computing, utility computing, networking, and software services. It provides a new service consumption and delivery model inspired by Consumer Internet Services. Cloud computing has many advantages such as cost savings, scalability, integration, reusability of services, or high availability, which make cloud computing interesting for many areas (Ismail, 2011).

The importance of cloud computing and its benefits for the public sector has a already been noticed by different sectors in many countries. For instance, European Commission explicitly refers to cloud computing in their digital agenda for 2020. It aims to strengthen the European internal market by taking the advantage of cloud computing benefits (Kuldeep, 2012).

This study is based on cloud computing and e-government. The use of cloud computing in the context of e-government has been described in detail in this study. The rest of paper is organized as follow. In Section 2, e-government and its benefits have been discussed. Section 3 provides an overview cloud computing. The benefits of using cloud computing analyzed in Section 4, while Section 5 discusses the applicability of the cloud computing in the context of e-government. Followed by the conclusion in Section 6.

2. E-GOVERNMENT

E-government is the application of information and communication technology in public administration to improve public services and democratic processes and to facilitate citizens and businesses. Through e-government, the internet is used for delivering information and services between government and customer (G2C), between government and business (G2B), between government agencies and business (G2B), and between government and government (G2G) (Safari et al., 2002).

Today, e-government is one of the most important areas of modern information technology. It helps simplify government processes and makes the access to government information more accessible for public sector agencies and citizens. In addition to its simplicity, e-democracy services can reduce the operations cost and time, and improving the efficiency of services and business productivity (Layne and Lee, 2001). E-government also allows for government transparency because it allows the public to be informed about what the government is working on as well as the policies they are trying to implement(Khan et al., 2011).

Table 1. Top 10 Countries in the UN-Survey 2014

Country	Index
Republic of Korea	0.9462
Australia	0.9103
Singapore	0.9076
France	0.8938
Netherlands	0.8897
Japan	0.8874
United States of America	0.8748
United Kingdom of Great Britain	0.8695
New Zealand	0.8644
Finland	0.8449

E-government has had a massive and permanent influence on our lives. It is changed the unidirectional (up to down) relationship into an interactive relationship between the government, businesses, institutions, citizens and cooperation with other governments (Wojciech and Sergiusz, 2009). Many countries have attempted to implement e-government to realize their goals with the principles mentioned above. Some of these countries have achieved remarkable successes in this area. Based on United Nations E-Government Survey(UN-Survey, 2014), which was presented in March 25,2014. Republic of Korea is at the forefront of the most successful countries in implementation of e-government. The top 10 countries in implementation of e-government ranked by the UN-Survey are listed in Table 1.

In UN-Survey, four main metrics used to rank the e-government development of countries in the world. These metric are: Online Service Index, Telecommunications Infrastructure Index, E-Participation Index and Human Capital Index. These indices collectively represent measurements of a nation's readiness in terms of: (1) telecommunication infrastructure, (2) maturity of e-services, (3) participation of citizens in decision making, and (4) human resource availability to meet the requirements of offering e-government services (UN-Survey,2014).

E-government progress in the world remains relatively fast and uneven. Table-2 provides the UN rankings of the top five Middle East countries in terms of their e-government readiness over a 6 year period(UN-Survey,2014). Of the five countries listed above, four are from the Gulf Cooperation Council (GCC), with only Jordan being a non GCC Arab country included.

Bahrain and the United Arab Emirate(UAE) were ranked top two respectively, followed by Saudi Arabia at 3th, Qatar at 4th and Jordan at 5th. It is also observed that there has been steady progress by Saudi Arabia in the field of e-government. Between 2012 and 2014, Saudi Arabia has made remarkable progress in terms of improving its UN e-government ranking, jumping 14 points up to rank 36 worldwide after being ranked at 50 in the UN e-government readiness Survey in 2012. UAE has also advanced from (49) to (32), and Qatar from (62) to (44), which is attributed, in general, to these countries further investment in IT infrastructure. On the other hand, the Jordan fell 28 points, slipping from 51st to79th while Bahrain fell by three ranks, moving from 13rd to 18th.

Table 2. UN Ranking of Middle East Countries

	Country	Ranking 2014	Ranking 2012	Ranking 2010	Ranking 2008
6.	Bahrain	18	13	42	53
7.	UAE	32	49	32	42
8.	Jordan	79	51	50	68
9.	Saudi Arabia	36	50	78	80
10.	Qatar	44	62	53	62

In general, the survey pointed out that e-government initiatives in GCC countries have helped support regulatory reform, while in Jordan still facing challenges.

Many countries still facing challenges such as financial problems, people with appropriate IT skills, reliability of information on the web, law for privacy, and hidden agendas of government groups that could influence and bias public opinions (Mälkiä,2004).

To reverse this trend, countries need to be innovative. One of the new inventions that can be useful for e-government is cloud computing. E-government with cloud computing offers integration management with automated problem solution, and helps enabling e-government services faster and cheaper. Cloud computing play a important role in enhancing the delivery of public services, enabling governments to respond to a wider range of challenges despite the difficulties in the global economy.

3. CLOUD COMPUTING

Cloud computing is currently one of the dominating topics in the IT sector. Cloud computing enables the provisioning of IT services such as computing power or data storage just on demand. Precisely, only those resources which have been effectively consumed are charged by a cloud service provider. Many scientists of the National Institute of Standards and Technology(NIST) that work on cloud computing in America define it as follows:"Cloud computing is a model for enabling ubiquitous, convenient, on-demand network access to a shared pool of configurable computing resources (e.g., networks, servers, storage, applications, and services) that can be rapidly provisioned and released with minimal management effort or service provider interaction" (Mell and Grance, 2012).

Based on NIST definition, cloud computing has the following features: Users can perform self-service according to their needs, access to any network device, share resources and redeployment tasks. Under the conditions of cloud computing, services and resources usage is constantly monitored, controlled and reported for fair pay-as-you-go model implementation.

Cloud computing has many facets and characteristics. Basically, cloud computing can be applied either in service or deployment models. Depending on the amount of self governance or control on resources by the renter, there mainly four types of cloud computing deployment model (Ismail, 2011). They are: Private, Community, Public and Hybrid. Private cloud is specific for an organization. When the computing infrastructures are not shared among any other organizations. When the cloud infrastructures are shared by many numbers of co-operated organizations is called community cloud. Community cloud supports a specific community that has a shared concern. In public cloud visibility and control over the computing infrastructures are available to the customer. The computing infrastructures are shared among many organizations. When both public and private cloud are working together is called hybrid cloud. In hybrid cloud, both public and private are separate cloud systems but are connected by interfaces that enable sharing or utilizing each other's data, application or computational resources(Xiong &Perros, 2009).

Depending on what resources are shared and delivered to public services, there are three types of services cloud computing models (Gurdev et al., 2011). They are:

- **Infrastructure as a Service (IaaS):** Infrastructure as a service virtualizes the hardware/ network and storage aspects of the datacenter. Cloud architectures present a common infrastructure for all applications to work which is easy to use and deploy(Shivani et al., 2011).
- **Platform as a Service (PaaS):** Cloud offers standard platforms in terms of providing different kinds of systems, middleware and integration systems. Government departments requiring resources can request and get resources instantly as compared to traditional methods where they have to wait till they purchase, deploy etc.(Kaylor et al., 2011).
- **Software as a Service (SaaS):** Cloud service provider offers complete software solutions as a service. Customers can access the software via a simple web browser and do not need local installations on their PC. In this case, cloud offers excellent services for e-government. Instead of each government department hosting software and applications, they can get a particular service immediately from the cloud provider (Zissis and Lekkas, 2012).

The selection of the cloud model to be applied for e-government applications in the cloud requires a careful and systematic analysis. In fact, some models might be easier applicable for e-government than others. However, the adoption of cloud computing in e-government is not only a vision, it already became reality. Many countries have already adopted cloud computing solutions in the public sector or are planning to do so. In the next section, the study analysis the benefits of adopting cloud computing in e-government

4. THE BENEFITS OF USING CLOUD COMPUTING FOR E-GOVERNMENT

Cloud computing is penetrating many areas because of its advantages. High scalability, low maintenance efforts, enormous cost savings potential, and several other benefits make cloud computing also interesting in e-government. Cloud computing have many benefits in different parts of e-government. literature view listed some of advantages of cloud computing for the public sector (Bertot et al., 2008; Mukherjee and Sahoo,2010; Aljawarneh, 2011; Grossman, 2011; Ismail, 2011; Antonio et al.,2014). Based on these findings, we list the most important advantages of cloud computing in the governmental sector:

- **Scalability:** The growing numbers and demands of citizens and businesses on the e-government systems are increasing day by day. Cloud computing is considered a scalable technology because it can dynamically add extra resources such as servers, hard drives to accommodate growing number of citizens and businesses.
- **Availability:** Citizens want the governmental information and services to be available 24/7 to them. Earthquakes, wars or internal troubles could cause the e-government applications not only loose data, but also make services unavailable. Thus, complete backup and recovery solutions

must exist in separated locations. This could make big problems. Applications and data should be available on a short time to switch from one data center to another center.

The use of clouds can increase availability of applications. Applications can be deployed in different cloud data centers, distributed around the world. In case of a breakdown of one data center, the application may still continue running in another cloud data center of the cloud provider.

- **Data Scaling:** For e-government, the databases should be scalable to deal with large data gathered over the working days(e.g. Election days e-procurement, tendering), which may have higher access rates in a limited time period.

Cloud databases could be scaled and can be used for such type of applications. Cloud databases available for deployment offer amazing level of scaling without effecting on the performance. It can absorb high load of e-government applications easily.

- **Traceability and Integrity:** Traceability to any changes to information content in e-government services is necessary. Corruption in government organizations is hard to be controlled. As a result, there is no guarantee regarding the security and integrity of any data or information stored or transmitted via the services or the internet. Cloud can help in analyzing enormous volumes of data and discovering any piracy. It can improve the availability and reliability of e-government applications by building and placing defense mechanisms to improve the security.
- **Efficiency:** Providing public services efficiently and effectively to citizens and businesses is one of the main benefits of e-government. So, a suitable model for implementing e-government is required to include system efficiency and user satisfaction. The use of cloud based e-government system makes the task easier for the government in order to improve e-services delivery. It is also possible to create new solutions which are not technically and economically feasible without the use of cloud services.
- **Flexibility:** Different cloud deployment models ensure that the cloud based e-government implementations can be aligned closely with business needs and ICT strategies of the organizations. Public sector organizations can easily choose hybrid cloud computing model and get benefits from both private and public cloud models.
- **Maintenance:** The use of cloud services also lowers maintenance tasks. Patch or update management can be fully handled by the cloud service provider, so no manual maintenance tasks, e.g. for updating operating systems or installing security patches, are required.
- **Cost Saving:** E-government system need to buy and install the ICT equipments and software on their own premises. It also need employ professional employees to manage and maintain these system. Cloud computing creates an opportunity to change from costs of investment to operating costs by eliminating the upfront capital costs.

Pay-as-you-go pricing model enables public services to save a lot of IT costs including: the elimination of the cost of power, cooling, floor space and storage as resources are moved to a service provider.

5. DISCUSSION AND RECOMMENDATIONS

Considering the benefits of cloud computing technology, this technology is now the best option for e-government, specially developing countries that have not yet fully implemented e-government. This will decrease costs and enhance the efficiency, data integrity, speeding up of processes and user satisfaction. Even though there are many drivers for movement to a cloud-based solution, cloud computing is not without disadvantages. A main disadvantage in cloud computing is that it is under the maintenance and supervision of a third party. Therefore, the privacy and security measures are less secure (Zissis and Lekkas, 2012).

Security plays an important role in establishing the trust of the users in e-government. Thus, it is important that e-government based on cloud computing should be secure. There are a number of security issues/concerns associated with e-government based on cloud computing. These issues fall into two wide groups: security issues faced by cloud providers (organizations providing software-platforms, or infrastructure-as-a-service via the cloud) and security issues faced by the e-governments itself (Takabi and Joshi, 2010).

The responsibility goes both ways. First, the provider must ensure that their infrastructure is secure and that their clients data and applications are protected. Second, the e-governments must trust that the provider has taken the proper security measures to protect their information. Trust is an act of firm belief in truth, reliability, faith, confidence, or strength of someone or something. It is a belief in the capabilities and skills of others that you think you can reasonably rely on them to care for your valuable assets(Soleimanian and Hashemi,2012). Trust is playing an important role in the success of e-government system. It is important for the success of e-government that governments should have trust in cloud computing providers.

In cloud computing data and information is not stored and processed locally at the enterprise premises. In fact third parties are responsible for storing and processing of data at their own sites. In a situation like that individuals are concerned about the privacy of their personal data and information. When third parties are processing important data stored at remote machines at various locations, it is obvious people would be worried about the privacy of their personal data because it is a human right to secure their private and sensitive information. Therefore, the need for a new laws and regulations between countries in data transfer field, to use of services provided by service providers to be possible for governments all over the world to secure their private and sensitive information.

6. CONCLUSION

Due to the rapid growth of technology, it seems that in future the cloud computing will support many information systems. E-government implemented on a cloud offers huge benefits to the government, businesses and citizens. Numerous benefits like flexibility, cost effectiveness, availability and accessibility that cloud computing provides, has converted it to an appropriate option for use in e-government. From this paper, it could be concluded that all governments around the world have critical need to create e-government to reduce costs and to provide coherence between the various administrative government units in order to achieve the sustainable development and the best way to accomplish this matter is the use of green and cheap technology which is the cloud computing.

REFERENCES

Alford, T. (2009). *The Economics of Cloud Computing*. Booz Allen Hamilton.

Aljawarneh, S. (2011). Cloud Security Engineering: Avoiding Security Threats the Right Way. *Cloud Applications and Computing, 1*(2), 64–70. doi:10.4018/ijcac.2011040105

Antonio, C., Mario, F., & Luca, F. (2014). VM consolidation: A real case based on openstack cloud. *Future Generation Computer Systems, 32*(1), 118–127.

Bertot, J., Jaeger, P., & Mcclure, C. (2008) Citizen-Centered E-Government Services: Benefits, Costs, and Research Needs. *9th Annual International Digital Government Research Conference* (pp.137-142). Academic Press.

Grossman, R. (2009). The Case for Cloud Computing. *IT Professional, 11*(2), 23–27. doi:10.1109/MITP.2009.40

Gurdev, S., Gaurav, G., & Harmandeep, S. (2011). The Structure of Cloud Engineering. *Computer Applications, 33*(8), 44–48.

Hashemi, S., Monfaredi, K., & Masdari, M. (2013). Using Cloud Computing for E-Government: Challenges and Benefits. *Information Science and Engineering, 7*(9), 987–995.

Ismail, N. (2011). Cursing the Cloud or Controlling the Cloud. *Computer Law & Security Report, 27*(3), 250–257. doi:10.1016/j.clsr.2011.03.005

Jeanna, M., Christofer, H., & Jeff, W. (2009). Virtual Machine Contracts for Datacenter and Cloud Computing Environments. *Workshop on Automated Control for Datacenters and Clouds* (pp.25-30). ACM.

Kaylor, C., Deshazo, R., & Van Eck, D. (2001). Gauging E-Government: A report on implementing Services Among American Cities. *Government Information Quarterly, 18*(4), 293–307. doi:10.1016/S0740-624X(01)00089-2

Khan, F., Zhang, B., Khan, S., & Chen, S. (2011). Technological Leap Forging E-Government Through Cloud Computing. *4th IEEE International Conference on Broadband Network and Multimedia Technology* (pp.201-206). IEEE.

Khazaei, H., & Misi, C. (2010). Performance of Cloud Centers with High Degree of Virtualization Under Batch Task Arrivals. *IEEE Transactions on Parallel and Distributed Systems, 9*(2), 111–117.

Kuldeep, V., Shravan, S., & Amit, R. (2012). A Review of Cloud Computing and E-Governance. *Advanced Research in Computer Science and Software Engineering*, *2*(2), 185–213.

Layne, K., & Lee, J. (2001). Developing fully functional e-government: A four stage model. *Government Information Quarterly*, *18*(2), 122–229. doi:10.1016/S0740-624X(01)00066-1

Lee, J. (2010) 10 year Retrospect on Stage Models of E-Government: A Qualitative Meta-Synthesis. *Government Information Quarterly*, *27*, 220-230.

Mälkiä, M., Anttiroiko, A., & Savolainen, R. (2004). *E-Transformation in Governance: New Directions in Government*. Hershey, PA: Idea Group Publishing. doi:10.4018/978-1-59140-130-8

Mell, P., & Grance, T. (2012). *The NIST definition of cloud computing*. National Institute of Standards and Technology. Special Publication 800-145. Retrieved April 12, 2014, from http://csrc.nist.gov/publications/nistpubs/800-145/SP800-145.pdf

Mukherjee, K., & Sahoo, G. (2010). Cloud Computing: Future Framework for E-Governance. *Computer Applications*, *7*(7), 975–8887.

Safari, H., Mohammadian, A., & Tamizi, A., Haki, K., & Moslehi, A. (2002). Iran's Ministry of Commerce E-Government Maturity Model. *Quarterly Journal of Knowledge Management*, *63*, 53–78.

Soleimanian, F., & Hashemi, S. (2012). Security Challenges in Cloud Computing. *Foundations of Computer Science & Technology*, *3*(2), 41–51.

Takabi, H., Joshi, G., & Ahn, G.-J. (2010). Security and Privacy Challenges in Cloud Computing Environments. *IEEE Security Privacy Magazine*, *8*(1), 24–43. doi:10.1109/MSP.2010.186

UN E-Government Survey. (2014). *E-Government For The Future We Want*. Retrieved May 19, 2014, from http://unpan3.un.org/egovkb#.VCg77fl_sro

Wojciech, C., & Sergiusz, S. (2009). E-Government Based on Cloud Computing and Service-Oriented Architecture. *3rd International Conference on Theory and Practice of Electronic Governance* (pp.5-10). ACM.

Zissis, D., & Lekkas, D. (2012). Addressing Cloud Computing Security issues. *Future Generation Computer Systems*, *28*(3), 583–592. doi:10.1016/j.future.2010.12.006

Chapter 3
Supply Chain in the Cloud:
Opportunities, Barriers, and a Generic Treatment

Goknur Arzu Akyuz
Atilim University, Turkey

Mohammad Rehan
Atilim University, Turkey

ABSTRACT

Cloud concept is directly related with the beyond-ERP integrity and collaboration across a number of heterogeneous Supply Chain (SC) partner infrastructures. The technology enables partners to form a collaborative SC community without the burden of significant IT investment. Cloud applications offer significant opportunities from SC perspective, and the assimilation of the Cloud Technology is not complete yet in the Supply Chain domain. It also involves various barriers from implementation perspective, as well as the concerns related with vendor lock-in, security, reliability, privacy and data ownership. This chapter provides a comprehensive coverage of the opportunities and barriers as well as the generic treatment from SC perspective. It also highlights how the cloud technology represents a perfect fit with the ideas of 'Collaborative Supply Chains', 'Business Process Outsourcing' and 'long-term strategic partnerships, which are the key themes characterizing the Supply Chains of today's era. This chapter reveals that the intersection of the topics 'Cloud computing' and 'Supply Chain' is a promising area for further research. Further studies in a multi-partner setting with respect to a variety of configurations, case studies and applications, as well as the security, reliability and data ownership issues are justified.

INTRODUCTION

In the IT domain, Cloud computing is one of the most recent paradigms, receiving more and more interest in the literature (Vaquera *et al.*, 2009; Sterling & Stark, 2009). Increasing opportunities for improving IT efficiency and performance through centralization of resources and the maturation of technologies such as SOA (Service-Oriented Architecture), virtualization, distributed computing, grid computing,

DOI: 10.4018/978-1-4666-8676-2.ch003

Copyright © 2015, IGI Global. Copying or distributing in print or electronic forms without written permission of IGI Global is prohibited.

networking and web services led to the natural outcome of what has become increasingly referred to as 'cloud computing' (Tiwari & Jain, 2013; Oracle, 2009). Basic motivations behind the technology are: (a) the need for rapidly scalable elastic computing infrastructures, (b) the increased cost of traditional IT infrastructure, and (c) increased focus on service orientation (Yousif, 2009; IBM, 2008).

Cloud computing represents outsourcing of IT (infrastructure, service, platform and business processes), and enables on-demand access to IT resources from external providers generally on a pay-for-use basis like a utility. This paradigm provides access to a shared pool of configurable resources (networks, servers, storage, applications and services) delivered over the Internet (Buyya, Broberg & Goscinski, 2011; Sterling & Stark, 2009; Gartner, 2008a, b; Sosinsky, 2011; Raines, 2009; Schramm, Wright, Seng & Jones, 2010).

The approach is inherently compatible with the service-oriented philosophy, enabling standardized access to IT resources for totally heterogeneous, diverse and distributed infrastructures without knowledge of the underlying system details. Cloud benefits from SOA, since cloud computing is directly related with provisioning and consumption of IT capabilities as a service over the web. Markz & Lozano (2010) emphasises this idea by mentioning that 'Cloud builds on the shoulders of SOA'. Thus, cloud logically builds on the concepts of services, organization and orchestration of which can be managed inside the cloud within a service-oriented architecture (Wang, Wang & Lee, 2009). Since the modularity, reusability, standardization of interfaces, interoperability, platform independence and scalability are the core issues, cloud approach can be considered as complementing the SOA paradigm, providing pay-for-use model for service oriented thinking (Sosinsky, 2011). This is also highlighted by Markz & Lozano, 2010, mentioning the 'double play' between cloud and SOA, cloud pulling new SOA initiatives through and SOA enabling cloud initiatives from business, IT and infrastructural perspectives.

Representing the virtualization of resources, cloud computing provides the illusion of infinite computing resources available on demand, offers highly customizable services, and enables access for IT services without significant investment (Sagawa *et al.*, 2009; Sterling & Stark, 2009; Sosinsky, 2011). It also provides: (a) the user to get rid of operating and maintenance costs in relation to IT, (b) flexible, dynamic and efficient use of IT resources, (c) instantly scalable infrastructure and load balancing, (d) rapid access to new resource capabilities without incurring the delays implicit in upgrading and expanding local resources to manage them,(e) responsive delivery of services, and f) higher service quality (Vaquera *et al.*, 2009; Sterling & Stark, 2009; IBM, 2008). In the SC domain, Web technologies appear as the greatest enabler of SC collaboration by enhancing information flow, avoiding information asymmetry and providing transparency and visibility among partners (Akyuz & Gursoy, 2011); and transition towards collaborating, web-enabled structures is well-supported (Ross, 2003; Akyuz & Gursoy, 2011). Connectivity and enterprise application integration of heterogeneous partner systems are involved across multiple partners within the supply networks. It is already well-proven that SOA paradigm and extant EAI (Enterprise Application Integration) platforms of major vendors offer significant solutions in this regard (Rehan & Akyuz, 2010). SOA paradigm received a certain degree of assimilation, however, cloud computing appears as a more recent technology. Its assimilation in SC domain is not mature yet, with cloud-based modelling efforts being only recent (Cheng *et al.*, 2011; Ryu Nakayama & Onari, 2011).

Hence, the reasons for selecting the intersection of cloud-SC domains for this study are multifold: a) investigating the state-of-the-art cloud technology from the perspective of recent collaborative SC paradigm, b) identifying cloud opportunities and barriers for multi actor connectivity and collaboration, and c) providing a cloud-based, generic representation for collaborative context. Therefore, this study is beneficial and addresses for the audience from both IT and SC domains.

The rest of the chapter is structured as follows: next focuses on cloud computing from SC perspective, discussing the advantages, opportunities, barriers and the enabler effect for SC s. Then a generic, cloud-based representation is given followed by a comprehensive discussion section. After further research suggestions, last section concludes.

CLOUD COMPUTING AND SUPPLY CHAIN: OPPORTUNITIES AND BARRIERS

According to Gartner, SCM (Supply Chain Management) applications have played a sizeable role in cloud computing and assimilation is growing dramatically (McCrea, 2012) However, the, literature supports that Cloud computing in SCM is a paradigm that is still immature (Wright, 2011). The highest adoption rates in the areas of collaborative sourcing, procurement and demand planning, involving various opportunities and barriers. This section provides a comprehensive treatment of the opportunities and barriers in relation to cloud computing for SCM.

Opportunities

Cloud infrastructure from SC perspective means an enterprise and its suppliers all participate in an external cloud-based SC network with a single database accessed by everyone. This offers normalised and cleansed data, eliminating the data quality problems and provides a single repository (Shacklett, 2010). Therefore, cloud gives the manufacturer the ability to share a single version of SC truth with its suppliers and business partners, since all parties work off the same, unified database of information resident on the cloud (Shacklett, 2011; Shacklett, 2012). The database maintained by the SC cloud provider has standardized access, which virtually allows any company to access the data through any means. Naturally each organization applies its own business, governance and security rules. Therefore, a cloud-based SC solution has the inherent capacity to allow users anywhere in the world to collaborate with other users since they are working off of the same server and data set (Cloud Standards Customer Council, 2014).

This provides high quality, single-source data for multi-agent collaboration with a focus on the standardization among trading partners. Reduced noise within the SC simplifies and speeds up the data exchange, and enables real time visibility, workflow automation and information symmetry among partners across the entire chain (Shacklett, 2011; Shacklett, 2012). This is the most fundamental and critical issue of SC collaboration and the literature at the intersection of IT and SC domains repeatedly highlights the enabling role of IT on SC collaboration by providing visibility and information symmetry among partners (Akyuz & Rehan, 2009; Akyuz & Gursoy, 2011). Thus, sharing a single version of truth across the network forms the basis of on-line, real-time decision making. With the basic data exchange and data quality problems overcome, partners now have the ability to focus on data warehousing and reporting aspects for multi-partner collaboration of business processes. By eliminating the compatibility problem using the same platform of access, cloud computing enables active and effective collaboration and real-time exchange of information with multiple-parties, and provides increased visibility and integrity across organizational boundaries among heterogeneous, distributed partner infrastructures (Hugos & Hulitzky, 2010; Jun & Wei 2011; Tiwari & Jain 2013; Truong, 2014).

With cloud computing technology, instantaneous access to a rich community of partners is made available (Shacklett, 2011; Shacklett, 2012). Manufacturer finds that a great percent of its supplier base is already on the cloud, and that many suppliers which are normally difficult to qualify are on-board

(Shacklett, 2012). Shippers, receivers and service providers all join the cloud-based community and readily connect to each other (Bentz, 2013). From sourcing perspective, this opens up tremendous opportunities for operational, tactical and strategic-level collaboration. Not only searching for alternative suppliers and making initial engagements are made faster, but also instant access to master data of multiple suppliers is made possible. This is a radical contribution to many enterprises struggling with critical master data compatibility problems across restricted e-procurement applications to provide a single version of truth.

Cloud computing provides affordable ways for suppliers of all sizes to link into the common database, avoiding initial investment barriers. This is especially attractive for small and medium sizes enterprises (SMEs) having restrictions on IT budgets (Domini, 2012). Hence, SMEs which would otherwise be content with their restricted, isolated IT infrastructures now obtain access to an entirely different level of IT services, and to a collaborative community.

From the partner perspective, cloud implementation means no servers to maintain, no IT infrastructure to setup, no upfront licensing fees, no software programs to install and maintain, and offsite software maintenance & updates (Shacklett, 2011; Shacklett 2012). The result is lower upfront investments, removal of the internal costs associated with running partners' own IT infrastructure, and faster implementation.

From the network perspective, cloud means: a) availability of a supplier portfolio of a variety of sizes, b) quick reconfiguration opportunities, c) flexibility and agility to respond to the changing conditions, and d) the ability of the complex network structure to accept new partners into the collaborative structure faster and more easily with standardized data, interfaces and business processes (Shacklett, 2011; Domini, 2012). This provides highly global, more dynamic, scalable and capable SC structure (Wright, 2011), which is the key to compete in today's competitive environment. Aral, Sundararajan & Xin (2010) also support that companies complementing cloud services with standardized infrastructure, data management, and business processes can isolate individual processes suitable to cloud services and employ cloud vendors' best practices more easily. A consolidated and standardized technical platform provides faster deployment. The propagation and the assimilation of standard ways of doing business gets faster, since new entrants have the chance of directly adopting the commonly accepted business processes. The speed of access to IT resources and capacity increase agility, improves visibility to data and analytics, make SCs more responsive, and make SCs more efficient by enabling multi-enterprise collaboration with suppliers, clients and business partners (Wright, 2011). The result is more speed, efficiency as well as adaptiveness, responsiveness and dynamic reconfiguration capabilities built into the network.

Again from the network perspective, Marks & Lozano (2010) highlight the concept of 'asymmetric competitor' as the most critical implication of cloud computing, enabling a host of new asymmetric competitors to enter various existing markets without installed, rigid IT infrastructures and legacy applications anchoring them to their accumulated, past investments. From strategic management perspective, this elevates the competition to a different dimension and represents a radical change in marketing.

Hence, cloud offers tremendous opportunities of business processes standardization and enables the concept of 'processes on the cloud' (Wright, 2011). Undoubtedly, accessing complete business processes is the foundation of joint process planning, control and execution, and it opens up infinite opportunities of collaborative process designs among multiple partners. The following SC processes are specifically highlighted in the literature as the prominent venues for cloud computing:

- Planning and Forecasting
- Logistics Management
- Inventory Management

- Sourcing and Procurement
- Collaborative Design and Development
- Service and spare parts management
- CRM (Customer Relationship Management)
- HR (Human Resources).

It is well-supported in the SC literature that sourcing, procurement and logistics -the key activities in SC domain (Akyuz & Gursoy, 2010)- are radically transformed by cloud computing (Wright 2011; Tiwari & Jain, 2013; Truong 2014). Multi-sourcing among heterogeneous systems gain new momentum, and consequently cloud computing has entered the arena of strategic sourcing and procurement as the redefining technology (Morrison & Foerster 2013; GEP Group, 2011). As such, cloud technology offers opportunities for the integrity of very basic material management activities across the network. This forms the base for establishing collaborative planning, forecasting and replenishment processes across the partners. Based on a recent study by SCM World, Columbus (2014) also highlights Sales & Operations Planning (S&OP), Transportation Management and Spare Parts Management among the processes that are most cloud-friendly, with the greatest potential to deliver the network effect throughout a SC. Transformative impact of the cloud is also seen across the enterprise in areas such as HR and CRM (KPMG International, 2013). In fact, at the application level, the first wave of cloud-based services falls broadly into the areas of CRM, Human Capital and Financial Management (Schramm, Wright, Seng & Jones, 2010). The second wave focuses on desktop productivity tools, including word processing, spreadsheets, e-mails and Web Conferencing. Third wave covers the core business applications becoming available as cloud solutions. This is the consolidation phase requiring collaboration and tighter integration. At the business process/industry level, this represents cloud-based solutions enabling business process outsourcing (Schramm, Wright, Seng & Jones, 2010). Along this line, SaaS ERP (Software as Service ERP) is growing rapidly among the SC solutions (Truong, 2014), offering complete functionality including CRM. Truong (2014) highlights that we are in the post-adoption phase, emphasising the fact that initial waves are over.

In short, cloud computing facilitates unlimited opportunities for collaboration and performance improvement for both individual partners and the overall SC.

Barriers

Despite all the aforementioned opportunities, cloud paradigm involves a number of difficulties and barriers regarding itsassimilation. Undoubtedly, issues of privacy, confidentiality, security, reliability and vendor lock-in stand out and well-supported as the major concerns regarding the technology (Buyya, Broberg & Goscinski, 2011; Sterling & Stark, 2009; Gartner, 2008; Sosinsky, 2011; Shacklett, 2011; Schramm, Wright, Seng & Jones, 2010).

Increased dependence on a certain provider, and obtaining and maintaining satisfactory service levels from the provider are repeatedly highlighted maybe as the most critical concern. Since tight couplings and dependencies are created between the service provider and the chain partner, vendor lock-in is created, which makes it hard to switch from one service provider to another. Currently, this appears as one of the most fundamental issues hindering the implementations. In this regard, governance of service level agreements appears as a key issue (KPMG International, 2011).

Issues of data ownership and privacy across multiple partners naturally form a barrier. The enterprise which is accustomed to work with on-premise systems suddenly loses control on the data, infrastructure and the IT environment, and starts interacting through tools provided by the vendor. This is a corporate culture shock, and especially difficult for sharing the confidential data which is required for strategic levels of collaboration (such as collaborative risk management or collaborative financial management).

The following are also supported as the main barriers to faster adoption of the technology: (a) lack of clarity in the definition and attributions of responsibilities, (b) achieving accountability across the cloud SC, c) the difficulties in performing internal and external due diligence, d) lack of clarity in Service Level Agreements, (e) lack of awareness and expertise (Cloud Standards Customer Council, 2014).

It is evident that negotiation, consensus-seeking culture, collaborative and strategic-level agreements, and sound contract management practices are needed across the network for overcoming such issues. Managerial skills as well as openness and trust become the vital soft aspects to ensure the continuity of the relationships. Since exchange of business processes at the network level is in question, agreement upon ways of doing business and managerial aspects are as much critical as the technical aspects of connectivity. Thus, achieving consensus on the workflows which are generally accepted in the network becomes crucial.

From implementation perspective, the following are the key issues highlighted in the literature:

- Organisations that have already embraced SOA paradigm are expected to experience an easier transition to cloud. Relevance of EAI and SOA to e-supply chain formation has already been discussed in Rehan & Akyuz (2010) with all the advantages from SC integration perspective. Since cloud computing embraces and complements the service orientation philosophy, all the discussions mentioned in this previous study are valid, with the additional advantages of pay-for-use and outsourcing characteristics inherent in the cloud philosophy. Accustomed to SOA-based, platform-independent exchange of information, organizations that have already assimilated SOA will absorb these additional cloud benefits more easily.

- Larger enterprises are less likely to use cloud for SCM than smaller businesses, preferring on-premises or hosted applications due to process complexity, data integration requirements, advanced analytics and the need for industry-specific functionality (Domini, 2012).

- Firms that have already excelled in managing external vendors adapt to the cloud services more effectively (Aral, Sundararajan & Xin, 2010). Since cloud services are based on distributed application platforms owned and operated by different organizations (so-called 'multi-tenant architecture'), companies must manage complex multilateral contractual relationships. This constrains firms' ability to audit cloud vendors' IT practices, and clients don't have much control over the future changes made to the system. After all, utilizing cloud technology means delegating the control of IT resources at varying degrees to the service provider, and this makes the cloud vendors a vital partner of the network. Thus, previous excellence in vendor and contract management eases the adoption of the technology. As such, success lies in well-defined service agreements and collaborative, win-win, long-term contractual relationships with the cloud vendors. This will alleviate the major concerns of security, data ownership and high provider dependence in relation to this technology.

- Complex and/or unique processes that require a heavy degree of customized processing, and processes that require heavy integration with either a physical flow or with other information systems do not appear as well-suited to cloud (KPMG International, 2013).

- Cloud is particularly helpful for fast-growing manufactures that are becoming more and more complex as they grow (Fuerst, 2014)
- Cloud computing adoption in SCs is heavily dependent on the legacy ERP systems already in place, as they provide the system of record corporate-wide. Based on SCM Research Report by Courtin (2013), Columbus 2014 reports that 56% of respondents have standardized on SAP ERP systems, followed by Oracle (including PeopleSoft & JD Edwards) 16%, and the remainder being multiple ERP systems.
- Organizations with the most successful ERP implementations are most likely to consider SaaS ERP deployments. Truogh (2014) supports that more than 44% of companies have decided to use SaaS ERP compared to 56% that use traditional licensed ERP. Large companies have tendency to use SaaS ERP more than small companies, and start moving away from traditional licensed ERP solutions.

A GENERIC, CLOUD-BASED TREATMENT OF SC

Previous section clearly put forward the relevance of cloud-computing to SCs, along with all the opportunities and barriers from SC connectivity and collaboration perspectives. It became evident that a totally dynamic and scalable structure is enabled, with tremendous number of configuration options for the complex supply networks.

Based on the basic service models of: Infrastructure as a Service (IaaS), Platform as a Service (PaaS), Software as a Service (SaaS) and Business Process as a Service (BPaaS), Figure 1 provides a generic, cloud-based representation of the chain.

In this figure, multiple partners are depicted, having different roles (manufacturer, customer, logistics provider etc.) and different levels of prior IT investments.

Manufacturer 1 represents a big brother, with significant prior IT investment, with in-house availability of infrastructure, platform, software and processes. Manufacturer m again has significant IT investment, with possible connectivity to manufacturer 1 via Enterprise Application Integration Platforms (e.g.: two different full ERP implementations talking to each other). These two manufacturers have access to the cloud provider, hence the single version of network-level truth, with minimum fee since they do not utilize resources from the cloud.

Supplier n represents a partner that does not maintain any rigid IT resources at all. It is connected to the network via the service provider, rents infrastructure, platform, software and its processes as a service. As such, it represents the partner with the highest level of dependency on the service provider for all the IT services, and does not allocate any in-house resources for the IT.

Other partners represent the connectivity options and IT investments lying in between these two extremes of the spectrum. For example, Supplier 1 has in-house infrastructure, platform and software but receives processes as service. Customer 1 receives processes and software as service from the service provider utilizing existing in-house platform and infrastructure (on top of the existing infrastructure, accessing standardized processes). Logistic provider depicted in this diagram is an example again utilizing its own in-house platform and infrastructure, while accessing software and processes as service.

It must be emphasised here that the types of connections and the degrees of in-house and cloud-based utilization depicted in this figure are intended as only samples to indicate different possibilities and levels of utilization. Depending on the initial levels of IT investments, maybe the logistics provider will be the partner having full prior IT investment.

Figure 1. A generic representation of cloud-based SC
(Source: Akyuz & Rehan, 2013)

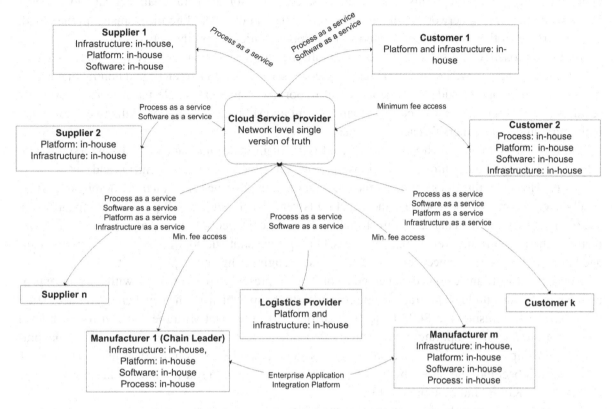

Figure 1. A generic representation of cloud-based SC (Akyuz&Rehan, 2013)

DISCUSSION

The generic depiction given in Figure 1 clearly represents all the advantages of cloud computing from SC perspective. This structure enables the formation of a collaborating network of n partners with totally different levels of prior IT utilization and investment. Besides the main suppliers and manufacturers, other stakeholders with different roles (such as logistic providers and service providers) become critical players of the SC. As indicated in the figure, any partner can access to the cloud with varying degrees of rental options. Consequently, a community of collaboration is formed including all stakeholders.

Such a structure enables the connectivity of totally different sizes and scales, since the entire logic is dependent on SOA. As such, a partner with a full-scale ERP system can connect to a supplier with a procurement-oriented application developed in-house. Thus, all the advantages of SOA are preserved, along with all the benefits of outsourcing.

From SC perspective, centralized type of connectivity assumes a critical importance especially for master data management and network-level consolidated reporting. This enables maintaining and accessing the single network-level version of truth by the community. This is totally compliant with the need for preserving, maintaining and reporting network-level performance and risk indicators for SC performance and risk management viewpoints. Besides, a centralized cloud-based approach does not restrict direct pair wise communication and collaboration between partners, as long as there is compatibility between their infrastructures. Still, a single version of truth for the overall network resides on the cloud and accessed centrally. This enables pair wise collaboration at operational, tactical and strategic levels while preserving network level analytics, reporting and dashboarding mechanisms in the cloud. This is perfect for the separation of concerns and responsibilities across the network.

In this approach, cloud service provider naturally becomes a binding resource on which the entire network is depends, as well as a critical player. Hence, service-level guarantees and contractual agreements with the cloud provider assume a critical importance for every single partner. This definitely requires successful collaborative contract management and strategic negotiation skills to establish and maintain long-term partnerships across the network.

The dominant partner, which can be interpreted as the chain leader, undoubtedly will have a significant effect for ensuring sound contractual relationships, guaranteed service level agreements and agreed-upon processes. However, this does not mean the creation of an environment in which the dominant partner totally overwhelms. On the contrary, the structure is very beneficial to small partners or laggards of a sector since they get the chance of direct inclusion and acceptance into a community probably more mature than their current level of doing business. Once proper strategic contractual agreements are managed, they obtain better chances for business process reengineering and improvement.

Consequently, it can be argued that cloud technology represents a perfect match with the concepts of collaboration, outsourcing and strategic, long-term partnership, which are the key themes characterizing the way of doing business in SCM today. It is also totally compliant with the spirit of network-level collaboration. Cloud computing creates strong dependencies, long-term partnerships and collaborative relationships with the IT service providers. As such, cloud becomes more than just very good IT economics. It becomes the means by which entirely new information sharing models become possible (Kefer, 2011; KPMG International, 2013).

Despite the barriers, utilization of cloud-based architectures will trigger supply network collaboration, and improved collaboration, in turn, will enable better contractual relationships, better partnerships with the cloud service provider and more successful cloud-based implementations.

FUTURE RESEARCH DIRECTIONS

This study revealed that the intersection of SC and cloud computing still appears as a promising research area. Case-based field research to measure the maturity levels of the implementation are definitely valuable. Further research related with the security and confidentiality issues as well as the reliability of the providers are critical unresolved issues in the area. Prospects for different configurations (such as presence of multiple cloud providers) and knowledge management on the cloud also appear as critical areas that deserves attention. The authors hold the opinion that both survey-based field studies and conceptual modeling efforts are valuable in the domain.

CONCLUSION

This study put forward a detailed discussion of cloud computing from SC perspective. Then, a generic representation of cloud-based supply chain is provided, highlighting the prospects of using cloud technology in supply networks. Inherently containing all the benefits of SOA technology, it became evident that cloud technology is offering: a) direct connectivity with networks of diverse trading partners regardless of their systems capabilities, through any-to-any data exchange, b) tremendous opportunities for platform-independent supply network collaboration, c) better and broader decision making abilities at individual partner and network-level, d) totally different IT and business process governance approach. The technology is shown to be promising especially for SMEs and laggard partners.

Undeniably, the issues of data ownership, security, vendor lock-in and overdependence on the cloud providers still remain as the main concerns for the assimilation and wide-spread use of the technology. When multi-partner, complex supply networks is in question, rules of the game should be set at the network level, and the resolution of such issues is possible only with: a) joint business process management and master data management practices across partners, b) sound strategic service level agreements and long-term contract management, and c) long-term, collaborative, trust-based relationships with the cloud providers.

In this approach, cloud provider turns into one of the main actors of the collaborative game; and a community culture with fewer barriers for entry and exit are created. It is evident that business-IT alignment for both the individual partners and the entire network is vital. Hence, network-level strategies and overall collaborative culture in which jointness, openness and communication are valued determines the success of the implementations. As a new technology for which assimilation in the SCM domain is not complete, success stories will definitely motivate and trigger the formation of more collaborative communities and the development of collaborative business processes. As these collaborative processes gain momentum, utilization of the technology will in turn accelerate.

REFERENCES

Akyuz, G. A., & Gursoy, G. (2010). Taxonomy of collaboration in supply chain management. In *Proceedings of VIII. International Logistics and Supply Chain Congress*. LODER.

Akyuz, G. A., & Gursoy, G. (2011). Role and importance of information technology (IT). In supply chain collaboration. In Proceedings of *IX. International Logistics and Supply Chain Congress*. LODER.

Akyuz, G. A., & Rehan, M. (2013). A Generic, cloud-based representation of supply chains. *International Journal of Cloud Applications and Computing*, *3*(2), 12–20. doi:10.4018/ijcac.2013040102

Aral, S., Sundararajan, A., & Xin, M. (2010). Developing competitive advantage in the cloud: Qualitative findings. *Harvard Business Review*. Retrieved April 20, 2013, from http://blogs.hbr.org/research/2010/12/developing-competitive-advanta.html

Bentz, B. (2013). *How cloud technology can transform supply chain performance?* Retrieved September 15, 2014, from http://www.cio.com/article/2385117/supply-chain-management/how-cloud-technology-can-transform-supply-chain-performance.html

Buyya, R., Broberg, J., & Goscinski, A. (2011). *Cloud computing: Principles and paradigms*. Hoboken, NJ: John Wiley & Sons. doi:10.1002/9780470940105

Cheng, F., Young, S. L., Akella, R., & Tang, X. T. (2011). A meta-modelling service paradigm for cloud computing and its implementation. *South African Journal of Industrial Engineering*, *22*(2), 151–160. doi:10.7166/22-2-22

Cloud Standards Customer Council. (2014). *The Supply chain cloud: Your guide to contracts standards solutions*. Retrieved September 5, 2014 from http://www.cloud-council.org/TheSupplyChainCloud.pdf

Columbus, L. (2014). *Where cloud computing is improving supply chain performance: Lessons learned from SCM world*. Retrieved September 9, 2014, from http://www.forbes.com/sites/louiscolumbus/2014/02/12/where-cloud-computing-is-improving-supply-chain-performance-lessons-learned-from-scm-world/

Courtin, G. (2013). Supply chain and the future of applications. *SCM World Research Report*. Retrieved September 5, 2014, from http://www.e2open.com/assets/pdf/papers-and-reports/SCMWorld-Supply-Chain-and-the-future-of-Applications.pdf

Domini, M. (2012). Impact of cloud computing on SCM. Gartner Group. *InformationWeek*. Retrieved January 20, 2013, from http://www.informationweek.in/cloud_computing/12-09 26/impact_of_cloud_computing_on_supply_chain_management.aspx

Fuerst, C. (2014). *Tips for evaluating cloud-based supply chain management software*. Retrieved September 13, 2014, from http://www.automation.com/automation-news/article/tips-for-evaluating-cloud-based-supply-chain-management-software

Gartner Group. (2008a). *How to identify cloud computing?* Research ID Number: G00158761. Retrieved 20 February, 2013, from http://www.gartner.com/id=705817

Gartner Group. (2008b). *Cloud computing: Defining and describing an emerging phenomenon*. ID Number: G00156220. Retrieved January 20, 2013, from http://www.gartner.com/id=697413

Group, G. E. P. (2011). *Strategic sourcing trends: Mid-year review 2011*. Retrieved January 15, 2014, from http://www.gep.com/Resources

Hugos, M. H., & Hulitzky, D. (2010). *Business in the cloud: What every business needs to know about cloud computing*. Hoboken, NJ: Wiley.

IBM. (2008). IBM Perspective on cloud computing: The "next big thing" or "another fad"? *IBM Whitepaper*. Retrieved January 25, 2013, from http://www-935.ibm.com/services/in/cio/pdf/ibm_perspective_on_cloud_computing.pdf

Jun, C., & Wei, M. Y. (2011). The Research of supply chain information collaboration based on cloud computing. *Procedia Environmental Sciences. 3rd International Conference on Environmental Science and Information Application Technology, ESIAT 2011* (*vol.10*, part A, pp. 875–880). ESIAT.

Kefer, G. (2011). *The cloud solves those lingering supply chain problems*. Retrieved September 5, 2014, from http://www.networkworld.com/article/2182683/tech-primers/the-cloud-solves-those-lingering-supply-chain-problems.html

KPMG International. (2011). *Embracing the cloud: 2011 Global cloud survey report*. Retrieved September 10, 2014, from http://www.kpmg.com/Global/en/IssuesAndInsights/ArticlesPublications/Documents/embracing-cloud.pdf

KPMG International. (2011). *The cloud: Changing the business ecosystem*. Retrieved September 18, 2014, from http://www.kpmg.com/IN/en/IssuesAndInsights/ThoughtLeadership/The_Cloud_Changing_the_Business_Ecosystem.pdf

KPMG International. (2013). *Breaking through the cloud adoption barriers.* Retrieved September 5, 2014, from https://www.kpmg.com/SG/en/IssuesAndInsights/ArticlesPublications/Documents/Advisory-ICE-Breaking-through-the-Cloud-Adoption-Barriers-Glob.pdf

Marks, E. A., & Lozano, B. (2010). *Executive's guide to cloud computing.* Hoboken, NJ: John Wiley & Sons.

McCrea, B. (2012, November). Cloud Breakthrough. *Logistics Management,* 36-40.

Morrison & Foerster LLP. (2013). *Global sourcing trends in 2013.* Global Surcing Group. Retrieved September 15, 2014, from http://www.mofo.com/files/Uploads/Images/130501-Global-Sourcing-Trends.pdf

Oracle. (2009). *Platform-as-a-Service private cloud with Oracle Fusion Middleware.* An Oracle Whitepaper. Retrieved February 5, 2013, from http://www.oracle.com/us/technologies/cloud/036500.pdf

Raines, G. (2009). *Cloud computing and SOA.* Systems Engineering at MITRE. Retrieved January 20, 2013 from http://www.mitre.org/work/tech_papers/tech_papers_09/09_0743/09_0743.pdf

Rehan, M., & Akyuz, G. A. (2010). EAI (Enterprise Application Integration), SOA (Service Oriented Architectures) and its relevance to e-supply chain formation. *African Journal of Business Management, 4*(13), 2604–2614.

Ross, D. (2003). *Introduction to e-supply chain management.* St. Lucie Press.

Ryu, S., Nakayama, K., & Onari, H. (2011). Strategic supply chain coordination scheme under cloud computing environment considering market uncertainty. *International Journal of Business Strategy, 11*(3), 47–57.

Sagawa, C., Yoshida, H., Take, R., & Shimada, J. (2009). Cloud computing based on service-oriented platform. *FUJITSU Science Tech. Journal, 45*(3), 283–289.

Schramm, T., Wright, J., Seng, D., & Jones, D. (2010). *Six questions every supply chain executive should ask about cloud computing.* Retrieved September 6, 2014, from http://www.accenture.com/SiteCollectionDocuments/PDF/10-2460-Supply_Chain_Cloud_PoV_vfinal.pdf

Shacklett, M. (2010). Is supply chain emerging from the cloud? *WorldTrade, 100*(April), 34–37.

Shacklett, M. (2011). A smarter supply chain: Can companies keep pace with the advances? *WorldTrade, 100*(August), 20–26.

Shacklett, M. (2012). Next generation cloud technology for supply chain. *WorldTrade 100, 25*(1), 18-23.

Sosinsky, B. (2011). *Cloud computing bible.* Wiley Publishing.

Sterling, T., & Stark, D. (2009). A High-performance computing forecast: Partly cloudy. *Computing in Science & Engineering, 11*(July/August), 42–49. doi:10.1109/MCSE.2009.111

Tiwari, A., & Jain, M. (2013). Analysis of supply chain management in cloud computing. *International Journal of Innovative Technology and Exploring Engineering, 3*(5), 152–155.

Truong, D. (2014). Cloud-based solutions for supply chain management: A post-adoption study. In *Proceedings of American Society of Business and Behavioral Sciences (ASBBS) 21st Annual Conference*. ASBBS.

Vaquero, L., Rodero-Merino, L., Caceres, J., & Lindner, M. (2009). Break in the clouds: Towards a cloud definition. *Computer Communication Review*, *39*(1), 50–55. doi:10.1145/1496091.1496100

Wang, G., Wang, Y., & Lee, Q. (2009). *Cloud computing: A perspective study*. Retrieved January 20, 2013 from http://ebookbrowse.com/cloud-computing-a-perspective-study-pdf-d198329934

Ward, T. (2012). Supply Chain World Souteast Asia: Cloud Computing and Supply Chain. *SCC*. Retrieved March 1, 2013, from http://supply-chain.org/f/Thomas%20Ward%20-%20Supply%20Chain%20and%20Cloud%20Computing_0.pdf

Wright, J. (2011). An Introduction to cloud computing in SCM. *Supply Chain Asia*, 8-11. Retrieved September 10, 2014, http://archive.supplychainasia.org/component/rsfiles/view.raw?path=Magazinc%2FSCA-Jan-Feb-11.pdf

KEY TERMS AND DEFINITIONS

Collaboration: Ability of two or more partners to engage in joint activities at strategic, tactical and operational levels to plan and execute SC operations towards a win-win agreement with greater success than when acting in isolation.

Enterprise Application: Software suits designed to integrate all processes of an enterprise and to provide linkages with customers, suppliers and other business partners.

Enterprise Resources Planning (ERP) System: Integrated management information system towards planning, execution and control of all enterprise resources, including money and human resources.

Generic: General, applicable to any sector or enterprise.

Service Level Agreemetns (SLAs): A contract between a network service provider and a customer that specifies, in measurable terms, what services the network service provider will offer.

Supply Chain (SC): Complex networked system of organizations, people, technology, activities, information and resources for moving a product or service from suppliers to customers. Includes channel partners, which can be suppliers, intermediaries, third-party service providers and customers, engaging in planning and management of all activities involved in sourcing, procurement, conversion, and all logistics management activities.

Visibility: Ability to trace all resources (including all physical items, data, information and knowledge) across entire processes and partners to provide a coherent view with a single version of truth across the network.

Chapter 4
System Benchmarking on Public Clouds:
Comparing Instance Types of Virtual Machine Clusters

Sanjay P. Ahuja
University of North Florida, USA

Kerwin E. Roslie
University of North Florida, USA

Thomas F. Furman
University of North Florida, USA

Jared T. Wheeler
University of North Florida, USA

ABSTRACT

There are several public cloud providers that provide service across different cloud models such as IaaS, PaaS, and SaaS. End users require an objective means to assess the performance of the services being offered by the various cloud providers. Benchmarks have typically been used to evaluate the performance of various systems and can play a vital role in assessing performance of the different public cloud platforms in a vendor neutral manner. Amazon's EC2 Service is one of the leading public cloud service providers and offers many different levels of service. The research in this chapter focuses on system level benchmarks and looks into evaluating the memory, CPU, and I/O performance of two different tiers of hardware offered through Amazon's EC2. Using three distinct types of system benchmarks, the performance of the micro spot instance and the M1 small instance are measured and compared. In order to examine the performance and scalability of the hardware, the virtual machines are set up in a cluster formation ranging from two to eight nodes. The results show that the scalability of the cloud is achieved by increasing resources when applicable. This chapter also looks at the economic model and other cloud services offered by Amazon's EC2, Microsoft's Azure, and Google's App Engine.

1. INTRODUCTION

The cloud is an emerging platform that is taking shape as more vendors offer services and researchers delve deeper into how to use it and how to measure it. Currently, reliance is placed upon the specifications that each cloud vendor publishes to judge price and performance comparisons. With more widely

DOI: 10.4018/978-1-4666-8676-2.ch004

Copyright © 2015, IGI Global. Copying or distributing in print or electronic forms without written permission of IGI Global is prohibited.

accepted benchmarking, these specifications may become easier to compare in a more direct manner. Performance is the one of the key factors for any enterprise when determining the true benefits of cloud computing. Cloud providers promise many services with corresponding service quality attributes to end user.

End users however require a vendor neutral means to assure that a certain level of performance will be achieved before they commit to hosting their applications and services in the cloud provided by a specific cloud provider. This is where benchmarks play a vital role. Benchmarking would allow enterprises to perform transparent and insightful comparisons to see how various types of applications run on different clouds with various kinds of instance configurations.

When examining the performance of cloud computing, it is worthwhile to note the many different varieties of performance testing that can be done. The evaluation of a cloud environment can vary widely depending on the hardware, hypervisor, guest operating systems, and applications used in the configuration (Ahuja & Sridharan, 2012). Policies set in place by the cloud provider can also have an effect in relation to how much of a priority over the system resources a virtual machine has. Each vendor that offers a cloud service will inarguably use a different setup and configuration that may lead to changes in performance.

The contents of this paper detail the benchmarking of the Amazon Elastic Compute Cloud using the STREAM benchmark for memory bandwidth, IOR benchmark for disk input and output, and NPB-EB benchmark for communication speed. Section two examines some example cloud platforms. Section three identifies previous work in cloud benchmarking, section 4 provides a sampling of system level benchmarks, and section five focuses on the benchmarking performed and its results. Section six draws conclusions.

2. PLATFORM

Current cloud computing offerings come from a number of service providers ranging from small local companies running 3rd party cloud OS software to offer up their hardware resources to other local businesses to some of the worlds largest companies running massive services running their own proprietary software to serve clients across the entire globe. The smaller providers are typically more focused on local business clients as their hardware infrastructure isn't large enough to scale for the needs of large national or international companies. For this reason we will focus on a subset of services offered by the three largest providers; Amazon Web Services (AWS) Elastic Compute Cloud (EC2) which was used in testing for this paper, as well as Microsoft Windows Azure (Azure) VM Roles, and Google Cloud Platform (GCP) App Engine (AE).

The Elastic Compute Cloud (EC2) by Amazon is an Infrastructure as a Service (IaaS) public cloud. EC2 is available, for an hourly fee, to the public. As an IaaS product, EC2 offers users a virtual machine and options of OS to be installed on it. This is to contrast against the Platform as a Service (PaaS) product, where an OS with middleware is rented to the user, or Software as a Service (SaaS), which provides an end-product or application for use. This makes EC2 flexible for use during peak hours or as a full time enhancement or replacement of the existing server infrastructure of a business.

The VM Roles from Windows Azure are very similar to the EC2 instances and are also IaaS services but are a less mature product and as such offer far fewer sizing options. AppEngine (AE) from Google in contrast is a PaaS and offers no options of operating system and even restricts the programming languages to Java (and others that compile to java byte code), Python, and currently experimentally, the Google Go language.

3. RELATED WORK

The paper by Folkerts, Alexandrov, Sachs, Iosup, Markl, & Tosun (2012) is one of the earliest systematic studies on the topic of cloud benchmarking. Based on general benchmark requirements, the authors describe what cloud benchmarking should or should not be. The paper points out the main challenges in building scenario-specific benchmarks for the cloud. The goal of cloud benchmarking is to help developers to predict the behavior of the targeted application and help users to know the performance offered by the target applications for comparison with other offerings. Benchmarking in the cloud computing world can help establishing a baseline of user's application ability to support business requirements. Many vendors/cloud providers do not reveal the details about the implementations of the services provided by them. So it helps organizations or end user to review the benchmarks and decide who (cloud provider) suites better to their needs.

With the increasing commercialization and use of the cloud, more research goes towards the benefits of the cloud, such as the operational and financial advantages of the cloud (Ahuja & Rolli, 2011). It has become a greater priority to accurately depict the performance of cloud services. To this end, benchmarking methodologies and benchmark comparisons across clouds has become a more common topic of concern. Another experiment was conducted between Amazon's EC2 platform and Microsoft's Windows Azure platform that analyzed the differences between the IaaS and PaaS environments with similar methodologies (Ahuja & Mani, 2013).

Salah, Al-Saba, Akhdhor, Shaaban, & Buhari (2011) examined benchmarking of EC2, Elastic Hosts, and BlueLock. The authors made use of the Simplex benchmark to measure CPU execution time, the STREAM benchmark for memory bandwidth, and FIO benchmark to determine average disk input and output. EC2 was benchmarked as having the lowest CPU performance, which the authors attribute to the limit EC2 imposes on how many cycles can be used by an instance, despite its CPU's faster clockrate. EC2 does, however, maintain the same performance when the benchmark is run across two virtual machines, indicating use of the second core made available. EC2 ranked lowest in the memory bandwidth benchmark, except its low standard deviation indicates that the bandwidth is predictable. In the FIO benchmark, EC2 was tested by a sequential read and write of one gigabyte without cache; EC2 outperformed the other two cloud platforms in both the read and the write categories.

Lenk, Menzel, Lipsky, Tai, & Offermann (2011) sought to determine if the performance indicators provided by cloud providers are accurate and comparable. They performed tests with the following benchmarks: Crafty, dcraw, eSpeak, HMMer, JTR, OFMM, OpenSSL, OSVD, OSVSP, OVSP, and Sudokut. The authors never directly indicate what each benchmark measures; however the units of measure and if the higher values or lower values are better are provided. The benchmarks were run across small, medium, and large EC2 instances, Flexiscale, and Rackspace. The direct comparisons are never made by the authors; however the paper indicates that the cloud providers' actual statistics varied from what would have been expected given the publicity materials. The authors did specifically point out that EC2's performance varied according to the architecture beneath the instances, which the user has no control over, therefore this impact is not completely known until the instance is spun up. Also, time of day did not seem to impact the performance of one virtual running without outside communications. Lenk, Menzel, Lipsky, Tai, & Offermann also pointed out that these benchmarks are synthetic, and therefore may not be completely indicative of a true business application's performance in the cloud.

The experiment to be described in this research is different from these previous two examples of other work in cloud benchmarking. While the experiment in Salah, Al-Saba, Akhdhor, Shaaban, & Buhari

(2011) uses the STREAM benchmark, like our research, it uses alternatives to the IOR and NPB-EB that we put in use. The work by Lenk, Menzel, Lipsky, Tai, & Offermann (2011) uses the benchmarking as a means to an end to determine how accurate cloud provider publicized details are, while our work seeks to benchmark EC2 for its own purpose. Also, neither of these experiments looked at the EC2 micro instance which we take advantage of in our benchmarking.

4. TRADITIONAL SYSTEM LEVEL BENCHMARKS

This section provides a sampling of existing system level benchmarks from traditional computing environments that could be leveraged for use in cloud environments. These benchmarks typically aim to capture CPU, memory, and I/O performance.

4.1 UnixBench

It is a benchmark suite that provides a basic indicator of the performance of a Unix-like system. The tests compare UNIX systems by comparing their results to a set of scores set by running the code on a benchmark system, which is a SPARCstation 20-61. UnixBench consists of a number of individual tests that are targeted at specific areas such as file I/O and CPU. A single comparable score is given based on results of various tests (http://code.google.com/p/byte-unixbench/).

4.2 PassMark

PassMark benchmark measures CPU performance with following metrics:

- **Integer Math:** Expressed in Millions of Operations per second. This metric is used to test the CPU speed to perform mathematical integer operations.
- **Floating Point Math:** Expressed in Millions of operations per second. This metric is used to test the CPU speed to perform mathematical floating operations.
- **Prime Number Test:** Expressed in Millions of primes per second. This metric tests the CPU speed to search for prime numbers (http://www.passmark.com/).
- **Multimedia Instructions:** Expressed in Millions of Matrices per second. It measures the Streaming SIMD Extensions (SSE) capabilities of a CPU.

4.3 CacheBench

This benchmark suite is designed to evaluate the performance of the memory hierarchy of computer systems with possibly multiple levels of cache present on and off the processor. Cachebench incorporates 8 benchmarks: Cache Read, Cache Write, Cache Read/Write/Modify, Hand tuned Cache Read, Hand tuned Cache Write, Hand tuned Cache Read/Write/Modify, memset(), and memcpy() (Mucci & London, 1998).

4.4 STREAM

It is a standard synthetic benchmark for the measurement of memory bandwidth expressed in MBs/sec and the corresponding computation rate for simple vector kernels. Details are provided in Section 5.2.

4.5 IOR Benchmark

IOR stands for Interleaved Or Random. This benchmark is used for testing the performance of parallel file systems using various interfaces and access patterns. IOR uses MPI for process synchronization. Details follow in Section 5.2.

5. RESULTS AND COMPARISONS

5.1 Test Bed

Amazon's EC2 offers a wide variety of hardware to be used for virtual machines (http://aws.amazon.com/ec2/). In this experiment, the three types of benchmarks were executed on micro-sized and small-sized virtual machines on Amazon's EC2 platform. The micro instance (t1.micro) utilizes a low amount of resources to provide for a short burst of computing capacity. The micro instance has 613 Megabytes of memory and up to two EC2 Compute Units usable for short periodic bursts. The M1small instance (m1.small) is similar to the micro instance in terms of resources. The small instance has 1.7 Gigabytes of memory but is limited to only one EC2 Compute Unit. An EC2 Compute Unit provides an equivalent CPU performance of a 1.0-1.2 GHz 2007 Opteron or 2007 Xeon processor (Perry, 2009).

To create the Amazon EC2 nodes and to manage the virtual machines, a program called StarCluster was utilized. StarCluster is a cluster-computing toolkit that allows the user to remotely spin up multiple virtual machines on Amazon's EC2 and have them automatically configured in a cluster. StarCluster is written in Python 2.7 and was released open-source under the LGPL license. StarCluster has several preset AMIs that define the operating system environment on the virtual machines (http://star.mit.edu/cluster). In this experiment, the ami-999d49f0 image was used to create a Linux environment using Ubuntu 11.10 64-bit.

5.2 Benchmarks and Metrics

Three types of benchmarks were used in this experiment. The benchmarks STREAM, IOR, and NPB-EP tested aspects in memory, I/O, and CPU performance respectively.

The STREAM Benchmark examines the performance of memory bandwidth within high performance computers. It performs four different operations that occur in memory (McCalpin, 1995). These operations are Copy, Scale, Add, and Triad. Each of the operations reported their results in terms of MB/s. The STREAM benchmark was written in C and FORTRAN and was created by John McCalpin (http://www.cs.virginia.edu/stream/ref.html).

The IOR benchmark was created to examine the I/O capabilities of a high performance computer. It performs two operations, Read and Write, and reports the results of them in MiB/s. The MiB/s metric is measuring the throughput of data when the virtual machine is either reading from or writing to a file. An important detail to observe when measuring I/O is to examine how performance is affected when multiple nodes are trying to read or write to the same file at the same time. The IOR benchmark is available for download on the SourceForge website (http://sourceforge.net/projects/ior-sio/).

The NAS Parallel Benchmarks (NPB) are a set of several different benchmarks that are targeted at evaluating the performance of high performance computers. The Embarrassingly Parallel (NPB-EP) benchmark used in this project measured the performance of the CPU by generating a large quantity of random numbers. The collected results were reported in the operation time in seconds and the total number of millions of operations per second (Mop/s). This benchmark program can be downloaded from NASA's open-source software website, or a preconfigured version is available on Github's website at (https://github/com/moutai/hpc-medley).

5.3 Research Methodology

To be able to use StarCluster, Python 2.7 must be installed on the host computer. StarCluster is necessary to create the nodes on Amazon's EC2 in a preconfigured cluster. It is critical that the configuration file for StarCluster is edited to have the correct information. The configuration file holds information on connecting to the AWS account, the proper encryption key to use, the type and number of nodes to create, and any of services needed to be used by the nodes on the cluster. Once the file has been properly configured, open a command prompt, navigate to the folder where StarCluster was installed, and use the following command to create the cluster:

```
starcluster start[name]
```

After this command is invoked, StarCluster will create the cluster and properly configure all of the nodes. One node will be assigned as the master and communicates with all of the other nodes within the cluster. Using either the StarCluster command or another program, like WinSCP, connect to the master node of the cluster and transfer all of the benchmark files over to /home/ec2-user folder. This folder is shared amongst all of the nodes, which is important when compiling the benchmarks.

To compile and run the STREAM benchmark, use the following commands from the STREAM-MPI folder:

```
Compile:
mpicc-DPARALLEL_MPI-03-o stream_mpi stream_mpi.c
Run:
mpiexec-host master, node001, node002, node003./stream_mpi > output/c1.m_n4.
1.txt
```

To compile and run the IOR benchmark, use the following commands from the IOR/src/C folder:

```
Compile:
make
```

```
Run:
mpiexec-host master, node001, node002, node003 ./IOR -b 4m -t 4m > output/
c1.m_n4. 1.txt
```

To compile and run the NPB-EP benchmark, use the following commands from the NPB-MPI folder:

```
Compile:
make EP NPROCS = 4CLASS =A
Run:
mpiexec -host master, node001, node002, node003 bin/ep.A.4 > output/ep.A.4_3.
txt
```

Each benchmark should be run ten times to acquire uniform results in the event of a result appearing to be skewed. Once all of the benchmarks have been processed, move all of the output files off of the master node. The cluster can be terminated from the same command prompt using the following command:

```
starcluster terminate[name]
```

This methodology should be repeated multiple times using 1, 2, 4, 6, 8 nodes and t1.micro & m1.small instance types. These parameters are specified in the StarCluster configuration file previously mentioned.

5.4 Results

After taking the data from the output files, the mean value for each metric was generated and used to create the eight figures on the next page. The figures display the results of 1, 2, 4, 6, 8 node clusters benchmarked on the micro instance type and small instance type. The figures can be used to find whether or not there are any patterns present as the number of nodes are scaled up in the cluster. Overall, the figures show that each benchmark has its own unique behavior.

The STREAM benchmark tested the bandwidth capability of the memory. Figure 1 [Copy], Figure 2 [Scale], Figure 3 [Add], and Figure 4 [Triad] all present the data results from this benchmark. Figure 1 shows a drop in performance on the small instance type whenever more nodes are added; however, the micro instance type cluster fluctuates around the same value. This fluctuating behavior can be observed on the other graphs as well for both the micro and small instance types. This behavior is probably attributed to the processing speed and not the actual memory. Both instance types must handle some form of overhead when more nodes are added, but the micro instance type is able to achieve bursts in performance to overcome the performance of the small instance type. Also, for this benchmark, the total capacity of the memory most likely does not matter as much as the speed of the memory. Nodes utilizing a faster memory module and processor will probably show increased performance over simply adding more nodes to the cluster.

The IOR benchmark was supposed to measure the average read and write times when testing the I/O functionality. Figure 5 [Write] and Figure 6 [Read] show the averages of all of the tests ran using this benchmark. However, due to the nature of the graphs, it is unlikely that they properly reflect the real performance of I/O on these clusters. When using only a single node, the average read and write times seemed standard; but on all of the multi-node clusters, the results plummeted and stagnated at very low

Figure 1. Data Transfer Rate of the Copy Operation in the Stream Benchmark across multiple cluster configurations.

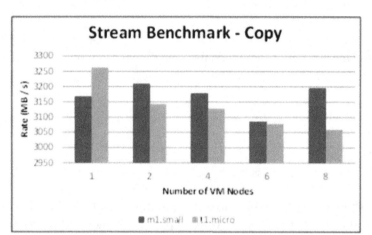

levels. It is not likely that these results were mere coincidence. These results were consistent for both micro and small instance types even running the benchmark on newly configured clusters during different times of the day and on multiple days. It is speculated that either the benchmark was not properly set up for this experiment and therefore is not running properly, or the overhead for utilizing more than one node in the cluster is so high for this benchmark that it negatively affects over all performance drastically. It would be worthwhile to attempt the testing of the I/O metric again using a different benchmark to see if these results are truly false.

Lastly, the NPB-EP benchmark shows promising results when testing the performance of the CPU. Figure 7 and Figure 8 respectively show the operation time of the benchmark in seconds and the total number of million operations per second. Here it is very clear that the increased nodes positively affect the performance of the benchmark. As more nodes are added, the time it takes to complete the benchmark decreases for both the micro and small instance types as shown in Figure 7. Likewise, Figure 8 shows

Figure 2. Data Transfer Rate of the Scale Operation in the Stream Benchmark across multiple cluster configurations.

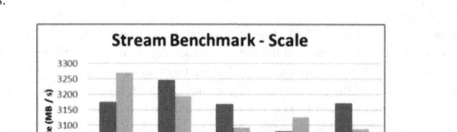

Figure 3. Data Transfer Rate of the Add Operation in the Stream Benchmark across multiple cluster configurations.

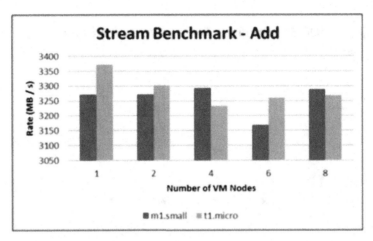

that the total number of operations completed increases gradually as well. It is important to note that the micro instance is utilizing its second EC2 Compute Unit to perform better than the small instance for this benchmark. The micro instance can gain a burst in performance when needed, whereas the small instance type is limited to its single EC2 Compute Unit.

5.5 Services

The services from AWS used for this paper include the EC2 compute service that gives customers the use of Virtual Machines on demand with nearly any operating system. EC2 instances can be created in a variety of sizes from the Micro which includes a single virtual core up to 2 ECU and only 613MiB of ram to the Eight Extra Large which offers 88 ECU and 244GB of ram. Also offered are cluster compute

Figure 4. Data Transfer Rate of the Triad Operation in the Stream Benchmark across multiple cluster configurations.

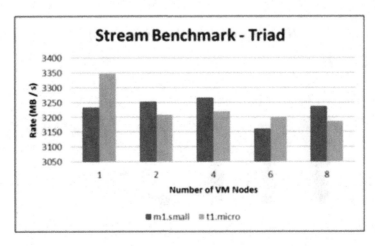

Figure 5. Average Speed of the Write Operation in the IOR Benchmark across multiple cluster configurations.

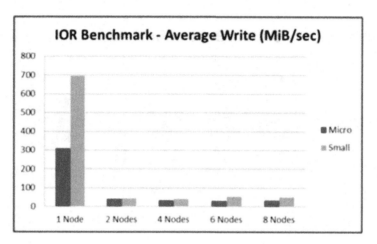

Figure 6. Average Speed of the Read Operation in the IOR Benchmark across multiple cluster configurations.

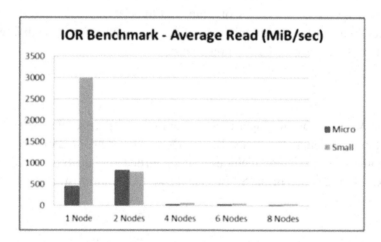

Figure 7. Operation Time (in seconds) of the NPB-EP Benchmark across multiple cluster configurations.

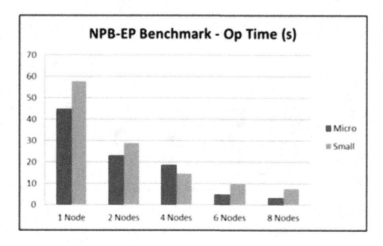

Figure 8. Million Operations per Second of the NPB-EP Benchmark across multiple cluster configurations.

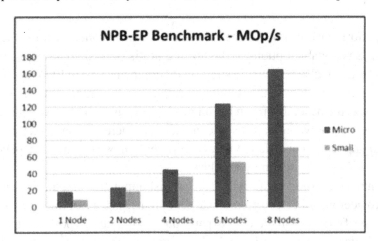

instances that give access to GPU compute as well as dedicated SSD storage for speed or a complete physical hard drive array of 24, 2TB HDD for massive storage capacity.

Windows Azure VM Roles offer an equivalent to the AWS Micro called an Extra small that includes shared compute capacity and 768MB of ram. However, they top out an Extra Large role that only has 8 cores and 14GB of ram (http://www.windowsazure.com/en-us/).

Google App Engine on the other hand is a platform service designed to scale horizontally automatically as needed and doesn't offer Virtual Machines to manage (https://developers.google.com/appengine/).

5.6 Economic Model

The EC2 service is part of the overall IaaS offering that AWS is built upon. The economic model around this service is pay for usage where that usage is computed based upon a combination of the instance size and the geographic location it is created/running in per hour or part thereof. The per hour usage cost can be reduced by computing your minimum usage requirements and reserving instances to meet that need. For batch processing that can be run at different times Amazon also offers spot instances where unused capacity is bid upon and becomes available for the bidders use when they are the highest bidder for the current time period and the capacity is available for their use. Other services offered by AWS vary from IaaS to PaaS type services and pricing models vary as well from the per usage hour type model the EC2 service has to pay per request or transaction (http://aws.amazon.com/ec2/pricing/).

This is a similar economic model to Azures Web, Worker, and VM Roles in which they can be used in an IaaS capacity and are paid for in a per hour of usage where the user determines the size of instance needed. Some of the other services offered in Azure similar to AWS have pay per request or transaction models as well.

In contrast to the usage per hour models of EC2 and VM Roles Google App Engine charges based on exact resources used. This means if your application is sitting idle there are no charges and when your application is processing the platform monitors exact compute cycles, network bandwidth, and other resources consumed and bills by the monitored amount used.

6. CONCLUSION

Our system level performance testing of the micro and small instances within the Elastic Compute Cloud shows that EC2 is a viable option for the hosting of distributed applications that may make use of multi node clusters. It can also be a viable solution for companies, or individuals, which wish to have dedicated virtual machines, with or without clustering, but do not want to invest in their own hardware.

The variability in performance from run to run on the same instance type running in the same data center from a single Cloud provider leads us to conclude that there are many factors that can affect the performance of your application in different ways at different times but can be, depending on the nature of your application, mitigated by scaling your cluster.

This set of benchmarks, testing memory, CPU, and disk input and output, was run on only a single service from one provider and only a very small subset of that service's options. We leave it up to future researchers to both verify our results and to expand our testing and hypothesis to more services and providers to gain a better understanding of whether or not the variability we experienced was due to temporary conditions, the provider we selected, or to the cloud service paradigm as a whole.

ACKNOWLEDGMENT

This research has been supported in part by the FIS Distinguished Professor in Computing Sciences Award to Dr. Sanjay P. Ahuja.

REFERENCES

Ahuja, S., & Mani, S. (2013). Empirical performance analysis of HPC benchmarks across variations of cloud computing. *International Journal of Cloud Applications and Computing, 3*(1), 13–26. doi:10.4018/ijcac.2013010102

Ahuja, S., & Rolli, A. (2011). Survey of the state-of-the-art of cloud computing. *International Journal of Cloud Applications and Computing, 1*(4), 34–43. doi:10.4018/ijcac.2011100103

Ahuja, S., & Sridharan, S. (2012). Performance evaluation of hypervisors for cloud computing. *International Journal of Cloud Applications and Computing, 2*(3), 26–67. doi:10.4018/ijcac.2012070102

Amazon.com Inc. (n.d.). *Elastic Compute Cloud.* Retrieved from http://aws.amazon.com/ec2/

Amazon.com Inc. (n.d.). *EC2 Pricing.* Retrieved from http://aws.amazon.com/ec2/pricing/

Amazon.com Inc. (n.d.). *EC2 Instance Types*. Retrieved from http://aws.amazon.com/ec2/instance-types/

Folkerts, E., Alexandrov, A., Sachs, K., Iosup, A., Markl, V., & Tosun, C. (2012). Benchmarking in the cloud: What it should, can, and cannot be. *4th TPC Technology Conference (TPCTC)*, (pp. 173-188). TPC.

Google Inc. (n.d.). *App Engine*. Retrieved from https://developers.google.com/appengine/

IOR Benchmark on SourceForge. (n.d.). Retrieved from http://sourceforge.net/projects/ior-sio/

Lenk, A., Menzel, M., Lipsky, J., Tai, S., & Offermann, P. (2011). What are you paying for? Performance benchmarking for infrastructure-as-a-service offerings. In *Proceedings of Cloud Computing (CLOUD), 2011 IEEE International Conference on*, (pp. 484-491). IEEE.

Massachusetts Institute of Technology. (n.d.). *StarCluster*. Retrieved from http://star.mit.edu/cluster/

McCalpin, J. D. (1995). *Memory bandwidth and machine balance in current high performance computers. In Proceedings of IEEE Computer Society Technical Committee on Computer Architecture (TCCA)* (pp. 19–25). IEEE.

Microsoft. (n.d.). *Windows Azure*. Retrieved from http://www.windowsazure.com/en-us/

Mucci, P. J., & London, K. (1998). *The CacheBench report*. Retrieved from http://www.cs.surrey.ac.uk/BIMA/People/L.Gillam/downloads/publications/Fair%20Benchmarking%20for%20Cloud%20Computing%20Systems.pdf

PassMark Software Inc. (n.d.). Retrieved from http://www.passmark.com/

Perry, G. (2009). *What are Amazon EC2 compute units? Thinking out cloud*. Retrieved from http://gevaperry.typepad.com/main/2009/03/figuring-out-the-roi-of-infrastructureasaservice.html

Salah, K., Al-Saba, M., Akhdhor, M., Shaaban, O., & Buhari, M. I. (2011). Performance evaluation of popular cloud IaaS providers. In *Proceedings of Internet Technology and Secured Transactions (ICITST), 2011 International Conference for*, (pp. 345-349). ICITST.

Taifi, M. (2012). *NPB Benchmark*. Retrieved from https://github.com/moutai/hpc-medley/

University of Virginia. (n.d.). *Stream Benchmark*. Retrieved from http://www.cs.virginia.edu/stream/ref.html

UnixBench. (n.d.). Retrieved from http://code.google.com/p/byte-unixbench/

KEY TERMS AND DEFINITIONS

Benchmarking: The process of measuring the performance of an application, platform, or communication medium.

Cloud Computing: The practice of hosting services on a remote server(s) which are accessible through the Internet. Connected users are able to access, store, manage, and process data utilizing the resources of the remote server instead of their local computer.

Cluster: A group of computers networked together so that they are able to share resources and function as a single, distributed entity.

Computing Services: Availability of resources to perform computational work via a third party. Typically in the form of data processing or application hosting through Cloud providers.

Infrastructure as a Service: The hosting of various hardware and hardware configurations by a third party in a remote location accessible over the Internet. Oftentimes highly scalable in terms of resources which can be adjusted on-demand for dynamic utilization.

Instance Type: Refers to the specifications of a virtual machine. The computational resources allocated to a virtual machine will determine its Instance Type. Large instance types will have more dedicated resources for the virtual machine to utilize.

Virtualization: Simulating the environment of a computer hardware platform, operating system, or application. To the end-user, the virtualized environment should be indistinguishable from a similar real environment.

Chapter 5
Approaches to Cloud Computing in the Public Sector:
Case Studies in UK Local Government

Jeffrey Chang
London South Bank University, UK

Mark Johnston
Julian Campbell Foundation, UK

ABSTRACT

Cloud computing refers to a scalable network infrastructure where consumers receive IT services such as software and data storage through the Internet on a subscription basis. Potential benefits include cost savings, simpler IT and reduced energy consumption. The UK government and local authorities, like commercial organisations, are considering cloud-based services. Concerns have been raised, however, over issues such as security, access, data protection and ownership. This study attempts to investigate the likely impact of cloud computing on local government based on a conceptual framework and case studies of four London borough councils. It reveals that the concept of cloud computing is new and not clearly understood. Local authorities, who face further cuts in government funding, welcome a cloud-based IT infrastructure which may lead to considerable savings. Yet local government is conservative, so with their risk-adverse attitude local authorities are more likely to adopt a hybrid approach to implementation.

INTRODUCTION

Cloud computing is held to offer a number of advantages to the organisations which utilise it. These include cost savings, scalable computing services, simpler IT infrastructure and reduced energy consumption. Theoretically the advantages offered are as relevant to public sector organisations as they are for the private sector. Within local government there are pressures, positive and negative, from a decline in IT budgets, a lack of adequate skills in public sector employees and from the centrally imposed e

DOI: 10.4018/978-1-4666-8676-2.ch005

Copyright © 2015, IGI Global. Copying or distributing in print or electronic forms without written permission of IGI Global is prohibited.

-Government agenda. As a result cloud-based delivery models are rapidly gaining the attention of government. Across the public sector, many IT leaders are carefully considering the implications of cloud utilisation. Software applications, hardware, infrastructure, platforms, services and storage or whether the government should develop its own cloud are issues which require careful consideration. Key concerns include issues such as the security and ownership of data, potential impact on employment within the client organisations and the structural and cultural implications of moving to cloud provision for large, complex and conservative government institutions. As yet, very little research has been carried out on the implications of utilising cloud services for local government. This study, through theoretical analysis using a conceptual framework and four case studies of London-based borough councils, attempts to explore the likely impact of cloud computing use within local authorities. Firstly, the conceptual framework is presented in the context of current literature relating to the subject. This will consider aspects such as driving and resisting forces and potential implementation issues arising within the public sector. Following on from this theoretical discussion case study data from the four boroughs will be analysed using the same framework considerations. Conclusions will be drawn and consideration given to potential next-steps in this specific field of research.

THE CONCEPT OF CLOUD COMPUTING

Cloud computing is a style of computing where IT capabilities are provided as a service delivered over the Internet to a customer's workplace, similar to utilities such as water and electricity which are 'piped' to the customer's premises. Although there is no universally agreed definition, cloud computing has five key attributes according to a group of researchers at Gartner: service-based, scalable and elastic, shared, metered by use and using Internet Technology (Plummer et al, 2009). These attributes are addressed as 'essential characteristics' by the National Institute of Standard and Technology (NIST, 2011).

The key advantages of cloud computing are held to be reduced costs, increased efficiency and a significant reduction in energy consumption leading to cost savings and greener IT (Catteddu, 2010; Armbrust et al, 2010; Foster et al, 2008; Luis et al, 2008; Aymerich et al, 2009; Grossman, 2009; Korri, 2009; Maggiani, 2009; Nelson, 2009). For potential customers cloud computing presents an attractive alternative to buying, setting up and maintaining their own in-house computing infrastructure (Korri, 2009). These advantages are theoretically as applicable to the public sector as to private organisations, and as set out in the Digital Britain (2009) report, the UK government sees the adoption of cloud computing as critical to the success of its plans to increase efficiency in the public sector.

In the private sector, concerns have been expressed both about the security of data management and loss of organisational control of a key resource (Takabi et al, 2010; Buyya et al, 2009; Grossman, 2009). Public sector clients (or potential clients) will be aware of these concerns. Given the confidential and sensitive nature of much of the data held by public institutions, this becomes a particularly important issue (Nelson, 2009).

So in considering the public sector use of cloud computing we see there are opposing forces; potential cost and efficiency savings verses potential, but difficult to quantify, risks to data security.

Figure 1. A conceptual framework of implementing cloud computing in local government (Chang, 2011)

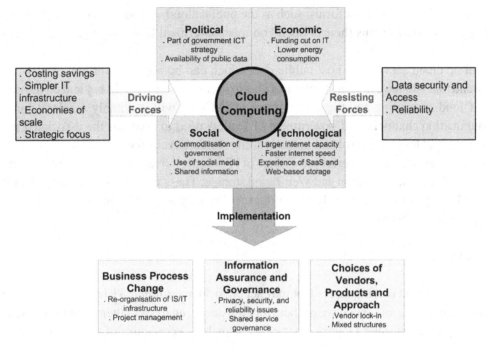

THE CONCEPTUAL FRAMEWORK FOR IMPLEMENTING CLOUD COMPUTING IN LOCAL GOVERNMENT

The conceptual framework (Figure 1) draws on two models for analysing the change process: Lewin's model (Lewin, 1947) and the PEST model which sorts attributes and consequences by four types: political, economical, social and technological. In the framework the key elements commonly associated with cloud computing, or commonly understood to be attributes or consequences of cloud computing implementation, are categorised using PEST. This provides a general background and sets out the relevance of cloud computing for government organisations. On top of this, through applying Kurt Lewin's change process model, driving forces and resisting forces are identified. This framework was developed as part of a theoretical paper (Chang, 2011) before the current empirical study was devised.

There are three client-side activities involved in the implementation of cloud computing; business process change, information assurance and governance, and choice of vendors, products, platform and approach. These implementation activities also form part of the conceptual framework.

Background

In the UK public sector the move towards cloud-based services is largely driven by the Westminister government's strategies for centralising ICT resources and for making more public services directly available online (Cabinet Office, 2010). It has been predicted that the adoption of the government cloud, known as the G-Cloud would result in some £3.2 billion savings. G-Cloud is considered to be an innovative development to meet demand for greater efficiency and a simpler IT infrastructure in the current economic situation where, even as the mainstream economy recovers, it is considered prudent policy to maintain low public spending, or even reduce it further. Government agencies need to prioritise their IT services and explore shared platforms, such as the public cloud, in order to achieve the required cost savings. They will have to focus their IT spend on mission-critical business areas (Das et al, 2011; Di Maio, 2009).

Using public cloud services to host public data which can be accessed through social media is an important trend that will have a significant impact both on citizen service delivery and on the government workplace. Cloud computing and the development of G-Cloud will inevitably accelerate and open up such communication channels, and government IT leaders need to consider the associated issues such as security, potential loss of control and accountability for data recovery.

Government agencies have experienced a range of IT solutions over past years including outsourcing, grid computing, SaaS, virtualisation and Web-based storage. These form a foundation for the implementation of cloud computing. Additionally, larger internet capacity and speed nowadays will ensure reliant and appropriate cloud service delivery.

Driving Forces

There are four significant driving forces that may act on local government IT leaders, prompting them to consider cloud computing and encouraging them forward during analysis of their IT options. These driving forces are cost savings, simpler IT infrastructure and flexibity, economies of scale and strategic focus.

Cost Savings

The cloud computing client should benefit from reduced investment in IT and much smaller servicing and maintenance costs because the requirement for 'owned' or 'in house' IT hardware will drop significantly (Wyld et al, 2010; Vaquero et al, 2008). They will also benefit financially because running less hardware means reduced energy consumption (AbdelSalam et al, 2009). Cloud users can also utilise their remaining 'in house' hardware more efficiently (Aymerich et al, 2008) thus freeing up internal resources.

Simpler IT Infrastructure/Flexibility

Cloud computing services are delivered through the Internet so, as stated above, there is no need for the client organisation to own and run a large and complex IT infrastructure. There is no need for capacity for changes in usage or software/technology. The cloud is easily flexible, providing an inherent ability to scale computing power up and down according to usage (Armbust 2010; McEvoy & Schulze, 2008). With cloud-based software services clients do not need to worry about updating or maintaining software, or with licensing issues. These aspects are dealt with by the vendor (Vining & Di Maio, 2009).

Economies of Scale

Cloud vendors have typically been reputable enough to offer customers a reliable service because they are large enough to provide the necessary resilience. With their large data centres and extensive computing capacity cloud providers can enjoy economies of scale impossible for individual clients, yet the benefits can be passed on to those clients (Marston et al, 2011; Grossman, 2009).

Strategic Focus

Having realised cost savings by using cloud based computing, and with a smaller in-house IT infrastructure, local authorities are able to re-focus their attention on strategic goals. Cloud computing should free them up to make better use of limited financial, IT and human resources (Low et al, 2011; Vining & Di Maio, 2009).

Resisting Forces

At the same time there are significant resisting forces that local government must consider during analysis of their IT options, and which may ultimately prevent them from adopting cloud computing. These resisting forces are security and access, and reliability and trust.

Security and Access

Customers of cloud computing do not know where the machines they use actually are. They do not know where their data is actually stored. Everything is somewhere in the cloud. This is a significant concern for local authorities because, to meet the requirements of current privacy legislation, government agencies must know exactly where their data is being stored and who is able to access it (Mishra et al, 2013; Buyya et al, 2008).

Reliability and Trust

The successful implementation of cloud computing relies largely on the trust between buyers and vendors, so local authority clients will need reassuring as to the service they will receive. In particular the vendor has to provide assurance over data security and privacy issues, which must be carefully written into the service level agreements (SLAs) agreed between the parties (Moreno-Vozmediano et al, 2013; Kandukuri et al, 2009). The cloud supplier must use encryption technologies to protect data in shared environments (Younis and Kifayat, 2013; Vining & Di Maio, 2009).

Implementation Issues

So we see that local authorities should carefully consider the benefits and risks of adopting a cloud based service model, and this will include start-up and ongoing 'rental' costs as well as long term savings. They must also consider which of the several service models on offer is appropriate for their needs. Once the decision to proceed has been taken it is important that they implement cloud computing as a business process change project, which requires senior management support (Bojanova et al, 2013; Scholl, 2003). Concerns have already been raised that local government is not used to running large IT projects and therefore the project failure rates are high (Gilbert, 2009). In the public sector successful cloud computing implementation does not just depend on solving the technical issues, such as broadband bandwidths. It will have considerable impact on the authority's IT infrastructure, on its staff, both in terms of numbers and required skills, and on the authority's service users. These aspects all need to be addressed to achieve successful implementation, and decisions taken now will have implications for how local government provides services well into the future.

According to Armbrust et al (2010) success in implementing cloud-based infrastructure depends on a careful comparative assessment of the various types of service delivery available, and the alternative price models. IT leaders should also consider the choice of public cloud or private cloud. Some of the pricing models on the market are quite complex and therefore total service costs may be difficult to predict. Vendor lock-in could potentially be a serious concern because it can be extremely difficult to change the interface when moving from one provider to another (Silva et al, 2013; Buyya et al, 2008). This may cause problems for authorities who have to comply with stringent public sector competition and 'value for money' tests. Another significant risk consideration will be future technology change costs if the provider discontinues the service (Foster et al, 2008).

Cloud computing generally is a relatively new service model. Considering this alongside the concerns over data security and privacy already discussed has lead to the suggestion that local government is more likely to adopt a staged approach to the implementation of cloud computing and to utilise a mixed service structure built on both public and private clouds (Tsohou et al, 2014; Di Maio, 2009).

RESEARCH QUESTIONS

Chang's conceptual model (Chang, 2011) sets out in theoretical terms the principle issues local authorities must address when considering cloud computing. By discovering some of the actual views and concerns held by real life stakeholders we can develop a more realistic assessment of potential implementation problems.

There are three main research questions:

1. To what extent are local authorities aware of cloud computing and the development of the government cloud (G-Cloud)?
2. What do stakeholders see as the main benefits for local authorities of adopting cloud computing and what do they see as the main disadvantages?
3. How might cloud computing be implemented by local authorities, in terms of business process change, information assurance and vendor selection?

RESEARCH METHOD AND DESIGN

As the aim of the research was to investigate key stakeholders' perceptions of cloud computing and the relative importance of contextual factors, a qualitative approach was used (Yin, 2009; O'Donnell & Stewart, 2007). Case study analysis was undertaken at four London based local authorities to determine if they were planning to move to cloud service utilization, and if so, how they were planning to achieve this change.

Interviews were held with the head of IT and members of the IT management team at each council between October 2011 and January 2012, seeking to gain a better understanding of how they viewed cloud service provision and the nature and purposes of the G-Cloud as well as opportunities for, and constraints on, its implementation in local authorities. The local authorities selected are all sufficiently large to be at the stage of considering cloud computing and may already have some experience of shared services. They were identified from press reports and government publications. Prior to commencing the interviewees were all give assurance that no mention would be made of their name or the organisation they represent in any of the findings/published material.

The results obtained from interviewing the four case study organisations have been comparatively analysed based on the conceptual framework previously proposed and using the three main research questions addressed in the study. The findings have then been analysed to identify the level of awareness of cloud computing in local government, perceived opportunities for its use, perceived constraints and threats and then to determine if there are any organisational factors which account for differences in response from one council to another. It will also be possible to gauge differences in central government's perception of the key issues and determine what actions need to be taken to address the concerns raised.

DISCUSSION

The four local authorities will be referred to as Council A, Council B, Council C and Council D. Although these local government organisations have yet to adopt cloud computing they are fully aware of cloud services currently available and the development of government cloud (G-Cloud) from various government publications. In particular Council B has intentions to implement cloud computing with an SME cloud provider and has included this in their strategic plans.

A brief introduction to each of the participating councils is given below:

Council A: Council A serves a population of 295,532 people, of which over 60 per cent are in employment with only 2.7 per cent registered unemployed. The council had a net budget of £200 million for 2012-13. Their strategic plan is to save more than £30 million over the three years to 2015. This is in addition to the £22 million the council saved in 2011-12. Therefore in total the council will be saving £50 million over a four year period. The council has already cut staffing costs saving over £3 million. At the time of interview they were in discussion with surrounding councils to look at potential shared services.

Council B: Council B serves a population of some 247,000, according to the 2011 census data. Residents aged 25-49 count for more than 42% of this total, while residents aged 50 and over comprise a smaller amount of the whole borough population (23%). The prevailing economic climate and central government funding cuts were placing considerable pressure on the council's budget, and this is likely to continue for the next few years. Efficiency savings had been a priority in addressing the budget cuts in order to minimise the effect on front-line services. Council B claims to be one of the first local authorities to be migrating email telephony and Microsoft technology to a cloud-based solution.

Council C: Council C serves a population of over 300,000, and has seen 6% population growth per annum since 1991. In that time the number of people aged below 16 has increased by 5%. The council's diversity is high and has also increased in recent years, with over than 40% of residents being classified as minority ethnic compared with 9.1% nationally. One the council's priorities from financial year 2012-13 onwards has been to deliver value for money in response to funding cuts, with an objective to save £85 million by April 2015. The council has supported the concepts of opening up public information and providing public services online, and a range of electronic forms has been developed. The council has adopted a 24-hour automated information service with the aim of reducing the need for unnecessary customer visits, with an appointment system for complex queries.

Council D: Council D serves a population of approximately 150,000, and is one of the richest and most densely populated districts in the United Kingdom. Notwithstanding this demographic the council, in line with the rest of the public sector, has suffered cuts in central government grant. They were actively seeking means of reducing management and operational costs at the time of the interviews. A major aspect of this was seeking to establish a new relationship with surrounding boroughs in the shared delivery of council services. With an objective to reduce management costs in shared services by 50% the council was expecting to save a total of £35 million a year by 2014-15. Council D adopts a hybrid approach to IT provision. Whilst the network server is developed and maintained in-house, many departmental information systems have been outsourced, one example being the human resources information systems.

Concept of Cloud Computing

The notion that cloud computing is not clearly defined is confirmed by all four local authorities. The lack of a universally agreed definition of cloud computing is expressed by Council A, "I think the first thing is that cloud computing isn't clearly defined, what people mean by cloud computing, do they mean hosted solutions accessible via the internet? …. I think there's a lot of hype around it, without going into detail about what they actually mean by it". Similar to Council A, Council C is concerned that "different people are using that term and meaning different things" and staff in the IT department believe, from a technical point of view, that cloud computing is, in a sense, software as a service (SaaS) on a subscription basis, while Council D refers cloud computing as hosting services "with a different kind of name". Council B, sharing the same view as other participating councils, further indicates that because of the confusion about what is really meant by cloud computing it is unclear how much cloud computing and the G-Cloud will assist the council to achieve the substantial gains it promises.

Background

Political

All four councils disagreed with the notion that cloud computing is driven by Central Government's ICT strategies. The reasoning behind this is that, regardless of Government's ICT strategies and e-initiatives, local authorities have already been looking into ways of saving costs which always includes rationalisation options for their IT provision. In Council B's own words, cloud computing is driven by "the provision of more cost-effective services and the private sector responding to that business model or new business model which it is beginning to do at the minute…". Similarly Council A believes that cloud's cost-saving abilities, and the potential to be 'infrastructure-free' are major advantages in terms of transforming the way the council operates and therefore it is an area that local government has been considering anyway, whether or not the Government had it in its IT strategy.

When asked specifically whether considering cloud computing has any correlation with the government's intentions to provide information and services online (Cabinet Office, 2010) the participants again disagree to some extent. Council B states that they can supply public service data online without necessarily subscribing to a cloud-based service, so the two are not inevitably linked. This argument is supported by Council C. Council D further explains that central government strategy is that by 2005 all services could be delivered electronically and that therefore local authorities - with this timeline in mind - had done a considerable amount of work to support the strategy. So this does indicate some driving influence from central government. However, they had not actually implemented cloud computing at the time of interviews because, as Council D indicates, "we do have concerns over where our data would reside for some of our sensitive data".

There are differing opinions between the interviewees when considering if councils should specifically include moving to a cloud-based infrastructure of future IT provision in their ICT plans. Council B, in support of the government's cloud strategy, confirms that a cloud-based infrastructure is in the council's ICT strategy. Council A, on the other hand, maintains that the broader aims of reducing costs and increasing the flexibility of IT provision in future years are what are addressed in the council's strategic plans, and they are not convinced that cloud would be mature enough in the current strategic timeframe.

Of the four participants only Council D agrees with the notion that the move to cloud-based IT provision and the development of G-Cloud come as a result of the Westminster government's intention to centralise IT resources. Aside from the issue of cloud computing, councils have already experienced the advantage of shared IT provision and recognise the need for collaboration among local authorities in a belief that it will lead to significant cost reduction and economies of scale. It is evident, according to Council A, that they have achieved a lower cost through jointly tendering for IT projects with a neighbouring council. Council C also points out that most local authorities are looking at ways of sharing their infrastructure or their key applications and hosted solutions, although again they do not consider such a practice to be cloud-driven.

Economic

All the participating councils have experienced significant cuts in IT budgets as a general result of the economic downturn of 2008 onwards, and specifically because of central governments ongoing tight public spending policies. Councils are proactively seeking ways of reducing IT costs and rationalising their existing infrastructure to sit within the available funding. With regard to cloud computing, however, Council A believes that G-Cloud is not the answer to the shrinking IT budget. The move to cloud-based services will make savings but it is not the only way of driving those savings. Conversely, savings may not be the only driver for change: Council C indicates that the council would not consider cloud computing purely for cost-saving purposes.

Although local councils generally support the development of the government cloud there is a level of suspicion in local government and the general attitude is to 'wait and see'. G-Cloud has been advocated by central government as an innovative ICT strategy for tomorrow's IT infrastructure model. The councils, however, consider both the innovation and the progress of the G-Cloud disappointing. According to Council D: "…. the whole G-cloud concept has been scaled back recently and kind of distilling down more to consolidating of data centres in the public centre really. Not much emphasis on the G-app side of it as there was before shall we say. …. I've attended various seminars, heard the spiel on G-Cloud, nothing much seems to be happening is my observation really, beyond the work they seem to be doing on data centre consolidation which seems generally sensible". The suspicion is that economic considerations have got in the way of central governments ambitious aspirations.

One of the held advantages of implementing cloud computing is that it is environmentally friendly and will reduce energy consumption in IT systems, therefore leading to reduced energy servicing costs (Vining & Di Maio, 2009; AbdelSalam et al, 2009). While greener IT is a top priority for many local authorities (Foster et al, 2008) the participating councils do not think that adopting cloud computing on its own will reduce energy consumption much more than the IT practices they are already implementing. For example, Council B points out that the third-party data centre they use has greatly enhanced efficiency both in terms of virtualisation of servers and the environmental efficiency of cooling, heating and the use of electricity. The cost savings achieved through running a highly efficient data centre is also confirmed by Council C who own their own data centre and believe that they may not achieve any further cost savings by opting for an external cloud-based data centre. When asked about the G-Cloud, Council C felt that if it is built in an energy efficient data centre using virtualisation technology then it will use less energy. However, they are not sure whether this is in fact the case, at least not yet.

Council D, taking a slightly different view, emphasises that actual realised reductions is energy consumption will depend entirely on how efficient the particular cloud provider is. It is suggested that, "yes it would reduce our energy consumption and in terms of the carbon reduction commitment that would be good for us as an organisation, it would reflect well on us, ...on the eco friendliness shall we say, of the provider, ...to watch from a purist point of view of the environmental impact of what you're delivering as a business, ...so you do need to watch the provider and make that your criteria..." This response also points to the fact that green technology issues are not just relevant to authorities as an economic factor. There are also political and social considerations.

Social

In the literature there is a general assumption that the development of cloud computing or G-Cloud is derived from the concepts of 'commoditisation of government' and 'open government data' through the use of social media (Bertot et al, 2014; Di Maio, 2009). The participating councils disagree with this assumption, arguing instead that cloud computing has nothing to do with social media. They hold that the concept of allowing the general public to access public data through the Internet had been proposed a while ago, and therefore bears no direct connection with the move to cloud services.

It has been suggested that with their previous experience of outsourcing, SaaS (Software as a Service) and virtualisation, local authorities would be well positioned to successfully implement cloud-based initiatives. From the case studies it is clear that local government does indeed have a great deal of experience in outsourcing. For example, Council A's IT infrastructure is heavily outsourced, including the IT helpdesk, servers and data networks and web-based back-up. Council C has virtually outsourced the entire IT management to a private sector service provider, and their applications run on hosted services from a variety of different vendors. When asked about implementing cloud computing from the perspective of building on their outsourcing experience, Council C said, "there's no great impediment to the council using cloud". However, as cloud computing and, more precisely, G-Cloud are still at an initial stage of development it seems from the interviewees that local authorities intend to wait until full benefits have been realised before considering implementation. As Council D comments, "We tend to be a risk averse organisation so we tend not to be on the leading edge, but we were an early adopter of virtualisation technology..."

Technological

It is held that one of the key features of cloud computing is simpler client-side infrastructure with a significantly reduced requirement for heavy IT investment, both hardware and upkeep costs (Han, 2013; Vaquero et al, 2008). This would be welcomed by local government when developing future IT strategies. After some years experience of outsourcing, the IT skills in Council B have been left undeveloped. There is therefore a 'skills gap' and the magnitude of that gap, or at least its significance as a problem, would be minimised by using cloud computing services and outsourcing various components on those services. Council D is the only one of the four case study participants to retain an in-house IT team. This team, they believe, has a lot of expert technical capability, so simpler infrastructure of itself would not be a factor to encourage them to move to cloud. That does not prevent them from considering cloud services for other reasons.

Flexibility is an important factor for local authorities when considering the cloud, specifically the ability to easily scale up and down the type and level of services provided sounds appealing (Herbst et al, 2013; McEvoy & Schulze, 2008). Scalability means that if the council buys the IT infrastructure and has it for five years, and in that time the organisation shrinks, or some specific processes in the organisation shrink, then the council would need less of that infrastructure. In practice Council A predicts that identifying the level of infrastructure takes some 'intelligence around storage'. Local councils tend not to be that flexible. Most things are known in advance, so the cloud's flexible scalability is not a significant advantage to the council. Council B reaches a similar conclusion but via a different argument: they point out that one of the selection criteria in choosing a vendor is that if the service provider is incapable of meeting the council's needs and adjust the level of services quickly the council would not consider it. As the participating councils have yet to have substantial experience of cloud computing it is unclear to them how the 'scalability' feature will work for local authorities.

Local councils have had lots of experience in appraising and choosing external IT vendors through their outsourcing and SaaS practices. For example, Council A do not own in-house developers at all; they buy packages off the shelf and the application is customised according to requirements. As Council A comments, "the biggest challenge is to modernise line of business applications and some of the suppliers are quite slow in terms of responding to things". When asked how the vendors' experience would benefit the provision of cloud services, Council C points out that they would certainly expect cloud vendors to have more skills than their own staff which is one of the reasons for migrating.

Driving Forces

Cost Savings

As already mentioned, cost-saving is perhaps the most important factor driving local government to consider cloud computing since local authorities are currently under enormous pressure to find cost-effective ways of restructuring IT infrastructure to reduce capital, servicing and staffing costs. Although none of the participating councils has fully implemented cloud computing it is felt that moving to cloud-based platforms and services brings the potential of massive savings. This supports Korri's argument (2009) that cloud computing presents an attractive alternative to building one's own computing infrastructure, which can be extremely costly.

Having already exhausted the cost saving potential of other IT changes it may be that councils now have to embrace cloud computing to realise the further savings demanded of them. Council A reveals that, "We run at very tight margins anyway and because we've been outsourced for a number of years so we've already taken the savings where we can. We've already cut quite a number of our costs through virtualization, through outsourcing, the rationalization of systems. I don't think there's a huge pot of money that we can save just because we're putting it out on the cloud but I'm hoping there's some savings there….. we've identified £30m worth of cuts which is approximately 20% of our overall budget. So staff will go, the numbers will be dramatically reduced, so how do you reduce staff without impacting the service, is self service the way to do it"?

Council B also predicts they could realise a cost saving of around 30% through cloud. Council C suggests that the G-Cloud would be potentially cheaper than using commercial cloud, and in addition it would be more secure. Council C's also see a double cost and security advantage in the G-Cloud; it could be seen as a secure private cloud, where councils share services with other local authorities, therefore achieving savings. It is built to be secure, because it is exclusively used by the public sector, which is a key factor for encouraging local government to move to cloud computing.

Economies of Scale

If the G-Cloud is to offer a platform where public organisations and local authorities can share IT resources and key applications, then a high level of economies of scale can be expected through sharing data centres and centralising ICT facilities and expertise (Grossman, 2009; Kliazovich et al, 2013). Many local authorities have experienced savings from collaboration between IT departments and joint tendering for IT contractors. According to Council A, joined-up data centres can significantly reduce cost round data centres across government. In essence that is cloud at its most basic level providing hosted solutions. Using common applications that provide greater flexibility is another way of keeping IT costs to the minimum. Many IT initiatives and local partnership schemes have already encouraged local authorities to work together in sharing common platforms and networks.

Strategic Focus

If local authorities no longer need to make large investments in IT infrastructure including hardware, software and staff then in theory considerable internal resource can be freed up (Aymerich et al, 2008). This enables the focus of attention and limited IT and human resources on 'mission-critical' areas (Low et al, 2011; Vining & Di Maio, 2009). First of all, only Council B has specific plans to launch cloud initiatives and therefore the other three were unable to comment on this particular point. Secondly, in the current tight funding situation one intended outcome of local government's IT strategy is a conscious move to a much smaller IT infrastructure. So after downsizing it's questionable whether there will be significant resource available to strategically focus elsewhere. Thirdly, it is suggested that the staff remaining following a rationalisation process would need to be re-trained to support areas of strategic importance and their job descriptions will be significantly altered.

Resisting Forces

Security and Reliability of Data

Security and reliability of data are clearly a concern for local government when considering a move to cloud because of the confidential and sensitive nature of data being stored in the public sector (Younis and Kifayat, 2013; Buyya et al, 2009; Grossman, 2009). There is legislation in data security which impact on the adoption of cloud, for example, Council B stresses that, "… our information can't be hosted outside the country … those set of considerations have to be brought to betterment; they're just as important as the reliability of the vendor or disaster recovery report, they all have to be right otherwise you wouldn't take the service out..."

With regards to how secure the data should be and how the level of safety can be measured, Council C explains: "Microsoft 365 is certified to impact level 2, protect level status as rated by Communications-Electronics Security Group (CESG) which means that it can carry personal information which if released incorrectly to the public domain might be an embarrassment but wouldn't cause harm. ... that is in effect G-cloud solution which is rated up to a higher security, that can carry confidential, secret information … although it's fine for Data Protection Act purposes because it's inside the European Union, it means it's not likely ever to be rated more than IL2 by UK government, it's outside of their control".

Council A offers a different opinion about cloud security. The council is not worried too much about security because it is such an obvious issue that it will have to be taken care of by cloud vendors in due course, both private and G-Cloud. Security policies and disaster recovery strategies are very much dependant on the reliability of the vendor and the contract negotiations (service level agreement). This argument is supported by Council D.

Privacy and Access

In a similar way to their views on the security and reliability of data, the participating councils are not particularly concerned about privacy of and access to data. Council A explains that, "I'm not so concerned about privacy and similar issues etc. because they're so obvious. Those are sort of hygiene factors I would absolutely expect them to be taken care of". Local councils have already had policies and strategies in place to ensure individual privacy, data security and information assurance, and now have vast experience in dealing with these issues at all scales. Council D expresses the same level of confidence commenting that, "Individual privacy I see that probably more of a perception of a problem rather than a real problem ….providing that you choose your vendors well it didn't ought to be a problem, because you know it would bad for their business if it was". These are seen to be such obvious stumbling blocks for the whole concept of cloud computing that the councils assume that the technical issues will have to be solved.

Service Level Agreements

As previously discussed, realising the potential benefits of cloud services very much depends on the detail of the Service Level Agreements (SLAs) drawn up between vendor and client. Council B provides a detailed account of what should be considered and included in a SLA, which is an important task for local authorities managing IT projects of outsourcing, SaaS and cloud: "... you can make assessment based on experience and knowledge, use that as a basis... but the whole field of defining an SLA and penalty clauses is very difficult one to do in any commercial contract because of course the supplier will construct that, see the penalty clauses that will be extremely difficult to ever implement or ever come into effect... there has to be clauses and definitions within the contract which negate and define what security the data is, we have to analyze the financial viability of the vendor to make sure that the supplier of those services is financially secure and able to continue to provide those services for the length of the contract. ...what the levels of access will be for that data and how will that data be protected". Local government works in a strict regulatory framework and is required to scrutinise and audit to a high level when spending public monies. This will impact on the drafting of the SLA.

Internet-Related Issues

Internet speed and bandwidth-related issues are held to be a concern when services are provided entirely through the Internet (Grossman, 2009). As Council D comments, "... when you were looking to go to cloud route for service you would obviously be looking at your network band capabilities and you could upgrade that capability if you needed to deliver through a provider or use efficiently through cloud mechanism. So it's just a cost factor to bear in mind if you're heading down a cloud route for something which you may need to upgrade your network bandwidth capability". The attitude of the council is not so much that this could be a resisting force, but that it is certainly a technical and cost issue to be addressed in the consideration and implementation of cloud computing.

Implementation Issues

Business Process Change

A number of business process change related issues have been identified by the participating councils. In general terms, however, it is felt that moving to a different business model of public services is very much an evolutionary, rather than revolutionary process. For example, Council A believes that the IT departments in local government will inevitably be downsized due to the need to rationalise business applications. This will not happen overnight but through a planned, staged approach to business process change.

Council B gives some forecast as to what will be changed in the next five to six years,

... we're moving our infrastructure to third parties, ...the CIO, the IT director, will become much more of a commissioner of services rather than runner of internal services or manager of internal services, defining those requirements and working with businesses technology partner and then procuring those services through the most cost-effective means which might mean full scale out-sourcing, through the third party, it could be considerable, substantial outsourcing and anything in-between depending on the needs of the organization.

Similarly Council D predicts the council to be of "fewer staff, ultimately... savings don't come in a sort of linear way, they come in a step way when it comes to staffing so initially I would see in the early days just a few services you'd probably make very little difference". The job descriptions of the existing IT staff would be significantly different. They would not be doing things such as storing and looking after databases. When cloud has become a commonly used platform in local government IT professionals will need to be re-trained and move to different areas and do whatever is required. Again, Council D supports the idea that the outlook and activities of the IT department will be altered but this will change gradually, not radically.

Project Management and Planning

The four councils were asked to comment on project management in relation to cloud computing, considering the role both of central government and of local authorities. Adequate project management and planning skills are held to be critical to the successful development and implementation of G-Cloud, for which the government has adopted a staged approach. According to Council A there is a history of unsuccessful IT projects and contract negotiations in the public sector (cf. Gilbert, 2009; Sandeep and Ravishankar, 2014). This explains a delay in central government advocating its G-Cloud to local authorities. Council D shares the same view, indicating that, "...I can't see that [G-cloud] happening at the moment. G-Cloud doesn't seem to be delivering anything useful yet". The issue of G-Cloud delay should also be considered in the context of reduced public funding as already discussed.

Regarding the success or failure of IT projects in local government specifically, Council C admits that failures are mostly likely for those projects where the council has attempted to develop applications in-house. As the head of IT comments, "...I doubt you'll find any development of specific coding going on, council can't afford it; too risky and incidents of projects failing are too high". The participating councils tend to agree that the success of providing cloud-based IT provision in local government relies mainly on the selection of vendors and contract negotiations. As noted already, councils have experience in managing outsourcing and SaaS contracts, but the interviewees suggest specific project management and planning skills required for the transition from traditional IT provision to cloud-based infrastructure need to be further identified.

Information Assurance and Governance

As already discussed, security and privacy will be a concern for local government when considering cloud-based services, although local authorities are very aware of information assurance and governance issues and are familiar with the relevant legislation. Council B mentions GCS6 standards where the council has encrypted laptops so that if they are lost the data will not be accessible. They emphasise that they cannot adopt cloud computing if the cloud service is not compliant with GCS6. Cloud vendors will have to provide some assurance in the SLA (Kandukuri et al, 2009; Moreno-Vozmediano et al, 2013). "If you start to house some of that data in the cloud you may have some problems with complying with that ..." As regards individual privacy, Council C argues information assurance and data security "are all part of any procurement we would do, they would be key requirements for whether it was cloud, traditional hosting or in-house. They are core considerations and they would be part of the evaluation process".

Choices of Vendors, Products, and Approach

A number of issues are addressed in the conceptual framework regarding the implementation of cloud computing: selection of vendors, vendor lock-in, approach and methods. The participating councils were invited to comment on these issues. When asked how to choose a vendor Council A provided the criteria that would be adopted by the council: functionality and price. This is similar to how Council D would select a cloud provider. However, Council D indicates that there should be a different cost model used for cloud services, taking into consideration revenue, budgets and the council's own operating costs. Council C, on the other hand, advises that they would select vendors through a competitive procurement process, just like any other types of procurement. EU and UK public sector procurement rules would in any case apply to any large competitive tender for supplying cloud services.

An interesting perspective is offered by Council B: in choosing a cloud partner they would go for medium-sized service providers, "big enough to meet our needs, small enough for us to be their significant client". An explanation is given, "… So that's the key principle going forward with our vendors, as we form partnership with them and we choose vendors that are the right size and the right flexibility to meet our needs".

Vendor lock-in is a concern, shared by all four councils. As Council A raises, "what would stop the vendor from pushing their prices up because I can't walk away very easily and because I wouldn't have local infrastructure anymore. So there really has to be tight contracts negotiated there". Moving from one supplier to another can be costly (Buyya et al, 2008; Satzger et al, 2013). This includes the cost of changing the technology once a vendor discontinues the service (Foster et al, 2008). Without the IT infrastructure, a key resource, can lead to a loss of organisational control, as warned by Buyya et al (2008). For this Council B proposes that a contract should be formulated "in the term that you want to have the right exit strategy in it… and that there are lots of protection and procedures to make migrating commoditised service from one supplier to another relatively straightforward".

Another implementation issue is integration with existing IT infrastructure, considered the biggest challenge by Council A. As previously mentioned local authorities are relatively conservative and are likely to employ a hybrid and staged approach to cloud computing (Di Maio, 2009; Leavitt, 2013). Such an attitude is evident in Council B's plans to implement cloud computing: "We'd like other people to take the risk first and depending on how they go, then we go for it" As with all public sector IT rationalisations (and also often in large private sector organisations) choice of product and supplier has to take account of the existing infrastructure and processes. There is just not the money available to go for an idealised 'everything new' strategy. Certain otherwise attractive suppliers may need to be discounted if they cannot hybridise with the authority's existing systems.

FUTURE RESEARCH DIRECTIONS

This explorative study is based around the viewpoint of four urban local authorities, each based in London, close to central government and other national resources and with large, dense and mobile populations. Future research can build on the findings from the present study to include councils with alternative geographical and demographic characteristics, whose views might be substantially different. Including views from authorities situated in rural areas would be especially relevant, as IT resources and skills might not be readily available, and the required council service outcomes may be very different. Interviewing a greater range of stakeholders such as IT directors, senior managers, IT technicians and users from different departments would also enrich the study, adding depth to the findings. A quantitative survey would be beneficial as concepts and beliefs can be generalised. The framework can also be expanded to include success/failure factors once enough local authorities have considered and implemented cloud computing.

Taking the study in a different direction, future research can adopt a longitudinal approach by undertaking an in-depth case study with a single council which has had a full experience in utilising the G-Cloud framework. In this way the issues identified in the current conceptual framework can be investigated in greater detail. This may involve looking into the physical design and implementation of a cloud-based infrastructure, the approach, type and business model used to integrate cloud with existing systems, an analysis of cost savings in financial terms, the impact of cloud on the authorities existing and future business and IT strategies, methods used by the council for monitoring and 'lessons learned', and how central government has supported the G-Cloud.

CONCLUSION

A conceptual framework is proposed by Chang (2011) to help analyse the impact of implementing cloud computing in local government. Key issues are identified in the framework, which form the basis for the present research to gauge the general attitude and perceptions of local authorities towards the application of cloud-based services. The importance of the subject area is justified by the UK government's ICT strategies and staged plans to implement the government cloud (G-Cloud) (Cabinet Office, 2010). The research attempts to investigate to what extent local authorities are aware of cloud computing and the development of G-Cloud, the main benefits, as well as constraints of adopting cloud computing to local councils and any concerns regarding implementation, in terms of business process change, relationships with cloud providers and issues relating to data security and information assurance. A case study methodology has been adopted because the subject area is relatively new. Four London-based borough councils are chosen and interviews of senior members of staff from both IT and business departments are carried out. Their views and opinions are analysed and compared which shed a light into the current strategies and future plans for cloud services and the G-Cloud.

There is no precise definition of cloud computing, a notion that has been confirmed by the case study organisations who offer views about what cloud computing is. It can be suggested that many current IT practices, such as SaaS, hosted services and virtualisation, form part of the so-called cloud computing. In fact, most local councils now do not have in-house developers. Public services are provided mostly online and much of the IT services are outsourced. There is need for clear and universally agreed definitions of cloud computing for the purposes of academic discussion and practical guidance.

There is only one council that supports the government's cloud strategy and has intentions to implement cloud computing in the near future. Other councils would prefer to wait until there is a clear evidence to suggest that all benefits of cloud computing can be realised. Such an attitude comes from local authorities being relatively cautious and conservative in adopting new ways of providing public services, and risk-adverse so that it is unwise to be the first to implement cloud computing.

Contrary to the belief that the move to cloud services is largely driven by the government's central ICT strategies, case organisations disagree that there are specific instructions from the government to implement G-Cloud. Local government are proactively seeking ways of reducing management and operational costs, due to decreasing grant and budgets, and many local councils have already undertaken measures to ensure that considerable savings can be made in the coming years. These include using the most energy-efficient data centres, providing public services online, collaborating with surrounding councils for shared IT systems and rationalising the existing IT infrastructure, whether cloud-based or not. The view from the participating organisations is clear: cloud computing has a potential in helping councils to reduce costs but it is not the only answer to the economic downturn and reduced funding. Savings on, for example energy consumption, will depend on how efficient the cloud provider is.

It has been suggested that cloud computing is driven by the government's intension to commoditise public information and services. And the development of government cloud is linked to the prevalence of social media and Internet technologies. These views are not specifically supported by the participating councils. On the other hand, local authorities have had many years of experience in outsourcing and using external service providers to customise applications based on requirements. Local authorities are aware that considerable savings can be achieved by employing virtual servers and web-based storage and recognise the importance of negotiating with vendors for a well-balanced SLA. A more serious concern, vendor lock-in, is shared by the case organisations because the promised benefits of moving to cloud could be compromised once the cloud provider is responsible for the entire IT infrastructure and demands a higher price. Local government is urged to think carefully about 'exit' strategy and rules and procedures to be included in the contract when formulating SLAs.

Cloud computing will transform the council's IT infrastructure, business processes and how the services are provided. Although not asked specifically about downsizing the participating councils admit that due to the economic downturn and the enormous pressure arising from reduced public funding local government has 'staged' plans for a much smaller-scaled IT department, self-service online facilities and collaboration between local authorities. IT directors will be more concerned about commissioning work and negotiating SLAs. The impact of such business process change to existing staff and job descriptions need to be investigated further.

One of the major concerns in cloud computing is data security, privacy and access. The requirement to host sensitive data in the country will prevent local authorities from considering cloud services because there are certain laws and regulations councils need to comply with, for example, those governed by the CESG. This concern may be overcome by the adoption of the G-Cloud which is developed by central government with adequate security measures that will satisfy legal requirements. In fact, local authorities already have strict information governance policies and strategies in place. They are not too concerned about data security and individual privacy when considering cloud because it is an obvious issue that would be taken care of by the service provider. Similarly, technical issues such as Internet speed and network capabilities should not be a problem, because they can be easily assessed and dealt with if councils are to adopt cloud services.

REFERENCES

AbdelSalam, H., Maly, K., Mukkamala, R., Zubair, M. &Kaminsky, D. (2009). Towards energy efficient change management in a cloud computing environment. *AIMS*, 161-166.

Amazon. (2010). *Amazon elastic compute cloud*, Retrieved February 15, 2010 from www.amazon.com

Armbrust, M., Fox, A., Griffith, R., Joseph, A. D., Katz, R., Konwinski, A., & Zaharia, M. (2010). A view of cloud computing. *Communications of the ACM*, *53*(4), 50–58. doi:10.1145/1721654.1721672

Aymerich, F. M., Fenu, G., & Surcis, S. (2008). An approach to a cloud computing network. In *1st International Conference on the Applications of Digital Information and Web Technologies*, (pp. 113-118). doi:10.1109/ICADIWT.2008.4664329

Bertot, J. C., Gorham, U., Jaeger, P. T., Sarin, L. C., & Choi, H. (2014). Big data, open government and e-government: Issues, policies and recommendations. *Information Polity, 19*(1), 5–16.

Bojanova, I., Zhang, J., & Voas, J. (2013). Cloud computing. *IT Professional, 15*(2), 12–14. doi:10.1109/MITP.2013.26

Buyya, R., Yeo, C. S., & Venugopal, V. (2008).Vision, hype and reality for delivering IT services as computing utilities. In *10th IEEE International Conference on High Performance Computing and Communications*, (pp. 5-13). IEEE.

Cabinet Office. (2010). *Government ICT Strategy: smarter, cheaper, greener*. London: Cabinet Office, January.

Catteddu, D. (2010). *Cloud Computing: benefits, risks and recommendations for information security*. Berlin: Springer.

Chang, J. (2011, October-December). A framework of analysing the impact of cloud computing on local government in the UK. *International Journal of Cloud Applications and Computing, 1*(4), 25–33. doi:10.4018/ijcac.2011100102

Das, R. K., Patnaik, S., & Misro, A. K. (2011). Adoption of cloud computing in e-governance. In *Advanced Computing* (pp. 161–172). Berlin: Springer. doi:10.1007/978-3-642-17881-8_16

Di Maio, A. (2009a, June). Cloud computing in government: private, public, both or none? *Gartner.*

Di Maio, A. (2009b, September). GSA launches Apps.gov: what it means to government IT leaders? *Gartner.*

Di Maio, A. (2009c, June). Government in the cloud: Much more than computing. *Gartner.*

Digital Britain. (2009). *Final report, presented to Parliament in June 2009*. London: The Stationery Office.

Foster, I., Zhao, Y., Raicu, I., & Lu, S. (2008). Cloud computing and grid computing 360-degree compared. In *Grid Computing Environments Workshop*. doi:10.1109/GCE.2008.4738445

Grossman, R. L. (2009). The case for cloud computing. IEEE Computer Society. Retrieved from computer.org/ITPro

Han, Y. (2013). On the clouds: A new way of computing. *Information Technology and Libraries, 29*(2), 87–92. doi:10.6017/ital.v29i2.3147

Herbst, N. R., Kounev, S., & Reussner, R. (2013, June). Elasticity in Cloud Computing: What It Is, and What It Is Not. ICAC, 23-27.

Kandukuri, B. R., Ramakrishna, P. V., & Rakshit, A. (2009). Cloud security issues. In *2009 IEEE International Conference on Services Computing*, (pp. 517-520). IEEE.

Kliazovich, D., Bouvry, P., & Khan, S. U. (2013). Simulation and Performance Analysis of Data Intensive and Workload Intensive Cloud Computing Data Centers. In Optical Interconnects for Future Data Center Networks, (pp. 47-63). New York: Springer. doi:10.1007/978-1-4614-4630-9_4

Korri, T. (2009). Cloud computing: utility computing over the Internet. Seminar on Internetworking, Helsinki University of Technology.

Leavitt, N. (2013). Hybrid clouds move to the forefront. *Computer, 46*(5), 15–18. doi:10.1109/MC.2013.168

Lewin, K. (1947). Frontiers in group dynamics: Concept, method, and reality in social science. *Human Relations, 1*(1), 5–42. doi:10.1177/001872674700100103

Low, C., Chen, Y., & Wu, M. (2011). Understanding the determinants of cloud computing adoption. *Industrial Management & Data Systems, 111*(7), 1006–1023. doi:10.1108/02635571111161262

Luis, M.V., Luis, R, Caceres, J., & Lindner, M. (2008). A break in the clouds: towards a cloud definition. *SIGCOMM Computer Communication Review, 39*(1).

Maggiani, R. (2009, November). Cloud computing is changing how we communicate. *IEEE Explore.*

Marston, S., Li, Z., Bandyopadhyay, S., Zhang, J., & Ghalsasi, A. (2011). Cloud computing—The business perspective. *Decision Support Systems, 51*(1), 176–189. doi:10.1016/j.dss.2010.12.006

McEvoy, G. V., & Schulze, B. (2008). Using clouds to address grid limitations. In *MGC '08: Proceedings of the 6th international workshop on Middleware for grid computing*, (pp. 1-6). New York: ACM.

Mell, P., & Grance, T. (2009). The NIST definition of cloud computing. *National Institute of Standards and Technology, 53*(6), 50.

Mishra, A., Mathur, R., Jain, S., & Rathore, J. S. (2013). Cloud Computing Security. *International Journal on Recent and Innovation Trends in Computing and Communication, 1*(1), 36–39.

Moreno-Vozmediano, R., Montero, R. S., & Llorente, I. M. (2013). Key challenges in cloud computing: Enabling the future internet of services. *IEEE Internet Computing, 17*(4), 18–25. doi:10.1109/MIC.2012.69

Nelson, M. R. (2009). The cloud, the crowd and public policy. *Issues in Science and Technology*, (Summer), 71–76.

O'Donnell, M., & Stewart, J. (2007). Implementing change in the public agency/leadership, learning and organisational resilience. *International Journal of Public Sector Management, 20*(3), 239–251. doi:10.1108/09513550710740634

Plummer, D.C., Smith, D.M., Bittman, T.J., Cearley, D.W., Cappuccio, D.J., Scott, D., Kumar, R., and Robertson, B. (2009, May). *Five refining attributes of public and private cloud computing.* Gartner.

Sandeep, M. S., & Ravishankar, M. N. (2014). The continuity of underperforming ICT projects in the public sector. *Information & Management, 51*(6), 700–711. doi:10.1016/j.im.2014.06.002

Satzger, B., Hummer, W., Inzinger, C., Leitner, P., & Dustdar, S. (2013). Winds of change: From vendor lock-in to the meta cloud. *IEEE Internet Computing, 17*(1), 69–73. doi:10.1109/MIC.2013.19

Scholl, H. J., & Klischewski, R. (2007). E-government integration and interoperability: Framing the research agenda. *International Journal of Public Administration, 30*(8-9), 889–920. doi:10.1080/01900690701402668

Silva, G. C., Rose, L. M., & Calinescu, R. (2013, December). Towards a Model-Driven Solution to the Vendor Lock-In Problem in Cloud Computing. In *Cloud Computing Technology and Science (Cloud-Com), 2013 IEEE 5th International Conference on* (pp. 711-716). doi:10.1109/CloudCom.2013.131

Takabi, H., Joshi, J. B., & Ahn, G. J. (2010). Security and Privacy Challenges in Cloud Computing Environments. *IEEE Security and Privacy*, *8*(6), 24–31. doi:10.1109/MSP.2010.186

Thomson, R. (2009, February 24). Socitm: Cloud computing revolutionary to the public sector. *Computer Weekly*.

Tsohou, A., Lee, H., & Irani, Z. (2014). Innovative public governance through cloud computing: information privacy, business models and performance measurement challenges. *Transforming Government: People, Process, and Policy*, *8*(2), 6–6.

Vaquero, L. M., Rodero-Merino, R., Caceres, J., & Lindner, M. (2008). A break in the clouds: towards a cloud definition. *SIGCOMM Computer Communication Review*, *39*(1).

Vining, J. & Di Maio,A. (2009, February). *Cloud computing for government is cloudy.* Gartner.

Wyld, D. C. (2010). The Cloudy future of government IT: Cloud computing and the public sector around the world. *International Journal of Web & Semantic Technology*, *1*(1), 1–20.

Yin, R. K. (2009). *Case Study Research: Design and Methods.* Sage Inc.

Younis, M. Y. A., & Kifayat, K. (2013). *Secure cloud computing for critical infrastructure: A survey.* Liverpool John Moores University.

KEY TERMS AND DEFINITIONS

Business Process Change: Business process change refers to a planned programme to redesign, update or integrate an organisation's business processes in order to achieve its business objectives. This may be in response to a specific change in the organisations business operating environment. It is an actively planned and analysed process enabling the organisation to re-think linkages between strategy, business processes and people.

Cloud Computing: Cloud computing refers to a scalable network infrastructure where consumers receive IT services such as software and data storage through the Internet on a subscription basis, like traditional utilities. Potential benefits include cost savings, simpler IT and reduced energy consumption. Areas of concern include security, access, data protection and ownership.

Data Centre: A data centre is a facility that houses and maintains computer, server and networking systems and their components as part of a company's IT infrastructure. In cloud computing the data centre is owned by the cloud service vendor.

Government Cloud (G-Cloud): The Government cloud in the UK, or G-Cloud, is an initiative developed by the central government to simplify the cloud procurement process for public organisations. The G-Cloud is a series of framework agreements with suppliers, from which public sector organisations can obtain services without needing to run a full, lengthy and complex tendering process. There is an online store called the "CloudStore" that allows public sector bodies to search for services that are approved by the G-Cloud frameworks.

IT Infrastructure: IT infrastructure refers to the set of IT hardware, software, networks and supporting facilities used by an organisation to develop, test, deliver, monitor, control or support IT services. It should be noted that users, processes and documentation are not part of the IT Infrastructure.

Outsourcing: Outsourcing is the practice whereby a business process is carried out by a vendor or service provider external to the client organisation. There are different types of outsourcing; sometimes it involves employees of the service provider working in the client company, or the other way round. It sometimes involves relocating a business function to another country to take advantage of lower labour rates. This is called offshore outsourcing. Cost savings are the main incentive to outsource business processes.

SaaS: Software as a Service, or SaaS, is a model of cloud computing in which software is licensed on a subscription basis. The term is sometimes referred as 'on-demand software'. The SaaS provider gives on-demand support to users and is responsible for software maintenance and upgrades. One of the selling points of SaaS is the client firm's reduction in IT support costs through outsourcing hardware and software maintenance to a reputable provider.

Service Level Agreements: A service-level agreement is an agreement between the client organisation and the service providers. It is the contract between two or more parties setting out the agreed services, performance measurement, timescales, warranties, disaster recovery and agreement termination procedures.

Vendor Lock-In: Vendor lock-in is a business practice whereby a service provider can make the client organisation solely dependent on them for a product or service, unable to user other vendors without paying substantial switching costs. This practice is sometimes referred as proprietary lock-in or customer lock-in. The behaviour itself encourages a monopoly in a market or industry.

Virtualisation: Virtualization is normally referred to creating a virtual, as opposed to actual version of a resource or device, such as a storage device, server, network or even an operating system. For example, server virtualization enables PCs to run multiple operating systems or applications making the IT infrastructure simpler and more efficient.

Chapter 6
A Mechanism for Securing Hybrid Cloud Outsourced Data:
Securing Hybrid Cloud

Abdullah El-Haj
University of Jordan, Jordan

Shadi Aljawarneh
Isra University, Pakistan

ABSTRACT

The existing research related to security mechanisms only focuses on securing the flow of information in the communication networks. There is a lack of work on improving the performance of networks to meet quality of service (QoS) constrains for various services. The security mechanisms work by encryption and decryption of the information, but do not consider the optimised use of the network resources. In this paper the authors propose a Secure Data Transmission Mechanism (SDTM) with Preemption Algorithm that combines between security and quality of service. Their developed SDTM enhanced with Malicious Packets Detection System (MPDS) which is a set of technologies and solutions. It enforces security policy and bandwidth compliance on all devices seeking to access Cloud network computing resources, in order to limit damage from emerging security threats and to allow network access only to compliant and trusted endpoint devices.

1. INTRODUCTION

The concept of cloud computing offers new methods and approaches for information pro-cessing and data transmission and however, the Federal CIO Vivek Kundra has emphasized that information security is still a top concern about cloud computing (Worthen, 2009). For instance, In Cloud, the data and associated software are not under their control (Aljawarneh, 2011).

In Devargas (1993) an overview of multi-processor scheduling algorithm is given without exploiting the two characteristics which are typi-cal in IPsec packet processing (see Section 3). Castanier et al

DOI: 10.4018/978-1-4666-8676-2.ch006

Copyright © 2015, IGI Global. Copying or distributing in print or electronic forms without written permission of IGI Global is prohibited.

(1995) discuss the problem of load balancing on multiple processors which could cause many problems in data transmission.

The SDTA presented in this paper allows scheduling packets to be processed either by the CPU or by the accelerators. This also enhances scalability: one may use an accelerator tailored for the bandwidth normally required for VPNs and use the CPU to have a further processing capability when a higher bandwidth is required. In this paper a SDTA in heterogeneous net-works IPSec-based is presented. Our goal is: to maximize the security to communications at the IP level, to minimize latency and, possibly, maximize throughput.

It is explained in Raghuram and Chakrabarti (2000) that how to obtain data independency among packets for AES. Our approach fully exploits these characteristics to achieve high security and better performance.

Wang and others (Wang, Li, Owens, & Bhargava, 2009) developed a mechanism to solve this issue in owner- write-users-read applications. They proposed to encrypt every data block with a different key so that flexible cryptography-based access control might be achieved. Through the adoption of key deriva-tion methods, the owner needs to maintain only a few secrets. In this mechanism, the data can be updated only by the original owner through authentication way. At the same stage, clients with various access rights need to read the information in an efficient and secure man-ner. Both data and client dynamics should be properly processed to preserve the performance and safety of the outsourced storage system.

Section 2 will explain the system archi-tecture; in Section 3 the Data Transmission Mechanism will be explained. The simulations and its result analysis will be explained in Sec-tion 4 and in Section 5 includes the conclusion and the future work.

2. SYSTEM ARCHITECTURE

The architecture of the developed SDTM is com-posed of generator computers, N cryptographic ac-celerators connected to the normal system bus of the gateway and distributed bandwidth negotiator as shown in Figure 1. We consider heterogeneous accelerators, i.e., accelerators implementing different cryptographic algo-rithms and allowing different processing speeds. CPU-memory communication is performed on a faster bus, as in most modern personal com-puters. The network card is also connected to the faster CPU bus. Only cryptography- related operations are offloaded to the accelerator(s). This means that all the IPSec header processing is done by the CPU.

2.1. The SDTM

The main goal of this research is to secure the data flow in heterogeneous networks in the Cloud. This can be achieved by detecting and preventing malicious packets, implementing various security strate-gies and investigating various security algorithms. The developed protocol provides security services and tries to treat the vulnerabilities in the previously used protocols as well as minimizes the hackers' and crackers' threats. The next stage of this research will look at secure data transmission mechanism in heterogeneous networks and to study a range of scenarios to see the impact of the developed scheme on network performance and behaviour.

Figure 1. Secure data transmission mechanism based on distributed bandwidth negotiator

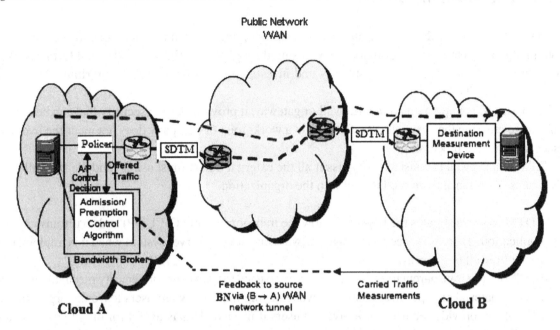

As shown in Figure 1 presenting the SDTM architecture which uses preemption control al-gorithm, each accelerator can support different sets of cryptographic algorithms (DES, 3DES, and AES…) and different processing speeds. A common application interface is needed to allow for uniformly access-ing all the cryptographic accelerators. This common application interface should also provide software implementations of the cryptographic algorithms as it is pos-sible in AES.

In this section we present the assump-tions made for the developed SDTM and their motivations, the description of our system and the MPDS.

2.2. Assumptions

Our algorithm is based on two fundamental assumptions: the first one is that the processing time for packets is known (at least approximate-ly) in advance. This is true for symmetric-key cryptographic algorithms which are normally used within the IPSec context: their process-ing time only depends on the number of data blocks to be processed. The only exception is for the software implementations of these algorithms. In this case the computation time may vary depending on the current CPU load. The second assumption is that each packet can be processed independently from the others (i.e., there are no data dependencies between different packets). This comes from IPSec specifications is that each packet must carry any data required for its processing (Anderson, 2001). In Devargas (1993) it is explained how to obtain data independency among packets for AES. Our approach fully exploits these assumptions to achieve high security and QoS.

2.3. Description of the SDTM

The main goal of our SDTM is to secure data transmission mechanism in heterogeneous networks and providing QoS data transmission such as maximising throughput, minimizing delay and lost packets by implementing the strongest security strategy and investigating various security algorithms. The main features of the SDTM:

When SDTM is implemented in a firewall or gateway, it provides strong security that can be applied to all traffic crossing the perimeter. Traffic within a workgroup or company does not incur the overhead of security –related processing.

SDTM in a firewall is resistant to bypass if all the external traffic must use IP, and the firewall is the only means of entrance from the Internet into the organization.

- SDTM as it investigates the IPsec is be-low the transport layer (TCP, UDP) and so is transparent to application. There is no need to change software on a user or server system when it is implemented in the firewall or gateway.
- SDTM can be transparent to end users. There is no need to train users on security mechanisms, issue keying material on a per-user basis, or revoke keying material when users leave the organization.
- SDTM can provide security for individual users if needed. This is useful for off site workers and for setting up a secure virtual sub network within an organization for sensitive application.
- SDTM can provide a quality of service data flow by possibly increasing throughput, decreasing delay and lost packets.

The main idea underlying the developed SDTM is to receive the packets generated by the host computers to be processed on the gateway (i.e., either one of the accelerators or the CPU) which can provide the shortest processing time. The developed SDTM processes each packet as follows:

- SDTM, implemented in a firewall or gateway, has a Malicious Packet Detection System (MPDS), which will analyze all the incoming packets and will decide to deny or pass the packets through the gateway.

For the passed packets from MPDS, accel-erators will be able to perform the cryptographic algorithm(s) required by the considered packet is selected.

The main goal of this research is to pro-vide the more secure path to data transmis-sion through the network, and so SDTM will investigate the IPsec as the future standard security protocol with Advanced Encryption Security (AES), which was already improved and chosen by National Institute of Security and Technology in USA as the more secure encryption algorithm.

2.4. The Malicious Packet Detection System (MPDS)

With the rapidly increasing threat to the network resources, it becomes very important to detect unauthorised packets on a network and estimate the damage they can cause to the legitimate us-ers. As the main goal of the developed SDTM is to secure data transmission mechanism in heterogeneous networks, so MPDS will ana-lyze all the incoming packets and try to pass only the trusted packets whilst discarding the malicious ones.

There are a number of commercial IDS's available. The description of some IDS's lists the types of unusual packets they captured dur-ing continuous operation (Lough & Krizman, 2003). And others give description of attacks based on individual malicious packets that can cause harm (Baghaei & Hunt, 2004). IEEE Std 802.11-1999 (1999) presents a statistical analysis of network packets characteristics, to enhance detecting network intrusions. After a global analysis of the nature of malicious packets, the fundamental assumption is that malicious packets tend to display UPD-like traffic behaviour and main-tain a high flow rate without alerting the flow identification (i.e., the source and destination addresses and port numbers) during the attack. On the other hand, legitimate flows such as TCP traffic are bursty in nature (IEEE Std 802.11-1999, 1999).

The main idea of our developed MPDS is characterised as follows:

- As the security is the main goal of our SDTM the MPDS is turned on with the operat-ing of the gateway and will start analyzing the kind of each packet.
- The MPDS will secure the data flow at the gateway against possible attacks that used invalid val-ues of IP and TCP headers fields through proper gateway configuration and filter out at least the following packets:
  ○ Packets carrying zero port number
  ○ Packets with private source or private destination IP address.
  ○ Packets carrying zero IP source address or destination address.
- MPDS will be modified in the future to detect all types of unauthorised packets.

3. SECURE DATA TRANSMISSION ALGORITHM WITH PREEMPTION CONTROL ALGORITHM

This Data transmission algorithm(DTA) as-sumes a distributed Bandwidth Negotiator (Barnet et al., 2000; Dasarathy et al., 2005) architecture, as depicted in the Figure 1. A Bandwidth Negotiator (BN) is located in each of the LANs interconnected by the public network backbone: BN is responsible for regulating traf-fic going into the public network. Suppose a host in Cloud A has a flow of traffic that needs to be sent to Cloud B, the requesting host in Cloud A would first make a request to the BN by sending the amount of requested bandwidth to BN. BN would run the CAC algorithm (to be described below) based on real-time measurements made on the existing traffic at the destination side. If an admit decision is made, the requesting host starts sending traffic, and the Policer is also informed to police the traffic. If a reject decision is made, the requesting host is notified about the decision. In addition, Policer is informed to prevent the rejected flow from entering into the public network (Dasarathy et al., 2005). In order for the source to quickly make an admis-sion/preemption decision, we believe the most valu-able piece of information is the amount of carried traffic, i.e. the amount of traffic that is successfully sent through the WAN backbone. Therefore, at Cloud B, a measurement device measures the amount carried traffic. Such measurements are done on a per Differentiated Services Code Point (DSCP) basis.

The measurements are periodically sent back to Cloud A, which are used for the CAC and preemp-tion algorithm. Suppose due to congestion in the public network, the bandwidth of a link along the path in the public network suddenly decreases to the extent that the link bandwidth is no longer able to support the amount of offered traffic. After a "congested" state is declared by the measurement device in Cloud B and the BN at Cloud A is notified, the preemption algorithm is triggered and a fraction of the ongoing traffic flows are preempted. Then both the affected hosts and Policer are notified by BN. Determination of the traffic flows to be preempted upon congestion or blockage is based on the carried traffic measurements, per-call requested bandwidth and a set of pre-defined policy (e.g. a policy based on MLPP described in *Developed draft strawman DSCP mapping for GIG enterprise IP networks* (n.d.)). Compared to the conventional Bandwidth Broker (BB), such as the one described in Soltwisch, Hogrefe, Bericht, and Gottingen (2004); IPSec Develop-ers Forum, n.d.), in which BB is assumed to have global knowledge about the network, this CAC utilizes a distributed architecture. Namely, each BN makes admission and preemption decision solely based on the feedback from the destina-tion, and there is no other inter BN information exchanged. In addition, BN is consulted only when a call needs to traverse through the public network. If a call originated from Cloud A does not need to go through the public network, BN will not be consulted. The detailed description of this algorithm is shown in the Figure 2 adopted from (IPSec Developers Forum, n.d.).

For UDP flow, the requested bandwidth is assumed to be the encoding rate of the codec. For TCP flows, the requested bandwidth is calculated as file size/speed of service require-ment. The result is then sent to PSM, where a leaky bucket algorithm is used to regulate the traffic. An alternative way to determine the requested bandwidth for TCP flows would be to deterministically assign a fixed value. We also note that the Preemption Algorithm is run as part of the data transmission mechanism. Suppose a high priority flow (e.g. a Flash Overwrite flow) requests for admission and the congested flag is on, lower priority flows may need to be preempted to accommodate the higher priority call, as mandated

Figure 2. Secure data transmission algorithm

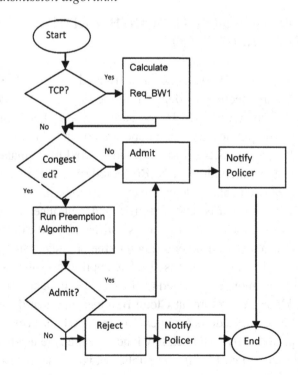

Figure 3. Preemption algorithm

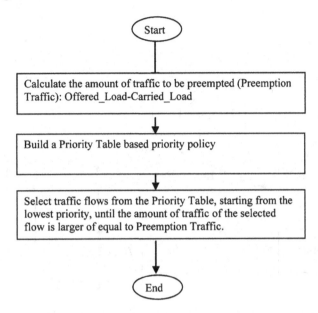

by the preemp-tion policy. When the "congested" flag is set by the measurement device, the preemption algorithm is triggered to preempt existing flows. Preemption algorithm is shown in Figure 3, in which two examples of preemption policy are presented. We note that the preemption policy can be set by the network operator dynami-cally, according to the need of the underlying mission.

By carefully observing Figure 2, we note that the data transmission algorithm shows a strong "reactive" nature, i.e. traffic will be admitted until congested state is declared. If the "available bandwidth" can be determined through bandwidth estimation techniques, the data transmission algorithm can be made more "proactive"; namely, traffic flows are rejected before congestion is observed. In a companion paper (Sucec, Samtani, & Bereschinsky, 2005), powerful bandwidth estimation techniques are presented such that the bottleneck link band-width (defined as the link with the smallest amount of bandwidth along the path) and avail-able bandwidth (defined as how much band-width "headroom" along the path for new traffic) are estimated. They can then be used in the data transmission, as shown in Figure 4. Our analysis showed that using bandwidth estimation; congestion avoidance can be ef-fectively achieved.

4. SIMULATION

To investigate the effectiveness of the data trans-mission /preemption algorithm, OMNET++ simulator was used to compare two different QoS setups, one with data transmission /preemp-tion algorithm and the other without. We used the same components of the model in Figure 1 to validate the SDTM, but with implementing data transmission algorithm/preemption algo-rithm and without data transmission/ preemption algorithm to study the behaviour of the system in both experiments.

Figure 4. Data transmission algorithm when available bandwidth can be obtained through bandwidth estimation techniques

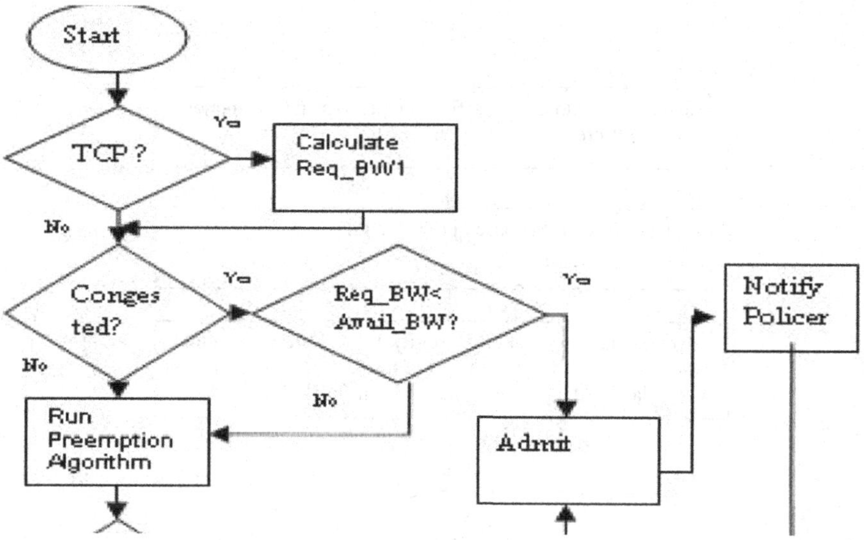

4.1. Simulation Results

4.1.1. Queuing Delay

Figure 5 shows the queuing delays as function of simulation time, with Data Transmission Algorithm (DTA) in red and without DTA in green. Figure 5. indicate that, as flow arrival rate increases over time, the queuing delay for the QoS scheme without DTA increases sig-nificantly, while as the average queuing delay with DTA stays low.

4.1.2. Throughput

Figure 6 compares the throughput performance between the two experiments with DTA in red and without DTA in green; one interesting observation is that with DTA, the network throughput is slightly less than without DTA.

Figure 6 shows that the simulation ex-periment with DTA yields a small network throughput decrease, especially when the net-work is heavily overloaded.

4.1.3. Packet Loss

Figure 7 shows once admitted, first-rate flows have a high chance of being delivered to their destination with DTA in red and without DTA in green. As we see from Figure 7 the packet loss performance without DTA is better than with DTA.

Figure 5. Queuing delay

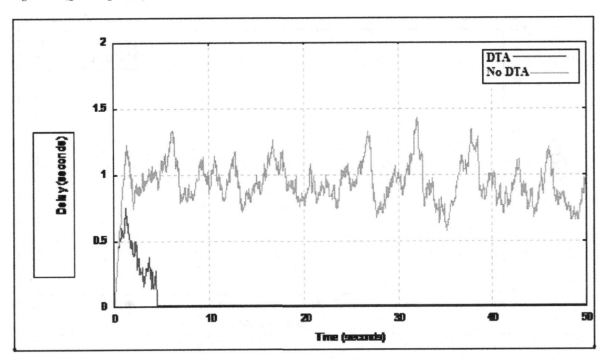

Figure 6. Throughput

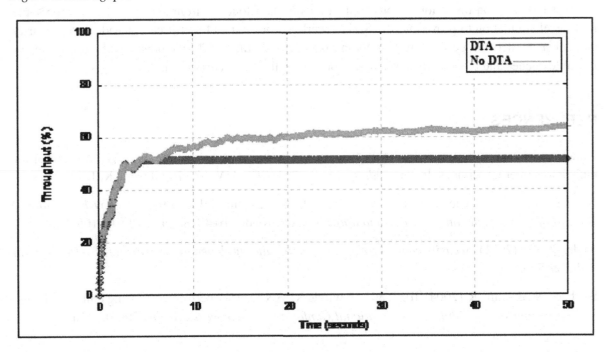

Figure 7. Packet loss

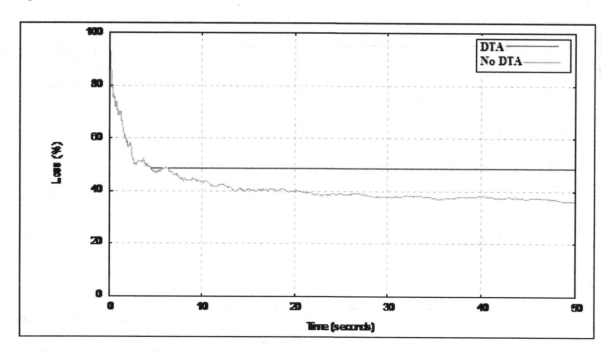

5. CONCLUSION AND FUTURE WORK

This paper has presented an investigation into the more secure protocols and security mecha-nisms to develop a Secure Data Transmission Mechanism (SDTM) with preemption control algorithm to combine between security and quality of service to improve the performance of networks to meet quality of service (QoS) constrains for various applications in the Cloud environment. We also provide some high-level simulation to prove that the SDTM works as desired and that it can provide good security and enhanced network performance. A comparison between the SDTM we presented here with one or multiple queues and other suitable security protocols will also be carried out.

REFERENCES

Alhaj, A., Mellor, J., & Awan, I. (2009). Performance evaluation of secure call admission control for mul-ticlass internet services. In *Proceedings of the 23rd IEEE-AINA'09*. Bradford, UK: IEEE.

Aljawarneh, S. (2011). Cloud security engineering: Avoiding security threats the right way. *International Journal of Cloud Applications and Computing, 1*(2), 64–70. doi:10.4018/ijcac.2011040105

Anderson, R. (2001). *Security engineering: A guide to building dependable distributed systems*. John Wiley & Sons.

Baghaei, N., & Hunt, R. (2004). IEEE 802.11 wireless LAN security performance using multiple clients. In *Proceedings of the 12th IEEE International Confer-ence on Networks* (ICON 2004). IEEE.

Barnet, Y., Ford, P., Yavatkar, R., Baker, F., Zhang, L., Speer, M., ... (2000). *A framework for integrated services operation over diffserv networks*. Retrieved from http://tools.ietf.org/html/rfc2998

Chang, K., Kim, G. T., Samtani, S., Staikos, A., Muzzelo, L., & Palumbo, J. (2006). A study on the call admission and preemption control algorithms for secure wireless ad hoc networks using IPSec tunneling. In *Proceedings of the MILCOM 2006*. doi:10.1109/MILCOM.2006.302177

Dasarathy, B., Gadgil, S., Vaidyanathan, R., Par-meswaran, K., Coan, B. A., Conarty, M., & Bhanot, V. (2005). Network QoS assurance in a multi-layer adaptive resource management scheme for mission-critical application using CORBA middleware framework. In *Proceedings of the 11th Real Time and Embedded Technology and Applications Symposium*. doi:10.1109/RTAS.2005.34

Devargas, M. (1993). *Network security*. Manchester, UK: NCC Blackwell.

Developed draft strawman DSCP mapping for GIG enterprise IP networks. (n.d.). Academic Press.

Hendry, M. (1995). *Practical computer network security*. Norwood, MA: Artech House.

IPSec Developers Forum. W.i.I. (n.d.). Retrieved January 2, 2005, from http://www-ip-sec. com5PSecinfoh.tml

Lough, D. L., & Krizman, K. J. (2003). *A short tuto-rial on wireless LANs and IEEE802.11*. Academic Press.

Moore, G. E. (1997). *An update on Moore's law*. Santa Clara, CA: Intel Corporation.

Raghuram, S. S., & Chakrabarti, C. (2000). A pro-grammable processor for cryptography. In *Proceedings of the IEEE International Symposium on Circuits and Systems (ISCAS 2000)*, (pp. 685–688). IEEE.

Soltwisch, R., Hogrefe, D., Bericht, T., & Gottingen, G.-a.-u. (2004). *Survey on network security - 2004. IEEE Std 802.11-1999 (1999). Part II: Wireless LAN medium access control (MAC) and physical layer (PHY) specifications*. IEEE.

Sucec, J., Samtani, S., & Bereschinsky, M. A. (2005, October 17-20). Resource friendly approach for es-timating available bandwidth in secure IP networks. In *Proceedings of the Military Communications Conference (MILCOM 2005)*. Academic Press.

Wang, W., Li, R., Owens, & Bhargava, B. (2009). Secure and efficient access to outsourced data. In *Proceedings of the 2009 ACM Workshop on Cloud Computing Security (CCSW '09)* (pp. 55-66). ACM. doi:10.1145/1655008.1655016

Worthen, B. (2009). Inside the head of Obama's CIO. *The Wall Street Journal Digits*.

Chapter 7
Optimal Resource Provisioning in Federated–Cloud Environments

Veena Goswami
KIIT University, India

Choudhury N. Sahoo
KIIT University, India

ABSTRACT

Cloud computing has emerged as a new paradigm for accessing distributed computing resources such as infrastructure, hardware platform, and software applications on-demand over the internet as services. Multiple Clouds can collaborate in order to integrate different service-models or service providers for end-to-end-requirements. Intercloud Federation and Service delegation models are part of Multi-Cloud environment where the broader target is to achieve infinite pool of resources. This chapter presents an optimal resource management framework for Federated-cloud environments. Each service model caters to specific type of requirements and there are already number of players with own customized products/ services offered. They propose an analytical queueing network model to improve the efficiency of the system. Numerical results indicate that the proposed provisioning technique detects changes in arrival pattern, resource demands that occur over time and allocates multiple virtualized IT resources accordingly to achieve application QoS targets.

1. INTRODUCTION

Cloud computing is a general term for system architectures that involves delivering hosted services over the Internet. Cloud computing services are offered on a pay-as-you-go basis and assure considerable reduction in hardware and software investment costs, as well as energy costs. These services are broadly divided into three categories: Infrastructure-as-a-Service (IaaS), which includes hardware, storage, servers, and networking components are made accessible over the Internet; Platforms-a-Service (PaaS), which

DOI: 10.4018/978-1-4666-8676-2.ch007

Copyright © 2015, IGI Global. Copying or distributing in print or electronic forms without written permission of IGI Global is prohibited.

includes computing platforms — hardware with operating systems, virtualized servers, and the like; and Software-as-a-Service (SaaS), which includes software applications and other hosted services. A cloud service differs from traditional hosting in three principal aspects. First, it is provided on demand, typically by the minute or the hour; second, it is elastic since the user can have as much or as little of a service as they want at any given time; and third, the service is fully managed by the provider (Brunette and Mogull, 2009; Mell and Grance, 2009; Vaquero et al., 2009).

Large service centers have been set up to provide comprehensive services by sharing the IT resources to clients. Companies often outsource their IT infrastructure to third party service providers to reduce the management cost. This extends to the efficient use of resources and a step-down of the operating costs. The service providers and their clients often negotiate utility based Service Level Agreements (SLAs) to manage its resources to maximize its profits. (Ardagna et al., 2005) proposed a Service level agreements (SLA) based profit optimization in multi-tier systems. Utility based optimization approaches provides, load balancing and obtain the best trade-off between job classes for Quality of Service levels.

Efficiently managing cloud resources and maintaining Service level Agreements for cloud services is an enormous challenge. Performance virtualization techniques have been employed to provide effective performance of computer service subject to QoS metrics such as response time, throughput, and network utilization, have been extensively studied in the (Slothouber, 1995; Karlapudi and Martin, 2004; Lu and Wang, 2005). Web server performance model using an open queueing network was employed to model the behavior of Web servers on the Internet (Slothouber, 1995). (Karlapudi and Martin, 2004) studied a Web application tool for the performance prediction of Web applications between specified end-points. Cloud centers as the enabling platform for dynamic and flexible application provisioning is facilitated by exhibiting data center's capabilities as a network of virtual services. Hence, users are able to access and deploy applications from any place in the Internet driven by the demand and Quality of Service (QoS) requirements (Buyya et al., 2009). IT companies are freed from the trivial task of setting up basic hardware and software infrastructures by using clouds as the application hosting platform. Thus, they can focus more on innovation and creation of business values for their application services (Armbrust et al., 2010). An optimal resource management framework for multi-cloud computing environment has been presented in (Goswami and Sahoo, 2013).

This chapter focuses on an analytical model through which Quality of service (QoS) is ensured by obtaining important performance indicators such as mean request response time, blocking probability, probability of immediate service and probability distribution of number of tasks in the system. This model allows cloud operators to tune the parameters such as the number of servers on one side, and the values of blocking probability and probability that a task request will obtain immediate service, on the other. Successful provision of cloud services and, consequently, widespread adoption of cloud computing necessitates accurate performance evaluation that allows service providers to dimension their resources in order to fulfill the Service Level Agreements with their customers.

The rest of this chapter is organized as follows. Section 2 contains a brief description of the system model and its analysis for the multi-cloud computing environments. Analytical model and its analysis is given in Section 3. Some important performance measures are presented in Section 4. Section 5 contains numerical analysis to show the effectiveness of the model parameters. Section 6 concludes the chapter.

2. SYSTEM DESIGN

We discuss different scenarios for the need of multi-cloud Environments.

1. **Multi-Cloud Environment Consisting of Multiple SaaS Cloud Services:** For the purpose of optimization, an organization may need to outsource a number of marginal functions to cloud services offered by different vendors. For example, it is highly likely that an enterprise may use Gmail for the email services and SalesForce.com for the HR service. This means that the many features (e.g. address book, calendar, appointment booking, etc.) in the email system must connect to the HR employee directory residing in the HR system. Here providers such as Gmail and SalesForce.com (Salesforce, 2009) need not be hosted on the same cloud rather are there in multi-cloud environment (Erdil, 2012; Tordsson et al., 2012).

2. **Multi-Cloud Environment Consisting of Multiple PaaS Cloud Services:** Enterprises with global operations can have multi-tiered applications hosted at multiple geographical locations. A typical example is Web applications using Service-Oriented-Architecture (SOA) model, involves middleware as well as persistence layers. Usually, each component runs in a separate virtual machine, which can be hosted in data centers that are owned by different cloud computing providers. Additionally, each plug-in developer has the freedom to choose which Cloud computing provider offers the services that are more suitable to run his/her plug-in. As a consequence, a typical web application is formed by hundreds of different services, which may be hosted by dozens of Cloud service providers around the world (Buyya et al., 2010; Rochwerger et al., 2011; Villegas et al., 2012).

3. **Multi-Cloud Environment Consisting of Private and Public Cloud Services:** To optimize the IT asset and computing resources, an organization often needs to keep in-house (private cloud) IT assets and capabilities associated with their core competencies while outsourcing marginal functions and activities (e.g. the human resource system) on to the public cloud. In this case, frequent communications between cloud services (the HR system), and on-premise systems (e.g. an ERP system on Private Cloud) becomes crucial and indispensable to run a business (Bojanova, 2011; Dillon, 2010).

Different Services supported by each Cloud-Service Layers (SaaS, PaaS, IaaS) with different Providers are represented in the Figure 1. All Cloud providers may not support services at all the SaaS, PaaS and IaaS layers.

4. **Multi-Cloud Environment Consisting of Multiple IaaS Cloud Services:** To deal with sudden spikes in capacity demand and to avoid over provisioning of resources, two or more independent cloud computing providers can join together to create a federated cloud. Federation participants who have excess capacity can share their resources, for an agreed-upon price, with participants needing additional resources. This sharing and paying model helps individual providers for scaling of applications across multiple vendor clouds (Sun et al., 2011; Khazaei et al., 2011; Clément et al., 2013; Nicolas et al., 2013; Adel et al.,2011).

Figure 1. Cloud Service Layers with Some Providers.

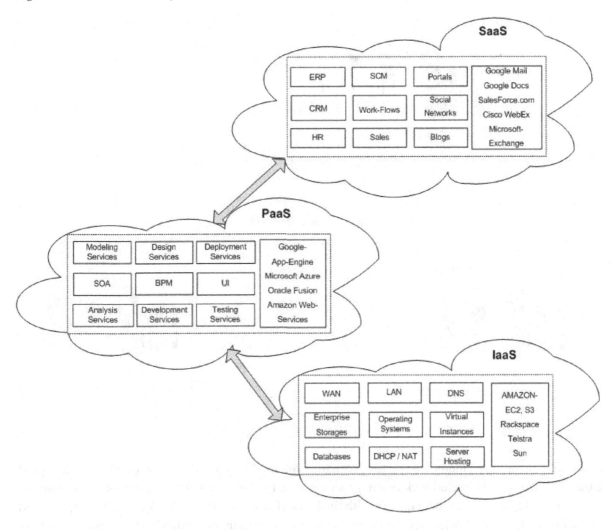

To meet aforementioned requirement for federation of cloud environments, the Figure 2 depicts the architecture diagram. This architecture is based on UDDI working mechanism. The core parts of this model are the Cloud Coordinator and Cloud Broker. Cloud Coordinators are part of each individual clouds which are basically responsible for exposing the cloud services based on load dynamically. Whereas Cloud Broker is responsible for mediating between service consumers and Cloud coordinators. Cloud Broker, plays the role of information service directory so that for finding available resources from the members of federation, providers send an inquiry to the Cloud Broker Service in case of shortage of local resources. The Cloud Broker is responsible for generating a list of providers with corresponding service rates that can handle the current request.

For the fulfillment of a request that is generated by an end-user to a designated Cloud (let us say Cloud-A) it might require either to be forwarded to another Cloud (let us say Cloud-B) or the response is directly sent back by Cloud-A. Again, when the forwarded-request is with Cloud-B then the response can be either directly sent back by Cloud-B or it can be redirected back to Cloud-A. This process can

Figure 2. Federation of Cloud services.

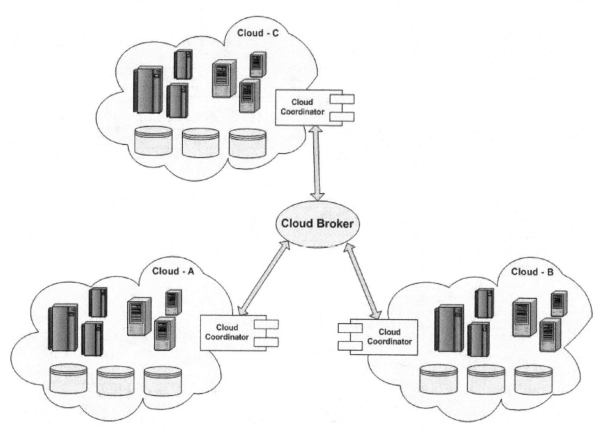

continue with multiple clouds in a real time scenario with n-Clouds forming the network and the request either forwarded or redirected back before generating the final response to the cloud service consumer. This can be depicted as Tandem queues with feedback (Hayes and Babu, 2004), which is represented in the Figure 3. For the buffer capacities, we consider two cases that is, either both buffers are finite or both are infinite.

Figure 3. Tandem queues with feedback.

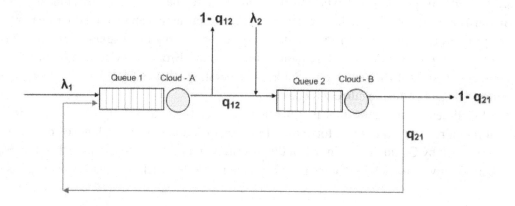

3. ANALYTICAL MODEL

3.1. Model 1, Both Buffers Are Infinite

Let us consider a network formed by two queues in tandem, each having an independent exponential server and infinite buffer. It is assumed that an external traffic arrives at each of two nodes according to a Poisson process with mean rates λ_1 and λ_2, respectively. The mean service rates are given by $1/\mu_1$ and $1/\mu_2$, respectively. The probability of routing between the queues is q_{12} and q_{21} as indicated. The total flow into each node of the network is Λ_1 and Λ_2 respectively. The total flow is composed of external arrival plus flows between queues. This can be represented with the help of traffic equation as

$$\Lambda_1 = \lambda_1 + q_{21}\Lambda_2, \tag{1}$$

$$\Lambda_2 = \lambda_2 + q_{12}\Lambda_1 \tag{2}$$

The state of the system is the number of requests at each of the nodes. Let us define the steady states of the system by P_{k_1,k_2} as the probability of k_1 and k_2 requests at the respective nodes. For the system under consideration, the Chapman-Kolmogorov forward differential equations at steady state can be written as

$$\lambda P_{0,0} = \mu_1(1-q_{12})P_{1,0} + \mu_2(1-q_{21})P_{0,01}, k_1 = k_2 = 0, \tag{3}$$

$$(\lambda+\mu_2)P_{0,k_2} = \lambda_2 P_{0,k_2-1} + \mu_1(1-q_{12})P_{1,k_2} + \mu_2(1-q_{21})P_{0,k_2+1} + \mu_1 q_{12}P_{1,k_2-1}, k_1 = 0, k_2 > 0, \tag{4}$$

$$(\lambda+\mu_1)P_{k_1,0} = \lambda_1 P_{k_1-1,0} + \mu_1(-q_{12})P_{k_1+1,0} + \mu_2(1-q_{21})P_{k_1,1} + \mu_2 q_{21}P_{k_1-1,1}, k_1 > 0, k_2 = 0, \tag{5}$$

$$
\begin{aligned}
(\lambda+\mu)P_{k_1,k_2} &= \lambda_1 P_{k_1-1,k_2} + \mu_1(-q_{12})P_{k_1+1,k_2} + \mu_1 q_{12}P_{k_1+1,k_2-1} + \mu_2 q_{21}P_{k_1-1,k_2+1} \\
&+ \lambda_2 P_{k_1,k_2-1} + \mu_2(1-q_{21})P_{k_1,k_2+1}, k_1, k_2 > 0,
\end{aligned}
\tag{6}
$$

where $\lambda = \lambda_1 + \lambda_2$ and $\mu = \mu_1 + \mu_2$. Now substituting the values of λ_1 and λ_2 from equations (1) and (2) in (3) and (6) yields

$$0 = -\Lambda P_{0,0} + \mu_1(1 - q_{12})P_{1,0} + \mu_2(-q_{21})P_{0,1} + (q_{12}\Lambda_1 + q_{21}\Lambda_2)P_{0,0}, k_1 = k_2 = 0, \tag{7}$$

$$0 = -(\Lambda + \mu_2)P_{0,k_2} + \mu_1 P_{1,k_2} + \mu_2 P_{0,k_2+1} + \Lambda_2 P_{0,k_2-1} + \mu_1 q_{12}P_{1,k_2-1} + (q_{12}q_{21}\Lambda_2)P_{0,k_2}$$
$$-q_{12}\Lambda_1 P_{0,k_2-1} - \mu_1 q_{12}P_{1,k_2} - \mu_2 q_{21}P_{0,k_2+1}, k_1 = 0, k_2 > 0, \tag{8}$$

$$0 = -(\Lambda + \mu_1)P_{k_1,0} + \mu_1 P_{k_1+1,0} + \mu_2 P_{k_1,1} + \Lambda_1 P_{k_1-1,0} + (q_{12}\Lambda_1 + q_{21}\Lambda_2)P_{k_1,0}$$
$$+\mu_2 q_{21}P_{k_1-1,1} - q_{21}\Lambda_2 P_{k_1-1,0} - \mu_1 q_{12}P_{k_1+1,0} - \mu_2 q_{21}P_{k_1,1}, k_1 > 0, k_2 = 0, \tag{9}$$

$$0 = -(\Lambda + \mu)P_{k_1,k_2} + \mu_1 P_{k_1+1,k_2} + \mu_2 P_{k_1,k_2+1} + \mu_1 q_{12}P_{k_1+1,k_2-1} + \mu_2 q_{21}P_{k_1-1,k_2+1} + \Lambda_1 P_{k_1-1,k_2}$$
$$+\Lambda_2 P_{k_1,k_2-1} + (q_{12}\Lambda_1 + \Lambda_2)P_{k_1,k_2} - q_{21}\Lambda_2 P_{k_1-1,k_2} - q_{12}\Lambda_1 P_{k_1,k_2-1} - \mu_1 q_{12}P_{k_1+1,k_2} - \mu_2 q_{21}P_{k_1,k_2+1}, k_1, k_2 > 0, \tag{10}$$

where $\Lambda = \Lambda_1 + \Lambda_2$. Equating pairs from each side of the above equation, we can generate two basic types as below.

$$\Lambda_1 P_{k_1,k_2} = \mu_1 P_{k_1+1,k_2}, \mu_2 P_{k_1,k_2+1} = P_{k_1,k_2}\Lambda_2.$$

Substituting $\rho_i = \Lambda_i / \mu_i$, for $i = 1, 2$ we get

$$P(k_1 + 1, k_2) = \rho_1 P_{k_1,k_2}, \tag{11}$$

$$P(k_1, k_2 + 1) = \rho_2 P_{k_1,k_2}. \tag{12}$$

Using equations (11) and (12) and applying normalizing condition $\sum_{k_1=0}^{\infty}\sum_{k_2=0}^{\infty} P_{k_1,k_2} = 1$, leads to the solution

$$P_{k_1,k_2} = \sum_{k_1=0}^{\infty}\sum_{k_2=0}^{\infty}(1 - \rho_1)(1 - \rho_2)\rho_1^{k_1}\rho_2^{k_2}, k_1, k_2 \geq 0, \tag{13}$$

3.2. Model 2, Both Buffers Are Finite

Let us define the probability

$$P(Q_1(t) = n_1, Q_2(t) = n_2) = P(n_1, n_2; t)$$

as the probability of n_1 and n_2 requests at the respective nodes (stations) at time t. The steady state probability for this Model where both buffers are finite is derived under the condition that the total buffer size in both the nodes is N where, $n_1 + n_2 \leq N$. This model differs from the model discussed in previous section that the capacity is N, that is, the maximum number of customers allowed in the queue (excluding those in service) at any time is N. Using the same arguments mentioned in previous section, we have the same set of equations in the case of finite buffer as those for infinite buffer, but equations (7) and (8) become

$$\lambda P_{0,0} = \mu_1(1 - q_{12})P_{1,0} + \mu_2(1 - q_{21})P_{0,1}, k_1 = k_2 = 0, \tag{14}$$

$$(\lambda + \mu_2)P_{0,k_2} = \lambda_2 P_{0,k_2-1} + \mu_1(1 - q_{12})P_{1,k_2} + \mu_1 q_{12}P_{1,k_2-1} + \mu_2(1 - q_{21})P_{0,k_2+1}, k_1 = 0, 0 < k_2 \leq N-1, \tag{15}$$

$$\text{(16)}$$

$$(\lambda + \mu_1)P_{k_1,0} = \lambda_1 P_{k_1-1,0} + \mu_1(1 - q_{12})P_{k_1+1,0} + \mu_2 q_{21}P_{k_1-1,1} + \mu_2(1 - q_{21})P_{k_1,1}, \\ 0 < k_1 \leq N-1, k_2 = 0, \tag{17}$$

$$\mu_1 P_{N,0} = \lambda_1 P_{N-1,0} + \mu_2(1 - q_{21})P_{N,1} + \mu_2 q_{21}P_{N-1,1}, \tag{18}$$

$$(\lambda + \mu)P_{k_1,k_2} = \lambda_1 P_{k_1-1,k_2} + \lambda_2 P_{k_1,k_2-1} + \mu_1(1 - q_{12})P_{k_1+1,k_2} + \mu_2(1 - q_{21})P_{k_1,k_2+1} \\ + \mu_1 q_{12}P_{k_1+1,k_2-1} + \mu_2 q_{21}P_{k_1-1,k_2+1}, k_1, k_2 > 0; k_1 + k_2 < N, \tag{19}$$

$$\mu P_{k_1,k_2} = \lambda_1 P_{k_1-1,k_2} + \mu_1 q_{12}P_{k_1+1,k_2-1} + \lambda_2 P_{k_1,k_2-1} + \mu_2 q_{21}P_{k_1-1,k_2+1}, \\ k_1, k_2 > 0; k_1 + k_2 = N \tag{20}$$

Following the procedure discussed for infinite buffer, we can obtain

$$P_{k_1,k_2} = \rho_1^{n_1} \rho_2^{n_2} P_{0,0} \tag{21}$$

Summing over k_1 and k_2 from 0 to N ($k_1 + k_2 \leq N$) and equating to unity give

$$P_{0,0} = \left[1 + \sum_{i=1}^{N} \sum_{j=0}^{N-i} P_{i,j} \right]^{-1} \tag{22}$$

4. PERFORMANCE MEASURES

In this section, we discuss some important operating characteristics in cloud system. In the case of infinite buffer, the marginal distribution for each node is, respectively,

P (node 1 has k_1 requests) =

$(1 - \rho_1)\rho_1^{k_1}, k_1 \geq 1.$

P(node 2 has k_2 requests) =

$(1 - \rho_2)\rho_2^{k_2}, k_2 \geq 1.$

The average number of requests in the node 1 $\left(L_1 \right)$ and in the node 2 $\left(L_2 \right)$ are respectively, given by

$$L_1 = \frac{\rho_1}{1 - \rho_1}, L_2 = \frac{\rho_2}{1 - \rho_2}$$

The average number of requests in the system $\left(L_s \right)$ is

$$L_s = \frac{\rho_1}{1 - \rho_1} + \frac{\rho_2}{1 - \rho_2}.$$

The mean waiting time of a task in the system can be obtained using Little's rule as

$$W_s = \frac{L_i}{\Lambda_i} = \frac{1}{\mu_1 - \Lambda_1} + \frac{1}{\mu_2 - \Lambda_2}$$

The intensity of the system, $\rho_{sys} = \dfrac{\Lambda}{\mu}$.

In the case of finite buffer, the average numbers of requests in the node 1 (L_1) and in the node 2 (L_2) are respectively,

$$L_1 = \sum_{k_1=1}^{N} k_1 \left(\sum_{k_2=0}^{N-k_1} P_{k_1,k_2} \right),$$

$$L_2 = \sum_{k_2=1}^{N} k_2 \left(\sum_{k_2=0}^{N-k_2} P_{k_1,k_2} \right).$$

The average number of requests in the system (L_s) is given by $L_s = L_1 + L_2$.

The average request being served is

$$\sum_{k_1=1}^{N} P_{k_1,0} + \sum_{k_2=1}^{N} P_{0,k_2} + \sum_{k_1=1}^{N}\sum_{k_2=1}^{N} P_{k_1,k_2}$$

The average number of requests in the queue $\left(L_q \right)$ is

$$L_q = \sum_{k_1=2}^{N}(k_1 - 1)P_{k_1,0} + \sum_{k_2=2}^{N}(k_2 - 1)P_{0,k_2} + \sum_{k_1=2}^{N-1}(k_1 - 1)P_{k_1,1} + \sum_{k_2=2}^{N-1}(k_2 - 1)P_{1,k_2}$$
$$+ \sum_{k_1=2}^{N-1}\sum_{k_2=2}^{N-1}(k_1 + k_2 - 2)P_{k_1,k_2}$$

The average waiting time in the queue $\left(W_q \right)$ can be obtained using Little's rule as $W_q = L_q / \lambda'$, where $\lambda' = \lambda(1 - PBL)$ is the effective arrival rate and $PBL = \sum_{k_1=0}^{N} P_{k_1,N-k_1}$ represents the probability of loss or blocking.

5. NUMERICAL RESULTS

In this section, we present the numerical studies of cloud computing environment as shown in Figure 1. The numerical results are obtained from the queueing models for both infinite and finite buffer given in Section 3. The performance measures of cloud are obtained from Section 4. We first consider a cloud when both buffers are infinite and the graphs are presented in Figures 4 to 7.

Figure 4 compares the effect of ρ_{sys} on the average waiting time in different Cloud Centers. It can be seen that as ρ_{sys} increases the average waiting time also increases. As it can be seen, the average waiting time in cloud center 1 is more than the average waiting time in cloud center 2.

Figure 5 illustrates the impact of ρ_{sys} (System Usage) on average number of jobs in different cloud centers. We observe that with the increase of the system usage the average number of jobs in cloud centers also increases. It can be observed that as the system usage increases, average number of jobs in cloud centers also increases. Again average number of jobs in the cloud center 2 yields the lowest.

The impact of ρ_{sys} on the cloud centers being busy is shown in Figure 6. It is seen that as ρ_{sys} increases usage of cloud centers also increases. It is also seen that in the multi-cloud system with the increase of ρ_{sys} the cloud centers being idle decreases.

Figure 7 also depicts this ρ_{sys} with respect to idle period of cloud centers in a multi-Cloud environment. From this figure we see that as system usage increases, the corresponding idle period of cloud

Figure 4. Impact of ρ_{sys} on average waiting Time

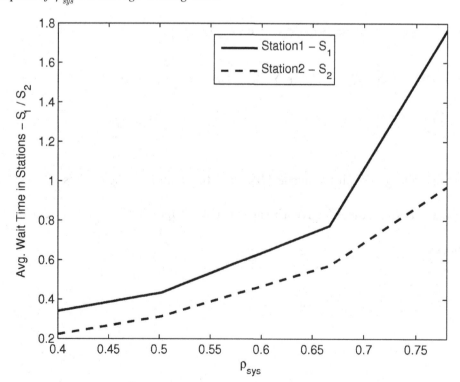

Figure 5. Impact of ρ_{sys} on average number of jobs

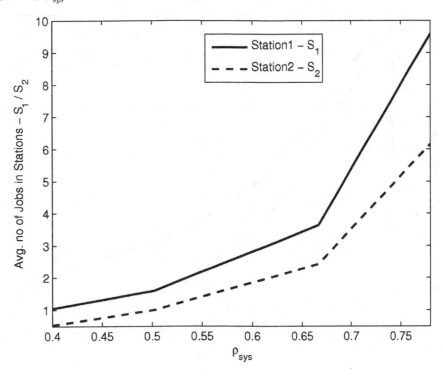

Figure 6. Impact of Stations being Busy on ρ_{sys}

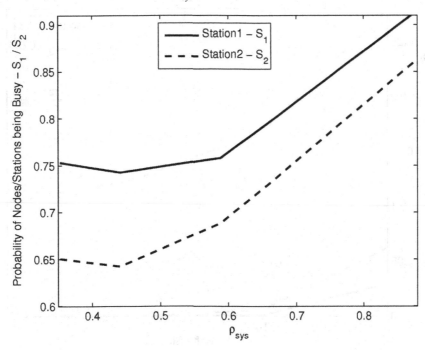

Figure 7. Impact of Stations being Idle on ρ_{sys}

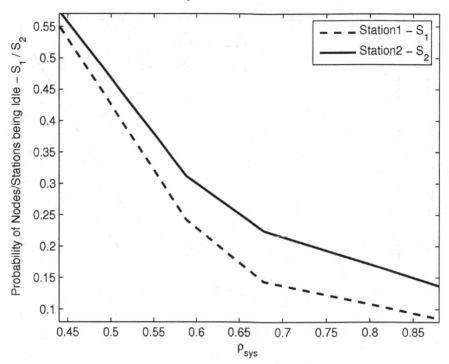

Figure 8. Impact of N on PBL

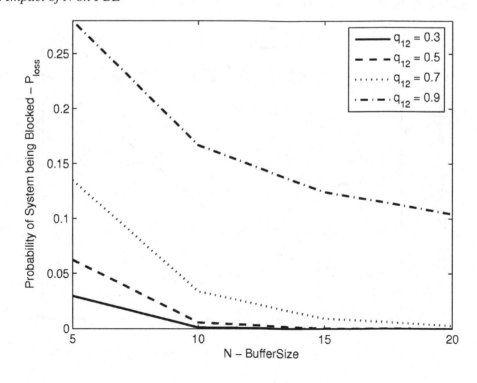

Figure 11. Impact of L_s *on* ρ_{sys}

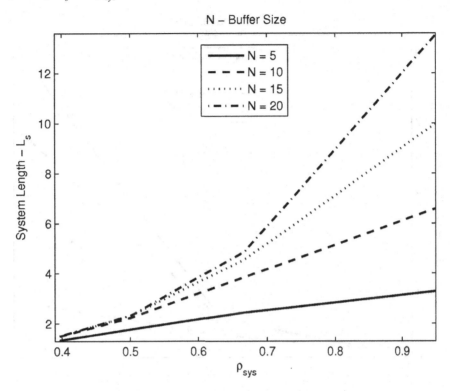

Figure 9. Effect of ρ_{sys} *on PBL*

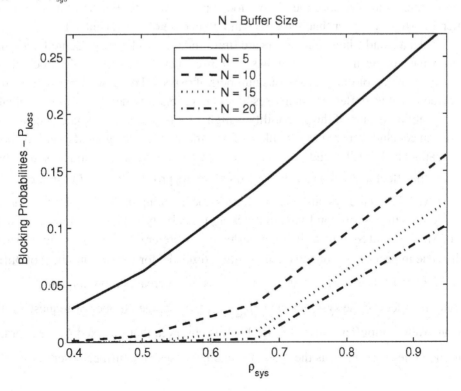

Figure 10. Impact of W_q on ρ_{sys}

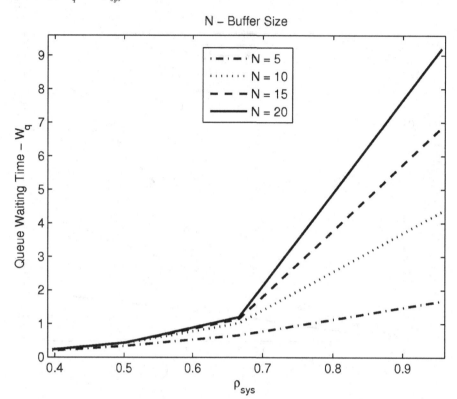

centers decreases monotonically until the idle period starts to saturate. Further, the idle period in case of cloud center 2 is slightly higher than the one obtained in case of cloud center 1.

Now, we consider a cloud when both buffers are finite and the graphs are presented in Figures 8 to 11 for various performance measures. Figure 8 shows the impact of buffer size (N) on the blocking probability (*PBL*), that is, system being blocked for various numbers of expected requests routed between two cloud centers. It is evident that as buffer size increases blocking probability decreases monotonically. Again, this blocking probability is more if the probability is higher for requests being routed between two cloud centers. So, we can conclude any request should be forwarded from a designated cloud to another cloud only if either it cannot be full filled end-to-end by the 1st-Center or there is serious resource bottle neck.

Figure 9 plots the effect of system usage $\left(\rho_{sys} \right)$ on blocking probability (*PBL*) for various buffer size N. It can be observed that as the system usage increases, the blocking probability also increases. But for larger buffer size N in the Multi-cloud system blocking probability is less in comparison with smaller buffer size. So, Multi-Cloud System with larger buffer size is preferable in order to minimize the blocking probability. The impact of ρ_{sys} on the queue waiting time W_q for various numbers of buffer sizes N is shown in the Figure 10. It is seen that as ρ_{sys} increases W_q increases monotonically.

We illustrate the effect of the system usage $\left(\rho_{sys} \right)$ on the average number of requests in the system $\left(L_s \right)$, for various values of buffer size, in Figure 11. It is observed that for fixed N, the average number of requests in the system increases as the system usage increases. We further observe that L_s become more evident for larger values of ρ_{sys}. When ρ_{sys} is kept fixed, the average number of requests in the system increases with the increase of *N*. To ensure minimum average number of requests in the system, we can carefully setup the value of system usage $\left(\rho_{sys}\right)$ and buffer size.

6. CONCLUSION

In this chapter, we have carried out an analysis of resource sharing and optimization of resource usage in multi-cloud computing environment. We have proposed analytical model for performance evaluation of a cloud computing center. The web applications are modeled as queues and the virtual machines are modeled as service centers in this queueing model. To maintain the QoS at an acceptable level is of great importance aspect of cloud computing which is essential for both cloud providers and customers. Various performance measures of cloud, the mean number of tasks in the system, mean response time, blocking probability, and the average number of requests in the queue have been discussed. We have conducted numerical studies to validate our model. Numerical results indicate that the proposed provisioning technique detects changes in arrival pattern, resource demands that occur over time and allocates multiple virtualized IT resources accordingly to achieve application Quality of Service targets.

Future work can be extended further in order to determine optimal number of virtual-machines (VMs) required within a federated cloud center which is supporting IaaS service layer. Also, how clustering of Cloud-centers can help further to minimize any disaster. Due to the existence of administrative boundaries and corporate ethics in organizations, multi-cloud (in particular in private clouds) based resource sharing approaches has got its own inherited limitations.

REFERENCES

Ardagna, D., Trubian, M., & Zhang, L. (2005). SLA based profit optimization in multi-tier systems. In *Proceedings of the 4th IEEE International Symposium on Network Computing and Applications*, (pp. 263–266). doi:10.1109/NCA.2005.48

Armbrust, M., Fox, A., Griffith, R., Joseph, A., Katz, R., Konwinski, A., & Zaharia, M. et al. (2010). A View of Cloud Computing. *Communications of the ACM, 53*(4), 50–58. doi:10.1145/1721654.1721672

Bojanova, I. (2011). Analysis of Cloud Computing Delivery Architecture Models. In *Proceedings of the IEEE Workshops of International Conference on Advanced Information Networking and Applications*, (pp.453–458). doi:10.1109/WAINA.2011.74

Brunette, G., & Mogull, R. (2009). *Security Guidance for critical areas of focus in Cloud Computing V2. 1', CSA (Cloud Security Alliance).* Retrieved from http://www.cloudsecurityalliance.org/guidance/csaguide.v2

Buyya, R., Ranjan, R., & Calheiros, R. N. (2010). 'InterCloud: Utility-Oriented Federation of Cloud Computing Environments for Scaling of Application Services', *Algorithms and Architectures for Parallel Processing. Lecture Notes in Computer Science, 6081*, 13–31. doi:10.1007/978-3-642-13119-6_2

Buyya, R., Yeo, C. S., Venugopal, S., Broberg, J., & Brandic, I. (2009). Cloud Computing and Emerging IT Platforms: Vision, Hype, and Reality for Delivering Computing as the 5th Utility. *Future Generation Computer Systems*, *25*(6), 599–616. doi:10.1016/j.future.2008.12.001

Dillon, T. (2010). Cloud Computing: Issues and Challenges. In *Proceedings of the 24th IEEE International Conference on Advanced Information Networking and Applications*, (pp.27–33). doi:10.1109/AINA.2010.187

Erdil, D. C. (2012). Autonomic cloud resource sharing for intercloud federations. *Future Generation Computer Systems*, *28*(2), 358–367.

Ferry, N., Rossini, A., Chauvel, F., & Solberg, A. (2013). Towards model-driven provisioning, deployment, monitoring, and adaptation of multi-cloud systems. In *Proceedings of 2013 IEEE Sixth International Conference on Cloud Computing*, (pp. 887 - 894). doi:10.1109/CLOUD.2013.133

Goswami, V., & Sahoo, C. N. (2013). Optimal Resource Usage in Multi-Cloud Computing Environment. *International Journal of Cloud Applications and Computing*, *3*(1), 45–57. doi:10.4018/ijcac.2013010105

Hayes, J. F., & Ganesh Babu, T. V. J. (2004). *Modeling and Analysis of Telecommunications Networks*. Wiley-Interscience Publication. doi:10.1002/0471643505

Karlapudi, H., & Martin, J. (2004). Web application performance prediction. In *Proceedings of the IASTED International Conference on Communication and Computer Networks*, (pp. 281–286). IASTED.

Khazaei, H., Misic, J., & Misic, V. B. (2011). Performance Analysis of Cloud Centers under Burst Arrivals and Total Rejection Policy. In *Proceedings of the IEEE International Conference on Global Telecommunications*, (pp.1–6). IEEE. doi:10.1109/GLOCOM.2011.6133765

Lu, J., & Wang, J. (2005). Performance modeling and analysis of Web Switch. In *Proceedings of the 31st Annual International Conference on Computer Measurement*, (pp. 665–672). Academic Press.

Mell, P., & Grance, T. (2009). *The NIST Definition of Cloud Computing*. Retrieved from http://www.nist.gov/itl/cloud/upload/cloud-def-v15.pdf

Quinton, C., Haderer, N., & Duchien, L. (2013). Towards multi-cloud configurations using feature models and ontologies. In *ACM, MultiCloud'13 Proceedings of the international workshop on Multi-cloud applications and federated clouds*, (pp. 21-26). doi:10.1145/2462326.2462332

Rochwerger, B., Breitgand, D., Epstein, A., Hadas, D., Loy, I., Nagin, K., & Tofetti, G. et al. (2011). Reservoir - When One Cloud Is Not Enough. *Computer*, *44*(3), 44–51. doi:10.1109/MC.2011.64

Slothouber, L. (1995). *A model of Web server performance*. Retrieved from www.geocities.com/webserverperformance

Sun, A., Ji, T., Yue, Q., & Xiong, F. (2011). IaaS Public Cloud Computing Platform Scheduling Model and Optimization Analysis. *International Journal of Communications, Network, and System Sciences*, *4*(12), 803–811. doi:10.4236/ijcns.2011.432098

Toosi, A. N., Calheiros, R. N., Thulasiram, R. K., & Buyya, R. (2011). Resource Provisioning Policies to Increase IaaS Provider's Profit in a Federated Cloud Environment. In *Proceedings of 2011 IEEE International Conference on High Performance Computing and Communications*, (pp. 279 – 287). doi:10.1109/HPCC.2011.44

Tordsson, J., Montero, R. S., Moreno-Vozmediano, R., & Llorente, I. M. (2012). Cloud brokering mechanisms for optimized placement of virtual machines across multiple providers. *Future Generation Computer Systems*, 28(2), 358–367. doi:10.1016/j.future.2011.07.003

Vaquero, L., Rodero-Merino, L., Caceres, J., & Lindner, M. (2009). A break in the clouds: Towards a cloud definition. *Computer Communication Review*, 39(1), 50–55. doi:10.1145/1496091.1496100

Villegas, D., Bobroff, N., Rodero, I., Delgado, J., Liu, Y., Devarakonda, A., & Parashar, M. et al. (2012). Cloud federation in a layered service model. *Journal of Computer and System Sciences*, 78(5), 1330–1344. doi:10.1016/j.jcss.2011.12.017

Chapter 8
Towards Future IT Service Personalization:
Issues in BYOD and the Personal Cloud

Stuart Dillon
University of Waikato, New Zealand

Florian Stahl
University of Münster, Germany

Gottfried Vossen
University of Münster, Germany

ABSTRACT

Cloud services are ubiquitous today and increasingly used for a variety of purposes, including personal and professional communication, social networking, media streaming, calendar management, file storage etc. In recent years, a fast evolution of cloud services from private applications to corporate usage has been observed. This has led to the question of how private and business cloud services can be dual-accessed through a single device, in particular a mobile device that is used as part of a BYOD (Bring Your Own Device) policy. This chapter considers the issues that arise from a consolidation of private and professional applications when accessed from a single device and introduces the term "personal cloud" to characterise such situations. It also surveys recent work in the field and finally presents an approach to cloud governance from a business perspective focusing in particular on security tokens, hardware keys and smart containers, thereby providing a glimpse into the future of IT service personalization.

INTRODUCTION

Cloud services are ubiquitous today and increasingly used for a variety of purposes, including personal and professional communication, social networking, media streaming, calendar management, file storage etc. Cloud sourcing and cloud computing are not new, but in particular for non-business uses and users have existed for many years; for business users they go back to the concept of application service

DOI: 10.4018/978-1-4666-8676-2.ch008

Copyright © 2015, IGI Global. Copying or distributing in print or electronic forms without written permission of IGI Global is prohibited.

provisioning (ASP), cluster computing, grid computing and the like already favoured in the 1980s and 1990s. However, in recent years we have observed an evolution of private cloud services to corporate/business applications, many of which overlap business and private domains. An online calendar for example will typically integrate private and professional appointments, and the employee may want to be able to access company files through a personal device, and vice versa. This chapter studies the issues that arise from such a merge of private and professional applications on a single device, introduces the term "personal cloud" for such scenarios, and presents an approach to govern such clouds from a company perspective.

With increasing market penetration of (mobile and) smart devices such as smartphones, tablets, or laptops and owing to the ubiquitous ("always-on") nature of these devices, meaning that they have continuous and uninterrupted Internet access, private applications such as social networks and e-mail will more and more reside on the same device as corporate documents or applications such as company spreadsheets or (interfaces to) proprietary software. Most commonly, both types of services are used interchangeably in both business and private environments, e.g., employees usually have a private and a corporate e-mail address, but both are accessed through a common interface or even using the same e-mail application. This observation is supported by the BYOD ("bring your own device") development, also known as IT consumerization (Castro-Leon 2014), where companies are allowing their employees to use their personal devices at work or for work-related purposes (Scarfo, 2012, Disterer & Kleiner, 2013). Of the many benefits BYOD offers (both to organizations and their employees), an increase in flexibility and efficiency as well as the ability to work at anytime from anywhere are considered key (Morrow, 2012). The underlying philosophy of BYOD is in line with Mark Zuckerberg's philosophy, implemented in Facebook, that every person has only one identity (as opposed to a private and a professional one). Indeed, in an interview with David Kirkpatrick for his book, "The Facebook Effect.," Zuckerberg is cited as saying "The days of you having a different image for your work friends or co-workers and for the other people you know are probably coming to an end pretty quickly. Having two identities for yourself is an example of a lack of integrity." (Zimmer, 2010)

Even though this statement is controversial from a privacy point of view, the lack of integrity is particularly pertinent, especially from a technological perspective. By way of an example which is a reality in many parts of the world today, consider the daily routine of a typical knowledge worker (e.g., a bank employee). While having breakfast she wants to check on her private and business e-mails. Today, it is very likely that she will do this on her smartphone, tablet, or on the rather new combination "phablet" (portmanteau from phone and tablet) using two different Web services, each with individual login. Also, a third and fourth application will be needed for calendar and (quality) news, all of which with potentially different credentials. In her office, after plugging her laptop into a docking station, she will access proprietary banking software, the same e-mail and calendar services, only via a different interface. She is likely to store some files on a company cloud storage solution. Heading for a customer presentation she grabs her laptop again which is obviously able to access the aforementioned cloud storage. Many interesting scenarios emerge from this setting: During a meeting, relevant company performance figures can be accessed; on the way home a presentation can be finalized on the train; during her lunch break a quick look can be taken at photos from a relative's vacation; during a free moment, the remainder of last night's movie can be watched. While this may still be viewed within the realms of science fiction to some, it is only the beginning of what will soon be everyday manifestations of our 24/7 hyper-connected world in which the distinction between private and professional life is vastly blurred (Schmidt and Cohen, 2013). In other words, people will soon be living in their "personal" cloud, a term that was first mentioned in a 2011 Forrester report in 2011 and also picked up by the Web blog rcadwriteweb.com around the same time.

A study reported in BITKOM (2013), the German *Federal Association for Information Economy, Telecommunication and New Media (Bundesverband Informationswirtschaft, Telekommunikation und Neue Medien e.V., abbreviated BITKOM)* shows that 43% of German IT and telecommunication companies allow their employees to connect their own devices to the company network. Almost 60% of these companies have established specific rules for this, 81% expect an increase in employee satisfaction, 74% expect increased productivity, while roughly 40% believe they will be perceived as a modern employer. On the other hand, 53% of the companies that were interviewed for this study declined the use of private devices in the workplace, mostly due to increased maintenance and security costs in the presence of a large variety of devices, differing operating systems, with all kinds of application software installed. We expect these figures to be similar in other parts of the Western world. Lance and Schweigert (2013) examine BYOD projects at IBM, Cisco, Citrix, and Intel to determine when and whether an implementation of this concept is successful.

Clearly, to make BYOD usage scenarios (such as the one outlined above) work, various issues need to be addressed, including but not limited to:

- Who owns the device(s)? An employee might be allow to use a private device for business-related purposes (BYOD), or the employer might provide the device (COPE).
- How are access rights managed on the various applications that reside on the same device, but are "owned" by different parties?
- How is a change of jobs or the termination of an employment handled?

More generally, issues relating to BYOD/COPE can be categorized into legal, economical, organizational, and technical issues, several of which will be elaborated upon in this paper; for an introduction to cultural and organizational impact, see Lofaro (2014). We look at current practice which reveals solutions already in use, and we point out research issues that need further study.

The remainder of this paper is organized as follows: To clarify what the personal cloud actually is, we describe and analyse the concept in the next section. Leading to the topic of governance, the subsequent section elaborates on the various forms of device ownerships models seen today. Thereafter, we present our suggestions on how data security and privacy can be achieved through Personal Cloud Governance. Finally, we conclude this paper. We mention that no explicit section on prior work is included in the paper, as prior work will be discussed throughout and wherever appropriate.

CHARACTERIZATION OF PERSONAL CLOUDS

In this section, we first define the notion and concepts on which this research is focused. BYOD (Bring Your Own Device) is a commonly used abbreviation for the situation where a mobile (or sometimes stationary) device is used within an organizational context, where that device is owned by an employee, not by the company, yet has access to IT resources of the company. The IT resources that are accessible through the device typically consist of software, in particular Web-based, as well as cloud-based services or applications. BYOD is different from what is commonly termed CYOD ("Choose Your Own

Device"), where an employee can choose from a (typically limited) variety of devices offered, yet the device chosen remains company property. CYOD is in turn very similar to COPE ("Corporate Owned, Personally Enabled"), where the company owns a device for which the employee has personal use. Both COPE and CYOD may or may not come with restrictions regarding the selection of devices. We will not distinguish CYOD and COPE in the remainder of this paper, and we will generally assume that for the latter private usage is accepted. COPE is more commonly discussed, so we will follow suit.

Independently of which model, BYOD or COPE, is used, it is obvious that the data and the services accessed via the device will partially be private (or for a private purpose) and partially be organizational (or for an organizational purpose). Some of the data and services will be installed locally on the device, while others (often the majority) will be available in, or accessible through, the cloud only; it is these data and services which together make up the personal cloud that we will focus on in this paper.

We note that a "definition" of personal clouds is currently flaky at best; perhaps a symptom of the embryonic state of the concept. Personal Clouds (2014) argues that, at present, users are at the mercy of cloud computing providers, as these are more or less in charge of the users' data as soon as it is handed over. This is easily substantiated by considering large providers of personal cloud services such as Apple or Google. In contrast to that, personal-clouds.org suggests a personal cloud where users can decide what *"data to put there and whom to share it with, where we [the users] decide which apps to run on it, and where we [the users] define the terms of service?"(Personal Clouds, 2014)*. Here they draw an analogy to personal computers which liberated users from mainframe operators. A different description is given by Forrester, as reported by Rowinski (2011). It can be seen that a personal cloud comprises both cooperate and personal services, which can be accessed through a number of devices. However, different services are still grouped like-for-like, otherwise separated when used in different contexts.

Following and extending this conceptualisation, we consider the personal cloud to be characterized by the following properties:

1. A personal cloud is conceptually a description of cloud exploitation by an individual user or, stated differently, a possibly structured collection of the cloud service an individual user is regularly referring to. As such, it is not a typical cloud in the strict sense, as established by Vossen et al. (2012).
2. It is a single point of access to all cloud services of a given user, i.e., the services and applications combined and gathered in a personal cloud are uniformly accessible through multiple and distinct devices in pretty much the same way. Moreover, they are integrated in such a way that a single service, even if used in multiple contexts, is always accessed through the same interface, where responsive design (Kadlec and Gustafson, 2012) is used for proper adaptation to varying devices.
3. Different devices do not limit the functionality of the personal cloud.
4. The content of applications and services comprising a personal cloud as well as the access to these applications and services are currently under the supervision and control of various individual providers, whereas device usage is at the device owners' discretion. This does not exclude the fact that some or all applications and services require the user to register or to exercise some form of access rights.

The above definition is illustrated in Figure 1 with a sample of relevant applications (e.g., e-mail, file management) either in the private (photos) or in the professional (corporate software) domain. We generally assume that both private data and company data is kept in the cloud; cases for which this is not

Figure 1. The Personal Cloud at the intersection of personal and professional data and services.

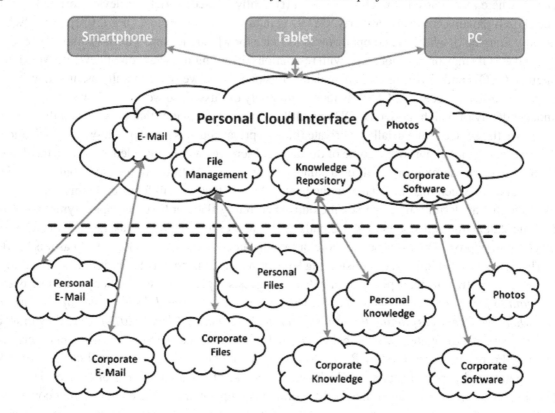

given are not considered here, since they typically do not have an "interference problem." In contrast to the personal cloud is the corporate cloud, which stores all information and services for a specific company. However, as might be expected, there is a significant overlap between the personal and corporate cloud.

At a more abstract level, a personal cloud has three main components as shown in Figure 2. These components are as follows:

- **Cloud Services:** Provide access to the cloud and can be provided in-house, i.e., by the enterprise in question itself (right border) or by an outside Cloud Service Provider (CSO, left border). CSPs other than the enterprise itself may provide services that are outside the scope of what the enterprise is doing, e.g., social networking, business process management software, etc.
- **Private as Well as Business Data (Storage):** Allows to access and store data from and to cloud services.
- **Synchronization ("Sync" or "Load" in Figure 2, Resp.):**
  - *Between access paths* it provides a consistent view of the data to the user regardless of the access paths s/he is using; i.e., the user needs to have the same data available on all devices/computers connected to a particular personal cloud.
  - *Between cloud software* provides a consistent deployment of the data across all cloud software, i.e., it does not force user to enter same data multiple times.

Figure 2. The core operations occurring in and around a personal cloud.

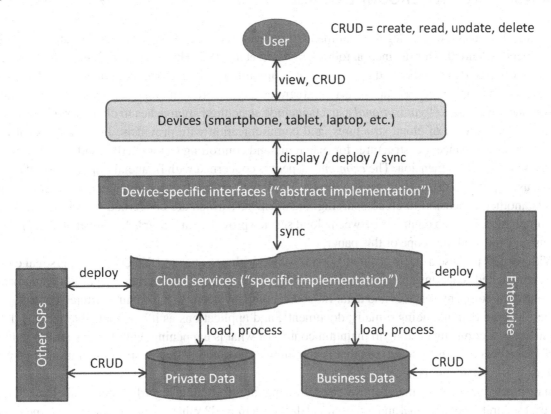

- ○ *(Down-) Load* ensures that the user has timely access to all relevant data whenever needed, taking into account the different capabilities of various access paths, e. g., regarding storage space, memory, processing power, bandwidth, energy, etc.
- ○ *(Up-) Load* transparently uploads changes into a user's Personal Cloud to store and sync them.

Figure 2 also shows a number of activities and operations that must be provided in order for this to work. In particular, there are deployment or display services for content delivered to the user, where content can originate from the enterprise the user is working for or from other cloud service providers (for personal content such as music). Most importantly, there must be a synchronization service between the collection of cloud services available to the user and the devices he or she is using; as will be seen in Section "Governance for Security and Privacy", control over this sync service is an essential governance component.

An interesting dimension of the personal cloud relates to the dual use of cloud based software in both work and private contexts. Facebook provides an ideal illustrative example of this. Increasingly, Facebook is being used for internal and external "communication" by businesses. However, the use of multiple identities is counterintuitive to the philosophy of Facebook (and not permitted anyway). Instead, Facebook provides the user with the option of linking multiple "pages" to a single profile, even if the profile is effectively for administrative purposes only.

DIMENSIONS OF A PERSONAL CLOUD

As previously noted, there are legal, economical, organizational, and technical aspects related to BYOD and the personal cloud. This distinction follows (Vossen et al. 2012; Haselmann & Vossen 2011), where they were discussed and elaborated upon for cloud computing and cloud sourcing in general. *Technical* aspects focus on topics such as data security, integratability of different cloud services, and the general performance of clouds. *Organizational* aspects include structured approaches to cloud service provider choice, documentation of cloud structures, and communication with providers. In the context of this paper, cloud governance, i.e. structures for managing and controlling (integrated) cloud services, is explicitly added to this dimension. The *economic* aspect is concerned with financial implications of cloud service usage, lock-in effects and pricing models used by cloud computing providers. We mention that there is another dimension to cloud sourcing, legal aspects, which are concerned with law obedience and compliance, but also contracts between cloud service providers and users (Vossen et al. 2012). This dimension is beyond the scope of this paper.

With respect to these aspects, it should first be obvious that the use of BYOD and the personal cloud can be unsolicited, since any enterprise is dependent on the employee's cooperation regarding monitoring and control of company services and data. Indeed, a company needs to have uninterrupted control over business-related data including e-mails, documents, and applications as it is responsible for this data. This includes a company needing to maintain control of what is happening with its data, and so that no interference occurs with personal data that is kept in the same cloud. Thus, a strict separation of private and business-related data is necessary.

In response to the issues noted above, the following questions arise regarding personal clouds: How can strict separation of personal and professional data be achieved? What special (data) security measures need to be taken in either case, and what security weaknesses do personal clouds have? Further, how can access be controlled and what exit strategies exists for personal cloud users and companies providing personal cloud services? Finally, how can a company retain its data and service provision once an employee leaves the company? Before we go into details here, we refer the reader to Koh et al. (2014) for a recent study on security threads as well as to Hernandez and Choi (2014) and Gupta et al. (2013).

We discuss some of the "physical" aspects regarding these questions in the following subsections, and will then turn to security as well as exit strategies and more conceptual considerations relating to governance in Section on "Governance for Security and Privacy". More specifically, the aspects we discuss next and how they relate to the aspects mentioned above are outlined in Table 1.

Table 1. Categorisation of Key Personal Cloud and BYOD Governance Issues.

	Device Ownership	Access Control	Security	Exit Strategies
Technical		X	X	X
Organizational	X		X	X
Economical	X			X

Device Ownership

BYOD eliminates the need to carry and use separate devices for private and work purposes. As shown in Figure 3, both BYOD (1) and COPE (2) have in common that the total cost of usage is carried by one entity (company in case of COPE, employee in case of BYOD). In reality, usage costs are likely to be shared such that the cost of work usage is paid for by the employer in case of BYOD or the cost of private usage is paid for by the individual (cases 4 and 3, respectively). In contrast to these forms is the traditional model of separate devices for professional and private usage (5). Whilst this is the most secure solution from a company perspective as the work device is controlled by it, it is also the most costly approach – at least if total cost is examined - because two devices have to be purchased and maintained. This is reversed with COPE or BYOD where less institutional control results in a greater security risk, while the total cost are smaller.

In terms of organizational processes, for each of these ownership models, it becomes necessary to specify what concrete actions will be taken when a new device is deployed or enabled. Furthermore, processes have to be defined that describe the actions to be taken in case a device is stolen or lost, when updates need to be physically deployed, or an employee leaves the company, as well as other eventualities.

Figure 3. Different forms of device ownership.

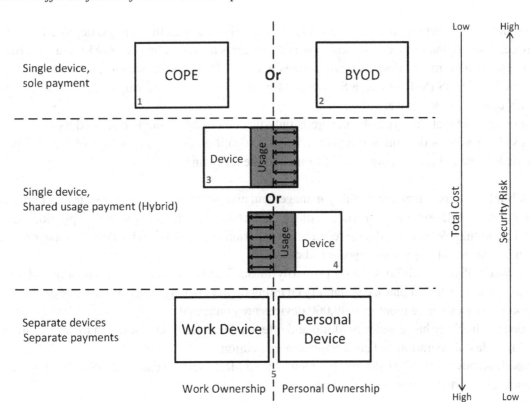

Access Control though MDM

It is eminently obvious that an appropriate form of security management is needed when company data ends up on personal devices, especially since this data will most likely be saved somewhere in the cloud and might get replicated around the world. The other obvious risk relates to potential theft or loss of the device. Since the trends that have led to the COPE model are unlikely to be reversed, there is a need to introduce ways to control them, instead of simply ignoring them or even forbidding usage of personal devices for work purposes, when such actions is likely to result in unauthorized, and indeed risky practices anyway.

A software solution to this problem is provided by *Mobile Device Management* (MDM) such as that described by Liu et al., 2010, which offers centralized management of all mobile devices that are used within an organizational context. MDM typically comes with features such as the following:

- Software distribution via an in-house app store, installation and maintenance via push apps
- Remote access for reading and setting possible configurations, push messages, switch-off (remote lock & wipe)
- Inventory management for keeping track of hardware, software, licenses, patch management
- Optional encrypted backup and restore
- "Containerization," i.e., strict differentiation between private and professional data and applications
- Protection against unauthorized access to enterprise services, jailbreak detection
- In general, conceptual issue include interfaces, SSO (single sign-on), architecture, standards.

To realize these functionalities, an *Enforcement Agent* (basically a client app) is deployed to the mobile device. Some of the latest devices and operating systems also offer an MDM-API as an alternative. From that point onward, the device communicates with an MDM server, which can be operated either o*n premise* or as SaaS (Software as a Service). Its main tasks are: monitoring of access, data storage, and configuration of the device.

Despite the fact that this type of software is only just emerging, a number of vendors exist. Forbes estimates about 80 vendors and Solutions Review has identified 20 main suppliers of MDM software (Solutions Review n.d.), including, but not limited to the following:

- MobileIron is specialized in mobility management and positions its software suite as a pure MDM solution. MobileIron has meanwhile deployed a portal that, in their own words, "provides an easy and customizable end user device registration experience and self-service device management." It can be reached at http://www.byodportal.com/).
- AirWatch offers its MDM solution primarily in SaaS form; however, on-premise installation is also possible. They emphasize scalability enabling them to manage large numbers of devices (they report on cases where more than 40,000 devices are connected).
- Good Technology has a wider portfolio and offers a dedicated MDM solution as well as software for mobile collaboration and enterprise communication.
- Fiberlink, now owned by IBM, offers a cloud-based MDM service called MaaS360 and has a large number of partners aiming for a global reach.

- Citrix XenMobile is an MDM tool that was originally created by Zenprise and that particularly emphasizes protection against data loss, besides offering a variety of functions pertaining to the mobile cloud.

We refer the reader to Schomm and Vossen (2013) for further details.

GOVERNANCE FOR SECURITY AND PRIVACY

While MDM is a viable solution and some features such as an in-house app store and SSO are demanded widely, this is particularly labor intensive and restricts users in the way they can actually use *their* device. In this section, we suggest alternative solutions and also look at the problem from a conceptual point of view; the reader is referred to Morrow (2012) and Miller et al. (2012) for an overview of relevant security (employer side) and privacy (employee side) challenges.

Essentially, two scenarios need to be considered:

1. **The Company Owns the Device (COPE):** In this case, the device needs different ways of being accessed: a personal domain, a company section, and a combined section, each with an individual user-chosen access code.
2. **The User Owns the Device (BYOD):** In case of a split, i.e., the user leaves the company and is no longer granted access to company data or services, the company disables access to any company application and the user returns the SIM card of the device in question (in particular if that card is not in his or her personal possession).

Clearly, the measures that need to be taken in either case vary slightly for different types of devices such as smartphones, tablets, or laptops and for cellular vs non-cellular devices. We ignore such differences in what follows.

Both scenarios can utilize any of the security measures discussed in the following subsections (security tokens, hardware keys, smart containers). Before we elaborate on these issues, we mention that an additional complication can arise depending on whether or not data is *replicated* on a user's device. Data replication necessitates identical copies existing at a central company-owned repository as well as on all devices that request access to that data. As is well-known, replica control, or making sure that all copies remain identical at all times, is a non-trivial problem (Weikum and Vossen, 2002), yet has the obvious advantage that data remains available in the presence of network failures. Conversely, if keeping replicas is not an option, data access depends on network availability. We consider replication a purely technical issue and therefore do not consider it any further here.

Chow et al. (2009) sketch the main topics from a general cloud computing perspective without presenting actual solutions: (1) Trusted Computing: "authenticate" hardware systems; allow computers to proof their compliance with certain requirements; make sure hardware is not tampered with. Question: How to adopt for virtual hardware in clouds? (2) Working on encrypted data: New approaches, such as searchable encryption, homomorphic encryption or private information retrieval can allow some operations, such as range queries, to be performed on ciphertext so that the Cloud Service Provider (CSP) never has to see the cleartext at all. Questions: How to make this easy-to-use for both CSP and cloud user? How to convince CSP to implement it and take on the additional computational effort? (3) Proofs of retrievability: CSP can prove that all data is stored as requested by client; client can be sure that provider actually stores data (and, e. g., not just pretends to be storing it); works without re-transmitting the original data, so it's feasible even for large data sets.

Tian et al. (2009) present a security requirements analysis as well as a security framework for personal clouds. Our considerations, presented next, try to be more precise with respect to practicality, as they build upon a variety of solutions nowadays available.

Security Tokens

Our first suggestion is along the lines of keyless entry systems for buildings or cars, including software features along with a hardware key.

Based on the assumption that company data will likely be stored securely on a potentially unsecure mobile device, software and data is encrypted on a company's server and then transferred securely to the company storage on the device. It builds the storage layer of the device together with the private storage. In order to secure the data stored in this layer, it is encrypted in a way that user authentication (Pin, Password, or biometric) is necessary to decrypt the data. However, to make the company data even more secure – and ensure that it cannot be accessed from the employee without the company's consent – access to enterprise data (which has been encrypted by the company onsite) requires the physical presence of a company security token (using for instance, time synchronized one-time keys or hash-chains) to be accessible. This is much like the SSAT (Single Sign-on Security Token) described by Tian, et al., 2011, as a "time limited, non-forgeable entity that is provided to cloud users. The architecture is depicted in Figure 4. While user authentication alone would be sufficient to protect the data, when the device is lost or stolen, the company would lose the control of its data in regard to its own employee. We note that recent wearable devices such as the Nymi (nymi, n.d.) which bases personal authentication on a person's unique cardiac rhythm may play a role in this context as well.

Figure 4. Device and Security Architecture.

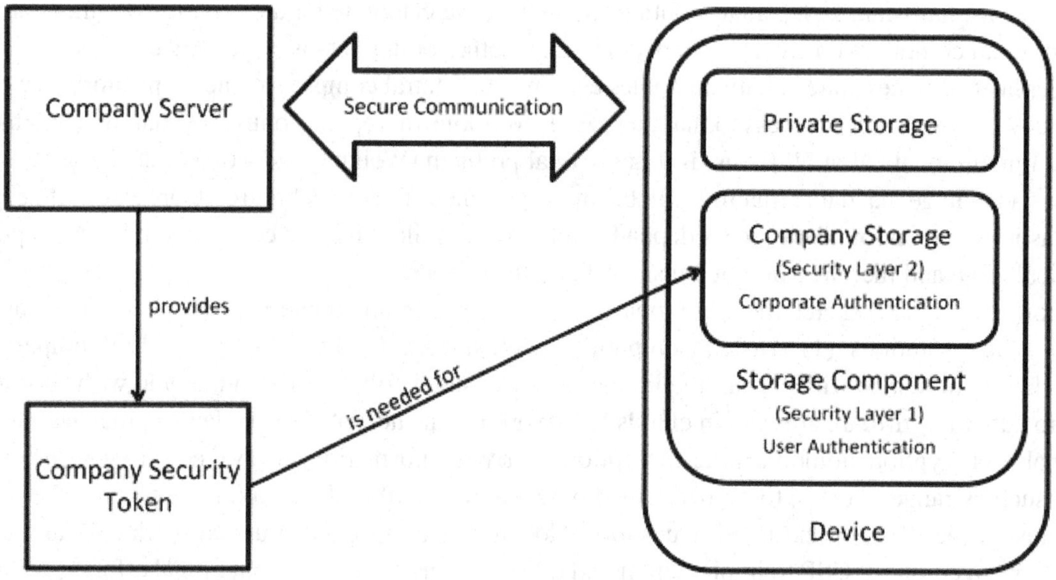

Besides a technical, infrastructure-based solution such as the one described, attention must also be given to appropriate organizational structures. Also, security key fobs need to be synchronized with / authorized by the company and distributed to the users. The appropriate mobile environment needs to be deployed to the devices which can be particularly challenging with a BYOD strategy as potentially a multitude of mobile operating systems will need to be supported.

Hardware Keys

Through the method just described it is relatively simple for a company to retain the sovereignty of their data which is particularly important if an employee leaves a company. In particular, if an employee is released or shall no longer have access a certain resource, the company has increased interested in protecting its knowledge assets. Therefore, we propose the additional usage of a hardware key such as a NFC, staff card, Bluetooth devices or alternative authentication via key fobs, as used by some banks, as TAN (transaction authentication number) generators: Opening an enterprise application (and enterprise data) on your own device requires a TAN which is dynamically created by the key fob. If the access shall be restricted or an employee leaves the company, all that needs to be done is seizing the key. Of course the data is still on the device but choosing appropriate encryption can make it inaccessible and minimize the risk of a successful attack. Also, if former employees would like to free space on their device they can simply delete what has become irrelevant, unreadable, data. This means leaving a company using this model does not have any negative consequences - the private cloud components will continue to function and appear in the way they used to, only company components cease functioning. From this it follows that the technical and organizational dimensions of exit strategies are closely linked (identical) to those of security. This strategy is also very economical as the data can remain at the device thus incurring no additional cost for either the company or the employee, as opposed to an approach where the device is not encrypted and had to be wiped entirely.

Smart Containers

We next offer an extension of the security token concept. Since the key question a company needs to address is how to enforce access rights on data once it is transmitted outside a company's sphere of control, we suggest that "data" is sent out, not only as mere records, but rather as a *smart container* of sorts, comparable to a smartcard. Only after presenting a valid authorization token, a user is granted access to the data within the container, as illustrated in Figure 5.

In an ideal world, a smart container would behave as follows: It can be handed to anybody – even untrusted parties – (and, thus, also be transmitted over insecure network connections) because the data is protected from unauthorized access. Only authorized individuals can gain access to the data inside the container. The authorization can be issued with an expiry timestamp so that the user must reauthorize at regular intervals. This also means that the company can choose to deny access to the user by the end of an authorization period. Data manipulation can be either outside the container ("low security level") or controlled by the logic of the container ("high security level"). The latter would provide for additional data protection as only certain actions are allowed on the data (e. g., only query aggregate values, not individual records), but would also expand the size and complexity of the container. If data manipulation is handled by the smart container, it can keep track of the changes and provide secure deltas that allow for efficient exchange of changes to the data. This is in a way comparable to homomorphic encryption

Figure 5. Interacting with a smart container.

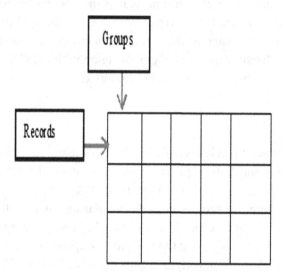

as described, for example, in Gentry (2009). The company can receive either a copy of the entire smart container or a set of secure deltas. In either case, the data is sufficient to sync back changes that the user made while "disconnected" from the main database.

Another way to implement smart containers is through virtualisation (Stallings, 2014) or derivations thereof. One such approach is Docker (see https://www.docker.com/), a means to run application on Linux machines in their own encapsulated environment. Though these concepts have not yet been applied to mobile devices on a large scale, they provide an ideal means of a smart container as we envision it. In this case the virtual machine would be installed as an app on the user's mobile device in an encrypted container. To use the machine users would need to log on which can either be verified through online communication, security tokens, or hardware keys described before. Both options leave employers in full control of who can access the data within the smart container, while at the same time leaving employees complete freedom with regard to the device they are using and where they use it.

CONCLUSION

Personal clouds can provide a number of new business opportunities and allow for new business models, in line with a growing consumerization of IT services (Castro-Leon, 2014). Instead of buying devices for new employees, a company can sponsor Bring Your Own Device (BYOD) campaigns, with the advantage that capital expenditure and the burden of maintenance is moved to the employee, with the minor drawback to the employer that the device cannot be taken away from employee. The company also needs to keep in mind that there will be some costs for infrastructure extensions (e.g., trusted computing, intelligent networking.) On the other hand, preliminary experience with the BYOD approach clearly shows increased employee satisfaction and productivity.

For the various technical challenges in BYOD implementation (e.g., interface design, data storage, service synchronization) we have described several solutions in this chapter, among them a two-factor authentication scheme and smart containers.

We envision that BYOD will become more relevant and widespread as we move from the Internet of Services to the Internet of Things (Atzori et al. 2010). As more and more "things" get an Internet presence, individuals will increasingly interact with them, and hence the personal clouds of these individuals will constantly grow or at least undergo changes, and the distinction between a private and a professional section within that personal cloud will continue to blur. This may also lead to a transition from BYOD to BYOA (Bring Your Own App). Having appropriate governance structures in place will then be even more relevant than it already is today.

REFERENCES

Atzori, L., Iera, A., & Morabito, G. (2010). The Internet of Things: A survey. *Computer Networks*, *54*(15), 2787–2805. doi:10.1016/j.comnet.2010.05.010

Castro-Leon, E. (2014). Consumerization in the IT Service Ecosystem. *IEEE IT Professional*, *16*(5), 20–27. doi:10.1109/MITP.2014.66

Chow, R., Golle, P., Jakobsson, M., Shi, E., Staddon, J., & Masuoka, R., Molina, & J. (2009). Controlling Data in the Cloud: Outsourcing Computation without Outsourcing Control, In *Proceedings of ACM Workshop on Cloud Computing Security (CCSW 2009)*. Chicago, IL: ACM. doi:10.1145/1655008.1655020

Clouds, P. (2014). *Personal Clouds*. Retrieved June 10, 2015, from http://personal-clouds.org/wiki/Main_Page

Disterer, G., & Kleiner, C. (2013). Using Mobile Devices with BYOD. *International Journal of Web Portals*, *5*(4), 33–45. doi:10.4018/ijwp.2013100103

Gentry, C. (2009). Fully homomorphic encryption using ideal lattices. In *Proceedings of 41st ACM Symposium on the Theory of Computing (STOC)*. Bethesda, MD: ACM.

Gupta, M. V., Sangroha, D., & Dhiman, L. (2013). An approach to implement Bring Your Own Device (BYOD) Securely. *International Journal of Electronics Communication and Computer Engineering*, *4*(2), 154–156.

Haselmann, T., & Vossen, G. (2011). Software-as-a-Service in Small and Medium Enterprises: An Empirical Attitude Assessment. In *Proceedings of 12th International Conference on Web Information Systems Engineering (WISE)*. Sydney, Australia: Springer. doi:10.1007/978-3-642-24434-6_4

Haselmann, T., Vossen, G., Lipsky, S., & Theurl, T. (2011). A Cooperative Community Cloud for Small and Medium Enterprises. In *Proceedings of 1st International Conference on Cloud Computing and Service Science (CLOSER)*. Noordwijkerhout, Netherlands: SciTePress Science and Technology Publications.

Hernandez, A., & Choi, Y. (2014). Securing BYOD Networks: Inherent Vulnerabilities and Emerging Feasible Technologies. In *Proceedings of ASE International Conferences on Big Data Science and Computing / Social Computing / Cyber Security*. Stanford, CA: Academy of Science and Engineering (ASE).

Informationswirtschaft, B. Telekommunikation und neue Medien (2013). *Bring Your Own Device*. Retrieved June 10, 2015, from http://www.bitkom.org/files/documents/20130404_LF_BYOD_2013_v2.pdf

Kadlec, T., & Gustafson, A. (2012). *Implementing Responsive Design: Building Sites for an Anywhere, Everywhere Web*. San Francisco, CA: New Riders Publishing.

Koh, E. B., Oh, J., & Im, C. (2014). A Study on Security Threats and Dynamic Access Control Technology for BYOD, Smart-work Environment. In *Proceedings of the International MultiConference of Engineers and Computer Scientists*. Hong Kong, China: Newswood.

Lance, D., & Schweigert, M. E. (2013). BYOD: Moving toward a More Mobile and Productive Workforce. *Business & Information Technology*. Paper 3. Retrieved June 10, 2015, from http://digitalcommons.mtech.edu/business_info_tech/3/

Liu, L., Moulic, R., & Shea, D. (2010). Cloud service portal for mobile device management. In *Proceedings of 7th IEEE International Conference on e-Business Engineering (ICEBE)*. Shanghai, China: IEEE Computer Society. doi:10.1109/ICEBE.2010.102

Lofaro, R. (2014). *The Business Side of BYOD: Cultural and Organizational Impacts*. Retrieved June 10, 2015, from http://www.amazon.com/business-side-BYOD-cultural-organizational/dp/1494844265

Miller, K., Voas, J., & Hurlburt, G. (2012). BYOD: Security and Privacy Considerations. *IT Professional*, *14*(5), 53–55. doi:10.1109/MITP.2012.93

Moreno-Vozmediano, R., Montero, R., & Llorente, I. (2013). Key Challenges in Cloud Computing. *IEEE Internet Computing*, *17*(4), 18–25. doi:10.1109/MIC.2012.69

Morrow, B. (2012). BYOD security challenges: Control and protect your most sensitive data. *Network Security*, *2012*(12), 5–8. doi:10.1016/S1353-4858(12)70111-3

Nymi (n.d.). *Nymi*. Retrieved June 10, 2015, from http://www.getnymi.com/

Rowinski, D. (2011). *The Personal Cloud Will Be A $12 Billion Industry in 2016*. Retrieved June 10, 2015, from http://readwrite.com/2011/06/06/the_personal_cloud_will_be_a_12_billion_industry_i

Scarfo, A. (2012). New security perspectives around BYO. In *Proceedings of 7th IEEE International Conference on Broadband, Wireless Computing, Communication and Applications (BWCCA)*. Victoria, Canada: IEEE Computer Society.

Schmidt, E., & Cohen, J. (2013). *The New Digital Age – Rapidly Shaping the Future of People, Nations and Business*. London: John Murray.

Schomm, F., & Vossen, G. (2013, Summer). Mobile Device Management in the IT Consumerization Age. *DOAG Business News*, 27-29.

Solutions Review. (n.d.), *Mobile Device Management Solution Directory and Buyer's Guide*. Retrieved June 10, 2015, from http://solutions-review.com/mobile-device-management/mdm-buyers-guide-directory/

Stallings, W. (2014). *Operating Systems: Internals and Design Principles* (8th ed.). Upper Saddle River, NJ: Prentice Hall.

Tian, Y., Song, B., & Huh, E. N. (2011). Towards the development of personal cloud computing for mobile thin-clients. In *Proceedings of 2011 IEEE International Conference on Information Science and Applications* (ICISA). Jeju Island, Republic of Korea: IEEE Computer Society.

Vossen, G., Haselmann, T., & Hoeren T. (2012). *Cloud Computing for Enterprises – Technical, Economical, Legal, and Organizational Aspects*. Heidelberg, Germany: dpunkt.verlag.

Weikum, G., & Vossen, G. (2002). *Transactional Information Systems – Theory, Algorithms, and the Practice of Concurrency Control and Recovery*. San Francisco, CA: Morgan Kaufmann.

Zimmer, M. (2010). *Facebook's Zuckerberg: "Having two identities for yourself is an example of a lack of integrity"*. Retrieved June 10, 2015, from http://www.michaelzimmer. org/2010/05/14/facebooks-zuckerberg-having-two-identities-for-yourself-is-an-example-of-a-lack-of-integrity/

KEY TERMS AND DEFINITIONS

Authorization Token: A hardware key such as a NFC, staff card, Bluetooth devices or alternative authentication via key fobs, as used by some banks, as TAN (transaction authentication number) generators, which may be required for opening an enterprise application or access corporate data.

Bring Your Own Device (BYOD): BYOD is a corporate mobile device management strategy, where companies allow their employees to use their personally owned devices for business purposes.

Choose Your Own Device (CYOD): CYOD is a corporate mobile device management strategy, where an employee can choose from a (typically limited) variety of devices offered, yet the device chosen remains company property.

Corporate Owned, Personally Enabled (COPE): COPE is a corporate mobile device management strategy, where the company owns a device for which the employee has personal use.

Mobile Device Management (MDM): MDM is a software solution, which offers centralized management of all mobile devices that are used within an organization.

Personal Cloud: A single point of access to all cloud serviced a user is regularly referring to, uniformly accessible through the same interface across multiple and distinct devices.

Smart Container: A data container which can only be accessed with a valid authorization token, which allows for transmitting it over insecure network connections.

Chapter 9
User Preference–Based Web Service Composition and Execution Framework

Bassam Al-Shargabi
Isra University, Jordan

Omar Sabri
Isra University, Jordan

ABSTRACT

the motivation behind this chapter is that Service Oriented architecture issued to compose an application as a set of services that are language and platform independent, communicate with each other, Therefore, user preferences rules in web service composition process plays crucial role and has opened a wide spectrum of challenge, In this chapter, an agent for composing web services based on user preferences was introduced to fulfill a certain process, where the user preferences are essential for determining which web service are to be selected. In other word, the agent designed to maintain the following function: an intelligent web services selection and planning based on user preferences(such as price or availability), along with web services execution, tracking and adaptation.

INTRODUCTION

Service-Oriented Architecture (SOA) is paradigm to build a distributed systems that bring application functionality as services to end-user applications (Booth, Hass, Mccabe, Newcomer, Champion, &Ferris, 2005). The basic idea of SOA is to compose an application as a set of services that are language and platform independent, communicate with each other using standardized messages like XML, Web services is a technology that realize the SOA.

A web service is a software system identified by a URL, whose public interfaces and bindings are defined and described using XML. Its definition can be discovered by other software systems (Booth, Hass, Mccabe, Newcomer, Champion, &Ferris, 2005). As individual web services are limited in their capability, which created the need for composing existing services to create new functionality in the form of composite service. However, the process of creating composite service is achieved by combin-

DOI: 10.4018/978-1-4666-8676-2.ch009

Copyright © 2015, IGI Global. Copying or distributing in print or electronic forms without written permission of IGI Global is prohibited.

ing existing elementary or complex services, possibly offered by different providers. For example, a travel plan service can be developed by combining several elementary services such as hotel reservation, ticket booking, car rental, sightseeing package, etc. In carrying out this composition task, one should be concerned with the efficiency and the QoS that the composed process will exhibit upon its execution (Chandrasekaran, Miller, Silver, Arpinar, &Sheth, 2003).

Some proposals are being made to enable dynamic composition of web services and execution monitoring frameworks (Al-Shargabi, El Shiekh, &Sabri, 2010). Few of these proposals address user QoS constraints: whether these constraints are locally on every individual web service or globally for the whole composition process according to (Al-Shargabi, El Shiekh, &Sabri, 2010).These constraints must be addressed to satisfy client requirements, such as price, availability, so it is necessary to represent required QoS in the selected and composed web services (Bakhshi,&. Hashem 2012,). Moreover, Evaluation of composition process: when the composer selects a web service, it is quite common that many web services have the same functionalities. So it is possible that the composer generates more than one composite service fulfilling the requirements. In that case, the composed web services are evaluated by their overall utilities using the information provided from the non-functional attributes. The most commonly used method is utility functions as in WSCE framework. The requester should specify weights to each QoS attribute and the best composite service is the one that is ranked on top. During the execution of composed web service, some web services may update their QoS properties others may become unavailable. A dynamic composition approach is needed, in which runtime changes in the QoS of the component services are taken into account(Chen, Ha& Zhang 2013). It is imperative to design a Web Service Composition and Execution (WSCE) framework that adapts to failure of web services or changes in their QoS offerings to satisfy user preferences or constraints, these issues already have been discussed in previous work by(Al-Shargabi, El Shiekh, &Sabri, 2010).

The remained of this chapter organized as follows: section 2 the User PreferencesWSCE framework is presented. Section 3 describes User Preferences WSCE agent functions. Section 4 presents domain registries. Section 5 the QoS certifier is presented. Section 6analysis and validation, and finally conclusion and future work in section7.

WSCE FRAMEWORK ARCHITECTURE

The User Preferences WSCE framework is aagent-based framework for the dynamic composition of web services as illustrated in Figure 1. The main motivation behind this framework is to build a User Preferences WSCE agent to make intelligent service selection decisions for composite service which fits with user preferences in his/her web process. The main functions of User Preferences WSCE agent include: execution tracking: User Preferences WSCE agent has a composition repository to record all feasible composition plans of composed services it is aware of, which QoS information of these composition plans are optimal or closer to user constraints. Dynamic service selection: This is the key function of User Preferences WSCE agent, when the WSCE agent selects web services to execute a web process according to the user-defined utility function, and user's QoS requirements. Dynamic service adaptation: In case of individual web service failure during execution of composite service, the WSCE agent either replaces the failed services or replaces the composition plan with an alternative plan. The WSCE agent either way can create a new composition plan from scratch. In this framework a QoS certifier is which is controlled by the UDDI registry to verify the claimed QoS attributes for the registration requests of web service provider.

Figure 1. WSCE Framework Architecture

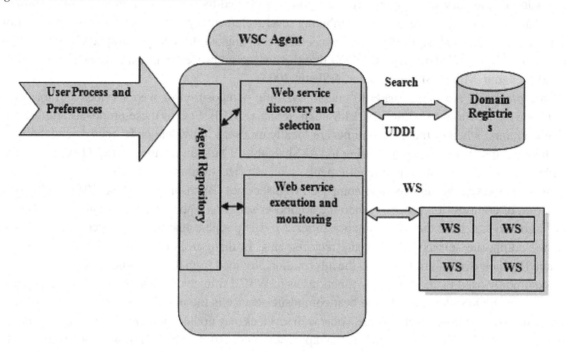

Web Process

The web process is a collection of related, structured activities or tasks that serve a particular goal for a particular customer or customers. Example of web process that is used in this chapter, Travel Planner Service process consists of three tasks, flight reservation, hotel reservation, and car rental. The three atomic tasks (which are not composed) will internally execute the travel planning process. Each task of the three tasks will be executed by 3 web services (execution of three services called composite service) in order to meet user preferences

Local User Preferences

In local user preferences, user can set preferences on each candidate web service to execute individual task, where the execution of service is isolated from other services. This chapter only emphasized on five user preferences constraints of web service (OMG Specification,2004), where the user can set constraint values in each individual web service to execute task of web process. User preferences evaluation criteria of web service and their meanings are as follows: (Anbazhagan, &Arun 2002; O'sullivan, Edmond, &Hofstede, 2002):

1. **Execution Price:** It is the price of executing a web service. The price is usually fixed for each individual web service, but may be changed according to the web service provider's business policy.
2. **Execution Duration:** It is the average time expected for executing a web service. Individual execution times upon the requests of the clients vary because the server loads change. Therefore, the average execution time should be updated continuously by the service provider.

3. **Availability:** It means the ratio of the time that web service is available for immediate use. It is measured as av = uptime/ (uptime + downtime) and updated by the service provider. The downtime includes the time to repair the web service that has failed.

4. **Reputation:** It is the average reputation score of web service evaluated by the clients. The individual reputation scores are likely to be subjective, but the average score becomes trustable as the total number of the usages increases. The reputation score is measured by rep = accumulated score/ total number of usages.

5. **Reliability:** The reliability of a web service is the probability that a request is correctly responded to within the maximum expected time frame indicated in the web service description. Reliability is a measure related to hardware and/or software configuration of web services and the network connections between the service requesters and providers.

Global User Preferences

In global user preferences, the users can put constraints on the execution of composite service as whole, not on every individual service of the composite service, e.g., price of composite service, and execution duration. The following user preferences are used in this framework: (Anbazhagan, &Arun 2002; O'sullivan, Edmond, & Hofstede, 2002)

1. **Execution Price:** The execution price of an execution plan of a composite service is the sum of the execution prices of the operations invoked over the services that participate in composite service. The WSCE framework the user can set a price for the whole composition of Flight, Hotel, and Car rental services. Also the user may wish to get the lowest prices of composed services.

2. **Execution Duration:** The execution duration of an execution plan of a composite service is the sum of the execution time of the web services that participates in composite service. In the WSCE framework the user can set the execution duration for the whole composition of Flight, Hotel, and Car rental services. Also the user may wish to get the lowest duration of composed services.

3. **Reputation:** The reputation of an execution plan of travel composite service is the average of the reputations of the web services that participate in travel composite service. Reputation constraints should have scaled value between (1-10).

4. **Reliability:** The reliability of execution plan of travel composite service is product of aggregated values of reliability for composed web services that participate in travel composite service.

5. **Availability:** The availability of execution plan of travel composite service is product of aggregated values of availability of composed web services that participate in travel composite service.

WSCE AGENT

In User Preferences WSCE framework, there is a WSCE Agent, which is the mediator between user and public registries and web service providers. WSCE agent is responsible for locating the candidate web service from Universal Description Discovery and Integration (UDDI) registries and returns their Web Service Description Language (WSDL) and URL. The WSCE Agent is provided with an intelligent selection and matching technique to select web services that meet user preferences based on QoS constraints, whether the constraints are local on each individual web service or the whole composition process. The WSCE Agent creates number of composition plans and only one plan will be selected for execution according to user preferences that are set up by user. WSCE Agent controls the execution of the composition plan and monitors the execution of web services and dynamically adapts to any change (e.g. service unavailable) as explained in following subsections.

Web Service Discovery Module

In order to find the right web services, it would be easier if the registries were categorized based on domains as in the WSCE framework, with each registry maintaining only the web services pertaining to that domain, the registries are specialized in certain domain (e.g. Flight domain, Hotel domain, and Car rental domain).That makes it possible to use domain specific ontology. As a result, all the web service definitions pertaining to that registry may be forced to conform to that ontology and search for services in that domain can be carried out in a relevant registry. The WSCE agent is responsible for web service discovery in public registry according to user requirements. The discovery process will result in a number of candidate web services. The consumer of a web service has a certain functional and QoS requirements, such as "execution duration ≤ 2 ms with execution price$< \$100$". Using the web service discovery module, the WSCE agent searches the UDDI registry for a web service with the required functionality as usual. User can also add constraints to the search operation. One type of constraint is the required QoS. If there were multiple web services in the UDDI registry with similar functionalities, then the QoS requirement would enforce a finer search in WSCE framework. The search would return a web service that offers the required functionality with the desired set of QoS. If there is no web service with these qualities, the WSCE agent sends feedback to user. The user can then reduce their QoS constraints or consider trade-offs between the desired QoS constraints.

The WSCE agent through using web service discovery module conducts a search for candidate web services for each atomic task in the composition process. For this purpose, the following two matching tasks are performed:

1. **Web Service Name Matching:** For each atomic task according to user requirement, the WSCE agent requests the URLs of WSDL documents of candidate web services. For the request, the WSCE agent sends the name of the atomic task to the UDDI. The UDDI will search, and will find group of web services by matching the name of the atomic task with service names in the business services of registered web services, and then returns the URLs of the WSDL documents of candidate web services to the WSCE agent.

2. **Operation Mode and Input/Output Matching:** The inputs and outputs of atomic task should correspond to the input and output messages of WSDL operation. That is, the numbers of input and output messages and the message syntax should be matched between the specification in the atomic process and that in the WSDL documents of the candidate web services. In addition, operation modes of the candidate web services specified in the WSDL documents, such as request-response, and solicit response should be matched with the message transfer type in the corresponding atomic process. This can be done without difficulty by checking the input and output information of the web service specified in the WSDL documents (Myoung,,Ouk Kim, & Hyun, 2008).

Selection and Planning Module

The main idea behind this module is to select web services for the composition process, and create number of plans, and select the plan that meet user constraints. First, the goal of the selection is to identify the best assignment of web service candidates to the tasks of the composition. The selection can be performed by either considering or ignoring the arrangement of the tasks. Web service selection based on user preferences can be done in two ways; by considering QoS constraints on every individual web service or the whole composition process which is called a global QoS constraints selection.

Web Service Selection Based on User Preferences

The selection of the web service that will execute a given task of web process is done at the last possible moment and without taking into account the other tasks involved in the web process. When a task actually needs to be executed, the WSEC agent through selection module collects the information about the QoS of each of the web services that can execute this task (namely the candidate web services for this task). After collecting this QoS information, a quality vector (equation 1) (Zeng, Benatallah, Dumas, Kalagnanam, &Cheng, 2004) is computed for each of the candidate webservices, and based on these quality vectors, WSEC agent selects one of the candidate web services by applying a Multiple Criteria Decision Making (MCDM) techniques (Ksalan & Zionts, 2001).

$$q\left(s,t\right) = \left(q_{pr}\left(s,t\right), q_{du}\left(s,t\right), q_{av}\left(s\right), q_{re}\left(s\right), q_{rep}\left(s\right)\right) \tag{1}$$

where s is candidate web service, t is web process task. This selection of web service is based on the weight assigned by the user to each criterion, and a set of user-defined constraints expressed using a simple expression language. Examples of constraints that can be expressed include availability, and price constraints. However, constraints can only be expressed on individual tasks, and not on combinations of tasks. In other words, it is not possible to express the fact that the sum of the durations for two or more tasks should not exceed a given threshold.

To illustrate the local user preferences web service selection approach, only 5 quality dimensions used (Anbazhagan &Arun, 2002). The dimensions are numbered from 1 to 5, with 1 = price, 2 = duration, 3 = availability, 4 = reliability, and 5 = reputation. Given a task tj in a composite service, there is a set of candidate webservices $S_j = \left\{S_{1j}, S_{2j}, ..., S_{nj}\right\}$ that can be used to execute this task. By merging the quality vectors of all these candidate web services, a matrix as in equation 2 $Q = \left(Q_{ij}; 1 \leq i \leq n; 1 \leq j \leq 5\right)$ is built, in which each row Q_{ij} corresponds to a Web service sij while each column corresponds to a quality dimension.

$$Q = \begin{pmatrix} Q_{1,1} & Q_{1,2} & \cdots & Q_{1,5} \\ Q_{2,1} & Q_{2,2} & \cdots & Q_{2,5} \\ Q_{n,1} & Q_{n,2} & \cdots & Q_{n,5} \end{pmatrix} \tag{2}$$

A Simple Additive Weighting (SAW) technique is used to select an optimal web service (Zeng, Benatallah, Dumas, Kalagnanam, & Sheng, 2003; Ksalan &Zionts, 2001). There are two phases in applying SAW:

- **Scaling Phase:** Some of the QoS attributes could be negative, i.e., the higher the value, the lower the quality, such as execution duration and execution price. Other QoS attributes are positive, i.e., the higher the value, the higher the quality such as reputation and reliability. For negative QoS attributes, values are scaled according to equation 3. For positive QoS attributes, values are scaled according to equation 4.

$$f(x) = \begin{cases} \dfrac{Q_j^{\max} - Q_{i,j}}{Q_j^{\max} - Q_j^{\min}} & if \quad Q_j^{\max} - Q_j^{\min} \neq 0 \\ 1 & if \quad Q_j^{\max} - Q_j^{\min} = 0 \end{cases} \tag{3}$$

$$f(x) = \begin{cases} \dfrac{Q_{i,j} - Q_j^{\min}}{Q_j^{\max} - Q_j^{\min}} & if \quad Q_j^{\max} - Q_j^{\min} \neq 0 \\ 1 & if \quad Q_j^{\max} - Q_j^{\min} = 0 \end{cases} \tag{4}$$

In the above equations, $Q_j^{\max}$ is the maximal value of QoS attribute in matrix Q, i.e., $Q_j^{\max}$ = Max (Q_i,j), $1 \leq i \leq$ n. While $Q_j^{\min}$ is the minimal value of QoS attribute in matrix Q, i.e $Q_j^{\min}$ = Min (Q_i,j), $1 \leq i \leq$ n. By applying equations 3, 4 on Q, QN matrix is obtained QN= (QNi;j; $1 \leq i \leq$ n; $1 \leq j \leq$ 5), in which each row QNj corresponds to a web service Sij while each column corresponds to a QoS attribute dimension.

- **Weighting Phase:** Equation (5) is used to compute the overall QoS score for each web service:

$$Scor(S_i) = \sum_{j=1}^{5} \sum \left(QN_{i,j} * W_j \right) \tag{5}$$

where $W_j \in (0, 1)$ and $\sum_{j=1}^{5} w_j = 1$ represents the weight of QoS attribute j that is set by user. As stated before, end user express their preference regarding QoS by providing values for the weights Wj. For a given task, the WSCE agent through selection module will choose the web service that has maximum score which satisfies the user constraints for that task. If there are several web services with the same maximum score, one of them is selected randomly. If no web service satisfies the user constraints for a given task, an execution exception will be raised and the WSCE agent will propose to the user to loosen up these constraints.

Web Service Selection Based on Global QoS Constraints

The basic idea of global web service selection based on QoS constraints (user preferences) is that several composition plans are identified and the optimal composition plan is selected that does satisfy user preferences. Assuming that for each task t_j in web process, there is a set of candidate web services $S_j = \left\{ {}_{1j}, S_{2j}, ..., S_{nj} \right\}$ that are available to which task t_j can be assigned. In order to assign a candidate web service S_{ij} to each task .., in Selection and Planning module: the WSCE agent will generate a set of composition plans P (equation7) along with its QoS information according to equation 6.Table1 provides aggregation functions for the computation of the QoS of each composition plan, which used by WSCE agent for the computation of QoS attributes of composed web services (CS).

$$(p) = \left(q_{pr}(p), q_{du}(p), q_{av}(p), q_{re}(p), q_{rep}(p) \right) \tag{6}$$

$$P = \left\{ p_1, p_2, ..., p_n \right\} \tag{7}$$

where P is the composition plans that are generated by the WSCE agent selection and planning module, n is the number of execution plans generated by the WSC Agent.

The WSCE agent needs to select an optimal composition plan. Selection process of composition plan uses MCDM approach. Once the QoS vector for each composition plan is derived, by accumulating all the composition plans' quality vectors, Q_p matrix is obtained as seen in equation (8), where each row represents an execution plan's quality vector.

Table 1. Aggregation functions for computing the QoS of composition plans

Criteria	Aggregation Function
Price	$CS_{pr}(p) = \sum_{i=1}^{n} Q_{pr}(s_i, t_i)$
Duration	$CS_{du}(p) = \sum_{i=1}^{N} (q_{du}(s_1, t_1), ... q_{du}(s_N, t_N))$
Reputation	$CS_{rep}(p) = \frac{1}{N} \sum_{i=1}^{N} q_{rep}(s_i)$
Reliability	$CS_{rel}(p) = \prod_{i=1}^{N} (e^{q_{rel}(s_i)*z_i})$
Availability	$CS_{av}(p) = \prod_{i=1}^{N} (e^{q_{av}(s_i)*z_i})$

(Zeng, Benatallah, Dumas, Kalagnanam, & Sheng, 2003)

$$Q_n = \begin{pmatrix} Q_{1,1} & Q_{1,2} & \cdots & Q_{1,5} \\ Q_{2,1} & Q_{2,2} & \cdots & Q_{2,5} \\ Q_{n,1} & Q_{n,2} & \cdots & Q_{n,5} \end{pmatrix} \qquad (8)$$

The selection of a composition plan relies on applying MCDM approach to the QoS matrix

$$Q_p = \left(Q_{pi}, j; 1 \le i \le n; 1 \le j \le 5 \right)$$

of generated composition plans. In this matrix, each row corresponds to the QoS vector of one possible composition plan for the execution of web process. As in the local QoS based selection approach, a SAW technique is used to select an optimal composition plan. The two phases of applying SAW are:

- **Scaling Phase:** As in the previous section, the needs for scaling the values of each QoS attribute. For negative QoS attribute, values are scaled according to equation 3. For positive QoS attribute, values are scaled according to equation 4. Note, the values of $Q_j^{\max}$ and $Q_j^{\min}$ can be computed without generating all possible composition plans. For example, in order to compute the maximum execution price (i.e., $Q_{pr}^{\max}$) of all the execution plans, we select the most expensive web service for each task and sum up all these execution prices to compute $Q_{pr}^{\max}$. In order to compute the minimum execution duration (i.e., $Q_{du}^{\min}$) of all the composition plans, we select the web service with the shortest execution duration for each task to compute $Q_{du}^{\min}$. The computation cost of $Q_j^{\max}$ and $Q_j^{\min}$ is thus polynomial. After the scaling phase, the matrix $Q' = (Q'$ i;j ; $1 \le i \le n$; $1 \le j \le 5$) is obtained. Q' Represents all composition plans generated by WSCE agent with its QoS attributes in order to be selected to execute web process.

$$Q' = \begin{pmatrix} Q'_{1,1} & Q'_{1,2} & \cdots & Q'_{1,5} \\ Q'_{2,1} & Q'_{2,2} & \cdots & Q'_{2,5} \\ Q'_{n,1} & Q'_{n,2} & \cdots & Q'_{n,5} \end{pmatrix} \qquad (9)$$

- **Weighting Phase:** Equation 10 is used to compute the overall QoS score for each composition plan in matrix Q' :

$$Scor\left(P_i\right) = \sum_{j=1}^{5} \left(Q'_{i,j} * W_j \right) \qquad (10)$$

where Wj ∈ (0,1) and $\sum_{j=1} w_j = 1$ represents the weight of QoS attributes. The user can set weights on QoS (i.e., balance the impact of the different QoS attributes) to select a desired composition plan by adjusting the value of Wj. As a final stage, the WSCE agent will choose the composition plan which has the maximum score.

If there is more than one composition plan that has the same score, then the WSCE Agent will select randomly a composition plan to execute the web process. Accordingly, if all composition plans do not meet user expectation or the determined constraints, then the user has to loosen up his QoS constraints or choose one of the available plans that are selected by the WSCE agent, the plans should be optimal or near optimal for user constraints. The selected composition plan is stored in a composition repository, which contain the web service included in the composition plan and the QoS information for each web service in a table containing this information. Whatever, the WSCE agent also sends the proceeding composition plan that has the second maximal score just in case if the web services of selected plan failed to deliver or any QoS violation that may occur during execution.

User Preferences

The selection of a composition plan is restricted by the user preferences (QoS attributes) and their weights, where the selected plan that has maximum score to execute user web process should not exceed the upper limits that are fed by the user according to equations11, 12.

$$q_{pr}(p) \leq PR \tag{11}$$

$$q_{dr}(p) \leq ED \tag{12}$$

where $q_{pr}(p)$ is the execution price of selected composition plan is, $q_{dr}(p)$ is the execution duration of the selected composition plan. The QoS constraints that the user wishes to have upper limits for are the execution price (PR), and execution duration (ED)of web process. Accordingly, the lower limits constraint that is fed by the user for e.g. availability, reputation, reliability according to equations 13, 14, 115.

$$q_{av}(p) \geq AV \tag{13}$$

$$q_{rel}(p) \geq REL \tag{14}$$

$$q_{rep}(p) \geq REP \tag{15}$$

where $q_{av}(p)$ is the availability of selected composition plan, $q_{rel}(p)$ is the reliability of selected composition plan, and $q_{rep}(p)$ is the reputation of selected composition plan. The QoS constraints that the user wish's to have lower limits for are the availability (AV), reliability (REL), and reputation (REP)of web process.

Accordingly, sometimes the generated composition plans for web process based on the available QoS information of web services does not meet the user preferences but they are close. The selection and planning module of WSCE agent, gives the ability for the user either to select the available composition plan or to change the user preferences, where the WSCE agent tries again to find a new optimal composition plan that fits the user new constraints.

Execution Modules

Right after the Selection and Planning, the selected composition plan for web process is sent to the Execution Module, which generates executable BPEL code of composition plan. The WSCE agent orchestrates the included web services to execute composite service. At run time, the WSCE agent monitors the execution of composed web services. If everything goes well, after successful complete executions, the WSCE agent reports the actual recorded QoS to composition repository of this composition and put them into the QoS Statistics table.

Monitoring and Adaptation Module

Due to the dynamicity of internet and some of web services may fail or become unavailable. At run-time, during the execution of selected composition plan the WSCE Agent monitor the QoS of composed services for any violations against user preferences and tries to react if any web service fail to deliver the intended result. If a web service problem occurs during execution, the WSCE agent through monitoring and adaptation module will look up for an alternative web service from the same domain or class in composition repository. If there is no alternative web service from the same class which meet the user preferences, the WSCE agent will react to this situation by using the web service discovery module and will look up for new web service that meet the user preferences. Either way, the WSCE agent can switch to the backup composition plan to continue execution if all web services on selected composition plan failed to deliver. At the same time, the WSCE agent will adopt the replacement plan for all new web services. The WSCE agent then reports the failure to composition repository. The WSCE agent can generate a new composition plan and replacement plan based on the newly deployed web services. The WSCE agent will update the QoS Statistics table (in composition repository) of corresponding QoS attribute values (such as reliability, availability, and execution duration.)

QoS Monitoring

The pattern-based aggregation can be applied during the execution of the composition process (Michael, Jaeger, Rojec, & Gero, 2004). With monitoring and adaptation module, the delivered QoS can be captured. If a centralized execution environment in a mediator-based structure executes the composition, the mediator in framework is WSCE Agent. In this framework the monitoring process is performed at run-time by the WSCE agent. It can be seen as history management (El Hadad, Manouvrier, & Rukoz, 2010; Michael, Jaeger, Rojec, &Gero, 2004) for the execution of composed web services as follows:

- **Recovery:** during the execution of selected composition plan the WSCE agent monitors if there is any detected QoS violations provided by web service which is against user preferences during the execution according to the QoS information of the selected composition plan, and notifications or recovery activities can be established. To establish recovery tasks when errors occur during the execution or to check the delivered QoS of individual web services, to analyze the performance of the composition plan, and to predict future characteristics for controlling purposes, the aggregation of QoS values can be performed to deliver a more accurate estimation of the delivered QoS.

- **QoS Analysis:** According to the metrics of the execution of selected composition plan, it is possible to check whether the selected services are delivered with the desired QoS. However, monitoring the QoS only applies to metrics that can be directly derived from the execution, such as execution duration or availability. For example, capturing the execution price during the execution depends on the payment method. Capturing the execution duration of the composition and the execution of individual services can be used to analyze the performance. This information is already verified by the QoS certifier in WSCE framework.
- **Controlling:** CONSIDERING composition as realizing of web process as whole or in parts. Controlling execution can benefit from up-to-date information about the progress. It can be determined by WSCE agent thought the aggregation of the QoS attributes of web services selected to execute web process, which can be stored in the composition repository and can be used later on for further execution of the same web process.

Dynamic Adaptation during Execution

Due to the dynamicity of internet and some of web service may fail to deliver result or become unavailable, the idea of QoS-based adaption is to keep re-planning in small scope. But there is still many occasions when re-planning is needed (Bixin et al., 2013), for example, if the failed component web service is the key task on the execution of composed service and there is no other suitable candidate service for this task, the WSCE agent will switch to other composition plan. Therefore, re-planning and how to re-plan are two critical challenges in QoS-based adaptation. Solutions to them are re-planning trigger and re-planning strategies, respectively.

The design of monitoring and adaptation module of the WSCE Agent is tightly bound to the QoS model. The quality values of the specified composition plan of composed service should be used to determine the thresholds. As mentioned above, to keep re-planning in limited scope. Therefore, the re-planning should be like a hill climbing process. If only a component web service fails, the WSCE Agent should save the rest of tasks on this composition plan, and check if there are suitable candidate web services for this task. If a suitable component web service is found, the WSCE Agent selects the suitable web service and substitutes the failed web service with the new one. If there is no suitable candidate web service found, the WSCE Agent should abandon the saved to-execute plan and turn to alternative composition plan. In worst case, the re-planning procedure has to start over from scratch.

Agent Repository

The WSCE agent has a composition repository to record all feasible web services it is aware of. The WSCE agent can also build new composition plans or update existing plans based on user requirements and newly discovered web services. Dynamic service adaptation: At run time, the WSCE Agent monitors the execution at every step, such as execution duration of each web service. If everything goes well, after successful complete executions; the WSCE agent reports the actual recorded QoS information to

QoS statistics table in composition repository. The composition repository contains number of composition plans according to pervious processes. The repository Table includes the following fields (both functional and QoS characteristics about the of web service):

1.   **ID:** A unique representation of the record;
2.   **Service Name:** Name of the web service;
3.   **URL:** Where the web service is located (usually it points to the WSDL file of the service);
4.   **Namespace URI:** The namespace used for definitions in the service WSDL document. Each web service needs a unique namespace for client applications to distinguish it from other services on the web;
5.   **Service Class:** Web services belong to different service classes. A Service Class is a group of services that provide similar functionalities with possibly different nonfunctional parameters (QoS);
6.   **Operation (with Input and Output Parameters):** The actual function provided by web service; e.g. weather report (input: zip code; output: temperature);
7.   **Description:** Description of the operation;
8.   **Execution Duration:** The time needed for web service to be executed;
9.   **Execution Price:** The price of invoking web service;
10. Availability;
11. Reliability.
12. Reputation.
13. **Composition Reference:** This is a web service pointer to which composition plan this web service belongs to.

DOMAIN REGISTRIES

In WSCE framework, the concept of Domain registry is used, where every UDDI registry only contain specific domain of services such as, Hotel booking, Weather forecasting. The structure of UDDI registry is same as the tModel (Blum, 2004; Zhou, Chia, & Lee, 2004) that was used to describe the functional and non-functional information of web services, tModels UDDI registries can be used to provide QoS information on <bindingTemplates>. Using tModel for QoS information for the binding template that represents a web service deployment is generated to represent QoS information. Each QoS metric, such as average response time or average throughput is represented by a <keyedReference> in tModel.

QoS CERTIFIER

The architecture of web services is presented in (Booth, Hass, Mccabe, Newcomer, Champion, & Ferris, 2005), where the web service provider publishes WSDL to UDDI registry. The discovery process is largely unregulated based on UDDI registries. 48% of the production UDDI registries have links that are unusable. These pointers contain missing, broken or inaccurate information (Ran, 2003). Therefore the ability of incorporating quality of service into service discovery and also to make sure all this claimed QoS information by web service provider must be tested and authenticated by the UDDI registry. To overcome these shortcomings the QoS Certifier is introduced in this framework.

The QoS certifier is managed by UDDI registry. The web service provider offers web service by publishing the service into the registry; the registry sends a request to the QoS certifier with the WSDL of web service provider to verify the QoS claims by provider. The QoS certifier verifies the claims of QoS for a web service by a trail invocation of the web service provider. The certifier then reports the recorded QoS information of the provider and compares them to the WSDL of provider. If they match, it sends back to the registry the recorded QoS information of that web service provider, the register then accepts the request of the provider with both functional description of the service and its associated QoS information.

ANALYSIS AND VALIDATION

Example and Experiments Results

The web process consists of three tasks flight reservation, hotel booking, and car rental, the web process can be realized by a new composite service, obtained by coordination of the available component services as follows first it allows the user to buy flight ticket, book a hotel room and to rent a car as illustrated in the activity diagram Figure 2.

The case of Travel Planner Service has three tasks flight booking, booking a Hotel room and Car rental task. Each task needs to be assigned to a web service to be executed. As illustrated in Figure 3 as described in (Al- Masri &Qusay, 2007), there are three different classes of registry, flight booking, hotel reservation, and Car rental class. In each class there are two services discovered by WSCE agent. The WSCE agent generates composition plans for the travel planner process. The composition plan that will be selected to execute composite service is the one that meet user constraints and satisfy his requirements.

The WSCE agent retrieves the candidate web services for each task as is shown in Figure 3. In the selection module, the WSCE agent generates a number of composition plans for the web process of travel planner service. Each composition plan has its own QoS information aggregated from individual

Figure 2. Travel planner process

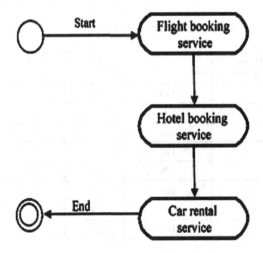

Figure 3. Different Classes of Web services

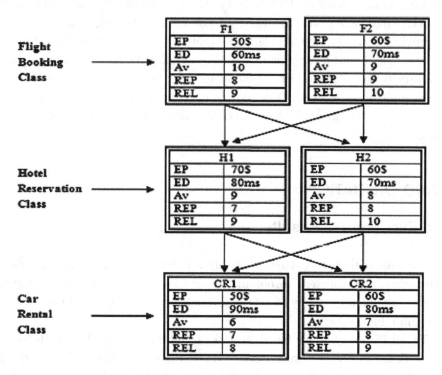

web services (Table 1: contain the aggregation functions for computing the QoS of composition plans) involved in the composition as is shown in Table 2.

Now in order to evaluate the multi-dimensional QoS of each composition plan in Table 2, the WSCE agent uses Simple Additive Weighting (SAW) technique for scaling QoS attributes values to allow a uniform measurement of the multi-dimensional service qualities independent of their units and ranges. The scaling processes that will be executed by the WSCE agent in selection module, where negative QoS attributes values are scaled according to equation 3. For positive QoS attributes, values are scaled according to equation 4. As is shown in Table 3.

Table 2. Composition plans with their QoS information

ID	QoS Attribute Composition Plan	EP	ED	AV	REP	
1	F1,H1,CR1	170	230	540	7.3	648
2	F1,H1,CR2	180	220	630	7.6	724
3	F1,H2,CR1	160	220	480	7.6	720
4	F1,H2,CR2	170	210	560	8	810
5	F2,H1,CR1	170	240	486	7.6	720
6	F2,H1,CR2	190	230	567	8	810
7	F2,H2,CR1	170	230	432	8	800
8	F2,H2,CR2	180	220	504	8.3	900

Table 3. Scaling process

ID	QoS Attribute Composition Plan	EP	ED	AV	REP	REL
1	F1,H1,CR1	0.67	0.33	0.55	0	0
2	F1,H1,CR2	0.33	0.67	1	0.3	0.30
3	F1,H2,CR1	1	0.67	0.24	0.3	0.29
4	F1,H2,CR2	0.67	1	0.65	0.7	0.64
5	F2,H1,CR1	0.67	0	0.27	0.3	0.29
6	F2,H1,CR2	0	0.33	0.68	0.7	0.64
7	F2,H2,CR1	0.67	0.33	0	0.7	0.60
8	F2,H2,CR2	0.33	0.67	0.31	1	1

Following scaling process is a weighting process (equation 10) for representing user priorities and preferences for each QoS attribute that matter the most for the user. Lets assumes that the weights for each QoS attribute that represents the user priorities as follows (EP=0.5,ET=0.4,AV=0.0,REP=0.1,REL=0.0}, using equation 8 To calculate the scores and the weights for each composition plan as it shown in Table 4.

According to Table 4, the WSCE agent will choose the composition plan which has the maximal value of score which is the composition plan number 4. If there is more than one composition plan which has the same maximal value of score, then the WSCE Agent will select randomly a composition plan to be executed. Accordingly, the process of selection of a composition plan is restricted by the user constraints, where the selected plan which has maximal score to execute web process should not exceed the upper limits or the lower limits according to equations 11.12.13, 14, and 15 that are fed by the user. As in the example used in this chapter, the WSCE agent selects the composition plan 4. The WSCE checks the user constraints (e.g EP≤170$, ET≤220ms,REP≥8). If composition plan with the higher score meet user constraints, then composition plan 4 meets user constraints which will be selected to execute web process of travel planner service. the selected composition plan along with the composition plan that has the second maximal score will be sent to be stored in composition repository with all its recorded QoS values along with WSDL, URI of involved web services of selected the composition plan, which will be used for further execution or used by WSCE agent to monitor the execution of composition plan

Table 4. Scores for composition plans

ID	Composition Plan	Score
1	F1,H1,CR1	0.467
2	F1,H1,CR2	0.465
3	F1,H2,CR1	**0.800**
4	F1,H2,CR2	**0.805**
5	F2,H1,CR1	0.365
6	F2,H1,CR2	0.202
7	F2,H2,CR1	0.537
8	F2,H2,CR2	0.535

during execution. The second composition plan is stored in composition repository in case of the selected composition plan execution failed to deliver. At run-time, the WSCE agent can either select the second plan 3 to execute user web process or re-plan the whole composition from scratch in case of failure of composition plan 4.

Analytical Hierarchy Process Validation

To validate the selection made by WSCE agent in the framework, Analytical Hierarchy Process (AHP) is used (Belton, & Stewart, 2002), which developed by Saaty in 1980. The goal of the AHP is to enable a decision maker to structure a multi-attribute decision making problem visually in the form of an attribute hierarchy. An attribute hierarchy has at least three levels: the focus or the overall goal of the problem on the top level, multiple criteria that define alternatives in the middle level, and competing alternatives in the bottom level. When criteria are highly abstract such as e.g. "well being", subcriteria (or sub-subcriteria) are generated subsequently through a multilevel hierarchy. As in the used example in this chapter, at level 1 the focus is to find an optimal composition plan for travel planner service to execute composite service, Level 2 comprises the QoS criteria that contribute to the decision making of which composition plan would be selected according to this criteria: Execution price (EP), Execution time (ET), Availability (AV), Reputation (REP), and Reliability (REL). Level3 consists of the eight possible composition plans: P1, P2, P3, P4, P5, P6, P7, and P8. Figure 4 shows the different levels in a hierarchy structure.

It is obvious that each criterion in level 2 should contribute differently to the focus. As seen in the example, the user sets which of these criteria are more important for him as follows, EP=0.5, ET=0.4, AV=0.0, REP=0.1, and REL=0.0 and these are values are the same values that used by the WSCE agent to select the optimal composition plan.

The next step for the decision maker is to make pair-wise comparisons of the eight alternatives in level 3 with respect to five criteria in level 2, the weight values of pair-wise comparison of eight alternative composition plans with respect to the weights of five criteria in level 2 are taken from Table 3. The results of pair-wise comparison of eight alternatives with 5 QoS criteria are shown in Table 5.

Table 5. Pair-wise comparison alternatives composition plans and QoS criteria

ID	EP	ED	AV	REP	REL
p1	0.67	0.33	0.55	0	0
p2	0.33	0.67	1	0.3	0.30
p3	1	0.67	0.24	0.3	0.29
p4	0.67	1	0.65	0.7	0.64
p5	0.67	0	0.27	0.3	0.29
p6	0	0.33	0.68	0.7	0.64
p7	0.67	0.33	0	0.7	0.60
p8	0.33	0.67	0.31	1	1
Sum	4.34	4	3.37	4	3.76

Figure 4. A hierarchy for choice of an Optimal Composition Plan

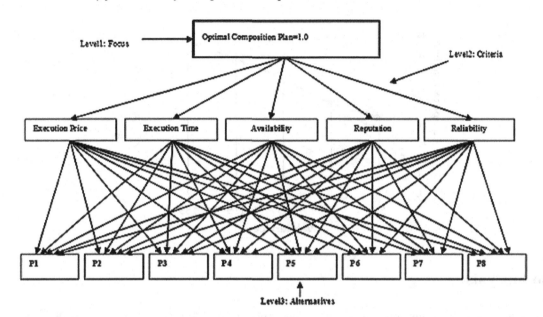

Figure 5. Priorities for each hierarchal level with Scores for composition plans

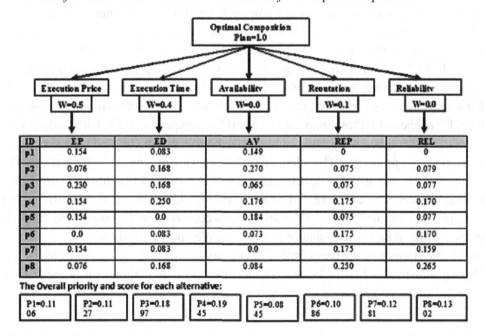

ID	EP	ED	AV	REP	REL
p1	0.154	0.083	0.149	0	0
p2	0.076	0.168	0.270	0.075	0.079
p3	0.230	0.168	0.065	0.075	0.077
p4	0.154	0.250	0.176	0.175	0.170
p5	0.154	0.0	0.184	0.075	0.077
p6	0.0	0.083	0.073	0.175	0.170
p7	0.154	0.083	0.0	0.175	0.159
p8	0.076	0.168	0.084	0.250	0.265

The Overall priority and score for each alternative:

P1=0.11 06	P2=0.11 27	P3=0.18 97	P4=0.19 45	P5=0.08 45	P6=0.10 86	P7=0.12 81	P8=0.13 02

The final stage of the AHP is to compute the contribution of each alternative to the overall goal which is the optimal composition plan by aggregating the resulting weights vertically (table inside Figure 5). The overall priority for each alternative is obtained by summing the product of the criteria weight and the contribution of the alternative, with respect to that criterion as illustrated in Figure 5 for the selection of composition plan. Therefore, the decision maker's choice would be plan P4, which has the maximal score among the other alternative composition plans, if the decision was only to be based on these criteria, which is the same composition plan selected by WSCE Agent.

Figure 6. Computational time of selecting composed web services based LUP and GUP

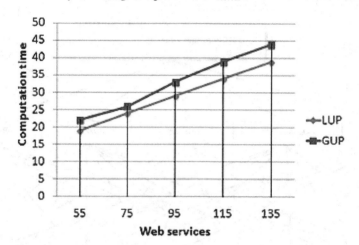

Time Analysis

Time analysis is used to measure the computational time required to select composed web services for web process as in Travel Plan process. Two experiments have been conducted to compute the overall time estimate for the two methods in WSCE framework, local user preferences selection of composed web services, and global user preferences selection of composed web services. The experiments were performed on a personal computer (Intel Corei5with 2.50 GHz CPU and 6 MB RAM).

Experiment 1 (LUP) is conducted for the three tasks (flight reservation, hotel booking, and car rental). For each task a different numbers of available candidate web services (55, 75, 95,115,135) to be composed, and each web service has different QoS properties. The selection in this experiment is based on Local User Preferences(LUP)of composed web services. Experiment 2 (GUP) is done for the same three tasks. A different number of available candidate web services (55, 75, 95,115, 135) to be composed along with different QoS properties. The selection in this experiment is based on Global User Preferences (GUP) of composed web services. Computational times of the two experiments increased directly as the number of candidate web services increased which is almost a linear increase as illustrated in Figure 6. As expected, the computational times for the selection of composed web services based on global user preferences are a little bit higher than that of local user preferences selection.

As expected, the computational times for the selection of composed web services based on GUP are a little bit higher than that of LUP selection. The average of computational times for experiment 1 is 29ms and 32.8ms for experiment 2.

CONCLUSION

This chapter introduced a user preferences based agent for web service composition, the main motivation of WSCE agent to make intelligent web service discovery, service selection decisions based on local user preferences for individual web service or global user preferences based selection for the whole composed web services with less computational time. Although, during the execution of the composed web services, some web services may update their QoS properties others may become unavailable, the

WSCE agent is provided with a QoS monitoring and adaptation for the composed web services during run-time to overcome such issue. QoS certifier controlled by the UDDI registry also introduced to verify the claimed QoS attributes for the registration requests of web service provider. Finally, an evaluation has been conducted to evaluate selection of composition plan using AHP and performance time analysis has been conducted.

ACKNOWLEDGMENT

I would like to thank everyone who contributed to the completion of this work.

REFERENCES

Al-Masri, E., & Qusay, H. (2007).QoS-based Discovery and Ranking of Web services. In Proceedings of the 16th International Conference on Computer Communications and Networks, IEEE (ICCCN 2007). Honolulu, HI: IEEE.

Al-Shargabi, B., El Shiekh, A., & Sabri, A. (2010). Web Service Composition Survey: State of the Art Review. *Recent Patent on Computer Science Journal, 3*(2), 91–107. doi:10.1109/ICCCN.2007.4317873

Anbazhagan, M. &Arun, N. (2002). *Understanding quality of service for Web services*. IBM Developer Works.

Bakhshi, M., & Hashemi, M. (2012). User-Centric Optimization for Constraint Web Service Composition using a Fuzzy-guided Genetic Algorithm System. *International Journal on Web Service Computing, 3*(3), 1–15. doi:10.5121/ijwsc.2012.3301

Bixin, L., Shunhui, J., Dong, Q., Hareton, L., & Gongyuan, G. (2013). Verifying the Concurrent Properties in BPEL Based Web Service Composition Process. Network and Service Management. *IEEE Transactions on, 10*(4), 410–424.

Belton, V., & Stewart, T. (2002). Multi Criteria Decision Analysis – An Integrated Approach. Kluwer.

Blum, A. (2004). UDDI as an Extended Web Services Registry: Versioning, quality of service, and more. *SOA World Magazine, 4*(6).

Booth, D., Hass, H., Mccabe, F., Newcomer, E., Champion, M., Ferris, C., & Orchard, D. (2005). *Web services architecture, W3C Working Group Note 11 February 2004', W3C Technical Reports and Publications*. Retrieved from http://www.w3.org/TR/ws-arch/

Chandrasekaran, S., Miller, J., Silver, G., Arpinar, B., & Sheth, A. (2003). Performance analysis and simulation of composite web services. *International Journal of Electron Commer Bus Media., 13*(2), 18–30.

Chen, L. P., Ha, W. T., & Zhang, G. J. (2013). Reliable execution based on CPN and skyline optimization for web service composition. *TheScientificWorldJournal, 2013*, 1–10. PMID:23935431

El Hadad, J., Manouvrier, M., & Rukoz, M. (2010). TQoS: Transactional and QoS-Aware Selection Algorithm for Automatic Web Service Composition. *IEEE Transactions on Services Computing.*, *3*(1), 73–85. doi:10.1109/TSC.2010.5

Ksalan, M., & Zionts, S. (2001). *Multiple Criteria Decision Making in the New Millennium*. Springer-Verlag. doi:10.1007/978-3-642-56680-6

Michael, C., Jaeger, G., Rojec, G., & Gero, M. (2004).QoS Aggregation for Web Service Composition using Workflow Patterns. In *Proceeding of 8th International Enterprise Distributed Object Computing Conference (EDOC 2004)*.Washington, DC: EDOC.

Myoung, J., Ouk-Kim, C., & Hyun, I. (2008). Quality-of-service oriented web service composition algorithm and planning. *Journal of Systems and Software*, *81*(11), 2079–2090. doi:10.1016/j.jss.2008.04.044

O'sullivan, J., Edmond, D., & Hofstede, A. T. (2002). What's in a service? *Distributed and Parallel Databases*, *12*(23), 117–133. doi:10.1023/A:1016547000822

Ran, S. (2003). A model for web sevices discovery with QoS. *ACM SIGEcomExch, 4*(1), 1–10.

UML Profile for Modeling Quality of Service and Fault Tolerance Characteristics and Mechanisms. (2004).*OMG Adopted Specification ptc/04-09-012*.Retrieved from www.omg.org/docs/ptc/04-09-01.pdf

Zhou, C., Chia, L., & Lee, B. S. (2004). QoS-Aware and Federated Enhancement for UDDI. *International Journal of Web Services Research*, *1*(2), 58–85. doi:10.4018/jwsr.2004040104

Zeng, L., Benatallah, B., Ngu, A. H. H., Dumas, M., Kalagnanam, J., & Chang, H. (2004). QoS-aware middleware for web services composition. *IEEE Transactions on Software Engineering*, *30*(5), 311–327. doi:10.1109/TSE.2004.11

Zeng, L., Benatallah, B., Dumas, M., Kalagnanam, J., & Sheng, Q. (2003). Quality driven web services composition. In *Proceedings of the 12th International Conference on World Wide Web (WWW 2003)*. Budapest, Hungary: Academic Press.

KEY TERMS AND DEFINITIONS

Analytical Hierarchy Process: A technique for analyzing and choosing a complex decision.

Quality of Service: It's the performance of service or network or computer program as perceived by users.

Service Composition: Set of services that can be composed to fulfill a certain process.

Service Oriented Architecture: A design pattern for developing independent software services.

Software Agent: A computer program that acts in behave of its user.

User Preferences: A set of properties that fits user need.

Web Services: A software function that be provided over network.

Chapter 10

Cloud Security Engineering Concept and Vision:
Concept and Vision

Shadi A. Aljawarneh
Jordan University of Science and Technology, Jordan

ABSTRACT

The research community found that a software system should be evolved once every few months to ensure it is adapted to the real-world environment. The system evolution requires regularly amendments that append, delete, or alter features. It also migrates or converts the software system from one operating platform to another. These amendments may result in requirements/ specifications that were satisfied in a previous release of a software system not being satisfied in the subsequent versions. As a result, software evolutionary changes violate security requirements, and then a system may become vulnerable to different kinds of attacks. In this paper, concepts and visions are presented to avoid/minimize the Cloud security issues.

INTRODUCTION

Due to lack of control over the Cloud software, platform and/or infrastructure, several researchers stated that a security is a major challenge in the Cloud. In Cloud computing, the data will be virtualized across different distributed machines, hosted on the Web (M. Taylor, 2010), (R. Marchany, 2010). In business respective, the cloud introduces a channel to the service or platform in which it could operate (M. Taylor, 2010).

Thus, the security issue is the main risk that Cloud environment might be faced. This risk comes from the shortage of control over the Cloud environment. A number of practitioners described this point. For example, Stallman (Ch. Arthur, 2010) from the Free Software Foundation re-called the Cloud computing with Careless Computing because the Cloud customers will not control their own data and software and then there is no monitoring over the Cloud providers and subsequently the data owner may not recognize where data is geographically located at any particular time.

DOI: 10.4018/978-1-4666-8676-2.ch010

Copyright © 2015, IGI Global. Copying or distributing in print or electronic forms without written permission of IGI Global is prohibited.

Threats in the Cloud computing might be resulted from the generic Cloud infrastructure which is available to the public; while it is possessed by organization selling Cloud services (R. Marchany, 2010), (R. Chow et al.,2009).

In Cloud computing, software and its data is created and managed virtually from its users and might only accessible via a certian cloud's software, platform or infrastructure. As shown in Figure 1, there are three Cloud models that describe the Cloud architecture for applications and services (M. Taylor, 2010), (R. Marchany, 2010):

1. **The Software as a Service (SaaS) Model:** The Cloud user rents/uses software for use on a paid subscription (Pay-As-You-Go).
2. **The Platform as a Service (PaaS) Model:** The user rents a development environment for application developers.
3. **The Infrastructure as a Service (IaaS) Model:** The user uses the hardware infrastructure on pay-per-use model, and the service can be expanded in relation to demands from customers.

Figure 1. Models of Cloud environment
Taken from (M. Taylor, 2010)

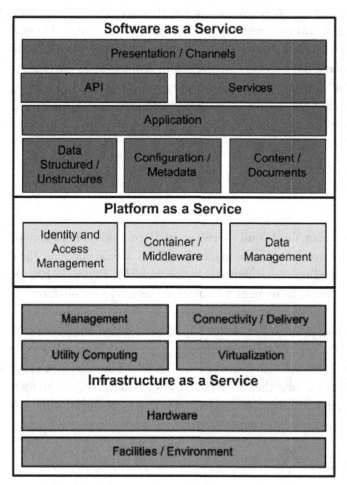

Figure 2. Cloud computing Security
Taken from (R. Marchany, 2010):

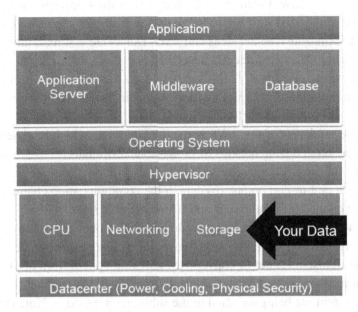

In spite of this significant growth, a little attention has been given to the issue of Cloud security both in research and in practice. Today, academia requires sharing, distributing, merging, changing information, linking applications and other resources within and among organizations. Due to openness, virtualization, distribution interconnection, security becomes critical challenge in order to ensure the integrity and authenticity of digitized data (RG. Cárdenas et al., 2005), (H. Wang et al., 2005).

Cloud opts to use scalable architecture. Scalability means that hardware units that are added bringing more resources to the Cloud architecture (M. Taylor, 2010). However, this feature is in trade-off with the security. Therefore, scalability eases to expose the Cloud environment and it will increase the criminals who would access illegally to the Cloud storage and Cloud Datacenters as illustrated in Figure 2.

Availability is another characteristic for Cloud. So the services, platform, data can be accessible at any time and place. Cloud is candidate to expose to greater security threats, particularly when the cloud is based on the Internet rather than an organization's own platform (M. Taylor, 2010).

Although the security is a risk in the Cloud environment, several companies are offering now Cloud services including Microsoft Azure Services Platform, Amazon Web Services, Google and open source Cloud systems such as Sun Open Cloud Platform for academic, customers and administrative purposes (M. Taylor, 2010). Yet, some organizations have not realized the importance of security for the Cloud systems. These organizations adopted some ready security and protection tools to secure their systems and platforms.

RELATED WORK

Amazon constructed Amazon Web Services (AWS) platform to secure the access for web services (Amazon, 2010). The AWS platform introduces a protection against traditional security issues in the Cloud network.

Physical access to AWS Datacenters is limited controlled both at the perimeter and at building ingress nodes by security experts to raise Video Surveillance (VS), Intrusion Detection Systems (IDS), and other electronic means. Authorized staff has to log in two authentication phases with restricted number of time for accessing to Amazon Web Services and AWS Datacenters at maximum (Amazon, 2010).

Note that Amazon only offers restricted Datacenter access and information to people who have a legal business need for these privileges. If the business need for these privileges is revoked, then the access is stopped, even though if employees continue to be an employee of Amazon or Amazon Web Services (Amazon, 2010).

However, one of the weakness of the AWS is the dynamic data which is generated from the AWS could be listened and penetrated from hackers or professional criminals.

Basically there are six areas for security vulnerabilities in cloud computing (Trusted Computing Group, 2010): (a) data at end-to-end points, (b) data in the communication channel, (c) authentication, (d) separation between clients, (e) legal issues and (f) incident response.

It has recently found that a software system should be evolved once every few months to ensure it is adapted to the real-world environment. The system evolution cloud requires amendments that append, delete, or alter features. It also migrates or converts the software system from one operating platform to another. These amendments may result in requirements/ specifications that were satisfied in a previous release of a software system not being satisfied in the subsequent versions. Note that the software evolutionary changes violate security requirements, and then a system may become vulnerable to different kinds of attacks (A. Nhlabatsi et al., 2012).

Nhlabatsi and others (A. Nhlabatsi et al., 2012) reviewed the current approaches to security requirements engineering and drawn that they lack explicit support for managing the effects of software evolution. Thus they suggested that a cross fertilization of the areas of software evolution and security engineering would address the problem of maintaining compliance to security requirements of software systems as they evolve.

Security requirements engineering deals with the protection of assets from potential threats that may lead to harm (Haley et al., 2008). Haley et al. studied that existing approaches to security requirements engineering have restricted capability for stopping or preserving security features that may be violated as a result of software evolution. In supporting this argument we surveyed the state-of-the-art in the literature of Cloud security software engineering and its software evolution.

This article is organized as follows: a study shows that the Cloud threats and an overview of existing cloud computing concerns are described in Section 2. In section 3, the proposed vision and strategies that might be improved to mitigate or avoid some of the concerns outlined in Sections 1 and 2. Finally conclusions future works are offered in Section 4.

CLOUD THREATS

However, security principles (such as data integrity, and confidentiality) in the Cloud environment could be lost (Amazon, 2010). For example, a criminal might penetrate the web system in many forms (RT. Snodgrass et al., 2004), (N. Provos et al., 2007). An insider adversary, who gains physical access to Datacenters, is able to destroy any type of static content in the root of a web server. It is not only physical access to Datacenter that can corrupt data. Malicious web manipulation software can penetrate servers and Datacenter machines and once located them such malicious software can monitor, intercept, and tamper online transactions in a trusted organization. The result typically allows a criminal full root access to Datacenter and web server application. Once such access has been established, the integrity of any data or software is in question.

There are several security products (such as Antivirus, Firewalls, gateways, and scanners) to secure the Cloud systems but they are not sufficient because each one has only specific purpose and hence, they are called ad-hoc security tool. For example, Network firewalls provide protection at the host and network level (B. Gehling et al., 2005). There are, however, five reasons why these security defences cannot be only used to secure the systems (B. Gehling et al., 2005):

- They cannot stop malicious attacks that perform illegal transactions, because they are designed to prevent vulnerabilities of signatures and specific ports.
- They cannot manipulate form operations such as asking the user to submit certain information or validate false data because they cannot distinguish between the original request-response conversation and the tampered conversation.
- They do not track conversations and do not secure the session information. For example, they cannot track when session information in cookies is exchanged over an HTTP request-response model.
- They provide no protection against web application/services attacks since these are launched on port 80 (default for web sites) which has to remain open to allow normal operations of the business.
- Previously, a firewall could suppose that an adversary could only be on the outside. Currently, with Cloud systems, an attack might originate from the inside as well, where firewall can offer no protection.

Note that the computer forensics has classified e-crime into three classes (G. Mohay et al., 2003): The computer is the target of the crime; data storage which is created during the commission of a crime; or a tool or scheme that used in performing a crime.

Figure 2 shows the data storage and Datacenters which are possibly targeted by the criminals. According to the computer forensics, the distrusted servers and Datacenters are the target of crime. Therefore, question should be attempted to answer is that whether data is safe and secure?

Data confidentiality might be exposed either from insider user threats or outsider user threats from (CPNI, 2010). For instance, Insider user threats might maliciously form from: cloud operator/provider, cloud customer, or malicious third party. The threat of insiders accessing customer data take place within the cloud is larger as each of models can offer the need for multiple users:

- **SaaS:** Cloud clients and administrators;
- **PaaS:** Application developers and testers;
- **IaaS:** Third party consultants.

A VISION AND STRATEGY TO MITIGATE OR AVOID CLOUD SECURITY CONCERNS

In this article, a vision is proposed to avoid the Cloud security threat at the SaS level. Our vision is that SaS is based on Service-oriented architecture. A service is a standard approach to make a reusable com-

Figure 3. The proposed strategy

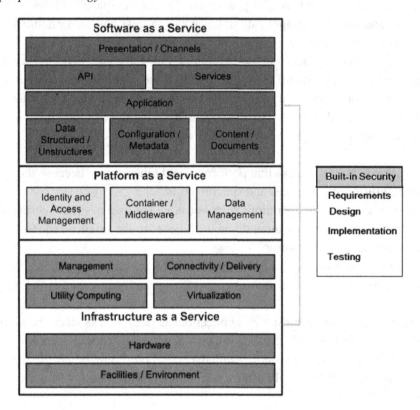

ponent available and could be accessible across the web or possible technology. Thus, service provision is independent of the application that using the service.

In reference to the article (S. Aljawarneh, 2011) a case study has been described to mention a number of significant threat vulnerabilities that can be introduced during all phases of the software (service) development life cycle.

For instance, number security vulnerabilities might be occurred at the requirements specification process cycle (SC. Bono et al., 2005), (DM. Cappelli et al., 2006):

- Ignoring to declare authentication and role-based access control requirements eased the insider and or outsider attacks.
- Ignoring to declare security requirements of duties for automated business processes provided a simplified method for attack.
- Ignoring to declare requirements for data integrity checks gave insiders the security of knowing their actions would not be detected.

The existing Cloud services face some security issues because a security design is not integrated into the Cloud architecture development process (W. Glisson et al., 2005). Thus, organizations should pay more attention to the insider threats to operational systems; it turns out that vulnerabilities can be accidentally and intentionally introduced throughout the development life cycle – during requirements definition, design, implementation, deployment, and maintenance (DM. Cappelli et al., 2006). Once business leaders are aware of these, they can implement practices that will aid in mitigating these vulnerabilities.

As illustrated in Figure 3, security should be built in all steps of the service development process to identify what a customer and an organization need for every stage of the software engineering principles. This proposed vision or strategy could help to detect the threats and concerns at each stage instead of processing them at the implementation stage. Consequently, our vision and strategies might help the Cloud developers, providers and administrators to eliminate the attacks or mitigate them if possible in the design stage not waiting for actual attacks to occur.

CONCLUSION

Cloud faces some security issues at the SaS, PaS, IaS models. One main reason is that the lack of control over the Cloud Datacenters and distributed servers. Furthermore, security is not integrated into the service development process.

Indeed, the traditional security tools alone will not solve current security issues and so it will be effective to incorporate security component upfront into the development methodology of Cloud system phases. In the next part of this article, we will propose a methodology that could help to mitigate the security concerns on the Cloud models.

REFERENCES

Aljawarneh, S. (2011, March). A web engineering security methodology for e-learning systems. *Network Security Journal, Elsevier, 2011*(3), 12–16. doi:10.1016/S1353-4858(11)70026-5

Aljawarneh, S. (2011). Cloud Security Engineering: Avoiding Security Threats the Right Way. *International Journal of Cloud Applications and Computing, 1*(2), 64–70. doi:10.4018/ijcac.2011040105

Amazon. (2010). *Amazon Web Services: Overview of Security Processes*. Retrieved from awsmedia. s3.amazonaws.com/pdf/AWS_Security_Whitepaper.pdf

Arthur, C. (2010). *Google's ChromeOS means losing control of data, warns GNU founder Richard Stallman*. Retrieved from http://www.guardian.co.uk/technology/blog/2010/dec/14/chrome-os-richard-stallman-warning

Bono, S. C., Green, M., Stubblefield, A., Juels, A., Rubin, A. D., & Szydlo, M. (2005). Security analysis of a cryptographically-enabled RFID device. In *SSYM'05: Proceedings of the 14th conference on USENIX Security Symposium*. Berkeley, CA: USENIX Association.

Cappelli, D. M., Trzeciak, R. F., & Moore, A. B. (2006). *Insider Threats in the SLDC: Lessions Learned From Actual Incidents of Fraud: Theft of Sensitive Information, and IT Sabotage, Carnegie Mellon University*.

Cárdenas, R. G., & Sanchez, E. (2005). Security Challenges of Distributed e-Learning Systems. *ISSADS: Springer, Series Lecture Notes in Computer Science, 3563*. Retrieved from http://dblp.uni-trier.de/db/conf/issads/issads2005.html#CardenasS05

Chow, R., Golle, P., Jakobsson, M., Shi, E., Staddon, J., Masuoka, R., & Molina, J. (2009). Controlling data in the cloud: outsourcing computation without outsourcing control. In *Proceedings of the 2009 ACM workshop on Cloud computing security* (CCSW '09). ACM. http://doi.acm.org/10.1145/1655008.1655020

CPNI. (2010). *Information security briefing 01/2010 cloud computing*. Retrieved from www.cpni.gov. uk/Documents/.../2010/2010007-ISB_cloud_computing.pdf

Gehling, B., & Stankard, D. (2005). eCommerce security. In *Proceedings of Information Security Curriculum Development (InfoSecCD) Conference*. Academic Press.

Glisson, W., & Welland, R. (2005). Web Development Evolution: The Assimilation of Web Engineering Security. In *Proceedings of the Third Latin American Web Congress*. Washington, DC: IEEE Computer Society. doi:10.1109/LAWEB.2005.48

Google. (2011b). *Google Trends: private cloud, public cloud*. Retrieved from http://www.google.de/trends?q=private+cloud%2C+public+cloud

Marchany, R. (2010). *Cloud Computing Security Issues: VA Tech IT Security*. Retrieved from www. issa-centralva.org/.../01-2010_CCSecIssues.ppt

Mohay, G., Anderson, A., Collie, B., & del Vel, O. (2003). *Computer and intrusion forensics* (p. 9). Boston, MA: Artech House.

Nhlabatsi, A., Nuseibeh, B., & Yu, Y. (2010). Security Requirements Engineering for Evolving Software Systems: A Survey. *International Journal of Secure Software Engineering*, *1*(1), 54–73. doi:10.4018/jsse.2010102004

Provos, N., McNamee, D., Mavrommatis, P., Wang, K., & Modadugu, N. (2007). The ghost in the browser analysis of web-based malware. In *HotBots'07: Proceedings of the RST conference on First Workshop on Hot Topics in Understanding Botnets*. Berkeley, CA: USENIX Association.

Ramim, M., & Levy, Y. (2006). Securing e-learning systems: A case of insider cyber attacks and novice IT management in a small university. *Journal of Cases on Information Technology*, *8*(4), 24–34. doi:10.4018/jcit.2006100103

Snodgrass, R. T., Yao, S. S., & Collberg, C. (2004). Tamper detection in audit logs. In *Proceedings of the Thirtieth international conference on Very large data bases*. VLDB Endowment. doi:10.1016/B978-012088469-8.50046-2

Taylor, M. (2010). *Enterprise Architecture – Architectural Strategies for Cloud Computing: Oracle*. Retrieved from http://www.techrepublic.com/whitepapers/oracle-white-paper-in-enterprise-architecture-architecture-strategies-for-cloud-computing/2319999

Trusted Computing Group. (2010). *Cloud Computing and Security –A Natural Match*. Retrieved from www.infosec.co.uk/.../Cloud_Computing_and_Security-A_Natural_Match_ TCG_Whitepaper_20.pdf

Wang, H., Zhang, Y., & Cao, J. (2005). Effective Collaboration with Information Sharing in Virtual Universities. IEEE Transactions, 21(6), 40-853.

Chapter 11
Fairness–Aware Task Allocation for Heterogeneous Multi–Cloud Systems

Sanjaya Kumar Panda
Indian School of Mines Dhanbad, India & VSS University of Technology Burla, India

Roshni Pradhan
VSS University of Technology Burla, India

Benazir Neha
VSS University of Technology Burla, India

Sujaya Kumar Sathua
VSS University of Technology Burla, India

ABSTRACT

Cloud computing is rapidly growing for its on-demand services over the Internet. The customers can use these services by placing the requirements in the form of leases. In IaaS cloud, the customer submits the leases in one of the form, namely advance reservation (AR) and best effort (BE). The AR lease has higher priority over the BE lease. Hence, it can preempt the BE lease. It results in starvation among the BE leases and is unfair to the BE leases. In this chapter, the authors present fairness-aware task allocation (FATA) algorithm for heterogeneous multi-cloud systems, which aims to provide fairness among AR and BE leases. We have performed rigorous experiments on some benchmark and synthetic datasets. The performance is measured in terms of two metrics, namely makespan and average cloud utilization. The experimental result shows the superiority of the proposed algorithm over the existing algorithm.

INTRODUCTION

The popularity of *Cloud Computing* is rapidly growing because of its advancement in virtualization technology (Buyya, Yeo, Venugopal, Broberg, & Brandic, 2009; Li et al., 2012; Huang et al., 2013). This technology facilitates the cloud service providers (CSPs) to create the virtual machines (VMs) instantly (Desmarais, 2013, pp. 18-24). Moreover, the VMs are deployed in a data center to access a service (Sotomayor, Montero, Llorente, & Foster, 2008). Thus, the CSP provides on-demand service over the internet. These services are delivered to customers on pay-per-use basis. But these services are

DOI: 10.4018/978-1-4666-8676-2.ch011

Copyright © 2015, IGI Global. Copying or distributing in print or electronic forms without written permission of IGI Global is prohibited.

limited to the capacity of a data center. In order to handle the customer's demands, some of the services are transferred to another data center (Forell, Milojicic, & Talwar, 2011). In Infrastructure-as-a-Service (IaaS) cloud, the services are demanded by customers in the form of leases. The lease may be submitted in one of the form, namely Advance Reservation (AR) or Best Effort (BE) (Sotomayor, Keahey, & Foster, 2006; Sotomayor, Montero, Llorente, & Foster, 2009; Li et al., 2012; Nathani, Chaudhary, & Somani, 2012).

AR lease is represented by a 3-tuple as follows.

$<S, E, N>$

where

S = Start time of a lease,
E = Execution time of a lease (Note that, End time $(ET) = S + E$), and
N = No preemption. (Note that, AR lease is non-preemptive in nature.)

In contrary, BE lease is also represented by a 3-tuple as follows.

$<E, ST, P>$

where

E = Execution time of a lease,
ST = Starvation time of a lease (i.e., how long a BE lease can wait), and
P = Preemption. (Note that, BE lease is preemptive in nature (Sotomayor, 2008)).

AR lease has higher priority over BE lease. Hence, AR lease can preempt BE lease on its arrival. Moreover, if the AR lease is remaining or arriving in the cloud systems, the BE lease cannot be executed. Thus, it leads to starvation among BE leases. Therefore, a significant problem is to schedule the AR and BE leases such that starvation among the leases is reduced up to some extent. This problem is referred as task (or lease) allocation problem in heterogeneous multi-cloud environment, which is not studied in the recent literatures. The primary objective of this problem is to find the execution order of the leases so that the starvation is reduced.

In this chapter, we address the above problem for heterogeneous multi-cloud environment and propose a novel algorithm Fairness-Aware Task Allocation (FATA). The algorithm allows few BE leases to schedule before AR leases in a regular interval. However, the interval depends on the arrival rate of AR and BE leases respectively. For example at time instance $t = 0$, eighty AR leases and twenty BE leases are arrived. If there is no fairness, it schedules eighty AR leases followed by twenty BE leases which leads to starvation among BE leases. From here onwards we will refer the no fairness (i.e., stated above) as existing algorithm. We also refer lease, workload and task interchangeably in this chapter. In order to overcome the starvation problem, we introduce FATA algorithm. We perform extensive experiments on the proposed algorithm using synthetic and benchmark data sets. The experimental results clearly show that the proposed algorithm outperforms existing algorithm. To the best of our knowledge, this is the first fairness work for heterogeneous multi-cloud environment.

Thus our major contributions can be summarized as follows.

- We present a fairness-aware task allocation algorithm for heterogeneous multi-cloud systems. This algorithm is suitable for both online and offline task scheduling, which allows quite a few BE leases to schedule before AR leases in order to avoid starvation.
- We test the algorithm with both synthetic and benchmark datasets.
- We compare the proposed task allocation algorithm with the existing task allocation algorithm in terms of two performance metrics, namely makespan and average cloud utilization.

The remainder of this chapter is organized as follows: Section 2 presents related work with their pros and cons. Section 3 describes the cloud model, problem statement and one motivational example. Section 4 presents the proposed algorithm followed by the performance metrics in Section 5. Section 6 presents the experimental results followed by the conclusion in Section 7.

RELATED WORK

Task allocation in a heterogeneous multi-cloud system is very challenging due to the dynamic arrival of leases, workloads or tasks (Bajaj & Agrawal, 2004, Xu, Hu, & Yihe, 2010). These leases are executed as per the service level agreement (SLA). However, the cloud service provider (CSP) aims to maximize the revenue by selecting high profit leases without violating the SLA (Beloglazov, Abawajy, & Buyya, 2012). It leads to starvation among the low profit leases. For instance, Haizea (Sotomayor et al., 2006; Panda & Jana, 2014; Panda & Jana, 2015) supports advance reservation (AR) and best effort (BE) leases. AR lease has more revenue than BE lease. Hence, a CSP may select all AR leases to maximize the revenue. However, it causes starvation (or dissatisfaction) among BE leases (or customers).

Li et al. (2012) have proposed two task scheduling algorithms, namely cloud list scheduling (CLS) and cloud min-min scheduling (CMMS). However, these algorithms cause starvation problem as BE leases (or tasks) can only be processed after the completion of AR leases. Chen et al. (2013) have presented user-priority guided min-min scheduling for cloud computing. Unlike Haizea, the task is categorized into VIP and ordinary service level. If there are so many VIP tasks and a few ordinary tasks then this algorithm causes starvation among ordinary tasks.

Ming and Li (2012) have extended a well-known algorithm known as max-min and proposed max-min spare time algorithm to reduce the expenses of the cloud services. However, the algorithm does not support the AR and BE leases. Hence, service level is not provided. Panda & Jana (2014) have proposed cloud normalized min-min max-min (CNXM) algorithm which supports the service level as used by (Sotomayor et al., 2006; Li et al., 2012; Chen, Wang, Helian & Akanmu, 2013). The service level is provided by placing the AR and BE leases into two different queues. However, starvation still remains among BE leases.

Shrivastava & Bhilare (2012) have introduced two algorithms. The first algorithm keeps track of the number of suspension of each BE lease. If it exceeds the maximum limit then it rejects the AR lease

Figure 1. Gantt chart for one AR lease and one BE lease

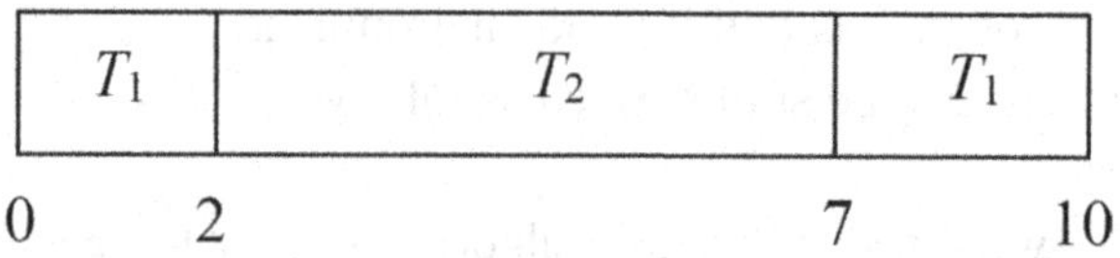

T_1	T_2	T_1

0   2   7   10

without agitating the BE lease. Hence, the starvation is reduced up to some extent. We call it post-starvation removal as the decision is taken after the maximum limit expires. The second algorithm makes a conversion of AR to BE leases due to lack of resources. However, the algorithms are not performing well when the cloud system has multiple requests of same type of leases.

In this chapter, we deal with above pitfalls by introducing fairness-aware task allocation (FATA) algorithm. The algorithm is completely different from the above literatures with respect to the following aspects.

- FATA dispatches AR lease followed by BE leases on a regular interval such that starvation is reduced to greater extent. The dispatch value (i.e., AR:BE ratio) purely depends on the arrival of AR and BE leases. It changes with respect to the time instance.

- FATA deals with the pre-starvation removal. Hence, we need not require counting the number of suspensions.
- FATA makes fairness among AR and BE leases.
- The algorithm is tested in benchmark as well as synthetic datasets.

MODELS AND PROBLEM STATEMENT

Motivational Example

Let us consider an illustration with a single VM. At $t = 0$, a BE lease $T_1 = <5, 50, P>$ is arrived. So, T_1 starts execution as there is no AR lease. However, at $t = 2$, an AR lease $T_2 = <2, 5, N>$ is arrived. Therefore, T_1 is preempted and its corresponding disk image is stored by the VM (Li et al., 2012). Once the AR lease T_2 completes its execution at $t = 7$, the BE lease T_1 is resumed subjected to no AR lease T_2 is arrived. T_1 completes its execution at $t = 10$. The corresponding Gantt chart is shown in Figure 1.

Let us assume that at $t = 7$, two BE leases, namely $T_3 = <3, 50, P>$ and $T_4 = <1, 60, P>$ and four AR leases, namely $T_5 = <8, 5, N>$, $T_6 = <15, 3, N>$, $T_7 = <18, 2, N>$ and $T_8 = <20, 3, N>$ are arrived. The corresponding Gantt chart is shown in Figure 2.

The above example clearly shows the unfairness of AR leases over BE leases. Moreover, starvation among the BE leases may happen. So, we present FATA to overcome the starvation and fairness problem.

Figure 2. Gantt chart for three BE leases and five AR leases

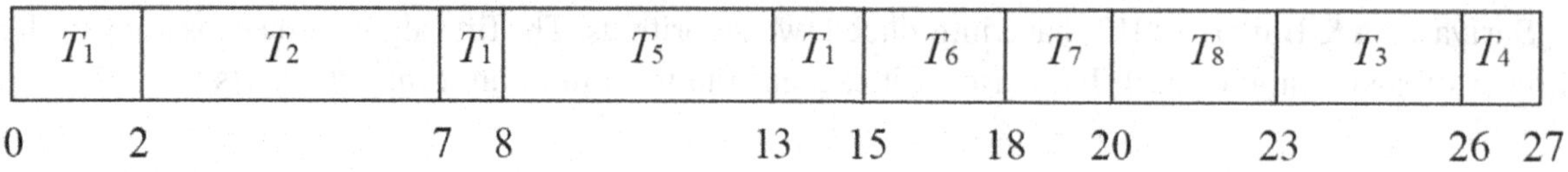

T_1	T_2	T_1	T_5	T_1	T_6	T_7	T_8	T_3	T_4

0   2   7 8   13   15   18   20   23   26   27

Assumptions

We assume AR and BE leases has two parameters, namely execution time and no preemption or preemption. The main rationale behind this is that we have to generate the expected time to compute (ETC) matrix (Maheswaran, Ali, Siegel, Hensgen, & Freund, 1999; Wang, Yan, Liao, & Wang, 2010) for AR and BE leases as generated by (Li et al., 2012). Moreover, the benchmark dataset does not have start time and starvation time of AR and BE leases respectively (Braun et al., 2001). These things are done for simplicity of experiments and lacuna of the AR and BE leases parameter in benchmark datasets. All these assumptions are made on the assumptions made in (Li et al., 2012).

Cloud Model

In our cloud model, we use the IaaS cloud system. We assume that there are two queues, namely waiting queue and execution queue. The waiting queue places the incoming AR and BE leases according to the arrival time. In other hand, the execution queue places the AR and BE leases according to our proposed algorithm. For instance, four AR leases and one BE lease (i.e., 4:1 ratio) are placed in order to achieve the fairness. In general, k: l ratio is achieved where k and l are the number of AR and BE leases respectively. Figure 3 clearly shows the above scenario where green and orange colors are used to represent AR and BE leases respectively.

When the tasks in execution queue are put in order, the tasks are mapped to different clouds in first come first serve (FCFS) order. In each cloud, VMs are created and deployed in the data center to provide on-demand service. However, our cloud model does not deal with how the VMs are created, managed or organized. Note that, each VM is of different types and characteristics (Panda & Jana, 2014). Each cloud has a manager server to keep tracks of information about the VMs. When sufficient number of VMs is not available, the tasks are transferred to other clouds. The disk image of the tasks is also transferred to other clouds as and when required. The major concern of this paper is to dispatch the AR and BE tasks from the execution queue such that 1) fairness is achieved and 2) starvation is removed.

Application Model and Problem Statement

Consider a set of m clouds $C = \{C_1, C_2, C_3, ..., C_m\}$, a set of k independent AR tasks $T_{AR} = \{T_1, T_2, T_3, ..., T_k\}$ and a set of l independent BE tasks $T_{BE} = \{T_{k+1}, T_{k+2}, T_{k+3}, ..., T_{k+l}\}$. A task set T is the permutation of the independent AR and BE tasks. For instance, $T = \{T_1, T_{k+l}, T_3, ..., T_{k+1}, T_{k+3}, T_{k+2}, T_k, ..., T_2\}$.

Figure 3. Waiting and execution queues for the proposed algorithm

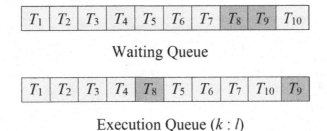

Waiting Queue

Execution Queue (k : l)

Therefore, $T = T_{AR} \cup T_{BE}$. The problem is to assign the AR and BE tasks to the clouds such that fairness among the tasks can be achieved. This problem is restricted to the following constraints. 1) $T_i \prec T_{i+1}$ where $1 \leq i \leq k$-1 and $A \prec B$ denotes A is executed before B. 2) $T_i \prec T_{i+1}$ where $k+1 \leq i \leq k+l$-1. 3) $T_i \prec \succ T_j$ where $1 \leq i \leq k, k+1 \leq j \leq k+l$ and $A \prec \succ B$ denotes A and B are executed in any order.

PROPOSED ALGORITHM

Fairness-Aware Task Allocation

Fairness-Aware Task Allocation (FATA) is a fairness algorithm to allocate the independent AR and BE tasks to the available clouds. The fairness is achieved by assigning BE tasks over the AR tasks on a regular interval. Let us assume that at time instance t = 0, p tasks are arrived in the waiting queue (WQ). The p tasks contain a set of k independent AR tasks and a set of l BE tasks. From now we will use C_{AR} and C_{BE} instead of k and l respectively. Therefore, the rate of arrival of AR tasks (R_{AR}) is defined as follows.

$$R_{AR} = \frac{C_{AR}}{C_{AR} + C_{BE}} \tag{1}$$

where C_{AR} = Total number of AR tasks in the WQ and C_{BE} = Total number of BE tasks in the WQ
Similarly, the rate of arrival of BE tasks (R_{BE}) is calculated as follows.

$$R_{BE} = \frac{C_{BE}}{C_{AR} + C_{BE}} \tag{2}$$

Based on the rate of arrival of AR and BE tasks, the cloud service provider sets the satisfaction rate. We define the satisfaction and dissatisfaction rate with some notable remarks as follows.

Definition 4.1: Satisfaction rate of BE tasks (or Dissatisfaction rate of AR tasks) are the amount of BE tasks preferred over AR tasks. Alternatively, it is an agreement between the cloud service provider and BE customer to satisfy the BE tasks over AR tasks.
Definition 4.2: Dissatisfaction rate of BE tasks are the amount of AR tasks preferred over BE tasks.
Remark 4.1: Satisfaction rate (of BE tasks) are directly proportional to dissatisfaction rate (of AR tasks).
However, satisfaction rate (of BE tasks) are inversely proportional to satisfaction rate (of AR tasks).
Remark 4.2: The satisfaction rate of BE tasks (denoted as τ) are the upper bound of $R_{BE.}$

Therefore,

$$R_{BE} = \begin{cases} \tau & if\ R_{BE} > \tau \\ R_{BE} & Otherwise \end{cases} \tag{3}$$

The R_{BE} is limited to τ constraint because the agreement between the cloud service provider and BE customer are to satisfy at least τ amount of BE tasks. Hence, the lower bound of the service provider is τ. In contrary, the upper bound of the customer is τ.

The above process is illustrated as follows.

Let us assume that at $t = 0$, four AR tasks (i.e., T_1, T_2, T_3 and T_4) and two BE tasks (i.e., T_5 and T_6) are arrived in the WQ. Therefore, R_{AR} and R_{BE} become 0.67 and 0.34 respectively (refer Equation 1 and Equation 2 respectively). Assume that the cloud service provider sets $\tau = 0.3$. It makes $R_{BE} = 0.3$ as the cloud service provider needs to satisfy 30% BE tasks as per the agreement (refer Equation 3). In order to achieve profit, the cloud service provider sets 0.3 as the lower bound. Alternatively, the customer sets 0.3 as the upper bound.

The rate of dispatch of AR tasks (R) is defined as follows.

$$R = \left\lceil \frac{R_{AR}}{R_{BE}} \right\rceil \tag{4}$$

Note that, R is the amount of AR tasks dispatch from the waiting queue (WQ) to the execution queue (Q). Similarly, the rate of dispatch of BE tasks (R') is calculated as follows.

$$R' = \begin{cases} \left\lceil \dfrac{\tau}{R_{AR}} \right\rceil & \text{if } R_{BE} > \tau \\[3mm] \left\lceil \dfrac{R_{BE}}{R_{AR}} \right\rceil & \text{Otherwise} \end{cases} \tag{5}$$

The above process is illustrated as follows.

Recall the previous example where $R_{AR} = 0.67$ and $R_{BE} = 0.3$. Therefore, R and R' becomes 3 and 1 respectively (refer Equation 4 and 5 respectively). Therefore, WQ dispatches three AR tasks (i.e., T_1, T_2 and T_3) followed by one BE task (i.e., T_5) to the execution queue in the first iteration. In the next iteration, WQ is trying to find three AR tasks. However, only one AR task is left in the WQ. Hence, it dispatches one AR task (i.e., T_4) followed by one BE task (i.e., T_6).

Remark 4.3: The proposed algorithm achieves fairness as it dispatches BE task(s) prior to the AR tasks on a regular interval. Therefore, we call the proposed algorithm as pre-starvation removal algorithm.

At last, the execution queue tasks are scheduled to one of the available cloud based on the task scheduling algorithm such as round robin (Rimal, Choi, & Lumb, 2009), CLS (Li et al., 2012) etc.

Pseudo Code for FATA

The pseudo code for FATA is shown in Figure 4. The algorithm uses two queues, namely WQ and Q. The WQ is used to keep both AR and BE tasks in the order of their arrival. The total number of AR and BE tasks are calculated by scanning WQ from left to right (Lines 3-9). Note that, C_{AR} and C_{BE} are used to

Figure 4. Pseudo code for FATA algorithm

```
1.   Set C_AR = C_BE = 0 and j = 1
2.   while WQ ≠ NULL do
3.       for i = 1, 2, 3, ..., |WQ|
4.           if WQ(i) == T_AR
5.               C_AR ← C_AR + 1
6.           else
7.               C_BE ← C_BE + 1
8.           end if
9.       end for
10.      R_AR = C_AR / (C_AR + C_BE)  and R_BE = C_BE / (C_AR + C_BE)
11.      if R_BE > τ
12.          R_BE = τ
13.      end if
```

```
14.      do
15.          R = ⌈R_AR / R_BE⌉  and R' = ⌈τ / R_AR⌉
16.          for i = 1, 2, 3, ..., |WQ|
17.              if WQ(i) == T_AR and R ≠ 0
18.                  Q(j) = WQ(i)
19.                  R ← R - 1 and j ← j + 1
20.              end if
21.          end for
22.          for i = 1, 2, 3, ..., |WQ|
23.              if WQ(i) == T_BE and R' ≠ 0
24.                  Q(j) = WQ(i)
25.                  R' ← R' - 1 and j ← j + 1
26.              end if
27.          end for
28.          Assign tasks from Q to the available resources
29.          Remove the T_AR and T_BE from the WQ and Q
30.          Update |WQ| and |Q|
31.      while(|WQ| ≠ NULL)
32. end while
```

count the number of AR and BE tasks respectively. Based on the count values, R_{AR} and R_{BE} are calculated (Line 10). In case the R_{BE} value exceeds the satisfaction rate of BE tasks (τ), the R_{BE} value is limit to the satisfaction rate (Lines 11-13). Thereafter, we calculate the dispatch value of AR and BE tasks (denoted as R and R') form the WQ (Line 15). Therefore, we again scan the WQ from left to right and dispatch R number of AR tasks (Lines 16-21) and R' number of BE tasks (Lines 22-27) respectively. These tasks are dispatched from WQ to Q. At last, the tasks in the Q is executed based on the task scheduling algorithm and the executed task is removed from WQ and Q respectively (Lines 28-30). This completes the first iteration. The above process iterates until WQ is empty.

Theorem 1: The number of iterations requires for dispatching tasks from WQ to Q is C_{BE} if and only if $R_{BE} \leq \tau$.

Proof:

Case 1: Let $C_{AR} = x$, $C_{BE} = y$, $x > y$ and $R_{BE} \leq \tau$. It results $R_{AR} > R_{BE}$, $R = \left\lceil \dfrac{x}{y} \right\rceil > 1$ and $R' = \left\lceil \dfrac{y}{x} \right\rceil = 1$.

Therefore, WQ dispatches R tasks followed by R' tasks in the first iteration. In the second iteration, R tasks followed by R' tasks are dispatched (Note that, it is applicable if and only if sufficient number of AR and BE tasks are available). In y^{th} iteration, WQ dispatches R tasks before R' tasks.

The number of AR tasks dispatched $= R + R + R + \dots$ (y times)

$$= \left\lceil \frac{x}{y} \right\rceil + \left\lceil \frac{x}{y} \right\rceil + \left\lceil \frac{x}{y} \right\rceil + \dots \left(y \ times \right) = y \times \left\lceil \frac{x}{y} \right\rceil = x \text{ (by ignoring ceiling)}$$

and the number of BE tasks dispatched

$$\left(C_{BE} \right) = R' + R' + R' + \dots (y \ times)$$

$$= \left\lceil \frac{y}{x} \right\rceil + \left\lceil \frac{y}{x} \right\rceil + \left\lceil \frac{y}{x} \right\rceil + \dots (y \ times) = x \times \left\lceil \frac{y}{x} \right\rceil = y \text{ (by ignoring ceiling)}.$$

So, the number of iterations (i.e., y) required for dispatching tasks from WQ to Q is C_{BE} (i.e., y). Hence, it is proved.

Note that, total number of tasks dispatched $=$

$$\left(y \times \left\lceil \frac{x}{y} \right\rceil + x \times \left\lceil \frac{y}{x} \right\rceil \right) = x + y \text{ (by ignoring ceiling)}.$$

Case 2: Let $C_{AR} = x$, $C_{BE} = y$, $x = y$ and $R_{BE} \leq \tau$. It results $R_{AR} = R_{BE}$, $R = 1$ and $R' = 1$. The proof is same as Case 1.

Case 3: Let $C_{AR} = x$, $C_{BE} = y$, $x < y$ and $R_{BE} \leq \tau$. It results $R_{AR} < R_{BE}$, $R = 1$ and $R' > 1$. The proof is same as Case 1.

Example: Let $C_{AR} = 80$, $C_{BE} = 20$, $x > y$ and $R_{BE} \leq \tau$. It results $R = 4$ and $R' = 1$. WQ dispatches 4 AR tasks followed by one BE task in the one iteration. Therefore, the number of iterations requires for dispatching tasks from WQ to Q is 20 which is same as C_{BE}.

Time Complexity Analysis

Let k be the number of AR tasks and l is the number of BE tasks. Therefore, $|WQ| = k + l$. Steps 1 to 2 require $O(1)$ time. To count the number of AR and BE tasks, steps 3 to 9 require $O(k + l)$ time. To set the satisfaction rate of BE tasks, steps 10 to 13 require $O(1)$ time. Again, step 15 requires $O(1)$ time. To calculate the dispatch value, steps 16 to 27 require $O(k + l)$ time. At last, steps 28 to 30 require $O(1)$ time to assign the tasks as well as update the queues. So, the overall time complexity of the proposed algorithm is $O(j \times (k + l))$ time as it invokes FATA j times.

PERFORMANCE METRICS

To evaluate the performance of the proposed algorithm, we use two parameters, namely cloud makespan and average cloud utilization. These metrics are especially used in scheduling (Xhafa, Barolli, & Durrresi, 2007; Panda & Jana, 2014; Panda & Jana, 2015). They are briefly defined as follows.

Cloud Makespan (*M*)

In a particular cloud, it is the completion time of last task (that may be AR or BE task). However, it refers to overall completion time required to execute all tasks in multi-cloud heterogeneous environment. It is worth mentioning that one or more cloud has equal completion time. Therefore, they together hold the makespan. It is mathematically defined as follows.

$$M = \max \left\{ \begin{array}{l} \sum_{i=1}^{m} ETC\left(i,1\right) \times F\left(i,1\right), \sum_{i=1}^{m} ETC\left(i,2\right) \times F\left(i,2\right), \\ \sum_{i=1}^{m} ETC\left(i,3\right) \times F\left(i,3\right), ..., \sum_{i=1}^{m} ETC\left(i,m\right) \times F\left(i,m\right) \end{array} \right\}$$

where $ETC(i, j)$ = Expected time to compute AR or BE task i on cloud j and

$$F\left(i,j\right) = \begin{cases} 1 & if\ T_i \rightarrow C_j \\ 0 & Otherwise \end{cases}$$

Here, $T_i \rightarrow C_j$ indicates that the task i is assigned to cloud j.

Remark 5.1: It is noteworthy that if the order of task allocation is rescheduled, then it may or may not give least makespan. However, it may give better fairness. In the proposed algorithm, we aim to get better makespan and fairness by rescheduling the task allocation (that is AR followed by BE).

Average Cloud Utilization (*U*)

Cloud utilization (CU) is the percentage time a particular cloud is busy for executing the AR or BE tasks. It is mathematically defined as follows.

$$CU(C_i) = \frac{M(C_i)}{M}$$

where $M(C_i)$ denotes the makespan of cloud *i*, $CU(C_i)$ denotes the utilization of cloud *i*.

The average cloud utilization (*U*) is the mean of all clouds utilization. Mathematically,

$$U = \frac{\sum_{i=1}^{m} CU(C_i)}{m}$$

Remark 5.2: Utilization of a cloud is 100% if and only if it holds the makespan.

Remark 5.3: Better makespan may not guarantee better average cloud utilization and vice-versa. In this chapter, we aim to get better average cloud utilization without compromising the makespan and fairness.

EXPERIMENTAL RESULTS

We evaluate the proposed algorithm through simulation run with some benchmark and synthetic datasets. The experiments are carried out using MATLAB R2014a version 8.3.0.532 on an Intel Core 2 Duo processor, 2.20 GHz CPU and 4 GB RAM running on Microsoft Windows 7 platform. The simulation results are presented as follows.

Benchmark Dataset

In this simulation, we used two different benchmark datasets generated by (Braun et al., 2001). The first dataset contains 512 independent tasks and 16 different clouds. The 512 independent tasks are to be executed by 16 different clouds in first come first serve (FCFS) basis. However, they will follow their respective modes (i.e., AR or BE). We denote this dataset by 512 × 16. In the same way, the second dataset holds 1024 independent tasks and 32 different clouds. We represent dataset by 1024 × 32. We assume that VMs are created in each cloud to execute the tasks. Though, we represent the execution time of the tasks for simplicity of experiment. Both 512 × 16 and 1024 × 32 has 12 different instances (i.e., *u_c_hihi, u_c_hilo, u_c_lohi, u_c_lolo, u_i_hihi, u_i_hilo, u_i_lohi, u_i_lolo, u_s_hihi, u_s_hilo, u_s_lohi* and *u_s_lolo*). Here, the general formation of these instances is *u_x_yyzz* where

u = uniform distribution to generate these instances
x = type of consistency (i.e., consistent (*c*), inconsistent (*i*) or semi-consistent (*s*))
yy = task heterogeneity (i.e., high (*hi*) or low (*lo*))
zz = cloud heterogeneity (i.e., high (*hi*) or low (*lo*))

These instances are especially used in scheduling (Xhafa et al., 2007; Panda & Jana, 2014; Panda, Agrawal, Khilar, & Mohapatra, 2014). To incorporate the mode of leases, we used two parameters, namely R_{BE} (the rate of arrival of BE tasks) and τ (satisfaction rate of BE tasks). We represent it by $[R_{BE}, \tau]$. It makes two different cases in our simulation which is discussed as follows.

Case A: $R_{BE} \leq \tau$ where $0.1 \leq R_{BE}, \tau \leq 0.4$
Case B: $R_{BE >} \tau$ where $0.3 \leq R_{BE} \leq 0.4$ and $\tau = 0.2$

Let us consider the 512×16 dataset. If $R_{BE} = \tau = 0.1$ (i.e., [0.1, 0.1]) then total number of BE tasks is 52 (i.e., 0.1×512) and the satisfaction rate allows 52 tasks out of 52 tasks. Therefore, 100% fairness is achieved.

Remark 6.1: In the above case, total number of AR tasks is $512 - 52 = 460$.

In contrary, if $RBE_{=} 0.3$ and $\tau = 0.2$ (i.e., [0.3, 0.2]) then total number of BE tasks is 154 (i.e., 0.3×512) and the satisfaction rate allows 103 tasks out of 154 tasks. Therefore, 66.88% fairness is achieved.

Remark 6.2: In the above case, total number of AR tasks is $512 - 154 = 358$.

Case A

In Case A, the comparison of cloud makespan for the existing and proposed algorithm is shown in Table 1 (512×16) and Table 2 (1024×32) respectively. For the sake of easy visualization, the graphical comparison of makespan is also shown in Figure 5 and Figure 6 respectively. Due to space limitation, we have shown the results when $R_{BE} = \tau$. The comparison results clearly show that 48 out of 48 instances

Table 1. Comparison of cloud makespan for existing and proposed algorithm in 512×16 benchmark datasets

Instances	Existing [0.1, 0.1]	Proposed [0.1, 0.1]	Existing [0.2, 0.2]	Proposed [0.2, 0.2]	Existing [0.3, 0.3]	Proposed [0.3, 0.3]	Existing [0.4, 0.4]	Proposed [0.4, 0.4]
u_c_hihi	1.1347e+07	1.1253e+07	1.1790e+07	1.1750e+07	1.1750e+07	1.1327e+07	1.1760e+07	1.1614e+07
u_c_hilo	1.8424e+05	1.8190e+05	1.8710e+05	1.8531e+05	1.8563e+05	1.8508e+05	1.8767e+05	1.8648e+05
u_c_lohi	3.8614e+05	3.8525e+05	3.8235e+05	3.7741e+05	3.8432e+05	3.7281e+05	3.8477e+05	3.7625e+05
u_c_lolo	6.2022e+03	6.1693e+03	6.2750e+03	6.2496e+03	6.3194e+03	6.1963e+03	6.3525e+03	6.2967e+03
u_i_hihi	4.2716e+06	4.1116e+06	4.1407e+06	4.1133e+06	4.1688e+06	4.1202e+06	4.1766e+06	4.1640e+06
u_i_hilo	9.3311e+04	9.2873e+04	9.7464e+04	9.3723e+04	9.4373e+04	9.3085e+04	9.6432e+04	9.6192e+04
u_i_lohi	1.5585e+05	1.4096e+05	1.5302e+05	1.4960e+05	1.6018e+05	1.5411e+05	1.5570e+05	1.5286e+05
u_i_lolo	3.1510e+03	3.1500e+03	3.2804e+03	3.1984e+03	3.2354e+03	3.2240e+03	3.2558e+03	3.2185e+03
u_s_hihi	6.4161e+06	6.2831e+06	6.4409e+06	6.2455e+06	6.1741e+06	6.1132e+06	6.6544e+06	6.5616e+06
u_s_hilo	1.2092e+05	1.2089e+05	1.2279e+05	1.2141e+05	1.2397e+05	1.2119e+05	1.2306e+05	1.2193e+05
u_s_lohi	1.8888e+05	1.8254e+05	1.8670e+05	1.7952e+05	1.9112e+05	1.8326e+05	1.9263e+05	1.8686e+05
u_s_lolo	4.4163e+03	4.3961e+03	4.4602e+03	4.2876e+03	4.4841e+03	4.4696e+03	4.4667e+03	4.3841e+03

Table 2. Comparison of cloud makespan for existing and proposed algorithm in 1024 × 32 benchmark datasets

Instances	Existing [0.1, 0.1]	Proposed [0.1, 0.1]	Existing [0.2, 0.2]	Proposed [0.2, 0.2]	Existing [0.3, 0.3]	Proposed [0.3, 0.3]	Existing [0.4, 0.4]	Proposed [0.4, 0.4]
u_c_hihi	3.2452e+07	3.2210e+07	3.2871e+07	3.2591e+07	3.2185e+07	3.2092e+07	3.2143e+07	3.1723e+07
u_c_hilo	3.2779e+06	3.1569e+06	3.2485e+06	3.2313e+06	3.3470e+06	3.3463e+06	3.2750e+06	3.2702e+06
u_c_lohi	3.0549e+03	3.0478e+03	3.0472e+03	3.0136e+03	3.0019e+03	2.9912e+03	3.0502e+03	2.9609e+03
u_c_lolo	3.3325e+02	3.3061e+02	3.1990e+02	3.1890e+02	3.2413e+02	3.2207e+02	3.3157e+02	3.2232e+02
u_i_hihi	7.9622e+06	7.7056e+06	8.3421e+06	8.0057e+06	8.2816e+06	7.6680e+06	7.5421e+06	7.3772e+06
u_i_hilo	7.1191e+05	7.0958e+05	7.2605e+05	7.0081e+05	7.4933e+05	7.3018e+05	7.0891e+05	6.7369e+05
u_i_lohi	8.1692e+02	7.8620e+02	7.5723e+02	7.3918e+02	7.6396e+02	7.4104e+02	7.7289e+02	7.6756e+02
u_i_lolo	7.5050e+01	7.4510e+01	7.5780e+01	7.2540e+01	7.5700e+01	7.4660e+01	7.5260e+01	7.2730e+01
u_s_hihi	2.0155e+07	1.9926e+07	1.9358e+07	1.8878e+07	1.9507e+07	1.8685e+07	1.8900e+07	1.8788e+07
u_s_hilo	1.8029e+06	1.7852e+06	1.8270e+06	1.8073e+06	1.8791e+06	1.8127e+06	1.7984e+06	1.7880e+06
u_s_lohi	1.8875e+03	1.8446e+03	1.9263e+03	1.8190e+03	1.8492e+03	1.8370e+03	1.9279e+03	1.8194e+03
u_s_lolo	1.9644e+02	1.9224e+02	1.9178e+02	1.8621e+02	1.8994e+02	1.8521e+02	1.9153e+02	1.8295e+02

Figure 5. Graphical comparison of cloud makespan for existing and proposed algorithm using 512 × 16 benchmark datasets

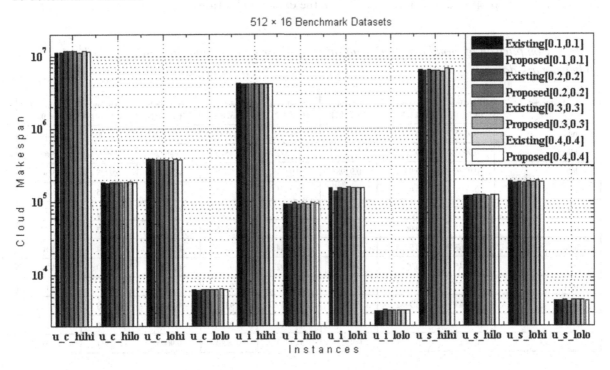

Figure 6. Graphical comparison of cloud makespan for existing and proposed algorithm using 1024 ×
32 benchmark datasets

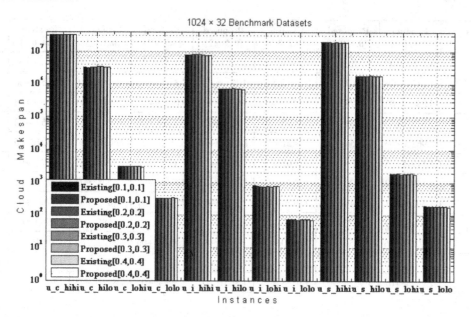

(i.e., 100%) in both 512 × 16 and 1024 × 32 dataset give better makespan for the proposed algorithm
FATA than the existing algorithm.

The average cloud utilization for the existing and proposed algorithm is shown in Table 3 (512 ×
16) and Table 4 (1024 × 32) respectively. It can be observed that 36 out of 48 instances (i.e., 77%) in
512 × 16 dataset and 47 out of 48 instances (i.e., 98%) in 1024 × 32 dataset give better average cloud
utilization for the proposed algorithm FATA than the existing algorithm.

Table 3. Comparison of cloud average cloud utilization for existing and proposed algorithm in 512 ×
16 benchmark datasets

Instances	Existing [0.1, 0.1]	Proposed [0.1, 0.1]	Existing [0.2, 0.2]	Proposed [0.2, 0.2]	Existing [0.3, 0.3]	Proposed [0.3, 0.3]	Existing [0.4, 0.4]	Proposed [0.4, 0.4]
u_c_hihi	0.9555	0.9682	0.9287	0.9458	0.9583	0.9682	0.9606	0.9499
u_c_hilo	0.9691	0.9812	0.9507	0.9572	0.9575	0.9627	0.9621	0.9635
u_c_lohi	0.9376	0.9409	0.9398	0.9431	0.9560	0.9443	0.9328	0.9308
u_c_lolo	0.9651	0.9815	0.9656	0.9681	0.9527	0.9500	0.9435	0.9480
u_i_hihi	0.9222	0.9528	0.9304	0.9356	0.9348	0.9414	0.9385	0.9567
u_i_hilo	0.9621	0.9626	0.9524	0.9700	0.9635	0.9673	0.9647	0.9494
u_i_lohi	0.9163	0.9725	0.9178	0.9284	0.9082	0.9096	0.9154	0.9108
u_i_lolo	0.9645	0.9704	0.9586	0.9702	0.9671	0.9641	0.9770	0.9774
u_s_hihi	0.9672	0.9515	0.9436	0.9460	0.9228	0.9387	0.9090	0.9157
u_s_hilo	0.9547	0.9482	0.9563	0.9539	0.9537	0.9630	0.9586	0.9512
u_s_lohi	0.9269	0.9530	0.9344	0.9620	0.9487	0.9592	0.9146	0.9196
u_s_lolo	0.9610	0.9741	0.9555	0.9782	0.9630	0.9600	0.9534	0.9588

Table 4. Comparison of cloud average cloud utilization for existing and proposed algorithm in 1024 × 32 benchmark datasets

Instances	Existing [0.1, 0.1]	Proposed [0.1, 0.1]	Existing [0.2, 0.2]	Proposed [0.2, 0.2]	Existing [0.3, 0.3]	Proposed [0.3, 0.3]	Existing [0.4, 0.4]	Proposed [0.4, 0.4]
u_c_hihi	0.9424	0.9523	0.9257	0.9423	0.9378	0.9548	0.9607	0.9605
u_c_hilo	0.9462	0.9519	0.9399	0.9492	0.9299	0.9388	0.9399	0.9412
u_c_lohi	0.9454	0.9557	0.9524	0.9546	0.9426	0.9525	0.9525	0.9573
u_c_lolo	0.9560	0.9576	0.9410	0.9475	0.9502	0.9514	0.9493	0.9512
u_i_hihi	0.8591	0.8714	0.8172	0.8673	0.8435	0.9031	0.9188	0.9209
u_i_hilo	0.9088	0.9180	0.9043	0.9377	0.8782	0.8949	0.9174	0.9452
u_i_lohi	0.8433	0.9027	0.9168	0.9177	0.9233	0.9318	0.9013	0.9154
u_i_lolo	0.9020	0.9093	0.8992	0.9378	0.8757	0.8919	0.8977	0.9127
u_s_hihi	0.8677	0.8877	0.9082	0.9144	0.9231	0.9429	0.9177	0.9287
u_s_hilo	0.9215	0.9364	0.9129	0.9386	0.8897	0.8980	0.9050	0.9177
u_s_lohi	0.9084	0.9368	0.9027	0.9317	0.9117	0.9366	0.8950	0.8995
u_s_lolo	0.8800	0.9226	0.8832	0.9170	0.9195	0.9235	0.9178	0.9299

Case B

In Case B, Table 5 (512 × 16) and Table 6 (1024 × 32) show the comparison of cloud makespan for the existing and proposed algorithm. The graphical comparison of makespan is shown in Figure 7 and Figure 8 respectively for clear visualization purpose. The comparison results clearly show that 24 out of 24 instances (i.e., 100%) in both 512 × 16 and 1024 × 32 dataset give better makespan for the proposed algorithm FATA than the existing algorithm.

Table 5. Comparison of cloud makespan for existing and proposed algorithm in 512 × 16 benchmark datasets

Instances	Existing [0.3, 0.2]	Proposed [0.3, 0.2]	Existing [0.4, 0.2]	Proposed [0.4, 0.2]
u_c_hihi	1.1819e+07	1.1521e+07	1.1511e+07	1.1336e+07
u_c_hilo	1.8898e+05	1.8435e+05	1.8728e+05	1.8665e+05
u_c_lohi	3.8808e+05	3.7888e+05	4.0516e+05	3.9415e+05
u_c_lolo	6.3097e+03	6.2886e+03	6.2648e+03	6.2171e+03
u_i_hihi	4.3432e+06	4.2537e+06	4.2883e+06	4.2359e+06
u_i_hilo	9.7849e+04	9.5784e+04	9.2697e+04	9.2687e+04
u_i_lohi	1.5064e+05	1.4730e+05	1.4944e+05	1.4385e+05
u_i_lolo	3.2220e+03	3.2029e+03	3.2215e+03	3.1866e+03
u_s_hihi	6.6271e+06	6.5701e+06	6.5899e+06	6.4990e+06
u_s_hilo	1.2230e+05	1.2170e+05	1.2346e+05	1.2340e+05
u_s_lohi	2.0907e+05	1.9719e+05	1.8838e+05	1.8612e+05
u_s_lolo	4.3697e+03	4.3572e+03	4.4532e+03	4.3995e+03

Table 6. Comparison of cloud makespan for existing and proposed algorithm in 1024 × 32 benchmark datasets

Instances	Existing [0.3, 0.2]	Proposed [0.3, 0.2]	Existing [0.4, 0.2]	Proposed [0.4, 0.2]
u_c_hihi	3.2445e+07	3.2027e+07	3.2783e+07	3.2525e+07
u_c_hilo	3.3183e+06	3.2838e+06	3.2782e+06	3.2239e+06
u_c_lohi	3.0691e+03	2.9792e+03	3.1229e+03	3.0424e+03
u_c_lolo	3.3197e+02	3.2980e+02	3.3098e+02	3.2900e+02
u_i_hihi	7.8985e+06	7.8826e+06	8.1518e+06	8.0209e+06
u_i_hilo	7.5650e+05	7.0475e+05	7.6862e+05	7.6385e+05
u_i_lohi	7.9159e+02	7.5884e+02	7.6396e+02	7.6359e+02
u_i_lolo	7.7060e+01	7.5020e+01	7.6590e+01	7.5120e+01
u_s_hihi	1.9253e+07	1.8823e+07	1.9660e+07	1.9454e+07
u_s_hilo	1.8182e+06	1.7820e+06	1.8225e+06	1.7847e+06
u_s_lohi	1.9061e+03	1.8144e+03	1.9204e+03	1.8692e+03
u_s_lolo	1.9641e+02	1.8887e+02	1.8754e+02	1.8492e+02

The average cloud utilization for the existing and proposed algorithm is shown in Table 7 (512 × 16) and Table 8 (1024 × 32) respectively. It can be observed that 16 out of 24 instances (i.e., 67%) in 512 × 16 and 15 out of 24 instances (i.e., 63%) in 1024 × 32 dataset give better average cloud utilization for the proposed algorithm FATA than the existing algorithm.

Figure 7. Graphical comparison of cloud makespan for existing and proposed algorithm using 512 × 16 benchmark datasets

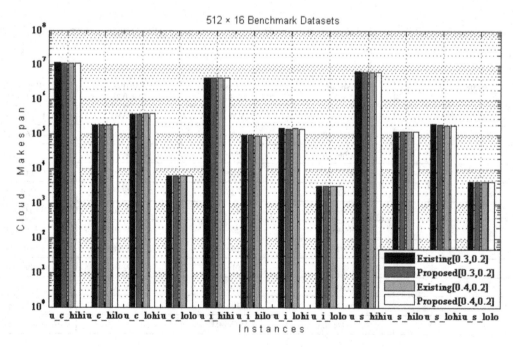

Figure 8. Graphical comparison of cloud makespan for existing and proposed algorithm using 1024 × 32 benchmark datasets

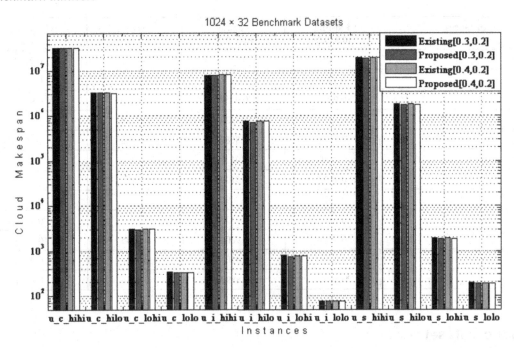

Table 7. Comparison of cloud average cloud utilization for existing and proposed algorithm in 512 × 16 benchmark datasets

Instances	Existing [0.3, 0.2]	Proposed [0.3, 0.2]	Existing [0.4, 0.2]	Proposed [0.4, 0.2]
u_c_hihi	0.9501	0.9503	0.9443	0.9602
u_c_hilo	0.9514	0.9607	0.9587	0.9624
u_c_lohi	0.9308	0.9411	0.9106	0.9186
u_c_lolo	0.9589	0.9615	0.9727	0.9686
u_i_hihi	0.9510	0.9583	0.9412	0.9328
u_i_hilo	0.9475	0.9780	0.9735	0.9720
u_i_lohi	0.9259	0.9251	0.9165	0.9441
u_i_lolo	0.9647	0.9645	0.9663	0.9614
u_s_hihi	0.9228	0.9286	0.9348	0.9369
u_s_hilo	0.9592	0.9610	0.9489	0.9422
u_s_lohi	0.8865	0.8974	0.9364	0.9370
u_s_lolo	0.9645	0.9605	0.9475	0.9570

Table 8. Comparison of average cloud utilization for existing and proposed algorithm in 1024 × 32 benchmark datasets

Instances	Existing [0.3, 0.2]	Proposed [0.3, 0.2]	Existing [0.4, 0.2]	Proposed [0.4, 0.2]
u_c_hihi	0.9497	0.9546	0.9663	0.9642
u_c_hilo	0.9373	0.9321	0.9511	0.9523
u_c_lohi	0.9383	0.9459	0.9314	0.9324
u_c_lolo	0.9326	0.9324	0.9435	0.9405
u_i_hihi	0.8777	0.8687	0.8702	0.8645
u_i_hilo	0.8730	0.9118	0.8355	0.8283
u_i_lohi	0.9092	0.9129	0.8927	0.9078
u_i_lolo	0.9019	0.9090	0.8677	0.8950
u_s_hihi	0.9217	0.9235	0.9181	0.9147
u_s_hilo	0.9081	0.9202	0.9345	0.9425
u_s_lohi	0.9147	0.9201	0.9027	0.9068
u_s_lolo	0.8995	0.8897	0.9136	0.9221

Synthetic Dataset

In this simulation, we used a dataset consisting of ten instances. These instances are generated using uniform distributed pseudorandom integer function randi() by MATLAB R2014a. The function takes four arguments, namely l, m, $imin$ and $imax$ as input and returns a 2-D array of size $[l, m]$ on the given interval $[imin, imax]$. For each instance (say 100 × 4), the first value (i.e., 100) denotes the number of tasks (l) and second value (i.e., 4) denotes the number of clouds (m).

Case A

The comparison of cloud makespan for the existing and proposed algorithm is shown in Table 9. For the sake of easy visualization, the graphical comparison is also shown in Figure 9. It is obvious to see that for all instances, the proposed FATA results better makespan than the existing algorithm. Alternatively, 40 out of 40 instances (i.e., 100%) give better makespan for the proposed algorithm.

The average cloud utilization for the existing and proposed algorithm is shown in Table 10. It is clearly shown that 39 out of 40 instances (i.e., 98%) give better average cloud utilization for the proposed algorithm than the existing algorithm.

Case B

In this case, the comparison of cloud makespan and average cloud utilization is shown in Table 11 and Table 12 respectively. The graphical comparison of cloud makespan is also shown in Figure 10. This time also for 20 out of 20 instances (i.e., 100%) in synthetic dataset produces better cloud makespan and 18 out of 20 instances (i.e., 90%) in average cloud utilization for the proposed algorithm than the exiting algorithm.

Table 9. Comparison of cloud makespan for existing and proposed algorithm in synthetic datasets

Instances	Existing [0.1, 0.1]	Proposed [0.1, 0.1]	Existing [0.2, 0.2]	Proposed [0.2, 0.2]	Existing [0.3, 0.3]	Proposed [0.3, 0.3]	Existing [0.4, 0.4]	Proposed [0.4, 0.4]
100×4	22362	21096	21957	20212	21633	21056	22062	21725
200×8	20367	20252	21353	20833	20432	20103	20621	20364
300×12	17108	16242	16946	16483	16425	15986	17161	16402
400×16	19788	19447	20342	20193	20036	20000	20348	19900
500×20	20425	20131	20091	20037	20110	19816	20240	19844
600×24	19843	19751	19757	19667	19440	19420	19921	19751
700×28	19869	19532	20020	19837	19323	19183	20495	20180
800×32	19816	19806	19882	19692	19647	19383	19519	19185
900×36	19796	19508	19756	19583	19554	19545	20120	20037
1000×40	20225	20187	19852	19836	19754	19534	19716	19516

Figure 9. Graphical comparison of cloud makespan for existing and proposed algorithm using synthetic dataset

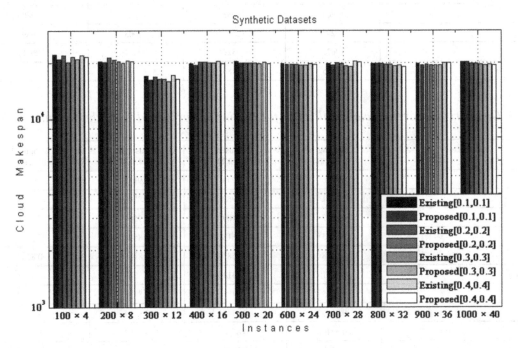

Table 10. Comparison of cloud makespan for existing and proposed algorithm in synthetic dataset

Instances	Existing [0.1, 0.1]	Proposed [0.1, 0.1]	Existing [0.2, 0.2]	Proposed [0.2, 0.2]	Existing [0.3, 0.3]	Proposed [0.3, 0.3]	Existing [0.4, 0.4]	Proposed [0.4, 0.4]
100 × 4	0.8510	0.9036	0.8631	0.9413	0.8785	0.9007	0.8615	0.8739
200 × 8	0.8670	0.8717	0.8250	0.8473	0.8619	0.8823	0.8585	0.8653
300 × 12	0.9289	0.9536	0.9501	0.9668	0.9381	0.9453	0.9420	0.9193
400 × 16	0.8552	0.8735	0.8318	0.8400	0.8432	0.8467	0.8313	0.8518
500 × 20	0.8197	0.8316	0.8342	0.8368	0.8322	0.8454	0.8285	0.8434
600 × 24	0.8365	0.8443	0.8412	0.8479	0.8557	0.8568	0.8341	0.8422
700 × 28	0.8320	0.8482	0.8254	0.8334	0.8559	0.8633	0.8081	0.8199
800 × 32	0.8302	0.8325	0.8285	0.8354	0.8373	0.8496	0.8443	0.8572
900 × 36	0.8283	0.8418	0.8311	0.8393	0.8393	0.8407	0.8168	0.8203
1000 × 40	0.8079	0.8104	0.8232	0.8255	0.8285	0.8383	0.8297	0.8379

Table 11. Comparison of cloud average cloud utilization for existing and proposed algorithm in synthetic dataset

Instances	Existing [0.3, 0.2]	Proposed [0.3, 0.2]	Existing [0.4, 0.2]	Proposed [0.4, 0.2]
100 × 4	19944	19477	20892	20508
200 × 8	20873	19759	20617	20263
300 × 12	17502	16506	17178	16560
400 × 16	20165	19630	19691	19535
500 × 20	20118	19521	20495	20387
600 × 24	20387	19973	20085	19818
700 × 28	19907	19533	19822	19806
800 × 32	20205	19736	19603	19597
900 × 36	19671	19529	20145	20111
1000 × 40	19725	19280	19597	19574

Table 12. Comparison of average cloud utilization for existing and proposed algorithm in synthetic dataset

Instances	Existing [0.3, 0.2]	Proposed [0.3, 0.2]	Existing [0.4, 0.2]	Proposed [0.4, 0.2]
100 × 4	0.9516	0.9744	0.9151	0.9299
200 × 8	0.8461	0.8962	0.8566	0.8728
300 × 12	0.9512	0.9409	0.9500	0.9478
400 × 16	0.8395	0.8613	0.8599	0.8696
500 × 20	0.8318	0.8583	0.8166	0.8223
600 × 24	0.8171	0.8318	0.8282	0.8391
700 × 28	0.8315	0.8481	0.8350	0.8365
800 × 32	0.8156	0.8345	0.8399	0.8419
900 × 36	0.8346	0.8400	0.8162	0.8169
1000 × 40	0.8299	0.8499	0.8347	0.8363

Figure 10. Graphical comparison of cloud makespan for existing and proposed algorithm using synthetic dataset

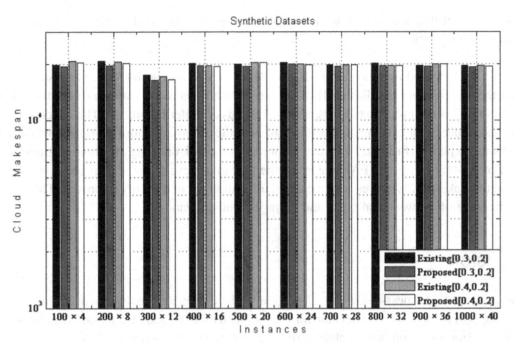

Figure 11. Task ordering for existing and proposed algorithm

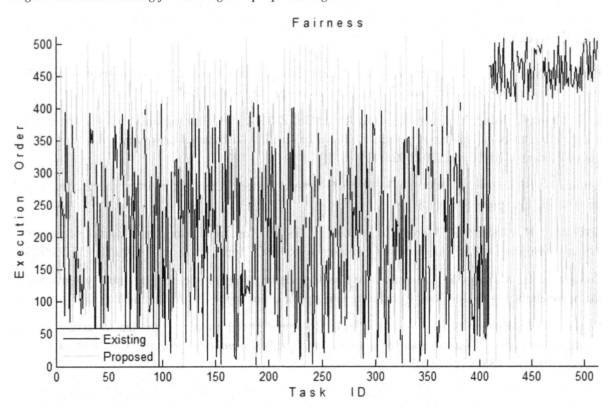

Discussion

The proposed algorithm achieves better cloud makespan, average cloud utilization and fairness. This is due to the following facts.

- Fairness is achieved by scheduling AR and BE tasks in a regular interval. For instance, assume that the total number of AR and BE tasks are 409 and 103 respectively. The existing algorithm orders the 409 AR tasks first followed by 103 BE tasks (Refer Figure 11). The red color indicates the task ordering of existing algorithm. However, the proposed algorithm schedules AR and BE tasks in a repetitive fashion. The green color shows the task ordering of proposed algorithm.
- Unlike existing algorithm, FATA reorders the task to achieve fairness. This reordering may lead to better makespan. However, average cloud utilization not necessarily improved. This is because of the trade-off between makespan and average cloud utilization.

CONCLUSION

We have presented a fairness-aware task allocation for heterogeneous multi-cloud systems. The algorithm is shown to run in $O(j \times (k + l))$ time for j iterations with k AR and l BE tasks. We have performed rigorous experimentation on two benchmark datasets and one synthetic dataset. The comparison results have clearly shown that the proposed algorithm outperforms the existing algorithm in terms of cloud makespan, average cloud utilization and fairness.

REFERENCES

Forell, T., Milojicic, D., & Talwar, V. (2011). Cloud management challenges and opportunities. In *IEEE International Symposium on Parallel and Distributed*. (pp. 881-889). IEEE.

Li, J., Qiu, M., Ming, Z., Quan, G., Qin, X., & Gu, Z. (2012). Online optimization for scheduling preemptable tasks on IaaS cloud systems. *Journal of Parallel Distributed Computing, Elsevier, 72*(5), 666–677. doi:10.1016/j.jpdc.2012.02.002

Sotomayor, B., Keahey, K., & Foster, I. (2006). Overhead matters: A model for virtual resource management. IEEE Computer Society, 1-8.

Sotomayor, B., Montero, R., Llorente, I., & Foster, I. (2009). Resource leasing and the art of suspending virtual machines. In *IEEE International Conference on HPCC* (pp. 1–9). doi:10.1109/HPCC.2009.17

Sotomayor, B., Montero, R., Llorente, I., & Foster, I. (2008). Capacity leasing in cloud systems using the opennebula engine. In Cloud Computing and Applications (pp. 1–5). Academic Press.

Sotomayor, B., Keahey, K., & Foster, I. (2008). Combining batch execution and leasing using virtual machines. In *17th ACM International Symposium on High Performance Distributed Computing* (pp. 87-96). doi:10.1145/1383422.1383434

Shrivastava, V., & Bhilare, D. (2012). Algorithms to improve resource utilization and request acceptance rate in iaas cloud scheduling. *International Journal of Advanced Networking and Applications*, *3*(5), 1367–1374.

Chen, H., Wang, F., Helian, N., & Akanmu, G. (2013). User-priority guided min-min scheduling algorithm for load balancing in cloud computing. In *National Conference on Parallel Computing Technologies* (pp. 1-8). Academic Press.

Panda, S., & Jana, P. (2014). An efficient task scheduling algorithm for heterogeneous multi-cloud environment. In *3ʳᵈ IEEE International Conference on Advances in Computing, Communications & Informatics* (pp. 1204-1209). doi:10.1109/ICACCI.2014.6968253

Panda, S., Nag, S., & Jana, P. (2014). A smoothing based task scheduling algorithm for heterogeneous multi-cloud environment. In *3rd IEEE International Conference on Parallel, Distributed and Grid Computing*. IEEE.

Nathani, A., Chaudhary, S. & Somani, G. (2102). Policy based resource allocation in IAAS cloud. *Future Generation Computer Systems, 28*, 94-103. doi:10.1109/PDGC.2014.7030716

Ming, G., & Li, H. (2012). An improved algorithm based on max-min for cloud task scheduling. In Recent Advances in Computer Science and Information Engineering, Lecture Notes in Electrical Engineering, 125 (pp. 217-223). doi:10.1007/978-3-642-25789-6_32

Braun. (n.d.). Retrieved from https://code.google.com/p/hcsp-chc/source/browse/trunk/AE/ProblemInstances/ HCSP/Braun_et_al/u_c_hihi.0?r=93

Haizea. (n.d.). Retrieved from http://haizea.cs.uchicago.edu/whatis.html

Rimal, B., Choi, E., & Lumb, I. (2009). A taxonomy and survey of cloud computing systems. In *International Joint Conference on INC, IMS and IDC* (pp. 44-51). doi:10.1109/NCM.2009.218

Buyya, R., Yeo, C., Venugopal, S., Broberg, J., & Brandic, I. (2009). Cloud computing and emerging it platforms: Vision, hype and reality for delivering computing as the 5ᵗʰ utility. *Future Generation Computer Systems*, *25*(6), 599–616. doi:10.1016/j.future.2008.12.001

Desmarais, R. (2013). *Adaptive solutions to resource provisioning and task allocation problems for cloud computing*. (Ph. D. Thesis). University of Victoria.

Huang, C., Guan, C., Chen, H., Wang, Y., Chang, S., Li, C., & Weng, C. (2013). An adaptive resource management scheme in cloud computing. *Engineering Applications of Artificial Intelligence, Elsevier*, *26*(1), 382–389. doi:10.1016/j.engappai.2012.10.004

Beloglazov, A., Abawajy, J., & Buyya, R. (2012). Energy-aware resource allocation heuristics for efficient management of data centers for cloud computing. *Future Generation Computer Systems, Elsevier*, *28*(5), 755–768. doi:10.1016/j.future.2011.04.017

Maheswaran, M., Ali, S., Siegel, H., Hensgen, D., & Freund, R. (1999). Dynamic mapping of a class of independent tasks onto heterogeneous computing systems. *Journal of Parallel and Distributed Computing*, *59*(2), 107–131. doi:10.1006/jpdc.1999.1581

Xu, Y., Hu, H., & Yihe, S. (2010). Data dependence graph directed scheduling for clustered vliw architectures. *Tsinghua Science and Technology, IEEE, 15*(3), 299–306. doi:10.1016/S1007-0214(10)70065-1

Xhafa, F., Barolli, L., & Durresi, A. (2007). Batch mode scheduling in grid systems. *International Journal Web and Grid Services, 3*(1), 19–37. doi:10.1504/IJWGS.2007.012635

Xhafa, F., Barolli, L., & Durresi, A. (2007). Immediate mode scheduling in grid systems. *International Journal Web and Grid Services, 3*(2), 219–236. doi:10.1504/IJWGS.2007.014075

Panda, S., Agrawal, P., Khilar, P., & Mohapatra, D. (2014). Skewness-based min-min max-min heuristic for grid task scheduling. In *4ᵗʰ IEEE International Conference on Advanced Computing and Communication Technologies* (pp. 282-289). IEEE.

Braun, T., Siegel, H., Beck, N., Boloni, L., Maheswaran, M., Reuther, A., & Freund, R. et al. (2001). A comparison of eleven static heuristics for mapping a class of independent tasks onto heterogeneous distributed computing systems. *Journal of Parallel and Distributed Computing, 61*(6), 810–837. doi:10.1006/jpdc.2000.1714

Bajaj, R., & Agrawal, D. (2004). Improving scheduling of tasks in a heterogeneous environment. *IEEE Transactions on Parallel and Distributed Systems, 15*(2), 107–118. doi:10.1109/TPDS.2004.1264795

Wang, S., Yan, K., Liao, W., & Wang, S. (2010). Towards a load balancing in a three-level cloud computing network. In *3ʳᵈ IEEE International Conference on Computer Science and Information Technology* (pp. 108-113). IEEE.

KEY TERMS AND DEFINITIONS

Advance Reservation: A kind of lease where the start and execution times are fixed.

Average Cloud Utilization: The average utilization of all clouds.

Benchmark Dataset: The dataset is generated by some standard rules.

Best Effort: A kind of lease where resources are provided as soon as possible basis.

Cloud Computing: The recent innovation in computing that provides on demand services to the customers over the Internet.

Cloud Service Provider: A company that offers computational resources, storage, memory and/or software as a service to the customers.

Makespan: The overall processing time needed to execute all the tasks.

Synthetic Dataset: The dataset is generated by any random function without following any specific rules.

Task Scheduling: The assignment of customers' tasks to the available clouds.

Chapter 12
Submesh Allocation in 3D Mesh Multicomputers Using Free Lists:
A Corner–Boundary Approach with Complete Recognition Capability

Saad Bani-Mohammad
Prince Hussein Bin Abdullah College for Information Technology, Al al-Bayt University, Jordan

Ismail Ababneh
Prince Hussein Bin Abdullah College for Information Technology, Al al-Bayt University, Jordan

Motasem Al Smadi
Prince Hussein Bin Abdullah College for Information Technology, Al al-Bayt University, Jordan

ABSTRACT

This chapter presents an extensive evaluation of a new contiguous allocation strategy proposed for 3D mesh multicomputers. The strategy maintains a list of maximal free sub-meshes and gives priority to allocating corner and boundary free sub-meshes. This strategy, which we refer to as Turning Corner-Boundary Free List (TCBFL) strategy, is compared, using extensive simulation experiments, to several existing allocation strategies for 3D meshes. In addition to allocation strategies, two job scheduling schemes, First-Come-First-Served (FCFS) and Shortest-Service-Demand (SSD) are considered in comparing the performance of the allocation strategies. The simulation results show that TCBFL produces average turnaround times and mean system utilization values that are superior to those of the existing allocation strategies. The results also reveal that SSD scheduling is much better than FCFS scheduling. Thus, the scheduling and allocation strategies both have substantial effect on the performance of contiguous allocation strategies in 3D mesh-connected multicomputers.

DOI: 10.4018/978-1-4666-8676-2.ch012

Copyright © 2015, IGI Global. Copying or distributing in print or electronic forms without written permission of IGI Global is prohibited.

1. INTRODUCTION

Mesh interconnection networks have been extensively employed in large-scale multicomputers due to their structural regularity, simplicity, ease of implementation and scalability (Ababneh, 2001; Bani-Mohammad, Ould-Khaoua, Ababneh, & Machenzie, 2006; Bani-Mohammad, Ould-Khaoua, Ababneh, & Machenzie, 2009; Bani-Mohammad & Ababneh, 2013; Foster, 1995; Kumar, Grama, Gupta, & Karypis 2003; Lo, Windisch, Liu, & Nitzberg, 1997; Seo & Kim, 2003; Zhu, 1992).

Effective processor allocation and job scheduling are critical if the full computational power of multicomputers is to be exploited properly (Choo, Yoo, & Youn, 2000; Yoo & Das, 2002). Processor allocation is responsible for determining the set of processors on which a parallel job is executed, whereas job scheduling is responsible for selecting the order in which jobs are selected for execution (Choo et al., 2000; De Rose, Heiss, & Linnert, 2007; Yoo & Das, 2002). The job scheduler selects the next job to execute, and then the processor allocator assigns free processors for executing the selected job (Choo et al., 2000; Windisch, 1997).

In mesh multicomputers, a parallel job is typically allocated a distinct contiguous sub-mesh for the duration of its execution, and the sub-mesh has the same general shape as the mesh multicomputer itself. Most contiguous processor allocation strategies proposed in the literature are for 2D meshes (Ababneh, 2009; Chuang & Tzeng, 1994; Kim & Yoon, 1998; Zhu, 1992). Although the 2D mesh has been used in a number of parallel machines, such as the Cray XE6m (Cray, 2010b), the iWARP (Peterson, Sutton, & Wiley, 1991) and the Touchstone Delta system (Intel, 1991), current multicomputers, such as the K-computer (Riken & Fujitsu, 2014), the Cray XE6 (Cray, 2010a) and the IBM BlueGene/L (Horn et al., 2014) utilize the 3D mesh or the 3D tori (Cray, 2010a; Horn et al., 2014; Riken & Fujitsu, 2014) as interconnection network due to their lower diameter, lower average communication distance, and higher connectivity and network degree (Athas & Seitz, 1988).

Contiguous allocation can lead to high external processor fragmentation, which occurs when the allocation strategy cannot allocate available processors to an incoming job because the available processors are not contiguous or they do not have the requested shape. Non-contiguous allocation can reduce processor fragmentation and improve system performance because a job can execute on multiple smaller sub-meshes. However, contiguous allocation is used in highly-parallel systems such as the IBM BlueGene/L because it isolates jobs from each other, which is useful for security and accounting reasons (Aridor, Domany, Goldshmidt, Moreira, & Shmueli 2005). Contiguous allocation for 3D meshes has been investigated in the literature (Ababneh, 2001; Bani-Mohammad et al., 2006; Bani-Mohammad et al., 2009; Choo et al., 2000; Mao, Chen, & Watson, 2005; Qiao & Ni, 1995).

Any allocation strategy must have good system performance. System performance is typically measured using overall performance parameters, such as the average job turnaround time and mean system utilization, where the job turnaround time is the time that the job spends in the system from arrival to departure, and system utilization is the percentage of processors that are utilized over time. A common issue with the few existing contiguous allocation strategies for 3D meshes (Ababneh, 2001; Bani-Mohammad et al., 2006; Bani-Mohammad et al., 2009) is that they have high processor fragmentation, which leads to low system performance. Performance of contiguous allocation is expected to improve if jobs are allocated corner sub-meshes or sub-meshes that are located on the periphery of the multicomputer. Giving priority to corner and boundary placements has for goal reducing processor fragmentation by leaving larger free sub-meshes for future allocation. Recently, we have proposed a contiguous allocation strategy for 3D mesh-connected multicomputers (Ababneh, Bani-Mohammad, & Al Smadi, 2015). This strategy gives priority to allocating a corner or peripheral sub-mesh. An internal sub-mesh is allocated only when no corner or boundary sub-mesh can accommodate the current request.

In evaluating this allocation strategy, we compare its performance with that of First-Fit Free List (FFFL), Turning First-Fit Free List (TFFFL) and Turning Busy List (TBL) for the scheduling strategies FCFS and SSD. In FCFS scheduling, the allocation request that arrived first is considered for allocation first. Allocation attempts stop when they fail for this request, while in SSD scheduling, the job with the shortest service demand is scheduled first.

Simulation results show that the new allocation strategy produces superior average turnaround times and mean system utilization as compared to previous allocation strategies. The results also reveal that the SSD scheduling strategy is much better than the FCFS scheduling strategy. That is, the scheduling and allocation strategies both have substantial effect on the performance of contiguous allocation strategies in 3D meshes.

The rest of the chapter is organized as follows: Section 2 presents preliminaries. Section 3 contains a brief summary of well-known contiguous allocation strategies proposed previously for the 3D mesh. Section 4 presents the TCBFL strategy. Section 5 contains a brief overview of the scheduling strategies considered. Simulation results are presented in Section 6. Finally, conclusions and future directions are given in Section 7.

2. PRELIMINARIES

The target system in this research is the 3D mesh-connected multicomputer. The target multicomputer's interconnection network is referred to as $M(W, D, H)$, where W is the width of the mesh, D is its depth and H is its height. Each processor is denoted by a coordinate triple (x, y, z), where $1 \leq x \leq W$, $1 \leq y \leq D$ and $1 \leq z \leq H$. A processor is connected by bidirectional communication links to its neighbour processors, as depicted in Figure 1. An internal node is directly connected to six neighbours. The eight mesh corner nodes have three neighbours each, mesh edge nodes have four neighbours each, and the remaining boundary nodes have five neighbours each. The size of the mesh, N, is the number of processors it has, where $N = W \times D \times H$.

Definition 1: A $w \times d \times h$ sub-mesh S in $M(W, D, H)$ is represented by $((x_b, y_b, z_b), (x_e, y_e, z_e))$, where (x_b, y_b, z_b) is the base (front lower-left corner) of S, (x_e, y_e, z_e) is its end (rear upper-right corner), $w = x_e - x_b + 1$, $d = y_e - y_b + 1$, $h = z_e - z_b + 1$, $1 \leq w \leq W$, $1 \leq d \leq D$ and $1 \leq h \leq H$.

Definition 2: A sub-mesh is free if all its processors are unallocated.

Example 1: In Figure 1, $((2, 1, 1), (3, 3, 2))$ represents the free 2×3×2 sub-mesh $S1$, where $(2, 1, 1)$ is the base node of $S1$ and $(3, 3, 2)$ is its end node.

Definition 3: A sub-mesh is busy if all its processors are allocated.

Example 2: In Figure 1, $((1, 1, 1), (1, 2, 1))$ represents the busy 1×2×1 sub-mesh.

Definition 4: A maximal free sub-mesh is a free sub-mesh that is not a proper subset of any other free sub-mesh.

Example 3: The maximal free sub-meshes in Figure 1 are $((2, 1, 1), (3, 3, 2))$, $((1, 1, 2), (3, 3, 2))$ and $((1, 3, 1), (3, 3, 2))$.

Figure 1. An example of a 3×3×2 3D mesh.

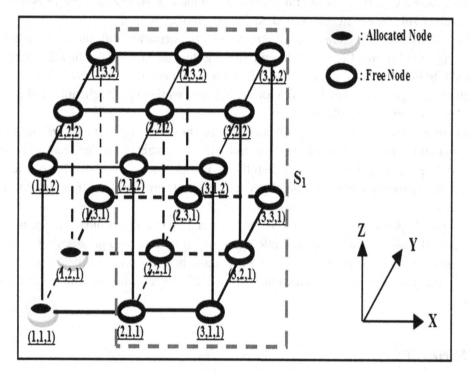

3. CONTIGUOUS ALLOCATION STRATEGIES

This section provides a brief overview of recent contiguous allocation strategies that have been proposed and investigated for 2D and 3D mesh-connected multicomputers (Ababneh, 2001; Ababneh, 2009; Bani-Mohammad et al., 2006; Qiao & Ni, 1995).

Maximal Peripheral Length (MPL) Strategy for 2D Meshes

This strategy (Ababneh, 2009) gives priority to allocating a sub-mesh with the largest number of processors located on the periphery of the 2D mesh multicomputer. This aims to decrease the number of sub-meshes that remain free after allocation, which is expected to increase their sizes and increase the probability of successful future allocation. For allocation, MPL uses a maximal free list that contains the maximal free sub-meshes. The simulation results in (Ababneh, 2009) show that MPL can improve system performance substantially.

First Fit (FF) and Best Fit (BF) for 3D Meshes

In these strategies (Ababneh, 2001), the free sub-meshes are scanned and FF allocates the first sub-mesh that is large enough for the job, whereas BF allocates the smallest such sub-mesh. Simulation results show that these strategies have comparable system performance; the performance of FF is close to that of BF. Therefore, we only consider the FF strategy for comparison in this research. The strategies FF and BF are not recognition-complete; an allocation request can be allocated only if there is a large enough sub-mesh with the same orientation $(\alpha \times \beta \times \gamma)$ as the allocation request, where α, β and γ are the width, depth and height of the job request.

Turning First Fit (TFF) for 3D Meshes

The problem of missing an existing possible allocation explained above is solved using TFF (Ababneh, 2001). The TFF strategy supports the rotation of the job request. It considers all orientations of the request, when needed. Let $(\alpha \times \beta \times \gamma)$ be the width, height and depth of a sub-mesh allocation request. The six permutations $(\alpha \times \beta \times \gamma)$, $(\alpha \times \gamma \times \beta)$, $(\beta \times \alpha \times \gamma)$, $(\beta \times \gamma \times \alpha)$, $(\gamma \times \alpha \times \beta)$ and $(\gamma \times \beta \times \alpha)$ are considered for allocation. If allocation succeeds for any of these permutations the process stops. For example, assume a free mesh (4×3×2) and the job requests (1, 3, 2), (2, 3, 2) and (3, 2, 1) arrive in this order. The third job request cannot be accommodated until it is changed to (1, 3, 2), as can be seen in Figure 2. Simulation results show that TFF can greatly improve performance in terms of average turnaround time and mean system utilization.

Busy List (BL) and Turning Busy List (TBL) for 3D Meshes

In these two strategies (Bani-Mohammad et al., 2006; Bani-Mohammad et al., 2009), allocation is based on maintaining a busy list of allocated sub-meshes (i.e., a list of all sub-meshes that are currently allocated to jobs). For accommodating a request, the list is scanned to determine all prohibited regions, where a prohibited region is a region consisting of nodes that cannot be used as base nodes for sub-meshes that can satisfy the request. TBL can identify a free sub-mesh of the requested size as long as it exists in

Figure 2. Allocation with switching to requests (1, 3, 2), (2, 3, 2), and (3, 2, 1).

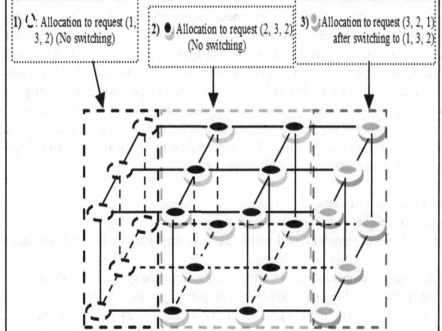

the mesh system. Simulation results show that the performance of TBL is at least as good as that of the promising strategies proposed previously in terms of average turnaround time and mean system utilization. Moreover, the allocation time of TBL is much lower than that of the previous strategies.

Turning First-Fit Free List Allocation Strategy (TFFFL)

This strategy (Qiao & Ni, 1995), proposed for 3D tori, is a first-fit strategy that uses a maximal free list and supports changing the orientation of request, when needed. The simulation results show that switching request orientation improves performance for 3D tori.

System utilization for all previous strategies proposed for 3D meshes and tori is low, and it is expected that it can be improved in 3D meshes by considering allocation in mesh corners and along mesh sides. Such principle is often used in placing furniture in rooms and offices.

4. TCBFL STRATEGY

In this strategy (Ababneh et al., 2015), the maximal free sub-meshes are determined after each allocation and de-allocation operation, and they are stored in an unordered maximal free list (*MFL*). Initially, *MFL* consists of the whole mesh system. For allocation, the *MFL* is scanned and a free sub-mesh that can accommodate the request in its initial orientation or any switched orientation is considered an allocation candidate. TCBFL gives priority to allocating a sub-mesh that is located at a corner of the mesh target system. When a mesh corner sub-mesh is subtracted from the whole system the number of leftover maximal free sub-meshes is two or three. This number is three, four or five for a peripheral non-corner (boundary) allocation, but it is six when the allocation is internal. When the number of free sub-meshes that results after an allocation operation is reduced, the size of these free sub-meshes will be increased overall. This increases the probability of successful future job allocation and improves system performance.

If an allocation candidate contains a single mesh corner, the request is placed in that corner, but if it contains multiple mesh corners, they are considered in the following order: front left-lower, rear left-lower, front left-upper, rear left-upper, front right-lower, rear right-lower, front right-upper, and rear right-upper. In all cases, the search process terminates when a mesh corner placement is found. If a mesh corner placement is not possible and there exists one or more non-corner peripheral allocation candidates, the first peripheral placement found is assigned to the request. Finally, allocation takes place in the front left-lower corner of the first candidate sub-mesh in *MFL* when all allocation candidates are internal sub-meshes. Allocation in TCBFL is implemented by the algorithm shown in Figure 3. In summary, TCBFL allocates sub-meshes in the following order:

1. The first mesh corner placement.
2. The first placement that is aligned with a mesh side.
3. The front left-lower placement found within the first large-enough internal free sub-mesh.

For example, to show the operation of TCBFL, let us assume the system state shown in Figure 4 and a request to allocate a 3×1×1 sub-mesh. The *MFL* corresponding to this state can consist of the following sub-meshes {((2, 2, 1),(3, 2, 2)), ((2, 1, 1),(2, 3, 2)), ((2, 1, 2),(3, 3, 2))}. The sub-mesh ((2, 2, 1),(3, 2, 2)) is not an allocation candidate because it is unable to accommodate the request in any of its orienta-

Figure 3. Outline of the TCBFL Contiguous Allocation Strategy.

Procedure *TCBFL_Allocate* (α, β, γ) {/* Allocation request for an $\alpha \times \beta \times \gamma$ sub-mesh. */

1. **if** (*free_pes* < $\alpha\beta\gamma$) /* *free_pes* is the number of free processors */
   return Failure;

2. *bd* = -1; /* used for reducing the number of searches, while giving priority to corner and peripheral placement */

3. **for** each free sub-mesh F_i ($w \times d \times h$) in *MFL* do {

4.   **if** ($wdh = \alpha\beta\gamma$) {

5.   **if** ($w=\alpha$ and $d=\beta$ and $h=\gamma$) or ($w=\alpha$ and $d=\gamma$ and $h=\beta$) or ($w=\beta$ and $d=\alpha$ and $h=\gamma$) or ($w=\beta$ and $d=\gamma$ and $h=\alpha$) or ($w=\gamma$ and $d=\alpha$ and $h=\beta$) or ($w=\gamma$ and $d=\beta$ and $h=\alpha$){ /* all rotations of $\alpha \times \beta \times \gamma$ at F_i */

6.   **if** F_i has a front left-lower, rear left-lower, front left-upper, rear left-upper, front right-lower, rear right-lower, front right upper, or rear right-upper mesh corner {
   allocate a corner sub-mesh to the request in the correct orientation, rebuild *MFL*, update *free_pes*, and return Success;
   }

7.   **else if** ($bd < 1$){
   if F_i has a side aligned with the left mesh side select allocation candidate *alloc_sub* at the front lower-left corner of F_i
   else if F_i is on the right side of the mesh select allocation candidate *alloc_sub* at the front lower-right corner of F_i
   else if F_i is at the bottom of the mesh select allocation candidate *alloc_sub* at the front lower-left corner of F_i
   else if F_i is on the top side of the mesh select allocation candidate alloc_sub at the front left-upper corner of F_i
   else if F_i is on the front side of the mesh select allocation candidate *alloc_sub* at the front lower-left corner of F_i
   else if F_i is on the rear side of the mesh select allocation candidate *alloc_sub* at the rear left-lower corner of F_i
   bd = 1;
   }

8.   **else if** ($bd < 0$) {/*here, F_i is an internal node*/
   select allocation candidate *alloc_sub* at the front left-lower corner of F_i;
   bd = 0;
   }
   }
   }
   } /* end for loop */

9. **if** ($bd = 0$) allocate *alloc_sub* to request in the correct orientation, rebuild *MFL*, update *free_pes*, and return Success;
   else
   return Failure;

}

Figure 4. An allocation example.

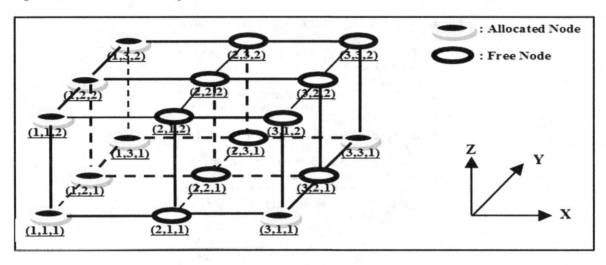

tions. The next free sub-mesh ((2, 1, 1), (2, 3, 2)) is an allocation candidate that has a side aligned with a mesh side. The sub-mesh ((2, 1, 1), (2, 3, 1)) is an allocation candidate after switching the request to 1×3×1. Finally, ((2, 1, 2), (3, 3, 2)) is a candidate sub-mesh with a mesh corner placement ((3, 1, 2), (3, 3, 2)) for the request in its 1×3×1 orientation. Even if there were other free sub-meshes, the allocation process would terminate here because a corner placement has been found for the request. After this allocation, *MFL* can be {((2, 1, 1), (2, 3, 2)), ((2, 2, 1), (3, 2, 1))}.

After each allocation, the allocated sub-mesh is added to the head of a busy-list. Upon de-allocation, the released sub-mesh is removed from the busy-list and *MFL* is rebuilt. The algorithm that builds *MFL* is a 3D variant of the algorithm proposed in (Kim & Yoon, 1998) for building the *MFL* in 2D meshes.

Free-List Construction

Several algorithms have been proposed for building the free-list in 2D mesh multicomputers. In (Kim & Yoon, 1998), allocation and de-allocation algorithms that use sub-mesh subtraction for finding all maximal free sub-meshes were proposed. The time complexities of these algorithms are in $O(f^2)$ and $O(b^3)$, respectively, where f is the number of free sub-meshes and b the number of busy (allocated) sub-meshes. In what follows, we present the time complexities obtained with a 3D free-list construction algorithm based on that proposed for 2D meshes in (Kim & Yoon, 1998). This construction algorithm is recognition-complete; that is, it detects all maximal free sub-meshes.

Complexity Analysis of TCBFL

In the worst case, the request placement in TCBFL is within the last free sub-mesh in *MFL*, which has complexity in $O(f)$. Also, the algorithm that rebuilds the free-list upon allocation has $O(f^2)$ time complexity. Therefore, the time complexity of allocation in TCBFL is in $O(f^2)$. When a job departs, the number of free processors, *free_pes*, is updated and *MFL* is rebuilt. The time complexity of the algorithm that rebuilds *MFL* upon a job departure is in $O(b^3)$, and because b and f are in the same order (Liu, Huang, Lombardi, & Bhuyan, 1995), the time complexity of de-allocation in TCBFL is in $O(f^3)$.

5. JOB SCHEDULING STRATEGIES

Job scheduling is responsible for determining the order in which jobs are selected for execution. Scheduling strategies can have significant effect on system performance (Bani-Mohammad, Ould-Khaoua, Ababneh, & Mackenzie, 2007a, b). In this research, the scheduling strategies used include FCFS and SSD. In FCFS scheduling, the allocation request that arrives first is considered for allocation first. Allocation attempts stop when they fail for the oldest waiting allocation request. In SSD scheduling, the job with the shortest service demand is scheduled first (Windisch, Miller, & Lo, 1995; Bani-Mohammad et al., 2007a, b).

Job scheduling is an important factor for processor allocation in multicomputers. For meshes, the results in (Windisch et al., 1995; Bani-Mohammad et al., 2009) have shown that SSD outperforms FCFS significantly. In this research, we show that SSD scheduling strategy could improve the system performance of allocation strategies in terms of average turnaround time and mean system utilization.

6. PERFORMANCE EVALUATION

In this section, the results from simulations that have been carried out to evaluate the performance of TCBFL are presented and compared to those of the existing strategies Turning Busy List (TBL) (Bani-Mohammad et al., 2006; Bani-Mohammad et al., 2009), Turning First-Fit Free List (TFFFL) (Qiao & Ni, 1995), and First-Fit Free List (FFFL) (Ababneh, 2001; Qiao & Ni, 1995). The simulation results in (Bani-Mohammad et al., 2006; Bani-Mohammad et al., 2009) show that TBL performs better than First-Fit (FF) and Busy List (BL) in terms of job turnaround times and mean system utilization. Also, the simulation results in this research show that the performance of TFF (Ababneh, 2001) is very close to that of TFFFL (Qiao & Ni, 1995). Therefore, only the TBL, TFFFL and FFFL allocation strategies are considered in this research.

The allocation and de-allocation algorithms for TCBFL along with the TFFFL and the FFFL allocation algorithm proposed in (Qiao & Ni, 1995) were implemented in the C language, and they were integrated into the ProcSimity simulation tool (Windisch et al., 1995; Windisch, 1997). This tool has been widely used for processor allocation and job scheduling in multicomputers.

The target system is a 3D mesh with width W, depth D, and height H. We assume jobs have exponential inter-arrival times, and they are served using either FCFS or SSD job scheduling. The FCFS strategy is selected because of its fairness and because it is widely used in similar studies (Ababneh, 2006; Bani-Mohammad et al., 2009; Seo & Kim, 2003), whereas SSD is optimal in single processor systems. Two distributions are used to generate the width, depth and height of job allocation requests. The first is the uniform distribution over the range from 1 to the corresponding mesh side length, where the width, depth and height of the job requests are generated independently. The second is a uniform-decreasing distribution. The latter distribution is governed by four probabilities p_1, p_2, p_3, and p_4, and three integers l_1, l_2, and l_3, where the probabilitics that the width/depth/height of a request falls in the ranges $[1, l_1]$, $[l_1+1, l_2]$, $[l_2+1, l_3]$, and $[l_3+1, L]$ are p_1, p_2, p_3, and p_4, respectively. The side lengths within a range are equally likely to occur. In this research, the simulations are for a cube with side-length $L = 16$, $p_1 = 0.4$, $p_2 = 0.2$, $p_3 = 0.2$, $p_4 = 0.2$, $l_1 = 2$, $l_2 = 4$, and $l_3 = 8$. The uniform-decreasing distribution represents the case where most jobs are small relative to the size of the system. These distributions have been used often in the literature (Ababneh, 2001; De Rose et al., 2007; Lo et al., 1997; Seo & Kim, 2003; Yoo & Das, 2002; Zhu, 1992).

The main performance parameters observed are the average turnaround time of jobs and mean system utilization. The turnaround time is the time that a parallel job spends in the mesh from arrival to departure. The utilization is the percentage of processors that are utilized over time.

The basic independent variable in the simulations is the system load. It is defined as the inverse of the mean inter-arrival time of jobs. Its values, from low to heavy loads, have been determined through experimentation with the simulator, allowing each allocation strategy to reach its upper limits of utilization. In the figures below, the *x*-axis represents the system load, while the *y*-axis represents the values of the performance metric of interest.

The notation <allocation strategy>(<scheduling strategy>) is used to represent the strategies in the performance figures. For example, TCBFL(SSD) refers to the Turning Corner-Boundary Free List allocation strategy under the Shortest-Service-Demand scheduling strategy.

Each simulation run consists of 1000 completed jobs. The simulation results are averaged over enough independent runs so that the confidence level is 95% that relative errors do not exceed 5% of the means. In the simulation experiments, the grand means are obtained along with several values, including the relative errors, as shown in Table 1 that corresponds to the results with FCFS scheduling strategy depicted in Figure 5 for the load 3.8 jobs/time unit.

In Figures 5 and 6, the average turnaround time of jobs is plotted against the system load for the uniform and uniform-decreasing job size distributions. It can be seen in the figures that the strategy with request switching that gives priority to allocating sub-meshes at the corners and boundaries of the mesh system under SSD scheduling strategy (TCBFL(SSD)) has superior performance as compared with the remaining strategies. This is bacause allocating corner and peripheral sub-meshes can leave larger free sub-meshes for future allocation. It can also be seen in the figures that the strategies with orientation switching (TFFFL(SSD)) and (TBL(SSD)) have almost identical performance, and that they are superior to (FFFL(SSD)). They are followed, in order, by the strategies TBL(FCFS), TFFFL(FCFS), and FFFL(FCFS). This is because switching the orientation of the allocation request increases the probability of successful allocation. When compared to TCBFL(SSD) in Figure 5, TBL(SSD) increases the average turnaround times by about 59% and 54% for the loads 3.4 and 3.8 jobs/time unit, respectively.

Table 1. The mean turnaround time of jobs and relative errors for 95% confidence interval under FCFS as shown in Figure 5 for the load 3.8 jobs/time unit.

Algorithm	TCBFL (FCFS)	TBL (FCFS)	TFFFL (FCFS)	FFFL (FCFS)
95% Confidence Interval	[27.28-28.58]	[41.12-43.26]	[40.29-43.38]	[95.66-98.10]
Mean turnaround time (time unit)	27.93	42.19	41.84	96.88
Relative Error	0.023	0.025	0.037	0.013

Figure 5. Average turnaround time vs. system load using the FCFS and SSD scheduling strategies for the uniform job size distribution in a 16x16x16 mesh.

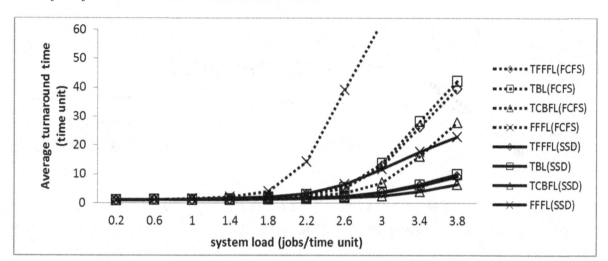

In Figure 6, the increases are by about 25% and 23% for the loads 34 and 38 jobs/time unit, respectively. It can also be seen in the figures that the average turnaround time of the strategy that depends on a free list approach (as in TFFFL) is very close to that of the strategy that depends on a list of allocated sub-meshes (as in TBL).

As has been reported above, the average turnaround time of the strategies with request switching (as in TCBFL, TFFFL, and TBL) is substantially superior to that of the strategy without switching (FFFL) because it is more likely that a suitable contiguous sub-mesh is available for allocation to a job when request orientation switching is allowed. It can also be noticed in the figures that the SSD scheduling strategy is much better than the FCFS scheduling strategy. This result show that the scheduling and al-

Figure 6. Average turnaround time vs. system load using the FCFS and SSD scheduling strategies for the uniform-decreasing job size distribution in a 16x16x16 mesh.

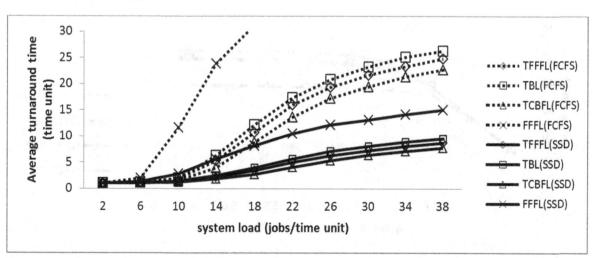

Figure 7. Mean System utilization using the FCFS and SSD scheduling strategies for the uniform job size distribution in a 16x16x16 mesh.

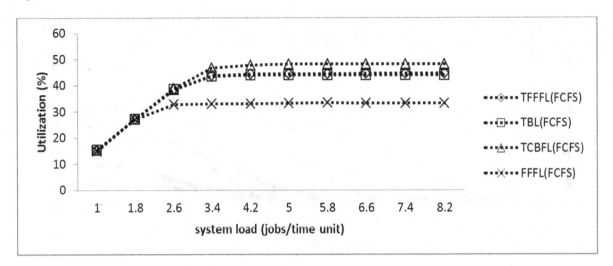

location strategies both have substantial effect on the performance of contiguous allocation strategies in the 3D mesh.

In Figures 7, 8, 9, and 10, the mean system utilization of the contiguous allocation strategies is plotted against the system load for the uniform and uniform-decreasing job size distributions under the FCFS and SSD scheduling strategies. The results show that switching request orientation and giving priority to allocating corner and boundary sub-meshes using SSD scheduling improves performance substantially. This is indicated by the superior mean system utilization of TCBFL(SSD) as compared with the other strategies. They are followed, in order, by the strategies TFFFL(SSD), TBL(SSD), TCBFL(FCFS), TFFFL(FCFS), TBL(FCFS), FFFL(SSD), and FFFL(FCFS). The system utilization of TCBFL(SSD)

Figure 8. Mean System utilization using the FCFS and SSD scheduling strategies for the uniform-decreasing job size distribution in a 16x16x16 mesh.

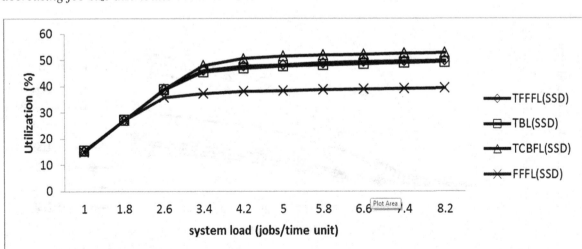

Figure 9. Mean System utilization using the FCFS and SSD scheduling strategies for the uniform-decreasing job size distribution in a 16x16x16 mesh.

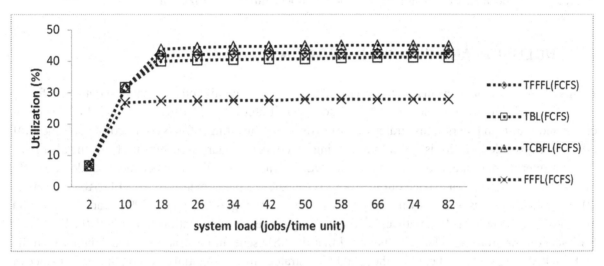

reaches 51% under the uniform-decreasing job size distribution and 53% under the uniform job size distribution. However, the system utilization of the allocation strategies with orientation switching (as in TFFFL(SSD) and TBL(SSD)) reaches 49% under the uniform-decreasing job size distribution and 50% under the uniform job size distribution. The utilization of FFFL(SSD) that does not support orientation switching reaches only 35% under the uniform-decreasing job size distribution and 39% under the uniform job size distribution. The system utilization achieved by the TCBFL allocation strategy based on the FCFS scheduling strategy (TCBFL(FCFS)) reaches 45% under the uniform-decreasing job size distribution and 49% under the uniform job size distribution.

Figure 10. Mean System utilization using the FCFS and SSD scheduling strategies for the uniform-decreasing job size distribution in a 16x16x16 mesh.

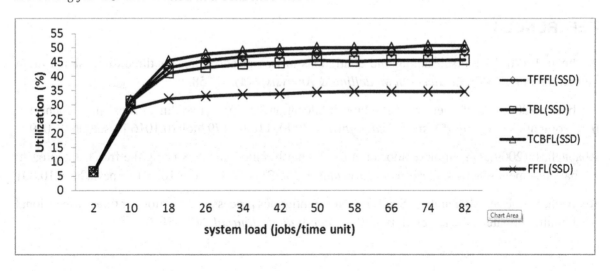

Higher system utilization is achievable under heavy loads because the waiting queue is filled very early, allowing each allocation strategy to reach its upper limits of utilization.

7. CONCLUSION AND FUTURE DIRECTIONS

In this chapter, we have evaluated the performance of a new contiguous allocation strategy, referred to as Turning Corner-Boundary Free List Allocation Strategy (or TCBFL for short), for 3D mesh-connected multicomputers. This strategy gives priority to allocating a free system corner sub-mesh. If this is not possible, priority is given to allocating a system boundary free sub-mesh. If this also fails, the first internal placement to be found is selected. Extensive simulation experiments under a variety of system loads have been carried out in order to compare the performance of TCBFL (Ababneh et al., 2015) against previous well-known contiguous allocation strategies (Ababneh, 2001; Bani-Mohammad et al., 2006; Qiao & Ni, 1995), with and without change of request orientation, under both the FCFS and SSD scheduling strategies. The results reveal that the SSD scheduling strategy is much better than the FCFS scheduling strategy, therefore, the scheduling strategy has substantial effect on the performance of contiguous allocation strategies in 3D meshes. The results also show that TCBFL(SSD) outperforms all other strategies considered in this research. When compared with TCBFL(SSD), TBL(SSD) increases the average turnaround times by up to 54% for high loads. Our results also show that TCBFL(SSD) achieves system utilization that reaches 51% for the uniform-decreasing job size distribution and 53% for the uniform job size distribution, but the allocation strategies with orientation switching (as TFFFL(SSD) and TBL(SSD)) can achieve system utilization of only 49% under the uniform-decreasing job size distribution and 50% under the uniform job size distribution, and the allocation strategy without orientation switching (FFFL(SSD)) can achieve system utilization of only 35% under the uniform-decreasing job size distribution and 39% under the uniform job size distribution.

As a continuation of this research in the future, it would be interesting to adapt TCBFL for non-contiguous allocation in 3D mesh-connected multicomputer. This is because previous results in (Ababneh & Bani-Mohammad, 2003) show that non-contiguous allocation for 3D mesh-connected multicomputers has superior performance than that of contiguous allocation.

REFERENCES

Ababneh, I. (2001). Job scheduling and contiguous processor allocation for three-dimensional mesh multicomputers. *AMSE Advances in Modelling & Analysis*, 6(4), 43–58.

Ababneh, I. (2006). An efficient free-list submesh Allocation Scheme for two-dimensional mesh-connected multicomputers. *Journal of Systems and Software*, 79(8), 1168–1179. doi:10.1016/j.jss.2006.01.019

Ababneh, I. (2009). On submesh allocation for 2D mesh multicomputers using the free-list approach: Global placement schemes. *Performance Evaluation*, 66(2), 105–120. doi:10.1016/j.peva.2008.10.001

Ababneh, I., & Bani-Mohammad, S. (2003). Non contiguous processor allocation for three-dimensional mesh multicomputers. *Advances in Modelling and Analysis Journal*, 8(2), 51–63.

Ababneh, I., Bani-Mohammad, S., & Al Smadi, M. (2015). Corner-Boundary Processor Allocation for 3D Mesh-connected Multicomputers. *International Journal of Cloud Applications and Computing, 5*(1), 1–13. doi:10.4018/ijcac.2015010101

Aridor, Y., Domany, T., Goldshmidt, O., Moreira, J., & Shmueli, E. (2005). Resource allocation and utilization in the BlueGene/L supercomputer. *IBM Journal of Research and Development, 49*(2/3), 425–436. doi:10.1147/rd.492.0425

Athas, W., & Seitz, C. (1988). Multicomputers: Message-passing concurrent computers. *IEEE Computer, 21*(8), 9–24. doi:10.1109/2.73

Bani-Mohammad, S., & Ababneh, I. (2013). On the performance of non-contiguous allocation for common communication patterns in 2D mesh-connected multicomputers. *Journal of Simulation Modelling Practice and Theory, 32*, 155–165. doi:10.1016/j.simpat.2011.08.007

Bani-Mohammad, S., Ould-Khaoua, M., Ababneh, I., Mackenzie, & Lewis, M. (2007a). An efficient processor allocation strategy thatmaintains a high degree of contiguity among processors in 2D mesh connected multicomputers. In *Proceedings of the ACS/IEEE International Conference on Computer Systems and Applications (AICCSA 2007)*. IEEE. doi:10.1109/AICCSA.2007.370743

Bani-Mohammad, S., Ould-Khaoua, M., Ababneh, I., Mackenzie, & Lewis, M. (2007b). A fast and efficient processor allocation strategy which combines a contiguous and non-contiguous processor allocation algorithms. Technical Report, TR-2007-229, DCS Technical Report Series, January, Department of Computing Science, University of Glasgow.

Bani-Mohammad, S., Ould-Khaoua, M., Ababneh, I., & Machenzie, L. (2006). A Fast and Efficient Strategy for Sub-mesh Allocation with Minimal Allocation Overhead in 3D Mesh Connected Multicomputers. *Ubiquitous Computing and Communication Journal, 1*(1), 26–36.

Bani-Mohammad, S., Ould-Khaoua, M., Ababneh, I., & Mackhenzie, M. (2009). Comparative evaluation of contiguous allocation strategies on 3D Mesh Multicomputers. *Journal of Systems and Software, 82*(2), 307–318. doi:10.1016/j.jss.2008.06.033

Choo, H., Yoo, S., & Youn, H.-Y. (2000). Processor scheduling and allocation for 3D torus multicomputer systems. *IEEE Transactions on Parallel and Distributed Systems, 11*(5), 475–484. doi:10.1109/71.852400

Chuang, P.-J., & Tzeng, N.-F. (1994). Allocating Precise Submeshes in Mesh Connected Systems. *IEEE Transactions on Parallel and Distributed Systems, 5*(2), 211–217. doi:10.1109/71.265948

Cray Inc. (2010a). *Cray XE6 Datasheet*. Retrieved September 9, 2014, form http://www.cray.com/Assets/PDF/products/xe/CrayXE6Brochure.pdf

Cray Inc. (2010b). *Cray XE6m Datasheet*. Retrieved September 9, 2014, form http://www.cray.com/Assets/PDF/products/xe/CrayXE6mBrochure.pdf

De Rose, C. A. F., Heiss, H.-U., & Linnert, B. (2007). Distributed Dynamic processor Allocation for Multicomputers. *Parallel Computing, 33*(3), 145–158. doi:10.1016/j.parco.2006.11.010

Foster, I. (1995). *Designing and Building Parallel Programs, Concepts and Tools for Parallel Software Engineering*. Boston, MA: Addison-Wesley Longman Publishing Co.

Horn, P. M., Gara, A., Goyal, A., Pulleyblank, B., Cotcus, P., Yaun, D., & Eleftheriou, M. (2014). *Blue Gene Project*. Retrieved September 9, 2014, from http://www.research.ibm.com/bluegene/index.html

Intel, C. (1991). *A Touchstone DELTA system description*. Intel Corporation.

Kim, G., & Yoon, H. (1998). On Submesh Allocation for Mesh Multicomputers: A Best-Fit Allocation and a Virtual Submesh Allocation for Faulty Meshes. *IEEE Transactions on Parallel and Distributed Systems*, *9*(2), 175–185. doi:10.1109/71.663881

Kumar, V., Grama, A., Gupta, A., & Karypis, G. (2003). *Introduction to Parallel Computing*. Redwood City, CA: Benjamin/Cummings publishing Company.

Liu, T., Huang, W.-K., Lombardi, F., & Bhuyan, L. N. (1995). A submesh allocation scheme for mesh-connected multiprocessor systems. In *Proc. Int'l Conference on Parallel Processing II* (vol. 2, pp. 159-163). Academic Press.

Lo, V., Windisch, K., Liu, W., & Nitzberg, B. (1997). Non-contiguous processor allocation algorithms for mesh-connected multicomputers. *IEEE Transactions on Parallel and Distributed Systems*, *8*(7), 712–726. doi:10.1109/71.598346

Mao, W., Chen, J., & Watson, W. (2005). Efficient Subtorus Processor Allocation in a Multi-Dimensional Torus. In *Proceedings of the 8th International Conference on High-Performance Computing in Asia-Pacific Region (HPCAS IA'05)*, (pp. 53-60). Beijing, China: Academic Press.

Peterson, C., Sutton, J., & Wiley, P. (1991). iWARP: A 100-MPOS, LIW microprocessor for multicomputers. *IEEE Micro*, *11*(3), 26–29, 81–87. doi:10.1109/40.87568

Qiao, W., & Ni, L. (1995). Efficient processor allocation for 3D tori. In *Proceedings of the 9th International Conference on Parallel Processing Symposium* (pp. 466-471). Washington, DC: Academic Press. doi:10.1109/IPPS.1995.395972

Riken & Fujitsu. (2014). *K computer*. Retrieved September 9, 2014, form http://www.olcf.ornl.gov/wp-content/events/lug2011/4-12-2011/230-300_Shinji_Sumimoto_LUG2011-FJ-20110407-pub.pdf

Seo, K.-H., & Kim, S.-C. (2003). Improving system performance in contiguous processor allocation for mesh-connected parallel systems. *Journal of Systems and Software*, *67*(1), 45–54. doi:10.1016/S0164-1212(02)00086-9

Windisch, K. (1997). *ProcSimity V4.3 User's Manual*. University of Oregon.

Windisch, K., Miller, J. V., & Lo, V. (1995). ProcSimity: an experimental tool for processor allocation and scheduling in highly parallel systems. In *Proceedings of the 5th Symposium on the Frontiers of Massively Parallel Computation (Frontiers'95)* (pp. 414-421). Washington, DC: Academic Press.

Yoo, B.-S., & Das, C.-R. (2002). A Fast and Efficient Processor Allocation Scheme for Mesh-Connected Multicomputers. *IEEE Transactions on Parallel and Distributed Systems*, *51*(1), 46–60.

Zhu, Y. (1992). Efficient processor allocation strategies for mesh-connected parallel computers. *Journal of Parallel and Distributed Computing*, *16*(4), 328–337. doi:10.1016/0743-7315(92)90016-G

KEY TERMS AND DEFINITIONS

Allocated Sub-Mesh: An allocated sub-mesh is a sub-mesh whose processors are allocated.

Busy List: The list of all sub-meshes that are currently allocated.

Free Sub-Mesh: A free sub-mesh is a sub-mesh whose processors are unallocated.

Job Scheduling: Job scheduling is responsible for determining the order in which jobs are selected for execution.

Job Turnaround Time: Job turnaround time is the time that the job spends in the system from arrival to departure.

Maximal Free List: A maximal free list is a list that contains the maximal free sub-meshes.

Maximal Free Sub-Mesh: A maximal free sub-mesh is a free sub-mesh that is not a proper subset of any other free sub-mesh.

Processor Allocation: Processor allocation is responsible for selecting the set of processors on which a parallel job is executed.

Processor Fragmentation: Processor fragmentation is of two types: *internal* and *external*; Internal fragmentation occurs when more processors are allocated to a job than it requires, whereas external fragmentation occurs when there are free processors sufficient in number to satisfy a pending allocation request, but they are not allocated because they are not contiguous.

System Utilization: System utilization is the percentage of processors that are utilized over time.

Chapter 13
Cloud Computing in the 21st Century:
A Managerial Perspective for Policies and Practices

Mahesh Raisinghani
Texas Woman's University, USA

Meghana Chekuri
Texas Woman's University, USA

Efosa Carroll Idemudia
Arkansas Tech University, USA

Kendra Fisher
Texas Woman's University, USA

Jennifer Hanna
Texas Woman's University, USA

ABSTRACT

The constant changes in technology has posed serious challenges to top management teams, employees, and customers on how to collect, store, and process data for competitive advantage and to make better decisions. In this chapter, to address this issue, we present the managerial perspective of cloud computing that provides the infrastructure and/or tools for decision making in the 21st century. Since the year 2000, the interest in cloud computing has had a steady increase. (Mason, 2002) Not only has cloud computing substantially lowered computing costs for corporations, it continues to increase their abilities for market offerings and to access customers' information with ease. Cloud computing has allowed managers to focus more on their business plans and bottom line to enhance competitive advantage.

INTRODUCTION

The constant changes in technology has posed serious challenges to top management teams, employees, and customers on how to collect, store, and process data for competitive advantage and to make better decisions. To address this issue, we present the managerial perspective of cloud computing that provides the infrastructure and/or tools for decision making in the 21st century. Since the year 2000, the interest in cloud computing has had a steady increase. (Mason, 2002) Not only has cloud computing substantially lowered computing costs for corporations, it continues to increase their abilities for market offerings

DOI: 10.4018/978-1-4666-8676-2.ch013

Copyright © 2015, IGI Global. Copying or distributing in print or electronic forms without written permission of IGI Global is prohibited.

and to access customers' information with ease. Cloud computing has allowed managers to focus more on their business plans and bottom line to enhance competitive advantage.

Imagining the Internet, we often think of a big cloud connected to network maps. Prior to the popularity of cloud computing, these network maps occupy physical spaces and would show routers, servers, users, mainframes, etc., connected to the Internet, which was represented by the big cloud. The cloud was also a representation of "everything else" that was on the Internet, outside of the corporate network. Essentially, cloud computing can employ processing power, storage, applications, cost efficient, almost unlimited storage space, easy access to information, and various services over the Internet. Cloud computing has become the way of organizing the "everything else" (i.e., data collection, data use, data storage, data processing, and so forth) on the Internet.

For cloud computing, the data storage and processing is done on a remote server. This means that the users don't have to install any software, store any data, or run programs, allowing for applications to be ran on a web browser. Thus, allowing users to access the information with ease from any part of the world. Most people using the Internet have likely used cloud computing. For example, most popular email providers like Gmail, Hotmail or Yahoo mail are all examples of cloud computing. This is also referred to as Software as a service (SaaS), or on-demand software that allows users to access applications over the Internet through automatic software integration. Hence, as long as the user has access to the Internet, they can connect to their applications and online data.

History and Evolution

The history of cloud computing can be dated back almost as early as computers themselves, when the ability for computers to connect through a mainframe was first introduced in academia and business corporations during the 1950s. At this time these terminal computers, or "static terminal" were only able to communicate, but did not possess any processing abilities relating to data collection, data storage, and data use for competitive advantage. These large-scale mainframes were very costly, occupies lot of space, produce lot of heat, and to improve cost efficiency and space availability users shared devices as well as time on the CPU-Central Processing Unit- so the devices were constantly being used. This practice became known in the industry as time-sharing, but in the 1970s was known as RJE-Remote Job Entry (Weik, 1961).

It was in the 1960s that John McCarthy stated that computation would be available to public someday to improve data collection and usage (Simson, 2011). It wasn't until the 1990s that telecommunication companies began offering Virtual Private Network (VPN) services to save cost. A VPN allows users to send private information and data across a public network, through means like encryption that would protect the information as though it were on a private network. However, it would have the benefit of superior functionality and services of a public network (Mason, 2002).

It was not until the year 2000 that cloud computing began gaining popularity because of cost efficiency, unlimited storage, and easy access to information. More and more corporations began utilizing cloud computing. Amazon was one of the first in the industry to implement cloud computing for competitive advantage. Like most other corporate computer networks, they were using a small fraction of their capacity to allow any jumps in activity. Amazon innovated their data centers, which allowed for less physical space needed and a smaller operating staff. They were able to extend cloud computing to their customers in 2006 with their launch of Amazon Web Services (AWS) (Hof, 2006). The AWS helps

Amazon to improve customers' loyalty and satisfaction because Amazon is able to address customers' immediate needs and wants.

IMPACT OF CLOUD COMPUTING

In less than twenty years cloud computing has revolutionized the way that not only large corporations utilize the Internet, but individual users as well. The impact of cloud computing in technology stretches from individual users to small and large businesses. Many are using cloud computing in our day-to-day lives, without even knowing the just how much. Mac users especially are using cloud computing for much of their data storage, use, and processes. All of our online collaboration is based in cloud computing going back to the early days of social networking on MySpace. Cloud Computing can also be found when routing our destinations in using the average day GPS system (Mather, Kumarasawmy & Latif, 2009). As we become more and more dependent on our mobile and smart devices, the more we utilize the impact of cloud computing to access information with ease and have unlimited space.

Cloud Computing Service Models

Many of the IT services accessible through cloud computing can be categorized into three main service models as shown in Figure 1; which are described as follows:

- **Infrastructure as a Service (IaaS):** In this model, cloud service providers (CSPs) host consumers' infrastructure. It provides fundamental building blocks such as hardware and storage so customers can create their own platform or individual services using the cloud infrastructure (Zissis & Lekkas, 2012). Customers possess complete responsibility for securing their applications deployed in the IaaS cloud and cannot expect any security assistance from CSPs other than firewall protection (Mather, Kumaraswamy & Latif, 2009).
- **Platform as a Service (PaaS):** In this service model, CSPs offer a platform that encompasses generic software modules, so consumers can build their own software programs or services. The consumers have no control over the underlying cloud infrastructure such as operating systems, network, and storage components. However, they do have control over the deployed applications and configurations of application hosting environment (Zissis & Lekkas, 2012).
- **Software as a Service (SaaS):** Within this service model, a cloud service provider offers application software with specific service features so consumers can host their software services on the cloud, and it is the most popular offering in the industry today. The SaaS providers are mainly responsible for securing the applications they offer customers. However, consumers are accountable for operational security functions. Similar to the PaaS service model, the consumer has no control over the underlying cloud infrastructure such as operating systems, networks, storage, and servers (Zissis & Lekkas, 2012).

Cloud Deployment Models

A cloud deployment model refers to a particular type of cloud environment, which can be differentiated by its size, proprietorship and access as shown in Figure 2. The four cloud deployment models that are identified within the cloud-computing infrastructure are described as follows:

Figure 1. The cloud computing stack
(Source: Voorsluys et al. 2011)

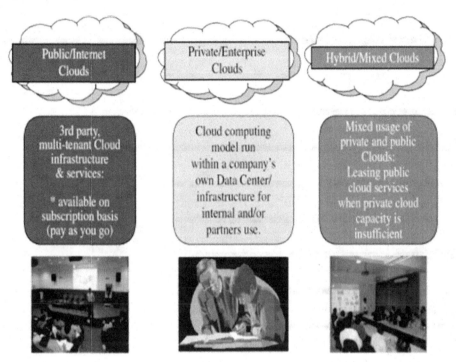

- **Private Cloud:** This particular cloud infrastructure is designed for an individual organization. It can be managed by the organization or the cloud service provider and may exist on-site or at a location remote to the organization's premises (Zissis & Lekkas, 2012).
- **Community Cloud:** This type of infrastructure is shared by several organizations in the community that have specific shared interests. This form of cloud can be managed by various organizations or by a third party provider, and may be deployed either on-site or off-site (Zissis & Lekkas, 2012).
- **Public Cloud:** This cloud infrastructure is accessible by general public or a large organization. It is generally owned by an organization that offers cloud services to public (Zissis & Lekkas, 2012).
- **Hybrid Cloud:** The hybrid cloud infrastructure is a combination of two or more clouds such as public, private, and community cloud. The two clouds are united by standardized or exclusive technology to enable portability of data and applications between the clouds (Zissis & Lekkas, 2012).

Benefits of Cloud Computing

Cloud computing provides a great example of how the Information Technology (IT) evolution is playing a crucial role in changing the way businesses operate today for competitive advantage. Organizations are utilizing cloud computing to boost their productivity, cost efficient, unlimited storage space, easy access to information, and overall performance. The benefits of cloud computing are numerous and some of the main benefits are listed below.

Figure 2. Types of clouds based on deployment models
(Source: Voorsluys et al. 2011)

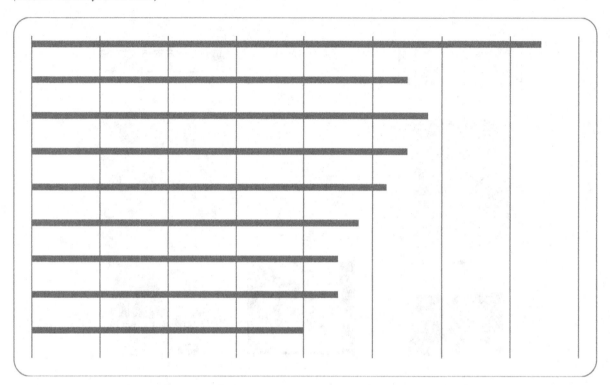

- **Reduced Costs and Better Financial Management:** Cloud computing helps an organization by decreasing or eliminating its upfront IT investments such as hardware and software purchases (Erl, Mahmood & Puttini, 2013). The organizations avoid heavy investment in hardware as the payments depend on the amount of cloud usage. As the infrastructure for hardware and software is rented and not bought, the costs are controlled and minimized. This in turn helps companies to start with a small investment, but can expand their IT resource allocation based on their requirements. Cloud computing reduces operational costs by avoiding unnecessary maintenance and electricity costs (Shivakumar & Raju, 2010). The reduction of up-front financial commitments and operational costs allows organizations to redirect the capital for essential business requirements leading to increased efficiency (Velte, Velte & Elsenpeter, 2010). Thus, it should be noted that cloud computing is the most efficient method to use, maintain, and update software and hardware. Cloud computing lower companies IT expenses and investment relating to licensing fees for multiple users using the systems.
- **Increased Scalability and Flexibility:** Cloud computing makes it easier for businesses to scale their service offerings that are increasingly reliant on accurate information, and subject to client's demand thus increasing customers' loyalty and satisfaction. Since the computing resources are managed through software, they can be deployed quick and efficiently as and when new requirements emerge. In fact, the central element to cloud computing is the ability to scale resources up or down, by dynamically managing them through software APIs with minimal service provider interaction (Marston et al., 2011). With the availability of pools of IT resources, along with associ-

ated tools and technologies designed to leverage them collectively, it makes it possible for clouds to almost instantly and dynamically allocate IT resources to cloud consumers, on-demand or via the cloud consumer's direct configuration. This empowers cloud consumers to not only scale their cloud-based IT resources, but also offers flexibility in terms of accommodating processing fluctuations and demand peaks automatically or manually (Erl, Mahmood & Puttini, 2013). With easy to install technology and increased flexibility, such as adding resources on demand, turning them off and reassigning as per business requirements costs, it further increases value proposition for consumers and attracts more companies to move to cloud (Shivakumar & Raju, 2010). Thus, cloud computing encourages automatic software integration for easy use.

- **Automation and Increased Storage Capacity:** The cloud can store much more data than a personal computer and provides unlimited storage space (Erl, Mahmood & Puttini, 2013). The companies need not worry about the amount of storage space availability or computer hardware upgrades. Moreover, backing up and recovery of data is simplified as all the information is stored on the cloud versus a physical device (Erl, Mahmood & Puttini, 2013). Automation is one of the attractive features of cloud computing. Automation helps businesses by not requiring dedicated teams to manage system updates and back-ups which in turn allow businesses to utilize the freed resources for other priority tasks (Shivakumar & Raju, 2010).

- **Mobile Business and Location Independence:** With cloud computing system, the workload has shifted significantly where the local computers are not required to do all the work (Shivakumar & Raju, 2010). The cloud providers operate from various locations which allow businesses to go mobile and decrease dependency on a specific location. In addition to traditional computers, cloud services can be accessed from various devices such as tablets, smart phones and other devices. Hence, consumers have increased flexibility with device options and easy access to data from anywhere in the world where there is an Internet connection (Erl, Mahmood & Puttini, 2013).

- **Better Business Support:** Time is one of the vital factors for any successful business. Cloud computing helps IT react quicker to the changing dynamics of a business by decreasing the time and effort required to launch new applications (Shivakumar & Raju, 2010). For instance, a project that usually takes 4 months to complete can be accomplished immediately or in less than 5 weeks utilizing cloud services. The decreased project turnaround time results in competitive advantage, as it helps cut overall costs,SS and improves operational efficiency.

Risks and Challenges Associated with Cloud Computing

Although cloud computing offers several benefits to the consumers, businesses need to be aware of the risks and challenges that comes with adopting cloud services. Some of the critical challenges involved with cloud computing are addressed below.

- **Greater Security Vulnerabilities:** Security is one of the primary concerns when considering cloud computing. Traditionally, companies feared connecting to any system outside of one's organization as it provided access to company's sensitive information (Zissis & Lekkas, 2012). This conceptual boundary protected an organization's information resources. However, shifting of business data to the cloud implies that a company's private information is shared with the cloud provider. With increasing cloud services, the conceptual boundary is becoming fuzzier and is requiring cloud consumers to expand trust boundaries (Erl, Mahmood & Puttini, 2013).

Figure 3. Cloud concerns (in percent)

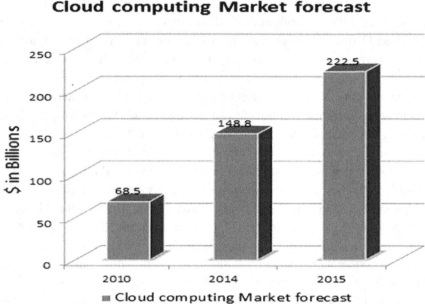

Establishing a secure architecture without introduction of vulnerabilities can be challenging as the trust boundaries overlap between the cloud consumer and cloud provider. In addition, cloud providers having access to cloud consumers data increases the chances of data exposure and makes it difficult to estimate the extent to which the data is secure. This overlapping of trust boundaries and increased chances of data exposure provide malicious users or hackers with greater opportunities to attack IT resources. Such malicious users can steal or destroy cloud consumer's personal data or a company's business data, thus increasing security threats (Erl, Mahmood & Puttini, 2013). A survey conducted by International Data Corporation (IDC) on cloud services showed that security is one of the main concerns. The following figure 3 illustrates the cloud concerns with security issue leading at 74.5percent (Velte, Velte & Elsenpeter, 2010). To address this issue relating to security in cloud, top management must be absolutely sure to choose the most reliable and reputable service providers that will help to keep company's information and data secure.

- **Decreased Administrative Control:** Cloud consumers are allowed a certain degree of governance control. However, it is lower than what consumers would enjoy with IT resources being on-premise (Erl, Mahmood & Puttini, 2013). This limited control can introduce risks depending on how a cloud provider operates one's cloud network. For example, if the geographic distance between the cloud provider and the cloud consumer is more, then it requires extra network hops, leading to delays in data transfer and eventually decreased efficiency. With cloud services being accessed remotely, certain features of the software might be inferior when compared to running it locally (Erl, Mahmood & Puttini, 2013).

- **Interoperability and Portability:** Migrating between different clouds, such as transferring of IT infrastructure resources from a private cloud to a public cloud, can be challenging (Mather, Kumarasawmy & Latif, 2009). In other words, the interoperability and portability of data from one cloud system to another plays a vital role in the adoption of cloud computing. Unfortunately, there are no mature standards for interoperability between different cloud systems. As a result, IT organizations fail to respond quickly to the dynamic business changes (Mather, Kumarasawmy & Latif, 2009).

- **Cloud Service Provider Dependency:** One of the main drawbacks of cloud computing is the dependency on a cloud service provider (Mather, Kumarasawmy & Latif, 2009). A cloud service provider (CSP) holds valuable information and may have certain business rules in place that makes it difficult or impossible for a cloud user to shift to a different cloud provider. When a particular CSP cannot match the changing needs of a business, then the cloud consumer might want to move to another cloud provider. However, this change can be problematic and cumbersome, as it requires transfer of huge data between the old and the new providers. This decreased flexibility can affect the overall business goals and decrease efficiency (Mather, Kumarasawmy & Latif, 2009).

- **Connectivity Dependency:** The complete potential of cloud computing is dependent on the availability of high-speed access to the Internet, which can be disadvantageous (Mather, Kumarasawmy & Latif, 2009). Cloud consumers have to be mindful of the fact that cloud service providers can experience cloud outage and downtime issues. If any connectivity or network problem arises then the whole system set up is worthless and ineffective (Velte, Velte & Elsenpeter, 2010).

- **Multi- Regional Compliance and Legal Issues:** Cloud service providers usually establish data centers in geographic locations that are inexpensive or convenient (Erl, Mahmood & Puttini, 2013). Cloud consumers are generally ignorant about where their IT resources and physical data actually resides. This variability in information can pose serious legal issues as organizations nowadays are expected to maintain privacy of personal data, such as HIPPA for the health care industry. Countries have certain laws in place that require selected data to be disclosed to the government. As a result of the US Patriot Act, the US governmental agencies can access a European cloud consumer's data positioned in the US cloud. On the contrary, European Union countries may not be able to access the US cloud consumer's data easily when hosted in the European Union. Although the information is held by the third party cloud provider, many regulatory frameworks require cloud consumer companies to safeguard personal data (Erl, Mahmood & Puttini, 2013). Hence organizations have to be knowledgeable about their accountability and mindful in considering cloud computing as an option.

Cloud Computing Security Best Practices

In an effort to counteract some of the security concerns within Cloud Computing, many strategies and best practices have come into play. Cloud providers and users alike are strongly encouraged to execute these best practices, as they present defense mechanisms against possible security and data breaches.

- **Policy:** Policy is a major best practice contributor to cloud security. Whether supplying the cloud or consuming it, ensuring there is a policy in place outlining the specific aspects of the cloud is a must. The policy should include the security information, and be assessable to the entire organization (Winkler, & Meine, 2011). This may sound like a common knowledge expectation, but ensuring all parties involved are aligned with the guidelines and regulations of the service play a vital role in securing the cloud. Once your policies are in place, a focus in risk management leadership should be established. Also, the policy should be updated regularly to address the constant changes in technology. It should be noted that most companies policy relating to BYOD or cloud computing are out of date because technology changes everyday/rapidly.

- **Risk Management:** The cloud is heavily used among many managers across many fields; however, one's ability to provide risk management is essential. To implement risk management as a best practice to securing the cloud is key to having a system in place, which reduces security risk in the cloud. Within risk management, one has to have a clear understanding of what types of security risk a particular cloud may present (Winkler, & Meine, 2011). This allows possible security measures to take place, which may counteract those risks. From this information, various types of securities are in place and then tested and monitored for their ability to secure (Winkler, & Meine, 2011). To emphasize how instrumental risk management is to securing the cloud, Winkler states that it is the "core activity around which your security practice revolves" (Winkler, & Meine, 2011). Also, companies should invest regularly on training relating to risk management associated with cloud computing.

- **Auditing:** Auditing is another type of best practice that is heavily used in the field. Auditing helps ensure the effects of current security systems are compliant. To ensure accurate auditing of the system, one should complete a series of specific steps. The first item within an audit includes a routine schedule check of any possible problems or weaknesses within the system (Winkler & Meine, 2011). With new risk arising daily, security controls should be checked to make sure they are up to date and current in their ability to control these risks. Policies in place as mentioned earlier should also go through audits to make sure they are still compliant (Winkler & Meine, 2011). To help identify any upgrades that should be made to the monitoring of security, system logs need to be audited occasionally by a manual review. There are many different auditing tools, which can be leveraged that include these best practices; yet, one should ensure they are choosing the right one. For example, those using platform as a service provider may find more challenges in using commercialized auditing programs due to their tenants having a bit less control (Winkler & Meine, 2011). Outside of this concern, commercialized audits allow a common interface and automation within the audit (Winkler & Meine, 2011).

- **Segregation of Duties:** Segregation of Duties is a best practice, which states the idea that privileges should not be given to individuals that are outside of their primary role (Winkler & Meine, 2011). Within this concept, privileges are only given and limited to what is needed for the completion of one's responsibilities and task. When one's access is limited only to their particular area, this allows for specific monitoring to take place. Segregation of duties goes as far as to limit sensitive material and task to what is known as the two-person rule, where access is given only to two specific individuals (Winkler & Meine, 2011).

As an attempt to continue creating best practices, many have joined together to find continued resolutions in helping secure the cloud (Subashini & Kavitha 2011). The Cloud Security Alliance (CSA) has taken the initiative to partner with providers among many others in helping identify the most secure processes to incorporate into cloud computing. They have founded the Open Web Application Security

Project (OWASP), which includes the top threats to cloud computing and is updated as security threats change in the field (Subashini & Kavitha 2011).

Changes to the Cloud

There are a few important aspects of the cloud that must also be taken into consideration outside of ensuring maximum security to the system. In an effort to overcome some of the challenges mentioned earlier, specific changes should be made to the cloud.

- **User Outage and Performance:** User outage and performance are two of the items which Cloud providers must take a closer look into making necessary alterations. Companies such as Amazon, and Google have already experienced such opportunities in their fields (Armbrust, et al., 2010). When consumers purchase or rent out their data within the cloud, they are expecting their information to be readily available at all times. It has been suggested to help avoid cloud outages; businesses should obtain their software stacks from multiple providers, as oppose to one or two (Armbrust, et al., 2010). The idea is that if one were to go down, it would not disrupt the flow of the entire entity. From here, the focus would be on the competition between the Cloud providers, their performance, and price, as businesses would look for the providers that would work best with their company's needs.
- **Data Lock-In:** Some companies have been hesitant to convert to cloud computing due to the fear in losing their data not only temporarily, but all together from data lock-in (Armbrust et al., 2010). Whether this is due to being locked into a company contract, or the inability to extract data from one provider to another, data lock-in can pose a major problem. A possible change to the current process could include incorporating service across multiple clouds, enabling users to pull their data as needed (Armbrust et al., 2010). Another advantage to this change includes the users ability to have their data at an alternate location, in the event that one provider looses their data permanently (Armbrust et al., 2010).

IMPLICATIONS FOR RESEARCH

The content within this paper in addition to other research on cloud computing can be used to help gain an understanding on cloud computing, and the technological advances it possesses. Although the information presented an overall framework on cloud computing, the research also offered ways to help compensate for some of its disadvantages. While conducting research on cloud computing, we found that when looking for scholarly or academic journals on the impact of cloud computing, the amount of research was not as extensive as first thought. Considering how fast cloud computing has grown within businesses and for private use, we would have liked to see a larger amount of academic resources supporting it.

There was also a major focus in research on the security concerns of the cloud. We were able to find other opportunities outside of security risk, but when looking for alternate solutions, the research was very limited. When one thinks of cloud computing concerns, their immediate thought may be security, yet as mentioned in our paper, there are several other opportunities that should equally be addressed.

Going forward, further research should be obtained on the opportunities of cloud computing outside of security risk, and how those opportunities should be addressed, in addition to the positive impact of cloud computing obtained from academic sources. Also, future research are encourage to investigate the specific factors that influence security vulnerability, administrative control, and portability relating to cloud computing to enhance competitive advantage.

IMPLICATIONS FOR MANAGEMENT

Managers should expand their knowledge on cloud computing and consider using cloud computing for their business. With the ability to conserve on expenses, and re-allocate task and responsibilities from systems to projects and strategies, this alone can help produce tangible results for the company. Managers should look at the advantages of cloud computing, and see how they would be of benefit to their company. From here, they should look at the specific items needed for their business, and align those to a provider who can meet those expectations. From the research gathered, managers should also ensure they are aware of the opportunities in cloud computing, and set the best practices in place to help them reduce the risk of security breaches, and the loss of data. For managers looking for more flexibility, the ability to cut expenses, free resources, and technically advance, cloud computing could be a great resource for businesses and managers. Finally, top management teams should invest on training relating to cloud computing; and should also make sure that their organization's policies for cloud computing are current and updated to enhance their organization's competitive advantage.

Figure 4. Cloud market forecast (in billions)

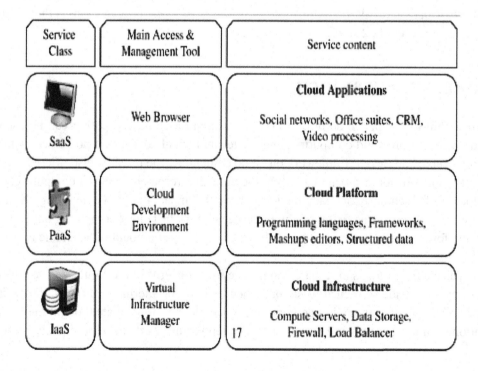

RECOMMENDATION

Our recommendation is for businesses and individuals alike to strongly consider using cloud computing based on the managerial perspective presented in our paper.

By 2015, cloud computing is expected to grow to a 222.5 billion dollar industry (Jayaprakash 2011). With that large of an industry, companies will be competing to see who can be a part of cloud computing first, and we suggest that everyone take advantage of the benefits now. With the ability to start your own cloud, join a provider individually, or have your entire company convert to cloud computing, the advantages are extensive relating to competitive advantage and establishing customers' loyalty and satisfaction.

CONCLUSION

The constant and daily changes in technology has posed serious challenges to top managements, employees, and customers on how to collect, store, and process big data for competitive advantage and to make better decision. To address this issue, we present the managerial perspective of cloud computing in the 21st century. From the research conducted, one can see how cloud computing has become the leading service in how we use the Internet. With one of the greatest advantages being cost, companies who use cloud-computing can look forward to operational cost reduction, flexibility in time and scaling, and an unlimited amount of data storage. It should be noted that cloud computing offers easy access to customers' current information and data to improve customers' services, loyalty, and satisfaction. Although there are some challenges and opportunities in cloud computing; and our study presents different resources and best practices that should be set in place to help compensate for those opportunities so one can reap the benefits of cloud computing. Cloud computing continues to grow daily and can enhance one's business, work, and personal life.

REFERENCES

Armbrust, M., Armando, F., Griffith, R., Joseph, A. D., Katz, R., Konwinski, A., & Zaharia, A. et al. (2010). A view of cloud computing. *Communications of the ACM, 53*(4), 50–58. doi:10.1145/1721654.1721672

Erl, T., Mahmood, Z., & Puttini, R. (2013). *Cloud computing: Concepts, technology & architecture.* Upper Saddle River, NJ: Prentice Hall.

Farber, D. (2008). *The new geek chic: Data centers.* CNET News.

Jayaprakash, G. (2011, September 15). Cloud computing security, is your seatbelt on? *Infosys.* Retrieved October 31, 2013, from http://www.infosysblogs.com/cloud/2011/09/

King, R. (2008). Cloud Computing: Small Companies Take Flight. *Business Week.*

Marston, S., Li, Z., Bandyopadhyay, S., Zhang, J., & Ghalsasi, A. (2011). Cloud computing- the business persepective. *Decision Support Systems, 51*(1), 176–189. doi:10.1016/j.dss.2010.12.006

Mason, A. G. (2002) Secure Virtual Private Network. Cisco Press.

Mather, T., Kumarasawmy, S., & Latif, S. (2009). *Cloud security and privacy* (1st ed.). Sebastopol, CA: O'Reilly Media, Inc.

Shivakumar, B. L., & Raju, T. (August 2010). Emerging role of cloud computing in redefining business operations. *Global Management Review, 4*(4).

Simson, G. (2011). *"The Cloud Imperative". Technology Review*. MIT.

Subashini, S., & Kavitha, V. (2011). A survey on security issues in service delivery models of cloud computing. *Journal of Network and Computer Applications, 34*(01), 1–11. doi:10.1016/j.jnca.2010.07.006

Velte, A. T., Velte, T. J., & Elsenpeter, R. (2010). *Cloud computing: A practical approach*. New York, NY: McGraw-Hill.

Voorsluys, W., Broberg, J., & Buyya, R. (February 2011). Introduction to Cloud Computing. In R. Buyya, J. Broberg, & A. Goscinski (Eds.), *Cloud Computing: Principles and Paradigms* (pp. 1–44). New York: Wiley Press. doi:10.1002/9780470940105.ch1

Weik, M. H. (1961). *A Third Survey of Domestic Electronic Digital Computing Systems*. Ballistic Research Laboratories.

Winkler, J. R., & Meine, B. (2011). *Securing the cloud*. Waltham, MA: Syngress.

Zissis, D., & Lekkas, D. (2012). Addressing cloud computing security issues. *Future Generation Computer Systems, 28*(3), 583–592. doi:10.1016/j.future.2010.12.006

KEY TERMS AND DEFINITIONS

Community Cloud: This type of cloud infrastructure is shared by several organizations in the community that have specific shared interests. It can be managed by various organizations or by a third party provider, and may be deployed either on-site or off-site.

Hybrid Cloud: The hybrid cloud infrastructure is a combination of two or more clouds such as public, private, and community cloud. The two clouds are united by standardized or exclusive technology to enable portability of data and applications between the clouds.

Platform as a Service (PaaS): In PaaS, cloud service provide offer a platform that encompasses generic software modules, so consumers can build their own software programs or services.

Private Cloud: A cloud infrastructure is designed for an individual organization. It can be managed by the organization or the cloud service provider and may exist on-site or at a location remote to the organization's premises.

Public Cloud: This cloud infrastructure is accessible by general public or a large organization. It is generally owned by an organization that offers cloud services to public.

Software as a Service (SaaS): In SaaS, a cloud service provider offers application software with specific service features so consumers can host their software services on the cloud.

Virtual Private Network (VPN): A VPN allows users to send private information across a public network, through means like encryption that would protect the information as though it were on a private network, albeit with the benefit of superior functionality and services of a public network.

Chapter 14
Bio-Inspired Private Information Retrieval System over Cloud Service Using the Social Bees' Lifestyle with a 3D Visualisation

Hadj Ahmed Bouarara
Tahar Moulay University of Saida, Algeria

Reda Mohamed Hamou
Tahar Moulay University of Saida, Algeria

Amine Abdelmalek
Tahar Moulay University of Saida, Algeria

ABSTRACT

In the last decade, a new paradigm had seen the light named Cloud Computing, which allows the delocalization of data and applications on a dematerialized infrastructure accessible from Internet. Unfortunately, the cloud services are facing many drawbacks especially in terms of security and data confidentiality. However, in a world where digital information is everywhere, finding the desired information has become a crucial problem. For the purpose to preserve the user privacy life new approaches and ideas had been published. The content of this chapter is a new system of bio-inspired private information retrieval (BI-PIR) using the lifestyle of social bees, which allows both to find and hid, the sensitive desired information. It is based on a multi-filters cryptosystem used by the server for the encryption of stored document and the retrieval model using a combination of filters by 3 types of workers bees (Purveyor, guardian and cleaner), the queen bee represents the query, and the hive represents the class of relevant documents. We have tested this system on the benchmark MEDLINE dataset with panoply of validation tools (recall, precision, f-measure, entropy, silence, noise, and accuracy) and a comparative study had been realized with other systems existed in literature. Finally, a 3D visualization tool had been developed in order to make the results in graphical format understandable by humans. Our objectives is to improve the services quality of cloud computing.

DOI: 10.4018/978-1-4666-8676-2.ch014

Copyright © 2015, IGI Global. Copying or distributing in print or electronic forms without written permission of IGI Global is prohibited.

INTRODUCTION AND BACKGROUND

Big data, Cloud Computing, and Data-Driven Decision-making are new concepts that had seen the light recently within the same area, the role of web in peoples' life. With more than 2.5 quintillion bytes of data created every day over the web; those concepts become a highly active domain of research in order to improve their services in many viewpoints such as security aspect (Aljawarneh, 2011).

The homomorphic encryption (HE), is the most useful security concept that is used in privacy preserving domain. With his ability of executing operations on ciphered data without need to decipher it. It gives opportunities to different domains starting from code obfuscation in the 90's until the PIR protocols in the recent few years. The HE uses complex mathematical concepts, such as bilinear applications and prime numbers theory, but this did not prevent the attackers and cryptanalysts to find weaknesses. In fact, some researches proved the inefficiency of this kind of schemes against hackers like in (Hervé, 2005), the authors presented a linear attack against TSZ cryptosystem called Anonymous Pirate Decoder (APD).

The concept of cloud computing offers a set of advantages, such as low cost payment for hard capacities of resources, and no need for cracks, patches or special software to access services...etc. In fact, cloud services present several problems and disadvantages, reside in the fact that it did not provide, neither information about data localisation during treatment (computing or storage), nor physical access to those data which pose problems in term of data confidentiality. As consequences of that, the evolution of cloud computing knows some criticism from users, especially the commercial ones concerning the security of computing and storage treatments.

However, the cloud services know a continuous growing in term of number of users and amount of data available online/offline that is counted by petabytes. The researches proved that 90% of the quantity of data stored on the web was created in last few years, precisely after the introduction of cloud computing. As result of that, the presence of system retrieval information SRI has becomes paramount, defined as a response to the need of user (query), by searching a sub set of documents that are closest to the query, from a wide range of documents that is useful to a claimant. The SRI is the basis of several application domain such as web, forums, and business. But the construction of an effective SRI, is a big challenge in the middle of the computer science and most of the classical methods present a several problems:

- **Diversity of Data:** The non-stable performance of the classical techniques caused by the multiplicity of data as multimedia, biological, medical, marketing, character recognition ... etc.
- **In Terms of Quality of Performance:** The classical algorithms are based only on simple functioning, for this reason they don't find the relevant documents.
- **The Difficulty to Select Parameters:** (Texts representation method, distance measurement metric), caused by the multitude of methods existed in the literature
- **Execution Time:** View the number of texts available on the web, the classical methods based on a single agent cannot analyse a large number of texts within a reasonable time.

Nature has a hundred million of experiments but humans have some years of industry, and consequently, draw inspiration from what nature has found (bio-mimicry technique), it's something interesting. The genius of nature is all around us, often in animals or plants that we encounter every day. There are three levels of bio-mimicry, we can inspire from forms, manufacturing process or ecosystems.

The first part of this chapter, is the development of a new bio-inspired private information retrieval system (BI-PRI), based on the social life of bees and their behaviour, using the distribution of tasks to

Figure 1. Positioning of our problematic

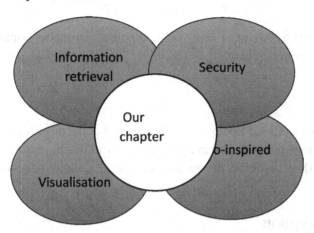

ensure the smooth functioning of the hive by the cleaning, the defence and the construction of honey. Each bee (queen, male or workers) permits the achievement of a precise task. The intelligence is distributed, in order to solve complex problems and have an optimal decision from the sum of individual interactions.

View the manner of results presentation for a query as a list organized or disorganized (semantics) has a real drawback. Most parts of the users consults only the first 2 or 3 pages. The solution to this problem is to introduce a method of visualization, to increase the space of representation and simplify the man-machine interface. This is the subject of the 2nd part of this chapter. Our problematic is positioned in the interaction of different areas as shown in Figure 1.

Objectives

In this chapter several objectives are fixed such as:

- Create a new system of bio-inspired private information retrieval (BI-PIR) system using the behaviour of bees by the development of:
  - A new encryption method called multilayer cryptosystem.
  - A new information retrieval model, called distances combination by social worker bees DC-SWB.
- Testing other classical encryption algorithms (TSZ, Water, Okamoto…... ect).
- The development of a new 3D visualization technique to have a good representation of results and facilitate the navigation and the interaction between users and system.
- Finding a perfect configuration for our private information system (distances combination, text representation and the encryption algorithm).
- Comparison between the performances of our system with the performance of a conventional technique existed in literature.
- Take decisions that will be the starting point for other researchers in the future.

STATE OF THE ART

Before going far in this chapter, we must give you a complete view about some essential concepts that we have used in our approach

Cloud Computing

There is no exact definition of Cloud Computing in literature, but the most common one is that the Cloud Computing allows the outsourcing of data treatment from local machines to distributed virtual servers in distance. It permits to share resources between several entities without dispute of data in secure, scalable and flexible way.

Homomorphic Encryption

The homomorphic encryption (HE), is a kind of cryptosystem that permits the conversion of a text into a form that can be analysed and worked with, as if it is in plaintext form. In other words, the homomorphic encryption allows complex mathematical operations to be performed on encrypted data without compromising the encryption.

Formally, the HE is a conventional cryptographic scheme based on three essential functions: setup for key generation, encryption step and decryption one. Some other resources divide the setup function into two functions: setup for public key generation and Key-Gen for secrete key generation. Such cryptosystem, is considered as homomorphic if it verifies the following property:

$$ENC\ (x) * ENC\ (y) = ENC\ (x + y) \tag{1}$$

with ENC is the encryption function and x and y are two plaintext.

Generally, the homomorphic cryptosystems use special information related to the owner of data. Those schemes are classified on three essential categories:

- **Identity Based Encryption (IBE):** The IBE uses the identity of the user,
- **Attribute Based Encryption (ABE):** The ABE uses a set of attributes related to the user
- **Predicate Based Encryption (PBE):** The PBE uses a specific predicate related to the user different from his identity.

Private Information Retrieval (PIR)

The PIR protocols consist, for hiding request and retrieve information from the server using a secure solution, such as homomorphic cryptography. This concept is now widely used for confidentiality of data in cloud services, such as multi computational services and retrieval models. The Figure 2 describes the general idea of PIR protocols.

1.   Firstly, the client sends his own information (att), used to generate the key (identity, attributes or predicate) to a specific server considered as a third part.

Figure 2. General framework of PIR protocol
As Figure 2 shows, the PIR protocol works as follows:

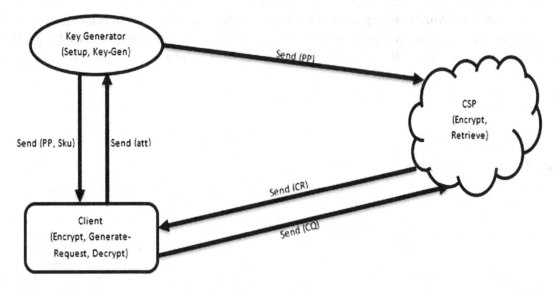

2. The server (key generator), executes setup function in order to generate public key, which is in homomorphic case (a set of parameter known by public parameters (PP)). The Key-Gen function was used to get a secrete key corresponding to a user (Sku) then send PP to both client and cloud service provider (CSP) and Sku to client only.

3. The client and CSP, execute encrypt function to encrypt their data (request for client and data for CSP).

4. The client, once he finished encrypting his request using PP, he sends the ciphered request CQ to the CSP.

5. The CSP in his turn applies CQ on his ciphered data and get ciphered results CR that will be sent to the client.

6. Finally, the client decrypt the CR and get a plaintext results that he want.

7. In our case, we eliminate the key generator and integrate his functions in client side.

Review of Literature

The protection of privacy within search protocols is now a highly active domain. Many systems were done over this as detailed in the next sections:

1. **Trusted Materials Protocols (TMP):** The TMP uses a third part material as trusted coprocessor (coprocessor consists of coordinating the server with the client by hiding the information). The TMP works in the fact that, the client doesn't know the received query by the server and the server know neither the query nor the answer. The main works following this principal are (Khan, 2013), (Reddema, 2012) and (Krzywiecki, 2010).

2. **Homomorphic Encryption Protocols (HEP):** The HEP based on the principal that the client is the one responsible about encryption of query, where he knows already the final query. Among the

main works in this field we mention (Li, 2012), (Bringer, 2011), and (Boneh, 2007) for the purpose to ensure the confidentiality of retrieving information.

3. **Encrypted Key-Word Protocols (EKWP):** The EKWP uses a set of key-words for the information retrieval. We can distinguish many works such as (Prevez, 2012), (Bringer, 2012), (Wang, 2010), (Liu, 2012), (Nourian, 2012) and (Wang, 2012). Figure 3 indicates the classification of known works by type of the protocol.

Figure 3. Works classification of PIR protocols

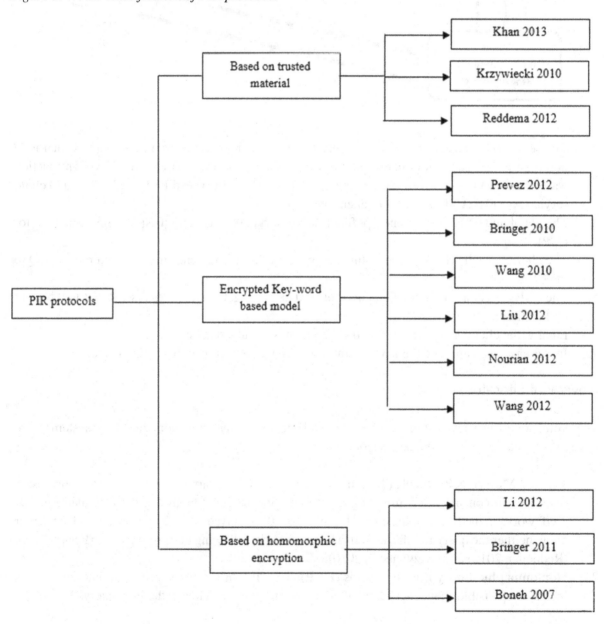

4. **Meta-Heuristic Private Information Retrieval Protocol:** From the known works in the area of applying the meta-heuristic models we mention (Zhang, 2013) where the authors present their paper consists of privacy preserving on retrieval models using an optimal solution resides in quasi-identifier techniques over indexation process. Also, we find (Lunde'98) that consists of combining mathematical simulation methods of biological processes in the image of Activated Sludge Model and knowledge-based models in order to get an optimized retrieval protocol. In (Tamine, 2002), the writers show their point of view concerning optimisation of pertinence of information retrieval system using a combination of genetic techniques, multimodal problems known by niching and query reformulation process in from of genetic relevance process in order to get an efficient optimisation of a retrieval model. Samatha and her friends present a paper in (Samatha, 2012) in which they discuss their optimisation approach using Query Optimization techniques for an efficient data retrieving in cloud storage services. The authors in (Bouarara[2], 2014) try to answer and discuss the attractive performance of the use of genetic algorithms in information retrieval systems. They study the efficiency of genetic algorithm in retrieving information under such conditions, reasons of its failures and ideas that can improve this efficiency. In (Ravinder, 2013) the authors present and discuss their approach of an efficient query construction and execution as a solution for an optimistic retrieval model in cloud computing.

MOTIVATION

We attempted in our proposed chapter, to consider a scientific research launched over a class of medical patients in a hospital Data Warehouse storage service. We were interested by, the information collecting and the online answering system to the specific symptoms and medical diagnostic evolving in time, which require from the users to derive all or some personal details as shown in Figure 4.

The first solution that comes to mind, is to store data in their encrypted form, which means that the encryption and decryption keys will be fixed from the beginning. This can presented an optimal solution at the beginning but as we said earlier; a network hacker fixes the keys all the time, which leads to another problem of performing operation on those data in their encrypted form to ensure privacy or decrypt them before then we cannot ensure the privacy over server side.

For that, we propose our system based on the idea of altering encryption keys with every generation of a query, using the private information retrieval protocol with specific attribute. The encryption depends on the username and password attribute. We also plan a periodic personal data encryption with each new query formulated by the Data Warehouse user. This encryption will use a new predicate generated from user information.

Our System

Our system consists of five parts as shown in Figure 5 where each step going to be seen in the following paragraphs with more details.

Figure 4. Health storage cloud service

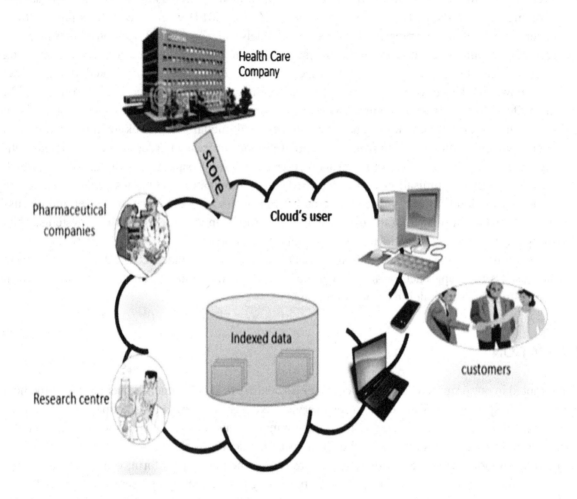

Authentication Part

Authentication part used to ensure the subscription and the connection of users to the system. This step consists of managing the users' personal information such as names, pseudo-names, passwords...etc., Figure 6 indicates the two principal processes of this part.

As Figure 6 indicates, the authentication part compound of two major processes: inscription process and connection process. For the inscription process that is presented in figure a), the user must first fill up a formula with his information (name, pseudo-name, password, mail...etc.) then send it to the server. The server in his turn will verify the existence of username in his users' database. The existence, means that there is already a count with this username; in that case an error message will be returned to the user asking him to change the username. Otherwise, the server hashes the password and stores the information in users' database.

For the connection that is presented in figure b), the user must be already subscribed in the system. To be connected, the user must send his username and password to the server. The server, recuperates the username and the corresponding hashed password from his database. After that, the server hashes

Figure 5. Architecture of our system

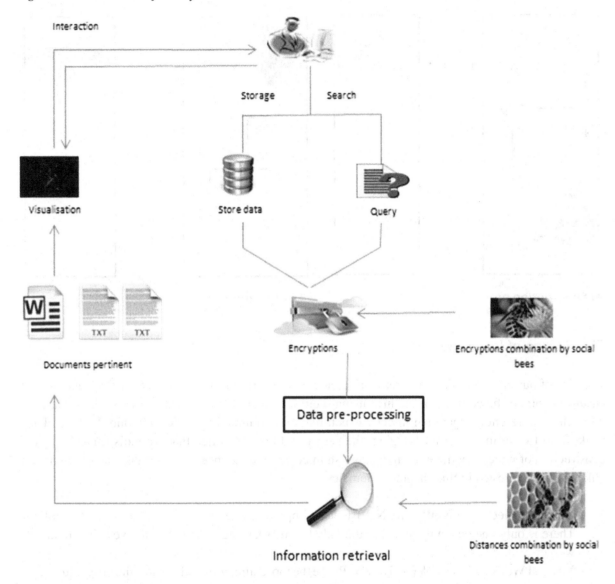

the received password and compares it with the one existed in the database. If the passwords are equals then the user passes automatically to the second part. Otherwise, an error message will be sent to the user informing him that there is an error on username or password.

Private Information Retrieval PIR (Profile Part)

The PIR protocol, represents the main field in which we implement our approach. The user, already well authenticated, can store data or retrieving information within the system in a safety mode. The strategy of this step is divided into two parts: i) information private phase using multilayers cryptosystem ii) information retrieval phase using distances combination by social worker bees. Before starting the description of this important phase we must give you the source of inspiration of each part.

Figure 6. Authentication part of our system

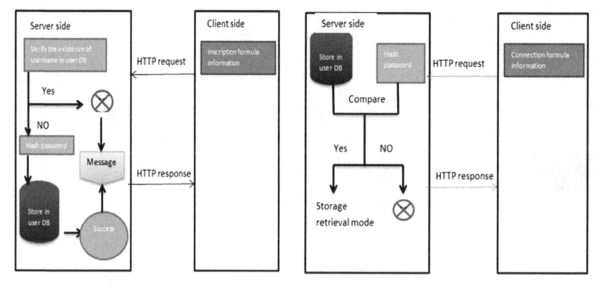

a) Subscription process　　　　　　　　　**b) connection process**

The Source of Inspiration

The idea of our private information retrieval protocol is inspired from the lifestyle of Bees and how to ensure the proper functioning of the hive using their antenna to communicate between them via their odor. Bees represent a vegetarian insects, which live in a community (society) within the hive. They walk, from flower to flower for foraging, the nectar and harvest pollen that are indispensable for the construction of honey (food). We can distinguish male and female, bees. But because the males are all alike, we are interested in this chapter by females' bees:

1. **Natural Queen Bee NQB:** The NQB is very important and ensures the renewal of the colony. There is only one queen by hive it is the only bee that lays eggs. The queen gives birth to all the workers of the hive.
2. **Natural Workers Bees NWBs:** The NWBs are the most numerous and ensures the proper functioning of the hive and changing work gradually as they grow older and they do this without learning from one activity to another.
    a. **Natural Cleaner Bee NCB:** The NCB represents the bee of the first three days carry out the cleaning cells of the hive.
    b. **Natural Handlers' Bee (NHB):** The NHB is responsible for storing pollen and nectar brought to the hive by bees.
    c. **Natural Guardian Bee (NGB):** The NGB has 18th to 21st day with a mission is to regulate the temperature inside the hive she is also the guardian of the hive.
    d. **Purveyor Bee (NPB):** The NPB roams the countryside around the hive to collect nectar, pollen and water for the production of honey indispensable to the survival of the hive.
3. **Natural Lifestyle of Social Bees:** Bees have two places where they can harvest food (flowers or garbage) where forager harvest nectar from flowers (sugar flowers) or sugar bins (fault flowers).

As previously detailed each bee had a specific role in the organisation of the colony. The communication between these bees make the optimal decision emerge (solution for a specific problem).

Multilayer Cryptosystems

In this section, we will describe the use of the inspiration source (natural life of bees) for the construction of multilayer cryptosystem, in order to ensure the security part of our system. As security improvement, we decided to use cryptosystems' combination in order to get security level as maximum as possible. Our idea resides in imitating the manner that the workers bees exchange information between them, for the construction of honey, and ensuring the safety of the hive. The Figure 7 illustrates the main idea of multilayer cryptosystem.

The hive represents the server, where the final encrypted document will be temporary stored until end of the retrieval process. Our system, generates and ciphers documents temporary for each new query, because the use of such cloud service means the use of materials with huge capacities. And that could help any attacker or the server itself to reduce time of attacking using dictionary or linear attack.

1. **The Nectar:** The nectar is the document of the user that will be stored
2. **Honey:** the honey is the document after passing through the boosting cryptosystem algorithm (three filters) it is an encrypted document

Figure 7. Cryptosystem combination framework of our system

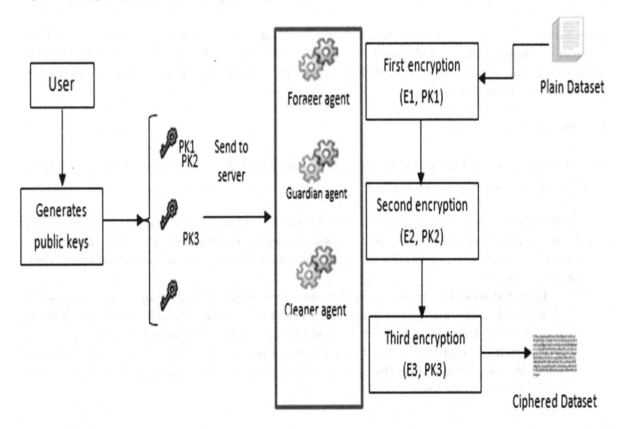

3. **Artificial Security Queen Bee (ASQB):** The ASQB is the main component of our system, characterized by the user because he can give birth to the workers agents, by means to generate keys. As we notice in the Figure 7, the user must execute the setup function of three different encryption schemes, in order to get three public keys that will be used to encrypt either, the query in user's side, and the dataset in server's side.

4. **Artificial Security Worker Bees ASWBs:** The ASWBs used to ensure a better document encryption, each artificial worker bee realizes an encryption using a key and following a homomorphic algorithm according to its level of security. In other words, we are faced with a multi security filtering, and each filter will be done by an officer worker, which represents a specific encryption scheme. For example filter 1 the forager bee uses the waters algorithm as cryptosystem.

5. **Artificial Security Lifestyle (ASL) Strategy:** However, the server, once he received the encryption keys, he start by encrypting the dataset basing on the bees worker agent (homomorphic cryptosystem used) using the:
    a. **First Public Key (PK1):** PK1 is done by forager agent that sends the encrypted data to the Guardian agent.
    b. **Second Public Key (PK2):** The Guardian agent encrypts the received data using PK2 and sends his own results to the Cleaner agent.
    c. **Third Public Key (PK3):** After that the artificial cleaner bee receives the encrypted data, she encrypts it using the PK3. This idea presents a major advantage resides in his security level, otherwise, using several encryption schemes requires a hard work to attack the system.

Distances Combination by Social Worker Bees DC-SWB for Information Retrieval

There are two type of documents, relevant (harvested from a flower) or irrelevant (collected from garbage). We must analyze each document in order to decide if it is relevant or not. For the realization of the second part of our system (information retrieval part), we use the inspiration source previously presented as exhibited in the Figure 8.

Text Preparation

In this phase, the query of the user and each document stored in the server must follow the next process in order to-have a unique representation.

1. **Text Segmentation (TS):** The TS based on the transformation of each text into a list of smaller units, called terms (term can be a set of characters, a word, sentence, concept..... ect), depending to the method used and the results that we want to achieve. The text representation techniques adopted in this chapter are:
    a. **Bag of Words:** This method is simple and oldest based on the division of text into a set of words (a word is a set of characters linked together separated by punctuations) several drawbacks were determined about this method views the Natural language ambiguity:
    b. **N-Gram Character:** It is based on a parameter N that represents a window of characters, which move in the text step by step and saving for each movement the capture window in a list, this technique has a several advantages:

Figure 8. Information retrieval using distance combination by social bees

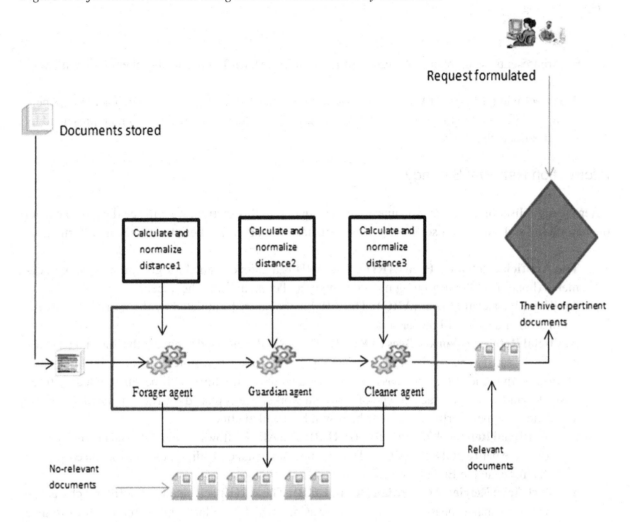

Text Coding TC: The TC uses a weighting technique to calculate the importance of each term in the text walled TF *IDF

$$\text{TF} \times \text{IDF} \,(\mathbf{D, T_i}) = \text{TF} \,(\text{T}_i, \text{D}) \times \text{IDF} \,(\text{T}_i)$$

where:

Term Frequency TF (T_i, Di)

= number of occurrence of term Ti in document Di.

$$P = \frac{number\ of\ relevant\ documents\ finding}{number\ of\ documents\ finding}$$

$$IDF\left(T\right) = \log \frac{|D|}{DF(T)}$$

DF(T) represents the number of documents that contain the term T and D the number of documents of

3. **Text vectoring TV:** The TV is the transformation of each text to a vector where each component vectors represent the position and the importance of each term and corpus will be represented by a matrix document*term.

Information Retrieval Strategy

After the digitalisation of textual documents and the query. In this section, we will see the passage from the natural life style of worker social bees to the artificial life of worker bees for retrieving information.

1. **The Artificial Retrieval Hive (ARH):** The ARH is a class designed for grouping relevant documents (honey). At the beginning must be empty and contains only the queen.
2. **Artificial Retrieval Queen (ARQ):** The ARQ is the query formulated by the user from which a set of worker agents will be generated.
3. **Artificial Retrieval Worker Bees (ARWB):** The ARWB were used to ensure the relevant research in order to satisfy the needs of users. Each artificial worker bee stores the TF * IDF of query. Starting with the idea that the class of relevant document (the hive) will be surrounded by three obstacles and in each obstacle a type of artificial worker bee is placed for filtering the documents. The different type of artificial worker bees will be detailed after:
    a. **Artificial Retrieval Forager Bee (ARFB):** The ARFB allows to calculate and normalizes the distance between the query Q and the document i distance 1 (di, Q) using a distance measure X1(for example Euclidian distance).
    b. **Artificial Retrieval Guardian Bee (ARGB):** The ARGB is located in the filter 2 characterized by distance measure X2 (for example csine), which calculates and normalizes the distance between the document di and query Q distance 2(di, Q).
    c. **Artificial Retrieval Cleaner Bee (ARCB):** The ARCB was located in the obstacle 3 (dam), it is the nearest artificial bee to the hive characterized by a distance measure x3 (for example Manhattan distance), which represents the last barrier that a document di must cross. The ARCB was designed to calculate and normalize the distance between the document di and the query Q distance 3 (di, Q). The distance measure used by each artificial retrieval worker bee must be different compared to the others.
4. **Normalization:** This is an essential point to ensure that all the distance will be in the same range because we work on a combination of distances for this we must unify these distances in order to not favour one by another. First, for each measure a matrix will be built q * Documents. We need to find the maximum and minimum value for each matrix and the normalization of distance must be as follows:

$$dis_X N = \frac{dis_X - dis_{\min}}{dis_{\max} - dis_{\min}}$$

5. **Adaptation Function AF:** The AF allows to take the decision if a document di is relevant or not. It represents the average distance AD between the three distances calculated by the worker agents

$$AD(Q, D_i) = \frac{dis_1 + dis_2 + dis3}{3}$$

6. **Procedure:** The pseudo code shown in Box 1 regroups the algorithm of information retrieval based on the social life of worker bees that represent a filter and the queen bee that represents the query.

7. **Ranking Documents:** In order to calculate the relevance degree of each document that will be presented as an ordered list from the most relevant documents to the least relevant. We will use the average distance AD criterion where the document with the lowest average distance is the most relevant and will be appointed as the head of the list.

Box 1. Information retrieval using artificial worker social bees

```
Input
Distances measures {X1,X2,X3}, Q: query, Dataset, Threshold.
Di: document number I
Begin
 Choose 3 distance measures (X1, X2, X3) and establish a distance matrix
 (Q*documents) for each one of them
 Find the the maximum distance dist     and the minimum distance dist      from the 3
                               max                                   min
distance matrix
```

$$\text{Normalization of the value distance } dis_X N = \frac{dis_X - dis_{min}}{dis_{max} - dis_{min}}$$

```
For each document Di do
    Calculate the average distance AD
```

$$AD(Q, D_i) = \frac{dis_1 + dis_2 + dis3}{3}$$

```
    If AD<threshold then the hive ← Di
     else Di is rejected (no-pertinent)
End
Return: The document of the hive
```

EXPERIMENTATION

Before presented the results we must define the documents collection used and the valuation metrics applied to measure the quality performances of our system.

MEDLARS (Medline) Benchmark

MEDLARS is a data set that contains 1033 documents written in English with a number of terms =8750, 30 queries and the list of relevant documents for each query. These documents were selected out of a large medical collection available at the national library of medicine, this project helped to develop the methodologies for the analysis and evaluation of information retrieval systems and establishing performance criteria such as recall and precision. All results are for a specific MEDLINE query "The crystalline lens in vertebrates includes humans" with size of 51 characters. The used query returns 37 pertinent documents among the whole corpus.

Validation Tools

The evaluation of information retrieval systems (IRS) is at the core of the problems of this study where the descents of the RI evaluation were prepared in the context of project crafield (Bouarara[1], 2014) we can cited several metrics were generally put up between 0 and 1 and the most used are f-measure and entropy, which are founded on the traditional measures recall and precision.
Recall:

$$R = \frac{number\ of\ relevant\ documents\ finding}{number\ of\ relevant\ documents}$$

Precision:

$$P = \frac{number\ of\ relevant\ documents\ finding}{number\ of\ documents\ finding}$$

F-measure is a measure that combined the recall and precision:

$$F = \frac{2 * R * P}{(R + P)}$$

Entropy is used to calculate the loss of information:

$$E(X) = -P(X) * \log(P(X))$$

Noise: this is when the irrelevant answers are selected by our system and delivered to the user as relevant

$$Noise(X) = 1 - P(X)$$

Silence is when relevant answers are not accepted by the system:

$$Silence(X) = 1 - R(X)$$

Result and Analysis

This section will be divided into two parts according to the protocol used (clear or private (encryption)):

Clear Protocol Results

Our first tests will be around the application of our approach distances combination by social worker bees DC-SWB for the information retrieval with clear protocol, without the application of cryptographic algorithms. View the number of representation methods existed in the literature and the Measures of distance that we can find. The question that arises what is the ideal setting for our approach?

To answer this question, we will use an experimental protocol by putting in confrontation the results obtained by our approach DC-SWB with the variation of the next parameters.

- Text representation (2,3, 4, 5-gram and bag of words).
- Distance combination used (EUClidian (EUC), minkowvsky (min3), Cosine (COS)) (Chebychev(CHEB), mink3, COS) (EUC,mink3,CHEB) (EUC,CHEB,,COS).
- Threshold between [0.1,0.9]

For each test we will fix two parameters and varied the third. After several tests, we have chosen to present to you in the Table 1 the most significant results that were obtained with the configuration ((EUC, THEB,, COS), threshold = 0.5) which allows to get the best performance.

Table 1. The best clear information retrieval result of our approach with configuration ((EUC,CHEB,,COS), threshold =0.5and variation of the text representation).

	2 Gram	3 Gram	4 Gram	5 Gram	Bag of Words
Precision	0.571	0.647	0.782	0.48	0.411
Recall	0.216	0.297	0.486	0.324	0.189
f-measure	0.313	0.407	0.599	0.386	0.25
Entropy	0.319	0.281	0.192	0.352	0.365
Silence	0.784	0.703	0.514	0.676	0.811
Noise	0.429	0.353	0.218	0.52	0.589

Figure 9. The best clear information retrieval result of our approach with configuration ((EUC,CHEB,,COS), threshold =0.5and variation of the text representation).

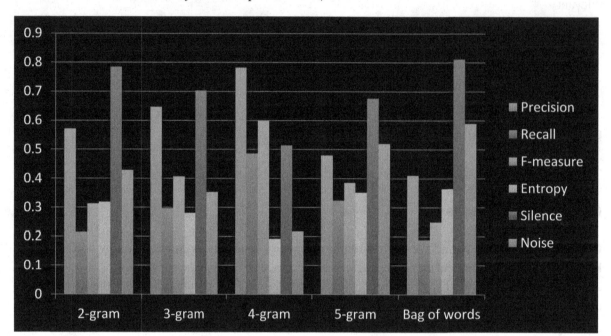

Discussion 1

After different tests presented in Table 1, we see that the variation of parameters have a very important role in the proper functioning and a great influence in the final results. We will explain the influence of each parameters and the change of result observed.

- **Influence of Text Representation:** By analyzing the results of the Table 1, we remark that the performance of the method DC-SB in terms of f-measure augment by increasing the value of N until N = 4, which has the optimum value because it generate a discriminant terms. This performance begins to relapse after for N=5. The bag of words text representation does not ensure the achievement of an efficient result because we did not use the linguistic processing caused by the ambiguity of natural language presented in the documents.

- **Influence of Distances Measures:** There is not a universal distance measure. Before trying to introduce an algorithm or technique for information retrieval we must select the distance measure used.

  Concerning our approach DC-SB based on the idea of combining the advantages of three distances where we had used four combinations as noticed in the experimental protocol but the best results are obtained with the combination (EUC THEB, COS) which confirms that these three distances measures can be used together and they are complementary.

- **In Term of Threshold, Recall and Precision:** The threshold parameter is a very difficult to adjust because it depends on several factors and requires several tests to be fixed. We discovered that if we increase the threshold, then the recall will increase and precision decrease because with a threshold = 0.9 or 1 all documents will be viewed as relevant which ensures that all real relevant documents will be delivered to the user and if the threshold is reduced to 0.1 or 0 then the number of documents retained going to be decreased and the precision will increase. The best results obtained are always held with a threshold of 0.5 which justify the high precision.

- **In Term of Noise and Silence:** Noise and silence bonded directly to recall and precision with silence = 0.514 which represents that half of really relevant documents are not returned by our system and with a noise = 0.218 indicates that the majority of documents retained by our system are really relevant.
- **In Term of f-Measure and Entropy:** The best outcomes are obtained with an f-measure = 0.599 as presented in the Table 1 (yellow boxes) which supports our idea of applying our model of distance combination by social bees to solve this problem and the performance of our system get close to the ideal outcome and with entropy = 0.192 which is apologized by the purpose of the method of dimension reduction which cause some loss of data.

We conclude with a decision and a response to the questions posed previously is that the ideal configuration for the information retrieval using DC-SB is ((EUC,CHEB,,COS), 4-gram characters, threshold =0.5).

Private Information Retrieval Result

The decision making after analyzing the previous results will be applied within the framework of a private information retrieval PIR with an encryption protocol. We will launch an experiment in two stages:

In order to test the effectiveness of our approach in the private protocol, we propose a comparison between the results obtained by the DC-SWB with the variation of the cryptosystem method (TSZ (Hervé, 2005), Okamoto-Uchiyama (Jason 2009), Waters (Khan, 2013), Goldwasser-Micali (Jason, 2009)). The results are grouped in the Table 2 and Figure 10.

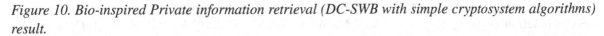

Figure 10. Bio-inspired Private information retrieval (DC-SWB with simple cryptosystem algorithms) result.

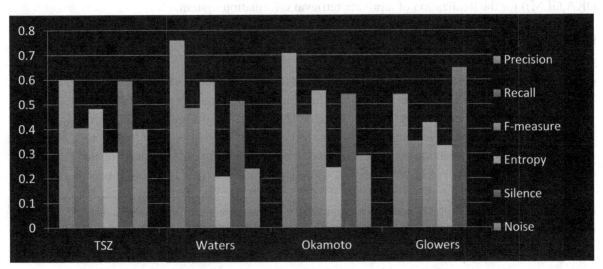

Table 2. Bio-inspired Private information retrieval (DC-SWB with simple cryptosystem algorithms) result.

Encryptions Algorithm	Private Information Retrieval			
	TSZ	Waters	Okamoto	Glowers
Precision	0.6	0.75	0.708	0.541
Recall	0.405	0.486	0.459	0.351
f-measure	0.483	0.589	0.556	0.426
Entropy	0.306	0.215	0.244	0.332
Silence	0.595	0.514	0.541	0.649
Noise	0.4	0.25	0.292	0.459

Discussion 2

- We notice that the integration of cryptographic schemes influenced the outcomes of the retrieval technique, because the content of the document will be changed after the encryption. Consequently the content of the query and the document Stored by the user will be changed according to the algorithm of cryptography farming.
- By analyzing the Table 2 and Figure 10, we see that the best result are given by the cryptosystem algorithm waters (yellow boxes). We note that the performance of our information retrieval system DC-SWB was increased with a precision = 0.75 (18 out of 24 returned no relevant document in the result) and a recall = 0.486 (18 from 37 records returned no actual document).
- The badly result are given by the glowers protocol (red boxes).
  - It is also noted that the result with waters algorithm can achieve a very close results compared to the clear protocol.

Second confrontation puts in competition the result of our algorithm DC-SB using our new boosting cryptosystem algorithm based on the combination of homomorphic algorithms with the variation of the combination cryptosystems ((OKA,GLM, WAT), (WAT, TSZ,OKA), (GLM, WAT,TSZ), (TSZ, OKA,GLM)) for the Realization of a private retrieval information system.

Discussion 3

- The cryptosystem boosting algorithm was a very interesting experience where we want to increase the degree of preservation of user private life through the use of three levels of filter and to combine the advantages of each cryptographic system. The Table 3 and Figure 11 show that waters and okamoto algorithms give better results and the combinations that contain (okamoto and waters) allow our method to obtain better performance. For our boosting cryptosystem the ideal combination is (OKA,GLM, WAT) yellow boxes with a precision = 0.642 (18 relevant papers among 28 returned 'by our system) and recall = 0.486 (18 relevant documents among 37 really relevant).
- After the analysis of Tables 2 and 3, we can classify the variances of our system using DC-SWB in term of cryptosystem applied as presents the podium in Figure 12.

Table 3. Bio inspired private information retrieval (DC-SWB with multilayer cryptosystem algorithms) results

Boosting Algorithm	Private Information Retrieval			
	(OKA,GLM, WAT)	**(WAT, TSZ,OKA)**	**(GLM, WAT,TSZ)**	**(TSZ, OKA,GLM)**
Precision	0.642	0.666	0.578	0.545
Recall	0.486	0.378	0.324	0.324
f-measure	0.553	0.482	0.415	0.406
Entropy	0.284	0.27	0.316	0.33
Silence	0.514	0.622	0.676	0.676
Noise	0.358	0.334	0.422	0.455

Comparison 1

The first comparison is to give our results a location and a reference by comparing the best performance obtained by DC-SB algorithm with the results of a conventional method (Salton, 1988) that was developed for this purpose applying in Clear and encryption protocol.

Figure 11. Bio inspired private information retrieval (DC-SWB with multilayer cryptosystem algorithms) results

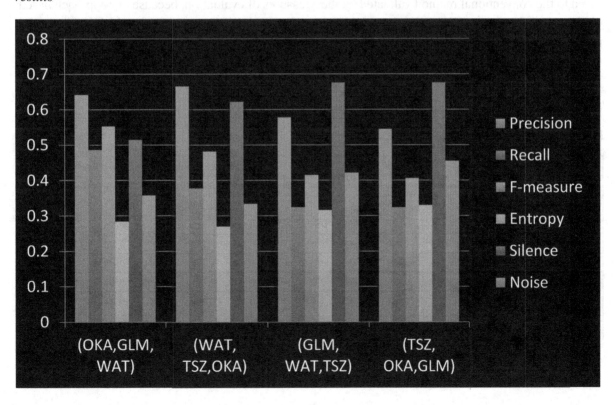

Figure 12. Podium of the best cryptosystem for the DC-SWB

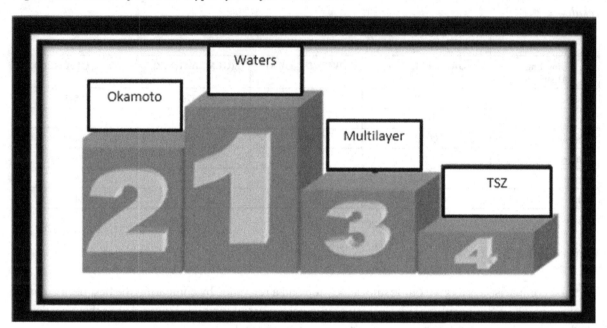

Discussion 4

The Table 4 shows Clearly that our model of information retrieval DC-SWB has a high priority compared to the conventional method validated by the Measures of evaluation, because our approach based on the principle of three filters and the combination of several distances measures which increases the precision and the number of relevant documents in, a clear and encryptions protocol.

Table 4. Comparison between our approach distance combination by social bees with a classical approach in clear and cryptosystem protocol

Validation Tools Cryptosystem	Classical Method						Distance Combination by Social Bees (DC-SB)					
	Recall	Precision	f-Measure	Entropy	Noise	Silence	Recall	Precision	f-Measure	Entropy	Noise	Silence
TSZ	0.35	0.61	0.444	0.301	0.39	0.65	0.405	0.6	0.483	0.306	0.4	0.595
Waters	0.27	0.8	0.403	0.178	0.2	0.73	0.486	0.75	0.589	0.215	0.25	0.514
Okamoto	0.37	0.71	0.486	0.243	0.29	0.63	0.459	0.708	0.556	0.244	0.292	0.541
Goldwassers micali	0.35	0.53	0.421	0.336	0.47	0.65	0.351	0.541	0.426	0.332	0.459	0.649
multilayer cryptosystem (OKA,GLM,WATERS)	0.243	0.5	0.327	0.365	0.5	0.757	0.486	0.642	0.553	0.284	0.514	0.358
Clear	0.27	0.7	0.39	0.249	0.3	0.73	0.782	0.486	0.599	0.192	0.514	0.218

Decisions

The ideal configuration of our system is:

- Cryptosystem waters
- Text representation 4-gram
- The distances combination (euc, cheb, cos)
- Threshold=0.5
  - Our encryption algorithm (multilayer cryptosystem) gives satisfactory results compared to conventional cryptosystem
- Our bio-inspired private information retrieval system gives better results than the conventional method.

Comparison 2

The Figure 13 illustrates a theoretical comparison of the cryptosystems that we used in our system. We defined a set of criteria for the evaluation. The scheme, it is a homomorphic system, Does it ensure the confidentiality of retrieving process, Does it ensure integrity of results Does the scheme use predicates (identity or other attributes) in order to generate the keys, and finally the size of the ciphered request(used).

Comparison 3

The third confrontation is a comparison between our approach model distance combination by social bees (DC-SB) and others models inspired by the behaviour of social insects like social ant Artificial Colony Optimization (Dorigo, 1996), genetic algorithm GAs (Holland,1973) and particle swarm optimization PSO(Kennedy, 1995) as presented in Figure 14 in order to summarize a theoretical analysis to exhibit their operating parameters, problems of application and the common points between these different techniques.

Figure 13. Theoretical comparison of cryptographic schemes

Cryptographic scheme	Homomorphic	Ensuring confidentiality	Ensuring integrity	Predicate Based algorithm (PBE)	Size of the request (character)
TSZ	Yes	Yes	No	Yes	252 603
Waters	Yes	Yes	Yes	Yes	266
Okamoto-Uchiyama	Yes	Yes	No	No	102
Paillier	Yes	Yes	No	No	146
Goldwasser-Micali	Yes	Yes	No	No	1 053

Figure 14. Summarization of a theoretical comparison, between the artificial social cockroaches (ASC) and others model inspired from the social insects.

	PSO	Genetic Algorithms	ACO	Our approach DC-SB
Parameters	Number of particles initial -Size of problem -Velocity maximum -Number of generation -Stopping criterion	- initial Population, chromosome, number of generation, probability of crossing , probability of mutation, - fitness function - Stopping criterion	-The choice of path to explore -Number of ant -Stopping criterion -Max-min ant system -importance of Strengthening	-Threshold -Selection method -The choice of filter for each bee worker agent -Stopping Criterion
Execution Time	Medium	Elevate	Medium	Elevate
Memory	Yes	Yes	Yes	No
Solution	randomly	Randomly	Unique	Depends on the choice of parameters
Operators	-initialisation of parameters. -evaluation and selection -updating	-Selection -Cross-over -Mutation	-Produce pheromone trails and solutions -Updating of pheromone path	-Filters -Worker agent -Queen agent
Problem application	Aerodynamics, exploration of March, clustering Image processing, , Social networks, link analysis purposes automatic summary, application web, knowledge extraction	The Traveling salesman problem (TSP) Knapsack problem , clustering, image processing, intrusion detection, plagiarism detection	The Traveling salesman problem (TSP) information retrieval Link analysis and social networks, test application, network routing, vehicle routing, quadratic assignment	Clustering, Gesture recognition and all bi class problem Security, protection of private life web service, dimension reduction problem, spam detection
Digitalisation	-Binary vector -Real vectors -matrix -structured data -vectors	Binary Tree Integer Real	Matrix of Binary Undirected graph	Vectors or matrix (D-dimensional)
Communication	Cooperation between particles	Transfer data between parent individual and son one	path pheromone	Odour pheromone
Objective	Collective decision	Evolution of the solution from generation to another	Find the shortest path	Ensures Proper functioning of the hive and production of the honey

3D VISUALISATION

This part of our system is the most interesting that provides a visualization of relevant documents and irrelevant documents as a cube 3d.

Whenever a new document identified as relevant, it will be stored in a box and the same for the non-relevant documents. Documents returned by our system as relevant are grouped together in boxes with

Figure 15. 3D Visualization of the results of PIR protocol

 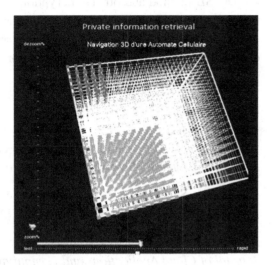

blue color and non-relevant documents are grouped in boxes with the color green as shown in Figure 15a this part was achieved by the Java 3D and characterized by a set of functionalities:

- Zoom (front and rear) to better view the documents in order to have a global and detailed view.
- The opportunity to see the results of different positions through the rotation (left or right).

We can know the information of each document and even his number as exhibited in the Figure 15.b by approaching the cursor to the box of the document.

CONCLUSION

In this chapter we had used the behavior of social bees for the construction of boosting cryptosystem based on the combination of three homomorphic algorithms and distance combination by social bees for information retrieval in order to develop a Private information retrieval system by imitating the cooperation between bees workers and queen bee in order to ensure the proper functioning of the hive.

The experimental results are positive and confirms the idea of testing this system and the evaluation tools used validate that our approach DC-SB with an ideal configuration ((EUC, THEB, COS), 4-gram and threshold = 0.5) for the part of information retrieval and a boosting cryptosystem using the configuration (OKA, GLM, WAT) for the encryption part gives better performance compared to the classical method. Nevertheless, our system presents a major drawback resides in the long time that is taken for encryption step because of the large number of operations executed by the cryptosystems. Our system allows a new presentation of the result in a 3D graphical form to be easily understandable and interpretable by users.

As future works we can apply others bio-inspired techniques for private information retrieval as social spiders, social ants, immune system, genetic algorithms, particle swarm optimization ….etc. for the optimizing the part of information retrieval or the process of cryptographic. We can also combine between these methods, using other methods of indexation like TFC. Tested others combinations of distances for the DC-SB method and others encryptions combination for the boosting cryptosystem. Also, another impediment of PIR protocols is that we can use neither a dictionary nor a thesaurus like wordnet because of the fact that the retrieval step is executed over encrypted data. For that, we will develop a framework consists of finding synonyms of words before encryption step in order to avoid language polysemy.

REFERENCES

Aljawarneh, S. (2011). Cloud security engineering: Avoiding security threats the right way. *International Journal of Cloud Applications and Computing, 1*(2), 64–70. doi:10.4018/ijcac.2011040105

Aljawarneh, S. (2011). A web engineering security methodology for e-learning systems. *Network Security, 1*(3), 12–15. doi:10.1016/S1353-4858(11)70026-5

Aljawarneh, S. (2011). Cloud security engineering: Avoiding security threats the right way. *International Journal of Cloud Applications and Computing, 1*(2), 64–70. doi:10.4018/ijcac.2011040105

Boneh, D., & Waters, B. (2007). Conjunctive, subset, and range queries on encrypted data. In *Theory of cryptography* (pp. 535–554). Springer Berlin Heidelberg. doi:10.1007/978-3-540-70936-7_29

Bouarara, H. A., Hamou, R. M., & Amine, A. (2014). Text Clustering using Distances Combination by Social Bees: Towards 3D Visualisation Aspect. *International Journal of Information Retrieval Research, 4*(3), 34–53.

Bouarara, H. A., Hamou, R. M., Rahmani, A., & Amine, A. (2014, 33). Rahmani, A., Abdelmalek A., Application of Meta-Heuristics Methods on PIR Protocols Over Cloud Storage Services. *International Journal of Cloud Applications and Computing, 4*(3), 1–19. doi:10.4018/ijcac.2014070101

Bouarara, H. A., Rahmani, A., Hamou, R. M., & Amine, A. (2014, June). Machine learning tool and meta-heuristic based on genetic algorithms for plagiarism detection over mail service. In *Computer and Information Science (ICIS), 2014 IEEE/ACIS 13th International Conference on* (pp. 157-162). IEEE. doi:10.1109/ICIS.2014.6912125

Bringer, J., & Chabanne, H. (2012). Embedding edit distance to enable private keyword search. *Human-centric Computing and Information Sciences, 2*(1), 1–12. doi:10.1186/PREACCEPT-1253053215890607

Dorigo, M., Maniezzo, V., & Colorni, A. (1996). Ant system: optimization by a colony of cooperating agents. Systems, Man, and Cybernetics, Part B: Cybernetics. *IEEE Transactions on, 26*(1), 29–41.

Hervé, C., Duong, H. P., & David, P. (2005). *Public Traceability in Traitor Tracing Schemes. Eurocrypt '05* (pp. 542–558). Aarhus, Denmark: Springer.

Holland, J. H. (1973). Genetic algorithms and the optimal allocation of trials. *SIAM Journal on Computing, 2*(2), 88–105. doi:10.1137/0202009

Jason, C. (2009). Cryptographically-enforced hierarchical access control with multiple keys. *Journal of Logic and Algebraic Programming, 76*(3), 690–700.

Kennedy, J., & Eberhart, R. (1995). "Particle Swarm Optimization". In *Proceedings of IEEE International Conference on Neural Networks* (vol. 4, pp. 1942–1948). IEEE. doi:10.1109/ICNN.1995.488968

Khan, A. N., Mat Kiah, M. L., Khan, S. U., & Madani, S. A. (2013). Towards secure mobile cloud computing: A survey. *Future Generation Computer Systems, 29*(5), 1278–1299. doi:10.1016/j.future.2012.08.003

Krzywiecki, Ł., Kutyłowski, M., Misztela, H., & Struminski, T. (2011, January). Private Information Retrieval with a Trusted Hardware Unit–Revisited. In *Information Security and Cryptology* (pp. 373-386). Springer Berlin Heidelberg.

Li, M., Yu, S., Lou, W., & Hou, Y. T. (2012, June). Toward privacy-assured cloud data services with flexible search functionalities. In *Distributed Computing Systems Workshops (ICDCSW), 2012 32nd International Conference on* (pp. 466-470). IEEE. doi:10.1109/ICDCSW.2012.41

Liu, Q., Tan, C. C., Wu, J., & Wang, G. (2012, March). Efficient information retrieval for ranked queries in cost-effective cloud environments. In INFOCOM, 2012 Proceedings IEEE (pp. 2581-2585). IEEE. doi:10.1109/INFCOM.2012.6195657

Lunde, R., & Dannenmann, P. (1998). Information Retrieval from Mathematical Models for Process Optimisation in Waste-Water Treatment. In *Proceedings of the 12th International Symposium "Computer Science for Environmental Protection"*. Metropolis.

Nourian, A., Maheswaran, M., & Maheshwari, V. (2012, December). Character-based search with data confidentiality in the clouds. In *Proceedings of the 2012 IEEE 4th International Conference on Cloud Computing Technology and Science (CloudCom)* (pp. 895-899). IEEE Computer Society.

Pervez, Z., Awan, A. A., Khattak, A. M., Lee, S., & Huh, E. N. (2013). Privacy-aware searching with oblivious term matching for cloud storage. *The Journal of Supercomputing, 63*(2), 538–560. doi:10.1007/s11227-012-0829-z

Ravinder, R. P., Sridhar, V. S., & RamaKrishna, V. (2013). An Optimistic Approach for Query Construction and Execution in Cloud Computing Environment. *International Journal of Advanced Research in Computer Science and Software Engineering, 3*(5), 237-241.

Reddemma, Y., Thirupathi, L., & Gunti, S. (2009). A Secure Model for Cloud Computing Based Storage and Retrieval. *SIGCOMM Computer Communication Review, 39*(1), 50–55.

Samatha N., Vijay Chandu K., Raja Sekhar Reddy P. (2012). Query Optimization Issues for Data Retrieval in Cloud Computing. *International Journal of Computational Engineering Research, 2* (5), 1361-1364.

Tamine, L., & Boughanem, M. (2002). Optimisation de la pertinence dans un SRI: Un problème multimodal approché sous l'angle de la génétique. In INFORSID (pp. 39-53). Academic Press.

Wang, C., Cao, N., Ren, K., & Lou, W. (2012). Enabling secure and efficient ranked keyword search over outsourced cloud data. Parallel and Distributed Systems. *IEEE Transactions on, 23*(8), 1467–1479.

Zhang, X., Liu, C., Nepal, S., & Chen, J. (2013). An efficient quasi-identifier index based approach for privacy preservation over incremental data sets on cloud. *Journal of Computer and System Sciences, 79*(5), 542–555. doi:10.1016/j.jcss.2012.11.008

KEY TERMS AND DEFINITIONS

3D Visualisation: It is a tool that allows to users to have a 3D navigation and present the results as images form in order to make the results easily interpretable and have a great space of outcome representation.

Bio-Inspired: This is a new paradigm that includes a set of algorithms based on the principle of imitating the lifestyle of living systems and natural phenomenon in order to solve complex problems in our life.

Cloud Service: A cloud service is any resource that is provided over the Internet.

Cryptographic Scheme: An algorithm that allows encryption and decryption of data according to a particular functioning.

Private Information Retrieval (PIR): It is a system that allows to the users to store and retrieve its data securely.

Social Bees: A set of insects which live in an organized colony. They communicate between them to ensure the good functioning of the hive.

Validation Tools: A set of measures which exist in literature. They are used to evaluate the performance of an information retrieval system.

Chapter 15
Performance Management on Cloud Using Multi-Priority Queuing Systems

A. Madankan
Yazd University, Iran

A. Delavar Khalfi
Yazd University, Iran

ABSTRACT

Cloud computing is known as a new trend for computing resource provision. The process of entering into the cloud is formed as queue, so that each user has to wait until the current user is being served. In this model, the web applications are modeled as queues and the virtual machines are modeled as service centers. M/M/K model is used for multiple priority and multiple server systems with preemptive priorities. To achieve that it distinguish two groups of priority classes that each classes includes multiple items, each having their own arrival and service rate. It derives an approximate method to estimate the steady state probabilities. Based on these probabilities, it can derives approximations for a wide range of relevant performance characteristics, such as the expected postponement time for each item class and the first and second moment of the number of items of a certain type in the system.

1. INTRODUCTION

Cloud computing has been an emerging technology for provisioning computing resource and providing infrastructure of web applications in recent years. Cloud computing greatly lowers the threshold for deploying and maintaining web applications since it provides infrastructure as a service (IaaS) and platform as a service (PaaS) for web applications. Consequently, a number of web applications, particularly the web applications of medium and small enterprises, have been built into a cloud environment. Meanwhile, leading IT companies have established public commercial clouds as a new kind of investment. For example, Amazon Elastic Compute Cloud (Amazon EC2) is a web service that provides resizable compute capacity in the cloud. It is designed to make web-scale computing easier for developers. Google App

DOI: 10.4018/978-1-4666-8676-2.ch015

Copyright © 2015, IGI Global. Copying or distributing in print or electronic forms without written permission of IGI Global is prohibited.

Engine enables enterprises to build and host web applications on the same systems that power Google applications. App Engine offers fast development and deployment; simple administration, with no need to worry about hardware, patches or backups; and effortless scalability. IBM also provides cloud options. Whether you choose to build private clouds, use the IBM cloud, or create a hybrid cloud that includes both, these secure workload solutions provide superior service management and new choices for deployment. We even can establish a private cloud with Ubuntu Enterprise Cloud to offer immediacy and elasticity in the infrastructure of web applications. In summary, both of the numbers of cloud applications and providers have kept gradually increasing for a couple of years. As a result, computing resource scheduling and performance managing have been ones of the most important aspects of clouding computing.

Since there is not any standard model has been widely accepted by industry yet, scaling up and down is an open issue for researchers. The cloud providers, such as Amazon, IBM, and Google have their own mechanisms which are commercial ones and inherited from their existing proprietary technology. The researchers from universities and institutes also have proposed some models and methods. For example, in (K. Xiong and H. Perros, 2009), the author introduces many outcomes on predicting system performance based on machine learning obtained in RAD lab of University of California at Berkeley. The existing solutions to scaling up and down are designed via various techniques, such as statistical methods, machine learning, and queuing theory.

Aware of the advantages and disadvantages of these solutions, we propose a queuing-based model for performance management on cloud. In this chapter, we show how the queuing model, M/M/K model is used for multiple priority and multiple server systems with preemptive priorities. To achieve that we distinguish two groups of priority classes that each classes includes multiple items, each having their own arrival and service rate. We derive an approximate method to estimate the steady state probabilities with an approximation error that can be made as small as desired at the expense of some more numerical matrix iterations. Based on these probabilities, we can derive approximations for a wide range of relevant performance characteristics, such as the expected postponement time for each item class and the first and second moment of the number of items of a certain type in the system.

A cloud computing is generally able to handle multiple incoming jobs priority, that we classify as either high priority or low priority job. Each job has its own arrival rate and service time distribution. As a consequence, we need to model cloud computing by a (multi-server) priority queuing system with two priority classes, where each class consists of multiple subclasses (item types). We develop our own algorithm in this chapter, assuming Poisson arrivals and exponential service times.

2. MODELING THE QUEUING

2.1 Definitions and Notations

We have assumed that jobs are processed according to a preemptive priority rule, i.e. when a high priority (hp) item arrives and no server is available, one of the low priority (lp) items in service (if there is one) is taken out of service (postponed) to allow the high priority item to be served. As preemption discipline we suppose that if preemption occurs each lp item in service is chosen with equal probability. When a server comes available again, one of the postponed items is taken back into the service (resumed). We also suppose a resume discipline with equal probability for each of the postponed items.

Because of the memory less property of the exponential distribution, it does not make a difference whether postponed jobs are resumed from the moment of interruption on or whether they are restarted completely. All servers are equal, and if multiple servers are available to process a job, each available server has an equal chance to get this job. We use to denote the utilization rates of high and low priority item classes in the system.

We characterize the system state by five vectors of dimensions and, where the components of each vector refer to the (high and low priority) subclasses. The first four vectors are obvious, i.e. vectors containing information about the items in queue and in service.

Next, we need one more vector to keep track of low priority items that have been withdrawn from service when a high priority item arrived. This vector is necessary since items with longer processing time will be withdrawn (postponed) more often and then the probability to have in front of server one of these slow moving items is higher. Thus, the systems state probabilities are denoted by $P_{m,n}(\overline{w}^h, \overline{s}^h, \overline{w}^l, \overline{s}^l, \overline{r}^l)$.

All notations that were used in this chapter and their description were gathered in table1. And also we define $PsTime_i^l$ as time spent by items of low priority subclass i in the postponed state, $SJTime_i^l$ as sojourn time of items of low priority subclass, $nrPreemptEvent_i^l$ as number of preemption events per low priority item of type i and $ReenterTime_i^l$ time between the moment a low priority item of type i is postponed and the moment when the service process is resumed again.

2.2 Stationary State Equations

In this section, we will write down the equilibrium state equations for the continuous time Markov chain. That is, the net exchange of probability in an infinitesimal interval from a given state with its neighbors has to be zero in an equilibrium situation. Neighbors of a state $(\overline{w}^h, \overline{s}^h, \overline{w}^l, \overline{s}^l, \overline{r}^l)$ with n clients of high priority and m clients of low priority are states to/from which a one-step transition is possible, either by an item arrival or by a service completion. According to the numbers n and m of items in the system, the system states (so the equilibrium equations) can be divided into three areas:

I. There is at least one high priority item in the queue $(n > k, m \geq 0)$,
II. All servers are busy, but there is no high priority item in the queue $(n \leq k, n + m \geq k)$,
III. There is at least one server available $(n + m < k)$,

All these subspaces have different equilibrium equations. Besides, we have to consider the equations for the two boundaries between the regions separately.

In area **I**, we have states with all servers occupied and high priority items in the queue, so no low priority items are in service $(\overline{s}^l = 0)$. Therefore the transitions from the neighbors of state $(\overline{w}^h, \overline{s}^h, \overline{w}^l, \overline{s}^l, \overline{r}^l)$ are due to:

1. The arrival of high and low priority jobs that enter the queue
2. The service completion of a high priority job, in this case, we consider all combinations (i, j) where i presents the subclass of the item for which service is completed and j is the subclass of the high priority item that enter service.

Table 1. All notations and their description

Notation	Description	Notation	Description
k	Number of servers	$\bar{w}^l$	Vector describing amounts of low priority items in the queue.
N^h	Number of high priority classes	$\bar{s}^h$	Vector describing amounts of high priority items in the service.
N^l	Number of low priority classes	$\bar{s}^l$	Vector describing amounts of low priority items in the service.
Λ^h	Total arrival rate of the high priority items, λ_i^h and arrival rate of the high priority subclass i. $\Lambda^h = \sum_{i=1}^{N^h} \lambda_i^h$	$\bar{r}^l$	Vector describing amounts of postponed low priority items.
Λ^l	Total arrival rate of the low priority items, λ_i^l and arrival rate of the low priority subclass i. $\Lambda^l = \sum_{i=1}^{N^l} \lambda_i^l$	$Z(\xi)$	Solution matrix of the states $(n > k)$, obtained as the solution of the equation (7)
a_i^h	Arrival fraction of the high priority subclass i.	P_n	Vector of servers states probabilities when there is a high priority items in the queue.
a_i^l	Arrival fraction of the low priority subclass i.	$\mathbb{P}_{\hat{i}}$	Vector of servers states probabilities when there is no high priority items in the queue.
μ^h	Average service rate of the high priority items, and μ_i^h - service rate of the high priority subclass i. $\mu^h = \Lambda^h / \sum_{i=1}^{N^h} \frac{\lambda_i^h}{\mu_i^h} = \frac{\Lambda^h}{k\rho^h}$	$v(\xi)$	Vector-function, which defines probabilities of system states with no high priority item in the queue.
μ^l	Average service rate of the low priority items, and μ_i^l - service rate of the low priority subclass i. $\mu^l = \Lambda^l / \sum_{i=1}^{N^l} \frac{\lambda_i^l}{\mu_i^l} = \frac{\Lambda^l}{k\rho^l}$	$\mathbb{H}(\xi)$	Matrix-function, which defines the vectors-function $v(\xi)$
γ	Fraction of general service rates of high and low priority items, i.e. $\gamma = \frac{\mu^l}{\mu^h}$.	q_i^l	Number of items of low priority subclass i in the queue.
δ_i^h	Permutation coefficient of service rate of high priority subclass i. $(1 + \delta_i^h) = \frac{\mu_i^h}{\mu^h}$	PS_i^l	Number of items of low priority subclass i in the postponed state.
δ_i^l	Permutation coefficient of service rate of low priority subclass i. $(1 + \delta_i^h) = \frac{\mu_i^l}{\mu^l}$	SR_i^l	Number of items of low priority subclass i in the service.

continued on following page

Performance Management on Cloud Using Multi-Priority Queuing Systems

Table 1. continued

Notation	Description	Notation	Description
n	Total number of the high priority items in the system, and n_i number of items of the high priority subclass i.	R_i^l	Number of items of low priority subclass i in the system.
m	Total number of the low priority items in the system, and m_i number of items of the low priority subclass i.	W_i^l	Waiting time of items of low priority subclass i.
$\hat{t}$	Total number of items in the system $\hat{t} = n + m$, and t - total number of items in the system minus number of items in service $t = \hat{t} - k$.	λ_i^{ps}	Arrival rate of a low priority item $i \cdot$ into postponed state
$\overline{w}^h$	Vector describing amounts of high priority items in the queue.		

Hence the equilibrium equations are:

$$(\Lambda^h + \Lambda^l + \overline{\mu}(\overline{s}^h, \overline{0}))P_{n,m}(\overline{w}^h, \overline{s}^h, \overline{w}^l, \overline{s}^l, \overline{r}^l) = \sum_{i=1}^{N^h} \lambda_i^h P_{n-1,m}(\overline{w}^h - \overline{e}_i^h, \overline{s}^h, \overline{w}^l, \overline{0}, \overline{r}^l)$$

$$+ \sum_{i=1}^{N^l} \lambda_i^l P_{n,m-1}(\overline{w}^h, \overline{s}^h, \overline{w}^l - \overline{e}_i^l, \overline{0}, \overline{r}^l)$$

$$+ \sum_{i=1}^{N^h} \sum_{j=1}^{N^l} \frac{w_j^h + 1}{|\overline{w}^h| + 1}(s_i^h + 1 - e_{ij}^h)\mu_i^h P_{n+1,m}(\overline{w}^h + \overline{e}_j^h, \overline{s}^h + \overline{e}_i^h - \overline{e}_j^h, \overline{w}^l, \overline{0}, \overline{r}^l)$$

where $\dfrac{w_j^h + 1}{|\overline{w}^h| + 1}$ characterizes the probability that the high priority item with class j is in front of the queue.

In area II the equilibrium equations are different for the internal states (i.e. $n < k, n + m > k$) and for the boundary states (i.e. $n = k, n + m > k$) for II-III and $n \leq k, n + m \geq k$ for I-II.

In the internal states of area II ($n < k, n + m > k$) all servers are busy, low priority items are in service and no high priority items are in the queue (i.e. $\overline{s}^l \neq 0$, $\overline{w}^h = 0$). So, the transitions from the neighbors of state $(\overline{0}, \overline{s}^h, \overline{w}^l, \overline{s}^l, \overline{r}^l)$ occur due to

1. The arrival of a low priority job that enters the queue,
2. The arrival of a high priority job that is served directly, thereby preempting a low priority job and changing the vector $\overline{r}^l$ we assume that low priority items to be withdrawn from service are selected randomly, so the probability that an item of subclass j is selected equals $\dfrac{s_j^l + 1}{|\overline{s}^l| + 1}$,

3. Service completion of a (high or low priority) item type i without postponed items in the queue $(\overline{r}^l = 0)$, so a new service of a low priority item type j is started, note that subclass j is at the front of the queue with probability $\dfrac{w_j^l + 1}{\left|\overline{w}^l\right| + 1}$.

4. Service completion of a (high or low priority) item type i with postponed items in the queue $(\overline{r}^l \neq 0)$, so the service of a postponed low priority item type j is continued, note that subclass j is at the front of the queue with probability $\dfrac{r_j^l + 1}{\left|\overline{r}^l\right| + 1}$.

When writing down the equilibrium equations, we use the fact that the service rates of the postponed items and the items in the queue are the same due to the memory less property of exponential distribution of the service times. Then, the equilibrium equations are:

$$
\begin{aligned}
(\Lambda^h + \Lambda^l + \overline{\mu}(\overline{s}^h, \overline{s}^l))P_{n,m}(\overline{0}, \overline{s}^h, \overline{w}^l, \overline{s}^l, \overline{r}^l) = &\sum_{i=1}^{N^l} \lambda_i^l P_{n,m-1}(\overline{0}, \overline{s}^h, \overline{w}^l - \overline{e}_i^l, \overline{s}^l, \overline{r}^l) \\
&+ \sum_{i=1}^{N^h} \sum_{j=1}^{N^l} \lambda_i^h \frac{s_j^l + 1}{\left|\overline{s}^l\right| + 1} P_{n-1,m}(\overline{0}, \overline{s}^h - \overline{e}_i^h, \overline{w}^l, \overline{s}^l + \overline{e}_j^l, \overline{r}^l - \overline{e}_j^l) \\
&+ I(\left|\overline{r}^l\right| = 0) \sum_{i=1}^{N^h} \sum_{j=1}^{N^l} \frac{w_j^l + 1}{\left|\overline{w}^l\right| + 1}\left(\overline{s}_i^h + 1\right) \mu_i^h P_{n+1,m}(\overline{0}, \overline{s}^h + \overline{e}_i^h, \overline{w}^l, \overline{s}^l + \overline{e}_j^l, \overline{0}) \\
&+ I(\left|\overline{r}^l\right| = 0) \sum_{i=1}^{N^h} \sum_{j=1}^{N^l} \frac{w_j^l + 1}{\left|\overline{w}^l\right| + 1}\left(\overline{s}_i^h + 1 - \overline{e}_{ij}^l\right) \mu_i^h P_{n,m+1}(\overline{0}, \overline{s}^h, \overline{w}^l + \overline{e}_j^l, \overline{s}^l + \overline{e}_i^l - \overline{e}_j^l, \overline{0}) \\
&+ \sum_{i=1}^{N^h} \sum_{j=1}^{N^l} \frac{r_j^l + 1}{\left|\overline{r}^l\right| + 1}\left(\overline{s}_i^h + 1\right) \mu_i^h P_{n+1,m}(\overline{0}, \overline{s}^h + \overline{e}_i^h, \overline{w}^l, \overline{s}^l - \overline{e}_j^l, \overline{r}^l + \overline{e}_j^l) \\
&+ \sum_{i=1}^{N^h} \sum_{j=1}^{N^l} \frac{r_j^l + 1}{\left|\overline{r}^l\right| + 1}\left(\overline{s}_i^l + 1 - \overline{e}_{ij}^l\right) \mu_i^h P_{n,m+1}(\overline{0}, \overline{s}^h, \overline{w}^l, \overline{s}^l + \overline{e}_i^l - \overline{e}_j^l, \overline{r}^l + \overline{e}_j^l)
\end{aligned}
$$

where $I(.)$ denotes the indicator function, so the value of the function is 1 if the statement between parentheses is true and 0 otherwise.

Then, we consider the border between the areas I and II $(n = k)$. That is, the number of high priority jobs in the system equals number of servers. So no high priority jobs are waiting in the queue and no low priority jobs are in service. Then the transitions to the state $(\overline{0}, \overline{s}^h, \overline{w}^l, \overline{s}^l, \overline{r}^l)$ are:

1. The arrival of a high priority job i that enters service immediately, thereby preempting the single low priority job j that was in service,

2. The arrival of a low priority job that enters the queue,

3. The service completion of a high priority job i, causing that the single high priority job in the queue (type j) is being served; note that a low priority job cannot be completed, since all servers are busy with high priority jobs.

So the equilibrium equations are:

$$(\Lambda^h + \Lambda^l + \bar{\mu}(\bar{s}^h, \bar{s}^l))P_{n,m}(\bar{0}, \bar{s}^h, \bar{w}^l, \bar{0}, \bar{r}^l) = \sum_{i=1}^{N^l} \lambda_i^l P_{n,m-1}(\bar{0}, \bar{s}^h, \bar{w}^l - \bar{e}_j^l, \bar{0}, \bar{r}^l)$$

$$+ \sum_{i=1}^{N^h} \sum_{j=1}^{N^l} \lambda_i^h P_{n-1,m}(\bar{0}, \bar{s}^h - \bar{e}_i^h, \bar{w}^l, \bar{e}_j^l, \bar{r}^l - \bar{e}_j^l)$$

$$+ \sum_{i=1}^{N^h} \sum_{j=1}^{N^l} (\bar{s}_i^h + 1 - \bar{e}_{ij}^h) \mu_i^h P_{n+1,m}(\bar{0}, \bar{s}^h + \bar{e}_i^h - \bar{e}_j^h, \bar{w}^l, \bar{0}, \bar{r}^l)$$

$$+ \sum_{i=1}^{N^h} \sum_{j=1}^{N^l} \frac{r_j^l + 1}{|\bar{r}^l| + 1} (\bar{s}_i^h + 1) \mu_i^h P_{n+1,m}(\bar{0}, \bar{s}^h + \bar{e}_i^h, \bar{w}^l, \bar{s}^l - \bar{e}_j^l, \bar{r}^l + \bar{e}_j^l)$$

Next, we consider the border between the areas II and III $n + m = k, n < k$. That is, all servers are occupied (with high and/or low priority jobs), the queue is empty and there is at least one low priority item in service. Then the transitions to the state $(\bar{0}, \bar{s}^h, \bar{w}^l, \bar{s}^l, \bar{0})$ are:

1. The arrival of a (high or low priority) job i that enters service immediately,
2. The service completion of a high priority job i, causing that a single low priority job in the queue (type j) is being served; note that a low priority job that is taken into service may be either a new service or a postponed service,
3. The service completion of a low priority job i, causing that the single low priority job in the queue (type i) is being served; again, a low priority job that is taken into service may be either a new or a postponed service; note that a high priority job cannot be in the queue if a low priority job is being served.

$$(\Lambda^h + \Lambda^l + \bar{\mu}(\bar{s}^h, \bar{s}^l))P_{n,m}(\bar{0}, \bar{s}^h, \bar{0}, \bar{s}^l, \bar{0}) = \sum_{i=1}^{N^l} \lambda_i^l P_{n,m-1}(\bar{0}, \bar{s}^h, \bar{0}, \bar{s}^l - \bar{e}_i^l, \bar{0})$$

$$+ \sum_{i=1}^{N^h} \lambda_i^h P_{n-1,m}(\bar{0}, \bar{s}^h - \bar{e}_i^h, \bar{0}, \bar{s}^l, \bar{0})$$

$$+ I(|\bar{r}^l| = 0) \sum_{i=1}^{N^h} \sum_{j=1}^{N^l} (\bar{s}_i^h + 1) \mu_i^h P_{n+1,m}(\bar{0}, \bar{s}^h + \bar{e}_i^h, \bar{e}_j^l, \bar{s}^l - \bar{e}_j^l, \bar{0})$$

$$+ I(|\bar{r}^l| = 0) \sum_{i=1}^{N^h} \sum_{j=1}^{N^l} (\bar{s}_i^l + 1 - \bar{e}_{ij}^l) \mu_i^l P_{n,m+1}(\bar{0}, \bar{s}^h, \bar{0}, \bar{s}^l + \bar{e}_i^l - \bar{e}_j^l, \bar{e}_j^l)$$

$$+ \sum_{i=1}^{N^h} \sum_{j=1}^{N^l} (\bar{s}_i^h + 1) \mu_i^h P_{n+1,m}(\bar{0}, \bar{s}^h - \bar{e}_i^h, \bar{0}, \bar{s}^l - \bar{e}_j^l, \bar{e}_j^l)$$

$$+ \sum_{i=1}^{N^h} \sum_{j=1}^{N^l} (\bar{s}_i^l + 1 - \bar{e}_{ij}^l) \mu_i^l P_{n,m+1}(\bar{0}, \bar{s}^h, \bar{0}, \bar{s}^l + \bar{e}_i^l - \bar{e}_j^l, \bar{e}_j^l)$$

Finally we consider probability states in area III. $(n + m < k)$ These states have empty queue and hence no items are postponed $(\bar{r}^l = 0)$. Now the transition from the neighbors of the state $(\bar{0}, \bar{s}^h, \bar{0}, \bar{s}^l, \bar{r}^l)$ becomes much simpler. They consist of:

1. The arrival of a high priority job that enters service immediatcly,
2. The arrival of a low priority job that enters service immediately,
3. The completion of a (high or low) priority job without starting a new job because the queue is empty.

Hence we find:

$$
(\Lambda^h + \Lambda^l + \bar{\mu}(\bar{s}^h, \bar{s}^l))P_{n,m}(\bar{0}, \bar{s}^h, \bar{0}, \bar{s}^l, \bar{0}) = \sum_{i=1}^{N^h} \lambda_i^h P_{n-1,m}(\bar{0}, \bar{s}^h - \bar{e}_i^h, \bar{0}, \bar{s}^l, \bar{0})
$$
$$
+ \sum_{i=1}^{N^l} \lambda_i^l P_{n,m-1}(\bar{0}, \bar{s}^h, \bar{0}, \bar{s}^l - \bar{e}_i^l, \bar{0})
$$
$$
+ \sum_{j=1}^{N^l} (\bar{s}_i^h + 1)\mu_i^l P_{n,m+1}(\bar{0}, \bar{s}^h, \bar{0}, \bar{s}^l + \bar{e}_j^l, \bar{0})
$$
$$
+ \sum_{i=1}^{N^h} (\bar{s}_i^h + 1)\mu_i^h P_{n+1,m}(\bar{0}, \bar{s}^h + \bar{e}_i^h, \bar{0}, \bar{s}^l, \bar{e}_j^l)
$$

In the next sections, we will show how we can solve these equilibrium equations thereby obtaining the exact system state probabilities.

3. SYSTEM STATES WITH HIGH PRIORITY ITEMS IN QUEUE

In this section we focus on area I, so there is at least one high priority item in the queue.

3.1 Reducing the Set of Equations

First, we note that we can rewrite these state probabilities by conditioning on the total number of high priority items in the queue. So,

$$
P_{n,m}(\bar{w}^h, \bar{s}^h, \bar{w}^l, \bar{0}, \bar{r}^l) \text{ is } P'_{n,m}\left(\left|\bar{w}^h\right|, \bar{s}^h, \bar{w}^l, \bar{0}, \bar{r}^l\right)
$$
$$
\times \Pr\{\text{distribution of high priority items in queue over subclasses} = \bar{w}^h \mid
$$
$$
\text{number of high priority items in queue} = \left|\bar{w}^h\right|\}
$$

Given the total number of high priority items in the queue, the items are distributed over the item subclasses according to a multinomial distribution $\left|\bar{w}^h\right|! \prod_{i=1}^{N^h} \frac{\left(a_i^h\right)^{w_i^h}}{w_i^h!}$. The expression $P'_{n,m}\left(\left|\bar{w}^h\right|, \bar{s}^h, \bar{w}^l, \bar{0}, \bar{r}^l\right)$ describes the probability that (1) the distribution of high priority items in service is given by the vector $\bar{s}^h$, (2) the low priority items in queue are given by the vectors $\bar{w}^l$ and $\bar{r}^l$, (3) no low priority items are in service, and (4) the total number of high priority items in the queue equals $\left|\bar{w}^h\right|$. Because it holds that $\left|\bar{w}^h\right| = n - k$, we see that this expression is in fact independent of $\left|\bar{w}^h\right|$. Therefore we can omit the parameter $\left|\bar{w}^h\right|$ and rewrite the equilibrium equations for the states with $n > k$ using the product form:

$$P_{n,m}(\overline{w}^h, \overline{s}^h, \overline{w}^l, \overline{0}, \overline{r}^l) = \left|\overline{w}^h\right|! \prod_{i=1}^{N^h} \frac{\left(a_i^h\right)^{w_i^h}}{w_i^h!} P'_{n,m}(\overline{s}^h, \overline{w}^l, \overline{0}, \overline{r}^l)$$

In this way, we reduce the number of state probabilities to be solved.

We substitute the relation (5) in equation (1) and we divide both sides by $k\mu^h$ to obtain equations that can be transformed in matrix form. This yields:

$$\left(1 + \overline{\delta}^h\left(\overline{s}^h, \overline{0}\right) + \overline{\rho}^h + \gamma\overline{\rho}^h\right)\left|\overline{w}^h\right|! \prod_{i=1}^{N^h} \frac{\left(a_i^h\right)^{w_i^h}}{w_i^h!} P'_{n,m}(\overline{s}^h, \overline{w}^l, \overline{0}, \overline{r}^l) = \overline{\rho}^h \sum_{i=1}^{N^h} a_i^h \left(\left|\overline{w}^h\right| - 1\right)! \frac{\left(a_i^h\right)^{w_i^h - 1}}{\left(w_i^h - 1\right)!} \prod_{j \neq i}^{N^h} \frac{\left(a_i^h\right)^{w_i^h}}{w_i^h!} P'_{n-1,m}(\overline{s}^h, \overline{w}^l, \overline{0}, \overline{r}^l)$$

$$+ \gamma\overline{\rho}^h \sum_{i=1}^{N^l} a_i^h \left|\overline{w}^h\right|! \prod_{j=1}^{N^h} \frac{\left(a_j^h\right)^{w_j^h}}{w_j^h!} P'_{n,m-1}(\overline{s}^h, \overline{w}^l - \overline{e}_i^l, \overline{0}, \overline{r}^l)$$

$$+ \sum_{i=1}^{N^l} \sum_{j=1}^{N^l} \left(\overline{s}_i^h + 1 - e_{ij}^h\right)\mu_i^h \frac{w_j^h + 1}{\left|\overline{w}^h\right| + 1} \frac{a_j^h\left(\left|\overline{w}^l\right| + 1\right)}{w_j^l + 1}\left|\overline{w}^h\right|! \prod_{q=1}^{N^h} \frac{\left(a_q^h\right)^{w_q^h}}{w_q^h!} P'_{n,m+1}(\overline{s}^h + \overline{e}_i^l - \overline{e}_j^h, \overline{w}^l, \overline{0}, \overline{r}^l)$$

where $\gamma = \dfrac{\mu^l}{\mu^h}$.

Because we use the product form (5), we have to sum up all the equations for the state probabilities satisfying $\sum_j w_j^h = \left|\overline{w}^h\right|$ Taking into account that $\sum a_j^h = 1$, we can write all equilibrium equation with the same n and m in a matrix form:

$$\left(\left(1 + \rho^h + \gamma\rho^h\right)I + \overline{\delta}^h\right)P_{n,m}(\overline{w}^l, \overline{0}, \overline{r}^l) = \rho^h P_{n-1,m}(\overline{w}^l, \overline{0}, \overline{r}^l) + \gamma\rho^h \sum_{j=1}^{N^l} a_j P_{n,m-1}(\overline{w}^l - e_j, \overline{0}, \overline{r}^l) + A P_{n+1,m}(\overline{w}^l, \overline{0}, \overline{r}^l)$$

where $P_{n+1,m}(\overline{w}^l, \overline{0})$ are vectors containing probabilities $P'_{n,m}(\overline{s}^h, \overline{w}^l, \overline{0}, \overline{r}^l)$ as component. The dimensions of vectors $P_{n+1,m}(\overline{w}^l, \overline{0})$ is equal to amount of different server states given that all servers are occupied with hp items, i.e. this dimension is equal to $d\left(N^h, k\right)\left(\sum_{i=0}^{k} d\left(N^h, i\right)\right)$, with $d\left(x, y\right) = \begin{pmatrix} x + y + 1 \\ y \end{pmatrix}$. $\overline{\delta}^h$ and A are linear operators on a $d\left(N^h, k\right)\left(\sum_{i=0}^{k} d\left(N^h, i\right)\right)$-dimensional linear space.

Solving this matrix equation we can find all state probabilities with $n > k$. To solve it, it is worth noticing that $\overline{r}^l$ only serves as an index, where equations with different indices $\overline{r}^l$ are decoupled. In the next lemma the structure of the solution of this equation is explained.

Lemma. Define the matrix-function $Z\left(\rho^h, \rho^l, \gamma; \xi\right)$ as the solution of

$$\left(\left(1 + \rho^h + \gamma\rho^h\right)I + \overline{\delta}^h\right) = \rho^h Z + \gamma\rho^h \xi + A Z^{-1}, \qquad \left|\sigma(Z)\right| > 1$$

Then

$$P_{n,m}(\overline{w}^h, \overline{s}^h, \overline{w}^l, \overline{0}, \overline{r}^l) = \left|\overline{w}^h\right|! \prod_{i=1}^{N^h} \frac{\left(a_i^h\right)^{w_i^h}}{w_i^h!} \left[\prod_{j=1}^{N^l} \frac{\left(a_j^l\right)^{w_j^l}}{w_j^l!}\right] \left(\frac{d}{d\xi}\right)^{\left|\overline{w}^h\right|} \times \left[\left(Z^{-1}\left(\xi\right)\right)^{n-k} C\left(\xi\right)\right]_{\xi=0} \left[\overline{s}^h, \overline{r}^l\right]$$

satisfies all equations for $m \geq 0, n > k$. The notation $\left[\overline{s}^h, \overline{r}^l\right]$ refers to the indicated vector component.

The probabilities of the system states constructed in this section have a differential form, therefore we will need derivatives of the matrix Z. To find these derivatives is not an easy task since we cannot derive an analytical form of the matrix Z, but we can use the equation (7) to find such derivatives iteratively.

4. SYSTEM STATES WITH NO HIGH PRIORITY ITEMS IN QUEUE

4.1 Reducing the Set of Equations

As in the previous section, we can reduce the set of equations by writing the state probabilities in product form, conditioning on the total number of low priority items in the queue $\left|\overline{w}^l\right|$. Given this total number, the number of jobs in the queue per low priority subclass has a multi nominal distribution with parameters $\left|\overline{w}^l\right|$ and $a_i^l = \dfrac{\lambda_i^l}{\Lambda^l}$, $i = 1, 2, ..., N^l$. So we can write:

$$P_{n,m}(\overline{w}^h, \overline{s}^h, \overline{w}^l, \overline{0}, \overline{r}^l) = \left|\overline{w}^h\right|! \prod_{i=1}^{N^l} \frac{\left(a_i^l\right)^{w_i^l}}{w_i^l!} P_{n,m}''(\overline{s}^h, \overline{s}^l, \overline{r}^l)$$

Note that we can omit two parameters, namely the number of high priority items in the queue per subclass (these are always zero) and the number of low priority items in the queue $\left|\overline{w}^l\right|$. For the latter, it holds that $\left|\overline{w}^l\right| = m - \left|\overline{s}^l\right| - \left|\overline{r}^h\right|$.

Again, we substitute this product form into the equations (2) for $n < k, m > k - n$, and next we sum up the equations for all system states having the total number of (non-postponed) low priority items in the queue equal to $\left|\overline{w}^l\right|$. After dividing the resulting equations by $k\mu^h$, we obtain the following equations for $P_{n,m}''(.,.)$:

$$\left(1 + \overline{\delta}^h\left(\overline{s}^h, \overline{s}^l\right) + \rho^h + \gamma\rho^h\right)\left(\sum_{i=1}^{N^l} a_i^l\right)^{\left|\overline{w}^l\right|} P_{n,m}''(\overline{s}^h, \overline{s}^l, \overline{r}^l) =$$

$$\rho^h \left(\sum_{i=1}^{N^l} a_i^l\right)^{\left|\overline{w}^l\right|} \sum_{i=1}^{N^h} a_i^h \sum_{j=1}^{N^l} \frac{s_j^l + 1}{\left|\overline{s}^l\right| + 1} P_{n-1,m}''(\overline{s}^h - e_i, \overline{s}^l + e_j, \overline{r}^l - e_j) + \left(\sum_{i=1}^{N^l} a_i^l\right)^{\left|\overline{w}^l\right|} \gamma\rho^l P_{n,m-1}''(\overline{s}^h, \overline{s}^l, \overline{r}^l)$$

$$= I\!\left(\left|\overline{r}^l\right| = 0\right)\left(\sum_{i=1}^{N^l} a_i^l\right)^{\left|\overline{w}^l\right|} \sum_{i=1}^{N^h} \sum_{j=1}^{N^l} \left(s_i^h + 1\right)\left(\delta_i^h + 1\right) a_j^l P_{n+1,m}''(\overline{s}^h + e_i^h, \overline{s}_j^l - e_j^l, \overline{0})$$

$$+ I\!\left(\left|\overline{r}^l\right| = 0\right)\left(\sum_{i=1}^{N^l} a_i^l\right)^{\left|\overline{w}^l\right|} \sum_{i=1}^{N^h} \sum_{j=1}^{N^l} \left(s_i^h + 1 - e_{ij}^h\right)\left(\delta_i^h + 1\right) P_{n,m+1}''(\overline{s}^h, \overline{s}^l + e_i^h - e_j^l, \overline{0})$$

$$+ \left(\sum_{i=1}^{N^l} a_i^l\right)^{\left|\overline{w}^l\right|} \sum_{i=1}^{N^h} \sum_{j=1}^{N^l} \left(s_i^h + 1\right)\left(\delta_i^h + 1\right) \frac{r_j^l + 1}{\left|\overline{r}^l\right| + 1} a_j^l P_{n+1,m}''(\overline{s}^h + e_i^h, \overline{s}_j^l - e_j^l, r^l + e_j^l)$$

$$+ \left(\sum_{i=1}^{N^l} a_i^l\right)^{\left|\overline{w}^l\right|} \sum_{i=1}^{N^h} \sum_{j=1}^{N^l} \left(s_i^h + 1 - e_{ij}^h\right)\left(\delta_i^h + 1\right) \frac{r_j^l + 1}{\left|\overline{r}^l\right| + 1} a_j^l P_{n+1,m}''(\overline{s}^h + e_i^h, \overline{s}^l - e_j^l, r^l + e_j^l)$$

where $\displaystyle\sum_{i=1}^{N^l} a_i^l = 1$ and $\gamma = \dfrac{\mu^l}{\mu^h}$.

Again this results in a matrix equation for $n < k, m \leq k - n$, namely:

$$D_{n,m}P_{n,m} = F_{n,m}P_{n-1,m} + E_{n,m}P_{n,m-1} + B_{n,m}P_{n+1,m} + G_{n,m}P_{n,m+1}$$

where $D_{n,m}, F_{n,m}, E_{n,m}, B_{n,m}$ and $G_{n,m}$ operate on the vector $\zeta\left[\overline{s}^h, \overline{s}^l\right]$.

The equilibrium equations (3) for $n = k$ have a similar form, with the only difference that these equations include the probabilities of the system states with one high priority item in the queue $(n = k + 1)$, which are equal to $\dfrac{1}{|\overline{w}^l|!}\left(\dfrac{d}{d\xi}\right)^{|\overline{w}^l|}\left[Z^{-1}(\xi)C(\xi)\right]$. So, we can aggregate all equations for states with no high priority items in queue $(n \leq k)$ and write them in matrix form. To this end, we write all vectors $P_{n,m}$ for the states with the same number of items in the system (i.e. $n + m$) into one vector $\mathbb{P}_{\hat{t}}$, with $\hat{t} = n + m$. For example, then the equations for the states with more items in the system than the number of servers $(\hat{t} > k)$ can be written as:

$$
\begin{pmatrix} D_{0,m} & & 0 \\ & \ddots & \\ 0 & & D_{k,m-k} \end{pmatrix}
\begin{pmatrix} P_{0,m} \\ \vdots \\ P_{k,m-k} \end{pmatrix} =
\begin{pmatrix} E_{0,m} & & & 0 \\ F_{0,m-1} & E_{1,m-1} & & \\ & \ddots & \ddots & \\ 0 & & F_{k,m-k+1} & E_{k,m-k} \end{pmatrix}
\begin{pmatrix} P_{0,m-1} \\ \vdots \\ P_{k,m-k-1} \end{pmatrix}
$$

$$
+ \begin{pmatrix} G_{0,m} & B_{1,m-1} & & 0 \\ & G_{1,m-1} & \ddots & \\ & & \ddots & B_{k-1,m-k+1} \\ 0 & & & G_{k,m-k} \end{pmatrix}
\begin{pmatrix} P_{0,m+1} \\ \vdots \\ P_{k,m-k+1} \end{pmatrix}
+ \begin{pmatrix} B_{0,m} \\ \vdots \\ B_{k,m-k} \end{pmatrix} m!\left(\dfrac{d}{d\xi}\right)^m\left[Z^{-1}(\xi)C(\xi)\right]_{\xi=0}
$$

The equations for $n + m \leq k$ have the same form, but they do not include the inhomogeneous term.

Rewriting these equations in a matrix form, where the vector $\mathbb{P}_{\hat{t}}$ is composed of the vectors $P_{n,m-n}$ we obtain:

$$\mathbb{D}_{\hat{t}}\mathbb{P}_{\hat{t}} = \mathbb{F}_{\hat{t}}\mathbb{P}_{\hat{t}-1} + \mathbb{G}_{\hat{t}}\mathbb{P}_{\hat{t}+1} + \mathbb{B}_{\hat{t}}\dfrac{1}{(\hat{t}-k)!}\left(\dfrac{d}{d\xi}\right)^{\hat{t}-k}\left[Z^{-1}(\xi)C(\xi)\right]_{\xi=0} \qquad \hat{t} \geq k$$

$$\mathbb{D}_{\hat{t}}\mathbb{P}_{\hat{t}} = \mathbb{F}_{\hat{t}}\mathbb{P}_{\hat{t}-1} + \mathbb{G}_{\hat{t}}\mathbb{P}_{\hat{t}+1} \qquad \hat{t} < k$$

where the matrices $\mathbb{D}_{\hat{t}}, \mathbb{F}_{\hat{t}}$ and $\mathbb{G}_{\hat{t}}$ are fixed for $\hat{t} \geq k$ and depend on $\hat{t}$ for $\hat{t} < k$.

So, we now have two systems of second order linear difference equations. One system (for $\hat{t} > k$) is an inhomogeneous system with a fixed dimension and with fixed coefficients. The second system (for

$\hat{t} < k$) has coefficients depending on $\hat{t}$. Also, the system dimension depends on ι. In the next sections we describe how we can construct the solution of these two systems.

4.2 States with Only Low Priority Items in Queue $\hat{t} \geq k, k \geq n$

The probabilities of the system states having only low priority items in queue satisfy the system of linear inhomogeneous difference equations of second order with fixed coefficients (10). However, the inhomogeneous term has a differential form, therefore the standard procedure of solving the inhomogeneous equations (solution of homogeneous + partial solution of inhomogeneous) is difficult to apply.

Therefore we will look for the solution in a differential form $\mathbb{P}_{\hat{t}+k} = \frac{1}{(\hat{t})!}\left(\frac{d}{d\xi}\right)^{t} v(\xi)_{\xi=0}$ where $t = \hat{t} - k$.

Now we can remove the derivatives from equation (10) and to obtain a new expression of the function $v(\xi)$ for any $t > 0$:

The function $C(\xi)$ can be expressed as a part of the vector-function $v(\xi)$, which corresponds to the states with k high priority items in the system $v_k(\xi)$ i.e. $C(\xi) = v_k(\xi)$.

In this way, we have defined a function $v(\xi)$ given the probability vectors $\mathbb{P}_k$ and $\mathbb{P}_{k-1}$ and next all probability vectors $\mathbb{P}_{\hat{t}}$ for $\hat{t} = k+1, ..., \infty$ follow from $\mathbb{P}_k$ and $\mathbb{P}_{k-1}$. However, an essential piece of information has not been used up to now. It is clear that we are looking for decaying solutions $\mathbb{P}_{\hat{t}}$ for $\hat{t} \to \infty$. As a consequence $v(\xi)$ should be analytic on a circle with radius $1 + \varepsilon$ for some $\varepsilon > 0$. Due to (15) extra conditions have to be satisfied at points ξ inside this circle where $H(\xi)$ is singular. It turns out that there are several such points in general. For example, $\xi = 0$ and $\xi = 1$ are points of this type. It is easy to check that in case $\xi = 0$ any vector with 0 entries whenever $|r^l| > 0$ is in the null space of $\mathbb{G}$. Using the the equilibrium property for subsystems with s^h, s^l, r^l fixed m arbitrary it is not difficult to check that $r^l 1^t = (1, 1, ..., 1)$ is a left eigen value of $\mathbb{H}(1)$ for the eigen value 0.

4.3 States with Empty Queue $(\hat{t} < k)$

The complete solution of the equilibrium equations for $\hat{t} < k$ can be represented as:

$$\mathbb{P}_{\hat{t}} = \mathbb{Q}_{\hat{t}-1}\mathbb{P}_{\hat{t}-1} = \mathbb{Q}_{\hat{t}-1}\mathbb{Q}_{\hat{t}-2}...\mathbb{Q}_0\mathbb{P}_0$$

where $\mathbb{Q}_{\hat{t}} = \left(\mathbb{D}_{\hat{t}} - \mathbb{G}_{\hat{t}}\mathbb{Q}_{\hat{t}}\right)^{-1}\mathbb{F}_{\hat{t}}$, $\hat{t} = k, ..., 1$.

The free constant $\mathbb{P}_0$ is determined by $\sum_{\bar{w}^h, \bar{s}^h, \bar{w}^l, \bar{s}^l, \bar{r}^l} P_{n,m}(\bar{w}^h, \bar{s}^h, \bar{w}^l, \bar{s}^l, \bar{r}^l) = 1$

5. PERFORMANCE MEASURES

In this section we will concentrate on the performance criteria for the low priority items in the system, since performance indicators for the high priority items can be calculated using the non-priority multi-class, multi-serve queue analysis by Van Harten and Sleptchenko (2003). The latter is possible due to the preemptive priority rule in our system, i.e. low priority items don't influence processing of high priority items and therefore they can be ignored.

We denote the number of low priority items of subclass i in the queue as q_i^l in the postponed state as PS_i^l and in the system as R_i^l. Such performance indicators role in spare part service networks as discussed in the introduction by Sherbrooke (1992) and Sleptchenko (2003). Other interesting performance measures are the expected number of postponements of per item of type i, the expected residential time of items of type i in service, queue and postponement, respectively.

The mean number of the low priority item i in the queue can be found as sum of all probability states with low priority items in the queue (i.e. zones I and II) multiplied by the number of low priority item i in the queue:

$$E\left[q_i^l\right] = -a_i^l \left\langle 1_{n>k}, \left(Z(1) - I\right)^{-1} Z'(1)\left(Z(1) - I\right)^{-1} v_k(1) \right\rangle$$
$$+ a_i^l \left\langle 1_{n>k}, \left(Z(1) - I\right)^{-1} Z'(1)\left(Z(1) - I\right)^{-1} v_k'(1) \right\rangle + a_i^l \left\langle 1_{i \geq k, k \geq n}, v_k'(1) \right\rangle$$

Here v_k refers to the vector components of v with $\left|\bar{s}^h\right| = k$. The notation 1 is used for a vector with components 1 of the dimension indicated by the subscript as introduced before.

The expected value of R_i^l is composed of these three terms:

$$E\left[R_i^l\right] = E\left[SR_i^l\right] + E\left[q_i^l\right] + E\left[PS_i^l\right]$$

where $E\left[SR_i^l\right] = \dfrac{\lambda_i^l}{\mu_i^l}$ and $E\left[PS_i^l\right] = \left\langle \chi_{n>k}^{r_i^l}, v_k(1) \right\rangle + \left\langle \chi_{i \geq k, k \geq n}^{r_i^l}, v_k(1) \right\rangle$.

Next Little's law can be applied to calculate performance indicators as the mean waiting time $E\left[W_i^l\right]$, the mean postponement time $E\left[PsTime_i^l\right]$ and the mean sojourn time $E\left[SJTime_i^l\right]$:

$$\lambda_i^l E\left[W_i^l\right] = E\left[q_i^l\right] \qquad\qquad \lambda_i^l E\left[PsTime_i^l\right] = E\left[PS_i^l\right]$$

$$\lambda_i^l E\left[SJTime_i^l\right] = E\left[R_i^l\right]$$

and, of course,

$$E\left[SJTime_i^l\right] = \frac{1}{\mu_i^l} + E\left[W_i^l\right] + E\left[PsTime_i^l\right]$$

Note that $E\left[PsTime_i^l\right]$ has to be interpreted as: the expected total time an item of type i spends in a postponed state between the moment it leaves the queue and the moment its service process is completed. Further, we should note that even though preemption occurs, the expected total service time equals $\dfrac{1}{\mu_i^l}$ due to Poisson character of the end of service events.

Comparing the number of preemption events with the number of arrivals over a long interval it is clear that number of preemption events per each item entering the system is equal to:

$$E\left[nrPreemptEvent_i^l\right] = \frac{\lambda_i^{ps}}{\lambda_i^l}$$

It is now also possible to compute the expected time between the moment an item of type i is postponed and the next moment when the service process was resumed again, i.e. the expected re-entrance into service time, $E\left[reenterTime_i^l\right]$. Using Little's law again, we obtain

$$\lambda_i^{ps} E\left[reenterTime_i^l\right] = E\left[PS_i^l\right]$$

6. CONCLUSION

In this chapter we propose a queueing-based model for performance management on cloud. We derived a method to analyze multi-class M/M/k priority queues with preemptive priority and two priority groups (high and low). Each group of priority can contain several classes of items with different arrival and service rates. The proposed method is based on solution of the stationary state equations. It uses an iteration algorithm. The computational effort to find good approximation depends on the number of types, number of servers and utilization rate.

REFERENCES

Amazon. (2010). *Amazon Elastic Compute Cloud (Amazon EC2)*. Available at: http://aws.amazon.com/ec2/

Armbrust, M., & Fox, A. (2009). *Above the Clouds: A Berkeley View of Cloud Computing*. Retrieved from http://www.eecs.berkeley.edu/Pubs/TechRpts/2009/EECS-2009-28.pdf

Armbrust, M., Fox, A., Griffith, R., Joseph, A. D., Katz, R., Konwinski, A., ... Zaharia, M. (2010). A view of cloud computing. *Commun. ACM, 53*, 50–58. Available: http://doi.acm.org/10.1145/1721654.1721672

Bharathi, Sandeep, Kumar, & Poornima. (2010). Performance factors of cloud computing data centers using M/G/m/m+r queuing systems. *IOSR Journal of Engineering, 2*(9), 6-10.

Buzen, J. P., & Bondi, A. B. (1983). The response times of priority classes under preemptive resume in M/M/m queues. *Operations Research*, *31*(3), 456–465. doi:10.1287/opre.31.3.456

Devis, R. H. (1966). Waiting time distribution of a multi-server priority queueing model. *Operations Research*, *14*(1), 133–136. doi:10.1287/opre.14.1.133

Gail, H. R., Hantler, S. L., & Taylor, B. A. (1988). Analysis of a non-preemptive priority multiserver queue. *Advances in Applied Probability*, *20*(4), 852–879. doi:10.2307/1427364

Gail, H. R., Hantler, S. L., & Taylor, B. A. (1992). On preemptive Markovian queue with multiple servers and two priority classes. *Mathematics of Operations Research*, *17*(2), 365–391. doi:10.1287/moor.17.2.365

Google. (2010). *Google App Engine*. Available at: http://code.google.com/intl/en/appengine/

Hooghiemstra, G., Keane, M. S., & van der Ree, S. (1988). Power series for stationary distributions of coupled processor models. *SIAM Journal on Applied Mathematics*, *48*(5), 1159–1166. doi:10.1137/0148069

Hu, Y., Wong, J., Iszlai, G., & Litoiu, M. (2009). Resource provisioning for cloud computing. In *Proceedings of the Conference of the Center for Advanced Studies on Collaborative Research*. ACM.

IBM. (2010). *IBM Smart Business Cloud Computing*. Available at: http://www.ibm.com/ibm/cloud/

Kanadia, A. S., Kazmi, M. F., & Mitchell, A. C. (1984). Analysis of a finite capacity non preemptive priority queue. *Computers & Operations Research*, *11*(3), 337–343. doi:10.1016/0305-0548(84)90022-4

Keller, A., & Ludwig, H. (2003). The wsla framework: Specifying and monitoring service level agreements for web services. *J. Netw. Syst. Manage.*, *11*, 57–81. Available: http://dl.acm.org/citation.cfm?id=635430.635442

Khazaei, Misic, & Misic, (2011). *Performance analysis of cloud centers under burst arrivals and total rejection policy*. IEEE Globecom.

Kimura, T. (1996). Optimal buffer design of an m/g/s queue with finite capacity. *Stochastic Models*, *12*(1), 165–180. doi:10.1080/15326349608807378

Kleinrock, L. (1975). Theory. *Queueing Systems*, *1*.

Ma, B. N. W., & Mark, J. W. (1998). Approximation of the mean queue length of an M/G/cqueueing system. *Operations Research*, *43*(1), 158–165. doi:10.1287/opre.43.1.158

Miyazawa, M. (1986). Approximation of the queue-length distribution of an M/GI/s queue by the basic equations. *Journal of Applied Probability*, *23*(2), 443–458. doi:10.2307/3214186

Roberts, J., Mocci, U., & Virtamo, J. (1996). *Broadband Network Teletraffic*. Springer.

Sherbrooke, C. C. (1992). *Optimal inventory modeling of systems: Multi-echelon techniques*. New York: Wiley.

Tijms, H. C. (1994). *Stochastic Models: An algorithmic approach*. Chichester, UK: Wiley.

Tijms & Wiley. (2003). *A first course in stochastic models* (Vol. 2). Wiley Online Library.

Ubuntu. (2010). *Private cloud: Ubuntu Enterprise Cloud*. Available at: http://www.ubuntu.com/cloud/private

Wagner, D. (1997). Analysis of mean values of a multi-server model with non-preemptive priorities and non-renewal input. *Communications in Statistics. Stochastic Models*, *13*(1), 67–84. doi:10.1080/15326349708807413

Xiong, K., & Perros, H. (2009). Service performance and analysis in cloud computing. In *Proceedings of IEEE 2009 World Conference on Services*. Los Angeles, CA. doi:10.1109/SERVICES-I.2009.121

Yang, B., Tan, F., Dai, Y., & Guo, S. (2009). *Performance evaluation of cloud service considering fault recovery*. Cloud Computing. doi:10.1007/978-3-642-10665-1_54

Zhang, Q., Cheng, L., & Boutaba, R. (2010). Cloud computing: State-of-the-art and research challenges. *Journal of Internet Services and Applications*, *1*(1), 7–18. doi:10.1007/s13174-010-0007-6

Chapter 16
An Efficient E–Negotiation Agent Using Rule–Based and Case–Based Approaches

Amruta More
Maharashtra Institute of Technology, India

Sheetal Vij
Maharashtra Institute of Technology, India

Debajyoti Mukhopadhyay
Maharashtra Institute of Technology, India

ABSTRACT

The research in the area of automated negotiation systems is going on in many universities. This research is mainly focused on making a practically feasible, faster and reliable E-negotiation system. The ongoing work in this area is happening in the laboratories of the universities mainly for training and research purpose. There are number of negotiation systems such as Henry, Kasbaah, Bazaar, Auction Bot, Inspire, Magnet. Our research is based on making an agent software for E-negotiation which will give faster results and also is secure and flexible. Cloud Computing provides security and flexibility to the user data. Using these features we propose an E-negotiation system, in which, all product information and agent details are stored on the cloud. This system proposes three conditions for making successful negotiation. First rule based, where agent will check user requirements with rule based data. Second case based, where an agent will see case based data to check any similar previous negotiation case is matching to the user requirement. Third bilateral negotiation model, if both rules based data and case based data are not matching with the user requirement, then agent use bilateral negotiation model for negotiation. After completing negotiation process, agents give feedback to the user about whether negotiation is successful or not. Using rule based reasoning and case based reasoning this system will improve the efficiency and success rate of the negotiation process.

DOI: 10.4018/978-1-4666-8676-2.ch016

Copyright © 2015, IGI Global. Copying or distributing in print or electronic forms without written permission of IGI Global is prohibited.

INTRODUCTION

Negotiation is basically a type of interaction in which a group of agents, with conflicting interests and a desire to cooperate try to come to a mutually acceptable agreement on the division of scarce resources. These resources do not only refer to money but also include other parameters like product quality features, guaranty features, mode of payment, etc. Electronic negotiations have gained heightened importance due to the development of the web and e-commerce. The rapid success of online auctions clearly shows that e-negotiation will eventually become the basis of e-commerce. Whether it is a case of B to B purchase or a case of online shopping, it is required to make the traditional negotiation pricing mechanism automated and intelligent. The automation saves human negotiation time and computational negotiators are better at finding deals in combinatorial and strategically complex settings. (Mukun, 2010)

Cloud Computing is technology for next generation Information and Software enabled work that is capable of changing the software working environment. It is an interconnection between the large-scale computing resources to effectively integrate and to computing resources as a service to users. Cloud computing allows users to use applications without installation of any application and easier access to their personal files and application at any system with internet or intranet access. Cloud computing is effectively the actual separation of physical and virtual services, a number of business services reduced costs, improved utilization of network resources. Cloud computing is a technology that uses the internet or intranet and central remote servers to maintain the data and applications. This technology allows for efficient computing by centralizing storage, memory, processing and bandwidth (Singh, Kumar and Khatn 2012).

Cloud Computing is innovation that uses advanced computational power and improved storage capabilities. Cloud computing is a new processing scheme in which computer processing is performed in the network. This means that users need not concern themselves with the processing details. Although Cloud computing enables more flexible, easier and faster computing. (Singh, Kumar and Khatn 2012).

Amazon, Microsoft, OpenStack, Google all these are cloud providers. Google Apps, Google Driver are the examples of cloud.

Case-based reasoning (CBR) is a problem solving paradigm where solution of new problem is based on solution of similar past problem. We use Rule based reasoning (RBR) concept, where there are some rules such as discount, festival offers etc.

In this paper, we are introducing an E-negotiation agent based system using rule based reasoning and case based reasoning. Due to the use of rule based reasoning and case based reasoning, system should improve the efficiency and success rate of the negotiation process. For making system faster and secure cloud computing concept is used.

The product details, Agent details, rule based data, case based data would be stored on the cloud. Seller and buyer select their respective agents through the cloud for negotiation. In this E-negotiation system agent act as a negotiator. Agent has user's (seller and buyer) details and their requirements for a particular product.

For making successful negotiation we use three ways for doing negotiation. The first way is rule based. In this way, agent checks users' requirement with rule based data which is stored on the cloud. If any rule is matched with users, then seller's agent and buyer's agent start negotiation through rule based data. The second way is case based. In this way, agent checks users' requirement with case based data which is stored on the cloud. If any similar case is matched with user's requirement, then seller's agent and buyer's agent start negotiation through case based data. The third way is bilateral negotiation.

If both rule based and case based data are not matched with users' requirements then both parties agent will start negotiation with each other using bilateral negotiation model.

After completing negotiation process, both parties agent will give feedback to their respective user whether negotiation is successful or not. If negotiation is successful, then agent will give bid price of particular product to their respective user.

This negotiation process will be stopped when both parties will come to final decision.

RELATED WORK

In this section, we are presenting literature survey related to rule based and cased reasoning. In previous paper (More, Vij and Mukhopadhyay, 2013), we have referred ten papers related to automated negotiation for literature survey.

Xiaowen and Jin (2012) introduced automated negotiation model for tourism industry. To improve the negotiation efficiency and success rate, this system proposed RBR and CBR. The model employs CBR method to support an automated negotiation by past successful negotiation cases used for those negotiation partners that have no contract rule existing in each other. This system does not support multi party multi issue negotiation.

Deochake, Kanth, Chakraborty and Mukhopadhyay (2012) propose that allows multi party multi issue negotiation system. This system focuses on the negotiation protocol to be observed. It also provides a platform for concurrent and independent negotiation on individual issues using the concept of multi threading.

Mukhopadhyay, Vij and Tasare (2012) present a new combinatory framework and architecture, NAAS. The feature of this framework is a component for prediction or probabilistic behavior pattern identification of a buyer, along with the other classical approaches of negotiation frameworks and architectures. Practically, negotiation is very complex activity to automate without human intervention. Therefore in the future they also intend to develop a new protocol. This protocol will facilitate automation of all the types of negotiation strategies like bidding, bargaining and auctions, under NAAS framework.

Vrbaski and Petriu (2012) proposed Context-aware systems which use rule-based reasoning engines for decision making without involving explicit interaction with the user. It is difficult to rank suitable solutions based on unclear, qualitative criteria with a rule- based approach, while rule-based systems excel in filtering out unsuitable solutions based on clear criteria.

Maes, Guttman, Moukas (1999) introduce a Kasbah negotiation system. In this system, agents can only negotiate over the single issue of price. However, B2B negotiations often involve multiple issues. Moreover, the Kasbah agents can only act according to one of their pre-defined negotiation strategies which may not lead to the optimal negotiation results.

Wurman, Wellman, Walsh (1998) present a Michigan Auction Bot negotiation system. The Michigan Auction Bot is a general purposed Internet- based auction server hosted by the University of Michigan. Sellers can create new auctions on Auction Bot by choosing from a set of pre-defined auction types and then enter their specific auction parameters such as clearing time, minimum bid increment and whether proxy bids are allowed. E-bay is the example of Auction Bot negotiation system.

Some of above papers support multi party, multi issue negotiation, rule based reasoning and case based reasoning. Our negotiation system is a bilateral, multi party, multi issue negotiation model. In this system, buyer and seller negotiate on multiple issues at a time and when both buyer and seller comes to final decision, then only negotiation process will be stopped.

PROPOSED SYSTEM

This section not only introduces problem definition of E- negotiation system but also give the solution to how to overcome problem of existing system. In this section we also present the mathematical model of bilateral E-negotiation system.

Problem Definition

In order to make some agreeable decision, two or more parties come together during the negotiation process. There are organizations to maintenance of product data as well as negotiation process data. But the maintenance of this data is a very tedious job. In order to reduce maintenance problem, all organizations product data is stored on cloud. Hence, security and maintenance cost of organizations data is reduced. To improve the efficiency and success rate of the negotiation process, we are using rule based reasoning and case based reasoning.

Mathematical Model

The given mathematical model is for bilateral negotiations where an agent can negotiate about multiple issues. It also supports learning from the previous negotiation round.

The mathematical model for the proposed work is as follows:

$$N = \{A, U, R, D, T\}$$

A: The set of agents that will participate in the negotiation.

$A = \{a_1, a_2, ..., a_n\}$ represents n number of agents.

U: The set of users that will participate in the negotiation. This set consists of both sellers and buyers.

$U = \{u_1, u_2, ..., u_m\}$ represents m number of users.

R: The set of requirements which are given by user to their respective agent. This set consists of both sides' seller side as well as buyer side requirements.

$R = \{r_1, r_2, ..., r_i\}$ represents i number of requirements that is 'R' represents total number of requirements which are available at current stage.

D : the set of database which is used for matching the users' requirement with rule based and case based database.

T : The time limit for negotiation process. Whole process of negotiation should complete before the time.

Constrains:

In previous we can use R for set of requirements but requirement of a single user can also become a constrain.

Algorithms:

A_1 = A single user gives his requirements to respective agent.

$N = \{A, U, R\}$

$A_1 = \{A_1, U_1, R_1\}$

Here, mapping of R_1 to R , A_1 to A , U_1 to U .

A_2 = Agent checks the user requirements with rule based and case based databases.

A_3 = After checking databases, agent will start actual negotiation process.

A_4 = Total time of negotiation process should be less than or equal to T .

$T \leq N_{time}$

Where, N_{time} is the total time of negotiation process.

Flow diagram of mathematical model of E-negotiation agent system is shown in Figure 1.

Figure 1. Flow Diagram of E-negotiation agent system

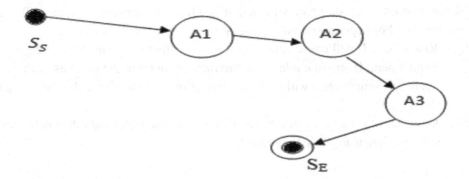

Figure 2. Architecture of E-negotiation Agent System

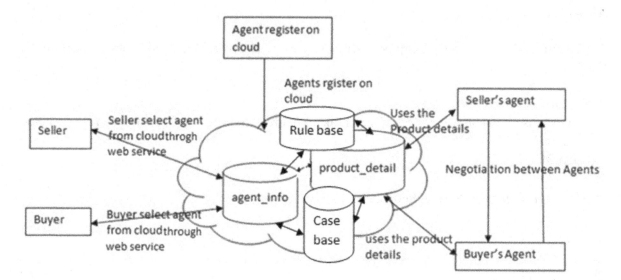

SYSTEM ARCHITECTURE

In this section we describe architecture of E-negotiation system using rule based and case based approaches. We can also discuss components of the system as well as flow chart of the system.

The architecture of E-negotiation agent system is shown in Figure 2.

Working:

1. Databases on cloud:
   i] Agent_info: used to store the agent details such as name, experience etc.
   ii] Product_detail: used to store organizations product detail like product_name, price, and quantity.
   iii] Case base: used to store experience of agent about negotiation process.
   iv] Rule base: used to store rules related to product like discount, festival offers.
2. Seller and Buyer: users of the system.
3. Agent: In this system an agent acts as a negotiator.
   i] Registration: Firstly, agent registers himself on cloud.
   ii] Select agent: Seller and Buyer select their respective agent through web service [REST]. And then, the seller and the buyer give their requirement to their agent using digital signature.
   iii] Negotiation Process: After receiving Sellers and Buyers requirement, agent will start negotiation process. For negotiation process, agent will check three conditions.
      a] Rule based: It will check rules based data whether any rule is matching with the user requirement. If any rule related requirement is found in the rule base data, then Buyers agent and Sellers agent will start the negotiation process with each other using rule based data.
      b] Case based: If users' requirements match with case based data then both parties agents are negotiate using case based data.

      c]   Bilateral Negotiation Model: In this model, both rule based and case based data are not matching with users' requirement. Then Buyers agent and Sellers agent will start the negotiation process with each other using Bilateral Negotiation model.

4.   Feedback: After completing negotiation process, agents give feedback to the user about whether negotiation is successful or not.

Components of the System

For this system, we can use three components. Using these components, system becomes easy to use and work efficiently.

1.   Store data on cloud and Agent registration: For storing data, we can use OpenStack cloud. OpenStack is a cloud computing project which is used to provide an infrastructure as a service (IaaS). In this module, agent detail and product information is stored on cloud in proper format. Only authorized can access product detail and cloud.
2.   Negotiation process: For negotiation process, seller and buyer select their agent respectively. After that they can give their requirement to agent in encrypted format that is generate the hash code of that requirement and encrypt that hash code using user's public key.

Buyer or seller requirement $= E = \left\{ H(m), U_{pk} \right\}$

Where, for generating hash function MD5 (Message Digest) algorithm is used.

U_{pk} is a user's public key.

We can use encryption for security purpose, in this process, we can use digital signature concept. Same as seller, Buyer can do same process for generating hash code of his requirement.

After getting the requirement, agent decrypts the hash code using his private key.

Calculate the hash code for checking whether this message comes from appropriate seller or buyer and whether it is modified or not.

Agent receive requirements$= D = \{A_{pri}, H(m)\}$

Where, A_{pri} is an agent's private key.

After completing decryption process, agent has user requirements. Agent checks user requirements with rule based and/ or case based data. If any rule or any similar previous case is found, then only seller's agent and buyer's agent will start negotiation process using decision function. (Rau, Chen and Shiang, 2009)

i.   Decision Function:

In the negotiation model, we use decision function concept for supplier and buyer.

The notation and assumptions which are required for decision function is shown in Table 1.

Table 1. Notation and Assumptions

B	Buyer
S	Supplier
A	Agent a, $a \in \{B, S\}$
J	Collection of issues for negotiation.
$x_J^{\,a \to b}(t_n)$	The proposal set of all issues and issues by agent a to agent b at time t_n.
$TP(t_n)$	Total profit at time t_n.
$TP(x_J^{\,a \to b}(t_n))$	Total profit for proposal $x_J^{\,a \to b}(t_n)$.
$TC(t_n)$	Total cost at time t_n.
$TC(x_J^{\,a \to b}(t_n))$	Total cost for proposal $x_J^{\,a \to b}(t_n)$.
t_{max}	Negotiation deadline.

Seller's agent responds at t_n to buyers agent offer sent at time t_{n-1} and total profit is defined as following equations.

$$D^s\left(t_n\right) = t_n > t_{max}$$

When this condition is satisfied then process will be terminate.

$$D^s\left(t_n\right) = TP(x_J^{\,B \to S}(t_{n-1})) \leq TP(x_J^{\,S \to B}(t_n))$$

If this condition is satisfied then seller accepts the proposal.

$$D^s\left(t_n\right) = x_J^{\,S \to B}(t_n)$$

Otherwise this proposal is accepted by supplier.
Using above decision function, a supplier can make decision.
Similarly, buyer's agent also has a decision function to respond at t_n to sellers agent offer sent at time t_{n-1} and total cost is shown in following equations.

$$D^B\left(t_n\right) = t_n > t_{max}$$

When this condition is satisfied then process will be terminate.

$$D^B\left(t_n\right) = TC(x_J{}^{S \to B}(t_{n-1})) \geq TC(x_J{}^{B \to S}(t_n))$$

If this condition is satisfied then buyer accepts the proposal.

$$D^B\left(t_n\right) = x_J{}^{B \to S}(t_n)$$

Otherwise this proposal is accepted by buyer.
The buyer uses above equations to decide whether he should accept suppliers' proposal or not.

ii.   *Bilateral Negotiation Model:* If both rules based data and case based data are not matching with the user requirement, then Buyer's agent and Seller's agent will start the negotiation process with each other using Bilateral Negotiation model.

For negotiation process, we can use The Bilateral Negotiation Model (Ateib, 2010)

Let x represents the buyer agent $\left(x \in \left\{x_1, x_2, ..., x_m\right\}\right)$ and y $\left(y \in \left\{y_1, y_2, ..., y_n\right\}\right)$ be the supplier agent. And let then i $\left(i \in \left\{i_1, i_2, ..., i_n\right\}\right)$ be the issues under negotiation, such as price, volume, duration, quality and so on. Each agent assigns to each issue i a weight W_i, denoting the relative importance of that issue to the agent.

Hence, W_i^x represents the importance of issue i to agent x, therefore the overall utility function of an offer O is

$$U(O) = \frac{\sum_{i=1}^{m} W_i u_i(x_i)}{\sum_{i=1}^{m} w_i}$$

Where the overall utility is denoted as $U(O)$ for the offer $O(= [O_1, ... O_m]T)$ and $u_i(x)$ is the individual utility function for issue i for $u_i \in [0,1]$ and the preference degree of an agent to an issue i is denoted as $W_i \in [0,9]$.

Each agent also specifies a minimum acceptable utility level $[U_{max}, U_{min}]$ to determine if an offer is acceptable.

Hence, for benefit-oriented, the utility function $U_i(x_i)$ is computed as follows:

$$U_i(x_i) = \frac{x_i - x_{\{min\}}}{x^i{}_{\{max\}} - x^i{}_{\{min\}}}$$

For cost oriented however, the utility function can be as follows:

$$U_i(x_i) = 1 - \frac{x_i - x_{\{min\}}}{x^i_{\{max\}} - x^i_{\{min\}}}$$

3. *Feedback:* When negotiation process was finished. Agent gives feedback to his appropriate seller or buyer about negotiation whether it is successful or not and also gives bid price of that particular product. Agent gives feedback to user through web service.

Flow chart of the E-negotiation agent system is shown in Figure 3.

1. User login himself/ herself. All login details are stored on the cloud.
2. User selects his/ her type either he/ she is buyer or seller.
3. After selecting type, user select agent from cloud.
4. Then user gives product requirements (Product name, quantity, price etc.) to respective agent.
5. Agent will check user requirements with rule base data and case base data.
6. If any rule is matched with user requirements and/or any previous similar case matched with user requirements then both parties agent start will negotiation using Decision Function.
7. If both rule base data and case base data are not matching with user requirements.
8. Then both parties agent will start negotiation process using Bilateral Negotiation model.

Figure 3. Flow chart of E-negotiation agent system

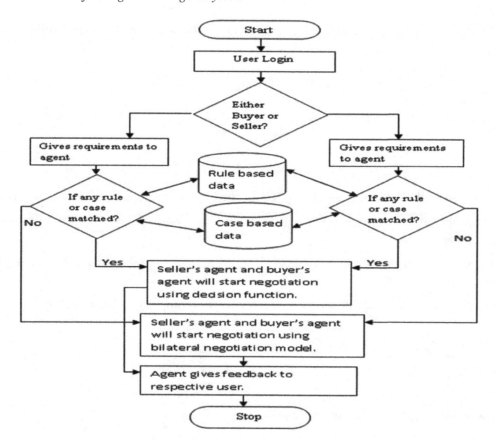

9.   After completing negotiation process, agent gives feedback to respective user whether negotiation is successful or not. If negotiation is successful, then agent gives bid price of that product to respective user.

RESULTS

This section contains results of E- negotiation system as well as performance analysis of system. For performance analysis we can compare our system with existing system on parameters of response time, memory utilizations.

We have worked on practical evaluation using the JAVA, J2EE. We have done implementation through the web application.

In this web application, users firstly select their agent for negotiation process and then select a product which they want either sell or buy. Then user gives his requirements (Expected price, quantity etc.) to respective agent.

Agent is in waiting state till another agent with same requirement is not available. When both agents are available then negotiation process will be start. This system uses three approaches for negotiation process as shown in Figure 4.

1.   Rule based approach- Before starting negotiation process agent check users' requirement with rule base data which is stored on the cloud. Rule base data consist of some rules such as if user buy some product (Pen drive, hard disk) more than 5 in quantity then they will get 10% discount on that product. These types of all rules are stored in rule base data.
2.   Case base Approach- If a user wants a HP v215b 16 GB Pen Drive and negotiation for same product with same features is already done, then agent does not need to do negotiation process once again for that product. Agent only gives bid price of previous negotiation round to respective user.
3.   Bilateral Approach- It is a normal negotiation approach. Here we can use utility function on quantity of product When both rules and case does not match with users' requirements then bilateral approach is used by this system.

Figure 4. Negotiation using Rule based, Case based and Bilateral Approaches.

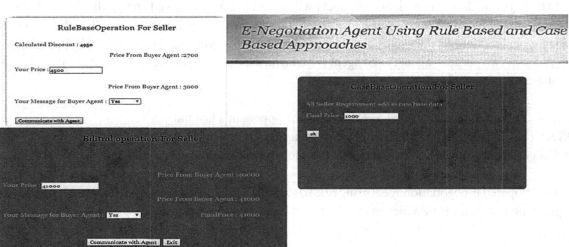

Figure 5. Comparison between rule based approach, case based approach and bilateral operation with respective to time

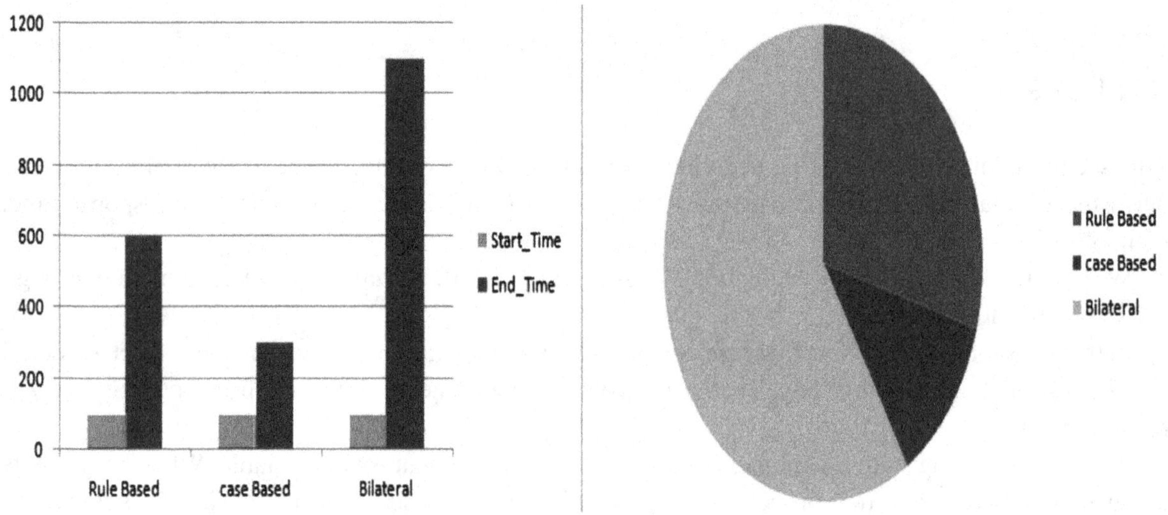

Figure 5 shows the two graphs. These graphs are runtime graph of E-negotiation agent system. First graph shows the start time and end time of negotiation process respectively rule based approach, case based approach and bilateral negotiation.

Second graph shows the total time required for each operation. In both graphs, case based approach required less time as compared to rule based approach and bilateral operation for negotiation process. Also rule based operation required less time as compared to bilateral operation for negotiation process.

Rule based approach provides some discount rules. Sometimes, users' expected price is higher than after getting discount price. In this case buyers' agents do not need to negotiate with sellers' agent. Hence this approach is requiring less time to complete negotiation process. Case based approach also required less time to complete negotiation process.

We can also compare E-negotiation agent with Automated Negotiation and Behavior Prediction (Bala and Vij, 2013) as an existing system.

Bala and Vij (2013) implemented an Automated Negotiation and Behaviour Prediction system.

In this system, during negotiation the agent will store the offers received and predict the preferences of the opponent based on these offers. The negotiation protocol determines the overall order of actions during a negotiation and the agents are obliged to stick to this protocol. In the bilateral alternating offers protocol two parties - agent A and agent B - take turns. Agent A starts the negotiation. Each turn an agent presents one of the three possible actions:

Accept: This action indicates that agent accepts the opponent's last bid.
Offer: This action represents the bid made by an agent.
EndNegotiation: This action indicates that the agent terminates the negotiation.

We compared E-negotiation agent using rule based and case based approaches system with Automated Negotiation and Behavior Prediction system based on response time.

Table 2. Response time values of E-negotiation agent system and Existing system

No. of Users	Response Time (E-negotiation agent)	Response Time (Existing system)
50	256	360
100	591	641
150	723	803
200	1138	1157
250	1364	1513
300	1681	1741

Table 2 shows the response time values of E-negotiation agent system and existing system. We calculated response time value of both the systems up to 300 users.

Figure 6 shows the comparison graph based on response time of both system

Therefore we can say that, using rule based and case based approaches E-negotiation process requires less time as compared to existing system.

In E-negotiation agent using rule based and case based approaches system, all

the data which is required for E-negotiation process such as product detail, rule base data, case base data is stored on cloud. Automated negotiation and Behavior Prediction system does not use cloud computing concept to store negotiation process.

We calculated Memory utilization (in percentage) of both systems up to 300 users.

Table 3 shows the memory utilization values of E-negotiation agent system and existing system.

Therefore we can say that, Due to use of cloud computing E-negotiation agent using rule based and case based approaches system requires less Memory utilization as compared to existing system.

Figure 6. Comparison graph based on Response Time

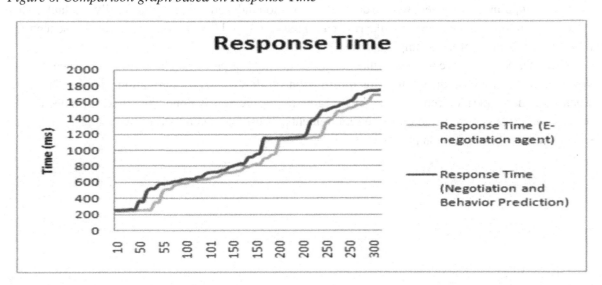

Table 3. Memory utilization values of E-negotiation agent system and Existing system

No. of Users	Memory% (E-negotiation agent)	Memory% (Existing system)
50	9%	12%
100	10%	13%
150	12%	16%
200	15%	19%
250	18%	23%
300	21%	27%

FUTURE RESEARCH DIRECTION

This section describes advantages and disadvantages of E-negotiation agent using rule based and case based approaches. This section also contains how to overcome the problem of this system as well as future research on this system.

The E-negotiation agent system is a bilateral negotiation model. In this system, negotiation is done between only two agents at a time on multiple issues. We can use cloud only for storing negotiation process data (product details, Agent information, case base data and rule base data). For rule based reasoning and case based reasoning we use decision function for negotiation process. In E-negotiation agent system we cannot predict behavior of agent.

So in future this system can be implemented as multilateral negotiation model and behavior prediction. It is also possible to use the concept of expert system for increasing success rate of negotiation process.

CONCLUSION

In this E-negotiation agent system, the product details, Agent details, rule based data, case based data would be stored on the cloud, it reduces the security cost and maintenance cost of data. Due to the use of cloud computing, this system will be device and location independent, flexible, easily available. This system also introduces new features like rule based reasoning and case based reasoning. These features make the negotiation process simple and faster.

In rule based data, there are some rules related to quantity of product. These rules make negotiation system faster. Case base data consist of information of all successful negotiation rounds. Therefore when agent has same requirements on which negotiation is previously done, then there is no need to do negotiation process once again on those requirements. These two features improve the efficiency and success rate of the negotiation process.

REFERENCES

Ateib, M. T. (2010). Agent Based Negotiation In E-cmmerce. *International Symposium on Information Technology 2010(ITSim 2010).* IEEE. doi:10.1109/ITSIM.2010.5561565

Bala, M. I., Vij, S., & Mukhopadhyay, D. (2013). Negotiation Life Cycle: An Approach in E-negotiation with Prediction. *48th Annual Convention of the Computer Society of India.CSI 2013 Proceedings, Visakhapatnam, India.* Springer-Verlag Germany.

Bala, M. I., & Vij, S. (2013). Automated Negotiation and Behavior Prediction. *International Journal of Engineering Research and Technology, 2*(6), 1832 – 1838.

Dastjerdi, A. V., & Buyya, R. (2012). An Autonomous Reliability-aware Negotiation Strategy for Cloud Computing Environments. *12th IEEE/ACM International Symposium on Cluster, Cloud and Grid Computing.* IEEE. doi:10.1109/CCGrid.2012.101

Deochake, S., Kanth, S., Chakraborty, S., Sarode, S., Potdar, V., & Mukhopadhyay, D. (2012). HENRI: High Efficiency Negotiation-based Robust Interface for Multi-party Multi-issue Negotiation over the Internet. *CUBE 2012 International IT Conference, Pune, India.* ACM Digital Library.

P. Maes, R. Guttman, A. Moukas (1999). Agents that buy and sell. *Communications of the ACM, 42*(3), 81 – 91.

More, A., Vij, S., & Mukhopadhyay, D. (2013). Agent Based Negotiation using Cloud - An Approach in E-Commerce. *48th Annual Convention of the Computer Society of India; CSI 2013 Proceedings, Visakhapatnam, India.* Springer-Verlag Germany.

Mukhopadhyay, Vij, & Tasare. (2012). NAAS: Negotiation Automation Architecture with Buyers Behavior Pattern Prediction Component. The Fourth International Conference on Web Semantic Technology, NeCoM, Chennai, India. Springer-Verlag.

Mukun, C. (2010). Multi-agent automated negotiation as a service. *7th International Conference on service System and Service Management (ICSSSM).* Tokyo: IEEE.

Pan, L. (2011). Towards A Ramework For Automated Service Negotiation In Cloud Computing. In *Proceedings of IEEE Cloud Computing and Intelligence System (CCIS).* doi:10.1109/CCIS.2011.6045091

Rau, H., Chen, C.-W., & Shiang, W.-J. (2009). Development of an Agent-based Negotiation Model for Buyer-supplier Relationship with Multiple Deliveries. *Proceedings of the 2009 IEEE International Conference on Networking, Sensing and Control.* doi:10.1109/ICNSC.2009.4919292

Singh, Kumar, & Khatn. (2012). Securing Storage data in Cloud using RC5 Algorithm. *International Journal of Advance Computer Research, 2*(4), 94–98.

Vrbaski, M., & Petriu, D. (2012). Tool Support for Combined Rule-Based and Goal-Based Reasoning in Context-Aware Systems. Requirement Engineering Conference 2012. IEEE.

Wurman, P., Wellman, M., & Walsh, W. (1998). The Michigan Internet AuctionBot: a configurable auction server for human and software agents. In *Proceedings of the Second International Conference on Autonomous Agents (Agents'98)*. ACM Press. doi:10.1145/280765.280847

Xiaowen, L., & Jin, Y. (2012). Hybrid Approach Using RBR and CBR to Design an Automated Negotiation Model for Tourism Companies. *International Conference on Management of e-Commerce and e-Government*. IEEE.

ADDITIONAL READING

Ateib, M. T. (2010). Agent Based Negotiation In E-cmmerce. *International Symposium on Information Technology 2010(ITSim 2010)*. volume 2- Engineering Technology, Piscataway. IEEE. 978-1-4244-6716/101. 861 – 868. doi:10.1109/ITSIM.2010.5561565

Bala, M. I., Vij, S., & Mukhopadhyay, D. (2013) "Negotiation Life Cycle: An Approach in E-negotiation with Prediction".*48th Annual Convention of the Computer Society of India.CSI 2013 Proceedings, Visakhapatnam, India.* Springer-Verlag Germany. ISBN 978-3-319-03107-1. 505 - 512.

Deochake, S., Kanth, S., Chakraborty, S., Sarode, S., Potdar, V., & Mukhopadhyay, D. (2012). HENRI: High Efficiency Negotiation-based Robust Interface for Multi-party Multi-issue Negotiation over the Internet. *CUBE 2012 International IT Conference, Pune, India.* ACM Digital Library, USA. ACM 978-1-4503-1185-4/12/09. 647-652.

Mohammad Irfan Bala, Sheetal Vij (2013). Automated Negotiation and Behavior Prediction. Published in International Journal of Engineering Research and Technology. Vol. 2 Issue 6. ISSN 2278 – 0181. IJERTV2IS60750. 1832 – 1838.

Rau, H., Chen, C.-W., & Shiang, W.-J. (2009). Development of an Agent-based Negotiation Model for Buyer-supplier Relationship with Multiple Deliveries. *Proceedings of the 2009 IEEE International Conference on Networking, Sensing and Control*, Okayama, Japan, March 26-29, 2009. 978-1-4244-3492-3. 308 - 312. doi:10.1109/ICNSC.2009.4919292

Vrbaski, M., & Petriu, D. (2012). Tool Support for Combined Rule-Based and Goal-Based Reasoning in Context-Aware Systems. Requirement Engineering Conference 2012, Chicago, Illinois, USA. IEEE. 978-1-4673-2785-5. 335 - 336.

Xiaowen, L., & Jin, Y. (2012). Hybrid Approach Using RBR and CBR to Design an Automated Negotiation Model for Tourism Companies. *International Conference on Management of e-Commerce and e-Government.*IEEE. 978-0-7695-4853-1. 197 - 201.

KEY TERMS AND DEFINITIONS

Automated Negotiation: In negotiation process two or more parties are come together to make some agreeable decision. When this negotiation process is combined with E-commerce then it is known as Automated Negotiation.

Cloud Computing: Cloud computing is a very popular technology. Cloud is a remote server where user can store or upload his data and access it when it is required from any location and from any device like laptops, tablet etc. Cloud computing is a "on demand service". It is a basis of pay per use.

Rule Based Data: In this E-negotiation system, rule based data is stored on cloud. This data consist of rule like discount, festival offers etc. All these rules are related to quantity of product. Suppose a user want more than 5 laptops, and then system gives 10% to user. Because there is a rule that give 10% discount on more than 5.

Case Based Data: Case based data is also stored on cloud. This data consist of experience of agent about previous negotiation round. Solution of new problem is depend on solution of previous similar problem is known as Case based reasoning. Bilateral: In negotiation process, all parties are come to final decision and then negotiation process will be stopped. This type of negotiation is known as Bilateral Negotiation.

Openstack: OpenStack is a cloud server. OpenStack is a free and open source platform.

Rest: REST stands for Representational State Transfer. REST is used as an architecture style for designing of network applications. REST depends on a client- server, stateless, cacheable communications protocol.

Device and Location Independent: User uploads data on cloud. User can upload his data from any device like tablet, laptop, mobile phones etc. an also access or retrieve data from cloud through any device and from any location.

Chapter 17
Domain–Based
Dynamic Ranking

Sutirtha Kumar Guha
Seacom Engineering College, India

Anirban Kundu
Netaji Subhash Engineering College, India

Rana Dattagupta
Jadavpur University, India

ABSTRACT

In this chapter a domain based ranking methodology is proposed in cloud environment. Web pages from the cloud are clustered as 'Primary Domain' and 'Secondary Domain'. 'Primary' domain Web pages are fetched based on the direct matching with the keywords. 'Primary Domain' Web pages are ranked based on Relevancy Factor (R_F) and Turbulence Factor (T_F). 'Secondary Domain' is constructed by Nearest Keywords and Similar Web pages. Nearest Keywords are the keywords similar to the matched keywords. Similar Web pages are the Web pages having Nearest Keywords. Matched Web pages of 'Primary' and 'Secondary' domain are ranked separately. A wide range of Web pages from the cloud would be available and ranked more efficiently by this proposed approach.

1. INTRODUCTION

1.1 Overview

Ever increasing e-population and associated services have led to an expansion of the world's domain. Role of Search Engine is invaluable in navigating through the vast expanse of the Web world to find the most relevant information. Web pages are resided in a cloud environment. In cloud environment, it is desirable to search Web pages from the cloud through the vast Web of information and rank the result so as to cater to the exact need of the user. The main function of search engine is to process the users'

DOI: 10.4018/978-1-4666-8676-2.ch017

Copyright © 2015, IGI Global. Copying or distributing in print or electronic forms without written permission of IGI Global is prohibited.

query, searching for a match within particular Web page of the relevant cloud, and to present the matching results in a ranked manner.

1.2 Motivations

Main functionality of a search engine is to match user query given as input with the extensive database of the search engine and display matched URLs in a chronological order. Most optimal and feasible result may not be obtained every time as the searching procedure is executed mechanically. It may happen that URL that may not tally fully with the user given query but match a few keywords may cater to users' requirements. However it is evident that URLs matching exactly with the users' query may also yield an optimal result.

1.3 Goal

In typical Search engine environment Web pages having matched keywords are fetched from the predefined database and ranked. Wide range of relevant Web pages having unmatched keywords are omitted in this procedure. Neglected Web pages having relevant information are covered by the proposed method. Relevant Web pages are fetched and displayed irrespective of keyword matching.

1.4 Methodology Applied

Relevance Factor and Turbulence Factor are introduced to rank the Web pages having matched keywords with respect to the user query. Hierarchical Web database is proposed to calculate the Relevance Factor. Turbulence Factor is calculated based on the effect on other Web pages of the same Web site. Relevant Web pages having unmatched keywords are collected by nearest keywords and similar Web pages concept as discussed in Section 3.2.

2. BACKGROUND

A regularization-based algorithm called ranking adaptation SVM (RA-SVM) is proposed in (Geng, Yang, Xu, & Hua, 2012) as a unique ranking model. Ranking adaptability measurement is proposed to quantitatively estimate if an existing ranking model can be adapted to a new domain (Geng et al., 2012). Different applications are also made based on the domain based ranking algorithm. A prototype application to demonstrate ranking model adoption using a novel ranking model meant for ranking the search results besides adapting to new domains is proposed in (Greeshma, Srinivasa Rao, & Krishnaiah, 2013). It is claimed by experimental results that in the paper that the proposed application is useful in searching data across the domains (Greeshma et all., 2013). It is observed that traditional search techniques fail to interpret the significance of geographical clues and unable to return highly relevant search results as users are interested in a set of location-sensitive topics. An innovative probabilistic ranking framework for domain information retrieval is proposed in (Li, H., Li, Z., Lee, W. C., & Lee D.L., 2009). The proposed method recognizes the geographical distribution of topic influence in the process of ranking documents and models it accurately using probabilistic Gaussian Process classifiers (Li et al., 2009). A framework is proposed to learn the aggregate votes of constituent rankers with domain specific expertise without supervision. The learning framework is applied to the settings of aggregating full rankings and aggregating top-k lists, demonstrating significant improvements over a domain-agnostic baseline in both cases (Klementiev, Roth, Small, & Titov, 2009).

Ranking of a Web page is measured by different parameters of the Web page as described in (Guha, Kundu, Bhadra, & Dattagupta, 2013). Session, Inlink-Outlink, Relevancy, traffic are considered as important parameters of a Web page to calculate the rank n (Guha et al., 2013). In (Guha, Kundu, & Dattagupta, 2012) a new technique is proposed for checking the relevancy of user sessions. Session of a Web page is considered as an important parameter for Web page ranking calculation, hence session relevancy inspection important to measure the ranking accurately. A longer session on a Web page may not yield high relevancy of the Web page, hence a threshold value (THV) is considered for individual Web page based on the contents to avoid the probable noise. The threshold value (THV) is calculated by Keyword Matching Index (K-index) and Data Transfer Speed of the client-server. The K-index is measured by implementing fuzzy logic on Pattern Matching of requirement and Web page contents. Field Matching information is fetched through hierarchical database (Guha et al., 2012).

Traditional ranking mainly focuses on one type of data source, and effective modeling still relies on a sufficiently large number of labeled or supervised examples. However, in many real-world applications ranking over multiple interrelated (heterogeneous) domains becomes a common situation, where in some domains we may have a large amount of training data while in some other domains we can only collect very little (Wangy, Tang, Fan, Chen, Yang, & Liu, 2009). Probability based ranking procedure is introduced in (Provost & Domingos, 2003). In this paper a comprehensive set of experiments, testing some straightforward methods for improving probability-based rankings conclude that probability estimation trees should be considered when rankings based on class-membership probability are required (Provost & Domingos, 2003). An innovative unsupervised method for automatic sentence extraction using graph-based ranking algorithms is introduced in (Mihalcea, 2004). The method is evaluated in the context of a text summarization task and the obtained results are compared favorably with previously published results on established benchmarks (Mihalcea, 2004).

The idea of automatically using the concepts of a thesaurus to improve search results is implemented in (Silveira & Ribeiro-Neto, 2004). The query terms are used to match concepts in the thesaurus. These concepts are then used to find other related concepts (narrow, broad, synonym), that are interpreted as independent sources of evidential knowledge. Each source of evidence is used to produce a separate concept-based ranking of the documents in the collection. These partial rankings are then combined into a final ranking (Silveira & Ribeiro-Neto, 2004). A new technique is proposed to using context in Web search that seeks to personalize the results of a generic search engine for the needs of a specialist community of users. In particular two separate evaluations are described in detail to demonstrate how the collaborative search method has the potential to deliver significant search performance benefits to end-users while avoiding many of the privacy and security concerns that are commonly associated with related personalization research (Freyne, Smyth, Coyle, Balfe, & Briggs, 2004). Graph-based ranking method is proposed in (Dom, Eiron, Cozzi, & Zhang, 2003) to rank email correspondents according to their degree of expertise on subjects of interest.

Figure 1. User query sent to the Web

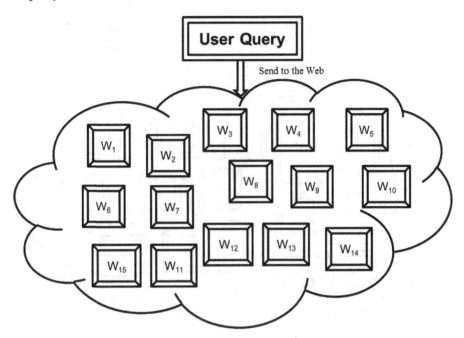

3. PROPOSED APPROACH

In real time scenario, it is observed that finite number of keywords is tagged with a particular Web page. The scope of a Web page could not be defined by limited number of 'words'. Hence, accuracy of searching is not assured by typical approaches. In this work, Web pages are categorized in two domains, such as 'Primary' and 'Secondary'. Web pages with unmatched keywords having relevant information are stored in 'Secondary' domain.

Definition 1: Domain - A Domain is defined as a cluster of Web pages. Mathematically, it is defined as follows:

Domain (W) = $\{w_1, w_2, w_3\}$

where, Domain W consists of Web pages w_1, w_2 and w_3;
User query is sent to the cloud as shown in Figure 1.
Web pages of cloud are classified in two domains, namely 'Primary Domain' and 'Secondary Domain' based on user query as shown in Figure 2.
Domain selection procedure is performed by different parameters. 'Primary Domain' is created by the matched Web pages. Matched Web pages are selected based on the similarity between user query and keywords of the Web pages as depicted in Figure 3.

Figure 2. Domain selection based on user query

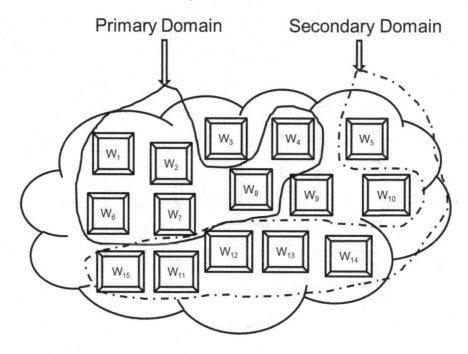

Figure 3. Primary Domain selection based on user query

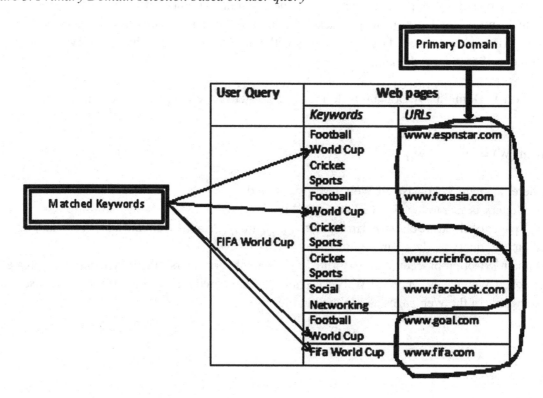

4.1 Primary Domain

In this paper, 'Primary Domain' Web ranking method is static in nature as the ranking depends on the relevance of Web pages with predefined cloud database. Hence, the ranking is called Static Rank (R_S).

Web pages of 'Primary Domain' are ranked based on Relevancy Factor (R_F) and Turbulence Factor. Relevancy measurement process proposed in (Guha, Kundu, Bhadra, & Dattagupta, 2013) is followed to calculate the R_F as shown in Equation 1. Relevancy Factor is measured based on hierarchical tree type Web database (Guha et al., 2013).

$$R_F(A) = \int_1^d Mfi \qquad \text{(1) (Guha et al., 2013)}$$

where, Mf = Successful Forward Movement of the Searching Pointer which is considered as the control that moves from one segment to another segment for continuation of the searching procedure.

Consider, a Web page W has 'n' number of neighbors (Web pages such as W_1, W_2, .., W_n). Neighbor Web pages are internally connected with the target Web page 'W'. Neighbor Web pages are visited by the user while visiting 'W' to satisfy user's requirement. If an important neighbor Web page is visited through 'W', then the importance of 'W' must be high. Turbulence Factor is measured as the impact of a particular user query towards all nearest Web pages of the target Web page.

Turbulence Factor (T_F) is measured by our proposed formula as shown in Equation 2.

$$T_F(A) = \sum_1^n (Session \times VisitedWebPageOfSameSite) \qquad (2)$$

Turbulence effect is the impact of a particular user query towards all nearest Web pages of the target Web page as explained in Figure 4.

Figure 4. Turbulence Effect for a Successful Hit in Web

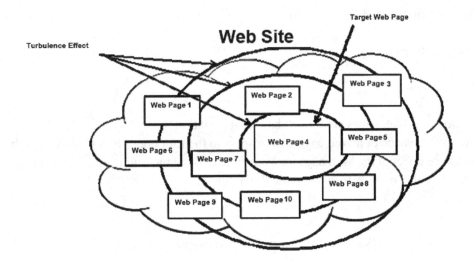

$R_S(W)$ is constructed by $R_F(W)$ and $T_F(W)$.

Hence, $R_S(W)$ is decomposed as follows:

$$R_S(W) = R_1(W) + R_2(W)$$

where, $R_1(W)$ is rank based on $R_F(W)$; and, $R_2(W)$ is rank based on $T_F(W)$;It is observed that a relevant Web page would have a better page ranking as follows:

$$R_1(W) \propto R_F$$

$$R_2(W) = (T_F \times B)$$

where, A is a constant, called weightage value of R_F;Similarly, Better Web page ranking would be reflected by better turbulence effect, mathematically,

$$R_2(W) \propto T_F$$

$$R_2(W) = (T_F \times B)$$

where, B is a constant, called weightage value of T_F;

$$R_S(W) = (R_1(W) + R_2(W))$$

$$R_S(W) = ((R_F \times A) + (T_F \times B)) \qquad (3)$$

where, $R_S(W)$= Static Rank of Web page W;

R_F= Relevancy Factor;

T_F= Turbulence Factor;

'Primary Domain' Web pages are ranked based on Equation 3.

Conceptually, relevance of a Web page with respect to the user query is considered much important than the turbulence effect of the Web page for Web page ranking measurement. Hence, weightage value of R_F is higher than that of T_F.A is mathematically defined as,

Table 1. Measurement of 'A'

Web Pages in Parent Domain	Rank of the Web Pages	Total Number of Web pages of Parent Domains	Value of A
www.abc.abc	3	7	2.4285
www.def.def	1		
www.ghi.ghi	5		
www.jkl.jkl	2		
www.mno.mno	1		
www.pqr.pqr	2		
www.stu.stu	3		

$$A = \left(\sum_{1}^{n} PR(WP_{PD}) \right) \div N_{WPPD} \qquad (4)$$

where, $PR(WP_{PD})$ = Page Rank of Web Pages of Parent Domain;

N_{WPPD} = Total Number of Web Pages residing in Parent Domain;

Consider, a Web page 'www.XYZ.xyz' resides in 'X' domain in a hierarchical database as proposed in (Guha et al., 2013). Page rank and number of Web pages residing in 'X' domain is shown in Table1.
Similarly, B is mathematically defined as,

$$B = \left(\sum^{n} PR_{AWP} \right) \div N_{AWP} \qquad (5)$$

where,

PR_{AWP} = Page Rank of the Affected Web Pages

N_{EWP} = Number of Affected Web Pages

Let, a Web page 'www.ABC.abc' is successfully hit for a particular user query. Page rank and number of effected Web pages is shown in Table 2.

4.2 Secondary Domain

'Secondary Domain' Web pages are ranked dynamically as ranking method depends on the request send to the server. It is evident that success or failure of sending request is directly related with the network activities. Hence the ranking method is non-deterministic in nature.

Table 2. Measurement of 'B'

Effected Web Pages	Rank of the Effected Web Pages	Total Number of Effected Web pages	Value of B
www.VXY.vxy	5	7	3.7142
www.ZAB.zab	7		
www.CDE.cde	1		
www.FGH.fgh	8		
www.IJK.ijk	2		
www.LMN.lmn	2		
www.OPQ.opq	1		

Secondary domain is constructed by the Web pages that have similar keywords with respect to the user query. These Web pages are selected based on nearest keywords and similar Web pages that are defined in Definition 2 and Definition 3.

Definition 2: Nearest Keywords – The keywords that attracts the same user query based on a particular field are known as nearest keywords to each other. Therefore, nearest keywords would be measured using similarity function as mentioned in Equation 6. (Kundu, Xu, & Ji, 2014)

$$SimilarityK(W(i),W(j)) = \left(ARoW(\operatorname{Re}W(W(i)) \cap \operatorname{Re}W(W(j))\right) \div \left(ARoW(\operatorname{Re}W(W(i)) \cup \operatorname{Re}W(W(j))\right)$$

(6)(Kundu et al.,2014)

where, W(n) = Web page n;

ARoW(n) = Function of "Amount of Request successfully responded by Web page n";

ReW(n) = Function of "Number of Requests made to the considered Web page";

SimilarityN() = Function of "Similarity Measurement between Web pages"; (Kundu et al.,2014)

Definition 3: Similar Web pages – The Web pages that satisfies the same user request based on a particular requirement are known as similar Web pages to each other. Therefore, similar Web pages would be measured using similarity function as mentioned in Equation 7. (Kundu et al., 2014)

$$SimilarityW(W(i),W(j)) = \left(ASRW(NRW(W(j)) \cap NRW(W(j))\right) \div \left(ASRW\left(NRW(W(i) \cup NRW(W(j))\right)\right)$$

(7) (Kundu et al., 2014)

where, W(n) = Web page n;

ASRW(n) = Function of "Amount of Successful Request met by the Web page n";

NRW(n) = Function of "number of Request made to the Web page n"; (Kundu et al.,2014)

Figure 5. 'Secondary Domain' Construction

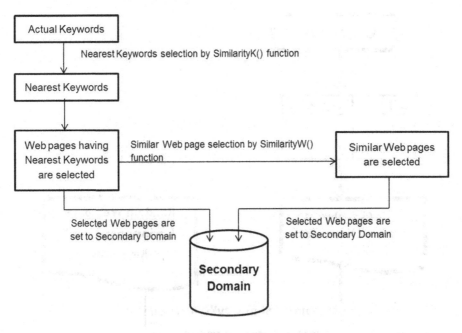

Nearest keywords (refer Definition 2) are responsible to locate the Web pages having similar keywords. Web pages similar to the selected Web pages are selected by similar Web pages (refer Definition 3). 'Secondary Domain' construction procedure is pictorially depicted in Figure 5.

Web pages having nearest keywords are collected by implementing 'SimilarityK()' on Web page n_1 and n_2, where n_1 is a Web page having matched keywords with respect to the user query and n_2 is considered Web page whose keywords are not exactly matched. Web page having nearest keywords selection method is depicted in Figure 6.

Similar Web pages are selected by implementing SimilarityW() functions on Web page n_1 and n_2, where n_1 is a Web page having similar keywords with respect to the exactly matched Web pages and n_2 is a randomly selected Web page. Similar Web page selection method is depicted in Figure 7.

It is evident that rank of a Web page is reflected from the amount of successful hit by the user query for a relevant Web page. Mathematically,

Web page rank $\propto$ Successful hit by the user query

Successful hit by the user query is decomposed as 'Request successfully responded by Web page' and 'Successful Request met by the Web page'.

Hence, Web pages of secondary domain are ranked based on Equation 8.

$$R_D(n) = ((\text{ARo}W(n) \div N_{RS}) + (\text{ASRW}(n) \div \text{ARo}W(n))) \qquad (8)$$

where, $R_D(n)$ = Dynamic Rank of Web page n;

Figure 6. Web page having nearest keywords selection

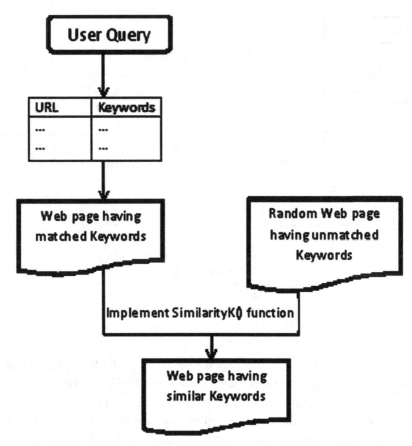

Figure 7. Similar Web page selection technique

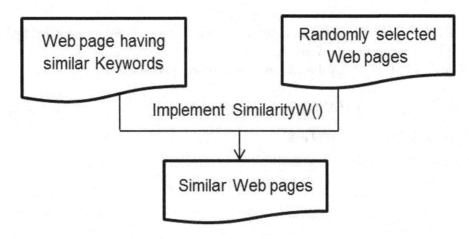

ARoW(n) = Function of "Amount of Request successfully responded by Web page n";

N_{RS} = Total Number of requests sent to the Web pages;

ASRW(n) = Function of "Amount of Successful Request met by the Web page n";

Wide range of Web pages is considered by our proposed approach. In typical search engine Web pages having matched keywords (W_1) with respect to the user query are displayed. Web pages having matched keywords (W_1) and Web pages having similar keywords (W_2) are analyzed.

Number of displayed Web pages in typical search engine = W_1

Number of displayed Web pages in by our proposed approach = $W_1 + W_2$

Hence, it is evident that number of displayed Web pages in by our proposed approach is greater than the number of displayed Web pages in typical search engines.

It is also evident that Web pages in 'Primary Domain' are selected based on the direct relation with the user query, whereas Web pages in 'Secondary Domain' are selected based on some assumption that keywords of a Web page may not be a perfect indicator of the Web page contents. Final ranking of the selected Web pages from 'Primary Domain' and 'Secondary Domain' is obtained by implementing fuzzy set theory. Final Web page ranking procedure is explained with case study in 'Analytical Study' section.

4. ANALYTICAL STUDY

'Primary' and 'Secondary' domain are selected independently, hence a particular Web page would be resided in 'Primary' as well as 'Secondary' domain. Different static and dynamic rank of the particular Web page is obtained for that particular instance. Fuzzy logic is used to determine the final ranking of those Web pages.

Let, user given query at time instance is 'Image Processing'. Predefined URL database and 'Primary Domain' and 'Secondary Domain' selection is shown in Figure 8.

Relevancy Factor($R_F(A)$), Turbulence Factor($T_F(A)$), value of weightage factor 'A and B' are calculated based on Equation 1, 2, 4 and 5. Calculated values are shown in Table 3.

Rank of 'Secondary Domain' is calculated based on Equation 8. Calculated values of ARoW, ASRW and N_{RS} and R_D of 'Secondary Domain' Web pages are shown in Table 4.

The membership function of the input 'R_S' and 'R_D' is shown in Table 5.

μ(Output) = { μ(R1), μ(R2), ..., μ(R108), μ(R109)}.

Let, consider crisp input for R_S and R_D for a Web page at any particular time instance are 0.035 and 0.125 respectively. Corresponding membership function of considered input values are shown in Figure 9.

Constructed rulebase for R_S and R_D with replaced membership values is shown in Table 6.

Final decision is rank of the Web page is 30% Rank 6.

Figure 8. 'Primary Domain' and 'Secondary Domain' construction for considered case study

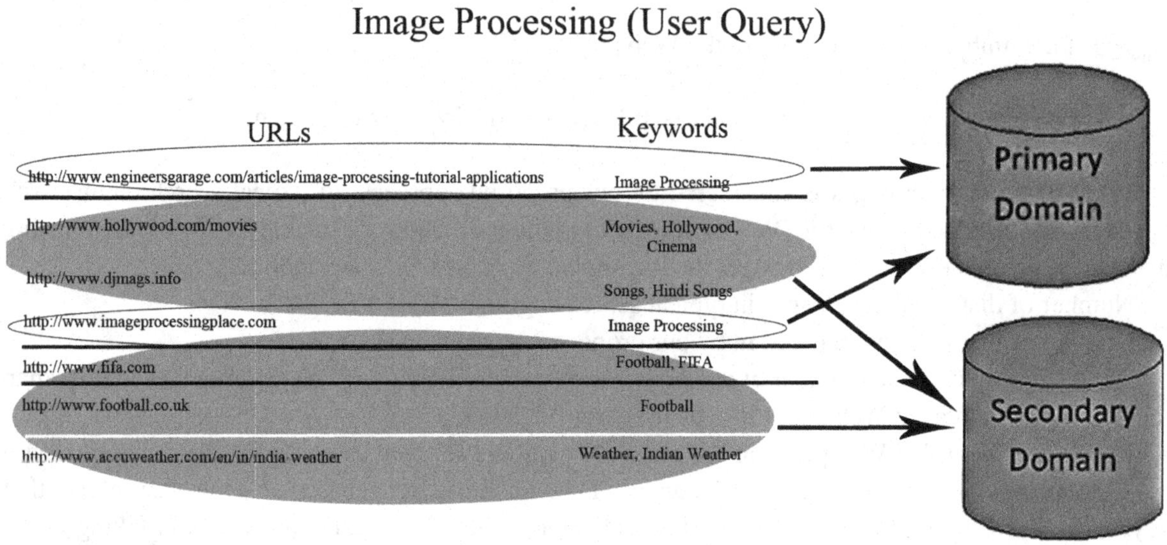

Table 3. R_S of 'Primary Domain' Web pages

Web page	$R_F(A)$	$T_F(A)$	Value of A	Value of B	$R_S(A)$ value	Rank
http://www.engineersgarage.com/articles/image-processing-tutorial-applications	6	7.23	3	5	54.15	01
http://www.imageprocessingplace.com/	4	5.34	4	5	42.7	02

Table 4. R_D of 'Secondary Domain' Web pages

Web page	ARoW	ASRW	N_{RS}	R_D Value	Rank
http://www.hollywood.com/movies/	12	7	20	1.18	03
http://www.djmaza.info/	10	8	20	1.30	01
http://www.fifa.com/	11	7	20	1.19	02
http://www.football.co.uk/	13	6	20	1.11	04
http://www.accuweather.com/en/in/india-weather	11	5	20	1.00	05

Table 5. Input Ranges of R_S and R_D

Inputs	Input Range Specification
Static Rank (R_S)	0.00-0.02 => R_S1 0.01-0.03 => R_S2 0.02-0.04 => R_S3 0.03-0.05 => R_S4 0.04-0.06 => R_S5 0.05-0.07 => R_S6 0.06-0.08 => R_S7 0.07-0.09 => R_S8 0.10-0.12 => R_S9 0.11-0.13 => R_S10 . . . . 0.97-0.99 => R_S99 0.98-1.00 => R_S100
Dynamic Rank (R_D)	0.00-0.02 => R_D1 0.01-0.03 => R_D2 0.02-0.04 => R_D3 0.03-0.05 => R_D4 0.04-0.06 => R_D5 0.05-0.07 => R_D6 0.06-0.08 => R_D7 0.07-0.09 => R_D8 0.10-0.12 => R_D9 0.11-0.13 => R_D10 . . . . 0.97-0.99 => R_D99 0.98-1.00 => R_D100

Table 6. Rulebase replaced with corresponding membership values

	R_D1	R_D2	R_D3	. . . . .	**0.5**	**0.5**	. . . . .	R_D99	R_D100
R_S1	R1	R1	R2	. . . . .	R5	R6	. . . . .	R50	R50
R_S2	R1	R2	R2	. . . . .	R6	R6	. . . . .	R50	R51
0.5	R2	R2	R3	. . . . .	**0.5**	**0.5**	. . . . .	. . . . .	. . . . .
0.5	R2	R3	R3	. . . . .	**0.5**	**0.5**	. . . . .	. . . . .	. . . . .
.	.	.	.	.	.	.	. . . .	.	.
.	.	.	.	.	.	.	. . .	.	.
.	.	.	.	.	.	.	. . . . .	.	.
R_S99	R50	R50	R51	. . . . .	R54	R55	. . . . .	R109	R109
R_S100	R50	R51	R51	. . . . .	R55	R55	. . . . .	R109	R110

Figure 9. Membership Functions of R_S and R_D with plotted input values

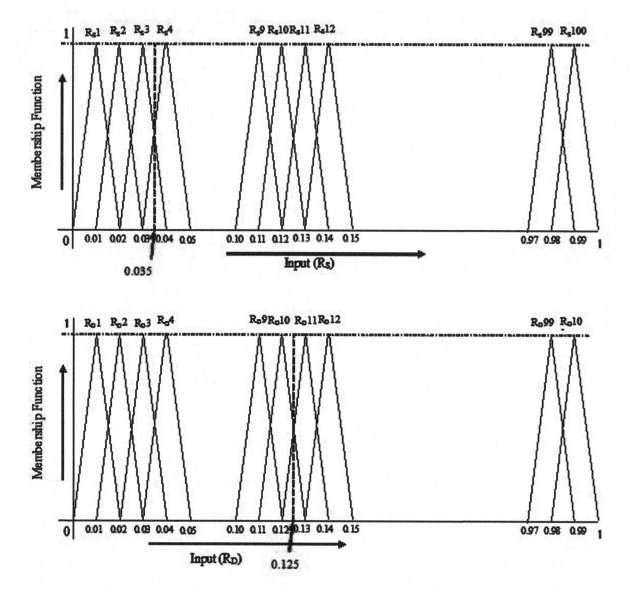

4.1 Discussion

In our work, R_S is calculated based on the contents of a particular Web page. R_D is measured based on the dynamic behavior of the Web pages, as amount of Request and number of requests at that particular moment is considered. Hence, rank of a Web page having R_S and R_D value is calculated based on the combination of the two values. A predefined set of input range is considered for R_S and R_D values. It is considered that R_S value is more stable and reliable compare to R_D. In our analytical case study considered R_S value 0.035 and R_D value 0.125 indicate different static and dynamic rank '3' or '4' and '10' or '11' respectively. It is depicted from the rank that particular Web page has relevant contents as the static rank is high but draws less user interest as dynamic rank is low. A combined rank value is obtained by implementing fuzzy set theory. Ideal rank must be not too low (as the Web page contains relevant information), not too high (as the Web page attracts less attention from the user).

5. FUTURE RESEARCH DIRECTIONS

It is obvious that fast and efficient searching and ranking procedure is desired in every sector. Data would be structured in domain based manner. Domain selection based on user based Web search trend, location based user behavior, event based user requirement would be introduced to provide more wide and user friendly searching in cloud based environment. This concept would be implemented in different electronic trading environment or online marketing. Domain based searching and ranking concept would be implemented in an environment where huge data is handled like cloud or Internet of Things (IOT).

6. CONCLUSION

In this paper Web pages are fetched from predefined database based on the user query. Fetched Web pages are classified as 'Primary Domain' and 'Secondary Domain'. 'Primary Domain' Web

pages are selected based on direct keywords matching. 'Secondary Domain' Web pages are nominated based on similar keywords and Web page selection. 'Primary Domain' and 'Secondary Domain' Web pages are ranked by two newly introduced equations as discussed in this chapter. Finally Web pages from two domains are ranked by implementing fuzzy set theory. Wide number of Web pages is selected and produced based on user query by the proposed approach.

REFERENCES

Dom, B., Eiron, I., Cozzi, A., & Zhang, Y. (2003). Graph-based ranking algorithms for e-mail expertise analysis. *Proceedings of the 8th ACM SIGMOD workshop on Research issues in data mining and knowledge discovery* (pp 42-48). San Diego, CA: ACM. doi:10.1145/882082.882093

Freyne, J., Smyth, B., Coyle, M., Balfe, E., & Briggs, P. (2004). Further Experiments on Collaborative Ranking in Community-Based Web Search. *Artificial Intelligence Review, 21*(3-4), 229–252. doi:10.1023/B:AIRE.0000036257.77059.40

Geng, B., Yang, Y., Xu, C., & Hua, X. S. (2012). Ranking Model Adaptation for Domain-Specific Search. *IEEE Transactions on Knowledge and Data Engineering, 24*(4), 745–758. doi:10.1109/TKDE.2010.252

Greeshma, L., Srinivasa Rao, M., & Krishnaiah, R. V. (2013). SVM and AdaBoost Based Ranking Model Adaptation for Domain Specific Search. *International Journal of Advanced Research in Computer and Communication Engineering, 2*(8), 3326–3329.

Guha, S. K., Kundu, A., Bhadra, S., & Dattagupta, R. (2013). Dynamic Web-page Ranking of Search Engine using Importance Increasing Factor. *International Journal of Digital Content Technology and its Applications, 7*(12), 28-39.

Guha, S. K., Kundu, A., & Dattagupta, R. (2012). Introducing Session Relevancy Inspection in Web Page. *Proceedings of Second International Conference on Computer Science, Engineering and Applications (ICCSEA 2012)* (pp. 181-192). Delhi, India, Springer. doi:10.1007/978-3-642-30111-7_18

Klementiev, A., Roth, D., Small, K., & Titov, I. (2009). Unsupervised Rank Aggregation with Domain-Specific Expertise. *Proceedings of 21st International Joint Conference on Artifical Intelligence (IJCAI'09)* (pp. 1101-1106). San Francisco, CA: Academic Press.

Kundu, A., Xu, G., & Ji, C. (2014). Data Specific Ranking in Cloud. *International Journal of Cloud Applications and Computing, 4*(4), 32–41. doi:10.4018/ijcac.2014100103

Li, H., Li, Z., Lee, W. C., & Lee, D. L. (2009). A probabilistic topic-based ranking framework for location-sensitive domain information retrieval. *Proceedings of 32nd international ACM SIGIR conference on Research and development in information retrieval* (pp 331-33). Boston: ACM. doi:10.1145/1571941.1571999

Mihalcea, R. (2004). Graph-based ranking algorithms for sentence extraction, applied for text summarization. *Proceedings of the ACL 2004 on Interactive poster and demonstration sessions (ACLdemo'04).* Stroudsburg, PA: ACL doi:10.3115/1219044.1219064

Provost, F., & Domingos, P. (2003). Tree Induction for Probability-Based Ranking. *Machine Learning, 52*(3), 199–215. doi:10.1023/A:1024099825458

Silveira, M. L., & Ribeiro-Neto, B. (2004). Concept-based ranking: A case study in the judicial domain. *Information Processing & Management, 40*(5), 791–805. doi:10.1016/j.ipm.2004.04.015

Wangy, B., Tang, J., Fan, W., Chen, S., Yang, Z., & Liu, Y. (2009). Heterogeneous Cross Domain Ranking in Latent Space. *Proceedings of 18th ACM Conference on Information and Knowledge Management (CIKM'09)* (pp 987-996). Hong Kong, China: ACM. doi:10.1145/1645953.1646079

ADDITIONAL READING

Guha, S., Kundu, A., Bhadra, S., & Dattagupta, R. (2013). Analytical Design of Feature based Ranking. *Proceedings of 1st International Conference on Computational Intelligence, Modelling, Techniques and Applications (CIMTA 2013).* West Bengal, India. Elsevier. pp. 773-780.

Guha, S. K., Kundu, A., & Dattagupta, R. (2014). Hierarchical Ranking in Search Engine Environment. *An Overview. Journal of Convergence Information Technology, 9*(5), 18–25.

He, C., Wang, C., Zhong, Y., & Li, R. (2008). A Survey on Learning to Rank. *Proceedings of Seventh International Conference on Machine Learning and Cybernetics.* Kunming. Agichtein, E., White, R., Dumais, S., & Bennett, P. (2012). *Proceedings of Search, Interrupted: Understanding and Predicting Search Task Continuation (SIGIR '12).* Portland, Oregon, USA.

Kundu, A., Banerjee, C., Guha, S. K., Mitra, A., Chakraborty, S., Pal, C., & Roy, R. (2010). Memory Utilization in Cloud Computing using Transparency. *ICCIT 2010.* Seoul, S. *Korea & World Affairs,* 22–27.

KEY TERMS AND DEFINITION

Dynamic Rank: It is defined as the rank that is calculated based on the real time data. Hence this rank value varies time to time based on the real time scenario.

Primary Domain: Primary domain is defined as the domain where Primary Web pages are resided.

Primary Web Pages: Primary Web pages are the Web pages that have direct matching with the user query.

Relevancy Factor: It is defined as a parameter to measure the relevancy of a Web page with a specific query.

Secondary Domain: Secondary domain is defined as the domain where secondary Web pages are resided.

Secondary Web Pages: Secondary Web pages are the Web pages that seem to have relevant information with respect to the user query but have no direct matching with the user query.

Static Rank: It is defined as the rank that is calculated based on some constant parameters. Hence this rank value would not change until major changes of constant parameters occur.

Turbulence Factor: It is defined as the parameter to measure the impact of a specific user query over a domain.

Web Page Ranking: It is defined as the ranking of the matched Web pages based on specific 'User Query'.

Chapter 18
An Approach on Cloud Disk Searching Using Parallel Channels

Saswati Sarkar
Adamas Institute of Technology, India

Anirban Kundu
Netaji Subhash Engineering College, India

ABSTRACT

In this chapter, Cloud disk searching technique is going to be proposed. Cloud based searching mechanism shows the utility of indexing, balancing, and data storage in cloud. The Chapter exhibits complexity of cloud based searching algorithms in real-time scenario. The proposed cloud based disk searching technique using parallel channels is searching data in less time consumption.Comparison graphs have been demonstrated for time difference realization in cloud. Parallel concepts have been introduced to facilitate searching the cloud. Sequential and several parallel situations have been compared using time graphsLoad balance monitoring, data searching and data accessing in less time have been introduced in this chapter.

1. INTRODUCTION

1.1. Overview

Cloudis typically a terminology used for describing a new class of network based computing that takes place over the internet.It is a step on from utility computing, collection/group ofintegrated and networked hardware, software and internet infrastructure / platform Internet is used for communication and transportationwhich provide hardware, software and networking services to customers in a global sense.Cloud computing is an abstractconcept used for internet based development and services.(as found in "http://www.johnhagel.com/cloudperspectives.pdf", Accessed 2009).

DOI: 10.4018/978-1-4666-8676-2.ch018

Copyright © 2015, IGI Global. Copying or distributing in print or electronic forms without written permission of IGI Global is prohibited.

Cloud storage is a service model in which data is maintained, managed and backed up remotely using advanced techniques of networking using internet. The cloud has become a new driving force for delivering resources such as computing and storage to customers on demand basis. Cloud is a new business model wrapped around new technologies such as server virtualization which takes advantage of economies of scale forminimizing cost of using information technology resources (as foundin"https://www.ogf.org/Resources/documents/CloudStorageForCloudComputing.pdf", Accessed 2009).

Cloud search is a fully-managed service in the cloud managing easy to set up, manage, and scale searching solutions for specific websites or applications. In cloud search, a user is ableto search large data collections such as web pages, document files, forum posts, product information, images, etc... A user could quickly add search capabilities without having expertise in searching.There is no need to know the details of hardware provisioning, setup, and maintenance of the server side resources. Cloud search scales to meet the need of users based on real time volume of data and traffic fluctuations (as found in "http://docs.aws.amazon.com/cloudsearch/latest/developerguide/what-is-cloudsearch.html" Accessed 2015).

Cloud disk searching(Mano M. M., 2009&IBM, 1980)is a powerful method for checking and/or verifying contents within specified sectors. It conveniently searches large numbers of text or ASCII based files in a proper sequence. Sequential(as found in "http://en.wikipedia.org/wiki/Hard_disk_drive_interface", Accessed2015), concurrent(as found in "http://en.wikipedia.org/wiki/Hard_disk_drive",Accessed 2015), parallel(as found in "http://www.fujitsu-ten.com/business/technicaljournal/pdf/20-3.pdf",Accessed 2003) methods have been introduced by several researchers. Web developers, computer professionals, programmers, system managers, and other demanding users are handling files or contents using various scheduling techniques (as found in "http://www.fujitsu-ten.com/business/technicaljournal/pdf/20-3.pdf", Accessed 2003).

Several approaches have been utilized in cloud based searching by researchers throughout the world. A lot of new methodologies have been invented to ease cloud searching in any situation. Binary search technique is one of the popular methods available in cloud based market. It helps to reduce time complexity of a searching operation.

Best fit approachis another well-known technique allocating the smallest cloud space which is big enough to accommodate a task within the specific memory space.Entire listis searched, unless the list is kept ordered by size. This strategy produces the smallest leftover hole (Knuth D., 1997).

The memory hierarchy consists of all storage devices used in computer systems of cloud and are also classified into specific groups, such as secondary memory, primary memory, cache memory, internal memory.Secondary memory is slow speed, low cost and high capacity device. Secondary memories are magnetic disk that is Hard disk, floppy disk and magnetic tape. These types of secondary memories are commonly used. This type of memory is used for storing all data. It is also used for storing programs. A program, residing out of main memory locations, could be in secondary memory that means when a program residing in secondary memory is needed to be executed;itis transferred from secondary memory to primary memory. On the other hand, if a program is not needed in main memory, then the program should be transferred to secondary memory providing free space for currently required programs and data. Hard disk is an example of secondary memory. It store data and information in bulk size (Mano M. M., 2009).

Main memory is a memory which communicates directly to CPU. Data and program which are needed to execute by the CPU reside in main memory. Main memory is a central position of total system which is able to communicate with CPU and with secondary memory device through Input/output processor.

Cache Memory is a special high-speed main memory. It mainly used to increase the speed of processing. Generally the CPU is much faster than main memory, thus resulting that processing speed is limited mainly by the speed of main memory. By the concept of cache memory, it is used to compensate the speed mismatch between main memory and CPU. Mainly to solve the speed mismatch between CPU and main memory, the concept of cache memory is introduced. Cache memory mainly is used for storing portions of programs which currently being executed in the CPU. Cache memory acts as a buffer between CPU and main memory .Data and program which are available in a rapid rate, possible to increases performance of the system.

Cache memory is mainly static RAM which is high speed memory. The cache memory is placed more than one level. There are two types of cache are available.L1 Cache which lies on the same chip with the processor. It is also called on-chip cache. L2 Cache which lies external to the processor chip in between the CPU and the main memory. L1 Cache is smaller in size but L2 cache larger in size.L1 cache is faster compare to L2 cache. Off–chip cache is also introduced .on-chip cache is slightly faster than off-chip cache.

The transfer of data as a block from main memory to cache memory is referred to as mapping process. There are three types of mapping are available. Direct mapping, Associative mapping, set associative mapping.

Direct mapping is mainly a particular block of main memory can be brought to be a particular block of cache memory. Direct mapping is mainly contains Tag, Block, and Word. It is not so flexible. Instead of storing total address information with data in cache memory, only part of address bits is stored along with data in the direct cache mapping.

In Associative mapping function block of main memory reside in any cache block. Associative mapping method contains Tag address and word. This mapping method is much more flexible and faster method. In this method both address and data of the memory word are stored. This method allows any location in cache to store any word from main memory. If cache memory contains 256 words and Main memory contains $64k = 64*1024$ bytes that are 16 address lines then from the above size of main memory CPU first sends a 16 bit address for a desired word. Associative memory is then searched for a matching address. If the address is found then 8 bit data word is send to CPU. If no match found then main memory start searching. The address brought to cache memory from main memory. If the Cache is full then replacement algorithm is used. Most used replacement algorithms are First-in-First-out that is FIFO algorithm, Least recently used that is LRU algorithm.First-in-First-out algorithm chooses the words that are exit in cache for a long time. In this algorithm, the word which is entered in the cache first, gets pushed out first.Least recently used algorithm chose the item for replacement that is used by the CPU minimum number of times in recent past.

In set associative mapping method, blocks of cache are grouped into sets and the mapping allows a block of main memory to reside in any block of a specified set. This set-associative mapping method is more flexible than direct mapping method and less flexible than Associative mapping method. Set-Associative mapping method contains Tag, set and word.There are two methods in writing into cache memory. Write through policy and Write back policy. Write through policy is a simplest procedure. It is more commonly used. This procedure is used to update the cache. In this technique when the cache memory is updated at the same time the main memory is also updated. Thus the main memory is always contains the same data that contain the cache memory. It is a slow process when main memory needs to be accessed. In Write back policy method, during the write operation only cache memory is updated. When update occurs, the location is marked by a flag .This flag is called dirty bit or modified bit. When the word is replaced from cache it is written into main memory if its flag bit is set. In this method, in write operation the words which exist in cache used several times which is called temporal locality of reference. This method reduces the number of reference to main memory. This method solve the problem of inconsistency due to different copies of the same data, one is cache and other in main memory.

Internal Memory is high speed a high speed memory. It is a high speed registers used inside the CPU. These registers hold temporary results. There is no speed disparity between the register and CPU because they are fabricated with the same technology. Registers is very expensive. Moreover the example of secondary memory is magnetic disk, optical disk. Example of main memory is DRAM, ROM. Example of cache memory is SRAM and example of internal memory is register. SRAM: - Such kind of RAM retains the stored information as long as the power is on. It is faster compare to DRAM. It is costly memory compare to DRAM.DRAM:-This kind if memory loses its stored information in a very short time or a few milliseconds even though the power supply is on. This memory is slower compare to SRAM and it is costly compare to SRAM. Memory capacity in decreasing order:-Secondary Memory, Main Memory, Cache Memory and Internal Memory.Memory speed in increasing order:-Registers Cache Memory, Main Memory, and Secondary Memory.Memory cost in increasing order:-Registers Cache Memory, Main Memory, and Secondary Memory.

The recording surface is divided into a number of circles called tracks and further tracks are divided into sections called sectors. There is a small inter-sector gap to distinguish between two consecutive sectors. There is also a small inter-track gap to distinguish between two consecutive tracks. The information is accessed from the tracks using movable read-write heads that move from the innermost to outer most tracks and vice-versa. Several identical disks have been arranged with specific separation called "disk pack". There is one read-write head per surface. Same radius tracks on different surface of disk are called cylinders (as found inhttp://dis-dpcs.wikispaces.com/6.2.1+Blocking,+Sectors,+Cylinders, +Heads.",Accessed 2015).A disk pack has n disks having 2n tracks per cylinder. Disk controller is the part of a disk having electronic circuitry to control the operation of disk within cloud.

1.2. Key Terms and Definitions

Definition1: Seek Time - Time taken by read/write head to get position over the correct track is known as seek time. It is denoted by 'ts' having range of"2-30 ns" (as found in "http://www.techopedia. com/definition/3558/seek-time", Accessed 2015).

Definition2: Latency Time - Time taken by read/write head to get position over the required sector to be accessed is known as latency time. It is denoted by 'tl' having range of "60-120 rotation"(as found in "http://whatis.techtarget.com/definition/latency ", Accessed 2015).

Definition 3: Access Time - Access time is the summation of seek time and latency time. Access time is calculated as "ts+tl"(as found in "http://dis-dpcs.wikispaces.com/2.1.5+Secondary+Memory", Accessed 2010).

Definition4: Data transfer Rate - Data transferring from one disk to another disk per time unit is called data transfer rate(as found in "http://ecomputernotes.com/fundamental/input-output-and-memory/ explain-secondary-storage-devices").

Definition5:Mean Time Feature - The reliability of disk measured by mean time to feature concept is known as mean time feature ("http://ecomputernotes.com/fundamental/input-output-and-memory/what-is-access-method-explain-different-type-of-access-methods").

1.3.Aim

Our aim is to search disk storage within cloud in less time for indexing, balancing and load balance monitoring, data searching and data accessing.

1.4. Scope

The scope of this chapter is only the knowledge discovery in database that is KDD within cloud, which consists of data selection, data transformation, and pattern searching, finding presentation and finding evaluation.

1.5. Organization

Rest of the chapter is organized as follows:Section 2 describes about Related Works; Section 3 discusses our proposed works; Section 4 shows experimental results; and finally Section 5 depicts the conclusion.

2. RELATED WORKS

2.1. Overview

Cloud based hard disks mainly storedata andsearching refers to the operation of finding location of particular data. There are many cloud searching algorithms which guide us to find specific data(as found in "http://docs.aws.amazon.com/cloudsearch/latest/developerguide/what-is-cloudsearch.html",Accessed2015). Binarysearch(SilberschatzA., Galvin P.B, Gagne G.,2011&Lipschutz S., 2006) and/orworst fit(as found in "http://www.cs.rit.edu/~ark/lectures/gc/03_03_03.html", Accessed 2001) and/or best fit algorithms are typically used for cloud based hard disk searching in industry(CormenT. H, Leiserson C. E, RivestR, SteinC., 2001). Binary search is applicable to find data in sorted array (IBM, 1964). In worst fit algorithm, largest hole means free and available memory is allocated by checkingentire list. In case of binary search, data would be previously sorted.

2.2. Binary Search Used in Cloud Based Hard Disk Searching

In binary search, values are typically considered as inputsin sequential order. Therefore, the complexity of binary search is $O \log(n)$.

Box 1.

```
intbinary_search(int *x,intn,int item)
{
      Declare integertype variables lb,ub,mid;
      Set lb to 0;
      Set ub to n-1;
      Process until lower boundary becomes less than or equal to upper boundary.
      {
            Set mid to (lower boundary +upper boundary /2);
            Check whetherx[mid] is identical with item or not.
            If x[mid] becomes identical with item then return the value of mid.
            If x[mid] becomes not identical with itemthen check whether item is greater than x[mid] or not.
            If item is greater than x[mid]then set lower boundary to(mid+1);
            If item becomes less than x[mid] then set upper boundary is mid plus 1;
      }
      If item is not found then return the value -1;
}
```

2.3. Worst Fit Memory Allocation Used in Cloud Based Hard Disk Searching

Entire list is to be searched, unless it is sorted by size. This strategy produces the largest leftover hole, which could be more useful than the smaller leftover hole from a best fit approach.

Typical procedure involved following steps in case of worst fit memory allocation:

Step1: Start
Step2: Sort holes by size in descending order
Step3: If the process is greater than first hole, then go to next hole and allocate particular hole for that particular process
Step4: Else if the process is less than first hole, then allocate that hole for the process
Step5: Stop

2.4. Best Fit Memory Allocation Used in Cloud Based Hard Disk Searching

Typical procedure involved following steps in case of worst fit memory allocation:

Step1: Start
Step2: Sort the holes by size in ascending order
Step3: If the process greater than first hole, then go to the next hole and allocate particular hole for that particular process
Step4: Else if, the process less than first hole,then allocate that hole for the process
Step5: Stop

Threshold should be at least [size (header) + 1] to leave room for header and link.Threshold could be set higher to combat fragmentation. Allocation time is $O(K)$, where K isthe number of blocks in free list. The complexity of best fit algorithm is $O(n^2)$.

Figure 1 is described about an arbitrary situation in memory before allocation and Figure 2 is described about an arbitrary situation in memory after allocation.

Figure 1. An arbitrary situation in memory before allocation.
("http://www.cs.rit.edu/~ark/lectures/gc/03_03_03.html")

Figure 2. An arbitrary situation in memory after allocation.
("http://www.cs.rit.edu/~ark/lectures/gc/03_03_03.html")

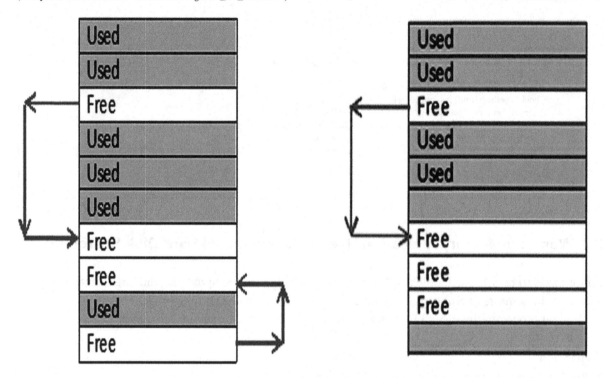

2.5. Other Data Search Methods in Cloud

Other data search methods involve B-Tree and Hashing First fit, B+ Tree.

B-tree: It is similar to m-way search tree and the number of access depends on the height of the tree. B-Tree is a tree structure. Data searching and sorting procedure is done by this method. This method allows sequential access, insertion and deletion in logarithmic time. It is mainly used in database system and file system-tree. It is a generation of binary search tree .It contains one node can have more than two children. In B-tree non-leaf nodes have variable number of child nodeswithin some pre-defined range-Number of child nodes changes when data is inserted or removed from a node. In order to maintain the pre-defined range, internal nodes may be joined or split. B-trees do not need re-balancing as frequently as other self-balancing searches trees. A range of child nodes is permitted, but it wastes some spaces. The lower and upper bounds on the number of child nodes are typically fixed for a particular implementation. Each internal node of a B-tree will contain a number of keys. The keys divide its sub trees.(as found in "http://en.wikipedia.org/wiki/B-tree", Accessed2014).

Hashing: Hashing is another data search technique. Hashing is a method which transform a string (combination of characters) of characters into a key (a fixed length value) which represent the original string. In this method the item is saved in key index table. In this technique one important term is Hash Function. Hash function is a method for computing table index from key. The main issues of hashing techniques are computing the hash function and equality test that is method for checking weather two cases are equal. Another important issue is collision resolution that is the algorithm and data structure to handle two keys that hash to the same index. There are different types of methods in Hashing. Division method, mid-square method, and folding method are available in hashing techniques (as found in "http://searchsqlserver.techtarget.com/definition/hashing", Accessed 2015). There are some popular hash functions are available .This hash functions can be easily and quickly evaluated by the computer.

Division method: Suppose a number a is larger than the number b of keys in k. Number a is chosen as a prime number or a is a number without small divisors, since this frequently minimize the number of collisions. The hash function H is defined by $H(k) = k(\bmod a)$ Or $H(k) = k(\bmod a) + 1$ .Here $k(\bmod a)$ denotes the remainder when k is divided by m. The second formula is used when we want the hash addresses to range from 1 to a rather than from 0 to $a - 1$

Mid-square Method: The key k is squared. The hash function H is defined by $H(k) = m$.

Where m obtained by deleting digits from both ends of k^2 .Same position of k^2 must be used for all of the keys.

Folding method: The key k is partitioned into a number of parts, $k_1, k_2 ......k_r$, where each part possibly the last, has the same number of digits as the requires address. Parts are added together and also ignore the last carry. $H(k) = k_1 + k_2 + ...k_r$

First fit searching: In first fit allocate searching technique allocate the first hole which is big enough. In this technique sort the holes by location. Searching can start at the beginning of the set of holes. Another way to start searching where the previous first fit searching technique is over. In the first-fit algorithm, the allocator keeps a list of free blocks (known as the free list) and, on receiving a request for memory, scans along the list for the first block that is large enough to satisfy the request. If the chosen block is larger than that requested block, then it is usually split, and the remainder added to the list as another free block. The first fit algorithm performs well, because it ensures that allocations are quickly done. Searching procedure is stopped when find the free hole that is big enough. First fit memory allocation suffer from external fragmentation. This technique is efficient to merge the adjacent free blocks but it is not fast for allocation or recycling. This procedure that is merging the free holes, reduce fragmentation. It also improve locality of reference. First fit allocation technique works fast. It is easy technique comparatively other searching technique. Memory is wastage more in this technique. But time is saved by this searching technique (as found in http://www.memorymanagement.org/mmref/alloc.html, Accessed 2015).

*B+ tree:*A B+ tree is ann-ary tree with a variable but often large number of children per node. A B+ tree contain root, internal nodes and leaves. The root may be either a leaf or a node with two or more children. A B+ tree contains keys and to which an additionallevel is added at the bottom with linked leaves.

3. PROPOSED WORK

The proposed system has been shown in Figure 3 for overall searching mechanism in cloud. Proposed system framework is divided into several parts as shown in the Figure 3. Each part represents distinct segments of our system to handle specific characteristics. Database search engines are included in our system to facilitate searching of stored data in disk in a typical cloud scenario. Table management has been executed using indexing mechanisms. Index manager is responsible for data indexing based on specified algorithms. They are also called indexing engines. These indexing engines are relatively limited in their ability to customize indexing formats that is compounding, normalization, transformation etc. Cloud based data search software has created a table in database for managing data and creating data indexes which is used for searching data. Table data are managed using table manager in the system.

Major parts of proposed system are mentioned as follows:

- **DBMS:** Database management system is typically used for various functions in case of table management, record management, and index management.
- **Table Management:** It helps to manage the table containing data. Table is constructed in the database and indexes are typically prepared for searching data.
- **Record Management:** Table is made in data database which contains data. Each line in the table is considered as record.
- **Index Management:** Search engine indexing is used for collection, parsing, and storage of data for facilitating fast and accurate information retrievalhttp://en.wikipedia.org/wiki/Information_retrieval. Searching procedure is done rapidly and is managed by index manager. It is also used to find out data from storage. Figure 4 is self-explanatory diagram which exhibits overall index management in our proposed framework. Keywords are searched in particular table, and then searched results of each keyword have been ranked allowing unique & relevant information. Figure 4 is described about proposed cloud based searching technique.
- **Table Data:** Data is stored in table format. Each row is considered as records, and column is considered as groups (refer Figure 5).
- **Index Data:** When the searching procedure is done, data search software compiles from table data, and indexes of data.
- **Load Balance Monitoring:** If data is overloaded in database, then load balance monitoring unit maintains the balance between nodes of our system. Figure 5 is described about Typical table structure that is used in our approach.

Pre-requisite of Algorithm 1: Elements are arranged in typical sorted manner.

Algorithm 1: Search_k
Input: 'n' number of elements
Output: Find specific item
Step 1: Start
Step 2: n number of elements is stored within an array 'x'
Step 3: Divide total number of elements into 'k' parts having 'n/k' elements.

Figure 3. Proposed framework in cloud.

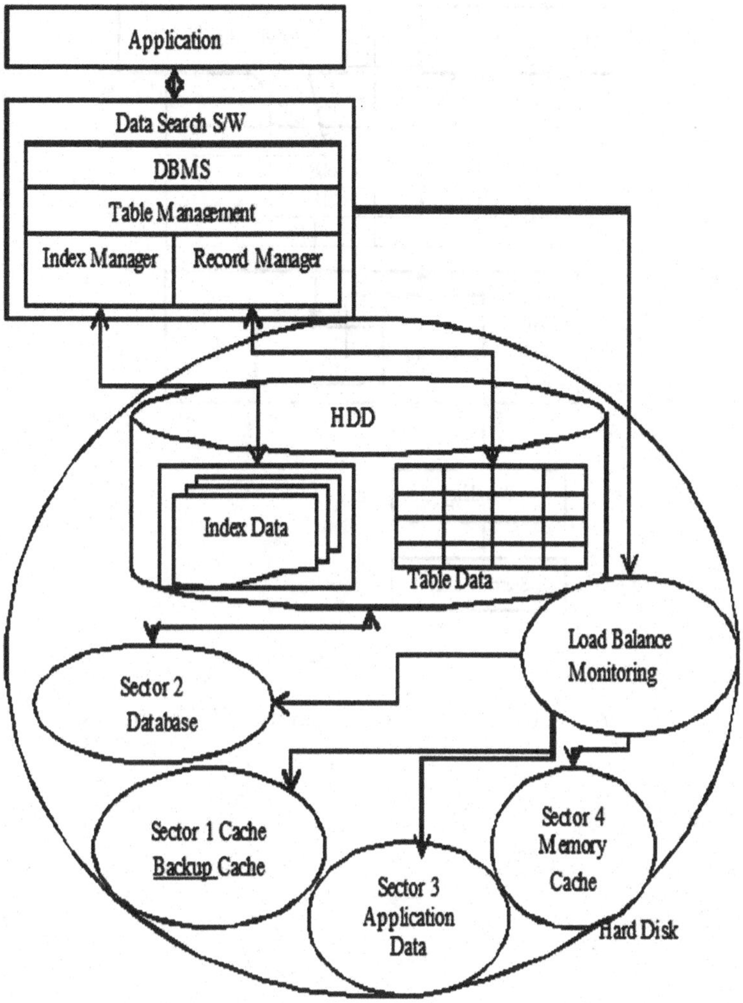

Step 4: Check (Range of Items)
Step 5: Fix a part in which the particular item is within range.
Step 6: If (Item found == TRUE), then Print (Position of particular item)
Step 7: Else, Print (Item not found)
Step 8: Stop

In this algorithm, n numbers of sorted elements are taken for finding specific items. Total elements are divided into k parts in which each part contains n/k elements. Check parts for the particular item. If item is found, then particular position of the item is located. Otherwise, it is concluded that the item is not found after searching.

Theorem 1: Execution Time $(T(n))$ is inversely proportional to the number of channels (k)

Figure 4. Proposed cloud based searching.

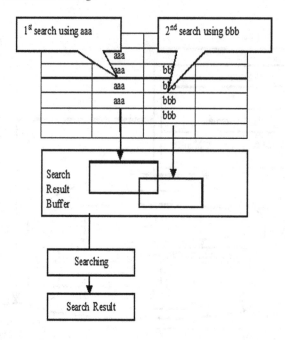

Proof: By the concept of binary search (number of channels $=2$), expression of execution time is as follows:

$$T(n) = 3n/4 + c$$

$$T(n) = (n(2^2 - 1))/2^2 + c$$

Figure 5. Typical table structure used in our approach.

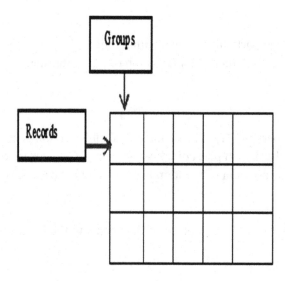

If k number of channels is considered,

$$T(n) = (n(2^k - 1) / 2^k) + c \; \forall k = 1, 2, 3....n$$

where, $T(n) =$ Execution time; $n =$ Data set; $c =$ Constant; $k =$ Number of channels;Now, $T(n) = (n(2^k - 1) / 2^k) + c$

$$\therefore T(n) = n - n / 2^k + c$$

$$\therefore T(n) = n(1 - 1 / 2^k) + c$$

Hence, it is proved that execution time is inversely proportional to number of channels.(End of Proof)

Theorem 2: Time complexity of proposed approach is better than existing approach.
Proof: In this chapter, time complexity of binary search (as an existing approach) for two channels is $(o(\log n))$

In proposed approach, we have following conditions based on number of channels:

Case 1: Number of channels $= 2$

$$T(n) = T(n / 2) + c$$

$$T(n) = n / 2 + T(n / 4) + c$$

$$T(n) = n / 2 + (n / 4) + T(n / 8) + c$$

$$T(n) = n / 2 + (n / 4) + (n / 8) + T(n / 16) + c$$

$$n(1 / 2 + 1 / 4 + 1 / 8 + 1 / 16 + ...n^{th} term$$

$$= 3n / 4 + c$$

$$\approx o(\log(n))$$

Case 2: Number of channels $= 4$

$$T(n) = T(n / 4) + c$$

$$T(n) = n/4 + T(n/8) + c$$

$$T(n) = n/4 + n/8 + T(n/16) + c$$

$$T(n) = n/4 + n/8 + (n/16) + T(n/32) + c$$

$$= n(1/2 + 1/4 + 1/8 + 1/16 + \ldots\ldots\alpha) + c$$

$$= n(1/2 + 1/4 + 1/8 + 1/16 + \ldots\ldots\alpha) + c$$

$$= 5n/16 + c$$

$$= \log(5/8) + \log(n/2) + c$$

$$\approx o(\log n/2)$$

Case 3: Number of channels = 8

$$T(n) = T(n/8) + c$$

$$T(n) = n/8 + T(n/16) + c$$

$$T(n) = n/8 + n/16 + T(n/32) + c$$

$$T(n) = n/8 + n/16 + n/32 + T(n/64) + c$$

$$T(n) = n(1/8 + 1/16 + 1/32 + \ldots\ldots\alpha) + c$$

$$= 9n/64 + c$$

$$= \log(9/16) + \log(n/4) + c$$

$$\approx o(\log(n/4))$$

Case 4: Number of channels = 16

$$T(n) = T(n/16) + c$$

$$T(n) = n/16 + T(n/32) + c$$

$$T(n) = n/16 + n/32 + T(n/64) + c$$

$$T(n) = n/16 + n/32 + n/64 + T(n/128) + c$$

$$T(n) = n(1/16 + 1/32 + 1/64 + \ldots \ldots \alpha)$$

$$= 17n/256$$

$$= \log(17/32) + \log(n/8) + c$$

$$\approx o(\log(n/8))$$

Case 5: Number of channels $= 32$

$$T(n) = T(n/32) + c$$

$$T(n) = n/32 + T(n/64) + c$$

$$T(n) = n/32 + n/64 + T(n/128) + c$$

$$T(n) = n(1/16 + 1/32 + 1/64 \ldots .\alpha) + c$$

$$= 33n/1024 + c$$

$$= \log(33/64) + \log(n/16) + c$$

$$\approx o(\log(n/16))$$

Hence, it is proved that, number of channels inversely proportional to time complexity. Therefore, our proposed approach is better than existing approach.(End of Proof)

4. EXPERIMENTAL RESULTS

Experimental setup is as follows:
Number of computers used in cloud – 100;
Nature of configurations – Homogeneous;
Processor - 2.70 GHz;
RAM - 2.00GB;
System Type - 32 bit Operating System;
Software used -VC++ Compiler;

4.1. Experimental Analysis

In Figure 6, 'X' axis is denoted by number of elements (n) and 'Y' axis is denoted by execution time $T(n)$.In this figure, curve represents $Y = \log(n)$

In Figure 7, 'X' axis is denoted by number of elements(n) and 'Y' axis is denoted by execution time $T(n)$. In this figure, curve represents $Y = \log(n / 2)$. Since, $\log(n / 2)$ is less than $\log(n)$, therefore in this particular graph, result of the curve shows better results than the graph represented in Figure 6. This case is valid for more than 2 elements $(n >= 2)$.

In Figure 8, 'X' axis is denoted by number of elements(n) and 'Y' axis is denoted by execution time $T(n)$. In this figure, curve represents $Y = \log(n / 4)$. As the log(n/4) is less than $\log(n / 2) < \log(n)$, so in that particular graph, the result of the curve shows better time complexity compared to the graph in Figure 6 and Figure 7. This case is valid for more than 4 elements$(n >= 4)$.

In Figure 9, 'X' axis is denoted by number of elements (n) and 'Y' axis is denoted by execution time $T(n)$.Inthisfigure,curverepresents $Y = \log(n / 8)$.Since $\log(n / 8) < \log(n / 4) < \log(n / 2) < \log(n)$, so in this particular case, the result of the curve shows better result than the graph represented in Figure 9. This case is valid for more than 8 elements $(n >= 8)$.

Figure 6. Results obtained using one channel.

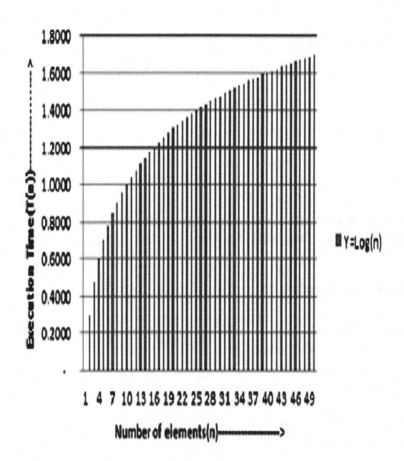

Figure 7. Results obtained using two channels.

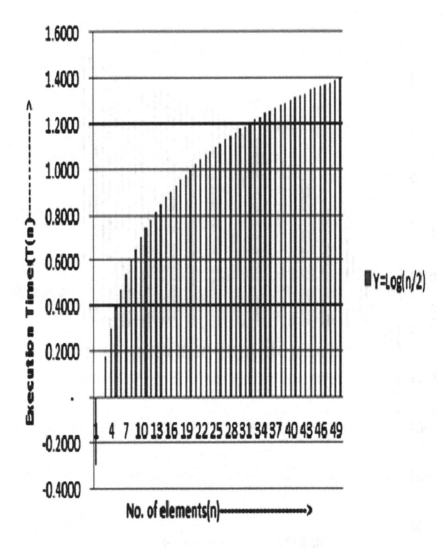

Figure 8. Results obtained using four channels.

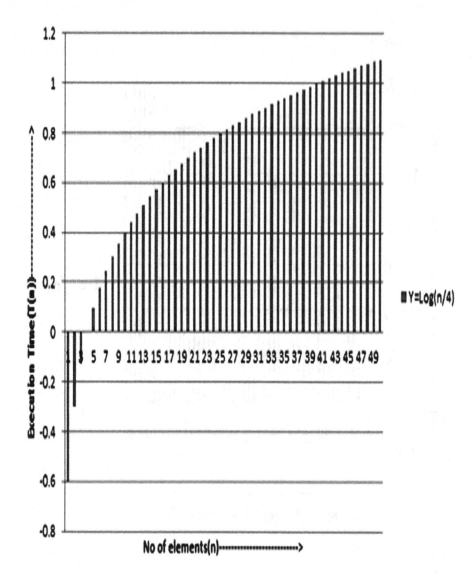

Figure 9. Results obtained using eight channels.

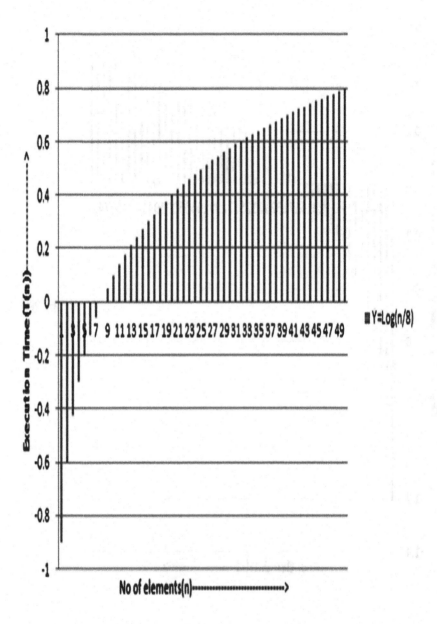

Figure 10. Results obtained using sixteen channels.

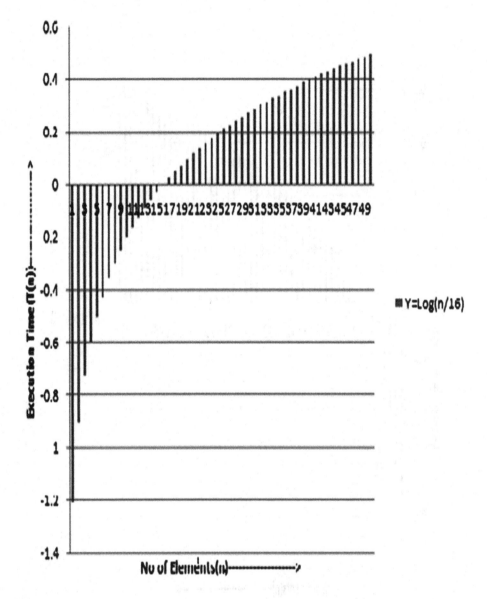

Figure 11. Comparative results achieved using proposed approach using different number of parallel channels.

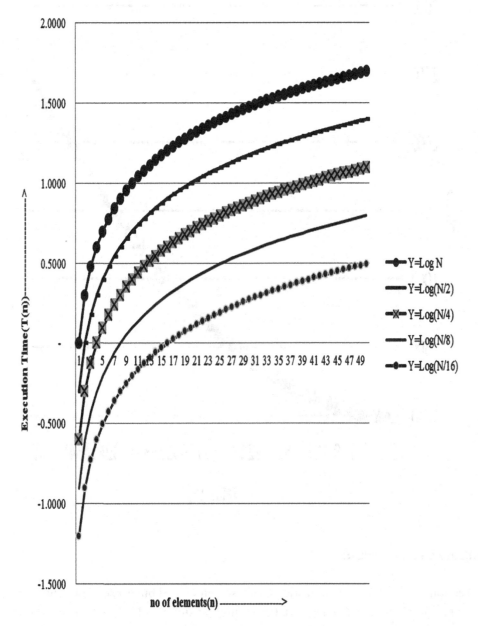

In Figure 10, 'X' axis is denoted by number of elements (n) and 'Y' axis is denoted by execution time $T(n)$. In this figure, the curve represents $Y = \log(n / 2)$. As $\log(n / 16) < \log(n / 8) < \log(n / 4) < \log(n / 2) < \log(n)$, so in this particular graph, the result of the curve shows better time consumption than the graph represented in Figure 9. This case is valid for more than 16 elements $(n >= 16)$.

In Figure 11, $\log(n / 16)$ curve exhibits better result than other curves. In this figure, we have compared all the curves having number of elements greater than 16.

Figure 12. Cloud based performance graph for best fit search.

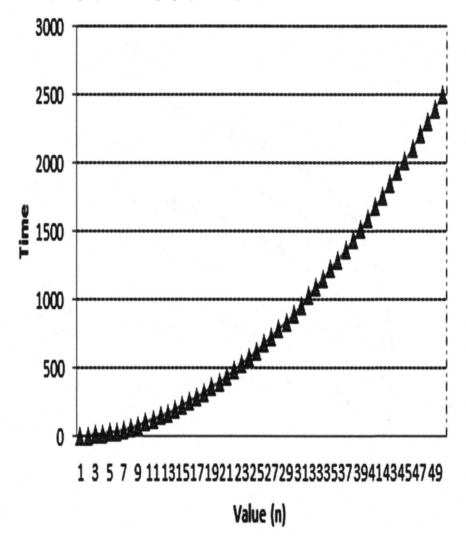

4.2. Comparative Analysis

In this sub-section, best fit memory allocation based searching and binary searching has been compared in a cloud scenario. It has been observed that best fit algorithm would exhibit better results compared to binary search algorithm, only if sorted array is not used.In Figure 12, 'X' axis is denoted by value (n) and 'Y' axis is denoted by time.The complexity of best fit algorithm is $O(n)$ .In Figure 13, 'X' axis is denoted by value (n) and 'Y' axis is denoted by time. The complexity of binary search is $O(\log n)$.

The complexity of bubble sort algorithm is $O(n^2)$ for sorting data, and it is used for data arrangement in sorted manner before executing binary search.

Therefore, total complexity is [$O(n^2)$ $+O(\log n)$].

We know, $O(n^2)$ $+O(\log n) > O(n^2)$.

Thus, best fit shows better results than binary search based approach in proposed cloud scenario.

Figure 13. Cloud based performance graph for binary search.

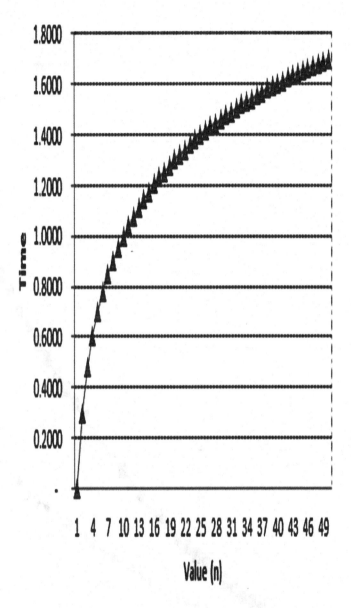

In Figure 14, 'X' axis is denoted by value (n) and 'Y' axis is denoted by time. It is a comparison graph between best fit and binary based approach. As per our experimental observations, best fit based approach shows less time complexity than binary search based method as we have considered initial sorting within binary search based approach in cloud.

In comparative analysis sub-section, two exiting searching techniques best fit and binary searchhave been depicted. It is shown that time complexity of best fit is less than the time complexity of binary search approach. In proposed approach, different numbers of parallel channels have been implemented within our cloud. Time complexity of proposed approach is less than existing approaches. So, proposed approach shows better results than existing approaches.

Figure 14. Comparison graph between best fit approach and binary search based approach in proposed cloud.

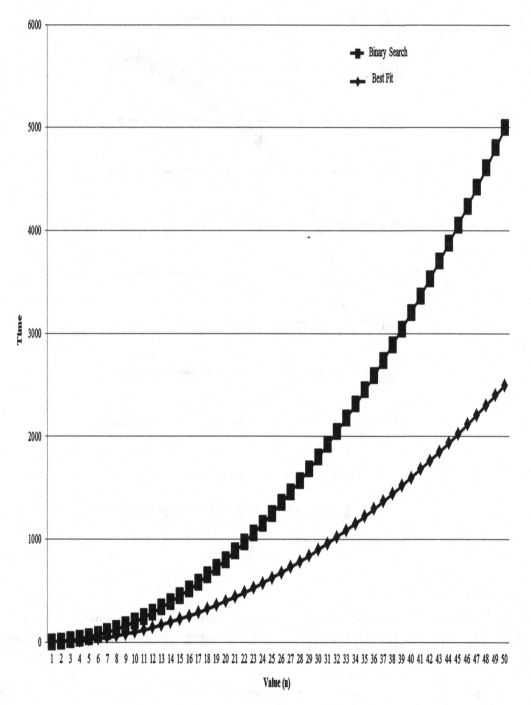

5. CONCLUSION

The proposed cloud based disk searching technique using parallel channels for facilitating data searching is achieved in less timeconsumption. This proposed approach has shown better results than existing search techniques.

REFERENCES

AcceassMethod. (n.d.). Retrieved from http://ecomputernotes.com/fundamental/input-output-and-memory/what-is-access-method-explain-different-type-of-access-methods

Algorithm, A. (2001). Retrieved from http://www.cs.rit.edu/~ark/lectures/gc/03_03_03.html

AmazonCloudsearch. (2015). Retrieved from http://docs.aws.amazon.com/cloudsearch/latest/developerguide/what-is-cloudsearch.html

B-tree. (2014). Retrieved from http://en.wikipedia.org/wiki/B-tree

Blocking, S., & Cylinders, H. (2015). Retrieved from http://dis-dpcs.wikispaces.com/6.2.1+Blocking,+Sectors,+Cylinders,+Heads

CloudStorageForCloudComputing. (2009). Retrieved from https://www.ogf.org/Resources/documents/CloudStorageForCloudComputing.pdf

Computing, C. (2009). Retrieved from http://www.johnhagel.com/cloudperspectives.pdf

Cormen, T. H., Leiserson, C. E., Rivest, R., & Stein, C. (2001). *Introduction to Algorithms*. McGraw-Hill.

Data Search Method for HDD. (2003). Retrieved from http://www.fujitsu-ten.com/business/technical-journal/pdf/20-3.pdf

Definition, H. (2015). Retrieved from http://searchsqlserver.techtarget.com/definition/hashing

Hard Disk Drive. (2015). Retrieved from http://en.wikipedia.org/wiki/Hard_disk_drive

Hard Disk Driveinterface. (2015). Retrieved from http://en.wikipedia.org/wiki/Hard_disk_drive_interface

IBM. (1964). *System/360, Model 30 1401 Compatibility Feature, A24-3255-1, "Mode status (System/360, Model 30, mode or 1401 compatibility mode) is set during the read-in of the compatibility initialization deck"*. IBM.

IBM. (1980). Reference Manual for IBM 2835 Storage Control and IBM 2305 Fixed Head Storage Module, Fifth Edition, GA26-1689-4. IBM.

Knuth, D. (1997). The Art of Computer Programming: Sorting and Searching (vol. 3). Pearson Education.

Lipschutz, S. (2006). *Data Structures*. The McGraw-Hill.

Mano, M. M. (2009). *Computer System Architecture*. Pearson Edition.

Memory, S. (2010). Retrieved from http://dis-dpcs.wikispaces.com/2.1.5+Secondary+Memory

Silberschatz, A., Galvin, P. B., & Gagne, G. (2011). *Operating System Concepts*. Willy-India Edition.

Technique, A. (2015). Retrieved from http://www.memorymanagement.org/mmref/alloc.html

Time, L. (2015). Retrieved from http://whatis.techtarget.com/definition/latency

Time, S. (2015). Retrieved from http://www.techopedia.com/definition/3558/seek-time StorageDevices. http://ecomputernotes.com/fundamental/input-output-and-memory/explain-secondary-storage-devices

Chapter 19
Data Intensive Cloud Computing:
Issues and Challenges

Jayalakshmi D. S.
M. S. Ramaiah Institute of Technology, Inida

R. Srinivasan
S. R. M. University, India

K. G. Srinivasa
M. S. Ramaiah Institute of Technology, India

ABSTRACT

Processing Big Data is a huge challenge for today's technology. There is a need to find, apply and analyze new ways of computing to make use of the Big Data so as to derive business and scientific value from it. Cloud computing with its promise of seemingly infinite computing resources is seen as the solution to this problem. Data Intensive computing on cloud builds upon the already mature parallel and distributed computing technologies such HPC, grid and cluster computing. However, handling Big Data in the cloud presents its own challenges. In this chapter, we analyze issues specific to data intensive cloud computing and provides a study on available solutions in programming models, data distribution and replication, resource provisioning and scheduling with reference to data intensive applications in cloud. Future directions for further research enabling data intensive cloud applications in cloud environment are identified.

INTRODUCTION

Massive amounts of data are being generated in scientific, business, social network, healthcare, and government domains. The "Big Data" so generated is typically characterized by the three Vs: Volume, Variety, and Velocity. Big data comes in large volumes, from a large number of domains, and in different formats. Data can be in structured, semi-structured or unstructured format, though most of the Big Data

DOI: 10.4018/978-1-4666-8676-2.ch019

Copyright © 2015, IGI Global. Copying or distributing in print or electronic forms without written permission of IGI Global is prohibited.

is unstructured; the data sets might also grow in size rapidly. There are many opportunities to utilize and analyze the Big Data to derive value for business, scientific and user-experience applications. These applications need to process data in the range of many terabytes or petabytes and are called data intensive applications. Consequently, computing systems which are capable of storing, and manipulating massive amounts of data are required; also required are related software systems and algorithms to analyze the big data so as to derive useful information and knowledge in a timely manner.

In this chapter we present the characteristics of data intensive applications in general and discuss the requirements of data intensive computing systems. Further, we identify the challenges and research issues in implementing data intensive computing systems in cloud computing environment. Later in this chapter, we also present a study on programming models, data distribution and replication, resource provisioning and scheduling with reference to data intensive applications in cloud.

Data Intensive Computing Systems

Data Intensive Computing is defined as "a class of parallel computing applications which use a data parallel approach to processing large volumes of data" ("Data Intensive Computing", 2012). They devote most of their processing time to I/O and manipulation of data rather than computation (Middleton, 2010). According to the National Science Foundation, data intensive computing requires a "fundamentally different set of principles" to other computing approaches. There are several important common characteristics of data intensive computing systems that distinguish them from other forms of computing(Middleton, 2010).

- Data and applications or algorithms are co-located so that data movement is minimized to achieve high performance in data intensive computing
- Programming models that express the high level operations on data such as data flows are used, and the runtime system transparently controls the scheduling, execution, load balancing, communications and movement of computation and data across the distributed computing cluster.
- They provide reliability, availability and fault tolerance.
- They are linearly scalable to handle large volumes of data.

Challenges and Research Issues for Data Intensive Computing Systems

Parallel processing using data-parallel approach is widely accepted as the way to architect data intensive applications. Many different system architectures such as parallel and distributed relational database management systems have been implemented for data intensive applications and big data analytics. However these assume that data is in structured form whereas most of the big data is in unstructured or semi-structured form.

Typical data intensive applications include scientific applications handling large amounts of geo-distributed data for which grid architectures have been used extensively. Hence, loosely coupled distributed systems with message passing are preferred over typical, tightly-coupled HPC systems. The challenge is to architect and implement applications that can scale to handle voluminous and geo-distributed data in different forms in a reliable manner, and in real time in some applications.

Cloud computing systems with their promise of seemingly infinite, elastic resources lend themselves to these requirements and hence data-intensive cloud applications are the focus of current research.

Building data-intensive applications in cloud computing environments is different due to the levels of scale, reliability, and performance.

- The first challenge is the type of data management solution. Data-intensive applications may be built upon conventional frameworks, such as shared-nothing database management systems (DBMSs), or new frameworks, such as MapReduce(Dean & Ghemawat, 2004), and so have very different resource requirements.
- New programming models needed are required to express data intensive computations in cloud to enable fast and timely execution.
- Since large-scale data-intensive applications use data-parallel approach on possibly geo-distributed data, scheduling and resource allocation should be done so as to avoid data transfer bottlenecks.
- Another challenge is to support effective scaling of resources.

The main research issues can be classified as platforms and programming model centric issues, data centric issues and communication centric issues (Shamsi, Khojaye, & Qasmi, 2013). Much research work is being carried out in solving these issues such as implementing efficient algorithms and techniques for storing, managing, retrieving and analyzing data, dissipation of information, placement of replicas, data locality, and data retrieval. The remainder of this chapter provides a study of the recent research in addressing these issues.

PROGRAMMING ABSTRACTIONS FOR DATA INTENSIVE APPLICATIONS

There are a number of programming paradigms and platforms available, each of them addressing different application characteristics. MapReduce is extensively used to implement large scale data processing in distributed systems. However it imposes restrictions on the way the processing is expressed by forcing them to be written as a map-reduce pair. There are also limitations to MapReduce in that the data set has to be staged in the local storage before processing, intermediate data has to be materialized in local files, and MapReduce is best suited for batch processing of data (Sakr, Liu, Batista, & Alomari, 2011).

MapReduce faces challenges in handling Big Data with respect to data storage (relational databases and NoSQL stores), Big Data analytics (machine learning and interactive analytics), online processing, and security and privacy (Grolinger et al., 2014). There have been many improvisations of the Apache Hadoop, the popular implementation of the basic MapReduce mode, hybrid implementations using SQL-like constructs on Hadoop and adapting Hadoop to process structured, graph and streaming data as well as perform iterative, interactive, and in-memory computations (Refer Table 1).

A large amount of computing power and resources are available to the end users by means of cloud computing, but they may not have the expertise to harness these effectively. They may not be able to express their computing workload in a manner which is intuitive in their subject domains, nor able to optimize the resource usage. The end users need to be provided with high-level programming abstractions that allow them to easily express their data intensive workloads as well as efficient execution of the workloads. Hence the challenges are to find programming abstractions that allow different types of data intensive computations on a common platform and allow application developers to express the application needs without concerns about the system management aspects. We now discuss some of the programming abstractions available to handle this issue (refer Table 2).

Table 1. Programming platforms for different data-intensive application types

Application Types	Available Solutions
Batch oriented models	
MapReduce based models	*Google MapReduce, Hadoop*
Dataflow based models	*Dryad, Sector/Sphere, HPCCloud, BSPCloud*
Streaming	*STORM*
Interactive	*Google Dremel/ BigQuery, Apache Drill*
Iterative	*HaLoop*
Graph-based	*Pregel*
Structured	*Hive, Tenzing*
Relational	*Map –Reduce- Merge*
In-memory	*Piccolo*

All-Pairs: An Abstraction for Data-Intensive Cloud Computing

All-Pairs(Moretti, Bulosan, Thain, & Flynn, 2008) is a programming abstraction that fits the needs of several data-intensive scientific applications such as biometrics and data mining. The objective is to provide abstractions that allow non-expert users to express large, data-intensive workloads so that resources are used effectively.

All-Pairs(set A, set B, function F) returns a matrix M and compares all elements of set A to all elements of set B via function F, yielding matrix M, such that M[i,j] = F(A[i],B[j]). In All-pairs the workflow is modeled so that execution can be predicted based on grid and workload parameters such as the number of hosts, and a spanning tree is used to distribute data to the compute nodes. Based on the

Table 2. Programming models for data-intensive cloud applications

Solution	Provides	Architecture supported	Programming model	Targeted application types
All-Pairs (Moretti, Bulosan, Thain, & Flynn, 2008)	Programming abstraction	Grid, Cloud	Multiple sequential programs with each being a Cartesian product of two objects with a custom comparison function	Batch processing
Meandre (Ács et al., 2011)	Application infrastructure	Cluster, Grids, Clouds	Component based directed multigraphs	Batch processing, interactive applications
Makeflow (Albrecht, M., Donnelly, P., Bui, P., & Thain, D., 2012).	Portable abstraction for running data –intensive scientific workflows	Grid, cluster, Cloud	Execution engine for complex workflows represented as graphs	Batch
Blue (Varshney, 2013)	Unified Programming model	Cluster, Cloud	Dependency graphs of component tasks	batch, interactive, iterative, relational, graph
epiC (Jiang, Chen, Ooi, Tan, & Wu, 2014)	Parallel computation for multi-structured data sets in a single system	Cluster	Concurrent programming	Batch, relational, graph

model, batch jobs are structured to provide good results and sent to the compute nodes. Once the batch jobs have completed, the results are collected into a canonical form for the end-user, and the scratch data left on the compute nodes is deleted. The workload's data requirement is served by implementing demand paging similar to a traditional cluster, and using active storage wherein data is pre-staged to local file systems on each compute node.

Problems in science and engineering can be expressed as variations of the All-Pairs problem. However, All-pairs is not a universal abstraction and it may be possible to express only few, specific applications using All-pairs. It also suffers from serious drawbacks in handling large data sets which do not fit into a single compute node. The model also makes assumptions on the homogeneity and availability of compute nodes which might not always hold true in a distributed environment. Also, the All-pairs state engine needs to use local state to ensure that it can complete the job within the local state limits, as well as clean the scratch data after the completion of the job.

Meandre Data-Intensive Application Infrastructure

Data driven execution revolves around the idea of applying transformation operations to a flow or stream of data when it is available. Meandre (Ács et al., 2011) provides semantic-driven data flow execution infrastructure to construct, assemble, and execute components and flows. Whereas MapReduce requires processes to be expressed as directed acyclic graphs, flows in Meandre are aggregations of basic computations tasks in a directed graph, cyclic or acyclic.

Meandre provides an application infrastructure including tools for creating components and flows, a high-level language to describe flows, and a multi-core and distributed execution environment based on a service-oriented architecture. The programming paradigm creates complex tasks by linking together a bunch of specialized components. Meandre's publishing mechanism allows components developed by third parties to be assembled in a new flow.

There are two ways to develop flows: – Meandre's Workbench visual programming tool and Meandre's ZigZag scripting language. Modeled on Python, ZigZag is a simple declarative language for describing data- intensive flows using directed graphs. Command-line tools allow ZigZag files to compile and execute. A compiler is provided to transform a ZigZag program (.zz) into Meandre archive unit (.mau). Mau(s) can then be executed by a Meandre engine. The Meandre server can mutate transparently from standalone to clustered mode without any extra effort providing scalability. It also uses virtualization techniques for rapid deployment in the cloud.

Makeflow: A Portable Abstraction for Data Intensive Computing on Clusters, Clouds, and Grids

Large scale distributed systems typically use a custom language for describing the application and the applications are not portable across systems. Makeflow, based on the Unix Make, provides a language for expressing highly parallel data intensive applications (Albrecht, M., Donnelly, P., Bui,P., & Thain, D., 2012). The Makeflow applications are portable and run without any modification on grids, HPC clusters and storage clouds. Makeflow scales in size of data, in time, across systems and across user-expertise.

Blue: A Unified Programming Model for Diverse Data-Intensive Cloud Computing Paradigms

Cluster manager frameworks such as Apache YARN (V. K. Vavilapalli, 2013) and Mesos (B. Hindman, 2011) introduce a resource management layer on which different application paradigms can be implemented. A unified programming framework called Blue (Varshney, 2013) introduces an intermediate layer between the resource management layer and the application layer and provides an abstraction for distributing computing to the cluster applications. It supports different computational paradigms such as batch processing, streaming, iterative, graph-based, structured, in-memory, etc.

The Blue Programming framework works under the assumptions of decomposability, determinism and parallelism. A cluster program is modeled as a collection of interconnected "tasks". For example, the Map Reduce program comprises of four tasks: reader, mapper, reducer, and writer. The tasks communicate by sending data over unidirectional links. The program, therefore, can be viewed as a directed graph. The links are represented as Output Queue and Input Queue at the source and destination processes, respectively.

The Blue model can be implemented by analyzing the graph and resources scheduled exploiting data and network locality. At runtime, the tasks are launched as processes and read data from input queues and write data to output queues as discrete records. Multiple processes on different machines are launched for a given task to provide parallelism. However, though program developers can control some high-level properties, they do not have control as to how data from output queues are assigned to the input queues.

Blue supports in-memory caching of data either explicitly by programmer or opportunistically by system thereby improving the latency and throughput of interactive and iterative programs. Finally, the Blue model provides simple and consistent semantics for fault-tolerance of acyclic as well as cyclic dependency graphs.

The Blue Framework is targeted for data-intensive computational problems and is not best suited for task parallelism. It is also not suited for query processing with bounded response delays, and message queue based architectures. The processes cannot reopen or rewind their input queues.For algorithms with cyclic dependencies, the processes cannot persist across iterations.

epiC: An Extensible and Scalable System for Processing Big Data

The MapReduce programming model manages unstructured data such as plain text data effectively, but it is found to be inconvenient and inefficient for processing structured and graph data, and iterative computation. Systems like Dryad [15] and Pregel [20] are built to process those kinds of analytical tasks.

The problem of data variety can be handled by a hybrid system. In a hybrid system with its dataset consisting of sub-datasets each of a different format, the multiple types in the data can be stored in a variety of systems based on types; for example, structured data can be stored in a database; unstructured data can be stored in Hadoop. These data can be processed by splitting the entire job into sub-jobs and executed on appropriate systems based on the data types. The final result can be obtained by aggregating all the results of the sub-jobs loaded into a single system, either Hadoop or database, with appropriate data conversions.

The complexity in a such a hybrid approach is in maintaining several clusters such as Hadoop cluster, Pregel cluster, database cluster,etc., and the overhead of frequent data formation and data loading for merging output of sub-jobs during data processing. However, the different systems (Hadoop, Dryad,

Database, Pregel) designed for different types of data all share the same shared-nothing architecture and decompose the whole computation into independent computations for parallelization. Therefore, epiC (Jiang, Chen, Ooi, Tan, & Wu, 2014) proposes an architecture that decomposes the computation and communication pattern and enables users to process multi-structured datasets in a single system. It provides a common runtime system for running independent computations and developing plug-ins for implementing specific communication patterns

epiC introduces a general "Actor-like concurrent programming model" for specifying parallel computations, independent of the data processing models. Users process multi-structured datasets by using appropriate data processing models for each dataset, mapping those data processing models into epiC's model and writing appropriate epiC extensions. Like Hadoop, programs written in this way can be automatically parallelized and the runtime system takes care of fault tolerance and inter-machine communications. Table 2 presents the different programming abstractions.

DATA DISTRIBUTION AND REPLICATION

The main issue with respect to data intensive applications is that the granularity of data partitions and placement of replicas is decided by the underlying distributed file system. Existing data parallel frameworks, e.g., Hadoop, or Hadoop-based clouds, distribute the data using a random placement method for simplicity and load balance.

Many data intensive applications exhibit interest locality which only sweep part of a big data set. That data are often accessed together results from their grouping semantics. Without taking data grouping into consideration, the random placement does not perform well and is way below the efficiency of optimal data distribution. When the semantic boundaries or interest locality are not considered, problems may arise in applications that read binary files like image, video, etc. The challenges lay in identifying optimal data groupings and re-organize data layouts to achieve the maximum parallelism per group subjective to load balance. DRAW (J. Wang, Xiao, Yin, & Shang, 2013) dynamically scrutinizes data access from system log files. It extracts optimal data groupings and re-organizes data layouts to achieve the maximum parallelism per group subjective to load balance.

The authors in (Guo, W., Luo, X., & Cui, L., 2014) use genetic algorithms to evolve a data placement strategy based on cost of distributed transactions. If a transaction needs to access two different slices of data stored on different data nodes, collaboration costs between the two data nodes are involved. This information, obtained through data log files and applications, is represented as a matrix. Genetic algorithm is used to find an optimal data slice placement strategy so as to minimize total collaboration costs while not exceeding the capacity limits of the data nodes.

With a large number of nodes in the cloud computing system, it is difficult to ask all nodes with the same performance and capacity in their CPUs, memory, and disks. If the nodes in a data center are not all homogeneous, it is possible that the data of a high-QoS application may be replicated in a low performance node with slow communication and disk access latencies. Later, if data in the node running the high-QoS application is corrupted, the data of the application will be retrieved from the low-performance node. Since the low-performance node has slow communication and disk access latencies, the QoS requirement of the high-QoS application may be violated.

The QoS-aware data replication (QADR) problem for data-intensive applications in cloud computing systems is addressed in (Lin, Chen, & Chang, 2013). The main goal of the QADR problem is to minimize the data replication cost and the number of QoS violated data replicas. To solve the QADR problem, the authors in (Lin, Chen, & Chang, 2013) propose a greedy algorithm, called the high-QoS first-replication (HQFR) algorithm. In this algorithm, if an application has a higher QoS requirement, it takes precedence over other applications to perform data replication. Since the HQFR algorithm could not achieve the above minimum objective, the optimal solution of the QADR problem was formulated as an integer linear programming (ILP) formulation. However, the ILP formulation involves complicated computation. Hence, to find the optimal solution of the QADR problem in an efficient manner, the QADR problem was transformed to the minimum-cost maximum-flow (MCMF) problem. Compared to the HQFR algorithm, the optimal algorithm takes more computational time. However, the two proposed replication algorithms run in polynomial time. Their time complexities are dependent on the number of nodes in the cloud computing system. To accommodate to a large scale cloud computing system, the scalable replication issue is considered by the use of node combination techniques to suppress the computational time of the QADR problem without linear growth as increasing the number of nodes.

Cloud computing is based on using commodity servers and hence failures of nodes in data centers is more a norm than an exception. When a failure occurs, the intermediate data of the workflow executed until the point of failure stored in the failed node is lost. To provide fault tolerance, the workflow is re-executed so that the lost intermediate data is recovered. CARDIO uses a trade-off between the cost of replicating intermediate data and the cost of re-executing a given a dataflow with a set of stages (Castillo, C., Tantawi, A.N., Arroyo, D., & Steinder, M., 2012). In CARDIO the minimum reliability cost problem is formulated as an integer programming optimization problem with nonlinear convex objective functions. CARDIO takes into account the probability of loosing data, the cost of replication, the storage capacity available for replication and potentially the current resource utilization in the system. CARDIO is implemented as a decision layer on top of Hadoop that makes intelligent replication decisions as the dataflow advances towards completion; CARDIO reconsiders its replication strategy at the completion of every stage in a workflow.

Geo-replication of data across multiple datacenters offers numerous advantages – improved accessibility and reduction in access latency to the user, fault tolerance and disaster recovery for the service providers. Simple static replica creation strategies that assign the same number of replicas to all data are not suitable in such scenario. To address this issue, Zhen Ye, et al. propose a two-layer geo-cloud based dynamic replica creation strategy called TGstag (Ye, Li, & Zhou, 2014). TGstag addresses the issue with two strategies: policy constraint heuristic inter-datacenter replication and load aware adaptive intra-datacenter replication. TGstag aims to minimize both cross-datacenter bandwidth consumption and average access time with constraints of policy and commodity node capacity.

Geo-replication of key-value stores is relatively easier as the atomicity of accesses is limited to a single key, whereas the traditional data management approach takes a holistic view of data, which makes it complex to scale commercial database management solutions (DBMSs) in a distributed setting. Google's Megastore, a storage system for interactive online services, provides a sharded data model which combines the scalability of a NoSQL datastore with the convenience of a traditional RDBMS (Baker et al., 2011). It provides both strong consistency guarantees and high availability. It provides fully serializable ACID semantics within fine-grained partitions of data. This partitioning allows synchronously replication of each write across a wide area network with reasonable latency using Paxos based replica consistency. It supports seamless failover between datacenters but suffers from poor write-throughput. Google's Spanner proposes to build globally distributed database over multiple datacenters (Corbett et al., 2012). It uses a sharded data-model and has a synchronous replication layer which uses Paxos. It

Table 3. Data placement and replication for data-intensive cloud systems

Task	Issue	Solution	Technique
Data placement	Interest locality and semantics boundary	DRAW (J. Wang, Xiao, Yin, & Shang, 2013)	Dynamically extracts optimal data groupings from system log files
	Cost of distributed transactions	(Guo, W., Luo, X., & Cui, L., 2014)	Minimizing collaboration costs between data nodes using genetic algorithms
Replication	QoS awareness	(Lin, Chen, & Chang, 2013)	High QoS First Replication, ILP and MCMF formulations with node combination techniques
	Minimizing reliability cost	CARDIO (Castillo, C., Tantawi, A.N., Arroyo, D., & Steinder, M., 2012)	Cost-benefit analysis of replication and regeneration costs
	Geo-replication of data across multiple data centres	TGStag (Ye, Li, & Zhou, 2014)	minimize both cross-datacenter bandwidth consumption and average access time with constraints of policy and commodity node capacity
	scalability of a NoSQL datastore with the convenience of a traditional RDBMS	Google Megastore (Baker et al., 2011)	Sharded data model with strong consistency guarantees, fully serializable ACID semantics, synchronous write replication across a wide area network with reasonable latency using Paxos based replica consistency, seamless failover between datacenters
	globally distributed database over multiple datacenters	Google Spanner (Corbett et al., 2012	sharded data-model, synchronous replication layer which uses Paxos, versioned data, supports SQL transactions as well as key-value read/writes, external consistency, automatic data migration across machines (even across datacenters) for load balancing and fault tolerance

provides versioned data, supports SQL transactions as well as key-value read/writes, external consistency, automatic data migration across machines (even across datacenters) for load balancing and fault tolerance. Table 3 presents some research work addressing data placement and replication related issues in data intensive cloud systems.

RESOURCE PROVISIONING

The main resource in contention in data intensive applications is the storage for large amount of data. Existing scheduling techniques focus on task scheduling based on processing time: storage needs need to be looked into as well. It is necessary to support this by scaling out for resources across the boundaries of the data centre into hybrid cloud, multi cloud or federated cloud scenarios. Both time and cost aware execution of data-intensive applications executed in such cloud settings is the need envisaged in the papers reviewed. The main challenges are therefore use of hybrid, multi- and federated clouds, topology aware resource allocation to minimize costs and QoS awareness.

The authors in (Lee, Tolia, Ranganathan, & Katz, 2011) propose an architecture called TARA for optimized resource allocation for data intensive workloads in Infrastructure-as-a-Service (IaaS)-based cloud systems. The idea is to allocate VMs considering network topology so as to route inter-VM traffic away from bottlenecked network paths. They use a "what if" methodology to guide allocation decisions taken by the IaaS. The architecture uses a prediction engine with a lightweight simulator to estimate the performance of a given resource allocation and a genetic algorithm to find an optimized solution in the large search space. The prediction engine is the entity responsible for optimizing resource allocation. When it receives a resource request, the prediction engine iterates through the possible subsets of available resources (each distinct subset is known as a candidate) and identifies an allocation that optimizes estimated job completion time. However, even with a lightweight prediction engine, exhaustively iterating through all possible candidates is infeasible due to the scale of IaaS systems. A genetic algorithm-based search technique allows TARA to guide the prediction engine through the search space intelligently.

A dynamic federation of data intensive cloud providers is proposed in (Hassan & Huh, 2011) to gain economies of scale and an enlargement of their virtual machine (VM) infrastructure capabilities (i.e., storage and processing demands) to meet the requirements of data intensive applications. They develop effective dynamic resource management mechanism based on game theory for data intensive IaaS cloud providers to model the economics of VM resource supplying in federating environment. Both co-operative and non-cooperative games using price–based resource allocation are analyzed.

Modern servers have multiple cores and a range of disk storage devices presented to the user as a single logical disk. Multiple parallel processes and virtual machines are provisioned on theses servers so as to efficiently utilize the computing power. However disk I/O resources are still scarce and the multiple parallel processes competing for I/O interfere with each other degrading the performance. The authors in (Groot, S., Goda, K., Yokoyama, D., Nakano, M., and Kitsuregawa, M., 2013) propose a model for predicting the impact of I/O interference which can be used for efficient resource allocation and scheduling for data intensive applications.

Jrad et al. (Jrad, Tao, Brandic, & Streit, 2014) propose a multi-dimensional resource allocation scheme to automate the deployment of data-intensive large scale applications in Multi-Cloud environments. A two level approach is used in which the target Clouds are matched with respect to the Service Level Agreement(SLA) requirements and user payment at first. In the next level, the application workloads are distributed to the selected clouds taking data locality into consideration while scheduling. Table 4 lists the various resource allocation strategies specifically targeting data intensive cloud systems.

Table 4. Resource allocation for data-intensive cloud systems

Task	Issue	Solution	Technique
Resource allocation	Support for inter-cloud architectures and topology aware resource allocation to minimize costs	TARA (Lee, Tolia, Ranganathan, & Katz, 2011)	Allocate VMs considering network topology so as to route inter-VM traffic away from bottlenecked network paths, a prediction engine with a lightweight simulator to estimate the performance of a given resource allocation and a genetic algorithm to find an optimized solution in the large search space.
	Support for economies of scale	(Hassan & Huh, 2011)	Dynamic resource management mechanism based on game theory to model the economics of VM resource supplying in federating environment.
	Scalability of data intensive applications due to I/O interference	(Groot, S., Goda, K., Yokoyama, D., Nakano, M., and Kitsuregawa, M., 2013)	model for predicting the impact of I/O interference on MapReduce application performance based on workload and hardware environment, and knowledge of the I/O behavior of the application
	Resource allocation based on SLA and budget in multi-cloud environments	(Jrad, Tao, Brandic, & Streit, 2014)	Two-level approach, select cloud based on SLA and cost first, distribute workload to selected cloud based on data locality.

SCHEDULING

The main issues in scheduling of data intensive application on cloud are

- Scheduling tasks efficiently with an awareness of data availability and locality.
- Supporting dynamic load balancing of computations and dynamic scaling of the compute resources.
- Coupling scheduling and replication to exploit data and process locality
- Decoupling compute and data scheduling for geographically distributed resources

Large-scale data centers leverage virtualization technology to achieve excellent resource utilization, scalability, and high availability. Ideally, the performance of an application running inside a virtual machine (VM) shall be independent of co-located applications and VMs that share the physical machine.

However, adverse interference effects exist and are especially severe for data intensive applications in such virtualized environments. TRACON (Chiang & Huang, 2011) is a novel **T**ask and **R**esource Allocation **CON**trol framework that mitigates the interference effects from concurrent data-intensive applications and greatly improves the overall system performance. TRACON utilizes modeling and control techniques from statistical machine learning and consists of three major components: the interference prediction model that infers application performance from resource consumption observed from different VMs, the interference-aware scheduler that is designed to utilize the model for effective resource management, and the task and resource monitor that collects application characteristics at the runtime for model adaption. The results presented indicate that TRACON can achieve up to 25 percent improvement on application throughput on virtualized servers.

In scientific applications such as high energy physics and bioinformatics, we encounter applications involving numerous, loosely coupled jobs that both access and generate large data sets. These data sets may be available at multiple, geo-distributed locations and an application might seek to use all these data sets. Data Grids make it possible to access geographically distributed resources for such large-scale data-intensive problems(Mansouri, 2014). Yet effective scheduling in such environments is challenging, due to a need to address a variety of metrics and constraints such as resource utilization, response time, global and local allocation policies.

It is a well known result in grid systems that while it is necessary to consider data locality while scheduling, job scheduling and data replication can be effectively decoupled (Ranganathan & Foster, 2002). Data intensive scientific workflows process files in the range of terabytes and generate voluminous intermediate data. Many recent works have focused on scheduling workflows so as to minimize data transfer costs. An evolutionary approach to task scheduling is proposed in (Szabo, Sheng, Kroeger, Zhang, & Yu, 2014) that considers and optimizes the allocation and ordering of tasks in the workflow such that the data transferred between tasks and the execution runtime are minimized together. A similar concept is used in (Xiao, Hu, & Zhang, 2013) wherein a novel heuristic called Minimal Data-Accessing Energy Path for scheduling data-intensive workflows aiming to reduce the energy consumption of intensive data accessing.

Data intensive applications need to process large intermediate data whereas schedulers typically consider processing demands of an application and ignore the storage needs. This can cause performance degradation and potentially increase costs. An integer linear program scheduler that considers disk storage scheduling besides the task scheduling based on processor time is proposed in (Pereira, W.F.,

Table 5. Scheduling data-intensive applications in the cloud

Task	Issue	Solution	Technique
Scheduling	interference effects from concurrent data-intensive applications co-located on VMs on a physical host	TRACON (Chiang & Huang, 2011)	collects application characteristics at the runtime for predicting interference
	scheduling workflows so as to minimize data transfer costs	(Szabo, Sheng, Kroeger, Zhang, & Yu, 2014)	Evolutionary approach
	Workflow using geo-distributed data and distributed web services	(Luckeneder & Barker, 2013)	the workflow orchestrator itself is moved to a location which is close to the data source and the web service nodes
	reduce the energy consumption of intensive data accessing	(Xiao, Hu, & Zhang, 2013)	Minimal Data-Accessing Energy Path
	Incorporate storage needs in scheduling decisions	(Pereira, W.F., Bittencourt, L.F., & da Fonseca, N.L.S.,2013)	An integer linear program scheduler that considers storage and processing needs

Bittencourt, L.F., & da Fonseca, N.L.S.,2013). The proposed scheduler aims to meet a deadline set by the user while minimizing costs.

When the scientific data intensive workflows process data which are geographically distributed and the web services used themselves are distributed, the workflow orchestrator itself is moved to a location which is close to the data source and the web service nodes (Luckeneder & Barker, 2013). Here the data transfer time is minimized in turn reducing execution times. There have been many attempts to bring the computation closer to geo-distributed data sources even in the Hadoop community. Many recent works have implemented MapReduce across data centres (L. Wang et al., 2013; Mattess, Calheiros, & Buyya,2013; Heintz et al., 2014). Table 5 lists some recent work on scheduling in data intensive applications in the cloud.

RESEARCH DIRECTIONS

Data Intensive computing is gaining a lot of attention due to the "Data Deluge". Apart from the works discussed here, a dispersed cloud infrastructure that uses voluntary edge resources for both computation and data storage is proposed in (Ryden, Oh, Chandra, & Weissman, 2014). The lightweight Nebula architecture enables distributed data- intensive computing through a number of optimizations including location-aware data and computation placement, replication, and recovery. There is a renewed interest in hybrid (Bicer & Chiu, 2012) and multi-cloud (Jung & Kettimuthu, 2014) architectures for data intensive cloud applications.

Deploying data intensive application in cloud environment is still fraught with many challenges. The complications arise due to the diverse nature of data intensive applications, the geographically distributed data sources and the legal jurisprudence issues over accessing and storing data. Each of the application types needs different type of application architecture and performance guarantees. Some of the possible research directions in this regard are identified as below.

- The geo-distribution of data sources can be handled by either taking the computation to the data or transferring data to the computation.
  - A single cloud might not have enough resources to hold the entire application data. Hence an inter cloud architecture – multi cloud, hybrid cloud or federated clouds, is an attractive option to process application data *in situ* avoiding costly data transfers.
  - Efficient data transfer techniques can be devised to enable large scale inter-datacentre data transfers across WAN. These techniques could also be useful in transferring data from its source to the cloud data centre also.
- Minimizing the overhead associated with data transfers by performing efficient, dynamic data replication across data centers.
- QoS-aware resource management and resource allocation within and/or across data centres.
- Providing simple and intuitive programming models to help ease application development across multiple data centres and interoperable clouds.

CONCLUSION

Data intensive computing provides enormous benefits in science, governance, social and business applications. The technology for data intensive cloud computing is constantly improving, but a large number of problems also are being encountered. This paper provides a study of the current work in the area of data intensive cloud computing. Some directions for further research enabling data intensive cloud applications in cloud environment are identified. The challenges are many and open a lot of opportunities for research in this area.

REFERENCES

Ács, B., Llorà, X., Capitanu, B., Auvil, L., Tcheng, D., Haberman, M., … Welge, M. (2011). Meandre Data-Intensive Application Infrastructure: Extreme Scalability for Cloud and / or Grid Computing. In New Frontiers in Artificial Intelligence (pp. 233–242). Academic Press.

Albrecht, M., Donnelly, P., Bui, P., & Thain, D. (2012). Makeflow: a portable abstraction for data intensive computing on clusters, clouds, and grids. In *Proceedings of the 1st ACM SIGMOD Workshop on Scalable Workflow Execution Engines and Technologies* (SWEET '12). doi:10.1145/2443416.2443417

Baker, J., Bond, C., Corbett, J., & Furman, J. (2011). Megastore: Providing Scalable, Highly Available Storage for Interactive Services. *CIDR*, 223–234.

Bicer, T., Chiu, D., & Agrawal, G. (2012). Time and Cost Sensitive Data-Intensive Computing on Hybrid Clouds. In *2012 12th IEEE/ACM International Symposium on Cluster, Cloud and Grid Computing (CCGrid'12),* (pp. 636-643). doi:10.1109/CCGrid.2012.95

Chiang, R. C., & Huang, H. H. (2014). TRACON : Interference-Aware Scheduling for Data-Intensive Applications in Virtualized Environments, *2011 International Conference for High Performance Computing, Networking, Storage and Analysis (SC)*, 25(5), 1-12. doi:10.1109/TPDS.2013.82

Corbett, J. C., Dean, J., Epstein, M., Fikes, A., Frost, C., Furman, J. J., … Woodford, D. (2012). Spanner : Google's Globally-Distributed Database. In *Proceedings of OSDI'12: Tenth Symposium on Operating System Design and Implementaton*, (pp. 251–264). doi:10.1145/2491245

Dean, J., & Ghemawat, S. (2004). MapReduce : Simplified Data Processing on Large Clusters. In *6th Symposium on Operating Systems Design and Implementation, OSDI '04*, (pp. 137–149). OSDI.

Grolinger, K., Hayes, M., Higashino, W. A., L'Heureux, A., Allison, D. S., & Capretz, M. A. M. (2014). Challenges for MapReduce in Big Data. In *Proc. of the IEEE 10th 2014 World Congress on Services (SERVICES 2014)*, (pp. 182-189). IEEE. doi:10.1109/SERVICES.2014.41

Groot, S., Goda, K., Yokoyama, D., Nakano, M., & Kitsuregawa, M. (2013). Modeling I/O interference for data intensive distributed applications. In *Proceedings of the 28th Annual ACM Symposium on Applied Computing - SAC '13*. ACM.

Hassan, M. M., & Huh, E. (2011). Resource Management for Data Intensive Clouds Through Dynamic Federation: A Game Theoretic Approach. In B. Furht & A. Escalante (Eds.), *Handbook of Cloud Computing* (pp. 169–188). Boston, MA: Springer US; doi:10.1007/978-1-4614-1415-5_7

Heintz, B., Member, S., Chandra, A., Sitaraman, R. K., Weissman, J., & Member, S. (2014). End-to-end Optimization for Geo-Distributed MapReduce. *IEEE Transactions on Cloud Computing, 7161*(c), 1–14. doi:10.1109/TCC.2014.2355225

Hindman, B., Konwinski, A., Zaharia, M., Ghodsi, A., Joseph, A. D., Katz, R. H., . . . Stoica, I. (2011, March). Mesos: A Platform for Fine-Grained Resource Sharing in the Data Center. *Proceedings of the 8th USENIX conference on Networked systems design and implementation* (NSDI'11). USENIX Association.

Jiang, D., Chen, G., Ooi, C., Tan, K., & Wu, S. (2014). epiC : An Extensible and Scalable System for Processing Big Data. *Proceedings of VLDB Endowment, 7*(7), 541–552. doi:10.14778/2732286.2732291

Jrad, F., Tao, J., Brandic, I., & Streit, A. (2014). Multi-dimensional Resource Allocation for Data-intensive Large-scale Cloud Applications. *Proceedings of the 4th International Conference on Cloud Computing and Services Science*, (pp. 691–702). doi:10.5220/0004971906910702

Jung, E., & Kettimuthu, R. (2014). Towards Addressing the Challenges of Data-Intensive Computing on the Cloud. *Computer, 47*(12), 82–85. doi:10.1109/MC.2014.347

Lee, G., Tolia, N., Ranganathan, P., & Katz, R. H. (2011). Topology-aware resource allocation for data-intensive workloads. *Computer Communication Review, 41*(1), 120. doi:10.1145/1925861.1925881

Lin, J., Chen, C., & Chang, J. (2013). QoS-aware data replication for data intensive applications in cloud computing systems. *IEEE Transactions on Cloud Computing, 1*(1), 101–115. Retrieved from http://ieeexplore.ieee.org/xpls/abs_all.jsp?arnumber=6562695

Luckeneder, M., & Barker, A. (2013). Location, Location, Location: Data-Intensive Distributed Computing in the Cloud. *2013 IEEE 5th International Conference on Cloud Computing Technology and Science*, (pp. 647–654). doi:10.1109/CloudCom.2013.91

Mansouri, N. (2014). Network and data location aware approach for simultaneous job scheduling and data replication in large-scale data grid. *Frontiers of Computer Science*, 8(3), 391–408. doi:10.1007/s11704-014-3146-2

Mattess, M., Calheiros, R. N., & Buyya, R. (2013). Scaling MapReduce Applications Across Hybrid Clouds to Meet Soft Deadlines. *2013 IEEE 27th International Conference on Advanced Information Networking and Applications (AINA)*, (pp. 629–636). doi:10.1109/AINA.2013.51

Middleton, A. M. (2010). 05 - Data-Intensive Technologies for Cloud Computing. In B. Furht & A. Escalante (Eds.), *Handbook of Cloud Computing* (pp. 83–136). Boston, MA: Springer US; doi:10.1007/978-1-4419-6524-0_5

Moretti, C., Bulosan, J., Thain, D., & Flynn, P. J. (2008). All-pairs: An abstraction for data-intensive cloud computing. *2008 IEEE International Symposium on Parallel and Distributed Processing*, (pp. 1–11). doi:10.1109/IPDPS.2008.4536311

Pereira, W. F., Bittencourt, L. F., & da Fonseca, N. L. S. (2013). Scheduler for data-intensive workflows in public clouds. *2nd IEEE Latin American Conference on Cloud Computing and Communications (LatinCloud)*, (pp. 41-46). doi:10.1109/LatinCloud.2013.6842221

Ranganathan, K., & Foster, I. (2002). Decoupling computation and data scheduling in distributed data-intensive applications. In *Proceedings 11th IEEE International Symposium on High Performance Distributed Computing* (pp. 352–358). IEEE Comput. Soc. doi:10.1109/HPDC.2002.1029935

Ryden, M., Oh, K., Chandra, A., & Weissman, J. (2014). Nebula: Distributed edge cloud for data-intensive computing. *2014 International Conference on Collaboration Technologies and Systems (CTS)*, (pp. 491–492). doi:10.1109/CTS.2014.6867613

Sakr, S., Liu, A., Batista, D. M., & Alomari, M. (2011). A Survey of Large Scale Data Management Approaches in Cloud Environments. *IEEE Communications Surveys and Tutorials*, 13(3), 311–336. doi:10.1109/SURV.2011.032211.00087

Shamsi, J., Khojaye, M. A., & Qasmi, M. A. (2013). Data-Intensive Cloud Computing: Requirements, Expectations, Challenges, and Solutions. *Journal of Grid Computing*, 11(2), 281–310. doi:10.1007/s10723-013-9255-6

Szabo, C., Sheng, Q. Z., Kroeger, T., Zhang, Y., & Yu, J. (2014). Science in the Cloud: Allocation and Execution of Data-Intensive Scientific Workflows. *Journal of Grid Computing*, 12(2), 245–264. doi:10.1007/s10723-013-9282-3

Varshney, M. (2013). *Blue: A Unified Programming Model for Diverse Data-intensive Cloud Computing Paradigms*. Technical Report #130005, Computer Science Department, University of California, Los Angeles. Retrieved May 5, 2013 from http://fmdb.cs.ucla.edu/Treports/blue.pdf

Vavilapalli, V. K. (2013). Apache Hadoop YARN: yet another resource negotiator. In *Proceedings of the 4th annual Symposium on Cloud Computing* (SOCC '13). ACM. doi:10.1145/2523616.2523633

Wang, J., Xiao, Q., Yin, J., & Shang, P. (2013). DRAW: A New Data-gRouping-AWare Data Placement Scheme for Data Intensive Applications With Interest Locality. *IEEE Transactions on Magnetics*, *49*(6), 2514–2520. doi:10.1109/TMAG.2013.2251613

Wang, L., Tao, J., Ranjan, R., Marten, H., Streit, A., Chen, J., & Chen, D. (2013). G-Hadoop: MapReduce across distributed data centers for data-intensive computing. *Future Generation Computer Systems*, *29*(3), 739–750. doi:10.1016/j.future.2012.09.001

Wikipedia. (2012). *Data Intensive Computing*. Retrieved November 23, 2014 from http://en.wikipedia.org/wiki/Data_Intensive_Computing

Xiao, P., Hu, Z.-G., & Zhang, Y.-P. (2013). An Energy-Aware Heuristic Scheduling for Data-Intensive Workflows in Virtualized Datacenters. *Journal of Computer Science and Technology*, *28*(6), 948–961. doi:10.1007/s11390-013-1390-9

Ye, Z., Li, S., & Zhou, J. (2014). A two-layer geo-cloud based dynamic replica creation strategy. *Applied Mathematics and Information Sciences*, *8*(1), 431–440. doi:10.12785/amis/080154

KEY TERMS AND DEFINITIONS

Data Placement: To store appropriate pieces of data locally at the node, rack, data centre, region or availability zone depending on the context; the aim is to allow the application to operate on data available locally, so as to avoid communication and data transfer costs.

Data Transfer: Large scale data movement across geographically distributed data centres using Wide Area Network (WAN).

Geo-Distributed Data: Data that is generated across countries from simulations, observations, experiments, etc, and are stored at their site of origin.

Intercloud: Globally interconnected clouds or a Cloud of clouds similar to definition of Internet as a network of networks. The common future use cases and functional requirements for Intercloud computing are published in a white paper by the Global Inter-Cloud Technology Forum (GICTF).

Multicloud: A type of Intercloud where the clouds operate independent of each other in contrast to federated clouds which have an agreement to use each other's resources.

Programming Models: An abstraction of computing systems that serves as an intermediary between the hardware architecture and the software layers available to applications; allows algorithms and data structures to be expressed independently of the programming language.

Replication: Creating multiple copies of a file, database or object with a view to increase data locality, availability and fault tolerance. In the cloud computing scenario, data replication techniques need to deal with consistency and lifetimes issue of replicas while keeping down storage and data transfer costs.

Scheduling: Allocating resources to jobs so that the work specified in the jobs are completed while maximizing throughput, and fairness among contending jobs as well as minimizing response time and latency.

Chapter 20
A Key–Based Database Sharding Implementation for Big Data Analytics

Sikha Bagui
University of West Florida, USA

Loi Nguyen
Development and Technology Center (NETPDTC), USA

ABSTRACT

In this chapter, we use MySQL Database Cluster to demonstrate and discover the capabilities of key based database sharding and provide the implementation details to build a key based sharded database system. After the implementation section, we present some examples of datasets that were sharded using our implementation. The sharded data is then used for data mining, specifically association rule mining. We present the results (association rules) for the sharded data as well as the non-sharded data.

1 INTRODUCTION

The dawn of Big Data entails the re-evaluation of data storage and analytical analysis. Traditional data storage techniques stored records as data, inserted via INSERT statements into database tables. Today, with the digital revolution, as tables have enormously grown in size storing petabytes of data, sifting through data for particular instances can consume a vast amount of resources (i.e. memory_target, sort_area_size). Data analytics is also facing new challenges. The idea of a centralized data storage has to be modified to accommodate availability, scalability, reliability and manageability. Higher performance and lower cost become a challenge. In this chapter we show how this is accommodated by database sharding.

The architecture of a sharded database is comprised of multiple computed nodes deployed across commodity servers to provide continuous uptime operation in the event of hardware or network failure. The commonly available sharding schemes are: vertical partitioning, range-based partitioning, key or hash based partitioning, and directory based partitioning. By leveraging on database sharding or horizontal partitioning, the database is divided into smaller chunks or shards across multiple data nodes in the

DOI: 10.4018/978-1-4666-8676-2.ch020

Copyright © 2015, IGI Global. Copying or distributing in print or electronic forms without written permission of IGI Global is prohibited.

cluster. Each node contains and is responsible for its own subset of the data to create a shared-nothing environment.

Unlike the shared-disk clustered database, where data can be accessed from all cluster nodes and thus can cause contention during simultaneous reads and writes, shared-nothing clustered database's nodes operate on their own subset of data. Data nodes are replicated to provide redundancy, and thus provide high availability and scalability. In a worst-case scenario, if a node, containing a subset data of a table, and the replicated node become unavailable, the other nodes, with a different subset of data, will remain online and available. The business application continues to perform transactions and access data from the remaining available data nodes. These database operations will execute successfully and transparently to the application if the application does not access the unavailable data node. The failed node can be examined, recovered, and rejoin the cluster when it is ready, without affecting any other nodes.

Due to economies of scale, the incurred cost of operating the database needs to be substantially reduced. Database sharding alleviates cost in two ways (1) cost of operation and maintenance - Total Cost of Ownership (TCO) and (2) cost of accessing and processing data. Instead of a centralized storage-area network (SAN), which introduces a single point of failure, database clustering addresses cost (1) by providing a shared-nothing environment that enables the database to scale horizontally on low cost commodity hardware. By wisely partitioning data rows horizontally in a cluster using range or hash partitioning, subsets of data can be accessed separately on each individual data node, which significantly influences the performance capacity while reducing the cost of accessing and processing the data.

Database sharding solves the issue of manageability by partitioning tables and indexes into more manageable units. Database administrators can use database sharding's Separation of Concerns design concept to pursue the management of data. Since each node is a representation of a portion of the data, maintaining the entire data table can be accomplished in succession for each individual node without affecting any other data nodes. For example, a typical usage for a database administrator is to archive or back up outdated data to save on storage. Rather than archiving the entire data table, a database administrator could archive a single data node containing the data for a particular partition, i.e. year. The archived data can be compressed and transferred to a less-expensive storage tier at a lower TCO cost.

For many years, the perception of gaining more database throughput was by building bigger and better database servers with supplementary multi-cores CPU, faster disk drives, and higher bandwidth and low latency memory. However, according to the law of diminishing returns, all three factors, CPU, disk drive, and memory, have to be added proportionally to provide maximum performance. If only one of the three factors is increased while the others remain constant, then the system will yield lower marginal returns. As business applications grow and are stored on the cloud, databases need to provide high performance to handle the increasing workloads. Not only does database sharding alleviate the TCO cost, but it is also a factor for gaining high performance. Since sharding divides the table into smaller partitions and distributes it across multiple data nodes, the number of records in each node is smaller than whole table. This technique improves searching performance by reducing the index size and limiting the number of records to be traversed.

In this chapter, we use MySQL Database Cluster to demonstrate and discover the capabilities of key based database sharding. We will provide the implementation details to build a key based sharded database system. After the implementation section, we present some examples of datasets that were sharded using our implementation. Then we used the sharded data for data mining, specifically association rule mining. We present the association rules for the sharded data as well as the non-sharded data.

The rest of the chapter is organized as follows. In section 2 we discuss related works. The implementation of a key based sharded database architecture is presented in Section 3. Section 4 presents results of this key based sharding. Section 5 is the data analytics section where we perform association rule mining on the sharded datasets and section 6 presents the discussion and conclusions.

2 RELATED WORKS

Traditional non-sharded databases are usually deployed on a single database server. If the server fails, the entire business applications crumbles and the system becomes unavailable. The concept of improving database reliability, high availability, maintainability, high performance, and dynamically adapting to increasing workloads has been around for decades. Several works have been done on database clustering and database sharding to address the above issues. Pattishall (2006) proposed his unorthodox approach to database design. Pattishall (2006) argued that by splitting the data among multiple servers, it would provide more write bandwidth as well as high availability. Since each shard of the data will be smaller than the full chunk, data will be faster to backup, recover, and easier to manage. While his work outlined the architecture for his database design, our work focuses on implementing a scalable database using sharding principles and providing experimental results to validate it.

Agrawal, et al. (2004) published techniques to optimize the performance of a database by incorporating both horizontal and vertical partitioning, in addition to indexes and materialized views, into the physical database design. Their approach differs from our work in the following key areas: (1) they implemented horizontal partitioning (sharding) on single-node partition while our work spreads the data across multiple nodes in the cluster. (2) They implemented their techniques and evaluated it on Microsoft SQL Server; whereas, we will use MySQL Cluster to evaluate our sharding model. (3) Our work does not include indexes, materialized views, and vertical partitioning. Instead we incorporate clustering architecture into our design to gain high availability with fault tolerance. (4) While their focus was only on scalable techniques for selecting candidate physical design structures, we provide implementation details for achieving horizontal partitioning (sharding) in a cluster environment.

With more and more data on the cloud, sharding has become a popular research topic for housing huge amounts data. Obasanjo (2009) discussed the challenges Facebook Inc. encountered with its data storage as it transitioned from a glorified online Harvard's yearbook, in 2004, to a 14 billion page views per month, in 2008. Obasanjo (2009) mentioned at some point during the development of Facebook, that the limitation on the physical capacity of their database server was at its maximum. In order to continue and expand the operation, Facebook had to either scale up by procuring bigger and better database servers with more RAM, higher CPU frequency and cores, and more storage capacity, or scale out by distributing their data across relatively cheap commodity database servers. The scenario presents sharding as the best alternative with regards to cost savings relative to the increased complexity of the system (Obasanjo, 2009). Obasanjo (2009)'s article presents some similarities with our work, such as the concept of key or hash based partitioning. However, our work extends Obasanjo (2009)'s work by providing the actual implementation details of a clustered and sharded database. We also address cross-shard joins and rebalancing, which were the known limitations in his article.

When Google, the world's largest search engine, needs a way to manage large arrays of data, they search for a solution that could distribute the data across multiple servers. Chang, et al. (2006) at Google Inc. wrote a white paper on their Bigtable storage system for structured data. Bigtable is a distributed storage system for managing structured data that is designed to scale to a very large size -- petabytes of data across thousands of commodity servers. The paper presented Bigtable as a sparse, distributed, persistent multidimensional-sorted map. The map is indexed by a row key, column key, and a timestamp; each value in the map is an uninterpreted array of bytes (Chang, et al., 2006). Bigtable and our work on MySQL Cluster have some components that overlap since both provide the ability to distribute data across multiple servers. Unlike our work, the implementation strategies of Bigtable do not fully support traditional ACID (Atomicity, Consistency, Isolation, Durability) database properties that guarantee reliable database transactions. Another challenge to overcome is the design nature of Bigtable. Since Bigtable is a proprietary distributed storage system created by Google to support their own products, it may not be easily integrated into mainstream commercial industry and quickly deployed across thousands of servers like MySQL Cluster.

The characteristics of database sharding is one of the enticing patterns in cloud computing. The ability to scale the data out horizontally is an important aspect to achieving a scalable and highly available database system in the cloud. Abadi (2009) highlighted five ideal characteristics or properties for data analysis in the cloud by evaluating MapReduce software and shared-nothing parallel databases. The five properties consist of efficiency, fault tolerance, heterogeneous environment, data encryption, and interfacing with business intelligence products. While Abadi (2009)'s paper discussed the theory of key components for a reliable cloud database system, our work will discuss the implementation aspects of such a system.

Krasuski and Szczuka (2011) proposed an idea of query sharding. Unlike database sharding, query sharding is taking a large query and decomposing it into a collection of smaller and simple queries. Krasuski and Szczuka (2011) proposed using Separation of Concerns design concept on the database table and processing it piece-wise. They suggested that a complex object, in this case a table, can process faster if it is divided into pieces that can be executed and optimized independently without distorting the global outcome. Each shard would contain information about an object in the data. Once the table has been sharded, calculations can be distributed among multiple threads on a single or multicore processor(s) or among several machines in a networked environment (Krasuski and Szczuka, 2011). However, in order for this scheme to execute successfully, the database system must support windowing functions. Windowing functions are new features introduced in SQL:2003 or sometimes refered to as SQL3 (Krasuski and Szczuka, 2011). These functions impose a limitation on a partition of a result set. Krasuski and Szczuka (2011)'s work and our work aim at improving query workload performance. However, that is the only similarity between their work and ours. Their concept of query sharding, *top-k* queries, resembles the idea of pagination with multithreading. Our work partitions the data to different data nodes across commodity servers. We are not limited by the availability of windowing functions. Although their work allowed the running of pieces of queries in parallel, relieving the overhead performance, it did not address the issues of scalability, fault tolerance and high data availability that our work on database sharding will offer.

CodeFutures (2010) provides a different view to database sharding. CodeFutures (2010) invented a unique product called dbShards. dbShards is a suite of database agnostic and management tools that facilitate critical features such as high availability and scalability (CodeFutures, 2010). Applying techniques such as database replication and database sharding to the database tier, dbShards seamlessly provides those critical features in an Application-Aware manner. DbShards differs from our work in the following key differences: (1) dbShards is a software layer that transforms a conventional Database Management System into a shared-nothing DBMS environment. Our work provides the actual implementation details of a shared-nothing environment at the database layer. (2) By using a custom database driver, dbShards composes the data shards and presents it as a single unit to the applications. Our work eliminates the needs for a custom driver since the sharded data stored in the data node will congregate by MySQL servers during SQL runtime execution.

With the augmentation of social networking sites and blogosphere sites, (Duong, et al., 2013) proposed sharding as a strategy to maintain scalable data infrastructures. In their study, they show different sharding strategies such as random sharding and de facto industry sharding standard are not optimal and ideal solution to shard social networks. They went further and introduced a scalable sharding algorithm that outperforms those techniques. Like us, they recognized and acknowledged as the popularity of social networks and blogospheres propagate, the surge of data will be difficult to manage if not distributed with properly. Their research compliments our work in one or more ways. (1) Both works present sharding in terms of improving performance. (2) Both works understand the fundamental necessity of storing data in a distributed, or sharded environment across commodity severs rather than single physical server. (3) Both works recognize the need to restructure the data to handle large internet-scale datasets. Even through there are similarity aspects in their work and ours; they did not present sharding as a method for data mining and data warehousing. We extend this chapter beyond sharding and discuss the interrelationship between the data using a data mining algorithm. We present the theory of sharding to aid in data mining, specifically association rule mining.

By exploring the related works and research papers in the database community, the realization of improving the traditional database performance and scalability has been perceived and pursued by many scholars. Many database properties have been proposed to initiate the database in a new direction. The advent of the cloud-computing platform validates the desire to deploy a database in a scalable, highly available, and fault tolerant ecosystem. In this chapter, we present the key properties as well as the implementation details to achieve a key based sharded database management system based on MySQL Cluster, which can be deployed in a public or private virtualization computing environment. After creating the architecture, we will use our implementation to create a few sharded databases, using some sample datasets.

3 KEY BASED SHARDING ARCHITECTURE

As the business commerce world expands and more and more data is stored on the cloud, demands for cheaper alternatives to store and provide data efficiently for data analytics and data management is on the rise. While configuring the database in a cluster environment provides scalability and high availability, it still depends on the underlying DBMS architecture to provide reliability, manageability, performance, and at the same time reduce cost. Database administrators often configure their databases in a cluster on top of shared-disk architecture. By deploying such a technique, DBAs are able to eliminate the complexity of a shared-nothing architecture while still maintaining redundancy. Shared-disk literally shares all data across all nodes on the cluster (Hogan, 2015). Since shared-disk share the same Storage Area Network (SAN) and/or Network Attached Storage (NAS), memory, and other resources, it is prone to single point of failure (SPOF). In this work we will build a scalable, highly available, and high performance database, an architecture that can be used for management of big data on the cloud.

We use MySQL Cluster to demonstrate and discover the capabilities of database sharding. MySQL Cluster is designed to solve the problems of availability, scalability, reliability, cost, manageability, and performance. It is a scalable, real-time, ACID-compliant transactional database, combining 99.999% availability with the low TCO of open source (Guide, 2011) and eliminates the need for expensive shared SANs storage. It employs a shared-nothing distributed data storage, multi-master architecture, to create a fail-tolerance system. The system consists of multiple nodes dispersed geographically across low commodity hardware to ensure high availability. With the ability of auto-sharding at the database tier, it eliminates complex custom sharding logic at the application layer and enables the database to scale horizontally to serve read and write-intensive workloads and high volume OLTP. The implementation of MySQL Cluster revolves around synchronization and replication of data storage. It integrates the standard MySQL server with an in-memory clustered storage engine called Network Database (NDB). The cluster is orchestrated by three types of nodes or processes: *Management nodes (ndb_mgmd), Application nodes or SQL nodes (mysqld), and Data nodes (ndbd)*. By definition, a cluster $C := \{M \cup A \cup D\}$, is a set of management nodes M, application nodes A, and data nodes D. These specialized nodes enable the cluster to seamlessly provide data services to clients.

Data node is the central key node in a cluster. It is a network database daemon (ndbd) process that is used to store and manage all the data in the tables within the cluster. The ndbd process empowers a data node to accomplish (MySQL, 2014):

- Data storage and management
- Distributed transactions
- Automatic or user-defined partition strategies
- Online backup
- Synchronous replication
- Self-healing recovery

To ensure continuous operation, each data node in the cluster is responsible for at least one fragment, a copy of a cluster partition data, in a node group. Data nodes in a node group communicate and keep track of the each other's status via heartbeat protocol. A given node group $G := (D/R: D/R := \{2n: n \in N\})$ is a function of data nodes D in the cluster divided by the number of replicas R such that D divided by R is equal to $2n$, where N is the set of all natural numbers, which is the set of all even natural numbers. For instance, if the cluster comprised of 4 data nodes and the number of replicas is set to 2 then $G = 4/2$, which equates to 2 node groups. Each data node in a node group contains a primary fragment and a backup fragment of the partition data. Therefore a cluster contains fragment $F := (P * R: R > 0)$. Figure 1 illustrates data partitioning to the data nodes within the cluster, in a shared-nothing environment.

As shown in figure 1, the data in the table is *sharded,* using the transaction ID, into four partitions, p0, p1, p2, and p3. Node group 0 consists of data node 1 and 2 and node group 1 consists of data node 3 and 4. Fragments of partitions 1 and 3 are in node group 0. Data node 1 contains the primary fragment of partition 3 and a backup fragment of partition 1. Data node 2 contains the primary fragment of partition 2 and a backup fragment of partition 3. Fragments of partition 0 and 2 are in node group 2 and follow the same distribution pattern as partition 1 and 3. By dispersing data in this pattern, as long as there is one active data node operating in each node group, the cluster has a complete copy of all data to endure high availability and sustainability. Data replication between data nodes in the cluster is performed synchronously. MySQL Cluster uses synchronous replication via atomic commit protocol to guarantee consistency and zero data loss. In an all or nothing environment, commit or abort, write process, and all copies of the data must be stored before signaling an acknowledgement to the SQL node

Figure 1. Data partitioning to data nodes[15]

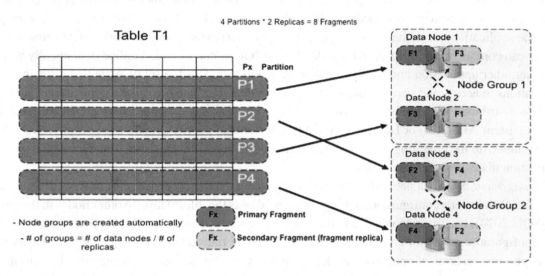

that it's ready to proceed with further processing (Stephens, 2007). The cluster ensures that the data is replicated simultaneously within all data nodes by implementing a concept called *two-phase commit protocol (2PC)* (Stephens, 2007). Gabriel (2002) described 2PC algorithm for *request-for-vote* message, in pseudocode, (Gabriel, 2002) as follows:

By relying on 2PC protocol, MySQL Cluster provides a fully ACID-compliant transactional database. It guarantees reliable database transactions while providing unparalleled scalable data nodes to achieve maximum data capacity and workload processing.

Figure 2. Two-phase commit algorithm (2PC)

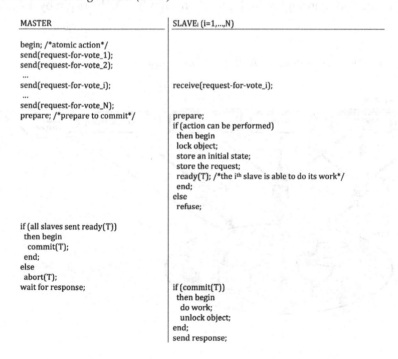

Application (SQL) node is a MySQL daemon process (mysqld), sometimes refered to as MySQL Server, which manages access to the data nodes within the cluster (MySQL, 2014). It provides a connecting path from the application tier to the databases, data tables, materialized views, and other data catalogues. A cluster can contain multiple application nodes and each node can be added online dynamically without affecting other application nodes. MySQL Cluster provides a flexible set of APIs that allow business applications to access and perform transactions on the data. For instance, a Java application can access the data distributed in the cluster by using a simple Java Database Connectivity (JDBC) connection, Java Persistent API (JPA) or Hibernate. MySQL Cluster also provides a powerful set of NoSQL APIs to accommodate the emerging of NoSQL technologies. Figure 3 illustrates the interaction between the application nodes and the data nodes.

Management node is a network database management daemon (ndb_mgmd) process that manages and scans the cluster's configuration settings and broadcasts the information to other nodes in the cluster (MySQL, 2014). It actively monitors and logs the cluster's activities and can be stopped or restarted with new configurations without affecting the current workload transactions. MySQL Cluster management server provides an array of options to check the cluster status. For instance, by executing the --print-full-config, -P command, the user will be able to retrieve extended cluster configuration details. Management node can also be served as an *arbitrator*. During a split-brain scenario, the *arbitrator* can decide which data node within the same node group should be the primary and remain online while the other nodes are restarted or shutdown to avoid contention. Figure 4 illustrates a complete interaction between the management node, application nodes, and the data nodes.

With this distributed architecture, where dependencies have been minimized, applications continue to run and data remains consistent, even if any one of the data, application (SQL), or management nodes fail.

As discussed above, the combination of the three specialized nodes constructs a cluster environment with automatic sharding throughout the data nodes. Our next step is to demonstrate the configuration of such systems along with our empirical findings. We will illustrate the ability to scale horizontally to simulate a geographically data dispersed pattern. The MySQL open source project allows us to take advantages of clustering and sharding technologies with a low TCO. We begin by downloading MySQL

Figure 3. Interaction between application nodes and data nodes[16]

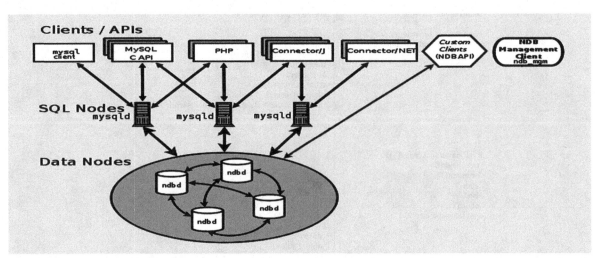

Figure 4. Interactions between management node, application nodes, and data nodes[16]

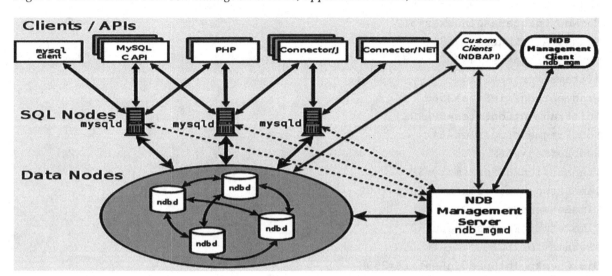

Cluster Generally Available (GA) release 7.3.6 from MySQL downloads site[1]. We create a directory called *mysql* under $HOME. Within this directory, we create *cluster/config, cluster/mysqld_data,* and *cluster/ndb_data*. We extract the downloaded MySQL Cluster into the *mysql* directory and call it *mysqlc*. In order to start the cluster, we need to properly configure MySQL's global configuration files. These files are critical in tuning and optimizing MySQL Cluster. The first file is called *config.ini*. This file is scanned and read by the *ndb_mgmd* process during the start-up phase (MySQL, 2014). It contains global configurations for MySQL Cluster, such as host and node information using INI format. As a deviation from the standard INI format, parameter values can be assigned to parameter names using either a colon ":" or and equal sign "=". We will define our global configuration as follows:

```
[tcp default]
SendBufferMemory=32M
ReceiveBufferMemory=32M
[ndb_mgmd]
NodeId=1
hostname=[NDB_Management_Server_IP]
[ndbd default]
noofreplicas=2
ServerPort=[PORT]
DataMemory=6144M
IndexMemory=1024M
LockPagesInMainMemory=1
Odirect=1
MaxNoOfConcurrentOperations=100000
MaxNoOfConcurrentTransactions=16384
StringMemory=25
MaxNoOfTables=4096
```

```
MaxNoOfOrderedIndexes=2048
MaxNoOfUniqueHashIndexes=512
MaxNoOfAttributes=24576
MaxNoOfTriggers=14336
#Params for REDO LOG
FragmentLogFileSize=256M
InitFragmentLogFiles=SPARSE
NoOfFragmentLogFiles=64
RedoBuffer=256M
TransactionBufferMemory=8M
TimeBetweenGlobalCheckpoints=2000
TimeBetweenEpochs=200
TimeBetweenEpochsTimeout=0
#Params for LCP
DiskCheckpointSpeedInRestart=250M
DiskCheckpointSpeed=32M
TimeBetweenLocalCheckpoints=23
CompressedLCP=1
#Heartbeating
HeartbeatIntervalDbDb=15000
HeartbeatIntervalDbApi=15000
#Params for BACKUP
BackupWriteSize=1M
BackupMaxWriteSize=6M
BackupLogBufferSize=4M
BackupDataBufferSize=16M
BackupMemory=20M
BackupReportFrequency=60
#Multithreading
MaxNoOfExecutionThreads=8
NoOfFragmentLogParts=4
[ndbd]
hostname=[Data_Node1_IP]
NodeId=3
[ndbd]
hostname=[Data_Node2_IP]
NodeId=4
[ndbd]
hostname=[Data_Node3_IP]
NodeId=5
[ndbd]
hostname=[Data_Node4_IP]
NodeId=6
[mysqld]
```

```
NodeId=60
hostname=[MySQL_Node_IP]
[mysqld]
NodeId=61
hostname=[MySQL_Node_IP]
```

Each specialized node must be assigned a unique node ID. The unique node ID is used as the node's address for all cluster internal messages (MySQL, 2014). Currently, MySQL Cluster can only support up to 48 data nodes; therefore, the node ID range for *ndbd* is 1- 48, inclusive (MySQL, 2014). However, the range for *ndb_mgmd* and mysqld is from 1-255, inclusive (MySQL, 2014). The configuration for each specialized node is declared in its own respective section. For instance, the *[ndbd]* section declares the configuration parameters for the data nodes. If the all the data nodes share common properties, they can be declared in a new section using the *default* keyword *[ndbd default]*. In order to optimize our MySQL Cluster, we tuned our data nodes with the following defaults:

```
#Memory parameters
DataMemory=6144M
IndexMemory=1024M
#Boolean parameters
LockPagesInMainMemory=1
Odirect=1
CompressedLCP=1
#LCP and GCP timing parameter
TimeBetweenLocalCheckpoints=23
TimeBetweenGlobalCheckpoints=2000
TimeBetweenEpochs=200
TimeBetweenEpochsTimeout=0
#Disk parameters
DiskCheckpointSpeed=32M
DiskCheckpointSpeedInRestart =250M
#Backup parameters
BackupWriteSize=1M
BackupMaxWriteSize=6M
BackupLogBufferSize=4M
BackupDataBufferSize=16M
BackupMemory=20M
BackupReportFrequency=60
#Logging
NoOfFragmentLogFiles=64
FragmentLogFileSize=256M
RedoBuffer=256M
#Multithreading
MaxNoOfExecutionThreads=8
```

Data Memory and *Index Memory* parameters allocate the volume of memory space and measure in bytes needed to store database records and the related indexes. This allocation should be proportional to the physical memory on the host. The *LockPagesInMainMemory* parameter is used to perform *paging*; therefore avoiding frequent swapping to a secondary storage medium such as disk drive. The value of 1 indicates locking should occur after the memory has been allocated to the process (MySQL, 2014). The host machine should have adequate memory to accommodate these parameters. Another setting to reduce Kernel swap daemon (*kswapd*) and CPU usage is the *Odirect* parameter. By enabling this feature, the network database (*ndb*) will attempt to use Linux's O_DIRECT writes for Local Checkpoints (LCPs), backups, and redo logs (MySQL, 2014). Since the data in the network database is stored in memory, it has to be able to write the data, including backups, and restore it during system recovery. To accomplish such task, MySQL Cluster provides two types of checkpoints: Local Checkpoint (LCP) and Global Checkpoint (GLP) (Davies and Fisk, 2006). A checkpoint is a snapshot at a specific point in time where all committed transactions are stored on disk. Local Checkpoint transfers all the data in the data node to the disk drive. Global Checkpoint saves the REDO-logs to the disk drive for future playback in the event of system failure (Davies and Fisk, 2006). These two checkpoints synchronize together in the network database storage engine to ensure a consistent view of the cluster's data. As a tradeoff between CPU cycles and space requirements, we can set the *CompressedLCP* to true to compress the LCP files to be saved on the disk. However, the compression process requires expenditure of CPU cycles. Therefore, this configuration should be set appropriately depending on the host's platform and environment. In order to avoid continuous LCP writes to disk, we can configure the *TimeBetweenLocalCheckpoints* parameter. Although the parameter name indicates the time interval between each LCP, the actual unit of measurement is base-2 logarithm of the number of 4-byte words (MySQL, 2014). For instance, setting the parameter value to 23 equates to $4 \times 2^{23} = 32MB$ of write operations before starting a new local checkpoint. During vast data import, this value should be set higher. The parameter *TimeBetweenGlobalCheckpoints* specifies the time elapse between global checkpoints, during which all nodes are synchronized and the transaction logs are flushed to disk. The default value for this parameter is 2000 milliseconds. The *DiskCheckpointSpeed* parameter is a quantitative measurement in bytes of the amount of data to be sent to disk during a local checkpoint (MySQL, 2014). The *DiskCheckpointSpeedInRestart* parameter is similar to the *DiskCheckpointSpeed*; however, it only occurs during a restart operation. The backup parameters section defines the allocation of buffer memory for online backups. Backup memories are defined accordingly to the formula (MySQL, 2014):

BackupMemory = BackupDataBufferSize + BackupLogBufferSize

BackupDataBufferSize >= BackupWriteSize + 188KB

BackupLogBufferSize >= BackupWriteSize + 16KB

BackupMaxWriteSize >= BackupWriteSize

We defined the default backup message size to 1 megabyte and set the other backup parameters respectively. We also defined the frequency of the backup status report to 60 seconds. By doing so, the backup status reports are written to the cluster log in 60 second intervals. When an unforeseen event happens and the system needs to be reinstated to a restoration point, MySQL Cluster uses the REDO log to replay all the past update transactions. Therefore setting the configuration for the REDO log is crucial to the system. The *NoOfFragmentLogFiles* is used to determine the number of files for REDO logging. The REDO log files are organized in a ring network topology and are allocated in a block of 64MB. The *FragmentLogFileSize* parameter specifies the size, in bytes, of the individual REDO log files. For instance, if the *FragmentLogFileSize* = 256M and *NoOfFragmentLogFiles* is 64 then there will be 64 set of two 256MB files for the total size of 32GB. Since the REDO log file is formulated in a ring, it is important that the first log file (head) and the last log file (tail) do not come close to each other; otherwise, the node begins aborting all transactions encompassing updates due to lack of space for new log records (Davis and Fisk, 2006). Once all the LCPs have been completed, the REDO log will be recycled; therefore, increasing *DiskCheckpointSpeed* value should also increase the *NoOfFragment-LogFiles* value, so that the head and the tail of the log files will not be in contention. Another parameter to be defined for REDO log is the *RedoBuffer*. The *RedoBuffer* parameter sets the size of the buffer in which the REDO log is written (MySQL, 2014). The last section in our configuration is preserved for multithreading. These settings specifically target the multi-thread version of the network database daemon (ndbd). The parameter *MaxNoOfExecutionThreads*[2] determines the number of available CPU threads to be allocated for the data node. For instance, if the host has an 8-core CPU, then the *MaxNoOfExecution-Threads* should be 8. For advanced multithreaded settings, such as assigning threads of different types to different CPUs, the *ThreadConfig* parameter is desired. Figure 5, from FROMDUAL site[3], illustrates the interaction between the Transaction Coordinator (TC), the Local Checkpoint (LCP) and the Global Checkpoint (GCP) with respect to the configuration file [3].

Figure 5.

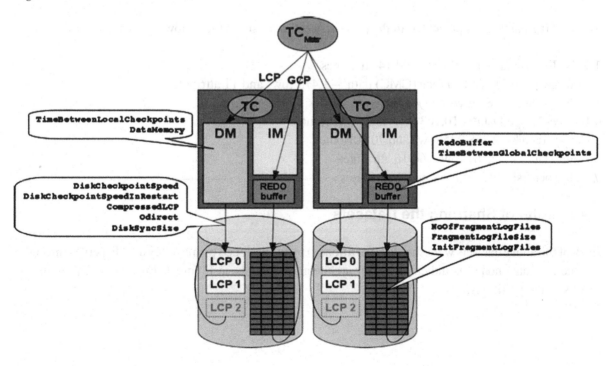

Our basic *config.ini* settings provide a quick and easy path to configure and deploy MySQL Cluster. There are more advance configurations defined by the MySQL Cluster documentation (MySQL, 2014) to tune and optimize the cluster.

Another important configuration file for MySQL Cluster is *my.cnf*. Each application node or SQL node requires a *my.cnf* file that provides two pieces of information: a ndb-connectstring that informs the location of the management node and a directive to notify the MySQL server on this host (the machine hosting the data node) to enable the NDBCLUSTER storage engine (MySQL, 2014). We defined our *my.cnf* file as follows:

```
[mysqld]
ndbcluster
server-id=60
port=5000
datadir=$HOME/mysql/cluster/mysqld_data
basedir=$HOME/mysql/mysqlc
ndb-connectstring=[NDB_Management_Server_IP]
```

As indicated by the configurations, we want to enable the ndbcluster storage engine and configure the application nodes to the active management server IP address. Along with the basic settings, we also need to set the *server-id* parameter. This parameter is linked to the NodeId of one of our application nodes (mysqld) in the *config*.ini file. The *port* parameter indicates the listened port of our MySQL Server as the *server-id* 60. The settings for this file are very basic but it should be adequate to start our cluster.

4 SHARDING THE DATASETS

We used the parameters presented in the previous section to shard the following datasets.

1 Solar Flare data[6] – 1,389 rows and 14 attributes
2 Contraceptive Method Choice (CMC) data[7] – 1,473 rows and 11 attributes
3 El Nino data[8] – 782 rows and 10 attributes
4 Internet Usage Data[9] – 10,103 rows and 73 attributes
5 Census data[10] – 2,458,285 rows and 70 attributes
6 Adult Data[11] – 32,561 rows and 16 attributes
7 Ants Species[12] – 1,776 rows and 7 attributes

4.1.Results of Sharding the Datasets

Each of the above datasets were sharded (partitioned) by the assigned primary key and dispersed throughout the four data nodes as indicated by our architecture diagram in Figure 1. Figures 6-12 present the results of the partitions.

Figure 6. Partitions for the Solar Flares dataset
--SOLAR FLARES --
Version: 1
Fragment Type: HashMapPartition
K Value: 6
Min Load Factor: 78
Max Load Factor: 80
Temporary Table: No
Number of Attributes: 14
Number of Primary Keys: 1
--Indexes –
Primary Key(id) – UniqueHashIndex
Primary(id) - OrderedIndex

-- SOLAR_FLARES -- -- Per partition info --						
Partition	**Row Count**	**Commit count**	**Frag fixed memory**	**Frag varsized memory**	**Extent_space**	**Free extent_space**
0	90	90	32768	32768	0	0
1	85	85	32768	32768	0	0
2	81	81	32768	32768	0	0
3	67	67	32768	32768	0	0

Figure 7. Partitions for the CMC dataset
--CMC –
Version: 1
Fragment Type: HashMapPartition
K Value: 6
Min Load Factor: 78
Max Load Factor: 80
Temporary Table: No
Number of Attributes: 11
--Indexes –
Primary Key(id) – UniqueHashIndex
Primary(id) - OrderedIndex

-- CMC -- -- Per partition info --						
Partition	**Row Count**	**Commit count**	**Frag fixed memory**	**Frag varsized memory**	**Extent_space**	**Free extent_space**
0	396	396	32768	32768	0	0
1	362	362	32768	32768	0	0
2	369	369	32768	32768	0	0
3	346	346	32768	32768	0	0

Figure 8. Partitions for the Elnino dataset
--ELNINO --
Version: 3
Fragment Type: HashMapPartition
K Value: 6
Min Load Factor: 78
Max Load Factor: 80
Temporary Table: No
Number of Attributes: 10
--Indexes --
Primary Key(id) -- UniqueHashIndex
Primary(id) - OrderedIndex

-- ELNINO --						
-- Per partition info --						
Partition	**Row Count**	**Commit count**	**Frag fixed memory**	**Frag varsized memory**	**Extent_space**	**Free extent_space**
0	189	189	32768	32768	0	0
1	187	187	32768	32768	0	0
2	177	177	32768	32768	0	0
3	179	179	32768	32768	0	0

Figure 9. Partitions for the Internet Usage dataset
--INTERNET USAGE --
Version: 5
Fragment Type: HashMapPartition
K Value: 6
Min Load Factor: 78
Max Load Factor: 80
Temporary Table: No
Number of Attributes: 73
--Indexes --
Primary Key(id) -- UniqueHashIndex
Primary(id) - OrderedIndex

-- INTERNET_USAGE --						
-- Per partition info --						
Partition	**Row Count**	**Commit count**	**Frag fixed memory**	**Frag varsized memory**	**Extent_space**	**Free extent_space**
0	237	237	32768	32768	0	0
1	219	219	32768	32768	0	0
2	226	226	32768	32768	0	0
3	210	210	32768	32768	0	0

Figure 10. Partitions for the CENSUS dataset

--CENSUS --

Version: 1
Fragment Type: HashMapPartition
K Value: 6
Min Load Factor: 78
Max Load Factor: 80
Temporary Table: No
Number of Attributes: 70
--Indexes –
Primary Key(id) – UniqueHashIndex
Primary(id) - OrderedIndex

-- CENSUS -- -- Per partition info --						
Partition	**Row Count**	**Commit count**	**Frag fixed memory**	**Frag varsized memory**	**Extent_space**	**Free extent_space**
0	407	407	32768	32768	0	0
1	371	371	32768	32768	0	0
2	352	352	32768	32768	0	0
3	370	370	32768	32768	0	0

Figure 11. Partitions for the ADULT CENSUS INCOME dataset

--ADULT_CENSUS_INCOME --

Version: 1
Fragment Type: HashMapPartition
K Value: 6
Min Load Factor: 78
Max Load Factor: 80
Temporary Table: No
Number of Attributes: 16
--Indexes –
Primary Key(id) – UniqueHashIndex
Primary(id) – OrderedIndex

-- ADULT_DATA8 -- -- Per partition info --						
Partition	**Row Count**	**Commit count**	**Frag fixed memory**	**Frag varsized memory**	**Extent_space**	**Free extent_space**
0	821	821	32768	65536	0	0
1	756	756	32768	65536	0	0
2	778	778	32768	65536	0	0
3	731	731	32768	65536	0	0

Figure 12. Partitions for ANTS dataset
--ANTS_SPECIES –
Version: 3
Fragment Type: HashMapPartition
K Value: 6
Min Load Factor: 78
Max Load Factor: 80
Temporary Table: No
Number of Attributes: 7
--Indexes –
Primary Key(id) – UniqueHashIndex
Primary(id) – OrderedIndex

-- ANTS -- -- Per partition info --						
Partition	**Row Count**	**Commit count**	**Frag fixed memory**	**Frag varsized memory**	**Extent_space**	**Free extent_space**
0	483	483	32768	32768	0	0
1	438	438	32768	32768	0	0
2	437	437	32768	32768	0	0
3	414	414	32768	32768	0	0

5 DATA ANALYTICS: MINING THE SHARDED DATASETS

As datasets grow to petabytes of data, data analytics is facing new challenges. The sharded datasets were used to perform data mining, specifically association rule mining.

5.1 Association Rule Mining

Association rule mining is used to discover interesting relationships hidden in large datasets. Association mining, originally developed by Agrawal, et al. (1993), can be stated as follows: Let $I = \{i_1, i_2, ..., i_n\}$ be a set of items and $D = \{t_1, t_2, ..., t_n\}$ be a transaction database, where $t_i (i \in [1,N])$ is a transaction and $t_i \subseteq I$. Every subset of I is called an itemset. If an itemset contains k items, then it is called a k-itemset. The support of an itemset l in D is defined as the percentage of transactions in D containing l, i.e. *support(l)* $= \|\{t \mid t \in D \wedge l \subseteq t\}\|/\|D\|$. If the support of an itemset exceeds a user-specified minimum support threshold, then the itemset is called a *frequent pattern*(Liu, et al., 2004).

5.2 Algorithm to Mine Association Rules

The most commonly used association mining rule algorithm, known as the Apriori algorithm, is an algorithm that finds frequent itemsets using an iterative approach based on candidate generation. Below we give the pseudocode for the Apriori algorithm, as presented in (Han, et al., 2011).

Box 1.

```
L₁:= {frequent 1-itemsets} D;
     for (k=2; Lₖ₋₁ ≠ ∅ ; k++)
     Cₖ = apriori_gen(Lₖ₋₁, min_sup);
     for each transaction t ∈ D { //scan D for counts
              Cₜ = subset(Cₖ, t); // get the subsets of t that are candidates
              for each candidate c ∈ Cₜ
                       c.count++;
}
     Lₖ = { c ∈ Cₖ | c.count ≥ min_sup}
}
return L= Uₖ Lₖ;
procedure apriori_gen(Lₖ₋₁; frequent(k-1)-itemsets; min_sup: minimum support threshold)
     for each itemset l₁ ∈ Lₖ₋₁
              for each itemset l₂ ∈ Lₖ₋₁
                       if (l₁[1] = l₂[1]) ∧ (l₁[2] = l₂[2]) ∧ ... ∧ (l₁[k-2] = l₂[k-2]) ∧ (l₁[k-1] = l₂[k-1])

then {
                                 c = l₁ |X| l₂ ; // join step: generates candidates
                                 if has_infrequent_subset(c, Lₖ₋₁) then
                                          delete c; //prune step: remove unfruitful candidate
                                 else add c to Cₖ;
     }
return Cₖ;
procedure has_infrequent_subset(c:candidate k-itemset; Lₖ₋₁: frequent (k-1)-itemsets);
              //use prior knowledge
     for each (k-1) – subset s of c
              if s ∉ Lₖ₋₁ then
              return TRUE;
              return FALSE;
```

This Apriori algorithm employs an iterative approach known as a level-wise search, where k-itemsets are used to explore $(k+1)$ – itemsets. First, the set of frequent 1-itemsets is found, denoted by L_1. All these frequent 1-itemsets have to have *support* above a user specified minimum. The frequent 1-itemsets are generated by counting item occurrences and then those that turn out to be frequent after computing their support are used.

L_1 is then used to find L_2, the set of frequent 2-itemsets, which is used to find L_3, and so on until no more frequent k-itemsets can be found. The size of the itemsets is incremented by one at each iteration, and the finding of each L_k requires one full scan of the database. This phase stops when there are no frequent itemsets.

The apriori_gen procedure performs two steps – a join and a prune. In the join part, L_{k-1} is joined with L_{k-1} to generate potential candidates. The prune portion employs the Apriori property to remove candidates that have a subset that is not frequent. The test for infrequent subsets is shown in procedure has_infrequent_subset (Han, et al., 2011).

5.3 Support and Confidence

The Apriori algorithm typically presents an enormous amount of association rules. We determine the significant rules using a rule's statistical significance, *support* and *confidence*. Support determines how often a rule is applicable to a given data set, while confidence determines how frequently items in Y appear in transactions that contain X (Tan, Steinbach & Kumar, 2006).

The rule $X \Rightarrow Y$ holds in the transaction set D with **support** s, where s is the percentage of transactions in D that contain $X \cup Y$ (that is, contain both X and Y).This is taken to be the probability, $P(X \cup Y)$. (Han, et al., 2011).

The rule $X \Rightarrow Y$ has **confidence** c in the transaction set D. The confidence c is the percentage of transactions in D containing X that also contain Y. This is taken to be the conditional probability, $P(X|Y)$. (Han, et al., 2011).

5.4 WEKA's Apriori algorithm

For this work, we used WEKA's Apriori algorithm[14]. First we ran the entire dataset using WEKA's Apriori algorithm and then we ran the individual partitions using WEKA's Apriori algorithm. We used a support percentage of 2%, 5%, and 10% to test the lower minimum support and a support percentage of 20%, 30%, 40%, 50% and 60% to test a relatively higher minimum support and the max support boundary. Tables 1 - 8 present the number of association rules generated by WEKA, for the whole dataset, and then for each partition at different levels of support and a confidence of 90% or greater.

From the results we can see that the individual partitions actually found more associations in the data.

Table 1. Support of 2% with confidence of 90% or greater (Using WEKA's Apriori association rule mining algorithm)

Dataset	No. of instances	No. of attributes	Full dataset results	Partition 0	Partition 1	Partition 2	Partition 3
Solar Flares	323	13	1813789	3053715	3786077	3278841	3441288
CMC	1 473	10	9085	24139	16326	16809	14554
Internet Usage	892	72	3611	9749	5756	5476	7291
El Nino	732	9	89	421	321	170	257
NASCAR	898	16	701	959	1028	989	1099
Adult Data	3 086	5	176	227	251	199	285
Ants	1 772	4	38	74	77	46	47

Table 2. Support of 5% with confidence of 90% or greater (Using WEKA's Apriori association rule mining algorithm)

Dataset	No. of instances	No. of attributes	Full dataset results	Partition 0	Partition 1	Partition 2	Partition 3
Solar Flares	323	13	589488	911518	1458211	846086	1096940
CMC	1 473	10	2215	5581	4430	3687	2685
Internet Usage	892	72	1118	1856	1472	1605	1332
El Nino	732	9	32	140	174	84	121
NASCAR	898	16	200	293	219	332	498
Adult Data	3 086	5	108	179	251	199	213
Ants	1 772	4	17	40	44	21	41

Table 3. Support of 10% with confidence of 90% or greater (Using WEKA's Apriori association rule mining algorithm)

Dataset	No. of instances	No. of attributes	Full dataset results	Partition 0	Partition 1	Partition 2	Partition 3
Solar Flares	323	13	248025	575584	318237	194485	371370
CMC	1 473	10	583	1520	1189	907	683
Internet Usage	892	72	411	604	351	486	423
El Nino	732	9	17	35	38	55	81
NASCAR	898	16	51	60	57	64	140
Adult Data	3 086	5	54	128	195	199	117
Ants	1 772	4	4	24	20	9	24

Table 4. Support of 20% with confidence of 90% or greater (Using WEKA's Apriori association rule mining algorithm)

Dataset	No. of instances	No. of attributes	Full dataset results	Partition 0	Partition 1	Partition 2	Partition 3
Solar Flares	323	13	17 709	163 896	47 274	23 026	48 653
CMC	1 473	10	119	338	258	172	113
Internet Usage	892	72	101	139	82	122	109
El Nino	732	9	5	5	16	36	50
NASCAR	898	16	6	9	8	7	15
Adult Data	3 086	5	20	78	171	199	26
Ants	1 772	4	2	9	10	2	11

Table 5. Support of 30% with confidence of 90% or greater (Using WEKA's Apriori association rule mining algorithm)

Dataset	No. of instances	No. of attributes	Full dataset results	Partition 0	Partition 1	Partition 2	Partition 3
Solar Flares	323	13	7562	29425	6224	5381	12169
CMC	1 473	10	29	85	71	55	33
Internet Usage	892	72	37	62	31	42	39
El Nino	732	9	2	1	2	36	31
NASCAR	898	16	1	1	2	1	2
Adult Data	3 086	5	5	8	151	134	2
Ants	1 772	4	0	4	4	2	6

Table 6. Support of 40% with confidence of 90% or greater (Using WEKA's Apriori association rule mining algorithm)

Dataset	No. of instances	No. of attributes	Full dataset results	Partition 0	Partition 1	Partition 2	Partition 3
Solar Flares	323	13	3753	14134	2284	2824	2779
CMC	1 473	10	9	28	23	20	10
Internet Usage	892	72	15	23	12	16	14
El Nino	732	9	1	0	1	36	16
NASCAR	898	16	1	1	1	1	0
Adult Data	3 086	5	0	6	20	50	0
Ants	1 772	4	0	2	2	0	3

Table 7. Support of 50% with confidence of 90% or greater (Using WEKA's Apriori association rule mining algorithm)

Dataset	No. of instances	No. of attributes	Full dataset results	Partition 0	Partition 1	Partition 2	Partition 3
Solar Flares	323	13	2124	6828	1336	1942	1549
CMC	1 473	10	5	13	8	9	5
Internet Usage	892	72	7	9	5	9	8
El Nino	732	9	0	0	0	12	8
NASCAR	898	16	0	0	0	0	0
Adult Data	3 086	5	0	5	10	50	0
Ants	1 772	4	0	0	0	0	1

Table 8. Support of 60% with confidence of 90% or greater (Using WEKA's Apriori association rule mining algorithm)

Dataset	No. of instances	No. of attributes	Full dataset results	Partition 0	Partition 1	Partition 2	Partition 3
Solar Flares	323	13	889	3650	831	1215	1012
CMC	1 473	10	2	6	4	4	3
Internet Usage	892	72	3	5	2	3	3
El Nino	732	9	0	0	0	7	7
NASCAR	898	16	0	0	0	0	0
Adult Data	3 086	5	0	3	8	36	0
Ants	1 772	4	0	0	0	0	0

The results substantiate that key based sharding, horizontal partitioning, is an effective method to mine data. From the results, for example, from table 7, the CMC dataset, we can see that partitions 0, 1, 2 and 3 returned 13, 8, 9, and 5 rules respectively, while the complete dataset only gave 5 rules. The sharding focuses the view on a particular partition of the data instead of the whole dataset. Database sharding allows mining to be more efficient and also more meaningful.

6 DISCUSSION AND CONCLUSION

In this work we illustrated and implemented key based sharded database prototypes using MYSQL Cluster version 7.3. Our sharding deployed across four data node clusters. While traditional horizontal partitioning techniques address performance by dividing the rows into different tables, these tables are separate tables and may not work together as a single logical unit. Even if the data is logically divided into horizontal partitions, the table still remains on a single shared everything storage area network (SAN). The data will be available and scalable in the event of unexpected disaster.

The data in our clusters dispersed and replicated amongst the data nodes. If a particular data node is down, the replicated data node will continue to deliver the content until that node is brought back online. This creates an ideal environment for high uptime and ease of adding more data nodes without affecting the database. The use of multiple SQL nodes allows for redundancy and avoids a single point of failure when accessing the data residing within the data nodes. Through replication and redundancy, the entire sharded architecture exhibits availability, scalability, and agility and will be very useful for big data management on the cloud. The results of our data mining work show that sharding can aid in data mining.

REFERENCES

Abadi, D. (2009). Data Management in the Cloud: Limitations and Opportunities. *Bulletin of the IEEE Computer Society Technical Committee on Data Engineering*, *1-2*, 5–9.

Agrawal, R., Imielinski, T., & Swami, A. (1993). Mining association rules between sets of items in large databases. In *ACM SIGMOD Conference*. ACM Press. doi:10.1145/170035.170072

Agrawal, R., & Srikant, R. (1994). Fast algorithms for mining association rules in large databases. In *Proceedings of the 20th VLDB Conference*. Morgan Kaufmann.

Agrawal, S., Narasayya, V., & Yang, D. (2004). Integrating Vertical and Horizontal Partitioning into Automated Physical Database Design. In *SIGMOD*, (pp. 359-370). ACM.

Chang, F., Dean, J., Ghemawat S., Hsieh, W., Wallach D., Burrows, M., Chandra, T., Fikes, A., & Gruber R., (2006). Bigtable: A Distributed Storage System for Structured Data, *OSDI*, *1*(4-5), 11-13.

Codd, F. (1970). A Relational Model of Data for Large Shared Data Banks. *Communications of the ACM*, *13*(6), 377–387. doi:10.1145/362384.362685

CodeFutures Corp. (2010). *Database Sharding Whitepaper*. Retrieved from http://www.dbshards.com/articles/database-sharding-whitepapers/

Davies, A., & Fisk, H. (2006). *MySQL Clustering*. Academic Press.

Duong, Q., Goel, S., Hofman, J., & Vassilvitskii, S. (2013). *Sharding Social Networks*. ACM VLDB Endowment. doi:10.1145/2433396.2433424

Gabriel, G. (2002). *Atomic Transactions in Distributed Systems*. Institute of Informatics and Applied Mathematics University of Berne.

Guide to Scaling Web Databases with MySQL Cluster: Accelerating Innovation on the Web. (2011). Retrieved from http://www.oracle.com/us/products/mysql/scaling-web-databases-461055.pdf

Han, J., Kamber, M., & Pei, J. (2011). *Data Mining: Concepts and Techniques*. Morgan Kaufmann Publishers.

Hogan, M. (2015). *Shared-Disk vs. Shared-Nothing: Comparing Architectures for Clustered Databases*. Academic Press.

Krasuski, A., & Szczuka, M. (2011). *Knowledge Driven Query Sharding*. Academic Press.

Liu, G., Lu, H., Lou, W., Xu, Y., & Yu, J. X. (2004). Efficient mining of Frequent Patterns Using Ascending Frequency Ordered Prefix-Tree. *Data Mining and Knowledge Discovery*, *9*(3), 249–274. doi:10.1023/B:DAMI.0000040905.52966.1a

MySQL Cluster. (2014). Retrieved from http://dev.mysql.com/doc/mysql-cluster-excerpt/5.5/en/index.html

MySQL Cluster Benchmarks. (2013). Retrieved from http://www.mysql.com/why-mysql/benchmarks/mysql-cluster/

Obasanjo, D. (2009). *Building Scalable Databases: Pros and Cons of Various Database Sharding Schemes*. Retrieved from http://www.25hoursaday.com/weblog/2009/01/16/BuildingScalableDatabasesProsAndConsOfVariousDatabaseShardingSchemes.aspx

Pattishall, D. (2006). *Unorthodox approach to database design part 1 and 2*. Retrieved from http://mysqldba.blogspot.com/2006/10/unorthodox-approach-to-database-design.html

Pei, J., Han, J., & Lakshmanan, L. V. S. (2004). Pushing Convertible Constraints in Frequent Itemset Mining. *Data Mining and Knowledge Discovery*, *8*(3), 227–252. doi:10.1023/B:DAMI.0000023674.74932.4c

Stephens, S., Kruckenberg, M., Bouman, R., Smith, S., & Chang, S. (2007). *MySQL 5.1 Cluster DBA Certification Study Guide, Lulu Enterprises*. UK Ltd.

Tan, P.-N., SteinBach, M., & Kumar, V. (2006). Introduction to Data Mining. Addison Wesley.

KEY TERMS AND DEFINITIONS

ACID: Atomicity, Consistency, Isolation, Durability of data.

Association Rule Mining: A data mining algorithm that finds which piece of data is associated with which other pieces of data.

Big Data Analytics: Used to analyze Big Data.

Big Data: Used to refer to data sets so large or complex that traditional data processing applications fall inadequate.

Database Clusters: Data Partitions.

Database Sharding: A method of partitioning large data.

Horizontal Data Partitioning: A method of partitioning the data into manageable chunks.

ENDNOTES

[1]   http://www.mysql.com/downloads/cluster/, retrieved 4/12/14.

[2]   http://dev.mysql.com/doc/refman/5.5/en/mysql-cluster-ndbd- definition.html#ndbparam-ndbmtd-maxnoofexecutionthreads, retrieved 4/12/14.

[3]   http://www.fromdual.ch/mysql-cluster-lcp-gcp, retrieved 4/12/14.

[4]   www.cs.waikato.ac.nz/ml/weka, retrieved 4/12/14.

[5]   http://archive.ics.uci.edu/ml/datasets.html, retrieved 4/12/14.

[6]   ftp://ftp.ics.uci.edu/pub/machine-learning-databases/solar-flare, retrieved 4/12/14.

[7]   http://archive.ics.uci.edu/ml/datasets/Contraceptive+Method+Choice, retrieved 4/12/14.

[8]   http://archive.ics.uci.edu/ml/datasets/El+Nino, retrieved 4/12/14.

[9]   http://archive.ics.uci.edu/ml/datasets/Internet+Usage+Data, retrieved 4/12/14.

[10]   http://archive.ics.uci.edu/ml/datasets/US+Census+Data+%281990%29, retrieved 4/12/14.

[11]   http://www.baybenthos.versar.com/data.htm, retrieved 4/12/14.

[12]   http://www.stat.ucla.edu/projects/datasets/seed-ant.dat, retrieved 4/12/14.
       http://www.stat.ucla.edu/projects/datasets/thatch-ant.dat, retrieved 4/12/14.
       http://www.stat.ucla.edu/projects/datasets/ant-explanation.html, retrieved 4/12/14.

[13]   http://www.wefeelfine.org, retrieved 4/12/14.

[14]   www.cs.waikato.ac.nz/ml/weka, retrieved 4/12/14.

[15]   http://www.slideshare.net/andrewjamesmorgan/mysql-cluster-introduction, retrieved 6/12/15.

[16]   https://dev.mysql.com/doc/refman/5.0/en/mysql-cluster-overview.html, retrieved 6/12/15.

Compilation of References

Ababneh, I. (2001). Job scheduling and contiguous processor allocation for three-dimensional mesh multicomputers. *AMSE Advances in Modelling & Analysis*, *6*(4), 43–58.

Ababneh, I. (2006). An efficient free-list submesh Allocation Scheme for two-dimensional mesh-connected multicomputers. *Journal of Systems and Software*, *79*(8), 1168–1179. doi:10.1016/j.jss.2006.01.019

Ababneh, I. (2009). On submesh allocation for 2D mesh multicomputers using the free-list approach: Global placement schemes. *Performance Evaluation*, *66*(2), 105–120. doi:10.1016/j.peva.2008.10.001

Ababneh, I., & Bani-Mohammad, S. (2003). Non contiguous processor allocation for three-dimensional mesh multicomputers. *Advances in Modelling and Analysis Journal*, *8*(2), 51–63.

Ababneh, I., Bani-Mohammad, S., & Al Smadi, M. (2015). Corner-Boundary Processor Allocation for 3D Mesh-connected Multicomputers. *International Journal of Cloud Applications and Computing*, *5*(1), 1–13. doi:10.4018/ijcac.2015010101

Abadi, D. (2009). Data Management in the Cloud: Limitations and Opportunities. *Bulletin of the IEEE Computer Society Technical Committee on Data Engineering*, *1-2*, 5–9.

AbdelSalam, H., Maly, K., Mukkamala, R., Zubair, M. &Kaminsky, D. (2009). Towards energy efficient change management in a cloud computing environment. *AIMS*, 161-166.

AcceassMethod. (n.d.). Retrieved from http://ecomputernotes.com/fundamental/input-output-and-memory/what-is-access-method-explain-different-type-of-access-methods

Ács, B., Llorà, X., Capitanu, B., Auvil, L., Tcheng, D., Haberman, M., ... Welge, M. (2011). Meandre Data-Intensive Application Infrastructure: Extreme Scalability for Cloud and / or Grid Computing. In New Frontiers in Artificial Intelligence (pp. 233–242). Academic Press.

Agrawal, R., Imielinski, T., & Swami, A. (1993). Mining association rules between sets of items in large databases. In *ACM SIGMOD Conference*. ACM Press. doi:10.1145/170035.170072

Agrawal, S., Narasayya, V., & Yang, D. (2004). Integrating Vertical and Horizontal Partitioning into Automated Physical Database Design. In *SIGMOD*, (pp. 359-370). ACM.

Agrawal, R., & Srikant, R. (1994). Fast algorithms for mining association rules in large databases. In *Proceedings of the 20th VLDB Conference*. Morgan Kaufmann.

Ahuja, S., & Mani, S. (2013). Empirical performance analysis of HPC benchmarks across variations of cloud computing. *International Journal of Cloud Applications and Computing*, *3*(1), 13–26. doi:10.4018/ijcac.2013010102

Ahuja, S., & Rolli, A. (2011). Survey of the state-of-the-art of cloud computing. *International Journal of Cloud Applications and Computing*, *1*(4), 34–43. doi:10.4018/ijcac.2011100103

Ahuja, S., & Sridharan, S. (2012). Performance evaluation of hypervisors for cloud computing. *International Journal of Cloud Applications and Computing*, 2(3), 26–67. doi:10.4018/ijcac.2012070102

Ajzen, I., & Fishbein, M. (1980). *Understanding Attitudes and Predicting Social Behavior*. Englewood Cliffs, NJ: Prentice-Hall.

Akyuz, G. A., & Gursoy, G. (2011). Role and importance of information technology (IT). In supply chain collaboration. In Proceedings of *IX. International Logistics and Supply Chain Congress*. LODER.

Akyuz, G. A., & Gursoy, G. (2010). Taxonomy of collaboration in supply chain management. In *Proceedings of VIII. International Logistics and Supply Chain Congress*. LODER.

Akyuz, G. A., & Rehan, M. (2013). A Generic, cloud-based representation of supply chains. *International Journal of Cloud Applications and Computing*, 3(2), 12–20. doi:10.4018/ijcac.2013040102

Albers-Miller, N. D.Albers –Miller. (1999). Consumer misbehaviour: Why people buy illicit goods. *Journal of Consumer Marketing*, 16(3), 273–287. doi:10.1108/07363769910271504

Albrecht, M., Donnelly, P., Bui, P., & Thain, D. (2012). Makeflow: a portable abstraction for data intensive computing on clusters, clouds, and grids. In *Proceedings of the 1st ACM SIGMOD Workshop on Scalable Workflow Execution Engines and Technologies* (SWEET '12). doi:10.1145/2443416.2443417

Alford, T. (2009). *The Economics of Cloud Computing*. Booz Allen Hamilton.

Algorithm, A. (2001). Retrieved from http://www.cs.rit.edu/~ark/lectures/gc/03_03_03.html

Alhaj, A., Mellor, J., & Awan, I. (2009). Performance evaluation of secure call admission control for mul-ticlass internet services. In *Proceedings of the 23rd IEEE-AINA'09*. Bradford, UK: IEEE.

Aljawarneh, S. (2011). Cloud Security Engineering: Avoiding Security Threats the Right Way. *Cloud Applications and Computing*, 1(2), 64–70. doi:10.4018/ijcac.2011040105

Aljawarneh, S. (2011, March). A web engineering security methodology for e-learning systems. *Network Security Journal, Elsevier*, 2011(3), 12–16. doi:10.1016/S1353-4858(11)70026-5

Al-Masri, E., & Qusay, H. (2007).QoS-based Discovery and Ranking of Web services. In Proceedings of the 16th International Conference on Computer Communications and Networks, IEEE (ICCCN 2007). Honolulu, HI: IEEE.

Al-Shargabi, B., El Shiekh, A., & Sabri, A. (2010). Web Service Composition Survey: State of the Art Review. *Recent Patent on Computer Science Journal*, 3(2), 91–107. doi:10.1109/ICCCN.2007.4317873

Altschuller, S., & Benbunan-Fich, E. (2009). Is music downloading the new prohibition? What students reveal through an ethical dilemma. *Ethics and Information Technology*, 11(1), 49–56. doi:10.1007/s10676-008-9179-1

Amazon. (2010). *Amazon Elastic Compute Cloud (Amazon EC2)*. Available at: http://aws.amazon.com/ec2/

Amazon. (2010). *Amazon elastic compute cloud*, Retrieved February 15, 2010 from www.amazon.com

Amazon. (2010). *Amazon Web Services: Overview of Security Processes*. Retrieved from awsmedia.s3.amazonaws.com/pdf/AWS_Security_Whitepaper.pdf

Amazon.com Inc. (n.d.). *EC2 Instance Types*. Retrieved from http://aws.amazon.com/ec2/instance-types/

Amazon.com Inc. (n.d.). *EC2 Pricing*. Retrieved from http://aws.amazon.com/ec2/pricing/

Amazon.com Inc. (n.d.). *Elastic Compute Cloud*. Retrieved from http://aws.amazon.com/ec2/

AmazonCloudsearch. (2015). Retrieved from http://docs.aws.amazon.com/cloudsearch/latest/developerguide/what-is-cloudsearch.html

Anbazhagan, M. &Arun, N. (2002). *Understanding quality of service for Web services.* IBM Developer Works.

Anderson, R. (2001). *Security engineering: A guide to building dependable distributed systems.* John Wiley & Sons.

Antonio, C., Mario, F., & Luca, F. (2014). VM consolidation: A real case based on openstack cloud. *Future Generation Computer Systems, 32*(1), 118–127.

Aral, S., Sundararajan, A., & Xin, M. (2010). Developing competitive advantage in the cloud: Qualitative findings. *Harvard Business Review.* Retrieved April 20, 2013, from http://blogs.hbr.org/research/2010/12/developing-competitive-advanta.html

Ardagna, D., Trubian, M., & Zhang, L. (2005). SLA based profit optimization in multi-tier systems. In *Proceedings of the 4th IEEE International Symposium on Network Computing and Applications,* (pp. 263–266). doi:10.1109/NCA.2005.48

Aridor, Y., Domany, T., Goldshmidt, O., Moreira, J., & Shmueli, E. (2005). Resource allocation and utilization in the BlueGene/L supercomputer. *IBM Journal of Research and Development, 49*(2/3), 425–436. doi:10.1147/rd.492.0425

Armbrust, M., & Fox, A. (2009). *Above the Clouds: A Berkeley View of Cloud Computing.* Retrieved from http://www.eecs.berkeley.edu/Pubs/TechRpts/2009/EECS-2009-28.pdf

Armbrust, M., Fox, A., Griffith, R., Joseph, A. D., Katz, R., Konwinski, A., . . . Zaharia, M. (2010). A view of cloud computing. *Commun. ACM, 53,* 50–58. Available: http://doi.acm.org/10.1145/1721654.1721672

Armbrust, M., Stoica, I., Zaharia, M., Fox, A., Griffith, R., Joseph, A. D., & Rabkin, A. et al. (2010). A view of cloud computing. *Communications of the ACM, 53*(4), 50–58. doi:10.1145/1721654.1721672

Arthur, C. (2010). *Google's ChromeOS means losing control of data, warns GNU founder Richard Stallman.* Retrieved from http://www.guardian.co.uk/technology/blog/2010/dec/14/chrome-os-richard-stallman-warning

Ateib, M. T. (2010). Agent Based Negotiation In E-cmmerce.*International Symposium on Information Technology 2010(ITSim 2010).* IEEE. doi:10.1109/ITSIM.2010.5561565

Athas, W., & Seitz, C. (1988). Multicomputers: Message-passing concurrent computers. *IEEE Computer, 21*(8), 9–24. doi:10.1109/2.73

Atzori, L., Iera, A., & Morabito, G. (2010). The Internet of Things: A survey. *Computer Networks, 54*(15), 2787–2805. doi:10.1016/j.comnet.2010.05.010

Aungst, S. G., & Wilson, D. T. (2005). A primer for navigating the shoals of applying wireless technology to marketing problems. *Journal of Business and Industrial Marketing, 20*(2/3), 59–69. doi:10.1108/08858620510583650

Aymerich, F. M., Fenu, G., & Surcis, S. (2008). An approach to a cloud computing network. In *1st International Conference on the Applications of Digital Information and Web Technologies,* (pp. 113-118). doi:10.1109/ICADIWT.2008.4664329

Baghaei, N., & Hunt, R. (2004). IEEE 802.11 wireless LAN security performance using multiple clients. In *Proceedings of the 12th IEEE International Confer-ence on Networks* (ICON 2004). IEEE.

Bajaj, R., & Agrawal, D. (2004). Improving scheduling of tasks in a heterogeneous environment. *IEEE Transactions on Parallel and Distributed Systems, 15*(2), 107–118. doi:10.1109/TPDS.2004.1264795

Baker, J., Bond, C., Corbett, J., & Furman, J. (2011). Megastore: Providing Scalable, Highly Available Storage for Interactive Services. *CIDR,* 223–234.

Bakhshi, M., & Hashemi, M. (2012). User-Centric Optimization for Constraint Web Service Composition using a Fuzzy-guided Genetic Algorithm System. *International Journal on Web Service Computing, 3*(3), 1–15. doi:10.5121/ijwsc.2012.3301

Bala, M. I., & Vij, S. (2013). Automated Negotiation and Behavior Prediction. *International Journal of Engineering Research and Technology, 2*(6), 1832 – 1838.

Bala, M. I., Vij, S., & Mukhopadhyay, D. (2013). Negotiation Life Cycle: An Approach in E-negotiation with Prediction. *48th Annual Convention of the Computer Society of India.CSI 2013 Proceedings, Visakhapatnam, India.* Springer-Verlag Germany.

Bandura, A. (1986). *Social Foundations of Thought and Action: A Social Cognitive Theory.* Prentice-Hall.

Bandura, A. (1989). Human agency in social cognitive theory. *The American Psychologist, 44*(9), 1175–1184. doi:10.1037/0003-066X.44.9.1175 PMID:2782727

Bandura, A., & Adams, N. (1977). Analysis of self-efficacy theory of behavioral change. *Cognitive Therapy and Research, 1*(4), 287–310. doi:10.1007/BF01663995

Bani-Mohammad, S., Ould-Khaoua, M., Ababneh, I., Mackenzie, & Lewis, M. (2007a). An efficient processor allocation strategy thatmaintains a high degree of contiguity among processors in 2D mesh connected multicomputers. In *Proceedings of the ACS/IEEE International Conference on Computer Systems and Applications (AICCSA 2007).* IEEE. doi:10.1109/AICCSA.2007.370743

Bani-Mohammad, S., Ould-Khaoua, M., Ababneh, I., Mackenzie, & Lewis, M. (2007b). A fast and efficient processor allocation strategy which combines a contiguous and non-contiguous processor allocation algorithms. Technical Report, TR-2007-229, DCS Technical Report Series, January, Department of Computing Science, University of Glasgow.

Bani-Mohammad, S., & Ababneh, I. (2013). On the performance of non-contiguous allocation for common communication patterns in 2D mesh-connected multicomputers. *Journal of Simulation Modelling Practice and Theory, 32,* 155–165. doi:10.1016/j.simpat.2011.08.007

Bani-Mohammad, S., Ould-Khaoua, M., Ababneh, I., & Machenzie, L. (2006). A Fast and Efficient Strategy for Sub-mesh Allocation with Minimal Allocation Overhead in 3D Mesh Connected Multicomputers. *Ubiquitous Computing and Communication Journal, 1*(1), 26–36.

Bani-Mohammad, S., Ould-Khaoua, M., Ababneh, I., & Mackhenzie, M. (2009). Comparative evaluation of contiguous allocation strategies on 3D Mesh Multicomputers. *Journal of Systems and Software, 82*(2), 307–318. doi:10.1016/j.jss.2008.06.033

Barnet, Y., Ford, P., Yavatkar, R., Baker, F., Zhang, L., Speer, M., ... (2000). *A framework for integrated services operation over diffserv networks.* Retrieved from http://tools.ietf.org/html/rfc2998

Beloglazov, A., Abawajy, J., & Buyya, R. (2012). Energy-aware resource allocation heuristics for efficient management of data centers for cloud computing. *Future Generation Computer Systems, Elsevier, 28*(5), 755–768. doi:10.1016/j.future.2011.04.017

Belton, V., & Stewart, T. (2002). Multi Criteria Decision Analysis – An Integrated Approach. Kluwer.

Bentz, B. (2013). *How cloud technology can transform supply chain performance?* Retrieved September 15, 2014, from http://www.cio.com/article/2385117/supply-chain-management/how-cloud-technology-can-transform-supply-chain-performance.html

Bertot, J. C., Gorham, U., Jaeger, P. T., Sarin, L. C., & Choi, H. (2014). Big data, open government and e-government: Issues, policies and recommendations. *Information Polity, 19*(1), 5–16.

Bertot, J., Jaeger, P., & Mcclure, C. (2008) Citizen-Centered E-Government Services: Benefits, Costs, and Research Needs.*9th Annual International Digital Government Research Conference*(pp.137-142). Academic Press.

Bharathi, Sandeep, Kumar, & Poornima. (2010). Performance factors of cloud computing data centers using M/G/m/ m+r queuing systems. *IOSR Journal of Engineering, 2*(9), 6-10.

Bicer, T., Chiu, D., & Agrawal, G. (2012). Time and Cost Sensitive Data-Intensive Computing on Hybrid Clouds. In *2012 12th IEEE/ACM International Symposium on Cluster, Cloud and Grid Computing (CCGrid'12),* (pp. 636-643). doi:10.1109/CCGrid.2012.95

Bixin, L., Shunhui, J., Dong, Q., Hareton, L., & Gongyuan, G. (2013). Verifying the Concurrent Properties in BPEL Based Web Service Composition Process. Network and Service Management. *IEEE Transactions on, 10*(4), 410–424.

Blocking, S., &Cylinders, H. (2015). Retrieved from http://dis-dpcs.wikispaces.com/6.2.1+Blocking,+Sectors,+Cylin ders,+Heads

Blum, A. (2004). UDDI as an Extended Web Services Registry: Versioning, quality of service, and more. *SOA World Magazine, 4*(6).

Bojanova, I. (2011). Analysis of Cloud Computing Delivery Architecture Models. In*Proceedings of the IEEE Workshops of International Conference on Advanced Information Networking and Applications,* (pp.453–458). doi:10.1109/ WAINA.2011.74

Bojanova, I., Zhang, J., & Voas, J. (2013). Cloud computing. *IT Professional, 15*(2), 12–14. doi:10.1109/MITP.2013.26

Boneh, D., & Waters, B. (2007). Conjunctive, subset, and range queries on encrypted data. In *Theory of cryptography* (pp. 535–554). Springer Berlin Heidelberg. doi:10.1007/978-3-540-70936-7_29

Bono, S. C., Green, M., Stubblefield, A., Juels, A., Rubin, A. D., & Szydlo, M. (2005). Security analysis of a cryptographically-enabled RFID device. In *SSYM'05: Proceedings of the 14th conference on USENIX Security Symposium.* Berkeley, CA: USENIX Association.

Booth, D., Hass, H., Mccabe, F., Newcomer, E., Champion, M., Ferris, C., & Orchard, D. (2005). *Web services architecture, W3C Working Group Note 11 February 2004', W3C Technical Reports and Publications.* Retrieved from http:// www.w3.org/TR/ws-arch/

Bouarara, H. A., Rahmani, A., Hamou, R. M., & Amine, A. (2014, June). Machine learning tool and meta-heuristic based on genetic algorithms for plagiarism detection over mail service. In *Computer and Information Science (ICIS), 2014 IEEE/ACIS 13th International Conference on* (pp. 157-162). IEEE. doi:10.1109/ICIS.2014.6912125

Bouarara, H. A., Hamou, R. M., & Amine, A. (2014). Text Clustering using Distances Combination by Social Bees: Towards 3D Visualisation Aspect. *International Journal of Information Retrieval Research, 4*(3), 34–53.

Bouarara, H. A., Hamou, R. M., Rahmani, A., & Amine, A. (2014, 33). Rahmani, A., Abdelmalek A., Application of Meta-Heuristics Methods on PIR Protocols Over Cloud Storage Services. *International Journal of Cloud Applications and Computing, 4*(3), 1–19. doi:10.4018/ijcac.2014070101

Bradshaw, S., Millard, C., & Walden, I. (2011). Contracts for clouds: Comparison and analysis of the terms and conditions of cloud computing services. *International Journal of Law and Information Technology, 19*(3), 187–223. doi:10.1093/ ijlit/ear005

Braun. (n.d.). Retrieved from https://code.google.com/p/hcsp-chc/source/browse/trunk/AE/ProblemInstances/ HCSP/ Braun_et_al/u_c_hihi.0?r=93

Braun, T., Siegel, H., Beck, N., Boloni, L., Maheswaran, M., Reuther, A., & Freund, R. et al. (2001). A comparison of eleven static heuristics for mapping a class of independent tasks onto heterogeneous distributed computing systems. *Journal of Parallel and Distributed Computing, 61*(6), 810–837. doi:10.1006/jpdc.2000.1714

Bringer, J., & Chabanne, H. (2012). Embedding edit distance to enable private keyword search. *Human-centric Computing and Information Sciences, 2*(1), 1–12. doi:10.1186/PREACCEPT-1253053215890607

Brunette, G., & Mogull, R. (2009). *Security Guidance for critical areas of focus in Cloud Computing V2. 1', CSA (Cloud Security Alliance).* Retrieved from http://www.cloudsecurityalliance.org/guidance/csaguide.v2

B-tree. (2014). Retrieved from http://en.wikipedia.org/wiki/B-tree

Buyya, R., Broberg, J., & Goscinski, A. (2011). *Cloud computing: Principles and paradigms.* Hoboken, NJ: John Wiley & Sons. doi:10.1002/9780470940105

Buyya, R., Ranjan, R., & Calheiros, R. N. (2010). 'InterCloud: Utility-Oriented Federation of Cloud Computing Environments for Scaling of Application Services', *Algorithms and Architectures for Parallel Processing. Lecture Notes in Computer Science, 6081,* 13–31. doi:10.1007/978-3-642-13119-6_2

Buyya, R., Yeo, C. S., Venugopal, S., Broberg, J., & Brandic, I. (2009). Cloud Computing and Emerging IT Platforms: Vision, Hype, and Reality for Delivering Computing as the 5th Utility. *Future Generation Computer Systems, 25*(6), 599–616. doi:10.1016/j.future.2008.12.001

Buyya, R., Yeo, C. S., & Venugopal, V. (2008).Vision, hype and reality for delivering IT services as computing utilities. In *10th IEEE International Conference on High Performance Computing and Communications,* (pp. 5-13). IEEE.

Buzen, J. P., & Bondi, A. B. (1983). The response times of priority classes under preemptive resume in M/M/m queues. *Operations Research, 31*(3), 456–465. doi:10.1287/opre.31.3.456

Cabinet Office. (2010). *Government ICT Strategy: smarter, cheaper, greener.* London: Cabinet Office, January.

Calder, B. J., Philips, L. W., & Tyhout, A. (1981). Designing research for application. *The Journal of Consumer Research, 8*(September), 197–207. doi:10.1086/208856

Cantisani, A. (2006). Technological innovation processes revisited. *Technovation, 26*(11), 1294–1301. doi:10.1016/j. technovation.2005.10.003

Cappelli, D. M., Trzeciak, R. F., & Moore, A. B. (2006). *Insider Threats in the SLDC: Lessions Learned From Actual Incidents of Fraud: Theft of Sensitive Information, and IT Sabotage, Carnegie Mellon University.*

Cárdenas, R. G., & Sanchez, E. (2005). Security Challenges of Distributed e-Learning Systems. *ISSADS: Springer, Series Lecture Notes in Computer Science, 3563.* Retrieved from http://dblp.uni-trier.de/db/conf/issads/issads2005. html#CardenasS05

Carusi, A., & De Grandis, G. (2012). The ethical work that regulations will not do. *Information Communication and Society, 15*(1), 124–141. doi:10.1080/1369118X.2011.634015

Castro-Leon, E. (2014). Consumerization in the IT Service Ecosystem. *IEEE IT Professional, 16*(5), 20–27. doi:10.1109/ MITP.2014.66

Catteddu, D. (2010). *Cloud Computing: benefits, risks and recommendations for information security.* Berlin: Springer.

Chandrasekaran, S., Miller, J., Silver, G., Arpinar, B., & Sheth, A. (2003). Performance analysis and simulation of composite web services. *International Journal of Electron Commer Bus Media.*, *13*(2), 18–30.

Chang, F., Dean, J., Ghemawat S., Hsieh, W., Wallach D., Burrows, M., Chandra, T., Fikes, A., & Gruber R., (2006). Bigtable: A Distributed Storage System for Structured Data, *OSDI*, *1*(4-5), 11-13.

Chang, J. (2011, October-December). A framework of analysing the impact of cloud computing on local government in the UK. *International Journal of Cloud Applications and Computing*, *1*(4), 25–33. doi:10.4018/ijcac.2011100102

Chang, K., Kim, G. T., Samtani, S., Staikos, A., Muzzelo, L., & Palumbo, J. (2006). A study on the call admission and preemption control algorithms for secure wireless ad hoc networks using IPSec tunneling. In *Proceedings of the MILCOM 2006*. doi:10.1109/MILCOM.2006.302177

Chan, S., & Lu, M. (2004). Understanding Internet banking adoption and use behavior: A Hong Kong perspective. *Journal of Global Information Management*, *12*(3), 21–43. doi:10.4018/jgim.2004070102

Charlesworth, A. (2012). Data protection, freedom of information and ethical review committees. *Information Communication and Society*, *15*(1), 85–103. doi:10.1080/1369118X.2011.637572

Chen, H., Wang, F., Helian, N., & Akanmu, G. (2013). User-priority guided min-min scheduling algorithm for load balancing in cloud computing. In *National Conference on Parallel Computing Technologies* (pp. 1-8). Academic Press.

Cheng, F., Young, S. L., Akella, R., & Tang, X. T. (2011). A meta-modelling service paradigm for cloud computing and its implementation. *South African Journal of Industrial Engineering*, *22*(2), 151–160. doi:10.7166/22-2-22

Chen, L. P., Ha, W. T., & Zhang, G. J. (2013). Reliable execution based on CPN and skyline optimization for web service composition. *TheScientificWorldJournal*, *2013*, 1–10. PMID:23935431

Chiang, R. C., & Huang, H. H. (2014). TRACON : Interference-Aware Scheduling for Data-Intensive Applications in Virtualized Environments, *2011 International Conference for High Performance Computing, Networking, Storage and Analysis (SC)*, *25*(5), 1-12. doi:10.1109/TPDS.2013.82

Chiu, C., Hsu, M., & Wang, E. (2008). Understanding knowledge sharing in virtual communities: An integration of social capital and social cognitive theories. *Decision Support Systems*, *42*(3), 1872–1888. doi:10.1016/j.dss.2006.04.001

Chonka, A., Xiang, Y., Zhou, W., & Bonti, A. (2011). Cloud security defence to protect cloud computing against HTTP-DOS and VML-DOS attacks. *Journal of Network and Computer Applications*, *34*(4), 1097–1107. doi:10.1016/j.jnca.2010.06.004

Choo, H., Yoo, S., & Youn, H.-Y. (2000). Processor scheduling and allocation for 3D torus multicomputer systems. *IEEE Transactions on Parallel and Distributed Systems*, *11*(5), 475–484. doi:10.1109/71.852400

Chow, R., Golle, P., Jakobsson, M., Shi, E., Staddon, J., & Masuoka, R., Molina, & J. (2009). Controlling Data in the Cloud: Outsourcing Computation without Outsourcing Control, In *Proceedings of ACM Workshop on Cloud Computing Security (CCSW 2009)*. Chicago, IL: ACM. doi:10.1145/1655008.1655020

Chow, R., Golle, P., Jakobsson, M., Shi, E., Staddon, J., Masuoka, R., & Molina, J. (2009). Controlling data in the cloud: outsourcing computation without outsourcing control. In *Proceedings of the 2009 ACM workshop on Cloud computing security* (CCSW '09). ACM. http://doi.acm.org/10.1145/1655008.1655020

Chuang, P.-J., & Tzeng, N.-F. (1994). Allocating Precise Submeshes in Mesh Connected Systems. *IEEE Transactions on Parallel and Distributed Systems*, *5*(2), 211–217. doi:10.1109/71.265948

Cloud Standards Customer Council. (2014). *The Supply chain cloud: Your guide to contracts standards solutions.* Retrieved September 5, 2014 from http://www.cloud-council.org/TheSupplyChainCloud.pdf

Clouds, P. (2014). *Personal Clouds.* Retrieved June 10, 2015, from http://personal-clouds.org/wiki/Main_Page

CloudStorageForCloudComputing. (2009). Retrieved from https://www.ogf.org/Resources/documents/CloudStorage-ForCloudComputing.pdf

Codd, F. (1970). A Relational Model of Data for Large Shared Data Banks. *Communications of the ACM, 13*(6), 377–387. doi:10.1145/362384.362685

CodeFutures Corp. (2010). *Database Sharding Whitepaper.* Retrieved from http://www.dbshards.com/articles/database-sharding-whitepapers/

Columbus, L. (2014). *Where cloud computing is improving supply chain performance: Lessons learned from SCM world.* Retrieved September 9, 2014, from http://www.forbes.com/sites/louiscolumbus/2014/02/12/where-cloud-computing-is-improving-supply-chain-performance-lessons-learned-from-scm-world/

Compeau, D., Higgins, C., & Huff, S. (1999). Social cognitive theory and individual reactions to computing technology: A longitudinal study. *Management Information Systems Quarterly, 23*(2), 145–158. doi:10.2307/249749

Computing, C. (2009). Retrieved from http://www.johnhagel.com/cloudperspectives.pdf

Coombs, R., Saviotti, P., & Walsh, V. (1987). *Economics and Technological Change.* Rownam & Littlefield.

Corbett, J. C., Dean, J., Epstein, M., Fikes, A., Frost, C., Furman, J. J., … Woodford, D. (2012). Spanner : Google's Globally-Distributed Database. In *Proceedings of OSDI'12: Tenth Symposium on Operating System Design and Implementaton,* (pp. 251–264). doi:10.1145/2491245

Cormen, T. H., Leiserson, C. E., Rivest, R., & Stein, C. (2001). *Introduction to Algorithms.* McGraw-Hill.

Courtin, G. (2013). Supply chain and the future of applications. *SCM World Research Report.* Retrieved September 5, 2014, from http://www.e2open.com/assets/pdf/papers-and-reports/SCMWorld-Supply-Chain-and-the-future-of-Applications.pdf

CPNI. (2010). *Information security briefing 01/2010 cloud computing.* Retrieved from www.cpni.gov.uk/Documents/.../2010/2010007-ISB_cloud_computing.pdf

Cray Inc. (2010a). *Cray XE6 Datasheet.* Retrieved September 9, 2014, form http://www.cray.com/Assets/PDF/products/xe/CrayXE6Brochure.pdf

Cray Inc. (2010b). *Cray XE6m Datasheet.* Retrieved September 9, 2014, form http://www.cray.com/Assets/PDF/products/xe/CrayXE6mBrochure.pdf

Dasarathy, B., Gadgil, S., Vaidyanathan, R., Par-meswaran, K., Coan, B. A., Conarty, M., & Bhanot, V. (2005). Network QoS assurance in a multi-layer adaptive resource management scheme for mission-critical application using CORBA middleware framework. In *Proceedings of the 11th Real Time and Embedded Technology and Applications Symposium.* doi:10.1109/RTAS.2005.34

Das, R. K., Patnaik, S., & Misro, A. K. (2011). Adoption of cloud computing in e-governance. In *Advanced Computing* (pp. 161–172). Berlin: Springer. doi:10.1007/978-3-642-17881-8_16

Dastjerdi, A. V., & Buyya, R. (2012). An Autonomous Reliability-aware Negotiation Strategy for Cloud Computing Environments.*12th IEEE/ACM International Symposium on Cluster, Cloud and Grid Computing.* IEEE. doi:10.1109/CCGrid.2012.101

Data Search Method for HDD. (2003). Retrieved from http://www.fujitsu-ten.com/business/technicaljournal/pdf/20-3.pdf

Davies, A., & Fisk, H. (2006). *MySQL Clustering*. Academic Press.

Davis, F. (1989). Perceived usefulness, perceived ease of use and user acceptance of information technology. *Management Information Systems Quarterly*, *13*(3), 319–339. doi:10.2307/249008

De Rose, C. A. F., Heiss, H.-U., & Linnert, B. (2007). Distributed Dynamic processor Allocation for Multicomputers. *Parallel Computing*, *33*(3), 145–158. doi:10.1016/j.parco.2006.11.010

Dean, J., & Ghemawat, S. (2004). MapReduce : Simplified Data Processing on Large Clusters. In *6th Symposium on Operating Systems Design and Implementation, OSDI '04*, (pp. 137–149). OSDI.

Definition, H. (2015). Retrieved from http://searchsqlserver.techtarget.com/definition/hashing

Deochake, S., Kanth, S., Chakraborty, S., Sarode, S., Potdar, V., & Mukhopadhyay, D. (2012). HENRI: High Efficiency Negotiation-based Robust Interface for Multi-party Multi-issue Negotiation over the Internet. *CUBE 2012 International IT Conference, Pune, India*. ACM Digital Library.

Desmarais, R. (2013). *Adaptive solutions to resource provisioning and task allocation problems for cloud computing.* (Ph. D. Thesis). University of Victoria.

Devargas, M. (1993). *Network security*. Manchester, UK: NCC Blackwell.

Developed draft strawman DSCP mapping for GIG enterprise IP networks. (n.d.). Academic Press.

Devis, R. H. (1966). Waiting time distribution of a multi-server priority queueing model. *Operations Research*, *14*(1), 133–136. doi:10.1287/opre.14.1.133

Di Maio, A. (2009a, June). Cloud computing in government: private, public, both or none? *Gartner*.

Di Maio, A. (2009b, September). GSA launches Apps.gov: what it means to government IT leaders? *Gartner*.

Di Maio, A. (2009c, June). Government in the cloud: Much more than computing. *Gartner*.

Digital Britain. (2009). *Final report, presented to Parliament in June 2009*. London: The Stationery Office.

Dillon, T. (2010). Cloud Computing: Issues and Challenges. In *Proceedings of the 24th IEEE International Conference on Advanced Information Networking and Applications*, (pp.27–33). doi:10.1109/AINA.2010.187

Disterer, G., & Kleiner, C. (2013). Using Mobile Devices with BYOD. *International Journal of Web Portals*, *5*(4), 33–45. doi:10.4018/ijwp.2013100103

Dom, B., Eiron, I., Cozzi, A., & Zhang, Y. (2003). Graph-based ranking algorithms for e-mail expertise analysis. *Proceedings of the 8th ACM SIGMOD workshop on Research issues in data mining and knowledge discovery* (pp 42-48). San Diego, CA: ACM. doi:10.1145/882082.882093

Domini, M. (2012). Impact of cloud computing on SCM. Gartner Group. *InformationWeek*. Retrieved January 20, 2013, from http://www.informationweek.in/cloud_computing/12-09 26/impact_of_cloud_computing_on_supply_chain_management.aspx

Dorigo, M., Maniezzo, V., & Colorni, A. (1996). Ant system: optimization by a colony of cooperating agents. Systems, Man, and Cybernetics, Part B: Cybernetics. *IEEE Transactions on*, *26*(1), 29–41.

Duong, Q., Goel, S., Hofman, J., & Vassilvitskii, S. (2013). *Sharding Social Networks*. ACM VLDB Endowment. doi:10.1145/2433396.2433424

El Hadad, J., Manouvrier, M., & Rukoz, M. (2010). TQoS: Transactional and QoS-Aware Selection Algorithm for Automatic Web Service Composition. *IEEE Transactions on Services Computing.*, *3*(1), 73–85. doi:10.1109/TSC.2010.5

Erdil, D. C. (2012). Autonomic cloud resource sharing for intercloud federations. *Future Generation Computer Systems*, *28*(2), 358–367.

Erl, T., Mahmood, Z., & Puttini, R. (2013). *Cloud computing: Concepts, technology & architecture.* Upper Saddle River, NJ: Prentice Hall.

Farber, D. (2008). *The new geek chic: Data centers.* CNET News.

Ferry, N., Rossini, A., Chauvel, F., & Solberg, A. (2013). Towards model-driven provisioning, deployment, monitoring, and adaptation of multi-cloud systems. In *Proceedings of 2013 IEEE Sixth International Conference on Cloud Computing*, (pp. 887 - 894). doi:10.1109/CLOUD.2013.133

Fishbein, M., & Ajzen, I. (1975). *Belief, Attitude, Intention, and Behavior: An Introduction to Theory and Research.* Reading, MA: Addison-Wesley.

Folkerts, E., Alexandrov, A., Sachs, K., Iosup, A., Markl, V., & Tosun, C. (2012). Benchmarking in the cloud: What it should, can, and cannot be. *4th TPC Technology Conference (TPCTC)*, (pp. 173-188). TPC.

Forell, T., Milojicic, D., & Talwar, V. (2011). Cloud management challenges and opportunities. In *IEEE International Symposium on Parallel and Distributed.* (pp. 881-889). IEEE.

Foster, I. (1995). *Designing and Building Parallel Programs, Concepts and Tools for Parallel Software Engineering.* Boston, MA: Addison-Wesley Longman Publishing Co.

Foster, I., Zhao, Y., Raicu, I., & Lu, S. (2008). Cloud computing and grid computing 360-degree compared. In *Grid Computing Environments Workshop.* doi:10.1109/GCE.2008.4738445

Freestone, O., & Mitchell, V.-W. (2004). Generation Y attitudes towards e-ethics and internet-related misbehaviours. *Journal of Business Ethics*, *54*(2), 121–128. doi:10.1007/s10551-004-1571-0

Freyne, J., Smyth, B., Coyle, M., Balfe, E., & Briggs, P. (2004). Further Experiments on Collaborative Ranking in Community-Based Web Search. *Artificial Intelligence Review*, *21*(3-4), 229–252. doi:10.1023/B:AIRE.0000036257.77059.40

Fuerst, C. (2014). *Tips for evaluating cloud-based supply chain management software.* Retrieved September 13, 2014, from http://www.automation.com/automation-news/article/tips-for-evaluating-cloud-based-supply-chain-management-software

Gabriel, G. (2002). *Atomic Transactions in Distributed Systems.* Institute of Informatics and Applied Mathematics University of Berne.

Gail, H. R., Hantler, S. L., & Taylor, B. A. (1988). Analysis of a non-preemptive priority multiserver queue. *Advances in Applied Probability*, *20*(4), 852–879. doi:10.2307/1427364

Gail, H. R., Hantler, S. L., & Taylor, B. A. (1992). On preemptive Markovian queue with multiple servers and two priority classes. *Mathematics of Operations Research*, *17*(2), 365–391. doi:10.1287/moor.17.2.365

Gartner Group. (2008a). *How to identify cloud computing?* Research ID Number: G00158761. Retrieved 20 February, 2013, from http://www.gartner.com/id=705817

Gartner Group. (2008b). *Cloud computing: Defining and describing an emerging phenomenon.* ID Number: G00156220. Retrieved January 20, 2013, from http://www.gartner.com/id=697413

Gehling, B., & Stankard, D. (2005). eCommerce security. In *Proceedings of Information Security Curriculum Development (InfoSecCD) Conference*. Academic Press.

Geng, B., Yang, Y., Xu, C., & Hua, X. S. (2012). Ranking Model Adaptation for Domain-Specific Search. *IEEE Transactions on Knowledge and Data Engineering*, 24(4), 745–758. doi:10.1109/TKDE.2010.252

Gentry, C. (2009). Fully homomorphic encryption using ideal lattices. In *Proceedings of 41st ACM Symposium on the Theory of Computing (STOC)*. Bethesda, MD: ACM.

Glisson, W., & Welland, R. (2005). Web Development Evolution: The Assimilation of Web Engineering Security. In *Proceedings of the Third Latin American Web Congress*. Washington, DC: IEEE Computer Society. doi:10.1109/LAWEB.2005.48

Godding, P., & Glasgow, R. (1985). Self-efficacy and outcome expectations as predictors of controlled smoking status. *Cognitive Therapy and Research*, 9(5), 585–590. doi:10.1007/BF01173011

Google Inc. (n.d.). *App Engine*. Retrieved from https://developers.google.com/appengine/

Google. (2010). *Google App Engine*. Available at: http://code.google.com/intl/en/appengine/

Google. (2011b). *Google Trends: private cloud, public cloud*. Retrieved from http://www.google.de/trends?q=private+cloud%2C+public+cloud

Goswami, V., & Sahoo, C. N. (2013). Optimal Resource Usage in Multi-Cloud Computing Environment. *International Journal of Cloud Applications and Computing*, 3(1), 45–57. doi:10.4018/ijcac.2013010105

Greeshma, L., Srinivasa Rao, M., & Krishnaiah, R. V. (2013). SVM and AdaBoost Based Ranking Model Adaptation for Domain Specific Search. *International Journal of Advanced Research in Computer and Communication Engineering*, 2(8), 3326–3329.

Grolinger, K., Hayes, M., Higashino, W. A., L'Heureux, A., Allison, D. S., & Capretz, M. A. M. (2014). Challenges for MapReduce in Big Data. In *Proc. of the IEEE 10th 2014 World Congress on Services (SERVICES 2014)*, (pp. 182-189). IEEE. doi:10.1109/SERVICES.2014.41

Groot, S., Goda, K., Yokoyama, D., Nakano, M., & Kitsuregawa, M. (2013). Modeling I/O interference for data intensive distributed applications. In *Proceedings of the 28th Annual ACM Symposium on Applied Computing - SAC '13*. ACM.

Grossman, R. L. (2009). The case for cloud computing. IEEE Computer Society. Retrieved from computer.org/ITPro

Grossman, R. (2009). The Case for Cloud Computing. *IT Professional*, 11(2), 23–27. doi:10.1109/MITP.2009.40

Group, G. E. P. (2011). *Strategic sourcing trends: Mid-year review 2011*. Retrieved January 15, 2014, from http://www.gep.com/Resources

Guha, S. K., Kundu, A., Bhadra, S., & Dattagupta, R. (2013). Dynamic Web-page Ranking of Search Engine using Importance Increasing Factor. *International Journal of Digital Content Technology and its Applications*, 7(12), 28-39.

Guha, S. K., Kundu, A., & Dattagupta, R. (2012). Introducing Session Relevancy Inspection in Web Page.*Proceedings of Second International Conference on Computer Science, Engineering and Applications (ICCSEA 2012)*(pp. 181-192). Delhi, India, Springer. doi:10.1007/978-3-642-30111-7_18

Guide to Scaling Web Databases with MySQL Cluster: Accelerating Innovation on the Web. (2011). Retrieved from http://www.oracle.com/us/products/mysql/scaling-web-databases-461055.pdf

Gupta, M. V., Sangroha, D., & Dhiman, L. (2013). An approach to implement Bring Your Own Device (BYOD) Securely. *International Journal of Electronics Communication and Computer Engineering, 4*(2), 154–156.

Gurdev, S., Gaurav, G., & Harmandeep, S. (2011). The Structure of Cloud Engineering. *Computer Applications, 33*(8), 44–48.

Haizea. (n.d.). Retrieved from http://haizea.cs.uchicago.edu/whatis.html

Han, J., Kamber, M., & Pei, J. (2011). *Data Mining: Concepts and Techniques.* Morgan Kaufmann Publishers.

Han, Y. (2013). On the clouds: A new way of computing. *Information Technology and Libraries, 29*(2), 87–92. doi:10.6017/ital.v29i2.3147

Harauz, J., Kaufman, L. M., & Potter, B. (2009). Data security in the world of cloud computing. *IEEE Security and Privacy*, (July/August), 61–64.

Hard Disk Drive. (2015). Retrieved from http://en.wikipedia.org/wiki/Hard_disk_drive

Hard Disk Driveinterface. (2015). Retrieved from http://en.wikipedia.org/wiki/Hard_disk_drive_interface

Harris, P., Rettie, R., & Kwan, C. C. (2005). Adoption and Usage of M-Commerce: A Cross-Cultural Comparison of Hong Kong and the United Kingdom. *Journal of Electronic Commerce Research, 6*(3), 210–224.

Haselmann, T., Vossen, G., Lipsky, S., & Theurl, T. (2011). A Cooperative Community Cloud for Small and Medium Enterprises. In *Proceedings of 1st International Conference on Cloud Computing and Service Science (CLOSER).* Noordwijkerhout, Netherlands: SciTePress Science and Technology Publications.

Haselmann, T., & Vossen, G. (2011). Software-as-a-Service in Small and Medium Enterprises: An Empirical Attitude Assessment. In *Proceedings of 12th International Conference on Web Information Systems Engineering (WISE).* Sydney, Australia: Springer. doi:10.1007/978-3-642-24434-6_4

Hashemi, S., Monfaredi, K., & Masdari, M. (2013). Using Cloud Computing for E-Government: Challenges and Benefits. *Information Science and Engineering, 7*(9), 987–995.

Hassan, M. M., & Huh, E. (2011). Resource Management for Data Intensive Clouds Through Dynamic Federation: A Game Theoretic Approach. In B. Furht & A. Escalante (Eds.), *Handbook of Cloud Computing* (pp. 169–188). Boston, MA: Springer US; doi:10.1007/978-1-4614-1415-5_7

Hayes, J. F., & Ganesh Babu, T. V. J. (2004). *Modeling and Analysis of Telecommunications Networks.* Wiley-Interscience Publication. doi:10.1002/0471643505

Heintz, B., Member, S., Chandra, A., Sitaraman, R. K., Weissman, J., & Member, S. (2014). End-to-end Optimization for Geo-Distributed MapReduce. *IEEE Transactions on Cloud Computing, 7161*(c), 1–14. doi:10.1109/TCC.2014.2355225

Hendry, M. (1995). *Practical computer network security.* Norwood, MA: Artech House.

Henry, J., & Stone, R. (1999). The impacts of end-user gender, education, performance, and system use on computer self-efficacy and outcome expectancy. *Southern Business Review, 25*(1), 10–16.

Herbig, P., Koehler, W., & Day, K. (1993). Marketing to the baby bust generation. *Journal of Consumer Marketing, 10*(1), 4–9. doi:10.1108/07363769310026520

Herbst, N. R., Kounev, S., & Reussner, R. (2013, June). Elasticity in Cloud Computing: What It Is, and What It Is Not. ICAC, 23-27.

Hernandez, A., & Choi, Y. (2014). Securing BYOD Networks: Inherent Vulnerabilities and Emerging Feasible Technologies. In *Proceedings of ASE International Conferences on Big Data Science and Computing / Social Computing / Cyber Security.*Stanford, CA: Academy of Science and Engineering (ASE).

Hervé, C., Duong, H. P., & David, P. (2005). *Public Traceability in Traitor Tracing Schemes. Eurocrypt '05* (pp. 542–558). Aarhus, Denmark: Springer.

Hesseldahl, A. (2010, February 22). The iPad: More than the sum of its parts', $270 more actually. *Business Week, 24.*

Hindman, B., Konwinski, A., Zaharia, M., Ghodsi, A., Joseph, A. D., Katz, R. H., . . . Stoica, I. (2011, March). Mesos: A Platform for Fine-Grained Resource Sharing in the Data Center. *Proceedings of the 8th USENIX conference on Networked systems design and implementation* (NSDI' 11). USENIX Association.

Hogan, M. (2015). *Shared-Disk vs. Shared-Nothing: Comparing Architectures for Clustered Databases.* Academic Press.

Holland, J. H. (1973). Genetic algorithms and the optimal allocation of trials. *SIAM Journal on Computing, 2*(2), 88–105. doi:10.1137/0202009

Hooghiemstra, G., Keane, M. S., & van der Ree, S. (1988). Power series for stationary distributions of coupled processor models. *SIAM Journal on Applied Mathematics, 48*(5), 1159–1166. doi:10.1137/0148069

Horn, P. M., Gara, A., Goyal, A., Pulleyblank, B., Coteus, P., Yaun, D., & Eleftheriou, M. (2014). *Blue Gene Project.* Retrieved September 9, 2014, from http://www.research.ibm.com/bluegene/index.html

Huang, C., Guan, C., Chen, H., Wang, Y., Chang, S., Li, C., & Weng, C. (2013). An adaptive resource management scheme in cloud computing. *Engineering Applications of Artificial Intelligence, Elsevier, 26*(1), 382–389. doi:10.1016/j.engappai.2012.10.004

Hugos, M. H., & Hulitzky, D. (2010). *Business in the cloud: What every business needs to know about cloud computing.* Hoboken, NJ: Wiley.

Hu, Y., Wong, J., Iszlai, G., & Litoiu, M. (2009). Resource provisioning for cloud computing. In *Proceedings of the Conference of the Center for Advanced Studies on Collaborative Research.* ACM.

IBM. (1964). *System/360, Model 30 1401 Compatibility Feature, A24-3255-1, "Mode status (System/360, Model 30, mode or 1401 compatibility mode) is set during the read-in of the compatibility initialization deck".* IBM.

IBM. (1980). Reference Manual for IBM 2835 Storage Control and IBM 2305 Fixed Head Storage Module, Fifth Edition, GA26-1689-4. IBM.

IBM. (2008). IBM Perspective on cloud computing: The "next big thing" or "another fad"? *IBM Whitepaper.* Retrieved January 25, 2013, from http://www-935.ibm.com/services/in/cio/pdf/ibm_perspective_on_cloud_computing.pdf

IBM. (2010). *IBM Smart Business Cloud Computing.* Available at: http://www.ibm.com/ibm/cloud/

Informationswirtschaft, B. Telekommunikation und neue Medien (2013). *Bring Your Own Device.* Retrieved June 10, 2015, from http://www.bitkom.org/files/documents/ 20130404_LF_BYOD_2013_v2.pdf

Intel, C. (1991). *A Touchstone DELTA system description.* Intel Corporation.

IOR Benchmark on SourceForge. (n.d.). Retrieved from http://sourceforge.net/projects/ior-sio/

IPSec Developers Forum. W.i.I. (n.d.). Retrieved January 2, 2005, from http://www-ip-sec. com5PSecinfoh.html

Ismail, N. (2011). Cursing the Cloud or Controlling the Cloud. *Computer Law & Security Report, 27*(3), 250–257. doi:10.1016/j.clsr.2011.03.005

Jaeger, P. T., Lin, J., & Grimes, J. M. (2008). Cloud computing and information policy: Computing in a policy cloud? *Journal of Information Technology & Politics, 5*(3), 269–283. doi:10.1080/19331680802425479

Jason, C. (2009). Cryptographically-enforced hierarchical access control with multiple keys. *Journal of Logic and Algebraic Programming, 76*(3), 690–700.

Jayaprakash, G. (2011, September 15). Cloud computing security, is your seatbelt on? *Infosys.* Retrieved October 31, 2013, from http://www.infosysblogs.com/cloud/2011/09/

Jeanna, M., Christofer, H., & Jeff, W. (2009). Virtual Machine Contracts for Datacenter and Cloud Computing Environments.*Workshop on Automated Control for Datacenters and Clouds* (pp.25-30). ACM.

Jiang, D., Chen, G., Ooi, C., Tan, K., & Wu, S. (2014). epiC : An Extensible and Scalable System for Processing Big Data. *Proceedings of VLDB Endowment, 7*(7), 541–552. doi:10.14778/2732286.2732291

Johnston, K., & Johal, P. (1999). The internet as a 'virtual cultural region': Are extant cultural classification schemes appropriate? *Internet Research: Electronic Networking Applications and Policy, 9*(3), 178–186. doi:10.1108/10662249910274566

Jrad, F., Tao, J., Brandic, I., & Streit, A. (2014). Multi-dimensional Resource Allocation for Data-intensive Large-scale Cloud Applications.*Proceedings of the 4th International Conference on Cloud Computing and Services Science*, (pp. 691–702). doi:10.5220/0004971906910702

Jun, C., & Wei, M. Y. (2011). The Research of supply chain information collaboration based on cloud computing. *Procedia Environmental Sciences.3rd International Conference on Environmental Science and Information Application Technology, ESIAT 2011 (vol.10*, part A, pp. 875–880). ESIAT.

Jung, E., & Kettimuthu, R. (2014). Towards Addressing the Challenges of Data-Intensive Computing on the Cloud. *Computer, 47*(12), 82–85. doi:10.1109/MC.2014.347

Kadlec, T., & Gustafson, A. (2012). *Implementing Responsive Design: Building Sites for an Anywhere, Everywhere Web.* San Francisco, CA: New Riders Publishing.

Kanadia, A. S., Kazmi, M. F., & Mitchell, A. C. (1984). Analysis of a finite capacity non preemptive priority queue. *Computers & Operations Research, 11*(3), 337–343. doi:10.1016/0305-0548(84)90022-4

Kandukuri, B. R., Ramakrishna, P. V., & Rakshit, A. (2009). Cloud security issues. In *2009 IEEE International Conference on Services Computing*, (pp. 517-520). IEEE.

Karlapudi, H., & Martin, J. (2004). Web application performance prediction. In *Proceedings of the IASTED International Conference on Communication and Computer Networks*, (pp. 281–286). IASTED.

Kaylor, C., Deshazo, R., & Van Eck, D. (2001). Gauging E-Government: A report on implementing Services Among American Cities. *Government Information Quarterly, 18*(4), 293–307. doi:10.1016/S0740-624X(01)00089-2

Kefer, G. (2011). *The cloud solves those lingering supply chain problems.* Retrieved September 5, 2014, from http://www.networkworld.com/article/2182683/tech-primers/the-cloud-solves-those-lingering-supply-chain-problems.html

Keller, A., & Ludwig, H. (2003). The wsla framework: Specifying and monitoring service level agreements for web services. *J. Netw. Syst. Manage., 11*, 57–81. Available: http://dl.acm.org/citation.cfm?id=635430.635442

Kennedy, J., & Eberhart, R. (1995). "Particle Swarm Optimization". In *Proceedings of IEEE International Conference on Neural Networks* (vol. 4, pp. 1942–1948). IEEE. doi:10.1109/ICNN.1995.488968

Keppel, G. (1991). *Design and Analysis: A Researcher's Handbook* (3rd ed.). Englewood Cliffs, NJ: Prentice-Hall.

Khan, A. N., Mat Kiah, M. L., Khan, S. U., & Madani, S. A. (2013). Towards secure mobile cloud computing: A survey. *Future Generation Computer Systems, 29*(5), 1278–1299. doi:10.1016/j.future.2012.08.003

Khan, F., Zhang, B., Khan, S., & Chen, S. (2011). Technological Leap Forging E-Government Through Cloud Computing. *4th IEEE International Conference on Broadband Network and Multimedia Technology* (pp.201-206). IEEE.

Khazaei, Misic, & Misic, (2011). *Performance analysis of cloud centers under burst arrivals and total rejection policy.* IEEE Globecom.

Khazaei, H., & Misi, C. (2010). Performance of Cloud Centers with High Degree of Virtualization Under Batch Task Arrivals. *IEEE Transactions on Parallel and Distributed Systems, 9*(2), 111–117.

Khazaei, H., Misic, J., & Misic, V. B. (2011). Performance Analysis of Cloud Centers under Burst Arrivals and Total Rejection Policy. In *Proceedings of the IEEE International Conference on Global Telecommunications*, (pp.1–6). IEEE. doi:10.1109/GLOCOM.2011.6133765

Kim, B. C., & Park, Y. W. (2012). Security versus convenience? An experimental study of user misperceptions of wireless internet service quality. *Decision Support Systems, 53*(1), 1–11. doi:10.1016/j.dss.2011.08.006

Kim, G., & Yoon, H. (1998). On Submesh Allocation for Mesh Multicomputers: A Best-Fit Allocation and a Virtual Submesh Allocation for Faulty Meshes. *IEEE Transactions on Parallel and Distributed Systems, 9*(2), 175–185. doi:10.1109/71.663881

Kimura, T. (1996). Optimal buffer design of an m/g/s queue with finite capacity. *Stochastic Models, 12*(1), 165–180. doi:10.1080/15326349608807378

King, R. (2008). Cloud Computing: Small Companies Take Flight. *Business Week.*

Kleinrock, L. (1975). Theory. *Queueing Systems, 1.*

Klementiev, A., Roth, D., Small, K., & Titov, I. (2009). Unsupervised Rank Aggregation with Domain-Specific Expertise. *Proceedings of 21st International Joint Conference on Artifical Intelligence (IJCAI'09)* (pp. 1101-1106). San Francisco, CA: Academic Press.

Kliazovich, D., Bouvry, P., & Khan, S. U. (2013). Simulation and Performance Analysis of Data Intensive and Workload Intensive Cloud Computing Data Centers. In Optical Interconnects for Future Data Center Networks, (pp. 47-63). New York: Springer. doi:10.1007/978-1-4614-4630-9_4

Knuth, D. (1997). The Art of Computer Programming: Sorting and Searching (vol. 3). Pearson Education.

Kock, N. (2004). The psychobiological model: Towards a new theory of computer-mediated communication based on Darwinian evolution. *Organization Science, 15*(3), 327–348. doi:10.1287/orsc.1040.0071

Koh, E. B., Oh, J., & Im, C. (2014). A Study on Security Threats and Dynamic Access Control Technology for BYOD, Smart-work Environment. In *Proceedings of the International MultiConference of Engineers and Computer Scientists.* Hong Kong, China: Newswood.

Korri, T. (2009). Cloud computing: utility computing over the Internet. Seminar on Internetworking, Helsinki University of Technology.

KPMG International. (2011). *Embracing the cloud: 2011 Global cloud survey report.* Retrieved September 10, 2014, from http://www.kpmg.com/Global/en/IssuesAndInsights/ArticlesPublications/Documents/embracing-cloud.pdf

KPMG International. (2011). *The cloud: Changing the business ecosystem.* Retrieved September 18, 2014, from http://www.kpmg.com/IN/en/IssuesAndInsights/ThoughtLeadership/The_Cloud_Changing_the_Business_Ecosystem.pdf

KPMG International. (2013). *Breaking through the cloud adoption barriers*. Retrieved September 5, 2014, from https://www.kpmg.com/SG/en/IssuesAndInsights/ArticlesPublications/Documents/Advisory-ICE-Breaking-through-the-Cloud-Adoption-Barriers-Glob.pdf

Krasuski, A., & Szczuka, M. (2011). *Knowledge Driven Query Sharding*. Academic Press.

Krzywiecki, Ł., Kutyłowski, M., Misztela, H., & Strumiński, T. (2011, January). Private Information Retrieval with a Trusted Hardware Unit–Revisited. In *Information Security and Cryptology* (pp. 373-386). Springer Berlin Heidelberg.

Ksalan, M., & Zionts, S. (2001). *Multiple Criteria Decision Making in the New Millennium*. Springer-Verlag. doi:10.1007/978-3-642-56680-6

Kuldeep, V., Shravan, S., & Amit, R. (2012). A Review of Cloud Computing and E-Governance. *Advanced Research in Computer Science and Software Engineering*, *2*(2), 185–213.

Kumar, V., Grama, A., Gupta, A., & Karypis, G. (2003). *Introduction to Parallel Computing*. Redwood City, CA: Benjamin/Cummings publishing Company.

Kundu, A., Xu, G., & Ji, C. (2014). Data Specific Ranking in Cloud. *International Journal of Cloud Applications and Computing*, *4*(4), 32–41. doi:10.4018/ijcac.2014100103

Kuratko, D. F., & Goldsby, M. G. (2004). Corporate entrepreneurs or rogue middle managers? A framework for ethical corporate entrepreneurship. *Journal of Business Ethics*, *55*(1), 13–30. doi:10.1007/s10551-004-1775-3

Lance, D., & Schweigert, M. E. (2013). BYOD: Moving toward a More Mobile and Productive Workforce. *Business & Information Technology*. Paper 3. Retrieved June 10, 2015, from http://digitalcommons.mtech.edu/business_info_tech/3/

LaRose, R., & Eastin, M. S. (2004). A social cognitive theory of Internet uses and gratifications: Toward a new model of media attendance. *Journal of Broadcasting & Electronic Media*, *48*(3), 358–372. doi:10.1207/s15506878jobem4803_2

Layne, K., & Lee, J. (2001). Developing fully functional e-government: A four stage model. *Government Information Quarterly*, *18*(2), 122–229. doi:10.1016/S0740-624X(01)00066-1

Leavitt, N. (2013). Hybrid clouds move to the forefront. *Computer*, *46*(5), 15–18. doi:10.1109/MC.2013.168

Lee, J. (2010) 10 year Retrospect on Stage Models of E-Government: A Qualitative Meta-Synthesis. *Government Information Quarterly*, *27*, 220-230.

Lee, G., Tolia, N., Ranganathan, P., & Katz, R. H. (2011). Topology-aware resource allocation for data-intensive workloads. *Computer Communication Review*, *41*(1), 120. doi:10.1145/1925861.1925881

Lee, S. M., & Peterson, S. J. (2000). Culture, Entrepreneurial Orientation, and Global Competitiveness. *Journal of World Business*, *35*(4), 401–416. doi:10.1016/S1090-9516(00)00045-6

Lenk, A., Menzel, M., Lipsky, J., Tai, S., & Offermann, P. (2011). What are you paying for? Performance benchmarking for infrastructure-as-a-service offerings. In *Proceedings of Cloud Computing (CLOUD), 2011 IEEE International Conference on*, (pp. 484-491). IEEE.

Lewin, K. (1947). Frontiers in group dynamics: Concept, method, and reality in social science. *Human Relations*, *1*(1), 5–42. doi:10.1177/001872674700100103

Leymann, F., Fehling, C., Mietzner, R., Nowak, A., & Dustdar, S. (2011). Moving applications to the cloud: An approach based on application model enrichment. *International Journal of Cooperative Information Systems*, *20*(3), 307–356. doi:10.1142/S0218843011002250

Li, M., Yu, S., Lou, W., & Hou, Y. T. (2012, June). Toward privacy-assured cloud data services with flexible search functionalities. In *Distributed Computing Systems Workshops (ICDCSW), 2012 32nd International Conference on* (pp. 466-470). IEEE. doi:10.1109/ICDCSW.2012.41

Li, H., Li, Z., Lee, W. C., & Lee, D. L. (2009). A probabilistic topic-based ranking framework for location-sensitive domain information retrieval. *Proceedings of 32nd international ACM SIGIR conference on Research and development in information retrieval* (pp 331-33). Boston: ACM. doi:10.1145/1571941.1571999

Li, J., Qiu, M., Ming, Z., Quan, G., Qin, X., & Gu, Z. (2012). Online optimization for scheduling preemptable tasks on IaaS cloud systems. *Journal of Parallel Distributed Computing, Elsevier, 72*(5), 666–677. doi:10.1016/j.jpdc.2012.02.002

Lin, J., Chen, C., & Chang, J. (2013). QoS-aware data replication for data intensive applications in cloud computing systems. *IEEE Transactions on Cloud Computing, 1*(1), 101–115. Retrieved from http://ieeexplore.ieee.org/xpls/abs_all.jsp?arnumber=6562695

Lin, C., & Huang, C. (2008). Understanding knowledge management system usage antecedents: An integration of social cognitive theory and task technology fit. *Information & Management, 45*(6), 410–417. doi:10.1016/j.im.2008.06.004

Lipschutz, S. (2006). *Data Structures.* The McGraw-Hill.

Liu, Q., Tan, C. C., Wu, J., & Wang, G. (2012, March). Efficient information retrieval for ranked queries in cost-effective cloud environments. In INFOCOM, 2012 Proceedings IEEE (pp. 2581-2585). IEEE. doi:10.1109/INFCOM.2012.6195657

Liu, T., Huang, W.-K., Lombardi, F., & Bhuyan, L. N. (1995). A submesh allocation scheme for mesh-connected multi-processor systems. In *Proc. Int'l Conference on Parallel Processing II* (vol. 2, pp. 159-163). Academic Press.

Liu, G., Lu, H., Lou, W., Xu, Y., & Yu, J. X. (2004). Efficient mining of Frequent Patterns Using Ascending Frequency Ordered Prefix-Tree. *Data Mining and Knowledge Discovery, 9*(3), 249–274. doi:10.1023/B:DAMI.0000040905.52966.1a

Liu, L., Moulic, R., & Shea, D. (2010). Cloud service portal for mobile device management. In *Proceedings of 7th IEEE International Conference on e-Business Engineering (ICEBE).* Shanghai, China: IEEE Computer Society. doi:10.1109/ICEBE.2010.102

Li, Y., Liu, Y., & Ren, F. (2007). Product innovation and process innovation in SOEs: Evidence from the Chinese transition. *The Journal of Technology Transfer, 32*(1-2), 63–85. doi:10.1007/s10961-006-9009-8

Lofaro, R. (2014). *The Business Side of BYOD: Cultural and Organizational Impacts.* Retrieved June 10, 2015, from http://www.amazon.com/business-side-BYOD-cultural-organizational/dp/1494844265

Lough, D. L., & Krizman, K. J. (2003). *A short tuto-rial on wireless LANs and IEEE802.11.* Academic Press.

Lo, V., Windisch, K., Liu, W., & Nitzberg, B. (1997). Non-contiguous processor allocation algorithms for mesh-connected multicomputers. *IEEE Transactions on Parallel and Distributed Systems, 8*(7), 712–726. doi:10.1109/71.598346

Low, C., Chen, Y., & Wu, M. (2011). Understanding the determinants of cloud computing adoption. *Industrial Management & Data Systems, 111*(7), 1006–1023. doi:10.1108/02635571111161262

Lu, J., & Wang, J. (2005). Performance modeling and analysis of Web Switch. In *Proceedings of the 31st Annual International Conference on Computer Measurement,* (pp. 665–672). Academic Press.

Luckeneder, M., & Barker, A. (2013). Location, Location, Location: Data-Intensive Distributed Computing in the Cloud. *2013 IEEE 5th International Conference on Cloud Computing Technology and Science,* (pp. 647–654). doi:10.1109/CloudCom.2013.91

Luftman, J., & Zadeh, H. S. (2011). Key information technology and management issues 2010-2011: An international study. *Journal of Information Technology, 26*(3), 193–204. doi:10.1057/jit.2011.3

Luis, M.V., Luis, R, Caceres, J., & Lindner, M. (2008). A break in the clouds: towards a cloud definition. *SIGCOMM Computer Communication Review, 39*(1).

Lu, J., Yu, C., Liu, C., & Yao, J. (2003). Technology acceptance model for wireless Internet. *Internet Research. Electronic Networking Applications and Policy, 13*(3), 206–222. doi:10.1108/10662240310478222

Lunde, R., & Dannenmann, P. (1998). Information Retrieval from Mathematical Models for Process Optimisation in Waste-Water Treatment. In *Proceedings of the 12th International Symposium "Computer Science for Environmental Protection"*. Metropolis.

Lundvall, B., & Borras, S. (1999). *The globalising learning economy: Implications for innovation policy.* Luxembourg: European Union.

Ma, B. N. W., & Mark, J. W. (1998). Approximation of the mean queue length of an M/G/cqueueing system. *Operations Research, 43*(1), 158–165. doi:10.1287/opre.43.1.158

Maggiani, R. (2009, November). Cloud computing is changing how we communicate. *IEEE Explore.*

Maheswaran, M., Ali, S., Siegel, H., Hensgen, D., & Freund, R. (1999). Dynamic mapping of a class of independent tasks onto heterogeneous computing systems. *Journal of Parallel and Distributed Computing, 59*(2), 107–131. doi:10.1006/jpdc.1999.1581

Malaviya, P., Kisielius, J., & Sternthal, B. (1996). The effect of type of elaboration on advertisement processing and judgement. *JMR, Journal of Marketing Research, 33*(4), 410–421. doi:10.2307/3152212

Malhotra, N., Hall, J., Shaw, M., & Crisp, M. (1996). *Marketing Research: An Applied Approach.* Sydney: Prentice-Hall.

Mälkiä, M., Anttiroiko, A., & Savolainen, R. (2004). *E-Transformation in Governance: New Directions in Government.* Hershey, PA: Idea Group Publishing. doi:10.4018/978-1-59140-130-8

Mano, M. M. (2009). *Computer System Architecture.* Pearson Edition.

Mansouri, N. (2014). Network and data location aware approach for simultaneous job scheduling and data replication in large-scale data grid. *Frontiers of Computer Science, 8*(3), 391–408. doi:10.1007/s11704-014-3146-2

Mao, W., Chen, J., & Watson, W. (2005). Efficient Subtorus Processor Allocation in a Multi-Dimensional Torus. In *Proceedings of the 8th International Conference on High-Performance Computing in Asia-Pacific Region (HPCAS IA'05)*, (pp. 53-60). Beijing, China: Academic Press.

Marchany, R. (2010). *Cloud Computing Security Issues: VA Tech IT Security.* Retrieved from www.issa-centralva. org/.../01-2010_CCSecIssues.ppt

Marks, E. A., & Lozano, B. (2010). *Executive's guide to cloud computing.* Hoboken, NJ: John Wiley & Sons.

Marston, S., Li, Z., Bandyopadhyay, S., Zhang, J., & Ghalsasi, A. (2011). Cloud computing—The business perspective. *Decision Support Systems, 51*(1), 176–189. doi:10.1016/j.dss.2010.12.006

Mason, A. G. (2002) Secure Virtual Private Network. Cisco Press.

Massachusetts Institute of Technology. (n.d.). *StarCluster.* Retrieved from http://star.mit.edu/cluster/

Mather, T., Kumarasawmy, S., & Latif, S. (2009). *Cloud security and privacy* (1st ed.). Sebastopol, CA: O'Reilly Media, Inc.

Mathieson, K. (1991). Predicting user intentions: Comparing the technology acceptance model with the theory of planned behaviour. *Information Systems Research, 2*(3), 173–191. doi:10.1287/isre.2.3.173

Matsuno, K., Mentzer, J. T., & Ozsomer, A. (2002). The Effects of Entrepreneurial Proclivity and Market Orientation on Business Performance. *Journal of Marketing, 66*(1), 18–32. doi:10.1509/jmkg.66.3.18.18507

Mattess, M., Calheiros, R. N., & Buyya, R. (2013). Scaling MapReduce Applications Across Hybrid Clouds to Meet Soft Deadlines. *2013 IEEE 27th International Conference on Advanced Information Networking and Applications (AINA),* (pp. 629–636). doi:10.1109/AINA.2013.51

May, R., Masson, M., & Hunter, M. (1991). *Applications of Statistics in Behavioral Research*. New York, NY: Harper and Row.

McCalpin, J. D. (1995). *Memory bandwidth and machine balance in current high performance computers. In Proceedings of IEEE Computer Society Technical Committee on Computer Architecture (TCCA)* (pp. 19–25). IEEE.

McCauley, J. M. (2011). Cloud computing- A silver lining or ethical thunderstorm for lawyers? *Virginia Lawyer, 59,* 49–54.

McCormick, M. J., & Martinko, M. J. (2004). Identifying leader social cognitions: Integrating the causal reasoning perspective into social cognitive theory. *Journal of Leadership & Organizational Studies, 10*(4), 2–11. doi:10.1177/107179190401000401

McCoy, S., Galletta, D. F., & King, W. R. (2007). Applying TAM across cultures: The need for caution. *European Journal of Information Systems, 16*(1), 81–90. doi:10.1057/palgrave.ejis.3000659

McCrea, B. (2012, November). Cloud Breakthrough. *Logistics Management,* 36-40.

McEvoy, G. V., & Schulze, B. (2008). Using clouds to address grid limitations. In *MGC '08: Proceedings of the 6th international workshop on Middleware for grid computing,* (pp. 1-6). New York: ACM.

McMahon, J. M., & Cohen, R. (2009). Lost in cyberspace: Ethical decision making in the online environment. *Ethics and Information Technology, 11*(1), 1–17. doi:10.1007/s10676-008-9165-7

Mell, P., & Grance, T. (2009). *The NIST Definition of Cloud Computing*. Retrieved from http://www.nist.gov/itl/cloud/upload/cloud-def-v15.pdf

Mell, P., & Grance, T. (2012). *The NIST definition of cloud computing*. National Institute of Standards and Technology. Special Publication 800-145. Retrieved April 12, 2014, from http://csrc.nist.gov/publications/nistpubs/800-145/SP800-145.pdf

Mell, P., & Grance, T. (2009). The NIST definition of cloud computing. *National Institute of Standards and Technology, 53*(6), 50.

Memory, S. (2010). Retrieved from http://dis-dpcs.wikispaces.com/2.1.5+Secondary+Memory

Michael, C., Jaeger, G., Rojec, G., & Gero, M. (2004).QoS Aggregation for Web Service Composition using Workflow Patterns. In *Proceeding of 8th International Enterprise Distributed Object Computing Conference (EDOC 2004).* Washington, DC: EDOC.

Microsoft. (n.d.). *Windows Azure*. Retrieved from http://www.windowsazure.com/en-us/

Middleton, A. M. (2010). 05 - Data-Intensive Technologies for Cloud Computing. In B. Furht & A. Escalante (Eds.), *Handbook of Cloud Computing* (pp. 83–136). Boston, MA: Springer US; doi:10.1007/978-1-4419-6524-0_5

Mihalcea, R. (2004). Graph-based ranking algorithms for sentence extraction, applied for text summarization.*Proceedings of the ACL 2004 on Interactive poster and demonstration sessions (ACLdemo'04)*. Stroudsburg, PA: ACL doi:10.3115/1219044.1219064

Miller, D. (1983). The correlates of entrepreneurship in three types of firms. *Management Science, 29*(7), 770–791. doi:10.1287/mnsc.29.7.770

Miller, K., Voas, J., & Hurlburt, G. (2012). BYOD: Security and Privacy Considerations. *IT Professional, 14*(5), 53–55. doi:10.1109/MITP.2012.93

Ming, G., & Li, H. (2012). An improved algorithm based on max-min for cloud task scheduling. In Recent Advances in Computer Science and Information Engineering, Lecture Notes in Electrical Engineering, 125 (pp. 217-223). doi:10.1007/978-3-642-25789-6_32

Mishra, A., Mathur, R., Jain, S., & Rathore, J. S. (2013). Cloud Computing Security. *International Journal on Recent and Innovation Trends in Computing and Communication, 1*(1), 36–39.

Miyazawa, M. (1986). Approximation of the queue-length distribution of an M/GI/s queue by the basic equations. *Journal of Applied Probability, 23*(2), 443–458. doi:10.2307/3214186

Moch, R., Merkel, A., Gunther, L., & Muller, E. (2011). The dimension of innovation in SME networks- A case study on cloud computing and Web 2.0 technologies in a textile manufacturing network. *International Journal of Innovation and Sustainable Development, 5*(2/3), 185–198. doi:10.1504/IJISD.2011.043067

Mohay, G., Anderson, A., Collie, B., & del Vel, O. (2003). *Computer and intrusion forensics* (p. 9). Boston, MA: Artech House.

Moore, G. E. (1997). *An update on Moore's law*. Santa Clara, CA: Intel Corporation.

More, A., Vij, S., & Mukhopadhyay, D. (2013). Agent Based Negotiation using Cloud - An Approach in E-Commerce. *48th Annual Convention of the Computer Society of India; CSI 2013 Proceedings, Visakhapatnam, India*. Springer-Verlag Germany.

Moreno-Vozmediano, R., Montero, R. S., & Llorente, I. M. (2013). Key challenges in cloud computing: Enabling the future internet of services. *IEEE Internet Computing, 17*(4), 18–25. doi:10.1109/MIC.2012.69

Moretti, C., Bulosan, J., Thain, D., & Flynn, P. J. (2008). All-pairs: An abstraction for data-intensive cloud computing.*2008 IEEE International Symposium on Parallel and Distributed Processing*, (pp. 1–11). doi:10.1109/IPDPS.2008.4536311

Morrell, R., & Chandrashekar, A. (2011). Cloud computing: New challenges and opportunities. *Network Security, 2011*(October), 18–19. doi:10.1016/S1353-4858(11)70108-8

Morrison & Foerster LLP. (2013). *Global sourcing trends in 2013*. Global Surcing Group. Retrieved September 15, 2014, from http://www.mofo.com/files/Uploads/Images/130501-Global-Sourcing-Trends.pdf

Morrow, B. (2012). BYOD security challenges: Control and protect your most sensitive data. *Network Security, 2012*(12), 5–8. doi:10.1016/S1353-4858(12)70111-3

Mucci, P. J., & London, K. (1998). *The CacheBench report*. Retrieved from http://www.cs.surrey.ac.uk/BIMA/People/L.Gillam/downloads/publications/Fair%20Benchmarking%20for%20Cloud%20Computing%20Systems.pdf

Mukherjee, K., & Sahoo, G. (2010). Cloud Computing: Future Framework for E-Governance. *Computer Applications, 7*(7), 975–8887.

Mukhopadhyay, Vij, & Tasare. (2012). NAAS: Negotiation Automation Architecture with Buyers Behavior Pattern Prediction Component. The Fourth International Conference on Web Semantic Technology, NeCoM, Chennai, India. Springer-Verlag.

Mukun, C. (2010). Multi-agent automated negotiation as a service.*7th International Conference on service System and Service Management (ICSSSM)*.Tokyo: IEEE.

Murphy, G. B., & Tocher, N. (2011). Gender differences in the effectiveness of online trust building information cues: An empirical examination. *The Journal of High Technology Management Research*, *22*(1), 26–35. doi:10.1016/j.hitech.2011.03.004

Myoung, J., Ouk-Kim, C., & Hyun, I. (2008). Quality-of-service oriented web service composition algorithm and planning. *Journal of Systems and Software*, *81*(11), 2079–2090. doi:10.1016/j.jss.2008.04.044

MySQL Cluster Benchmarks. (2013). Retrieved from http://www.mysql.com/why-mysql/benchmarks/mysql-cluster/

MySQL Cluster. (2014). Retrieved from http://dev.mysql.com/doc/mysql-cluster-excerpt/5.5/en/index.html

Nathani, A., Chaudhary, S. & Somani, G. (2102). Policy based resource allocation in IAAS cloud. *Future Generation Computer Systems, 28*, 94-103. doi:10.1109/PDGC.2014.7030716

Nelson, M. R. (2009). The cloud, the crowd and public policy. *Issues in Science and Technology*, (Summer), 71–76.

Nhlabatsi, A., Nuseibeh, B., & Yu, Y. (2010). Security Requirements Engineering for Evolving Software Systems: A Survey. *International Journal of Secure Software Engineering*, *1*(1), 54–73. doi:10.4018/jsse.2010102004

Nourian, A., Maheswaran, M., & Maheshwari, V. (2012, December). Character-based search with data confidentiality in the clouds. In *Proceedings of the 2012 IEEE 4th International Conference on Cloud Computing Technology and Science (CloudCom)* (pp. 895-899). IEEE Computer Society.

Nunnally, J. (1978). *Psychometric Theory*. New York, NY: McGraw-Hill.

Nymi (n.d.). *Nymi*. Retrieved June 10, 2015, from http://www.getnymi.com/

O'Donnell, M., & Stewart, J. (2007). Implementing change in the public agency/leadership, learning and organisational resilience. *International Journal of Public Sector Management*, *20*(3), 239–251. doi:10.1108/09513550710740634

O'sullivan, J., Edmond, D., & Hofstede, A. T. (2002). What's in a service? *Distributed and Parallel Databases*, *12*(23), 117–133. doi:10.1023/A:1016547000822

Obasanjo, D. (2009). *Building Scalable Databases: Pros and Cons of Various Database Sharding Schemes*. Retrieved from http://www.25hoursaday.com/weblog/2009/01/16/BuildingScalableDatabasesProsAndConsOfVariousDatabaseShardingSchemes.aspx

Oracle. (2009). *Platform-as-a-Service private cloud with Oracle Fusion Middleware*. An Oracle Whitepaper. Retrieved February 5, 2013, from http://www.oracle.com/us/technologies/cloud/036500.pdf

Osterman, S., Iosup, A., Yigitbasi, N., Prodan, R., Fahringer, T., & Epema, D. (2010). A performance analysis of EC2 cloud computing services for scientific computing. *Cloud Computing*, *34*, 115–131.

P. Maes, R. Guttman, A. Moukas (1999). Agents that buy and sell. *Communications of the ACM, 42*(3), 81 – 91.

Panda, S., & Jana, P. (2014). An efficient task scheduling algorithm for heterogeneous multi-cloud environment. In *3rd IEEE International Conference on Advances in Computing, Communications & Informatics* (pp. 1204-1209). doi:10.1109/ICACCI.2014.6968253

Panda, S., Agrawal, P., Khilar, P., & Mohapatra, D. (2014). Skewness-based min-min max-min heuristic for grid task scheduling. In *4th IEEE International Conference on Advanced Computing and Communication Technologies* (pp. 282-289). IEEE.

Panda, S., Nag, S., & Jana, P. (2014). A smoothing based task scheduling algorithm for heterogeneous multi-cloud environment. In *3rd IEEE International Conference on Parallel, Distributed and Grid Computing*. IEEE.

Pan, L. (2011). Towards A Ramework For Automated Service Negotiation In Cloud Computing. In *Proceedings of IEEE Cloud Computing and Intelligence System (CCIS)*. doi:10.1109/CCIS.2011.6045091

PassMark Software Inc. (n.d.). Retrieved from http://www.passmark.com/

Pattishall, D. (2006). *Unorthodox approach to database design part 1 and 2*. Retrieved from http://mysqldba.blogspot.com/2006/10/unorthodox-approach-to-database-design.html

Pei, J., Han, J., & Lakshmanan, L. V. S. (2004). Pushing Convertible Constraints in Frequent Itemset Mining. *Data Mining and Knowledge Discovery*, *8*(3), 227–252. doi:10.1023/B:DAMI.0000023674.74932.4c

Pereira, W. F., Bittencourt, L. F., & da Fonseca, N. L. S. (2013). Scheduler for data-intensive workflows in public clouds.*2nd IEEE Latin American Conference on Cloud Computing and Communications (LatinCloud)*, (pp. 41-46). doi:10.1109/LatinCloud.2013.6842221

Perry, G. (2009). *What are Amazon EC2 compute units? Thinking out cloud*. Retrieved from http://gevaperry.typepad.com/main/2009/03/figuring-out-the-roi-of-infrastructureasaservice.html

Pervez, Z., Awan, A. A., Khattak, A. M., Lee, S., & Huh, E. N. (2013). Privacy-aware searching with oblivious term matching for cloud storage. *The Journal of Supercomputing*, *63*(2), 538–560. doi:10.1007/s11227-012-0829-z

Peterson, C., Sutton, J., & Wiley, P. (1991). iWARP: A 100-MPOS, LIW microprocessor for multicomputers. *IEEE Micro*, *11*(3), 26–29, 81–87. doi:10.1109/40.87568

Pincus, J. (2004). The consequences of unmet needs: The evolving role of motivation in consumer research. *Journal of Consumer Behaviour*, *3*(4), 375–387. doi:10.1002/cb.149

Plummer, D.C., Smith, D.M., Bittman, T.J., Cearley, D.W., Cappuccio, D.J., Scott, D., Kumar, R., and Robertson, B. (2009, May). *Five refining attributes of public and private cloud computing*. Gartner.

Provos, N., McNamee, D., Mavrommatis, P., Wang, K., & Modadugu, N. (2007). The ghost in the browser analysis of web-based malware. In *HotBots'07: Proceedings of the RST conference on First Workshop on Hot Topics in Understanding Botnets*. Berkeley, CA: USENIX Association.

Provost, F., & Domingos, P. (2003). Tree Induction for Probability-Based Ranking. *Machine Learning*, *52*(3), 199–215.. doi:10.1023/A:1024099825458

Qiao, W., & Ni, L. (1995). Efficient processor allocation for 3D tori. In *Proceedings of the 9th International Conference on Parallel Processing Symposium* (pp. 466-471). Washington, DC: Academic Press. doi:10.1109/IPPS.1995.395972

Quinton, C., Haderer, N., & Duchien, L. (2013). Towards multi-cloud configurations using feature models and ontologies. In *ACM, MultiCloud'13 Proceedings of the international workshop on Multi-cloud applications and federated clouds*, (pp. 21-26). doi:10.1145/2462326.2462332

Raghuram, S. S., & Chakrabarti, C. (2000). A pro-grammable processor for cryptography. In *Proceedings of the IEEE International Symposium on Circuits and Systems (ISCAS 2000)*, (pp. 685–688). IEEE.

Raines, G. (2009). *Cloud computing and SOA*. Systems Engineering at MITRE. Retrieved January 20, 2013 from http://www.mitre.org/work/tech_papers/tech_papers_09/09_0743/09_0743.pdf

Ramim, M., & Levy, Y. (2006). Securing e-learning systems: A case of insider cyber attacks and novice IT management in a small university. *Journal of Cases on Information Technology*, 8(4), 24–34. doi:10.4018/jcit.2006100103

Ran, S. (2003). A model for web sevices discovery with QoS. *ACM SIGEcomExch, 4*(1), 1–10.

Ranganathan, K., & Foster, I. (2002). Decoupling computation and data scheduling in distributed data-intensive applications. In *Proceedings 11th IEEE International Symposium on High Performance Distributed Computing* (pp. 352–358). IEEE Comput. Soc. doi:10.1109/HPDC.2002.1029935

Ratten, V. (2008). Technological innovations in the m-commerce industry: A conceptual model of mobile banking intentions. *The Journal of High Technology Management Research*, 18(2), 111–117. doi:10.1016/j.hitech.2007.12.007

Ratten, V. (2011). Ethics, entrepreneurship and the adoption of e-book devices. *International Journal of Innovation and Learning*, 10(3), 310–325. doi:10.1504/IJIL.2011.042083

Ratten, V. (2013a). Social e-entrepreneurship and technological innovations: The role of online communities, mobile communication and social networks. *International Journal of Social Entrepreneurship and Innovation*, 2(5), 476–483. doi:10.1504/IJSEI.2013.059322

Ratten, V. (2013b). Cloud computing: A social cognitive perspective of ethics, entrepreneurship, technology marketing, computer self-efficacy and outcome expectancy on behavioural intentions. *Australasian Marketing Journal*, 21(3), 137–146. doi:10.1016/j.ausmj.2013.02.008

Ratten, V. (2014). Indian and US consumer purchase intentions of cloud computing services. *Journal of Indian Business Research*, 6(2), 170–188. doi:10.1108/JIBR-07-2013-0068

Ratten, V. (2015). International consumer attitudes towards cloud computing: A social cognitive theory and technology acceptance model perspective. *Thunderbird International Business Review*, 57(3), 217–228. doi:10.1002/tie.21692

Ratten, V., & Ratten, H. (2007). Social cognitive theory in technological innovation. *European Journal of Innovation Management*, 10(1), 90–108. doi:10.1108/14601060710720564

Rau, H., Chen, C.-W., & Shiang, W.-J. (2009). Development of an Agent-based Negotiation Model for Buyer-supplier Relationship with Multiple Deliveries.*Proceedings of the 2009 IEEE International Conference on Networking, Sensing and Control*. doi:10.1109/ICNSC.2009.4919292

Ravinder, R. P., Sridhar, V. S., & RamaKrishna, V. (2013). An Optimistic Approach for Query Construction and Execution in Cloud Computing Environment. *International Journal of Advanced Research in Computer Science and Software Engineering, 3*(5), 237-241.

Reddemma, Y., Thirupathi, L., & Gunti, S. (2009). A Secure Model for Cloud Computing Based Storage and Retrieval. *SIGCOMM Computer Communication Review*, 39(1), 50–55.

Rehan, M., & Akyuz, G. A. (2010). EAI (Enterprise Application Integration), SOA (Service Oriented Architectures) and its relevance to e-supply chain formation. *African Journal of Business Management*, 4(13), 2604–2614.

Riken & Fujitsu. (2014). *K computer*. Retrieved September 9, 2014, form http://www.olcf.ornl.gov/wp-content/events/lug2011/4-12-2011/230-300_Shinji_Sumimoto_LUG2011-FJ-20110407-pub.pdf

Rimal, B., Choi, E., & Lumb, I. (2009). A taxonomy and survey of cloud computing systems. In *International Joint Conference on INC, IMS and IDC* (pp. 44-51). doi:10.1109/NCM.2009.218

Roberts, J., Mocci, U., & Virtamo, J. (1996). *Broadband Network Teletraffic*. Springer.

Rochwerger, B., Breitgand, D., Epstein, A., Hadas, D., Loy, I., Nagin, K., & Tofetti, G. et al. (2011). Reservoir - When One Cloud Is Not Enough. *Computer, 44*(3), 44–51. doi:10.1109/MC.2011.64

Ross, D. (2003). *Introduction to e-supply chain management*. St. Lucie Press.

Rowinski, D. (2011). *The Personal Cloud Will Be A $12 Billion Industry in 2016*. Retrieved June 10, 2015, from http://readwrite.com/2011/06/06/the_personal_cloud_will_be_a_12_ billion_industry_i

Rycroft, R.W. (2006). *Time and technological innovation: Implications for public policy*. Academic Press.

Ryden, M., Oh, K., Chandra, A., & Weissman, J. (2014). Nebula: Distributed edge cloud for data-intensive computing.*2014 International Conference on Collaboration Technologies and Systems (CTS)*, (pp. 491–492). doi:10.1109/CTS.2014.6867613

Ryu, S., Nakayama, K., & Onari, H. (2011). Strategic supply chain coordination scheme under cloud computing environment considering market uncertainty. *International Journal of Business Strategy, 11*(3), 47–57.

Safari, H., Mohammadian, A., & Tamizi, A., Haki, K., & Moslehi, A. (2002). Iran's Ministry of Commerce E-Government Maturity Model. *Quarterly Journal of Knowledge Management, 63*, 53–78.

Sagawa, C., Yoshida, H., Take, R., & Shimada, J. (2009). Cloud computing based on service-oriented platform. *FUJITSU Science Tech. Journal, 45*(3), 283–289.

Sakr, S., Liu, A., Batista, D. M., & Alomari, M. (2011). A Survey of Large Scale Data Management Approaches in Cloud Environments. *IEEE Communications Surveys and Tutorials, 13*(3), 311–336. doi:10.1109/SURV.2011.032211.00087

Salah, K., Al-Saba, M., Akhdhor, M., Shaaban, O., & Buhari, M. I. (2011). Performance evaluation of popular cloud IaaS providers. In *Proceedings of Internet Technology and Secured Transactions (ICITST), 2011 International Conference for*, (pp. 345-349). ICITST.

Samatha N., Vijay Chandu K., Raja Sekhar Reddy P. (2012). Query Optimization Issues for Data Retrieval in Cloud Computing. *International Journal of Computational Engineering Research, 2* (5), 1361-1364.

Sandeep, M. S., & Ravishankar, M. N. (2014). The continuity of underperforming ICT projects in the public sector. *Information & Management, 51*(6), 700–711. doi:10.1016/j.im.2014.06.002

Sasikala, P. (2011). Cloud computing: Present status and future implications. *International Journal of Cloud Computing, 1*(1), 23–36. doi:10.1504/IJCC.2011.043244

Satzger, B., Hummer, W., Inzinger, C., Leitner, P., & Dustdar, S. (2013). Winds of change: From vendor lock-in to the meta cloud. *IEEE Internet Computing, 17*(1), 69–73. doi:10.1109/MIC.2013.19

Scarfo, A. (2012). New security perspectives around BYO. In *Proceedings of 7th IEEE International Conference on Broadband, Wireless Computing, Communication and Applications (BWCCA)*. Victoria, Canada: IEEE Computer Society.

Schiffman, L., & Kanuk, L. (2000). *Consumer Behavior* (7th ed.). New Jersey: Prentice-Hall.

Schmidt, E., & Cohen, J. (2013). *The New Digital Age – Rapidly Shaping the Future of People, Nations and Business*. London: John Murray.

Scholl, H. J., & Klischewski, R. (2007). E-government integration and interoperability: Framing the research agenda. *International Journal of Public Administration, 30*(8-9), 889–920. doi:10.1080/01900690701402668

Scholnikoff, E. B. (2001). International governance in a technological age. In J. De la Mothe (Ed.), *Science, Technology and Governance*. New York: Continuum Press.

Schomm, F., & Vossen, G. (2013, Summer). Mobile Device Management in the IT Consumerization Age. *DOAG Business News*, 27-29.

Schramm, T., Wright, J., Seng, D., & Jones, D. (2010). *Six questions every supply chain executive should ask about cloud computing*. Retrieved September 6, 2014, from http://www.accenture.com/SiteCollectionDocuments/PDF/10-2460-Supply_Chain_Cloud_PoV_vfinal.pdf

Seo, K.-H., & Kim, S.-C. (2003). Improving system performance in contiguous processor allocation for mesh-connected parallel systems. *Journal of Systems and Software*, *67*(1), 45–54. doi:10.1016/S0164-1212(02)00086-9

Shacklett, M. (2012). Next generation cloud technology for supply chain. *WorldTrade 100*, *25*(1), 18-23.

Shacklett, M. (2010). Is supply chain emerging from the cloud? *WorldTrade*, *100*(April), 34–37.

Shacklett, M. (2011). A smarter supply chain: Can companies keep pace with the advances? *WorldTrade*, *100*(August), 20–26.

Shamsi, J., Khojaye, M. A., & Qasmi, M. A. (2013). Data-Intensive Cloud Computing: Requirements, Expectations, Challenges, and Solutions. *Journal of Grid Computing*, *11*(2), 281–310. doi:10.1007/s10723-013-9255-6

Sheeshka, J., Woolcott, D., & MacKinnon, N. (1993). Social cognitive theory as a framework to explain intentions to practice healthy eating behaviors. *Journal of Applied Social Psychology*, *23*(19), 1547–1573. doi:10.1111/j.1559-1816.1993.tb01047.x

Sherbrooke, C. C. (1992). *Optimal inventory modeling of systems: Multi-echelon techniques*. New York: Wiley.

Sherif, M., & Sherif, C. W. (1967). *Attitude, Ego, Involvement and Change*. New York: John Wiley.

Sheth, J., Mittal, B., & Newman, B. (1999). *Consumer Behavior: Consumer Behavior and Beyond*. Austin: Dryden Press.

Shivakumar, B. L., & Raju, T. (August 2010). Emerging role of cloud computing in redefining business operations. *Global Management Review*, *4*(4).

Shrivastava, V., & Bhilare, D. (2012). Algorithms to improve resource utilization and request acceptance rate in iaas cloud scheduling. *International Journal of Advanced Networking and Applications*, *3*(5), 1367–1374.

Silberschatz, A., Galvin, P. B., & Gagne, G. (2011). *Operating System Concepts*. Willy-India Edition.

Silva, G. C., Rose, L. M., & Calinescu, R. (2013, December). Towards a Model-Driven Solution to the Vendor Lock-In Problem in Cloud Computing. In *Cloud Computing Technology and Science (CloudCom), 2013 IEEE 5th International Conference on* (pp. 711-716). doi:10.1109/CloudCom.2013.131

Silveira, M. L., & Ribeiro-Neto, B. (2004). Concept-based ranking: A case study in the judicial domain. *Information Processing & Management*, *40*(5), 791–805. doi:10.1016/j.ipm.2004.04.015

Simson, G. (2011). *"The Cloud Imperative"*. Technology Review. MIT.

Singh, Kumar, & Khatn. (2012). Securing Storage data in Cloud using RC5 Algorithm. *International Journal of Advance Computer Research*, *2*(4), 94–98.

Sinkula, J. M., Baker, W., & Noordewier, T. G. (1997). A framework for market-based organisational learning: Linking values, knowledge and behaviour. *Journal of the Academy of Marketing Science*, *25*(Fall), 305–318. doi:10.1177/0092070397254003

Slothouber, L. (1995). *A model of Web server performance.* Retrieved from www.geocities.com/webserverperformance

Snodgrass, R. T., Yao, S. S., & Collberg, C. (2004). Tamper detection in audit logs. In *Proceedings of the Thirtieth international conference on Very large data bases.* VLDB Endowment. doi:10.1016/B978-012088469-8.50046-2

Snowden, S., Spafford, J., Michaelides, R., & Hopkins, J. (2006). Technology acceptance and m-commerce in an operational environment. *Journal of Enterprise Information Management, 19*(5), 525–539. doi:10.1108/17410390610703657

Soleimanian, F., & Hashemi, S. (2012). Security Challenges in Cloud Computing. *Foundations of Computer Science & Technology, 3*(2), 41–51.

Soltwisch, R., Hogrefe, D., Bericht, T., & Gottingen, G.-a.-u. (2004). *Survey on network security - 2004. IEEE Std 802.11-1999 (1999). Part II: Wireless LAN medium access control (MAC) and physical layer (PHY) specifications.* IEEE.

Solutions Review. (n.d.), *Mobile Device Management Solution Directory and Buyer's Guide.* Retrieved June 10, 2015, from http://solutions-review.com/mobile-device-management/mdm-buyers-guide-directory/

Sosinsky, B. (2011). *Cloud computing bible.* Wiley Publishing.

Sotomayor, B., Keahey, K., & Foster, I. (2006). Overhead matters: A model for virtual resource management. IEEE Computer Society, 1-8.

Sotomayor, B., Keahey, K., & Foster, I. (2008). Combining batch execution and leasing using virtual machines. In *17th ACM International Symposium on High Performance Distributed Computing* (pp. 87-96). doi:10.1145/1383422.1383434

Sotomayor, B., Montero, R., Llorente, I., & Foster, I. (2008). Capacity leasing in cloud systems using the opennebula engine. In Cloud Computing and Applications (pp. 1–5). Academic Press.

Sotomayor, B., Montero, R., Llorente, I., & Foster, I. (2009). Resource leasing and the art of suspending virtual machines. In *IEEE International Conference on HPCC* (pp. 1–9). doi:10.1109/HPCC.2009.17

Sparks, J. R., & Pan, Y. (2010). Ethical judgments in business ethics research: Definition, and research agenda. *Journal of Business Ethics, 91*(3), 405–418. doi:10.1007/s10551-009-0092-2

Stallings, W. (2014). *Operating Systems: Internals and Design Principles* (8th ed.). Upper Saddle River, NJ: Prentice Hall.

Stephens, S., Kruckenberg, M., Bouman, R., Smith, S., & Chang, S. (2007). *MySQL 5.1 Cluster DBA Certification Study Guide, Lulu Enterprises.* UK Ltd.

Sterling, T., & Stark, D. (2009). A High-performance computing forecast: Partly cloudy. *Computing in Science & Engineering, 11*(July/August), 42–49. doi:10.1109/MCSE.2009.111

Subashini, S., & Kavitha, V. (2011). A survey on security issues in service delivery models of cloud computing. *Journal of Network and Computer Applications, 34*(01), 1–11. doi:10.1016/j.jnca.2010.07.006

Sucec, J., Samtani, S., & Bereschinsky, M. A. (2005, October 17-20). Resource friendly approach for es-timating available bandwidth in secure IP networks. In *Proceedings of the Military Communications Conference (MILCOM 2005).* Academic Press.

Sun, A., Ji, T., Yue, Q., & Xiong, F. (2011). IaaS Public Cloud Computing Platform Scheduling Model and Optimization Analysis. *International Journal of Communications, Network, and System Sciences, 4*(12), 803–811. doi:10.4236/ijcns.2011.432098

Szabo, C., Sheng, Q. Z., Kroeger, T., Zhang, Y., & Yu, J. (2014). Science in the Cloud: Allocation and Execution of Data-Intensive Scientific Workflows. *Journal of Grid Computing, 12*(2), 245–264. doi:10.1007/s10723-013-9282-3

Taifi, M. (2012). *NPB Benchmark*. Retrieved from https://github.com/moutai/hpc-medley/

Takabi, H., Joshi, G., & Ahn, G.-J. (2010). Security and Privacy Challenges in Cloud Computing Environments. *IEEE Security Privacy Magazine*, *8*(1), 24–43. doi:10.1109/MSP.2010.186

Tamasjan, A., Strobel, M., & Welpe, I. (2011). Ethical leadership evaluations after moral transgression: Social distance makes the difference. *Journal of Business Ethics*, *99*(4), 609–622. doi:10.1007/s10551-010-0671-2

Tamine, L., & Boughanem, M. (2002). Optimisation de la pertinence dans un SRI: Un problème multi-modal approché sous l'angle de la génétique. In INFORSID (pp. 39-53). Academic Press.

Tan, P.-N., SteinBach, M., & Kumar, V. (2006). Introduction to Data Mining. Addison Wesley.

Taylor, M. (2010). *Enterprise Architecture – Architectural Strategies for Cloud Computing: Oracle*. Retrieved from http://www.techrepublic.com/whitepapers/oracle-white-paper-in-enterprise-architecture-architecture-strategies-for-cloud-computing/2319999

Taylor, S., & Todd, P. (1995). Understanding information technology usage: A test of competing models. *Information Systems Research*, *6*(2), 144–176. doi:10.1287/isre.6.2.144

Technique, A. (2015). Retrieved from http://www.memorymanagement.org/mmref/alloc.html

Thomson, R. (2009, February 24). Socitm: Cloud computing revolutionary to the public sector. *Computer Weekly*.

Tian, Y., Song, B., & Huh, E. N. (2011). Towards the development of personal cloud computing for mobile thin-clients. In *Proceedings of 2011 IEEE International Conference on Information Science and Applications* (ICISA). Jeju Island, Republic of Korea: IEEE Computer Society.

Tijms & Wiley. (2003). *A first course in stochastic models* (Vol. 2). Wiley Online Library.

Tijms, H. C. (1994). *Stochastic Models: An algorithmic approach*. Chichester, UK: Wiley.

Time, L. (2015). Retrieved from http://whatis.techtarget.com/definition/latency

Time, S. (2015). Retrieved from http://www.techopedia.com/definition/3558/seek-time StorageDevices.http://ecomput-ernotes.com/fundamental/input-output-and-memory/explain-secondary-storage-devices

Tiwari, A., & Jain, M. (2013). Analysis of supply chain management in cloud computing. *International Journal of Innovative Technology and Exploring Engineering*, *3*(5), 152–155.

Toosi, A. N., Calheiros, R. N., Thulasiram, R. K., & Buyya, R. (2011). Resource Provisioning Policies to Increase IaaS Provider's Profit in a Federated Cloud Environment. In *Proceedings of 2011 IEEE International Conference on High Performance Computing and Communications*, (pp. 279 – 287). doi:10.1109/HPCC.2011.44

Tordsson, J., Montero, R. S., Moreno-Vozmediano, R., & Llorente, I. M. (2012). Cloud brokering mechanisms for optimized placement of virtual machines across multiple providers. *Future Generation Computer Systems*, *28*(2), 358–367. doi:10.1016/j.future.2011.07.003

Truong, D. (2014). Cloud-based solutions for supply chain management: A post-adoption study. In *Proceedings of American Society of Business and Behavioral Sciences (ASBBS) 21st Annual Conference*. ASBBS.

Trusted Computing Group. (2010). *Cloud Computing and Security –A Natural Match*. Retrieved from www.infosec.co.uk/.../Cloud_Computing_and_Security-A_Natural_Match_ TCG_Whitepaper_20.pdf

Tsohou, A., Lee, H., & Irani, Z. (2014). Innovative public governance through cloud computing: information privacy, business models and performance measurement challenges. *Transforming Government: People, Process, and Policy, 8*(2), 6–6.

Ubuntu. (2010). *Private cloud: Ubuntu Enterprise Cloud.* Available at: http://www.ubuntu.com/cloud/private

UML Profile for Modeling Quality of Service and Fault Tolerance Characteristics and Mechanisms. (2004). *OMG Adopted Specification ptc/04-09-012.* Retrieved from www.omg.org/docs/ptc/04-09-01.pdf

UN E-Government Survey. (2014). *E-Government For The Future We Want.* Retrieved May 19, 2014, from http://unpan3.un.org/egovkb#.VCg77fl_sro

University of Virginia. (n.d.). *Stream Benchmark.* Retrieved from http://www.cs.virginia.edu/stream/ref.html

UnixBench. (n.d.). Retrieved from http://code.google.com/p/byte-unixbench/

Vaquero, L. M., Rodero-Merino, R., Caceres, J., & Lindner, M. (2008). A break in the clouds: towards a cloud definition. *SIGCOMM Computer Communication Review, 39*(1).

Vaquero, L. M., Rodero-Merino, L., & Buyya, R. (2011). Dynamically scaling applications in the cloud. *ACM Siqcomm Computer Communication Review, 41*(1), 45–49. doi:10.1145/1925861.1925869

Vaquero, L. M., Rodero-Merino, L., & Moran, D. (2011). Locking the sky: A survey on IaaS cloud security. *Computing, 91*(1), 93–118. doi:10.1007/s00607-010-0140-x

Vaquero, L., Rodero-Merino, L., Caceres, J., & Lindner, M. (2009). Break in the clouds: Towards a cloud definition. *Computer Communication Review, 39*(1), 50–55. doi:10.1145/1496091.1496100

Varshney, M. (2013). *Blue: A Unified Programming Model for Diverse Data-intensive Cloud Computing Paradigms.* Technical Report #130005, Computer Science Department, University of California, Los Angeles. Retrieved May 5, 2013 from http://fmdb.cs.ucla.edu/Treports/blue.pdf

Vavilapalli, V. K. (2013). Apache Hadoop YARN: yet another resource negotiator. In *Proceedings of the 4th annual Symposium on Cloud Computing* (SOCC '13). ACM. doi:10.1145/2523616.2523633

Velte, A. T., Velte, T. J., & Elsenpeter, R. (2010). *Cloud computing: A practical approach.* New York, NY: McGraw-Hill.

Venkatesh, V., & Davis, F. D. (1996). A model of the antecedents of perceived ease of use: Development and test. *Decision Sciences, 27*(3), 451–482. doi:10.1111/j.1540-5915.1996.tb01822.x

Villegas, D., Bobroff, N., Rodero, I., Delgado, J., Liu, Y., Devarakonda, A., & Parashar, M. et al. (2012). Cloud federation in a layered service model. *Journal of Computer and System Sciences, 78*(5), 1330–1344. doi:10.1016/j.jcss.2011.12.017

Vining, J. & Di Maio,A. (2009, February). *Cloud computing for government is cloudy.* Gartner.

Voorsluys, W., Broberg, J., & Buyya, R. (February2011). Introduction to Cloud Computing. In R. Buyya, J. Broberg, & A. Goscinski (Eds.), *Cloud Computing: Principles and Paradigms* (pp. 1–44). New York: Wiley Press. doi:10.1002/9780470940105.ch1

Vossen, G., Haselmann, T., & Hoeren T. (2012). *Cloud Computing for Enterprises – Technical, Economical, Legal, and Organizational Aspects.* Heidelberg, Germany: dpunkt.verlag.

Vouk, M. A. (2008). Cloud computing- issues, research and implementations. *Journal of Computing and Information Technology, 16*(4), 235–246.

Vrbaski, M., & Petriu, D. (2012). Tool Support for Combined Rule-Based and Goal-Based Reasoning in Context-Aware Systems. Requirement Engineering Conference 2012. IEEE.

Wagner, D. (1997). Analysis of mean values of a multi-server model with non-preemptive prioritiesand non-renewal input. *Communications in Statistics. Stochastic Models, 13*(1), 67–84. doi:10.1080/15326349708807413

Wang, G., Wang, Y., & Lee, Q. (2009). *Cloud computing: A perspective study*. Retrieved January 20, 2013 from http://ebookbrowse.com/cloud-computing-a-perspective-study-pdf-d198329934

Wang, H., Zhang, Y., & Cao, J. (2005). Effective Collaboration with Information Sharing in Virtual Universities. IEEE Transactions, 21(6), 40-853.

Wang, S., Yan, K., Liao, W., & Wang, S. (2010). Towards a load balancing in a three-level cloud computing network. In *3rd IEEE International Conference on Computer Science and Information Technology* (pp. 108-113). IEEE.

Wang, W., Li, R., Owens, & Bhargava, B. (2009). Secure and efficient access to outsourced data. In *Proceedings of the 2009 ACM Workshop on Cloud Computing Security (CCSW '09)* (pp. 55-66). ACM. doi:10.1145/1655008.1655016

Wang, C., Cao, N., Ren, K., & Lou, W. (2012). Enabling secure and efficient ranked keyword search over outsourced cloud data. Parallel and Distributed Systems. *IEEE Transactions on, 23*(8), 1467–1479.

Wang, J., Xiao, Q., Yin, J., & Shang, P. (2013). DRAW: A New Data-gRouping-AWare Data Placement Scheme for Data Intensive Applications With Interest Locality. *IEEE Transactions on Magnetics, 49*(6), 2514–2520. doi:10.1109/TMAG.2013.2251613

Wang, L., Tao, J., Ranjan, R., Marten, H., Streit, A., Chen, J., & Chen, D. (2013). G-Hadoop: MapReduce across distributed data centers for data-intensive computing. *Future Generation Computer Systems, 29*(3), 739–750. doi:10.1016/j.future.2012.09.001

Wangy, B., Tang, J., Fan, W., Chen, S., Yang, Z., & Liu, Y. (2009). Heterogeneous Cross Domain Ranking in Latent Space.*Proceedings of 18th ACM Conference on Information and Knowledge Management (CIKM'09)*(pp 987-996). Hong Kong, China: ACM. doi:10.1145/1645953.1646079

Ward, T. (2012). Supply Chain World Souteast Asia: Cloud Computing and Supply Chain. *SCC*. Retrieved March 1, 2013, from http://supply-chain.org/f/Thomas%20Ward%20-%20Supply%20Chain%20and%20Cloud%20Computing_0.pdf

Weik, M. H. (1961). *A Third Survey of Domestic Electronic Digital Computing Systems*. Ballistic Research Laboratories.

Weikum, G., & Vossen, G. (2002). *Transactional Information Systems – Theory, Algorithms, and the Practice of Concurrency Control and Recovery*. San Francisco, CA: Morgan Kaufmann.

Wikipedia. (2012). *Data Intensive Computing*. Retrieved November 23, 2014 from http://en.wikipedia.org/wiki/Data_Intensive_Computing

Windisch, K. (1997). *ProcSimity V4.3 User's Manual*. University of Oregon.

Windisch, K., Miller, J. V., & Lo, V. (1995). ProcSimity: an experimental tool for processor allocation and scheduling in highly parallel systems. In *Proceedings of the 5th Symposium on the Frontiers of Massively Parallel Computation (Frontiers'95)* (pp. 414-421). Washington, DC: Academic Press.

Winkler, J. R., & Meine, B. (2011). *Securing the cloud*. Waltham, MA: Syngress.

Wojciech, C., & Sergiusz, S. (2009). E-Government Based on Cloud Computing and Service-Oriented Architecture.*3rd International Conference on Theory and Practice of Electronic Governance* (pp.5-10). ACM.

Woodward, B., Davis, D. C., & Hodis, F. A. (2007). The relationship between ethical decision making and ethical reasoning in information technology students. *Journal of Information Systems Education, 18*(2), 193–202.

Worthen, B. (2009). Inside the head of Obama's CIO. *The Wall Street Journal Digits.*

Wright, J. (2011). An Introduction to cloud computing in SCM. *Supply Chain Asia,* 8-11. Retrieved September 10, 2014, http://archive.supplychainasia.org/component/rsfiles/view.raw?path=Magazine%2FSCA-Jan-Feb-11.pdf

Wurman, P., Wellman, M., & Walsh, W. (1998). The Michigan Internet AuctionBot: a configurable auction server for human and software agents. In *Proceedings of the Second International Conference on Autonomous Agents (Agents'98).* ACM Press. doi:10.1145/280765.280847

Wyld, D. C. (2010). The Cloudy future of government IT: Cloud computing and the public sector around the world. *International Journal of Web & Semantic Technology, 1*(1), 1–20.

Xhafa, F., Barolli, L., & Durresi, A. (2007). Batch mode scheduling in grid systems. *International Journal Web and Grid Services, 3*(1), 19–37. doi:10.1504/IJWGS.2007.012635

Xhafa, F., Barolli, L., & Durresi, A. (2007). Immediate mode scheduling in grid systems. *International Journal Web and Grid Services, 3*(2), 219–236. doi:10.1504/IJWGS.2007.014075

Xiao, P., Hu, Z.-G., & Zhang, Y.-P. (2013). An Energy-Aware Heuristic Scheduling for Data-Intensive Workflows in Virtualized Datacenters. *Journal of Computer Science and Technology, 28*(6), 948–961. doi:10.1007/s11390-013-1390-9

Xiaowen, L., & Jin, Y. (2012). Hybrid Approach Using RBR and CBR to Design an Automated Negotiation Model for Tourism Companies.*International Conference on Management of e-Commerce and e-Government.* IEEE.

Xiong, K., & Perros, H. (2009). Service performance and analysis in cloud computing. In *Proceedings ofIEEE 2009 World Conference on Services.* Los Angeles, CA. doi:10.1109/SERVICES-I.2009.121

Xu, Y., Hu, H., & Yihe, S. (2010). Data dependence graph directed scheduling for clustered vliw architectures. *Tsinghua Science and Technology, IEEE, 15*(3), 299–306. doi:10.1016/S1007-0214(10)70065-1

Yang, C., Liu, S., Wu, L., Yang, C. & Meng, X. (2011). The application of cloud computing in textile order service. *International Journal of Digital Content Technology and its Applications, 5*(8), 222-233.

Yang, B., Tan, F., Dai, Y., & Guo, S. (2009). *Performance evaluation of cloud service considering fault recovery.* Cloud Computing. doi:10.1007/978-3-642-10665-1_54

Ye, Z., Li, S., & Zhou, J. (2014). A two-layer geo-cloud based dynamic replica creation strategy. *Applied Mathematics and Information Sciences, 8*(1), 431–440. doi:10.12785/amis/080154

Yin, R. K. (2009). *Case Study Research: Design and Methods.* Sage Inc.

Yoo, B.-S., & Das, C.-R. (2002). A Fast and Efficient Processor Allocation Scheme for Mesh-Connected Multicomputers. *IEEE Transactions on Parallel and Distributed Systems, 51*(1), 46–60.

Younis, M. Y. A., & Kifayat, K. (2013). *Secure cloud computing for critical infrastructure: A survey. Liverpool John Moores University.*

Yu, J., & Cooper, H. (1983). A quantitative review of research design effects on response rates to questionnaires. *JMR, Journal of Marketing Research, 20*(1), 36–44. doi:10.2307/3151410

Zeng, L., Benatallah, B., Dumas, M., Kalagnanam, J., & Sheng, Q. (2003). Quality driven web services composition. In *Proceedings of the 12th International Conference on World Wide Web (WWW 2003).* Budapest, Hungary: Academic Press.

Zeng, L., Benatallah, B., Ngu, A. H. H., Dumas, M., Kalagnanam, J., & Chang, H. (2004). QoS-aware middleware for web services composition. *IEEE Transactions on Software Engineering*, *30*(5), 311–327. doi:10.1109/TSE.2004.11

Zhang, Q., Cheng, L., & Boutaba, R. (2010). Cloud computing: State-of-the-art and research challenges. *Journal of Internet Services and Applications*, *1*(1), 7–18. doi:10.1007/s13174-010-0007-6

Zhang, X., Liu, C., Nepal, S., & Chen, J. (2013). An efficient quasi-identifier index based approach for privacy preservation over incremental data sets on cloud. *Journal of Computer and System Sciences*, *79*(5), 542–555. doi:10.1016/j.jcss.2012.11.008

Zhou, C., Chia, L., & Lee, B. S. (2004). QoS-Aware and Federated Enhancement for UDDI. *International Journal of Web Services Research*, *1*(2), 58–85. doi:10.4018/jwsr.2004040104

Zhu, Y. (1992). Efficient processor allocation strategies for mesh-connected parallel computers. *Journal of Parallel and Distributed Computing*, *16*(4), 328–337. doi:10.1016/0743-7315(92)90016-G

Zimmer, M. (2010). *Facebook's Zuckerberg: "Having two identities for yourself is an example of a lack of integrity"*. Retrieved June 10, 2015, from http://www.michaelzimmer.org/2010/05/14/facebooks-zuckerberg-having-two-identities-for-yourself-is-an-example-of-a-lack-of-integrity/

Zissis, D., & Lekkas, D. (2012). Addressing Cloud Computing Security issues. *Future Generation Computer Systems*, *28*(3), 583–592. doi:10.1016/j.future.2010.12.006

About the Contributors

Shadi Aljawarneh is a researcher and an associate professor, Software Engineering, at Isra University. He holds a BSc degree in Computer Science from Jordan Yarmouk University, a MSc degree in Information Technology from Western Sydney University and a PhD in Software Engineering from Northumbria University-England. He is currently an associate professor in faculty of IT in Isra University, Jordan, where he has worked since 2008. His research is centered in web and network security, e-learning, bioinformatics, Cloud Computing and ICT fields. Aljawarneh has presented at and been on the organizing committees for a number of international conferences and is a board member of the International Community for ACM, Jordan ACM Chapter, ACS, and others. A number of his papers have been selected as "Best Papers" in conferences and journals.

* * *

Ismail Ababneh received the BS degree in electromechanical engineering from the National Superior School of Electronics and Electro-mechanics of Caen, France, in 1979, the MS degree in software engineering from Boston University in 1984, and the PhD degree in computer engineering from Iowa State University in 1995. From 1984 to 1989, he was a software engineer with Data Acquisition Systems, Boston, Massachusetts. He is presently a full professor in the Department of Computer Science at Al al-Bayt University, Jordan. He is a member of Tau Beta Pi and Eta Kappa Nu. His current research interests include processor allocation in multicomputers, and ad hoc routing algorithms.

Sanjay P. Ahuja has a M.S. and Ph.D. in Computer Science and Engineering from the University of Louisville. He is a Full Professor and the FIS Distinguished Professor in Computer and Information Sciences in the School of Computing at the University of North Florida. He is a Senior Member of the IEEE and a member of the SPEC Research Group (RG) and the SPEC RG Cloud Working Group. He is the faculty advisor to the Upsilon Pi Epsilon Computer Science Honor Society. His research interests include Cloud Computing, performance evaluation and benchmarking, modeling, and simulation of Computer Networks and Distributed Systems.

Goknur Arzu Akyuz received her Bs degree from Industrial Engineering Department, Middle East Technical University. She has 12 years of experience in Production Planning and Control, Material Management and Enterprise Resources Planning (ERP) in different sectors (Military Electronics, Wooden, Power Transmission, Medical and Metal). She holds an MSc degree in Computer Engineering and a PhD degree in MODES (Modelling and Design of Engineering Systems) from Atilim University. Her research interests include Production Planning and Control, Enterprise Resources Planning Systems, Web-based Supply Chain Management, Cloud Computing and Quality Management. Her published papers in refereed Journals and Conferences are on Supply Chain Performance Management, e-Supply Chain, Service Oriented Architectures and Cloud Computing. Akyuz is faculty member of Atilim University, Industrial Engineering Department.

Abdullah Alhaj is an assistant professor at University of Jordan/Aqaba Branch since 5 years. His research interests range from security, cloud, networks and e-learning. He has published a number of conferences and journals papers.

Motasem Al Smadi received the BS degree in computer information systems from Al al-Bayt University, Jordan in 2008, the MS degree in computer science from Al al-Bayt university, Jordan in 2013. He is presently working as a teacher at ministry of education in Jordan. His research interests include processor allocation and job scheduling in multicomputers.

Thamer Al-Rousan is an Assistant Professor of Software Engineering at Isra University, Jordan. He holds a PhD in Software Engineering from University Sains Malaysia (USM). His research is centered in Web Engineering, Cloud Computing, Risk Management, Design and Architectures, Software Metrics and Quality Assurance. Thamer Al-Rousan has number of published papers in different Software Engineering topics. He is also a reviewer in different software engineering journals and conferences.

Bassam Al-Shargabi got his BSc in computer science from the Applied Science University (Jordan) in 2003 and his MSc in Computer Information System (CIS) from the university of Arab Academy for Banking and Financial Sciences (AABFS) in 2004. He got his PhD in Computer Information System in 2009 from the university of Arab Academy for Banking and Financial Sciences (AABFS). He is currently an Associated professor at Computer information system department at the School of IT in Isra university Amman-Jordan. His research expertise include: Web Services Composition, Natural Language Processing, Software Engineering and software Quality, E-Governments models.

Abdelmalek Amine received an engineering degree in Computer Science, a Magister diploma in Computational Science and PhD from Djillali Liabes University in collaboration with Joseph Fourier University of Grenoble. His research interests include data mining, text mining, ontology, classification, clustering, neural networks, and biomimetic optimization methods. He participates in the program committees of several international conferences and on the editorial boards of international journals. Dr. Amine is the head of GeCoDe-knowledge management and complex data-laboratory at UTM University of Saida, Algeria; he also collaborates with the "knowledge base and database" team of TIMC laboratory at Joseph Fourier University of Grenoble.

Sikha Bagui is a Professor and Chair of the Department of Computer Science and Director of Center for Cybersecurity at the University of West Florida, USA. Dr. Bagui's areas of research are database and database design, data mining, pattern recognition and statistical computing.

Saad Bani-Mohammad received the BSc degree in computer science from Yarmouk University, Jordan in 1994, the MSc degree in computer science from Al al-Bayt university, Jordan in 2002, and the PhD degree in computer science from University of Glasgow, U.K., in 2008. From 2002 to 2005, he was a lecturer in the Department of Computer Science at Al al-Bayt University in Jordan. He is presently an Associate Professor in the Department of Computer Science at Al al-Bayt University, Jordan. He is a member of IEEE Computer Society. His research interests include processor allocation and job scheduling in multicomputers. Dr. Bani-Mohammad has over 35 scientific papers and projects either presented or published. Most of his research is supported by Al al-Bayt University, Jordan and University of Glasgow, U.K. His findings were published (over 35 publications) in world leading journals and also in prestigious and top quality international conference proceedings.

Hadj Ahmed Bouarara received a licence degree in computer Science and Master diploma in computer modeling of knowledge and reasoning from the Computer Science department of Tahar Moulay University of Saida Algeria. Now Hadj Ahmed BOUARARA is a PhD student in Web and Knowledge Engineering in Dr. Tahar Moulay University. His research interests Data Mining, Knowledge Discovery, Metaheuristic, Bio-inspired techniques, Retrieval Information, Cloud Computing and images processing.

Jeffrey Chang is principal lecturer in strategic management at London South Bank University, UK. His research and teaching interests range from information systems management, electronic commerce, organisational change and behavior to small and medium sized-enterprises. He has published papers in these subject areas in journals such as Information Systems Journal and Knowledge and Process Management, and has attended conferences such as ECIS and UKAIS. Apart from his academic work Jeffrey is Programme Director of Postgraduate Informatics Studies within the University responsible for managing and developing courses, coordinating teaching tutoring responsibilities and maintaining the quality of regulations and procedures.

Meghana Chekuri was a graduate student in the Executive MBA program at Texas Woman's University.

Rana Dattagupta received the METeIE and PhD degree from Jadavpur University and the PhD degree from Brunel University, UK. He was Professor, Computer Science and Engineering Department, Jadavpur University, Kolkata, India. Currently he is an AICTE Emeritus Fellow.

Ali Delavarkhalafi was born 1967 in Tehran. He is faculty member of applied mathematics department of Yazd University. He graduated in Ph.D from optimal control department of Moscow State University. His interest in optimal control, differential games and queuing theory in computer networks. He is associate Prof of Yazd University.

Stuart Dillon is Associate Professor and Chairperson of the Department of Management Systems at the University of Waikato Management School in Hamilton, New Zealand. He has a PhD in Decision Science, however much of his research is in the area of electronic commerce and Information Technology Project Management. Past and current relevant research includes work on e-government, consumer perceptions on e-tailing, and data curation. He has published his research in academic journals such as MIS Quarterly, International Journal of Public Sector Management, and Journal of Global Information Management. He is an active member of the European Center for Information Systems (ERCIS) of which the University of Waikato is the sole New Zealand institutional member.

Jayalakshmi D. S. received her M.Sc.(Engg.) in Computer and Information Sciences from Visvesvaraya Technological University, India in 2009. She is currently an Associate Professor in the Department of Computer Science & Engineering, M.S. Ramaiah Institute of Technology, Bengaluru, India and is pursuing doctoral studies in the area of Cloud Computing from S.R.M. University, India.

Kendra Fisher was a graduate student in the Executive MBA program at Texas Woman's University.

Thomas F. Furman is a graduate student pursuing a Master's Degree in Computer and Information Sciences in the School of Computing at the University of North Florida. He is a member of the ACM and Upsilon Pi Epsilon. He is the Vice-President of the local student chapter of ACM at the University of North Florida. His research interests include cloud computing, general purpose GPU computing, and performance evaluation.

Veena Goswami is currently a Professor in the School of Computer Application, KIIT University, Bhubaneswar, India. She received her PhD degree from Sambalpur University, India, and then worked as a Research Associate at the Indian Institute of Technology, Kharagpur for two years. Her current research interests include continuous- and discrete-time queues, and performance analysis of mobile and ad-hoc networks. She has published research articles in INFORMS Journal on Computing, Computers and Operations Research, RAIRO Operations Research, Computers and Mathematics with Applications, Computers and Industrial Engineering, Applied Mathematical Modelling, Applied Mathematics and Computation, Journal of Systems Science and Systems Engineering.

Sutirtha Kumar Guha completed his B.Tech in Computer Science and Engineering. He completed his M.Tech in the same domain in 2008. He has many international journal and conference publication. He is also part of many international conference technical committee. Presently Prof. Guha is working as Assistant Professor in Seacom Engineering College

Reda Mohamed Hamou received an engineering degree in computer Science from the Computer Science department of Djillali Liabes University of Sidi-Belabbes-Algeria and PhD (Artificial intelligence) from the same University. He has several publications in the field of BioInspired and Metaheuristic. His research interests include Data Mining, Text Mining, Classification, Clustering, computational intelligence, neural networks, evolutionary computation and Biomimetic optimization method. He is a head of research team in GecoDe laboratory. Dr. Hamou is an associate professor in technology faculty in UTMS University of Saida-Algeria.

Jennifer Hanna was a graduate student in the Executive MBA program at Texas Woman's University.

Efosa C. Idemudia, an internationally known scholar, is conducting his Fulbright during the Summer of 2014 at the Lagos Business School. Dr. Idemudia is a full time faculty member and coordinator of the Business Data Analytics program at Arkansas Tech University. Prior to that, he was a visiting scholar at Georgia State University, working in their Computer Information Systems Department; this department is ranked in the top ten by the US News & World Report. At Georgia State University, Dr. Idemudia taught both graduate and undergraduate students. For six years, he was a faculty consultant to the Educational Testing Services (ETS) for the College Board's AP computer science reading program.

Currently, Dr. Idemudia is a member of the editorial board for the International Journal of Technology Diffusion and Journal of the Southern Association for Information Systems. His papers have been published and presented worldwide in leading IS conferences, such as America's Conference on Information Systems and Hawaii International Conference on Systems Sciences. Dr. Idemudia's manuscripts have been published in the Journal of Business Administration Online, Inf Syst E-Bus Manage Journal, International Journal of Education Administration and Policy Studies, International Journal of Technology Diffusion, Journal of Business Administration and Education, and the International Journal of Online Marketing. Dr. Idemudia holds degrees from universities located on three different continents: he holds a PhD in Management Information Systems from Texas Tech University, a Master's in Computer Information Systems from the University of Texas at El Paso, and an MBA in International Business from the Helsinki School of Economics and Business Administration. Dr. Idemudia is a member of Strathmore Who's Who of Professionals.

Mark Johnston obtained his MSc degree in Information Systems Management at London South Bank University, UK, in 2012. His academic interests are strategic management of information systems, enterprise modelling for systems support and project management. Currently he works for a mental health charity, Julian Campbell Foundation, as a project manager.

Anirban Kundu is an Associate Professor in Information Technology (IT) department of Netaji Subhash Engineering College, India. He is also holding the research head position in the Innovation Research Lab (IRL), India. He holds a B.E. Mechanical from Islamiah Institute of Technology, Bangalore University (1999). He had also received a Post Graduate Diploma in Financial Management from Management Studies Promotion Institute (2001), an M.Tech. (IT) from Bengal Engineering and Science University (2004), and a Ph.D (Engg.) in Computer Science from Jadavpur University (2009). Dr. Kundu completed his Post Doctorate in Computer Science from Kuang-Chi Institute of Advanced Technology, Shenzhen, P. R. China (2014).

Ali Madankan earned his Bachelor of Applied Mathematics from Tarbiat Moallem University (Iran) in 2003. He received his Master of Science degree in Numerical analysis in 2005 from The University of Sistan and Balouchestan (Iran). He worked as a lecturer for the department of Computer Science in University of Zabol (Iran) from 2005 to 2013. In 2013 he joined the doctoral program In Applied Mathematics at The Yazd University (Iran). Mr. Madankan's dissertation, Queuing System and Cloud Computing, is supervised by Dr. Delavar Khalfi.

Amruta More holds a BE (Computer Engineering) and pursuing an ME (Computer Engineering) from the University of Pune.

Debajyoti Mukhopadhyay is the Dean (R&D) and Professor & Head of Information Technology at Maharashtra Institute of Technology Pune. During 2008-2010 for almost 3 years, he was Professor & Head of the Information Technology & MIS at Calcutta Business School. He was a Visiting Scholar at George Mason University USA in 2014. He is a Distinguished Adjunct Professor at Curtin University, Australia. He also holds Adjunct Professorship at Monarch Business School, Switzerland. Earlier, he was a full Professor of Computer Sc & Engg at the West Bengal University of Technology during 2001-2008. He was a Visiting Professor at Chonbuk National University, Korea in 2006-2007. He had also taught at Stevens Institute of Technology, New Jersey, USA, 1982-1984 and at Bengal Engineering College. He had worked at Bell Communications Research, New Jersey, USA in its Computing Systems and Architecture Lab. He holds a B.E. (Electronics) from the University of Calcutta, a D.C.S. in Computer Science from The Queen's University of Belfast, an M.S. (Computer Science) from Stevens Institute of Technology, and a Ph.D.(Engineering) (Computer Science) from Jadavpur University.

Benazir Neha is currently pursuing her Master's in Information and Communication Technology from Veer Surendra Sai University of Technology, Burla. Her research interests focus on resource management and scheduling workflows in clouds.

Loi Nguyen works for the Naval Education and Training Professional Development and Technology Center (NETPDTC) in Pensacola, FL, USA. His areas of research are cluster database, distributed database design, data warehouse, data mining, business intelligence modeling, service component architecture, and web-oriented architecture.

Sanjaya Kumar Panda is currently working as an Assistant Professor at Veer Surendra Sai University of Technology (VSSUT) (Formerly, University College of Engineering (UCE)), Burla, Odisha, India. He is also pursuing his Ph. D. degree in Computer Science and Engineering (CSE) at Indian School of Mines (ISM), Dhanbad, Jharkhand, India. He received his M. Tech. degree in CSE from National Institute of Technology (NIT), Rourkela, Odisha, India and B. Tech. degree in CSE from VSSUT, Burla, Odisha, India. He received two silver medal awards for best post-graduate (CSE) and best graduate (CSE) in 2014 and 2011 respectively. He has published more than 22 papers in journals and conferences. He is the editorial board member of American Journal of Computer Science and Information Engineering, USA, International Journal of Sensors and Sensor Networks, USA and International Journal of Wireless Communications and Mobile Computing, USA. His current research interests include Cloud Scheduling, Grid Scheduling, Fault-Tolerance, Parallel Algorithms, Interconnection Network, List Accessing Problem and CPU Scheduling.

Roshni Pradhan was born in India in 1990. She received the Engineering degree from VSSUT, Burla in 2013 and is currently a M.Tech research scholar in the department of Information Technology of VSSUT, Burla. Her current research interest include task scheduling in heterogeneous cloud, cloud computing and cloud services.

Mahesh S. Raisinghani, is a professor in the Executive MBA program at the TWU School of Management. Dr. Raisinghani was awarded the 2008 Excellence in Research & Scholarship award and the 2007 G. Ann Uhlir Endowed Fellowship in Higher Education Administration. His research has been published in several academic journals such as IEEE Transactions on Engineering Management, Information & Management, Information Resources Management Journal, International Journal of Innovation and Learning, Journal of E-Commerce Research, International Journal of Distance Education Technologies, Journal of IT Review, Journal of Global IT Management, and Journal of IT Cases and Applications Research among others, and international/national conferences. Dr. Raisinghani serves as the Editor in Chief of the International Journal of Web based Learning and Teaching Technologies; on the board of Global IT Management Association; and as an advisory board member of the World Affairs Council.

He is included in the millennium edition of Who's Who in the World, Who's Who among Professionals, Who's Who among America's Teachers and Who's Who in Information Technology.

Vanessa Ratten is an Associate Professor of Entrepreneurship and Innovation in the Department of Management, La Trobe Business School at La Trobe University, Melbourne, Australia. She teaches Entrepreneurial Business Planning, Managing Innovation in Organisations and Entrepreneurship. Dr Ratten has previously been on the business faculty of Duquesne University, the University of Queensland, Queensland University of Technology and Deakin University. She has won a Vice Chancellors award for community engagement with innovation and entrepreneurship programs.

Mohammad Rehan is Associate Professor of Information Systems Engineering Department at Atilim University, Ankara Turkey. His area of interest are MIS, SCM, eSCM, e-commerce, eGovernment, eProcurement, Public eProcurement and Cloud computing. He has extensive experience of consultation and training programs in MIS and Business management courses. He is the author of "eProcurement: Supply Chain Management" book. He is also involved in book-reviews related to Database, and publications (research work) in referred journals and conferences including International Journal of Production Research.

Kerwin E. Roslie is a graduate student seeking a Master's Degree in Computer and Information Sciences. He received a Bachelor's Degree in Computer and Information Sciences in the School of Computing at the University of North Florida. He is a member of Upsilon Pi Epsilon.

Omar Sabri got his BSc in computer science from the University of Jordan (Jordan) in 2002 and his MSc in Computer Information System (CIS) from the university of Arab Academy for Banking and Financial Sciences (AABFS) in 2005. He got his PhD in Management Information System(MIS) in 2011 from the university of Arab Academy for Banking and Financial Sciences (AABFS). He is currently an Assistant Professor in Management Information System(MIS) department at the School of Business Administration. His research expertise includes Knowledge Management, E-government subjects, Web Services Composition, Natural Language Processing, Culture and Information System.

Saswati Sarkar has completed M.TECH in Computer Science & Engineering. She is currently working in an engineering college under West Bengal University of Technology with the teaching experience of 8 years. She has expertise on Computer Organization, Operating System with keen interest on Cloud Computing. She has contributed research on Bioinformatics and Search Engine and also has presented papers in different conferences.

Choudhury N. Sahoo has done his Masters in Computer Applications from National Institute of Technology, Jamshedpur, India, in 2002 and is currently pursuing doctoral studies in the area of Cloud Computing from KIIT University, India. His areas of interests include Cloud Computing, Big Data/ Hadoop and Performance Evaluation in Web-based applications.

Sujaya Kumar Sathua is currently working as an Assistant Professor at Veer Surendra Sai University of Technology (VSSUT) (Formerly, University College of Engineering (UCE)), Burla, Odisha, India. He received his M. Tech. degree in CSE from National Institute of Technology (NIT), Rourkela, Odisha,

India and B. Tech. degree in IT from VSSUT, Burla, Odisha, India. His current research interests include Cloud Scheduling, List Accessing Problem and CPU Scheduling.

Florian Stahl holds a BA in Business Administration (Giessen University, Germany) an MSc in E-Business and Information System (Newcastle University, UK) and a PhD in Information Systems from Münster University, Germany. He is currently a research assistant at the Information Systems department of Münster University, working in the Databases and Information Systems (DBIS) Group. His current research focus is on efficient on demand provisioning of data and information tailored to users' needs as well as on finding appropriate pricing models for such services.

K. G. Srinivasa received his PhD in Computer Science and Engineering from Bangalore University in 2007. He is the recipient of All India Council for Technical Education – Career Award for Young Teachers, Indian Society of Technical Education – ISGITS National Award for Best Research Work Done by Young Teachers, Institution of Engineers(India) – IEI Young Engineer Award in Computer Engineering, Rajarambapu Patil National Award for Promising Engineering Teacher Award from ISTE – 2012, IMS Singapore – Visiting Scientist Fellowship Award. He has published more than hundred research papers in International Conferences and Journals. He has visited many Universities abroad as a visiting researcher – He has visited University of Oklahoma, USA, Iowa State University, USA, Hong Kong University, Korean University, National University of Singapore are few prominent visits. He has authored two books namely File Structures using C++ by TMH and Soft Computer for Data Mining Applications LNAI Series – Springer. He has been awarded BOYSCAST Fellowship by DST, for conducting collaborative Research with Clouds Laboratory in University of Melbourne in the area of Cloud Computing. He is the principal Investigator for many funded projects from UGC, DRDO, and DST. His research areas include Data Mining, Machine Learning and Cloud Computing.

R. Srinivasan received the degree Doctor of Science, Electrical Engineering (electronics) from Washington University in St. Louis in 1974 and received his Master of Science (M.S.), degree in Electrical and Electronics Engineering from the East-West Center, Hawaiian Islands in 1971. He has a distinguished career of more than 35 years in the National Aerospace Laboratories, Bengaluru, India where he retired as the Deputy Director. He is an active member and a past-president of the Computer Society of India and since 1995 he is working in academia. Currently he is Professor Emeritus in the Directorate of Research, S. R. M. University, India and in M. S. Ramaiah Institute of Technology, Bengaluru, India.

Sheetal Vij holds a BE (Computer Engineering) and an ME (Computer Engineering) from the University of Pune. Currently she is working as an Assistant Professor at Maharashtra Institute of Technology, Pune.

Gottfried Vossen is a Professor of Computer Science in the Department of Information Systems at the University of Muenster in Germany. He is a Fellow of the German Computer Science Society and an Honorary Professor at the University of Waikato Management School in Hamilton, New Zealand. He received his master's and Ph.D. degrees as well as the German Habilitation in 1981, 1986, and 1990, resp., all from the Technical University of Aachen in Germany. He was a visiting professor at the University of California in San Diego, USA, from 1986 to 1988 and thereafter at several German universities including the Hasso-Plattner-Institute for Software Systems Engineering in Potsdam near Berlin, at Karlstad University in Sweden, at Marmara University in Istanbul, Turkey, and at The University of Waikato in

Hamilton, New Zealand. He was an Associate Professor at the University of Gießen in Germany from 1991 to 1993, and was appointed Full Professor at the University of Muenster in 1993. His current research interests include conceptual as well as application-oriented challenges concerning databases, information systems, social business process modeling, and Web 2.0 applications, cloud computing, and big data.

Jared T. Wheeler is a graduate student working towards a Master's Degree in Computer and Information Sciences in the School of Computing at the University of North Florida. He is a member of the ACM and Upsilon Pi Epsilon and President of the student chapters for each society at the University of North Florida. His research interests include linked data, artificial intelligence, and cloud computing.

Index

A

ACID 312, 324, 345
Advance Reservation 147-149, 170
allocated sub-mesh 178, 187
Analytical Hierarchy Process 134, 138
association rule mining 321-323, 325, 338, 345
authorization token 113, 117
Automated Negotiation 245, 247, 256-257, 261
average cloud utilization 147, 156-157, 160, 162, 164, 168, 170

B

Benchmark Dataset 151, 157, 170
benchmarking 37-40, 50
Best Effort 147-149, 170
best fit search 300
Big Data 199, 202, 305-307, 310-311, 321, 325, 343, 345
binary search 281, 284, 287, 290-291, 299-302
bio-inspired 201-202, 219, 225, 228
Bring Your Own Device (BYOD) 114, 117
B-tree 287
business process change 53, 55, 64, 67-68, 71
Busy List 173, 175, 179, 187
BYOD 102-105, 108-109, 113-115, 117

C

case based data 245-247, 251, 258, 261
case based reasoning 245-248, 258, 261
Choose Your Own Device (CYOD) 117
Cloud concerns 194
cloud governance 102, 104, 108
Cloud market forecast 198
cloud platforms 14, 37-39
Cloud Security Alliance 196

cloud service 2, 8, 18, 32, 37-38, 48, 54, 56, 65, 72, 85, 87-88, 107-108, 111, 147, 149, 152-153, 170, 200-201, 208, 211, 228
Cloud storage 103, 141, 281
cluster 37, 41-48, 50, 103, 305, 309-310, 321-329, 331-332, 334, 343
collaboration 24-33, 36, 59, 62, 68, 190, 311
community cloud 18, 200
computing services 1-3, 5, 7-8, 16, 50-51, 54, 61, 84
contiguous allocation 171-174, 177, 182, 184
COPE 104-105, 109-110, 117
Corporate Owned, Personally Enabled (COPE) 117
Cryptographic Scheme 204, 228
Cyberinfrastructure 2, 14

D

database clustering 322-323
Database Clusters 345
database sharding 321-325, 343, 345
data centre 2, 59-60, 72, 313, 320
Data Intensive computing 305-306, 309, 316-317
data placement 311, 313, 320
data transfer 21, 44-45, 264, 315-316, 320
data transmission 73-80, 82
Device and Location Independent 258, 261
distributed computing 16, 24, 84, 305
Dynamic Rank 273, 276, 279

E

e-government 15-21
Enterprise Application 25, 30, 36, 113, 117
Enterprise Resources Planning (ERP) System 36

F

free sub-mesh 175-176, 178, 184, 187

G

G-Cloud 53-54, 56-60, 62-63, 65, 67-68, 72
generic 24-26, 30-32, 36, 140, 200, 264
geo-distributed data 306, 316, 320
government cloud (G-Cloud) 57, 67, 72
government IT 54, 65

H

hashing 287
Horizontal Data Partitioning 345
hybrid cloud 19, 73, 200, 230, 313

I

information retrieval 111, 201-202, 204, 207, 209-
    210, 212-214, 216-219, 221-222, 225, 228, 263
Infrastructure as a Service 2, 30, 38, 50, 229
instance type 43, 45, 48, 50
Intercloud 84, 320
Internet applications 2, 14
Internet of Things 115, 277
IT consumerization 103
IT infrastructure 17, 25, 27, 51, 53-55, 59-62, 66-68,
    72, 85

J

job scheduling 171-172, 179, 187, 315
Job turnaround time 172, 187

L

local government 51-65, 67-68

M

makespan 147, 156-165, 167-168, 170
Malicious Packets Detection System (MPDS) 73
maximal free list 174, 176, 187
maximal free sub-mesh 187
mobile commerce 1-2, 14
Mobile Data 5, 14
Mobile Device Management (MDM) 110, 117
Multicloud 320
multi-cloud 84-86, 94, 98-99, 147-149, 156, 168,
    314, 316
multi-server 230

O

On-Demand Services 14, 147
OpenStack 246, 261
outsourcing 2, 24-25, 28, 31-32, 54, 60-65, 68, 72,
    204

P

personal cloud 102-108, 115, 117
Platform as a Service (PaaS) 2, 30, 38, 200, 229
Primary Domain 262, 265-268, 273-274, 277, 279
Primary Web pages 279
private cloud 18-19, 56, 62, 103, 113, 200, 230
private information retrieval 111, 201-202, 204, 207,
    209-210, 219, 221, 225, 228
Processor allocation 172, 179, 187
Processor fragmentation 172, 187
programming models 305-306, 320
public cloud 18, 37-38, 54, 56, 200
public sector 15-16, 19, 51-53, 55-56, 62-63, 65-66,
    72

Q

quality of service 73, 82, 85, 99, 130, 138
queueing 84-85, 94, 99

R

Relevancy Factor 262, 267, 273, 279
replication 111, 305-306, 311-313, 315-316, 320,
    324, 326, 343
resource 17, 25, 32, 52, 62, 66, 72, 84-85, 98-99,
    113, 198, 228-230, 305-307, 310, 312-315
rest 16, 26, 85, 129, 173, 261, 284, 323
rule based data 245-246, 258, 261
rule based reasoning 245-248, 258

S

SaaS 2, 28, 30, 37-38, 54, 58, 60-61, 63, 65, 67, 72,
    85-86, 110, 189, 200
scheduling 73-74, 149, 153-154, 156, 158, 170-173,
    179-184, 187, 230, 281, 305-306, 313-316, 320
Secondary Domain 262, 265, 269-271, 273-274,
    277, 279
Secondary Web pages 279
Secure Data Transmission Mechanism (SDTM) 73,
    82

security breaches 198
Service Composition 118-119, 136, 138
service level agreement 63, 149, 314
Service Oriented Architecture 118, 138
Service Personalization 102
simulation 79-80, 82, 157-158, 164, 171, 173-176, 179-180, 184
smart container 113-114, 117
social bees 201, 213-214, 223, 225, 228
Software Agent 138
Software as a Service (SaaS) 2, 30, 38, 58, 189, 200
Static Rank 267-268, 276, 279
Supply Chain (SC) 24, 36
switching request orientation 176, 182
synthetic dataset 164-165, 167-168, 170
system utilization 171-173, 175-176, 179-180, 182-184, 187

T

task scheduling 149, 153-154, 170, 313, 315
technology marketing 3, 5, 7

time complexity 156, 178-179, 281, 291, 293-294, 300
Turbulence Factor 262-263, 267, 273, 279
turnaround time 172, 175-176, 179-181, 187

U

user preferences 118-123, 125, 127-128, 135-136, 138

V

Validation Tools 201, 216, 228
vendor lock-in 24, 28, 33, 56, 65-66, 68, 72
virtualisation 54, 60, 67, 72, 114
Virtual Private Network (VPN) 189, 200
visibility 18, 25-27, 36

W

Web page ranking 264, 268, 273, 279
web service 118-125, 127-131, 135-136, 229, 316

Become an IRMA Member

Members of the **Information Resources Management Association (IRMA)** understand the importance of community within their field of study. The Information Resources Management Association is an ideal venue through which professionals, students, and academicians can convene and share the latest industry innovations and scholarly research that is changing the field of information science and technology. Become a member today and enjoy the benefits of membership as well as the opportunity to collaborate and network with fellow experts in the field.

IRMA Membership Benefits:

- **One FREE Journal Subscription**

- **30% Off Additional Journal Subscriptions**

- **20% Off Book Purchases**

- Updates on the latest events and research on Information Resources Management through the IRMA-L listserv.

- Updates on new open access and downloadable content added to Research IRM.

- A copy of the Information Technology Management Newsletter twice a year.

- A certificate of membership.

IRMA Membership $195

Scan code to visit irma-international.org and begin by selecting your free journal subscription.

Membership is good for one full year.

www.irma-international.org

Printed in the United States
By Bookmasters